Munich Studies on Innovation and Competition

Volume 21

The Munich Studies on Innovation and Competition present fundamental research on legal systems that have been created with the objective of promoting and safeguarding innovation and competition as the most important factors for economic growth and prosperity. Accordingly, this series will include monographic works in English in the different fields of intellectual property and competition law such as patent, trademark and copyright law, as well as unfair competition and antitrust law. Rather than describing what the law is, the series strives to contribute to the scholarship on how these legal systems should develop so as to promote innovation and competition. Therefore, its outlook is both international, by not focussing on any specific national legal system, and interdisciplinary. In particular, studies are encouraged that also incorporate the methods and findings of other disciplines such as economics, sociology and anthropology.

Fabian Böttger

CAFTA-DR, European Free Trade Agreements and the Industrial Property System in Central America

A Contribution to the TRIPS-plus Debate

Springer

Fabian Böttger
Munich, Germany

ISSN 2199-7462 ISSN 2199-7470 (electronic)
Munich Studies on Innovation and Competition
ISBN 978-3-031-93439-1 ISBN 978-3-031-93440-7 (eBook)
https://doi.org/10.1007/978-3-031-93440-7

This Springer imprint is published by the registered company Springer Nature Switzerland AG
The registered company address is: Gewerbestrasse 11, 6330 Cham, Switzerland

To my father Dr. jur Hans-Peter Böttger in loving and grateful memory

Acknowledgments

This book is based on my doctoral thesis which was written at the Faculty of Law of the Ludwig Maximilian University in Munich and the Max Planck Institute for Innovation and Competition, which supported my research with a generous scholarship.

I would like to express my deepest gratitude to my Doctoral Supervisor Prof. Dr. Josef Drexl, LL.M. (UC Berkeley), Managing Director of the Max Planck Institute for Innovation and Competition for his outstanding support and supervision, as well as his patience throughout the project. I am also very thankful to my second referee Prof. Dr. Dr. h.c. Reto M. Hilty, Director Emeritus for his highly valuable comments. I could not have started this journey without the supportive recommendation of the late Prof. Dr. Dr. h.c. mult. Gerhard Schricker.

I am greatly indebted to Sibylle Schlatter, my academic advisor, who provided exceptional support and personal encouragement in relation to this work and helped me prepare my field trip to Central America. My research benefitted from the valuable discussions with and support and encouragement from current and former Senior Research Fellows at the Institute, in particular Dr. Eva-Marina Bastian, Dr. Beatriz Conde Gallego, Prof. Dr. Henning Grosse Ruse-Khan and Prof. Dr. Dr. Mark-Oliver Mackenrodt, LL.M. (NYU), as well as the administrative staff of the Institute and particularly its library.

The research benefitted immensely from the field research and about 35 interviews with IP practitioners conducted in October and November 2008 in Central America. I thank especially Ana Catalina Monge Rodríguez and Néstor Morera in Costa Rica, Diana Hasbún and Carlos Castillo in El Salvador, Gabriela Contreras Aguilera and Ninoshka Urrutia in Guatemala and Ricardo Bendaña in Nicaragua, who agreed to be quoted in this thesis. They helped me greatly to better understand the realities of the industrial property law system in the region.

On a personal level, I am deeply grateful to my mother Brigitte, my godfather Wilfried Floeck and my brother Sebastian for their support and encouragement. My wife Arpi and our children Arno Peter and Ellen Sara were my constant source of happiness and dealt as amiable as they could with the seclusion I needed to work on this book. Arpi also provided valuable comments of my draft text and we engaged in many fruitful discussions. Arno helped me with cross-checking some reference sections. I love them more than I can say.

This book combines my interest in Latin America, which I owe to my friend Peter Hölzl, and my commitment to the practice of law, which I inherited from my father Hans-Peter. To him I dedicate this book in loving and grateful memory.

Munich, Germany
November 2024

Fabian Böttger

Contents

Abbreviations[1]

ABS	Access and Benefit Sharing
ACARG	Central American Agreement on Access to Genetic and Biochemical Resources and Related Traditional Knowledge (*Acuerdo Centroamericano de Acceso a los Recursos Genéticos y Bioquímicos y al Conocimiento Tradicional Asociado*)
ACP	African, Caribbean and Pacific Group of States
AIA	America Invents Act
ALBA	Bolivarian Alternative for the Americas (*Alianza Bolivariana para los Pueblos de Nuestra América*)
AmCham	American Chamber of Commerce
ASEAN	Association of Southeast Asian Nations
Biodiversity Directorate	Directorate General of Natural Resources and Biodiversity of the Ministry of the Environment and Natural Resources (Nicaragua)
Biotech Directive	European Directive 98/44/EC of 6 July 1998 on the legal protection of biotechnological inventions
BIT	Bilateral Investment Treaty
Brussels I Regulation	Council Regulation 44/2001 on jurisdiction and the recognition and enforcement of judgments in civil and commercial matters
CA	Central America
CACM	Central American Common Market
CAFTA-FTC	CAFTA-DR Free Trade Commission
CARICOM	Caribbean Community
CARIFORUM	Caribbean Forum

[1]The abbreviations and acronyms of international and bilateral agreements and national laws of Central America are stated in the Table of Legislation.

CBD	Convention on Biological Diversity
CBI	Caribbean Basin Initiative
CCAD	Central American Commission for Environment and Development (*Comisión Centroamericana de Ambiente y Desarrollo*)
CCSS (CR)	Costa Rican Social Security Fund (*Caja Costarricense de Seguro Social*)
ccTLD	Country Code Top-Level Domain
CEPAL	United Nations Economic Commission for Latin America and the Caribbean (*Comisión Económica para América Latina*)
CJEU	Court of Justice of the European Union
CLIP	Conflict of Laws in Intellectual Property
CNR	National Centre of Registers (*Centro Nacional de Registros*)
COMEX	Ministry of Foreign Trade (*Ministerio del Comercio Exterior*)
CONAGEBIO	National Commission for the Management of the Biodiversity (Costa Rica) (*Comisión Nacional para la Gestión de la Biodiversidad*)
CONAP	National Council of Protected Areas (Guatemala) (*Consejo Nacional de Áreas Protegidas*)
CR	Costa Rica
CSJ	Supreme Court of Justice (*Corte Suprema de Justicia*)
CUSTA	Canada-United States Free Trade Agreement
DO	Dominican Republic (abbreviation used in the PCT)
Doha Declaration	Doha Declaration on the TRIPS Agreement and Public Health
DR	Dominican Republic (CAFTA-DR abbreviation and TLD)
DRM	Digital Rights Management
ECLAC	United Nations Economic Commission for Latin America and the Caribbean
EFTA	European Free Trade Association
EPA	Economic Partnership Agreement
EPC	European Patent Convention
EPO	European Patent Office
EUIPO	European Intellectual Property Office (formerly "Office for the Harmonization of the Internal Market," OHIM)
FDI	Foreign Direct Investment
FTA	Free Trade Agreement
FTAA	Free Trade Agreement of the Americas (*Acuerdo de Libre Comercio das Americas*)
GATS	General Agreement on Trade in Services

GATT	General Agreement on Tariffs and Trade
GDP	Gross Domestic Product
GIZ	German Society for International Cooperation (*Deutsche Gesellschaft für Internationale Zusammenarbeit (GIZ) GmbH*)
GMO	Genetically Modified Organisms
GT	Guatemala
HN	Honduras
ICANN	Internet Corporation for Assigned Names and Numbers
ICSID	International Centre for Settlement of Investment Disputes
IFAC-3	Industrial Functional Advisory Committee on Intellectual Property to the USTR (*previous title of the committee*) (see ITAC 15)
ILO	International Labor Organization
IMF	International Monetary Fund
IMPACT	International Medical Products Anti-Counterfeiting Taskforce
INBio	National Biodiversity Institute (Costa Rica) (*Instituto Nacional de Biodiversidad*)
IMPI	Instituto Mexicano de la Propiedad Industrial
IP	Intellectual Property
IP Register	Industrial/Intellectual Property Register (*Registro de Propiedad Industrial/Intelectual*)
IPR	Intellectual Property Rights
ISI	Import Substitution Industrialization
ITAC 15	Industry Trade Advisory Committee on Intellectual Property (*current title of the committee*) (see IFAC-3)
LDC	Least Developed Countries
Mercosur	Southern Common Market (*Mercado Común del Sur*)
MFN	Most Favored Nation
MINAE	Ministry of Environment and Energy (*Ministerio del Ambiente y Energía*)
MINAET	Ministry of Environment, Energy and Telecommunications (*Ministerio del Ambiente, Energía y Telecomunicaciones*)
Ministerio Público	Public prosecution agency
NI	Nicaragua
OECD	Organisation for Economic Cooperation and Development
ONPI	National Industrial Property Office of the Dominican Republic (*Oficina Nacional de la Propiedad Industrial*)
Patent Examiner Manual	Manual for the Organization and Examination of Patent Applications (*Manual de Organización y Examen de*

	Solicitudes de Patentes de Invención de las Oficinas de Propiedad Industrial de los paises del Istmo Centroamericano y la República Dominicana)
PhRMA	Pharmaceutical Research and Manufacturers of America
PIC	Prior Informed Consent
PTO	Patent and Trademark Office
R&D	Research and Development
Sala IV	Constitutional Chamber of the CSJ of Costa Rica
SCCR	WIPO Standing Committee on Copyright and Related Rights
SCT	WIPO Standing Committee on the Law of Trademarks, Industrial Designs and Geographical Indications
SICA	Central American Integration System (*Sistema de la Integración Centroamericana*)
SME	Small and Medium-Sized Enterprise
SSFFC	Substandard, spurious, falsely labelled, falsified and counterfeit (medicines)
SV	El Salvador
TCB Committee	Committee on Trade Capacity Building (established under CAFTA-DR)
TLD	Top-Level Domain
TPA	Trade Promotion Agreement
TRA	Administrative Register Tribunal (*Tribunal Registral Administrativo*) (Costa Rica)
Trademark Directive	Directive (EC) 2008/95/EC of 22 October 2008 to approximate the laws of the Member States relating to trade marks, as amended by Directive (EU) 2015/2436 of 16 December 2015
Trademark Manual	Harmonized Manual regarding Trademark Criteria (*Manual armonizado en materia de criterios de marca*)
Trademark Regulation	Regulation (EC) 207/2009 of 26 February 2009 on the Community trademark, as amended by Regulation (EU) 2015/2424 of 16 December 2015
TPP	Trans-Pacific Partnership
TTIP	Transatlantic Trade and Investment Partnership
U.S.C.	United States Code
UCR	University of Costa Rica
UDRP	Uniform Domain-Name Dispute-Resolution Policy
UNCTAD	United Nations Conference on Trade and Development
UNED	National University for Distance Education (*Univerisdad Estatal a Distancia*)
UPOV	International Union for the Protection of New Varieties of Plants

USAID	United States Agency for International Development
USD	United States Dollars
USDOS	United States Department of State
USPTO	United States Patent and Trademark Office
USTR	United States Trade Representative
WHO	World Health Organization
WTO	World Trade Organization

List of Figures

List of Tables

Chapter 1
Introduction

1.1 Central America in the TRIPS-plus Era

In the 1990ies, the shift in international economic policy toward free trade and the end of the cold war opened up the global economic system. One important consequence of this change was the establishment of the World Trade Organization (WTO). Its members not only concluded agreements to liberalize trade in goods and services (GATT, GATS), but also the *Agreement on Trade-Related aspects of Intellectual Property Rights* (TRIPS). Subsequently, the USA and the EU started to sign bilateral free trade agreements (FTAs) with other countries, in particular developing countries, to further liberalize trade and raise the level of intellectual property (IP) protection in these countries, which was considered still insufficient by US and European businesses, beyond TRIPS.[1] This type of increased IP protection, therefore, became known as "TRIPS-plus". It made the protection of IP rights an issue on the international political agenda and was invoked by critics as one of the main examples of the problematic way in which globalization progressed. This discussion about the right level of IP protection was and remains quite intense, because its front line runs particularly between developed and developing countries.[2] Many legal and economic scholars as well as non-governmental organizations (NGOs) argue that strong IP protection, especially the patent law and data exclusivity provisions in such FTAs, benefited only the developed countries. In particular, they claim that these rules would result in higher, "unaffordable" prices for life-saving drugs.[3] Also, these rules are expected by critics to prevent developing

---

[1] See Sect. 1.4.

[2] Cornish et al. (2013) at Nr 1-36.

[3] See, e.g., economist and Nobel laureate *Joseph Stiglitz*, Stiglitz (2006), p. 7.

F. Böttger, *CAFTA-DR, European Free Trade Agreements and the Industrial Property System in Central America*, Munich Studies on Innovation and Competition 21, https://doi.org/10.1007/978-3-031-93440-7_1

countries from "closing the knowledge gap" by restricting the transfer of technology from industrial to developing countries.[4]

These issues were raised also with regard to the *Dominican Republic – Central America – United States Free Trade Agreement* (CAFTA-DR) between Costa Rica, El Salvador, Guatemala, Honduras, and Nicaragua (the Central American countries), the Dominican Republic and the USA. In Central America, after several economically and politically "lost decades" marked by internal conflicts and foreign interventions, relative social and political stability was restored in the early 1990ies. The internal economic opening in the region coincided with global economic developments, and all countries of the region became members of the WTO, and, therefore, TRIPS in 1995. Almost ten years later, in August 2004, the United States, Costa Rica, the Dominican Republic, El Salvador, Guatemala, Honduras, and Nicaragua signed CAFTA-DR, which includes rules on IP rights typical for "TRIPS-plus" FTAs.

While in most Central American countries the ratification process was swift, in Costa Rica, the fierce opposition by public interest groups and local businesses forced the government to hold a referendum, on 7 October 2007, on the ratification of CAFTA-DR, the second referendum ever held in this country, after the referendum on independence in 1822. Critics of the agreement focused in particular on patent protection and its effect on public health, the impact of the new IP regime on the country's efforts to protect and exploit its biodiversity and the implementation of the International Convention for the Protection of New Varieties of Plants (UPOV Convention), which allegedly "enslaves" local farmers.[5] Supporters on the other hand hailed CAFTA-DR as the new benchmark of international trade policy[6] and suggested that the IP provisions should be the new "base line" for future IP-related agreements.[7] This intense public debate on IP issues in Costa Rica was somewhat surprising, because of the technical nature of the subject and the fact that IP rights, especially patents, have traditionally been of limited practical importance in Central America.[8]

Subsequently, the Central American countries concluded bilateral FTAs with the European Union, on the one hand the Dominican Republic and other Caribbean

---

[4] Stiglitz (2006), p. 57.

[5] The negotiation history of CAFTA-DR is further discussed in Sect. 2.2.1.

[6] "A Trade Agreement for the Digital Age: state-of-the-art protection and non-discriminatory treatment are provided for digital products such as U.S. software, music, text, and videos. Protections for U.S. patents, trademarks and trade secrets are strengthened", USTR, CAFTA Policy Brief (2005).

[7] In the introduction to its report to the USTR, the Industry Functional Advisory Committee on IPR for Trade Policy Matters (IFAC-3) expressed its expectation that the level of IP rights protection reached in CAFTA-DR be made the new precedent no less than six times on four pages: "the agreement establishes a number of key precedents", "model FTA IP text", "strong precedents", "clear precedents", "set a new base line for all future FTAs", "establishes precedents", see IFAC-3 (2004), pp. 3–6.

[8] See in particular the statistics on patent applications and registrations in the region, see Sect. 3.1.7.

countries the EU-CARIFORUM-EPA, which is applicable since 2008, and on the other hand the Central American countries (including Panama) the EU-CA-AA, which is applicable since 2013 (collectively the EU-FTAs).[9]

Now, the statutory reforms caused by CAFTA-DR and the EU-CARIFORUM-EPA have been in place for more than fifteen years, and the statutory reforms caused by the EU-CA-AA for about ten years. This thesis attempts an assessment of the long-term impact of these FTAs in Central America, taking into account studies published on their practical effects on intellectual property, trade, public health.

This study analyses the implementation of these FTAs in all Central American countries that are parties to CAFTA-DR to provide a detailed picture of different ways in which FTAs are actually transformed in practice. Furthermore, it will assess not only the statutory, but also the regulatory, institutional and practical implementation, in order to make it a comprehensive contribution to the TRIPS-plus debate. As this study will show, the practical effect of a TRIPS-plus provision in a certain country can be very different from what the text of the respective FTA might require or suggest.

1.2 Focus, Scope and Methodology of the Study

1.2.1 Study Focus on CAFTA-DR and Its Institutional and Practical Effects

1.2.1.1 General Focus

Following this introduction (Chap. 1), Chap. 2 of this study discusses the general legal and institutional framework of IP protection in Central America, as a basis for the following analysis. Chapters 3 to 7 analyze the protection and enforcement of IP rights as provided for by CAFTA-DR and the EU-FTAs and their implementation in Central America. Chapter 8 summarizes the main findings and provides recommendations based on the evaluation of these findings, followed by a brief overall conclusion.

This study analyzes primarily the IP rules in CAFTA-DR and their implementation in Central America. The IP chapters of the EU-CARIFORUM-EPA and the EU-CA-AA are also discussed, however, in less detail. These agreements provide less material regarding the TRIPS-plus issue, because they resulted in much less implementation activities in Central America on both the statutory and institutional level and they are more recent. Therefore, their practical impact is more difficult to assess.

Most of the legal research conducted on "TRIPS-plus" focuses on the review of the text of the respective FTAs, without considering the practical consequences in the affected countries, providing only an "aerial view". Some observers, for instance,

[9] See Sect. 2.3.

support stronger statutory protection and easier enforcement because they focus on high levels of copyright piracy and trademark counterfeiting in consumer product markets (namely fashion apparel, software and entertainment content), often without analyzing whether statutory reforms improve the position of the right holders in practice and whether there are “collateral” effects of stronger enforcement in other areas, *e.g.*, on health care, because the new enforcement options are also available for patents. Conversely, some commentators oppose any increase in protection in developing countries based on a static competition point of view, without taking into account that insufficient IP protection in developing countries may also have negative impact, not only on global innovation, but also on domestic consumers and/or public interest (*e.g.*, in case of counterfeit pharmaceuticals).

However, this approach provides only an incomplete picture. This study, therefore, approaches the TRIPS-plus issues by also taking into account the legislative, institutional and practical implementation in each country. This implementation took place over a long period of time. CAFTA-DR was concluded in 2004 and became effective in most Central American countries in 2006 (by which time most countries had passed the implementation legislation), but in Costa Rica only in early 2009. The EU-CARIFORUM-EPA was provisionally applied in late 2008, the EU-CA-FTA was provisionally applied in 2013. All of these FTAs led to legislative and institutional implementation measures (of varying scope) over a period of several years. Therefore, the full implementation period for the FTAs analyzed in this study spans roughly the decade from 2005 to 2015. It is naturally difficult to monitor all legislative and institutional activities in all Central American countries in relation to all issues addressed in this study, and therefore gaps cannot be fully excluded. However, this long-term view provides a more complete, and hopefully more accurate, picture of the full effect the IP chapters of CAFTA-DR and the EU-FTAs in Central America.

Over the years, for example, it became clear that many legislative changes based on TRIPS were not followed-up by the necessary regulatory or institutional changes and therefore remained practically inoperable, such as test data protection in the Dominican Republic.[10] On the other hand, patent linkage was practically a non-issue in Costa Rica when the legislation was created in 2008, because no pharmaceutical patents had been granted for years; however, in 2013 to 2014, around 100 patents were granted annually, including pharmaceutical patents, which made patent linkage more practically relevant.[11]

1.2.1.2 Research Questions

The overarching question for the analysis of the IP chapter in CAFTA-DR and its implementation in Central America is whether including TRIPS-plus rules in FTAs

---

[10] See Sect. 3.4.2.

[11] For the statistics related to patent applications and grants see Sect. 3.1.7.

is an effective and appropriate approach to shape national IP systems in developing countries or whether this approach should be modified or replaced. This study addresses in particular the following research questions, which can be divided into two groups.

The first group of questions relates to the negotiation of the IP chapter of the FTAs:[12]

- Is the combination of market access and IP rules in a bilateral FTA an effective and appropriate "trade deal"? In particular, (i) what was the impact of negotiating and implementing IP rules as part of a *trade* agreement and (ii) did the Central American countries obtain the expected trade benefits to compensate for the IP concessions?
- Was the negotiation process of the IP chapter fair, transparent and inclusive?
- Did the FTAs lead to a more harmonized IP system?
- Do the FTAs provide for adequate review and change (re-negotiation) procedures?

The second group of questions relates to the implementation and content of the IP chapter of the FTAs:[13]

- How are the IP requirements under the FTAs implemented into the national statutory framework?
- Is the focus of the IP chapter of the FTAs on the statutory protection of IP appropriate and effective in practice? Does it sufficiently address the institutional and practical factors necessary for an effective IP system?
- Does the level of protection in the IP chapter of the FTAs and its implementation support core IP policy objectives and align with related policy objectives (*e.g.*, public health and biological diversity)?
- Do the FTAs provide for an appropriate balance between minimum protection and flexibilities?

1.2.2 *Legal Scope*

1.2.2.1 IP Rights

In terms of *subject matter*, this study addresses IP in the broad sense, based on the scope of TRIPS, but focuses primarily on the IP rights included in CAFTA-DR and (in less detail) the EU-FTAs. CAFTA-DR contains no definition of the term "intellectual property" or "industrial property", unlike some Central American laws.[14] Its scope is to be inferred from the subject matter regulated in the substantive

[12] These questions are discussed in more detail in Sect. 1.5.

[13] These questions are discussed in more detail in Sect. 1.6.

[14] E.g., Article 1(2) IP LAW (SV).

provisions.[15] Accordingly, it comprises trademarks, geographical indications, domain names, copyright, patents and test data.

This study focuses on industrial property and excludes copyright and related rights (including liability of internet service providers), which are also covered by the IP chapter of CAFTA-DR, to allow a more focused and in-depth analysis of the industrial property sections.

CAFTA-DR does not include provisions on utility models, trade names, unfair competition, designs and undisclosed information (other than test data), even though these rights are generally considered part of industrial property. However, this study also, more briefly, discusses these IP rights as well as the enforcement of these rights. On the one hand, as this study will show, some rights which are not affected by TRIPS-plus provisions, while of less importance for the international trade arena, play a significant practical role in Central America. On the other hand, TRIPS-plus provisions do not stand alone, but are applied within the context of the broader IP system and cannot be analyzed adequately without the context of other IP rights. Practitioners in Central America, for instance, sometimes prefer to enforce trademarks and even patents in unfair competition proceedings.[16] Furthermore, design law may overlap with trademark and patent law, so its protection indirectly bears on these rights as well. Therefore, in this study the following areas of IP law are addressed:

- inventions (patents and utility models), plant varieties and test data;
- distinctive signs (trademark, well-known marks, collective and certification marks, geographical indications, *brands*,[17] slogans, distinctive products,[18] domain names, trade names and emblems);
- design law, protection of topographies and unfair competition,
- protection of genetic resources and traditional knowledge, as an area of law not traditionally viewed as part of IP law, but closely connected with patent protection and particularly relevant in Central America, and
- enforcement of IP rights.

1.2.2.2 Substantive and Procedural Aspects of Protection

The specific IP rights will be analyzed according to a common structure. While CAFTA-DR, like TRIPS, does not contain rules on all of these aspects of protection, they nevertheless need to be discussed to give a comprehensive picture of the level of

---

[15] Articles 15.2 through 15.10 CAFTA-DR.

[16] See Sect. 5.4.5.

[17] Brands (*marcas de ganado*) are a region-specific element of the Central American IP system. They protect signs of cattle ranchers burned on the skin of cattle, *i.e.*, serve as brands in the original sense of the word, see Sect. 4.5.

[18] Chapter 3, Article E CAFTA-DR establishes “Bourbon Whiskey” and “Tennessee Whiskey” as “distinctive products” of the USA, creating in effect a special kind of IP right, see Sect. 4.7.

protection established for IP rights in Central America. Also, a coherent structure will make the analysis more easily accessible to the reader. Each section discusses policy considerations and the international and national legislative background of the respective IP right as well as its practical relevance, and the following substantive and procedural topics:

- subject matter (including exceptions),
- requirements (including statutory bars and ownership),
- procedure (application and registration, opposition and cancellation, judicial review),
- term of protection,
- rights (right to use, transfer and contractual licenses, infringement) and exceptions and limitations (*e.g.*, fair use and compulsory licenses).

1.2.2.3 The Term "Intellectual Property"

A brief comment on the "intellectual property" terminology: The protection of "intellectual property" or "industrial property" in international agreements has also been criticized on a fundamental terminological level. The expression *intellectual* or *industrial property rights* has been challenged because the term *property* supposedly creates a terminological link to physical property.[19] As the protection of physical property may be perceived as stronger than that of immaterial rights,[20] the use of the expression *property* is seen as an attempt to promote stronger protection for such rights.[21] Indeed, stronger IP protection has been justified based on the analogy with physical property.[22] But from a legal point of view the term *property* merely indicates that IP rights are absolute rights, with both positive (use) and negative (exclusion) elements, without pre-determining the scope of these rights. Physical property is also subject to its social function, including legal limitations and the possibility of administrative takings (expropriations),[23] therefore the terminological analogy does not preclude any restriction based on social policy considerations.

[19] The discussion is commonly about the broader concept of "intellectual property rights", which encompasses in addition also copyright and neighboring rights. However, this does not affect the point of the discussion.

[20] In Germany, where historically the term "immaterial goods" (*Immaterialgüterrechte*) has been dominant, the adoption of the modern term intellectual property has been opposed by some scholars for this very reason; on this discussion see Götting (2004), pp. 731–736.

[21] Díaz (2008), p. 19.

[22] For example, Straus and Klunker (2007), p. 919, propose the harmonization of patent protection globally based on the "discriminatory treatment of intellectual property rights compared to tangible goods" and implicitly advocate a limitation of the principle of territoriality; for a critical assessment of this line of reasoning see Heath (2008), p. 214.

[23] See, e.g., Article 45 Constitution (CR).

It is also argued that IP should not be considered a *right*, but rather a “privilege” that “has to be argued for”.[24] In this critique, the term *right* refers to *human rights* or “natural rights”, *i.e.*, rights that are “naturally” protected and beyond the grasp of policy-makers, while IP rights are only granted for utility reasons. However, historically the idea that there is a natural right, *e.g.*, with regard to inventions and, therefore, to patents, has been an important justification for IP protection. In many legal systems, including Central America, these rights have a personal (human) right component to it.[25] But even if one pronounces the human rights component *vis-à-vis* the utilitarian objective, the use of the term “right” does not prejudice the possibility to balance or restrict these rights with conflicting human rights or other policy goals.

This discussion is not only of a legal, but also of a political nature, because it affects the “balance between private control and public access”.[26] This issue was particularly controversial in relation to developing countries since the 1960ies, within the context of the “New International Economic Order”, especially in Latin America. At the time, multinational corporations and local economic elites could be found more on the side of “private control”, while many international organizations and scholars could be found more on the side of “public access”. Today, the controversy relates to compulsory licenses instead of expropriations, and the farmer's privilege to utilize protected plant seeds instead of land reform.[27] This historic context and the fact that the sustainable social balance has not yet been found in Central America, even with regard to physical property and social policy in general, sometimes also burdens the discussion about IP policy. Therefore, the term “IP” should be considered politically neutral, and is used as such in this study.

It should also be noted that the term “industrial property” is generally used in Central America when discussing patents and trademarks, whereas the term intellectual property (*propiedad intelectual*) traditionally refers only to copyright law, not to IP law in the wider sense, in which this term is used on the international level. Therefore, in local sources is it always necessary to clarify whether the term “intellectual property” is used in the narrow or wider sense.

---

[24] Ruth Chadwick, cited in EPO (2006), p. 8.

[25] For example, Article 42 Constitution (GT) recognizes “the author’s right and the inventor’s right [...] in their work or invention [...]”.

[26] Díaz (2008), p. 19.

[27] A good example is the UN-Organization for Latin America, CEPAL, which in the 1960 argued for the expropriation of foreign investment and since the 1990ies argues for limitations of foreign IP rights. While the organization publishes few statements itself on the issue, the studies it commissions frequently advocate a restrictive approach to IP policy. A paper published by CEPAL claimed that compulsory licenses are a tool that “must” be used to ensure access to medicines, see Fleury (2013), p. 12.

1.2.3 Geographical Scope and FTAs Covered

Geographically, this study covers the Central American countries that are parties to CAFTA-DR, *i.e.*, Costa Rica, the Dominican Republic, El Salvador, Guatemala, Honduras and Nicaragua.

It also analyzes the two FTAs concluded between the EU and the Central American CAFTA-DR parties, *i.e.*, the EU-CA-AA and the EU-CARIFORUM-EPA. However, these agreements are discussed in less detail than CAFTA-DR, because they had significantly less impact on IP legislation in Central America. The analysis of the EU-FTAs focuses on the comparison with CAFTA-DR and addresses the implementation issues which arose mainly in relation to geographical indications.

The analysis aims at reviewing the legal situation on each topic for all these countries, not least to show (as will be discussed in more detail below) that, despite the goal of CAFTA-DR and the EU-FTAs to create legal harmonization, the legal practice in general and implementation of CAFTA-DR in particular varies substantially in each jurisdiction. However, because of this variety, and the fact that sources are not available in equal measure in each country, not every jurisdiction merits or permits a discussion in equal detail on every issue. For instance, the implementation of certain trademark rules of CAFTA-DR, together with other factors, created a particularly complex statutory regime in Guatemala, which merits a more in-depth analysis, as an example of the unintended consequences of IP "harmonization".[28] Also, while Costa Rica has established an elaborate system of statutory and practical protection of genetic resources, the respective systems in other countries are rudimentary and, therefore, do not provide enough substance for an equally detailed discussion.[29]

1.2.4 Methodology

1.2.4.1 Sources

The starting point of this study is Chapter 15 CAFTA-DR, which contains the IP provisions. Legally, both the English and Spanish texts of the agreement are authentic and equally relevant for interpretation.[30] In this study, the English version was used for the analysis of the TRIPS-plus character of its provisions, the Spanish version for the comparison with the implementation laws.[31]

---

[28] See Sect. 4.1.8.

[29] See Sect. 6.

[30] Article 1 CAFTA-DR.

[31] Generally, there are few differences between the two texts, because most of the specific terminology is literally the same.

The national statutory sources serve as the second basis of this study. International agreements and the pre-existing legislation in Central America were easily and timely available in electronic form online. The reform laws implementing CAFTA-DR became available electronically in local legislative databases or the websites of the IP Registers, and some were made available, with some delay, on the WIPO legislative database. However, consolidated versions of the reformed laws often do not exist. In addition, in Honduras, the IP rules in the CAFTA-DR implementation law did not modify existing provisions and, therefore, exist in parallel to the basic IP laws. In other countries, official consolidated versions are not always available and practitioners sometimes manufactured "consolidated" versions of the IP laws themselves either electronically or by hand (in on instance, as observed by the author, by gluing new sections into their copies of the laws).[32] The direct reference to and use of the reform laws creates the additional problem that new provisions are sometimes referred to by the respective reform law article, not by the original article they amend.

Judicial and administrative decisions are also often not easily accessible. There are projects to collect and publish case-law, but the existing publications and electronic databases are not comprehensive.[33] In addition, there are no local law reviews reporting regularly on developments in jurisprudence. Nevertheless, important decisions of constitutional courts and some decisions of lower courts on IP issues are reported in the local media or by practitioners in legal journals, websites and other sources.

The legal profession in Central America faces significant problems with regard not only to the scarcely available case-law, but also to few secondary sources. Practitioners note "the lack of a culture of reading" and the absence of significant law journals, also because there are few full-time law professors.[34] As a consequence, there is little legal writing by either scholars or practitioners, in particular with regard to IP.[35] The only widely circulated comprehensive publication on industrial property in Central America is the "*Curso en Propiedad Industrial*" by *Bendaña-Guerrero* from Nicaragua, published in 1998, which analyzes primarily Nicaraguan law based on the Central American Convention (Trademarks) and, naturally, addresses neither the TRIPS reforms of 2000 nor the CAFTA-DR reforms.[36] In some countries the basic concepts of trademark law, which is probably the most practically relevant area of IP law in Central America, are sometimes

[32] Observation by the author in 2008.

[33] In Costa Rica, however, the exists a rather comprehensive electronic database with legislation and case-law that can be researched by keyword see https://nexuspj.poder-judicial.go.cr/ (accessed 2 Nov 2024).

[34] Many professors also work in private practice in parallel.

[35] Interestingly, there is a significant number of masters theses and academic papers by law students on specific matters. However, these typically focus on the historical context and comparisons with other jurisdictions, and less on the local legal practice.

[36] This obviously limits the utility of this significant contribution to regional IP law for current practitioners, even though it is still often cited by other authors in the region.

described in commercial law textbooks.[37] This scarcity of publications is partly a consequence of the legal practice, which at least in the field of IP relies to a considerable extend on extrajudicial settlements or agreements and on oral arguments rather than precedent and legal analysis. After CAFTA-DR, however, the number of publications on IP has increased, not least regarding the analysis of CAFTA-DR and its implementation.[38] Helpful sources on Central American law, which are available online, are reports by local practitioners, mostly attorneys publishing legislative updates online, and representatives of the IP Registers or judges, during WIPO regional meetings, which summarize relevant case law in the field of IP. Also, some master theses written at local universities provide information on the current practical status of IP issues in Central America, which are also often available online.

The usefulness of academic publications is often limited—from the perspective of someone trying to research local legal practice—by the fact that authors often focus more on foreign doctrine and legal theory than domestic case-law and doctrine, which is somewhat understandable given the scarcity of the latter.[39] This scarcity is especially felt in an area of law such as IP, which plays only a secondary role in Central American legal practice.[40] Therefore, the lawyers turn to foreign and international sources, especially from Spanish-speaking countries such as Argentina, Colombia and Spain.[41] Spanish doctrine has the advantage—in addition to the language—that the Central American legal system developed out of the legal system of colonial Spain and, therefore, the two legal systems share common principles. This is combined with legal training, e.g., for local IP Register personnel, provided primarily by or even at foreign institutions such as the Spanish Patent and Trademark Office or the USPTO.[42] In sum, the legal literature available in Central America often addresses the national legislation in a cursory way, limiting the practical impact of national laws as well as its reforms.

Because of the relative scarcity of local publications, also unpublished information has been used for this analysis, such as unreported decisions by patent offices, personal interviews with private practitioners, judges, IP Register lawyers and other experts in Costa Rica, El Salvador, Guatemala and Nicaragua as well as personal observations by the author during a study visit to Central America.

---

[37] Observation by the author in 2008.

[38] A good example is Retana Chinchilla (2007), who like Bendaña-Guerrero (1999) discusses case-law and compares the legal system of the various Central American countries.

[39] This problem exists throughout Latin America; it can be noted also in, e.g., Guatemala's neighboring country Mexico, see Grave (2002), p. 19.

[40] As noted above, there are typically no monographies on intellectual property law in Central America. This contrasts with other areas of business law such as corporoate or commercial law, where textbooks are available in each country (observation by the author in 2008).

[41] This approach has been observed by the author in most regional legal literature.

[42] See Sect. 2.5.3.

1.2.4.2 Special Note on References to National Laws and Institutions

As just discussed, this study analyzes the legislative and institutional implementation of the bilateral FTAs in each Central American country in relation to a broad range of IP rights. Accordingly, there are numerous references to national laws and institutions. The title of these laws and institutions are often identical in the different countries. This study uses a simply system of abbreviations to clearly identify which national law or institution these citations and references refer to, but also simplify these citations and references.

Each country is identified by a two letter-acronym, i.e., "CR" for Costa Rica, "DR" for the Dominican Republic, "GT" for Guatemala, "HN" for Honduras, "NI" for Nicaragua and "SV" for El Salvador. Each national law is given an abbreviated title, followed by the country's acronym in brackets. The full title and further information on each law can be found in Sect. 2.4. The Costa Rican Law on Marks and other Distinctive Signs, for example, is referred to as "Trademark Law (CR)". Similarly, the Intellectual Property Register (*Registro de Propiedad Intelectual*) of Guatemala is referred to as "IP Register (GT)".

1.2.4.3 Economic Approach

This study focuses not only on legal analysis, but also on policy and economic considerations. The evaluation of FTAs like CAFTA-DR depends strongly on the assumptions regarding the benefits of (strong) IP protection underlying the respective evaluation. However, the economically most efficient balance and level of protection of IP rights, especially with regard to developing countries, is highly controversial. *Peter Beattie* even suggests that because the results of economic research can usually not be tested, they should be no basis for evaluation.[43] The difficulties relating to the economic analysis have been repeatedly noted by researchers attempting empirical analysis: One meta-study of several economic studies conducted in relation to IP infringement criticized that many studies were unreliable because of "a lack of appreciation [for] principles of measurement and assessment of scale", were "usually contingent on particular technologies and/or sector perspectives", lacked "transparency in the methodologies and data used to form the basis of claims" and were "designed [...] to support the position of the particular commissioning body".[44] Such problems also exist with regard to the estimates of empirical studies, *e.g.*, on the loss of sales due to the infringement of

[43] Beattie (2007), pp. 6 and 14.

[44] Collopy et al. (2014), p. 1.

patents and trademarks.[45] Similar concerns were raised regarding studies on other areas of IP law, namely copyright.[46]

The following problems in particular limit the usefulness of economic analysis: First, many economists use the term "intellectual property" very broadly in their studies, both as regards terminology and as regards the data used: Terminology is used inconsistently or even incorrectly. It is often unclear whether "intellectual property" refers to patents, trademarks, copyright or other rights specifically or collectively. Sometimes it is not made clear whether statistics from patent offices include utility models or trademarks.[47] Second, it is very difficult in empirical economic studies to isolate the effect of specific legal tools. Especially in Central America, the political, social and educational framework has changed so significantly that it is hard to evaluate the effect of, *e.g.*, post-TRIPS patent protection specifically. It is, therefore, necessary to rely on theoretical models, too. Finally, the empirical basis for evidence relating to specific policy measures is relatively small, especially regarding countries of the size and level of development comparable to Central America. A significant restriction to economic analysis is the small size of the samples.[48] This problem is even more acute for studies with specific regard to developing regions such as Central America. A reliable study requires a large enough sample, and in the case of developing countries, there are often few countries sufficiently comparable for analysis which implemented similar IP policies. Also, there exists (not least because of the relatively short time TRIPS and CAFTA-DR have been implemented) little empirical research on the effect of TRIPS protection, and almost none on TRIPS-plus protection in Central America. Furthermore, the Central American countries are often neglected in regional studies on IP protection and/or international trade. Most studies on Latin America focus on larger countries, namely Brazil, Mexico, Argentina, Colombia, Chile and Peru. There are very few publications on the economic effects of the implementation of CAFTA-DR, which have been analyzed in this study, but it is, of course, difficult to validate the findings of one study without additional sources.

---

[45] For example, the Special 301 Report 2005 states that "losses to U.S. industries alone are estimated at $200-$250 billion per year", see USTR Special 301 Report (2005), p. 3; a study by the OECD and the EUIPO estimated losses to counterfeiting in 2013 of 461 billion USD or 2,5% of global trade, see OECD/EUIPO (2016).

[46] The difficulties in the related copyright field can be reviewed in the controversy over alleged losses of the US music industry, see the study by IPI (2007) and a critical review of the study by iRights.info, available at https://irights.info/artikel/neue-us-studie-zu-den-folgen-der-bdquomusikpiraterie/6319 (accessed 2 Nov 2024).

[47] For this section, both patent-specific and general intellectual property-related literature was used.

[48] Lederman and Maloney (2003), p. 13, point out that there are generally "very few studies of the determinants of R&D across countries" and caution that such studies "suffer from small samples and, as result, inconsistent estimates due to inability to deal with country-specific effects" (the authors refer to, e.g., the studies of Varsakelis (2001) and Bebczuk (2002)).

1.3 Putting Central America on the Map

Before discussing the TRIPS-plus issue and the specific research questions in more detail (Sects. 1.5 and 1.6), this chapter provides geographic, historic and socio-economic background on Central America, which is important to understand the context of CAFTA-DR and its implementation.

1.3.1 Geography

Geographically, Central America is the thin land bridge (the "isthmus") between North and South America. It consists of the seven countries (from North to South) Belize, Guatemala, Honduras, El Salvador, Nicaragua, Costa Rica and Panama. In this study, the term "Central America" refers only to Costa Rica, El Salvador, Guatemala, Honduras and Nicaragua, the parties to CAFTA-DR (and usually also includes the Dominican Republic). The position as the geographical link between North and South America, the Pacific Ocean and the Caribbean Sea (and the Atlantic) makes it an important geographic building block in the Western hemisphere. The topography of Central America is dominated by small valleys and tall volcanic mountain ranges, compartmentalizing the countries. This "challenging geography" complicates interstate trade and the creation of a regional market and infrastructure.[49]

The climate is favorable to agriculture and enables large-scale production of coffee, cocoa, bananas, sugar, corn and other foodstuff. As a consequence, the economies traditionally rely strongly on such agricultural commodities.[50] These can be easily traded across the oceans (Fig. 1.1).

Belize and Panama are often considered not to be part of Central America in the narrow politically sense, and both are not parties to CAFTA-DR. Belize used to be part of Guatemala, but was colonized by English and Scottish settlers and became *de facto* and later *de jure* part of the British Empire. It remained a British colony until 1981 and is still part of the Commonwealth.[51] Panama did not become a member of the Central American Federation in 1823, because it was at that time still a part of Colombia.[52] The Panama Canal connecting the Pacific Ocean and the Caribbean Sea led to a distinct economic and political development in this country and a strong presence of the USA, including interventions supporting an independence movement, which caused ultimately the separation of Panama from Colombia.[53] However, while Panama is no CAFTA-DR party, it is party to the EU-CA-AA.

---

[49] Reid (2007), p. 24.

[50] Reid (2007), pp. 83–84.

[51] For more information on the history of Belize see Booth et al. (2006), p. 4 and p. 48.

[52] On the Central American Federation, see Sect. 1.3.

[53] Reid (2007), p. 88; Booth et al. (2006), p. 48 and p. 178.

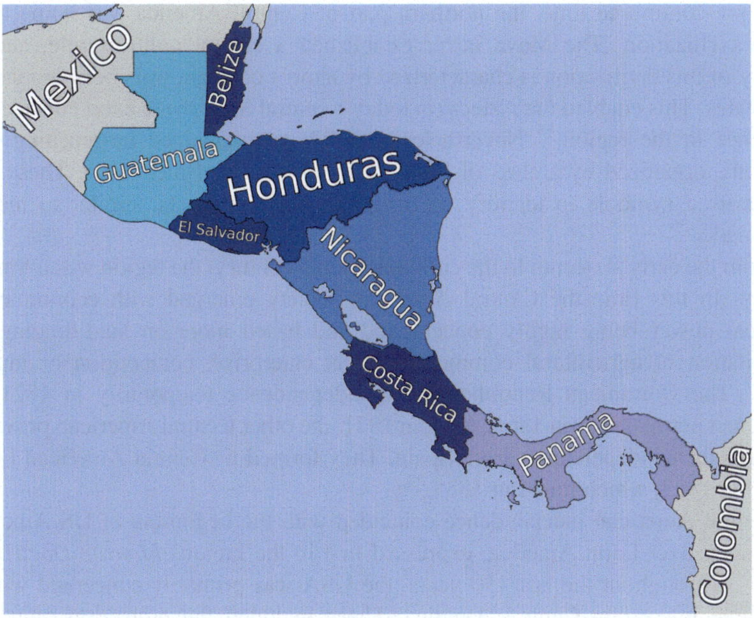

Fig. 1.1 Map of Central America. (Luveha, 2019). CC BY-SA 4.0

Geographically and historically, the Dominican Republic is part of the Caribbean region and not of Central America. It is the eastern part of the island of Hispaniola, the western part of which is Haiti. It was included among the members of CAFTA-DR because it is economically more developed than other Caribbean countries and similar to Central America. However, it is not a member of the EU-CA-AA, but is part of the group of Caribbean countries which concluded the EU-CARIFORUM-EPA with the EU. For simplification, the term "Central America" in this study includes the Dominican Republic as well, unless noted otherwise.

1.3.2 History

In his highly instructive book "Forgotten Continent: The Battle for Latin America's Soul", *Michael Reid* comments that "Guatemala is the saddest country in Latin America".[54] This provocative remark, which could similarly be applied to other Central American countries, refers to the opportunities for development which existed in the region earlier in history, but which were missed because of internal conflicts and foreign interventions in the twentieth century and their detrimental effects on economic and social development.

[54] Reid (2007), p. 81.

In pre-columbine time, the northern part of Central America was home to the Maya civilization. The Maya never established a central political rule, and the history of this civilization is characterized by almost constant wars between various city-states. This enabled the Aztecs (in today's central Mexico) to exert considerable influence in the region.[55] Nevertheless, the Maya maintained far-reaching trade relations, organized by a class of influential and respected merchants. These merchants used symbols to identify the origin of their products, similar to modern trademarks.[56]

From the early sixteenth to the early nineteenth century, the region was a Spanish colony. In this time the Central American society emerged with economic and political power being highly concentrated and based more on land-holding and exploitation of agricultural commodities than enterprise, competition or innovation.[57] The Dominican Republic gained independence temporarily in 1821 and 1844, and permanently in 1865. Also, in 1821, the other Central American provinces declared their independence from Spain. They formed a "Central American Federation" in 1823, which failed in 1838.[58]

Central American independence coincided with the beginning of US-American hegemony over Latin America, expressed first in the famous *Monroe Doctrine* of 1823.[59] Throughout the last 150 years, the USA was primarily concerned with its economic interest in Central America. These included the protection of trading enterprises such as the United Fruit Company and preventing competition from third countries.[60] But during the twentieth century, the USA also frequently intervened in almost all Central American countries, primarily to prevent communist satellite states. Central America experienced autocratic or military rule in the Dominican Republic (1930–1961 and 1966–1996) and Honduras (1957–1982),[61] and civil wars or internal conflicts in the Dominican Republic (1965–1966), El Salvador (1980–1992), Guatemala (1960–1996) and Nicaragua (1979–1990).[62]

---

[55] For more information, see the entry on Pre-Columbian Central in the Encyclopaedia Britannica, available at https://www.britannica.com/place/Central-America/Pre-Columbian-Central-America (accessed 2 Nov 2024).

[56] On many pottery products from the Mayan era there are stamps from the manufacturer, which were, according to the staff of the anthropology museum of San Salvador, used in trade as the identification of the origin of the product for the consumer, much like modern trademarks (observations by the author in 2008). However, some observers consider the use of distinctive symbols in Central America in pre-colonial times as merely decorative, because the economic structure did not require or permit the use of trademarks, see Lobos Luna (2012), pp. 8 and 32.

[57] Reid (2007), pp. 83–84.

[58] Perez-Brignoli (1989), p. XI. However, this period survives in the reference "in Central America" in the codes of arms of Costa Rica, El Salvador and Nicaragua.

[59] Reid (2007), pp. 86–88.

[60] Reid (2007), p. 84.

[61] On Honduras, see Booth et al. (2006), p. 135; on the Dominican Republic, see Reid (2007), p. 99.

[62] On the Dominican Republic, see Reid (2007), p. 99; on Guatemala, see Reid (2007), p. 85; the current view in Guatemala is that the conflict was not only a political civil war, but also included

Only Costa Rica enjoyed relative political stability and democracy during the second half of the twentieth century.[63] The most recent intervention occurred during the 1980ies in Nicaragua, when the USA financed the right-wing military opposition (the *Contras*) against the socialist Sandinista government, which was led by *Daniel Ortega* (partly with money from an *extralegal* arms sale to Iran).[64] *Daniel Ortega* was President of Nicaragua from 1985 to 1990 and was re-elected President in 2007, which—incidentally—made him the President to sign CAFTA-DR. The conflict ended with a peace plan known as the *Esquipulas II Accord*, which was signed in Guatemala City by the five Central American presidents on 7 August 1987. The plan was created by *Óscar Arias*, who was the President of Costa Rica from 1986 to 1990 and again from 2006 to 2010, during which time he also signed CAFTA-DR.

When the danger of the emergence of communist satellite states in the region disappeared after 1989, the USA sought political influence and regional stability again primarily through economic cooperation and integration, including free trade agreements.[65] During the 1990ies, political stability increased throughout the region. The economic transformation was accompanied by democratic debates and peaceful changes of government. Nevertheless, the military and economic interventions by the USA had profound consequences on the Central American countries. They affected the political and social development and created an ambivalent political relationship towards the USA, marked on the one side by skepticism and opposition, which also affects the implementation of CAFTA-DR in practice, but on the other hand a desire to comply with US-American interests at least on the surface to avoid conflict.[66]

The nation-building and democratization process is still ongoing. Especially in Guatemala and El Salvador, the strong tensions between different social and ethnic groups continue.[67] The difficult situation is evidenced by the high annual murder rate, which exceeded 100 (per 100.000 inhabitants) in El Salvador in 2015, making it the highest rate in the world at the time; by 2021 the rates have gone down to 20 (per 100.000 inhabitants) in Guatemala and El Salvador, which nevertheless is high by international standards.[68] In Honduras, on 28 June 2009, President *Manuel Zelaya*

---

ethnic elements in relation to the indigenous Maya population; the history of this conflict was analyzed in detail in Comisión para el Esclarecimiento Histórico (1999).

[63] Booth et al. (2006), p. 57; notably, in 1949, the President dissolved the armed forces, see Reid (2007), p. 273.

[64] See Reid (2007), p. 101.

[65] The National Security Strategy of the United States of America (September 2002), p. 18, specifically refers to FTAs in the Western Hemisphere as part of the USA's "national security through global prosperity" policy, available at https://2009-2017.state.gov/documents/organization/63562.pdf (accessed 2 Nov 2024).

[66] See Sect. 2.2.1.2.

[67] Regarding Guatemala, see e.g. Booth et al. (2006), pp. 128–131; regarding El Salvador, see e.g. Booth et al. (2006), p. 113.

[68] See data provided by the World Bank, available at https://data.worldbank.org/indicator/VC.IHR.PSRC.P5?locations=HN-SV-GT (accessed 2 Nov 2024).

was forced out of office by a parliamentary-military coalition after he had started to prepare a referendum to have the constitution changed to enable him to serve for a second term. This event led to (temporary) international isolation, one consequence of which was the temporary suspension of the EU-CA-AA negotiations between the EU and the Central American countries.[69] Following the 2013 parliamentary elections and political improvements, the EU-CA-AA was implemented.[70]

The security situation also improved in Honduras as shown by the reduction of the murder rate from around 85 (per 100.000 inhabitants) in 2010–2013 to around 60 (per 100.000 inhabitants) in 2014–2015 (making it the second highest rate in the world after El Salvador at the time) and by 2021 the rate has gone down to 20 (per 100.000 inhabitants).[71]

Costa Rica and the Dominican Republic remain politically more stable. The stability and the economic development earned Costa Rica the nickname "Switzerland of Central America". Fundamental political reforms in the 1940ies paved the way for this success story. The dissolution of the military freed financial resources which were allocated by the constitution to be used for education. Social programs also promoted education and equality.[72] The relatively well-educated workforce and the political stability helped the country in its technological and social development. This development attracted many immigrants from Nicaragua, who constitute about 7% of the country's population (as reported in 2024) and create new social and also economic tensions.[73]

1.3.3 General Socio-Economic Framework

As just noted, the geographical proximity enabled the USA to obtain and increase political, economic and military influence in the region throughout the late nineteenth and the twentieth century, in order to protect its interests. Some observers in Central America, based on this experience, perceive CAFTA-DR as another measure of the USA to exert its influence in the region. This influence is based on the relatively small size and the lower level of economic development of Central America, which means that the respective markets differ and which impacts the bargaining power the Central American countries had during the negotiations of CAFTA-DR. As a comparison, as shown in Table 1.1, the per capita GDP of the USA is 6–8 times higher than Costa Rica's and the Dominican Republic's, about

[69] See European Parliament (2011), p. 15.

[70] See Sect. 2.3.1.

[71] See data provided by the World Bank, available at https://data.worldbank.org/indicator/VC.IHR.PSRC.P5?locations=HN-SV-GT (accessed 2 Nov 2024).

[72] Booth et al. (2006), p. 57.

[73] On this issue see Reid (2007), p. 221; for data see https://www.cia.gov/the-world-factbook/countries/costa-rica/ (accessed 2 Nov 2024).

Table 1.1 Basic Data on Central America

Country	Population (in millions)	Territory (in sq. km.)	Annual GDP (in billion USD)	Annual GDP (per capita, in USD)
Costa Rica	5.1	51,000	65	12,700
Dominican R.	11.1	48,000	94	8500
El Salvador	6.3	21,000	29.5	4700
Guatemala	17	109,000	86	5100
Honduras	10.3	112,000	28.5	2800
Nicaragua	6.8	129,000	14	2100
Central America (total)	56,6	470,000	314	5600
USA	332	9,000,000	23,315	70,200

The data is rounded and current as of 2021 (the most recent available year); data was obtained from the World Bank database, available at https://data.worldbank.org/country/. Accessed 2 Nov 2024

Table 1.2 GDP Growth in Central America in Billion USD, based on data provided by the World Bank, available at https://data.worldbank.org/country/ (accessed 2 Nov 2024)

	GDP 2005	Growth rate 2005–2010	GDP 2010	Growth rate 2010–2014	GDP 2014
Costa Rica	20.0	81,5%	36.3	36,4%	49.5
Dom. Rep.	34.0	58,5%	53.9	18,7%	64.0
El Salvador	17.1	25,1%	21.4	17,3%	25.1
Guatemala	27.2	51,8%	41.3	42,1%	58.7
Honduras	9.6	64,6%	15.8	22,8%	19.4
Nicaragua	6.3	38,1%	8.7	35,6%	11.8
USA	13.000	15,4%	15.000	15,3%	17.300

15 times higher than El Salvador's and Guatemala's and about 25 times higher than Honduras' and Nicaragua's per capita GDP. In total, the size of the US economy is about 75 times the size of the combined economies of the Central American countries (including the Dominican Republic).

Trade between the USA and Central America is strong, not least because the economic structure is partly complementary. Central America was the second largest destination of US exports in Latin America (after Mexico) before the entry into force of CAFTA-DR and remains one of the major trade partners of the USA in Latin America.[74] The regional economy experienced significant economic growth in the decade after CAFTA-DR entered into force, as shown in Table 1.2. However, there is neither conclusive evidence that CAFTA-DR had a significant impact on this growth nor that it did not. Table 1.2 shows that the economic development varies

[74] See data available at https://ustr.gov/trade-agreements/free-trade-agreements/cafta-dr-dominican-republic-central-america-fta (accessed 2 Nov 2024).

significantly among the CAFTA-DR members, which is partly due to significant differences in the growth rate of the population.

All Central American CAFTA-DR countries are considered developing countries, but not "Least Developed Countries" (LDC); according to the OECD, Costa Rica and the Dominican Republic are "Upper Middle Income Countries" and the four other countries "Lower Middle Income Countries".[75] The per capita GDP of Costa Rica or the Dominican Republic is several times that of Nicaragua or Honduras.[76] Inflation remains a problem in several countries. In response, El Salvador adopted the US dollar as the official currency in 2001 (El Salvador is probably most closely linked to the US in terms of trade) and other countries introduced the US dollar as a secondary currency.[77]

The migration within Central America and from Central America to third countries has profound economic consequences. Almost 7% of Nicaraguans are estimated to live in Costa Rica.[78] In 2007, between 20% and 30% of Guatemalans and Salvadoreans lived in the USA, and an increasing number in Mexico and Spain.[79] For many years, this eased the demographic pressure in Central America, and the monetary remittances became an important source of income in several Central American countries, almost equal to revenues from exports, making up, in 2007, between 20 % and 35% of the national GDP (depending on the country).[80] By 2021 this situation had not significantly changed, with remittances to Honduras being an estimated 25% and to Guatemala being an estimated 18% (no later data was available).[81]

Apart from these remittances, the main export and source of income of Central American countries are agricultural and other primary sector products, especially coffee and bananas, but also other fruits, sugar, and palm oil, as well as gold and copper.[82] The share of primary sector exports (agricultural products and natural resources) between 2005 and 2020 was 20–30% in the Dominican Republic, about 35–45% in Costa Rica, about 35% in El Salvador, about 65–70%) in Honduras, about 55–60% in Guatemala and 55% (until 2011)—85% (since 2012) in Nicaragua.[83]

---

[75] A list of LDC can be found on the UN website, available at https://www.un.org/development/desa/dpad/wp-content/uploads/sites/45/publication/ldc_list.pdf (accessed 2 Nov 2024).

[76] See Sect. 1.3.1.

[77] Rodlauer and Schipke (2005), p. 4, Box 1.1.

[78] As of 2016, the last year for which data could be found, see https://www.cia.gov/the-world-factbook/countries/costa-rica/ (accessed 2 Nov 2024).

[79] Colburn and Cruz (2007), p. 55.

[80] Ibid.

[81] The data was obtained from the World Bank database, available at https://data.worldbank.org/country/ (accessed 2 Nov 2024).

[82] The main "non-primary" exception is medical equipment; see the data available at https://www.statista.com (accessed 2 Nov 2024).

[83] See the data available at https://www.statista.com (accessed 2 Nov 2024).

Only Costa Rica and the Dominican Republic have a more diverse economy, because of the more developed tourism sector and especially in Costa Rica the manufacturing industry, enabled by the better qualified workforce in these countries. For many years, microprocessors were one of Costa Rica's biggest export goods, after Intel invested several hundred million USD to build a microprocessor plant in the town of Heredia in 1997.[84] A series of investments by US companies and domestic undertakings made medical products another major export.[85] The Intel microprocessor plant was closed in 2014 and the manufacturing was moved to Southeast Asia, but shortly afterwards Intel established an R&D unit in Costa Rica for microprocessor development.[86] While the latter did not compensate fully the job loss and economic impact, it could be a sign of Costa Rica making inroads into the knowledge-based economy. By contrast, several countries created free trade zones to attract foreign business and create jobs, but the work in the factories in these zones (called *maquilas*) is basic and sometimes paid below the minimum wage and in addition seems not to have led to any transfer of the technologies used in production.[87] The pharmaceutical industry is of particular relevance in relation to the TRIPS-plus debate and particularly the access to medicines. In Central America, *e.g.*, Costa Rica, the Dominican Republic and Guatemala have developed a domestic generic drug industry, which heavily opposed the ratification and implementation of CAFTA-DR.[88]

1.3.4 IP-Related Socio-Economic Framework

In Central America, the technological and socio-economic framework inhibits local innovation. Probably the most important factor influencing the capacity to innovate and the feasibility of technology transfer and imitation is education. The educational framework providing the skills to develop and absorb new technologies should complement the legal framework.[89] Studies show that education influences cross-country differences in innovation.[90] It is not surprising that there is also empirical evidence that the quality of public research institutions affects innovation.[91] The

[84] See http://www.ticotimes.net/2014/04/08/intel-to-close-costa-rica-chip-assembly-plant-lay-off-1500-workers (accessed 2 Nov 2024).

[85] CIA, World Factbook, Costa Rica, available at https://www.cia.gov/the-world-factbook/countries/costa-rica/ (accessed 2 Nov 2024).

[86] *The Economist*, Intel Outside, 19 April 2014, available at http://www.economist.com/news/americas/21600985-chipmaker-shuts-factory-slicing-away-one-fifth-countrys-exports-intel-outside (accessed 2 Nov 2024).

[87] See https://dailybrief.oxan.com/Analysis/DB116827 (accessed 2 Nov 2024).

[88] See Sect. 3.1.1.4.

[89] See, e.g., Stiglitz (2006), pp. 32–33.

[90] Jaramillo and Lederman (2005), p. 4.

[91] Lederman and Maloney (2003), p. 4.

development both in Europe and the USA and the newly developed countries in Asia underlines the important role of public promotion and funding of research and innovation.[92] Conversely, the underdevelopment of such institutions limits the possibility of innovation, irrespective of the legal protection of IP rights. The World Bank identified education and research as the most important elements that needed improvement in Central America.[93] Literacy rates in the region are relatively low compared to other countries in Latin America.[94]

Technological advance in Central America occurs in particular in the agricultural sector, but even there, the professional utilization of innovations or protection of inventions is not developed.[95] An additional problem is the fact that much technology going into the agricultural sector is not appropriately measured by R&D statistics and innovation relating to agricultural technology is not adequately assessed. Therefore, one might underestimate the relevance of patents and innovation in agrarian economies, even though there are studies suggesting that innovation in this sector might increase productivity more than in manufacturing.[96] Central America is a good example, because inventions in the agricultural field is not strategically protected and exploited. This can reinforce the perception that the region is not innovative and Central American countries should focus on policies enabling imitation of foreign technology. However, the relationship between patents, innovation and agriculture is important, because the Central American economies strongly depend on the primary sector.[97] Much of the respective research done in Central America is not protected by patents and economically exploited by the inventor or the research institution, because of reservations within the local scientific community. In the context of CAFTA-DR, it is important to remember that the competitiveness of US agricultural exports is not only based on subsidies, but also higher, technology-based productivity.[98]

In the pharmaceutical industry, particularly affected by the TRIPS-plus provisions in CAFTA-DR, there is little innovative capacity in the Central America countries. In, e.g., Costa Rica and Guatemala, there exists a significant domestic generic pharmaceutical industry, but even in Costa Rica, arguably the most advanced country in terms of manufacturing capabilities, there is little capability of manufacturing pharmaceutical compounds, and in Guatemala only formulation of

[92] Stiglitz (2006), p. 27.

[93] Jaramillo and Lederman (2005), p. 10; for further analysis and recommendations see Rodlauer and Schipke (2005), pp. 3 and 5.

[94] According to data collected by the World Bank, the literacy rate is around 80% in Guatemala and Nicaragua compared to, e.g., around 95% in Mexico, see data.worldbank.org (accessed 2 Nov 2024).

[95] Interviews with *Ana Catalina Monge Rodríguez* and *Carlos Castillo*.

[96] Lederman and Maloney (2003), p. 19, citing UNESCO, Statistical Yearbook 1980, p. 743.

[97] See Sect. 1.3.3.

[98] Lederman and Maloney (2003), p. 13.

imported pharmaceutical compounds is possible.[99] The primary material must typically be imported from third countries (especially India).[100] Therefore, Central American companies or universities benefit little from patent protection, and less from the additional protection created by CAFTA-DR through patent term extensions, patent linkage and test data protection.

Another challenge is that during decades of internal conflicts in the region, power was not always channeled through legal institutions like property, contracts, courts and lawyers, which make the exercise of power transparent and foreseeable, but sometimes rested with "factual powers", e.g., militias which turned into criminal organizations after the end of these conflicts, which engage in, e.g., (narcotic) drugs and weapons trade and relies on political patronage and corruption.[101] But organized crime groups sometimes also engage in (trademark) counterfeiting activities, *e.g.*, by manufacturing or selling counterfeit brand products.[102]

While the extent of this connection is disputed, there is at least one noteworthy alleged connection between organized crime, corruption, and trademark counterfeiting in Guatemala. Several international shoe manufacturers released public statements claiming that one of the businesses of a family member of a former president served as a front for the importation and distribution of pirated athletic shoes.[103] He was arrested in 2018 on corruption charges.[104]

However, the counterfeiting industry is not always linked to organized crime, but is often run by "cottage industries" in remote rural areas.[105] The workshops often consist of a few sowing machines in the back room of an apartment, hidden from law enforcement as much as from competitors or gangs looking to extort "protection money", and the families running such businesses operate carefully and

---

[99] In Costa Rica, around 2015–2016 there were few local manufacturers capable of manufacturing and even developing drugs, see the report by The Central American Group, available at https://www.thecentralamericangroup.com/pharmaceutical-manufacturing-costa-rica/ (accessed 2 Nov 2024); a study published in 2022 found that several countries exported pharmaceuticals, vaccines (mainly Nicaragua) and biologics (mainly Costa Rica), but from the data provided it is unclear if these exports related to locally produced products or came from regional distribution centers, see Vargas (2022), p. 14.

[100] India was the largest foreign supplier of pharmaceutical products to Central America other than "originator" countries like the US, Germany and Switzerland (and Mexico) in 2016, see https://www.centralamericadata.com/en/product/inteligenciaComercialReporte/7067995 (accessed 2 Nov 2024).

[101] Regarding the current situation of organized crime in Central America see United Nations Office on Drugs and Crime, Transnational Organized Crime in Central America and the Caribbean: A Threat Assessment, September 2012, available at https://www.unodc.org/documents/data-and-analysis/Studies/TOC_Central_America_and_the_Caribbean_english.pdf (accessed 2 Nov 2024).

[102] OECD (2007), p. 17.

[103] Thomas (2011), pp. 64–65.

[104] See the report by *Prensa Libre*, https://www.prensalibre.com/guatemala/justicia/rey-del-tenis-sergio-roberto-lopez-villatoro-capturado-magistrado-giovanni-orellana-donis-mp-cicig-corrupcion/ (accessed 2 Nov 2024).

[105] See Sect. 4.1.9.

secretively.[106] The informal economy plays an important role in all Central American countries, also with regard to products protected by IP rights (including copyright). IP piracy is a widely accepted practice on the local level.[107] The street vendors in Guatemala have sold counterfeit goods such as tennis shoes, handbags, pharmaceuticals, CDs and DVDs and "cloned" books.[108] This business structure creates challenges to IP enforcement and makes it difficult to enforce IP rights "at the source". The size of the counterfeit market and the resulting problems for the enforcement of rights make it a great concern for practitioners and business representatives.[109] This practice may in many cases not be a consumer protection issue, because purchasers of "pirated" apparel on street markets are often aware that the goods are not original.[110] However, while this system might seem to provide poor people with cheap products, there are significant side effects. In particular, the sale of some counterfeit goods, especially medicines, creates a significant risk for consumer health and safety.[111] Addressing counterfeiting of medicines is, therefore, a focus of local law enforcement.[112]

Moreover, the state loses millions in value added tax (VAT).[113] This is a significant problem, because VAT is an important source of income in the chronically under-funded Central American countries.[114] Also, the official stores loose sales and often do not survive the competition with street vendors selling counterfeit products, which means that regular jobs are lost and are replaced by street jobs without economic or social safety.[115] In addition, many children are employed as street vendors. Because of the low margins and competition, they make little money, but forsake schooling and thus any chance for decent employment later on.

---

[106] Thomas (2011), p. 29.

[107] Thomas (2011), pp. 64–65.

[108] Observation by the author in 2008; see also Thomas (2011), p. 65.

[109] The estimate regarding the economic scope is around several hundred million USD, e.g., USTR Special 301 Report (2005), p. 3, and Thomas (2011), p. 3.

[110] Thomas (2011), p. 3 (fn 4).

[111] Matthews (2011), p. 51.

[112] For example, according to USTR Special 301 Report (2011), the interagency working group on IP rights in Guatemala focuses its training efforts on counterfeit medicines; see also the enforcement action related to counterfeit medicines in the Dominican Republic, Sect. 7.1.2.2.

[113] On this issue see Frontier Economics, The economic impacts of counterfeiting and piracy, p. 48, available at https://www.inta.org/wp-content/uploads/public-files/perspectives/industry-research/2017_Frontier_Report.pdf (accessed 2 Nov 2024); see further references in Thomas (2011), p. 69.

[114] In Guatemala, taxes and other revenues of the state account for 10.0% of GDP in 2020 (the last year for which data was available), which is among the lowest shares in the world; according to the CIA World Factbook, Guatemala ranks 197 out of 222, see https://www.cia.gov/the-world-factbook/countries/guatemala/#economy (accessed 2 Nov 2024).

[115] OECD (2007), p. 17.

According to estimates, Guatemala ranks first in Central America in sales of pirated goods.[116] This is not surprising because it is the largest market. Some data regarding copyright piracy, based on information of the Guatemalan *Ministerio Público*, illustrates the size of such activities: in 2005, 500.000 pirated CDs were seized and decommissioned. In one raid, the *Ministerio Público* found in a backroom five computers with 48 attached CD burners.[117] Regarding trademark counterfeiting in Guatemala, a field study of *Kedron Thomas* concluded: "(Local) manufacturers themselves report that as much as 80 percent of apparel (…) involves the use of pirated brands (…). Manufacturers say that pirated logos, labels, and tags are easy to obtain".[118] Nevertheless, enforcement activities are generally still low.[119] This can be attributed to the limited resources of the enforcement agencies, who must deal with other areas of crime and face budget constraints.[120] In addition, many practitioners point out that the view of the public regarding the enforcement of IP rights, in particular trademarks, is sceptical, because it is seen as only benefitting foreign companies. This scepticism contributes to the lack of incentive for enforcement actions on the local level.[121] Also, bearing in mind the low level of economic development and widespread poverty, many people simply cannot afford to buy original goods.[122]

1.4 Emergence of TRIPS-Plus Rules in Bilateral FTAs

With regard to IP rights, the debate about bilateral FTAs focuses on the problem of the so-called "TRIPS-plus" level of IP protection. This section discusses the origin of the TRIPS-plus concept, to provide some background for the analysis of the IP provisions of CAFTA-DR, the EU-CA-AA and the EU-CARIFORUM-EPA and their implementation in Central America.

1.4.1 Background

Since the 1980ies the USA (and other developed countries) experienced a growing trade deficit. It was concluded by the USA that this was (at least partly) due to the fact that, because of the different level of IP protection in other countries, US firms

[116] Menocal (2005).

[117] Ibid.

[118] Thomas (2009), p. 4.

[119] USTR Special 301 Report (2016), pp. 58–60.

[120] See Sect. 2.5.4.

[121] See Sect. 8.3.2.

[122] Thomas (2012), p. 788.

could not operate on a level playing field together with "third world" competitors.[123]

IP law is based on the principle of territoriality.[124] Protection is limited in legal and geographical scope to the country where the respective right is registered (or exists by law without registration).[125] Rights are independent from equivalent rights in other countries.[126] The nature of IP as an easily accessible global public good makes the protection in third countries an issue for the international trade system.[127] Therefore, the solution of the US government was to raise international and foreign protection of IP rights to its domestic level by means of international agreements. The Trade Promotion Authority Act of 2002, giving the US government the authority to conclude bilateral FTAs, states as the "principle negotiating objective" to ensure "that the provision of any multilateral or bilateral trade agreement governing IP rights entered into by the United States reflect a standard of protection similar to that found in United States law".[128]

This objective of stronger protection was achieved initially by TRIPS and preceding multilateral agreements, which included minimum standards of protection.[129] These agreements raised the level of protection in most developing countries. This mechanism also increased the harmonization of international IP law, at least as long as it was used in multilateral treaties.[130] TRIPS incorporated the principle of "minimum standards" protection established already by the Paris Convention, according to which parties may implement more extensive protection or enforcement than required by TRIPS in their domestic law, but not less.[131] Together with the incorporation of earlier multilateral agreements on IP[132] this created a "Paris-plus" base line of protection.[133] But TRIPS is not a fixation of the level of protection, i.e., it does not provide for maximum levels of IP protection, and, therefore, allows for further increases of protection under bilateral agreements

[123] This idea was expressed, e.g., in the "Young Report" of the President's Commission on Industrial Competitiveness in 1985, which recommended to protect US businesses against the "misappropriation of intellectual property", see President's Commission on Industrial Competitiveness, Report, 1985, p. 21; on this report and its effects on the international policy strategy of the USA see, for example, Díaz (2008), p. 71. On the implications of this concept for the TRIPS negotiations see Drexl (2016), pp. 54–59.

[124] Stoll, Peter-Tobias in Busche et al. (2013), Introduction 1, Nr 6 and Article 1, Nr 16; Cornish et al. (2013), at 1–31.

[125] Stoll, Peter-Tobias in Busche et al. (2013), Introduction 1, Nr 6.

[126] Cornish et al. (2013), at 1–31.

[127] Stoll, Peter-Tobias in Busche et al. (2013), Introduction 1, Nr 4.

[128] 19 U.S.C. § 3802(b)(4)(A)(i)(II); this provision obliged the USTR to include IP protection on the level valid in the US itself into the bilateral trade agreements; on this issue see Drexl (2016), p. 60.

[129] Stoll, Peter-Tobias in Busche et al. (2013), Introduction 1, Nr 7.

[130] The limits of the harmonization are discussed by Stoll, Peter-Tobias in Busche et al. (2013), Introduction 1, Nr 9.

[131] Article 1(1) TRIPS; see Stoll, Peter-Tobias in Busche et al. (2013), Introduction 1, Nr 7.

[132] Article 2(2) TRIPS.

[133] Koul (2006), p. 459.

(other further multilateral agreements).[134] While IP law was regulated as an autonomous or stand-alone regime under earlier agreements, with the inclusion of TRIPS into the GATT/WTO system, IP rules were linked to the international trade regime. In this way, developed countries secured higher levels of protection in developing countries in exchange for lower tariffs and better enforcement through the WTO dispute settlement regime.[135]

Following TRIPS, developed countries tried to further raise the level of IP protection, but encountered resistance from other countries during multinational negotiations.[136] As a result, the USA (and similarly the EU) started to use bilateral FTAs as a strategic tool to systematically raise the foreign and indirectly the international level of IP protection, because the goal of raising IP protection across the globe to the level of US law could not be fully achieved under TRIPS, and successive multilateral negotiations had almost come to a standstill.[137] Therefore, TRIPS turned out to be not the end, but rather the starting point for the development of the international IP system through a network of bilateral FTAs, which in turn also incorporated new specific multilateral IP agreements. These new bilateral FTAs contain provisions granting more extensive protection than TRIPS.[138] As these provisions increase TRIPS protection, they became known as "TRIPS-plus". The two ways used (often cumulatively) to achieve "higher standards of IP protection [are] by incorporating standards from WIPO (post-TRIPS) treaties as substantive obligations [...] and by seeking accession to those treaties".[139] Substantive obligations can consist of the introduction of new rights, *e.g.*, test data protection related to pharmaceuticals, or the strengthening of existing rules, *e.g.*, the facilitation of enforcement measures.

1.4.2 CAFTA-DR and the EU-FTAs

Central America is a good example for this TRIPS-plus mechanism. Before CAFTA-DR was concluded, US companies repeatedly complained about weak protection of their IP rights in Central America, especially in Guatemala, Costa

[134] See e.g. Koul (2006), p. 458.

[135] This was the result of efforts of knowledge-based companies in the developed countries, especially in the USA. After the conclusion of TRIPS and the growing difficulties of achieving multilateral agreements, the focus shifted to bilateral free trade agreements, see, e.g., Collins-Chase (2008), p. 780, with further references, and Drexl (2016), pp. 54 and 60–61.

[136] See, e.g., Collins-Chase (2008), p. 780, with further references.

[137] See, e.g., Drexl (2016), pp. 54–56 and 61.

[138] Bilateral FTAs necessarily establish TRIPS-plus protection, because the principle of minimum standards only permits provisions granting more protection, but not less.

[139] USTR Special 301 Report (2007), p. 9.

Rica and the Dominican Republic.[140] When the USTR initiated negotiations for the bilateral FTA with Central America, one of the primary goals was to "provide adequate and effective protection and enforcement of IP rights in each Party's territory".[141] CAFTA-DR also incorporates the characteristic "minimum standards" approach. Article 15.1(1) CAFTA-DR repeats literally the TRIPS provision on minimum protection.[142] This makes the level of protection established by CAFTA-DR the new "base line". It was the explicit goal of industries supporting CAFTA-DR that this mechanism of raising the minimum level of protection should be continuously used. Other countries or regions have also begun to use this method.[143] The European Union, European Free Trade Association (EFTA) and Japan have also introduced TRIPS-plus rules in their FTAs. However, as will be shown in this study with regard to the EU-CA-AA and the EU-CARIFORUM-EPA, they did so to a lesser degree than CAFTA-DR. The "softer" IP rules used in FTAs concluded by the European Union stand in contrast to the US approach. Interestingly, the EU-CA-AA is visibly more similar to US-FTAs and contains fewer and vaguer rules on, for instance, cooperation and the protection of genetic resources and biodiversity than the EU-CARIFORUM-EPA.

1.4.3 The Term "TRIPS-Plus"

Before turning to the specific research questions, a brief comment on the "TRIPS-plus" terminology: Supporters of TRIPS-plus protection claim that the increased levels of IP protection are an improvement from a policy perspective and defend the IP provisions in FTAs arguing that, at least in part, they serve as an interpretation and "clarification" of "vague" TRIPS provisions, not necessarily as an increase of the level of protection.[144] Some critics point out that the term "TRIPS-plus" as such implies that the new rules are better. This study uses the term "TRIPS-plus" because it has become the standard term in the discussion about IP protection in modern bilateral FTAs and in the sense that TRIPS-*plus* expresses the fact that *more* IP protection is legally required, but not because such protection is necessarily *better* in terms of IP policy. Whether this is actually the case, at least in relation to Central America, is part of the question this study will try to answer.

---

[140] This focus is expressed, e.g., in the Special 301 Report 2007, which shows that the main concerns are not the countries with the absolutely lowest level of protection, but the identification of countries were weak protection causes the most economic harm to US businesses, see USTR Special 301 Report (2007), p. 38.

[141] Article 1.2 (e) CAFTA-DR.

[142] Article 1(1) TRIPS.

[143] IFAC-3 (2004), p. 3.

[144] See, e.g., IFAC-3 (2004), pp. 5–6; critically Liebig (2007), pp. 2–3.

1.5 Research Questions Regarding the Negotiation of Bilateral FTAs

This and the following section identify the main topics of the TRIPS-plus debate relating to the negotiation, implementation and the substantive rules of the IP chapter of bilateral FTAs, which form the basis for the specific research questions of this thesis. The criticism raised in relation to TRIPS-plus rules in bilateral FTAs relates broadly speaking to two areas. Procedurally, the negotiation of such rules as part of bilateral FTAs is considered by critics to be imbalanced and not transparent and to create a harmonized and unchangeable global framework of IP protection (further discussed in this Sect. 1.5). Substantively, the scope of protection established by TRIPS-plus rules is criticized as detrimental to the objectives of IP protection and to deprive developing countries of necessary flexibilities and limitations of protection (discussed in Sect. 1.6). The following two sections provide an overview regarding the state of the discussion. The findings in relation to these topics based on the analysis of the implementation of bilateral FTAs in Central America will be evaluated in Sect. 8.

1.5.1 *Impact of the* Trade Deal *Structure on Negotiating TRIPS-plus Rules*

On the international level, starting with TRIPS, IP law was no longer regulated only in specific IP agreements (as was the case previously, *e.g.*, in the Paris and Berne conventions), but became part of a broader trade agenda. On the bilateral level, in the FTAs concluded after TRIPS by the USA (and also by the EU), privileged market access and other trade advantages were granted to developing countries in exchange for stronger IP provisions (and other commitments, *e.g.*, in relation to labor rights).[145] The *trade deal* approach can impact the policy making process on several levels. This approach is criticized because (in particular) the better access to the markets of the USA (and the EU) can work as a "carrot" during the negotiations of bilateral FTAs. The market access incentivizes developing countries to accept the TRIPS-plus provisions contained in such FTAs, without much leverage to negotiate them, irrespective of the effect of these provisions on domestic policy priorities.[146] In addition, the prospective market access can create pressure to implement the IP rules quickly on the *statutory level*, because an FTA usually becomes fully effective, and the market access and other benefits operational, only after the IP obligations (as well as other requirements) under the respective FTA have been implemented

[145] MPI Principles (2013), Nr. 1; Roffe (2013), p. 934.

[146] *Pedro Roffe* notes that "IP is not high on [the developing countries'] negotiating agenda", Roffe (2013), p. 934.

into national law and the implementation is deemed successful by the FTA partner country. This process can restrict the capacity of the country implementing the respective IP rules, *e.g.*, to conduct an assessment on the national level of the utilization of the flexibilities remaining under the FTA or engage in a discussion with the affected stakeholders on the most appropriate way to implement the FTA requirements.[147]

The *institutional and practical changes* to the national IP system on the other hand are largely in the discretion of the respective implementing country, because the IP chapters in CAFTA-DR, and similar FTAs concluded by the USA (and also the EU), contain mainly statutory obligations which must be implemented into national legislation.[148] However, the adaptation of the institutional and practical national IP framework to the new statutory system strongly influences whether the right holders really benefit from the increased statutory protection. Accordingly, one would expect the USA (and similarly the EU) and the right holders to leverage the trade incentives under an FTA not only during the negotiation and statutory implementation of IP obligations, but also in relation to the adaptation of the institutional and practical IP framework. However, the question whether the inclusion of IP rules in a trade deal leads to changes on the institutional and practical framework of IP protection, or whether there is pressure to make such changes by the FTA partner country and right holders, is not much discussed in the context of the TRIPS-plus debate. One reason is that institutional and practical aspects are largely beyond the scope of the FTAs concluded by the USA. Accordingly, the analysis of TRIPS-plus issues often focuses on the (statutory) requirements contained in the respective FTAs. Another reason may be that the analysis of the institutional and practical implementation needs to be conducted over a longer period of time and requires access to sources that are only available locally or at least only in the local language.[149] Nevertheless, this study will also analyze the institutional implementation and the impact of the *trade deal* structure on it, because of its impact on the practical effectiveness of TRIPS-plus rules.

1.5.2 *Economic Benefits Under a* Trade Deal

Another controversial topic, in addition to the impact of the trade incentives on the *process* of negotiating and implementing IP rules, is whether developing countries obtain the expected economic benefits under bilateral FTAs. This is primarily an economic and not a legal question, but this study will nevertheless address the main consideration relating to this topic and analyze the situation in Central America

[147] On these flexibilities, see Sect. 1.6.3.

[148] A notable exeption to the general statutory focus of bilateral FTAs is the registration of Established Geographical Indications under the EU-CA-AA, see Sect. 4.4.6.

[149] For the difficulties related to obtaining and using local sources, see Sect. 2.2.4.

briefly, as this topic influences the overall evaluation and possible justification of the use of TRIPS-plus rules in FTAs.

1.5.2.1 Economic Benefits Based on Market Access

It is disputed whether developing countries are practically able to reap economic benefits under bilateral FTAs. Many critics argue that, in addition to the detrimental effect of stronger IP protection, bilateral FTAs also fail to provide the alleged trade benefits to developing countries. According to this view, developing countries grant stronger IP protection to right holders from developed countries *and* are not compensated for the concessions in relation to IP protection and, therefore, loose on both sides of the *trade deal* equation.[150]

One factor potentially limiting the trade benefits granted under such FTAs is that these benefits can diminish over time, because developed countries conclude subsequent FTAs which grant the same or greater trade benefits to other countries. Accordingly, the competitive advantage obtained under earlier FTAs could decrease or even disappear ("erosion of trade benefits" or "domino effect").[151] In addition, developing countries may not be able to exploit lower tariffs as effectively as they anticipate, *e.g.*, because they cannot overcome other trade restrictions.[152]

The opposing view expects free trade agreements to have a positive economic effect on developing countries, because of the better market access by reducing tariffs and the resulting domestic economic growth.[153] Supporters argue that the tariff reductions provided under CAFTA-DR will benefit the Central American countries more than the USA, and that the improved access to the US market provides benefits to Central America that more than compensate any potential economic or welfare losses resulting from stronger IP protection.[154] In other words, even if stronger IP protection under TRIPS was detrimental for developing countries, it is justified as part of a global WTO *trade deal* in which developed countries open their markets in exchange for stronger IP protection.[155] This consideration is extended to bilateral FTAs concluded between the USA and Latin American countries.[156]

---

[150] See the review of studies showing no or limited economic benefits of FTAs in Stevens et al. (2015), pp. 17–23.

[151] MPI Principles (2013), Nr. 19; this issue is discussed further in Sect. 2.2.2.

[152] Tharin (2008).

[153] See the review of studies showing substantial economic benefits of FTAs in Stevens et al. (2015), pp. 17–23.

[154] For a detailed optimistic prognosis of the economic benefits for Central America see Jaramillo and Lederman (2005), p. 58.

[155] Pacón (1995), p. 875; Petersmann (1996–1997), p. 442.

[156] Pacón (1995), p. 875.

1.5.2.2 Economic Benefits Based on Legal Harmonization

Some observers argue that, irrespective of the possible immediate trade benefits, FTAs provide economic advantages by harmonizing the trade and IP legal framework. FTAs could produce economic benefits through *trade harmonization* by generally reducing tariffs and harmonizing market access rules. FTAs are considered to increase trade openness and specifically, within the framework of "open regionalism", support regional economic integration.[157] Also the "domino effect" of several countries in one region concluding FTAs with the USA or Europe in quick succession, in order to level the benefits of the neighboring countries under such FTAs, might increase legal and tariff harmonization among the countries involved, which might be an intermediate step leading to a new level of global integration.[158] On the other hand, critics submit that, conversely, the proliferation of FTAs is a threat to regional or global trading systems.[159] *Granados* and *Cornejo* argue that the "aggressive proliferation" of bilateral FTAs in the Americas and the "decentralized and uncoordinated process" threatens the hemispheric trading system.[160] They may result in a restriction of trade on aggregate, because of the large number of agreements and the differences these agreements contain in relation to market access rules.[161]

Trade benefits could also result from the *harmonization of IP rules*. The global harmonization of IP legislation is considered to be a necessary corollary of economic integration, because IP rights apply specifically to the respective country granting protection[162] and differences in IP protection can, therefore, function as trade barriers.[163] Under this view, the international harmonization of the IP system reduces the differences in the standard of IP protection in any given country and thereby reduces the impact of the IP system on the decision of allocating resources, *e.g.*, research, development and production resources. Other factors, such as the size of the respective market and the level of education of the workforce, would then become more important.[164]

1.5.3 Fair, Transparent and Inclusive Negotiations

The IP provisions in TRIPS represent a balance between minimum standards and flexibilities, because they are the result of a compromise of all TRIPS members.[165]

[157] Díaz (2008), p. 22.
[158] On the "domino effect" see in more detail Sect. 2.2.2.
[159] Granados and Cornejo (2006), p. 857.
[160] Ibid.
[161] The effects of the FTAs on trade harmonization are summarized in Sect. 8.2.2.
[162] This principle is known in German as the *Territorialitätsgrundsatz*.
[163] Hassemer (2000), p. 23.
[164] Drexl (2006–2007), p. 533.
[165] MPI Principles (2013), Nr. 4.

The IP rules under FTAs, however, have been criticized by legal scholars, developing countries and NGOs, because they are considered to be the result of unfair, non-transparent and non-inclusive negotiations. Negotiations are viewed as "unfair", because the smaller, less developed FTA partner countries and their stakeholders cannot effectively influence the negotiations.[166] Developed countries like the USA (or regions like the EU) possess superior bargaining power and knowledge with regard to the negotiation of such rules. Therefore, the negotiations are considered asymmetrical and biased in favor of developed countries.[167] With regard to bargaining power, the USA has several advantages over the small developing countries in the negotiations of FTAs. Unlike in multilateral negotiations, where large developing countries like Brazil and China can organize opposition to the interests and proposals of the developed countries, in bilateral negotiations the influence of developing countries is more limited. Also, FTAs are often concluded between the USA and relatively small developing countries. The USA grants better access to its huge market in exchange for concessions of developing countries in other areas, *e.g.*, with regard to IP protection. The bias towards the USA results from the fact that it is often by far the most important trading partner for these countries, whereas the developing countries are of much less importance to US trade.[168] This analysis applies similarly to the trade agreements concluded by the EU. Furthermore, there are information asymmetries especially in the very complex area of IP protection. The developing countries are viewed by some observers as lacking the knowledge and experience of their "developed" counterparts regarding the international legal framework and the practical consequences of IP protection. Thus, they may not know exactly what legal positions they are conceding in these areas.[169]

Secondly, this situation is compounded by the lack of transparency in the negotiations caused by the fact that during the negotiations of an FTA, the text is often kept confidential. This makes it difficult for stakeholders or third party observers to contribute to the drafting of the respective agreement.[170] In particular, the draft text of an agreement cannot be publicly discussed in such situations and in particular parliaments, therefore, cannot influence the negotiations.[171] They only have the possibility to vote on the final text. Such "backroom negotiations" are considered undemocratic.[172] One solution that has been recommended as part of a transparent and inclusive negotiations process, to ensure a more equitable outcome

[166] E.g., MPI Principles (2013), Nr. 14 and 15; Roffe (2013), p. 935; vocal critics of the IP provisions of CAFTA-DR described these rules as "neo-imperialist" or "colonial-style" methods of the USA in the tradition of earlier economic and military interventions, see, e.g., citations from Hugo Guiliani Cury in Guiliani: DR-Cafta fue mal negociado, available at https://www.bilaterals.org/?guiliani-dr-cafta-fue-mal (accessed 2 Nov 2024).

[167] See, e.g., Roffe (2013), p. 935.

[168] Drexl (2006–2007), p. 529.

[169] Roffe and Genovesi (2011), p. x (introduction).

[170] Roffe and Genovesi (2011), p. 103 in relation to the US-Peru-TPA.

[171] MPI Principles (2013), Nr. 10.

[172] Stiglitz (2006), p. 56.

of the negotiations, is to make the scope and subject matter of the negotiations available to the public, to provide a meaningful opportunity for stakeholders and interested third parties to raise concerns and influence the negotiation process.[173]

Thirdly, another point of criticism relates to inclusiveness, i.e., the disproportionate influence of certain groups of stakeholders on the negotiations of FTAs on the one hand and the failure to include significant stakeholders in the process on the other hand. These negotiations should enable all (potentially) affected stakeholders in the respective countries to participate in the negotiations in an open and nondiscriminatory manner and, in particular, to comment on drafts of the FTA.[174] However, in practice certain stakeholders and special interests are considered to have a disproportionate influence during this process. As summarized by *Josef Drexl*, "IP systems rely on a balance of a multitude of conflicting interests that are not, or not sufficiently, taken into account in international trade negotiations".[175] The "economics" of political decision-making often favor "big business". Already in the early 1970ies, *Mancur Olson* argued that (even) in a democracy, smaller groups tend to be more successful than larger groups in a political competition. Provided that a fixed economic interest is concerned, smaller groups are politically more effective because their incentive per person (or entity) is higher. Therefore, they are willing to invest significant time and money into political activities. Conversely, the incentive per person in a large group may be too small to generate any meaningful level of political activity.[176] In a way, this effect can be considered the *tragedy of the commons* on a political level. Applied to the negotiations of CAFTA-DR and the EU-FTAs, the possibility of better access to the US and EU markets and stronger IP protection benefits a relatively small number of businesses to a high degree. Conversely, lower levels of IP protection and, as a result, easier access to foreign technology, drugs, plant varieties (and similarly copyright content) benefit many members of the Central American societies, but each individual only to a small degree. The disproportionate influence of certain stakeholders already applies before the negotiations start. The standard set of IP rules in CAFTA-DR, as in similar FTAs, established before the start of the negotiations largely reflects the policy priorities of right holders of developed countries. In the USA, IP-focused industries are often well organized, which enables them to maintain politically influential industry associations. The influence of such industry groups is often bigger than that of groups advocating for more access and competition, because the "diffuse" public interests are politically less effective, even if they potentially benefit more people. For instance, pharmaceutical companies, relying on strong patent protection, were considered to have been very influential in the CAFTA-DR negotiations.[177] This could

[173] MPI Principles (2013), Nr. 12.

[174] MPI Principles (2013), Nr. 14 and 15.

[175] Drexl (2016), pp. 62 and 75–77.

[176] Olson (1971), p. 128; similarly, Drexl (2016), pp. 75–77.

[177] Public Citizen's Global Trade Watch (2006), p. 30.

explain, *e.g.*, the favorable provisions regarding test data and plant variety protection in CAFTA-DR.[178]

In addition, *Mancur Olson* found that smaller groups are better able to take action than larger, diffuse groups, irrespective of the economic incentive.[179] Applied to, *e.g.*, CAFTA-DR, this suggests that the few members of the ITAC 15 committee (which advises the USTR) can formulate specific IP policy objectives and draft wording for a bilateral FTA more easily than global NGOs or individual members of the legislature in an FTA partner country. In the field of IP, the economic interest of the right holders in exclusivity and of the public in access are a case in point. There are typically few right holders and many users, which suggests that more efforts will be made and more success will be achieved by the right holders. One can consider the controversial example of data exclusivity: The question whether *de facto* patent protection is extended through data exclusivity decides whether the patent-holder gains an additional monopoly rent or whether the users (health agencies and patients) save this amount because of cheaper generic competition. As there are many potential users, the incentive per person may be below the minimum necessary to trigger political activity, whereas the right holder has a strong incentive to push for the inclusion of data protection.

Fourthly, in the TRIPS-plus discussion, the focus of the criticism regarding transparency and participation of stakeholders is the negotiation phase of FTAs. However, as will be explored in detail in this study, the development of the set of IP rules proposed by developed countries before negotiations begin and the implementation of the IP rules after the conclusion of the negotiations play an at least as important role during the policy-making process as the actual negotiations. Therefore, the transparency and inclusiveness issues will also be analyzed with regard to these phases.

1.5.4 Legal Harmonization

1.5.4.1 Background

In addition or as a substitute to regional or international integration of the IP system (*e.g.*, the establishment of international patent and trademark registration procedures), the harmonization of IP legislation can be a useful corollary of economic integration, because IP rights have generally national effect and can thus function as trade barriers.[180] The international harmonization of substantive IP rules by FTAs could, therefore, reduce distortions of competition and be beneficial from a policy perspective. The harmonization could mean that the standards of IP protection in any

[178] See Sects. 3.3 and 3.4.

[179] Olson (1971), p. 55.

[180] Hassemer (2000), p. 23.

given country matter much less when it comes to the decision of allocating research, development and production.[181]

For a long time, this harmonization, usually in the form of increased IP protection, was achieved through multilateral agreements. After TRIPS, this approach became more difficult, because many developing countries opposed such an increase. As a consequence, developed countries (mainly the USA and the EU) began to "sidestep" the multilateral process. They started to utilize bilateral FTAs as a vehicle for raising the level of IP protection in third countries, because bilateral negotiations are faster and more flexible than multilateral negotiations.[182] Also, the USA and EU have been able to use their greater bargaining power to develop a "fitting" set of rules. Most FTAs concluded by the USA build on a template IP chapter and the recurring use creates a precedent for future bilateral agreements and extends the rules of the IP chapter to a growing number of countries. In addition, the US- and EU-FTAs require the other countries to ratify a number of multilateral agreements, which so far had been rejected by many developing countries. Therefore, the IP rules introduced under such FTAs could contribute to the harmonization of statutory IP protection on the national level and could spread the higher level of protection existing in developed countries around the globe.

Specifically regarding Central America, CAFTA-DR and the EU-FTAs are expected to increase the regional harmonization of the national IP systems in Central America. Article 141 EU-CARIFORUM-EPA states as policy goals the "further harmonization of IP laws" and "creation and management of regional intellectual property rights".[183]

1.5.4.2 National Treatment, Most-Favored-Nation Treatment and "Multilateralization"

However, these rules can also feed back into the multilateral IP system. They may subsequently be included in or at least influence other bilateral or multilateral agreements. The interaction between bilateral and multilateral IP activities has been described as the "global IP ratchet" (*Peter Drahos*),[184] the "multilateralization" of bilateral rules (*Josef Drexl*)[185] and the "three-dimensional

[181] As noted in Sect. 2.5.2, other factors, like market size or education, could become more important, see Drexl (2006–2007), p. 533; see also Drexl (2016), p. 80.

[182] See, e.g., Yu (2008), p. 936; Ostry (2000), p. 154.

[183] Other measures of harmonization include the Patent Examiner Manual of the IP Registers of Central America (including Panama) and the Dominican Republic (2006), see Sect. 2.5.2.3.

[184] Drahos (2003), p. 1.

[185] Drexl (2016), p. 63; see also Drexl (2018), Nr 112.

form" of bilateral, regional and multilateral processes (*Alfredo Corral*).[186] *Sylvia Ostry's* "(…) metaphor is the game of dominoes; the use of [bilateral FTAs] as part of a broader, evolving geo-economic policy template. The ultimate objective is to broaden and deepen the global system (…)".[187] *Sylvia Ostry* has analyzed this "domino effect" for the inclusion of service and investment rules in CUSTA, GATS and NAFTA.[188] Legally, the "multilateralization" may, on the one hand, result from the principle of national treatment in Article 3 TRIPS.[189] It requires members to "*accord to the nationals of other Members treatment no less favourable than that it accords to its own nationals with regard to the protection of intellectual property*".[190] It may result on the other hand from the most-favored-nation clause in Article 4 TRIPS.[191] It provides that "*any advantage (…) granted by a member to the nationals of any other country shall be accorded (…) to the nationals of all other members*". This "Most Favored Nation" (MFN) treatment requirement is a novelty compared to the Paris Convention and was designed to restore the "uniformity of the multinational trade environment".[192] Unlike the most-favored-nation clause in Article I (1) GATT, it applies to all FTAs without exception. As a result, parties to any agreement have to provide the same level of protection for all other WTO members.[193] As such bilateral agreements are covered by the national treatment and MFN principles of TRIPS, their IP rules can be enforced through WTO panel and appellate body dispute settlement. By means of the application by WTO bodies, they indirectly become part of WTO law. This might also force the WTO members to support the adoption of the CAFTA-DR level of protection in multilateral agreements, as a result of a practical "estoppel" situation: To the extent Central American countries are required to provide for minimum protection or maximum limitations under CAFTA-DR, they could not implement any restrictions of protection in contravention of such requirements, even if they were included in a multilateral agreement, and, therefore, are less likely to support any multilateral project in such direction. The concern of some observers is that this "multilateralization" will in the end lead to stronger protection on the multilateral level and the creation of a "TRIPS II" agreement.[194]

---

[186] Corral, Alfredo, Tratados de Libre Comercio en Iberoamérica – Derechos de Propiedad Intelectual e Industrial, in Flanzbaum (2005), pp. 106–107.

[187] Ostry (2000), p. 154.

[188] Ostry (2000), p. 159.

[189] Nadde-Phlix (2014), p. 138.

[190] Article 3(1) TRIPS.

[191] Nadde-Phlix (2014), p. 138.

[192] Koul (2006), p. 459; see also Cornish and Liddell, (2016), pp. 27–28.

[193] Drexl (2018), Nr 112.

[194] Yu (2008), p. 937.

1.5.4.3 Challenges and Concerns

In Central America, as in other regions, the proliferation of bilateral FTAs also challenges the legal harmonization. First, as these FTAs all provide for slightly different levels of protection, only national, not international uniformity is guaranteed. Second, even on the national level problems emerge, *e.g.*, in case of conflict between different FTAs of the USA and the EU.[195] While CAFTA-DR harmonizes IP protection on a high level, several issues still differ among the parties, as the Dominican Republic is bound by the EU-CARIFORUM-EPA while the other Central American countries have to comply with the EU-CA-AA. The trademark rules, for example, in CAFTA-DR could be incompatible with the protection of geographical indications in the EU-FTAs. This issue is not often discussed in the context of TRIPS-plus rules, because it focuses more on the legal ramifications of TRIPS and because for a long time there were only a handful of countries with several "layers" of IP obligations under FTAs. However, this number continues to increase, because the large economies and trade blocks continue to broaden their "FTA portfolio".[196] Central America is one of these cases and this study will, therefore, also assess the harmonizing effects of FTA on the IP system (or lack thereof) from this perspective. Third, the (increasing) level of IP protection required by FTAs may conflict with flexibilities or maximum protection ("ceilings") contained in existing multilateral agreements. TRIPS, for example, provides for flexibilities that support designing domestic IP systems to be "conducive to social and economic welfare".[197] Critics argue that the TRIPS-plus rules in FTAs conflict with the flexibility necessary for developing countries to pursue such policy goals.[198] The increasing use of flexibilities by countries unrestricted by TRIPS-plus rules and the increasing IP protection in countries subject to one or more FTAs could further reduce legal harmonization in the IP field.

1.5.5 Review and Change Procedures

The IP chapters in FTAs establish statutory requirements which fix a certain level of IP protection. However, both the global IP system and national policy need to evolve over time. Therefore, it has been suggested that IP obligations in FTAs should include a review clause, for example an option for re-negotiating IP provisions in

[195] This situation is analyzed with respect to the conflicting protection of trademarks in CAFTA-DR and geographical indications in the EU-CARIFORUM-EPA, respectively, see Sect. 4.4.6.

[196] The increasing number of bilateral FTAs and their overlap is discussed in more detail in Sect. 2. 1.2.

[197] Article 7 TRIPS; on this issue see MPI Principles (2013), Nr. 5.

[198] MPI Principles (2013), Nr. 6.

light of an impact assessment.[199] There are several cases in which adjustment of IP rules should be considered. If, for instance, IP rules are part of *trade deals* like CAFTA-DR, the countries which are party to the respective FTA may not enjoy the expected trade benefits in the long term, while the IP requirements remain in place and part of the national legislative regimes. A formal review and change procedure could provide several benefits: It would enable the respective parties to consider introducing either permanent modifications to the IP rules or "emergency" IP restrictions, similar to the existing "emergency" trade restrictions. Such mechanism could help level the playing field between the FTA partners. In effect, it might work as a mechanism to alleviate trade imbalances, similar to the possibility of "cross-retaliation".[200] Such a procedure could also permit countries to request the extension of concessions regarding exceptions and limitations obtained by other countries in similar situations. In effect, this might establish a "most favored nation" mechanism with regard to flexibilities or limitations relating to IP protection.[201] Finally, such a procedure could provide a mechanism for assessing the implementation of IP obligations contained in FTAs.[202] This could restrict the ability of developed countries to withhold trade benefits based on a unilateral determination that FTA partners did not comply with certain IP obligations.

1.6 Research Questions Regarding the Implementation and Effects of TRIPS-plus Rules

The substantive criticism regarding TRIPS-plus rules focuses on the scope of protection established by TRIPS-plus rules, which is considered detrimental to the objectives of IP protection and depriving developing countries of necessary flexibilities and limitations. The criticism typically assumes that TRIPS-plus rules are fully and effectively implemented into the national legal system. It is necessary to analyze to what extent this is actually the case.

1.6.1 Implementation on the Statutory and Institutional Level

The implementation of the IP rules of FTAs on the statutory level receives less attention within the context of the TRIPS-plus debate than the wording of the FTA itself. The TRIPS-plus rules are usually evaluated at "face value", *i.e.*, it is assumed

[199] MPI Principles (2013), Nr. 22.

[200] See Sect. 2.2.6.2; on the possibility of "cross-retaliation" in the field of IP see von Lewinski (2016), pp. 613-618.

[201] MPI Principles (2013), Nr. 26.

[202] MPI Principles (2013), Nr. 29.

that these rules are fully implemented on the national legislative level. However, as will be analyzed further in this study, the implementation is not as straightforward as it may seem. The institutional and practical impact of the implementation of IP rules of FTAs in developing countries was initially not the focus of much research conducted on the issue of TRIPS-plus protection. Subsequently the implementation phase has come more into focus.[203] The analysis of TRIPS-plus rules typically assumes that the national legislation is effectively applied in practice.[204] *Roffe*, for example, notes that "the new obligations [in a bilateral FTA] often require a substantial reinforcement of the country's institutional base in terms of recruiting competent staff to meet the stipulations of the agreement, and employing professionals duly qualified in the management of the system".[205] However, as will be discussed in detail in this study, first, the FTAs to not *legally* require such institutional measures, and the fact that the effective implementation of the obligations *practically* requires such institutional measures does not mean that the respective countries necessarily take them. Often, the institutional aspects of the IP system are not considered, which is understandable, because bilateral FTAs such as CAFTA-DR contain predominantly provisions relating to the statutory, but few if any institutional and practical level. If institutional aspects are considered, the focus of the discussion is on the financial and human resources required by FTAs and the burden the implementation of the FTA places on the legislative, administrative and judicial infrastructure.[206] In particular the TRIPS-plus enforcement provisions are criticized as requiring developing countries to invest disproportionate resources for IP enforcement and thus neglect other important policy areas. In order to alleviate the burden placed on developing countries, it has been suggested that the developed FTA parties should provide financial and technical support for implementing IP obligations.[207] Usually not discussed is the question whether the statutory changes required by bilateral FTAs are practically effective or not. However, the impact of TRIPS-plus rules on the IP system in Central America can only be evaluated if the effects on the institutional and practical level are also taken into consideration. Increased statutory protection does not necessarily lead to increased practical protection, in particular because of the institutional challenges that IP systems in Central America face.

[203] MPI Principles (2013), Nr. 23–30; Roffe (2013), p. 937.

[204] For example, Shaikh (2016), pp. 193–208, assesses the national implementation of test data requirements under FTAs in Central America almost exclusively based on the implementation legislation (with the exception of citing one article on practical effects of the CAFTA-DR implementation in Guatemala).

[205] Roffe (2013), p. 937.

[206] MPI Principles (2013), Nr. 9.

[207] MPI Principles (2013), Nr. 27.

1.6.2 Impact of TRIPS-plus Rules on the Objectives of IP Protection

1.6.2.1 Introduction

Whether one places the foundation of IP protection on natural rights or utilitarian considerations, the design of the IP system and the evaluation of specific IP policy measures, such as the introduction of TRIPS-plus protection, is only possible based on the objectives the IP system is supposed to achieve. Many international agreements, *e.g.*, Articles 7 and 8 TRIPS and the Doha Declaration, and national constitutions and laws, *e.g.*, the Costa Rican Constitution, state objectives of IP protection.[208] Also some FTAs refer to their objectives in relation to IP, *e.g.*, the EU-CARIFORUM-EPA.[209] Notably, CAFTA-DR is one of the few texts in which objectives are not included, in contrast to earlier US-FTAs, *e.g.*, the US-Chile-FTA.[210] The basic argument of the critics of TRIPS-plus rules, as introduced by CAFTA-DR and similar FTAs, is that the level of IP protection required under such FTAs does not promote the objectives of IP protection and other public policy goals, *e.g.*, public health.[211] Supporters on the other hand argue that stronger protection and enforcement rules are necessary to promote innovation and achieve the objectives of IP protection.[212] The analysis of CAFTA-DR and its implementation in Central America provides a practical example for TRIPS-plus rules in bilateral FTAs and their effects on the objectives of IP protection in developing countries. The evidence from this example will help evaluate the practical validity of some of the concerns put forward with regard to TRIPS-plus, at least with regard to Central America. The objectives and the underlying legal and economic considerations regarding the protection of specific IP rights are only briefly described here, to provide the context of the TRIPS-plus debate, and are discussed in more detail in the substantive sections in relation to the specific IP rights.

1.6.2.2 Innovation and Dynamic Competition

Concept of Dynamic Competition

Among the main objectives of IP protection are the promotion of competition, innovation and technology transfer, detailed by Article 7 and 8 TRIPS as "the

[208] Article 5(a) Doha Declaration; Article 47 Constitution (CR).

[209] Article 131 (2) EU-CARIFORUM-EPA.

[210] Preamble to Chapter 17 US-Chile-FTA: "[...] Emphasizing that the protection and enforcement of intellectual property rights is a fundamental principle of this Chapter that helps promote technological innovation as well as the transfer and dissemination of technology to the mutual advantage of technology producers and users, and that encourages the development of social and economic well-being [...]".

[211] See Sect. 1.1.

[212] IFAC-3 (2004), pp. 3–4.

promotion of technological innovation and (…) the transfer and dissemination of technology, to the mutual advantage of producers and users" and "technological development".[213]

There is an evolving discussion about the relationship between IP and competition law and the balancing of IP protection to achieve these objectives. The traditional view was based on the idea that the protection of right holders excludes competitors and, therefore, always limits competition, and that both fields are, therefore, mutually exclusive (sometimes described as the "inherency doctrine").[214] The modern approach assumes that these regimes are complementary, because they both promote allocation efficiency and dynamic (or innovative) competition.[215] This view today is expressed by the courts,[216] adopted by the antitrust agencies[217] and supported by many competition law scholars.[218] The WIPO put it simple: "the two branches of law (are) the two sides of the same coin: competition policy".[219] In other words, both IP law and competition law are necessary to protect the broad objective of "dynamic competition".[220]

The main benchmark for any type of IP protection, therefore, is the question whether the restriction of direct or static competition and the resulting welfare loss is compensated by the welfare gains resulting from dynamic competition. The protection of both distinctive signs and inventions shall overcome market failures caused by unrestricted, "imperfect" competition.[221] In a broad sense, these rights restrict the appropriation of certain business efforts by third parties to ensure an ongoing incentive to develop and provide innovative quality products. In other words, they

[213] On these objectives see, e.g., Díaz (2008), p. 19.

[214] On this view see, e.g., Drexl (2004), p. 792.

[215] Drexl (2004), p. 792.

[216] The CAFC expressed this concept as follows: "[T]he aims and objectives of patent and antitrust laws may seem, at first glance, wholly at odds. However, the two bodies of law are actually complementary, as both are aimed at encouraging innovation, industry and competition", *Atari Games Corp. v. Nintendo of America, Inc.*, 897 F.2d 1572, 1576 (Fed. Cir. 1990).

[217] According to the Antitrust Guidelines for the Licensing of Intellectual Property, issued by the U.S. Department of Justice and the Federal Trade Commission, 6 April 1995, section 1, subparagraph 3, "(t)he intellectual property laws and the antitrust laws share the common purpose of promoting innovation and enhancing consumer welfare"; the European Commission stated the concept of complementarity in para. 7 of the Guidelines on the application of Article 81 EC Treaty to technology transfer agreements, OJ EC No. C 101 of 27 April 2004, at 2.

[218] Drexl (2004), p. 792; see also Drexl et al. (2006), p. 561.

[219] WIPO, Public Policy-related Assistance - Flexibilities, available at http://www.wipo.int/ip-development/en/policy/flexibilities.html (accessed 2 Nov 2024).

[220] This term was used in the Guidelines to the application of Article 81 of the EC Treaty to technology transfer agreements, OJ EC2004 No. C 101, p. 2, para. 7; see also Kolstad (2008), p. 5.

[221] Regarding inventions, see Sect. 3.1.1.1, regarding trademarks see Sect. 4.1.1.1.

restrict static competition and present welfare gains to create dynamic competition and future welfare gains.[222] The balance between static and dynamic competition requires a system of protection that avoids both over- and under-protection. Insufficient protection can harm technological and economic development, because of the lack of economic incentives to be innovative. Over-protection can restrict competition excessively and negatively impact socio-economic policy goals. Patent law ideally compensates the short-term limitation of competition based on the exclusive right by providing an incentive for inventions, which will lead to better competition in the long term. If, for instance, a new drug cannot be patented at all or the patent cannot be enforced against illegal copies in Central America (and similar tropical countries) and R&D costs cannot be recovered, pharmaceutical companies have little incentive to invest in R&D for diseases endemic to the respective countries. But also too broad, excessive protection of IP rights can lead to restrictions of competition and thus harm the goals these rights are supposed to serve; for example, the right holder might set excessive prices or use licensing practices which restrict competition beyond the scope of the respective right and limit technology transfer.[223] The protection of trademarks and other distinctive signs is directed at protecting fair competition, however, such distinctive signs enable the consumer to identify better, innovative products in a competitive marketplace and incentivize the trademark owner to invest in improved products.[224] In this way trademarks and other distinctive signs also contribute to innovation.

Opponents of TRIPS-plus levels of IP protection take the view that the proliferation of TRIPS-plus rules creates excessive IP protection, which in effect limits, rather than facilitates, the core objective of promoting innovation.[225] Stronger IP protection on the international level or in bilateral FTAs is considered by critics as benefitting mainly the industries of developed countries[226] and taking from developing countries the possibility to use foreign technology and denying them their competitive advantage.[227] This argument is based on the assumption that developing countries have only a limited capacity to invent and, therefore, must absorb foreign inventions for technological development.[228]

---

[222] Article 40 TRIPS implies the idea that competition is an underlying objective of IP protection by enabling members to prevent or control the abuse of intellectual property rights having an adverse effect on competition.

[223] Article 40(2) TRIPS addresses this issue by allowing members to "[specify] in their legislation licensing practices or conditions that may in particular cases constitute an abuse of intellectual property rights having an adverse effect on competition [and to] adopt […] appropriate measures to prevent or control such practices, which may include for example exclusive grantback conditions, conditions preventing challenges to validity and coercive package licensing".

[224] On the quality function and investment function of trademarks see Stöbele et al. (2018), Introduction pp. 81–82, with references to CJEU case-law on these functions.

[225] MPI Principles (2013), Nr. 3; Roffe (2013), p. 934.

[226] Bennett (1994), p. 35.

[227] Davis and Neacsu (2000–2001), section III.A.

[228] The issue of innovation by imitation is further discussed in Sect. 3.1.2.2.

According to supporters, the TRIPS-plus provisions in CAFTA-DR not only protect US businesses, but also benefit the Central American businesses, because stronger patent protection creates an incentive for innovation and CAFTA-DR increases this incentive in Central America. The US IP-based industry argues that "high levels of [intellectual property] protection benefit indigenous creators and inventors in the same manner as they do in developed countries".[229] At first glance, this seems plausible. R&D spending has a measurably positive effect on economic growth especially for developing countries, because these can achieve greater increases in productivity (the more underdeveloped, the greater the return of investment).[230] Accordingly, more domestic innovation could have a significant positive impact on the Central American economies. But like Latin American countries in general, Central American countries have been under-performing in terms of R&D spending relative to their level of development.[231] Therefore, incentives for private investment into R&D are of particular importance in the region.

However, the claim of some US industry groups stating "that [the Central American] countries found it in their interest to significantly increase their levels of IP protection beyond that required by TRIPS is testament to the principle that high levels of protection benefit indigenous creators and inventors in the same manner as they do in developed countries"[232] is practically questionable. It does not account for the trade deal dynamics of CAFTA-DR and the lack of bargaining power of the Central American countries during the FTA negotiations. The Central American countries accepted the increase of IP protection as a trade-off for lower tariffs, whether they found it in their interest or not.[233]

Global Innovation

Some economic scholars argue that it is *economically and fiscally* beneficial for developing countries to imitate rather than protect foreign IP, because the cost and price reductions achieved by increased competition offset the lost innovation resulting from the reduced incentive to innovate for lack of IP protection. *Klaus Liebig* calculated the effects of patent protection in small markets on the global incentive to innovate. He concluded that because of the limited effect of small countries on the global market for new technology, the welfare loss because of reduced innovation would be more than compensated by the improved access to

---

[229] IFAC-3 (2004), pp. 3–4.

[230] Lederman and Maloney (2003), p. 13.

[231] Lederman and Maloney (2003), p. 28, fig. 2b, have analyzed this specifically for Costa Rica, but it can be assumed that it is also true for its less developed Central American neighbors; "development" in this context is equal to a country's GDP per captia.

[232] IFAC-3 (2004), pp. 3–4.

[233] See Sect. 2.2.1.

technology in such countries.[234] However, this analysis is based only on the competitive and innovative effect in the respective developing countries and their national welfare gain only, and does not take into account the "costs" of the lost innovation (the "welfare loss") in third countries. In other words, free-riding by developing countries leads to welfare gains, if one looks only at the specific country, *i.e.*, free-riding is beneficial from a national perspective, but could still lead to global welfare losses.[235]

The activities and investments of, e.g., large pharmaceutical companies suggest that the markets of developing countries are of, albeit limited, relevance for their commercial and research activities, and, therefore, insufficient IP protection could have a negative impact on innovation. If these markets didn't matter from an economic perspective because the potential revenues are too small, these companies might not invest human and financial resources into the protection of their patents and the marketing of their drugs in these countries. In addition, part of the reason why developing countries may be of lesser importance as markets for innovative drugs could be the fact that originator companies often face generic competition due to a lack of patent protection.[236]

Supporters of stronger IP protection in developing countries also invoke fiscal considerations. They consider it inequitable if developing countries enjoyed the benefits of innovation for free, while the costs are borne exclusively by the societies of developed countries which effectively protect IP. This issue was raised, for example, with regard to drugs, which are financed to a large extent by the public social (medical) systems of developed societies, while (allegedly) developing countries and their patients reap "free-riding" benefits without making a contribution to the research and development of the drugs.[237] It is seen as legitimate to demand that at least "middle-income" countries, like Costa Rica, share some of the costs of global innovation, and to ensure such sharing through international agreements. To prevent such behavior, just as IP rules are necessary on the national level to prevent individual free-riding, they are necessary in multilateral or bilateral agreements to prevent - or manage an acceptable level of - national free-riding.[238]

---

[234]Liebig (2005), pp. 95–100.

[235]In a nutshell, Klaus Liebig established that national free-riding is beneficial for an individual (small) country. However, this conclusion is not surprising, to the contrary, the fact that national free-riding is beneficial from the perspective of a single country is exactly the reason why multilateral and bilateral agreements in the IP field were established; this conclusion had already been drawn by Penrose (1951), pp. 112–127, in particular 113, and 226–227. From a global perspective, a negative impact on global welfare because of national free-riding can only be excluded in cases in which small and/or developing markets have no effect at all on the decision-making process regarding global investment into research. This may well be the case in relation to diseases also common in developed countries, where developing countries only constitute a small share of the global market, but may be different in relation to diseases endemic to Central America.

[236]Böttger (2008), p. 884.

[237]The issue of free-riding in relation to pharmaceutical innovation is discussed generally by Straus and Klunker (2007), p. 920; for a critical assessment of their reasoning see Heath (2008), p. 212.

[238]See Straus and Klunker (2007), p. 920.

Technology Transfer

Supporters of TRIPS-plus provisions claim that insufficient IP protection would negatively affect the *transfer of technology*, *e.g.*, by creating a disincentive for licensing activities, while "TRIPS-plus" levels of protection would increase the transfer of technology and foster also other forms of foreign direct investment.[239] Critics argue that developing countries must build the capacity to absorb technology and be allowed a period of free imitation (or at least lower levels of patent protection) to be able to technologically "catch up".[240] There is also no clear empirical evidence for a positive effect of stronger IP protection on technology transfer and foreign direct investment (FDI). Theoretically, better IP protection has "the potential of promoting" FDI by creating the necessary legal certainty for transferring technology to domestic licensees.[241] However, *Frederick Abbott* concluded that empirically "countries with the weakest levels of IPRs protection [...] have routinely been the recipients of the largest net FDI inflows".[242]

1.6.2.3 Social Policy Objectives

IP protection should also support broader socio-economic policy goals. Article 7 and 8 TRIPS express this idea by explicitly referring to economic objectives, such as *economic welfare* and *development* and social objectives, including "*social (...) welfare*". Specific socio-economic objectives are public health, nutrition and social development. Unlike CAFTA-DR, Article 3(2)(a) EU-CARIFORUM-EPA expresses these policy considerations by mandating that the "*agreement shall fully take into account the (...) social, health and environmental best interests of their respective population and future generations*".

Critics argue that TRIPS-plus protection does not significantly contribute to the objectives of innovation or competition, if at all, but negatively affects indirect, social objectives. In particular, it increases the potential for conflicts with public health, the environment, biological diversity, food security, access to knowledge and human rights.[243]

Public Health

Regarding such socio-economic policy goals, critics consider TRIPS-plus provisions to be particularly detrimental to the special social needs of developing countries in

[239] See Straus and Klunker (2007), p. 917; on this issue see also the references in Collins-Chase (2008), p. 780.

[240] Heath (2008), p. 212.

[241] Drexl (2016), p. 73.

[242] Abbott (1996), p. 474; see also Collins-Chase (2008), p. 782.

[243] MPI Principles (2013), Nr. 3; Roffe (2013), p. 934.

the area of *public health*. The provisions of CAFTA-DR in the IP field that were most strongly criticized in this regard were the patent and test data provisions. Stronger patent protection was seen as enabling the patent owners to prevent or delay market entry of generic drugs in Central America and maintain higher prices, thereby limiting access to medicines.[244] On the other hand, better protection and stricter enforcement of trademarks and effective protection of consumers against unfair competition could have a significant positive effect on public health by reducing the sale of counterfeit drugs.[245] In Central America (as in many other countries), enforcement laws apply to all IP rights and therefore trademark-specific enforcement rules would not easily align with the general structure of IP legislation. However, this does not exclude the possibility that IP enforcement agencies prioritize using the new enforcement rules in relation to counterfeit drugs.[246] Stronger patent protection could also increase the incentive for medical research, especially on diseases endemic to Central America and similar countries.[247]

Other Issues

The stronger protection of plant varieties is criticized for restricting traditional business models of local farmers, privatizing elements of nature and fostering monocultures which threaten *biodiversity*.[248] In addition, in Latin America sometimes a *human rights* (or anthropological) argument is put forward against IP protection. It is claimed that IP is a legal concept introduced by the European colonists and alien to the indigenous population, *e.g.*, in Central America the allegedly "commons-based" Mayan societies. Therefore, it is argued that IP protection should be restricted or even (partly) abolished, because it violates the rights of indigenous communities to follow their legal traditions.[249] Supporters of increased IP protection argue that it not only benefits the right holder, but also the consumer.[250] The underlying rationale of this view is that IP helps protect consumers against confusion and unfair competition as well as counterfeit products, and therefore increased IP protection also increases *consumer protection*. Protection against coun-

[244] See, e.g., Correa (2006), p. 402.

[245] Regarding Central American IP enforcement legislation in general and trademark counterfeiting in particular, see Sect. 7.1.2.

[246] In practice, local criminal enforcement agencies appear to focus on falsified medicines, see Sect. 8.8.3.

[247] See Sect. 3.1.1.4.

[248] See Sect. 6.1.2.3.

[249] See the references in Grave (2002), p. 20.

[250] USTR, TPP Chapter Summary Intellectual Property, pp. 2 and 6; regarding the relationship between trademarks and consumer protection in particular, see Sect. 4.1.1.1.

terfeit products is of special relevance if one considers that in Central America not only fashion clothes and DVDs are counterfeit, but also pharmaceuticals.[251] This rationale raises the question, which is analyzed in the following chapters, whether the increased protection of right holders practically really does translate into increased protection of consumers as well. Some researchers even contemplate a positive effect of stricter enforcement of IP rights on the *rule of law* in general, by making law enforcement more effective.[252] Such an effect could be particularly relevant for countries like El Salvador and Guatemala with widespread organized crime groups, which (sometimes) are also financed by the sale of counterfeit apparel and pharmaceuticals.[253]

1.6.3 Minimum Protection and Flexibilities

1.6.3.1 The Minimum Protection Mechanism

Multilateral Agreements

The structure of an FTA is that of an agreement that details the rights and obligations of the parties, *e.g.*, with regard to IP protection and enforcement based on the principle of "minimum protection". Accordingly, the IP chapters in FTAs typically do not contain rules regarding issues which are not relevant to right holders, especially mandatory exceptions and limitations. Accordingly, the balance between the obligations of the FTA and public interest must be achieved in the implementation of the agreement in the national legislation. Multilateral agreements such as the Paris Convention or TRIPS, on the other hand, are drafted as "model laws" and provide for a more comprehensive, balanced structure of IP protection and do not only contain minimum standards of IP protection.[254] This balance forms part of the negotiated consensus of all WTO Members.[255] Accordingly, TRIPS also includes provisions that place limitations on IP protection. *E.g.*, TRIPS provides for flexibilities that support designing domestic IP systems to be "conducive to social and economic welfare".[256] Such limitations can protect the balance of the IP system against the expansion of minimum protection. They have been described as "max-

[251] See Sect. 8.8.3.

[252] On the possible spill-over effects of bilateral FTAs on procedural law in general see Powell (2005), p. 88.

[253] See Sect. 2.5.5.

[254] MPI Principles (2013), Nr. 4.

[255] MPI Principles (2013), Nr. 4.

[256] Article 7 TRIPS; see MPI Principles (2013), Nr. 5.

imum protection",[257] "ceilings"[258] or "substantive maxima".[259] Critics argue that the principle of minimum protection creates ever-increasing levels of protection and ultimately "over-protection". Accordingly, they maintain that "enough is enough" and minimum protection rules should be balanced by flexibilities and maximum protection rules ("ceilings").[260] For clarification, the term "minimum protection" does not imply that the level of protection is low. To the contrary, such "minimum protection" represents, even compared to some industrial countries, an expansion of IP rights in favor of right holders over users.[261]

Bilateral FTAs

Increasing levels of minimum protection required under TRIPS-plus rules in bilateral FTAs create conflicts with the flexibilities and maximum protection ("ceilings") contained in TRIPS and other multilateral agreements. Critics argue that the TRIPS-plus rules in bilateral FTAs restrict the flexibilities under TRIPS and other multilateral agreements, encroach upon the multilateral balance and the ability of developing countries to pursue such policy goals. They demand that the level of IP protection required by FTAs should consider all international obligations of the parties of the FTA with regard to public policy goals, such as biological diversity and public health, and provide for the flexibilities necessary for the parties to include corresponding exceptions and limitations in their national IP laws.[262] Accordingly, critics maintain that bilateral FTAs should take international development principles, the WIPO Development Agenda and the level of development of their negotiating partner into account,[263] and in particular, that bilateral FTAs should provide for appropriate transition periods.[264] Also, this "ever increasing" base line of minimum protection established by an FTA is considered to be "cast in stone" and to create a "policy freeze" on the national level, which limits the possibility to adapt the national IP framework to changing economic, technological or other societal needs, even if such adaptation reflects an emerging international policy consensus.[265] Finally, ever increasing minimum levels of protection may have an *anti-competitive effect.* The increased protection tends to strengthen the market power of right holders and can restrict dynamic and innovation-oriented competition.[266]

---

[257] MPI Principles (2013), Nr. 4.

[258] Kur and Grosse Ruse-Khan (2008), p. 5.

[259] Dinwoodie (2006), p. 214.

[260] See, e.g., Kur and Grosse Ruse-Khan (2008), p. 5.

[261] See Finger (2000), p. 430, in relation to minimum standards under TRIPS.

[262] MPI Principles (2013), Nr. 20.

[263] MPI Principles (2013), Nr. 11.

[264] MPI Principles (2013), Nr. 22.

[265] MPI Principles (2013), Nr. 8; Roffe (2013), p. 937.

[266] Drexl (2007), p. 19.

1.6.3.2 Flexibilities and Differentiation of the Level of Protection

Concept

One solution often suggested to avoid the problems associated with minimum protection is the inclusion of flexibilities in multilateral agreements and bilateral FTAs. On the multilateral level, *TRIPS* recognizes different types of flexibilities, namely the differentiation of the level of protection depending on the level of development,[267] the reference to public policy goals,[268] optional protection and transitional periods.[269] The international criticism to some TRIPS provisions on patent law has resulted in an interpretation of TRIPS in the Doha Declaration, reaffirming flexibilities in relation to compulsory licenses, which also differentiates between high-, middle- and low-income countries.[270] Another solution could be the differentiation of the level of IP protection according to the level of technological and economic development of the respective country. This differentiation reflects the recognition, already included in TRIPS, that "one size does not fit all" and that with regard to IP protection, flexibilities and *differentiations* are necessary. The diverging realities in developed and developing countries with regard to the different ability to innovate and absorb technology and other social needs require different solutions in developing countries. With regard to the term of patent protection, for instance, "one size fits all" may not be suitable and it may be preferable from a public policy perspective to differentiate between developed and developing countries, different industries and between developing countries in different stages of development.[271]

The European Patent Office conducted an extensive study on the possible developments of international IP policy from 2005 to 2025, based on interviews with experts from practice, politics, academia and civil society. The results were four "scenarios" for the IP system, which differed substantially with regard to the role and level of IP protection and enforcement depending on the level of economic and technological development.[272]

In addition, it is argued that countries should have some discretion to adapt their legal system to the development policy they prefer and not be forced to implement specific levels of rights or limitations, because there is no generally accepted development theory. National legislators should retain sufficient policy space in the field of IP without being subject to dispute resolution schemes.[273] If IP protection and limitations are regulated in detail in multilateral agreements and bilateral FTAs,

[267] Article 66 TRIPS.

[268] Articles 7 and 8 TRIPS.

[269] Article 66 TRIPS.

[270] See the special rights granted to least-developed countries in Nr. 7 Doha Declaration.

[271] See, e.g., Barton (2007), p. 14; this is reflected, e.g., in the Doha Declaration, which differentiates between low-income and middle-income countries.

[272] European Patent Office (2006).

[273] See Liebig (2007), pp. 2–3.

policy issues such as human rights or access to medicines may ultimately be determined by a Dispute Settlement Body of the WTO or similar dispute resolution institution.[274] However, a country might need special limitations to IP rights for social reasons (*e.g.*, access to medicines or fair use) or create special systems of IP protection for their traditional knowledge or genetic resources.[275] Finally, it is argued that while there seems to be a broad consensus that patent protection contributes to innovation, without conclusive evidence as to the optimal level of patent protection, countries should not lose the "freedom to determine patent protection levels in accordance with economic development".[276]

Risks

However, while flexible and differentiated rules can help balance the "minimum protection" approach, there are certain risks associated with such flexibility. First, a policy approach based on flexibilities, enabling and possibly even encouraging diverging implementation on the national level, could inhibit further substantive IP law harmonization. Second, flexibilities in international agreements may not be used effectively by developing countries.[277] The analysis of national law implementing TRIPS found that many developing countries have not fully utilized flexibilities regarding, *e.g.*, compulsory licenses, limits on data protection and research exemptions in their legislation.[278] This behavior may have been caused by a lack of the time and expertise needed to draft balanced legislation.[279] If this is correct, then international agreements will only contribute to a meaningful improvement of national competition legislation if they provide more specific guidance. However, as *Josef Drexl* cautions, considerable divergence also exists between developed jurisdictions as to the most appropriate balancing rules, *e.g.*, regarding anti-competitive use of IP rights.[280] Other examples for open policy issues are compulsory licenses (modified by the *Doha Declaration* in 2001) and limitations to test data protection by the *Bipartisan Trade Deal* in 2007, both of which were substantially revised a few years after being incorporated into bilateral FTAs. In such cases, a

---

[274] TRIPS rules are interpreted by the WTO dispute settlement bodies in accordance with the Vienna Convention on the Law of Treaties, see Kaiser, Karen / Frick, Norman, in Busche et al. (2013), Article 64, Nr 38–46.

[275] There is yet no consensus on best practices for, e.g., protecting genetic resources and traditional knowledge (see Sect. 8.8.6). Therefore, policy flexibility should be maintained on the national level.

[276] Heath (2008), p. 212; "IP-demanding" countries should also be mindful that the process of technological development historically started for many countries with a period of imitation of foreign innovation, be it Germany and the USA in the nineteenth or Japan and Korea in the twentieth century; on this issue, in particular the specific design of the Japanese and Korean IP systems to support the diffusion of technology, see Maskus (2004), pp. 26–26.

[277] See, e.g., Shaikh (2016), p. 207.

[278] Musungu and Oh (2005), p. 32 (regarding the Bolar Exception) and p. 36 (regarding test data).

[279] Finger correctly points out that implementation requires time, Finger (2000), p. 426.

[280] Drexl (2007), p. 21.

more open approach to flexibilities should be used, *i.e.*, instead of including specific flexibilities in the text of an agreement, which could preempt a discussion on the national level as to the appropriate scope of the limitation, the agreement could clarify that it does not affect the policy space of the national legislator in the respective field.

Flexibilities also create the risk of under-protection by countries which, because of their level of development, are expected to provide a certain level of protection, but instead opt to implement national "free riding" policies. Good examples are activities of several countries in relation to compulsory licenses for patents. Under Article 31 TRIPS, a country may impose compulsory licenses for any purpose.[281] In case of a "national emergency", the respective government is even exempted from trying to obtain a commercial license from the right holder.[282] The term "national emergency" is a flexible rule, because each country is free to define the circumstances that constitute such a national emergency, including general public interest considerations. There is an inherent problem when "public interests" are pursued by reducing IP protection on the national level. Countries reduce the costs for their national health budget or increase the competitiveness of domestic industries by lowering their levels of protection and thus externalizing research costs, while profiting from the research results financed by other countries.[283] This reduces the global investment into research, which could lead to less research and less innovation. In the end, flexibilities for the national law might recreate the "tragedy of the commons" that the international law was designed to avoid. Such opportunistic behavior is less problematic with regard to lower-income or least-developed countries. However, as previous examples of compulsory licenses show, flexibilities are also utilized by middle-income and even developed countries, *e.g.*, Brazil, the USA[284] and Germany.[285] In these cases, it was not entirely clear that there existed really a national emergency.

---

[281] Except with regard to semiconductor technology, Article 31(c) TRIPS.

[282] Article 31(b) TRIPS.

[283] Straus (2003), pp. 130–131.

[284] The USA issued a compulsory license for a patent of the German pharmaceutical company Bayer to address the Athrax threat, based on the claim that there was the risk of a shortage of supply, even though Bayer insisted on being able and willing to provide the entire amount of medicine required by the US government. Brazil passed a law creating a compulsory license for a patent to *Efavirenz* relating to second-generation HIV drugs, claiming that the costs of the patented drug prevented the Brazilian government from providing healthcare to all HIV patients; this justification was not based on any emergency, but merely referred to fiscal considerations. Brazil claimed that it had to be considered a developing country and could, therefore, not be held to the standards of patent protection of developed countries. This two-tier claim disregards the multiple tiers of development used under TRIPS and the Doha Declaration to differentiate the level of IP protection. However, because of the flexibilities existing in Article 31 TRIPS, Brazil's action was compliant with its international legal obligations, even if it was not in the spirit of TRIPS; on these cases see in detail Böttger (2008), pp. 881–891; see also Abbott (2007), p. 9.

[285] In Germany, the Federal Patent Court granted a compulsory license in a preliminary decision to Merck for an HIV drug of Shionogi in 2016, see the report on the decision in GRUR-Prax 2017, 105.

Finally, flexibilities often evolve into mandatory rules. In other words, today's flexibility may be tomorrow's minimum protection, either because of increased TRIPS-plus requirements in international agreements or because of excessive implementation. Bilateral FTAs frequently provide for mandatory protection in areas that were explicitly optional under TRIPS.[286]

1.6.3.3 Maximum Protection or "Ceilings"

Maximum protection provisions could be created to balance the continually increasing minimum protection and supplement flexibilities. They could "immunize" developing countries in negotiations of bilateral FTAs.[287] However, including maximum protection provisions in bilateral FTAs could be "politically" difficult, because "IP-demanding" countries have no incentive to include such provisions which typically restrict the protection of "their" right holders. The FTA partner countries who may wish to include such clauses typically do not have the necessary bargaining position in trade deal negotiations to achieve such a goal. Therefore, it seems more likely that provisions establishing mandatory limitations can be agreed upon on the multilateral level.[288] On the TRIPS level, there have been several initiatives by developing countries in this respect, in addition to the Doha Declaration: By the summer of 2006, a number of WTO members had proposed moving towards text-based negotiations on the disclosure of origin requirement in patent applications and subsequently in June 2006, a proposal for an amendment of TRIPS by inserting a new Article 29*bis* TRIPS was presented by Brazil, China, Cuba, India, Pakistan, Peru, Thailand and Tanzania.[289] There are business sectors and international companies interested in balancing IP protection, *e.g.*, the generic pharmaceutical industry working against originator companies with strong patent portfolios, who support corresponding policy initiatives.[290] Another interesting initiative (which relates to limitations of copyright for educational purposes and is, therefore, not further analyzed here)

[286]Examples from CAFTA-DR are further discussed in Sect. 8.9.2.

[287]Kur and Grosse Ruse-Khan (2008), p. 14; the authors correctly qualify this expectation by observing that countries may still be forced, in the framework of bilateral FTAs, to implement rules conflicting with the provisions of other FTAs or regional agreements to which they are party, giving the conflicting trademark and geographical indication rules under CAFTA-DR and the EU-FTAs as an example. This issue will be discussed in detail in Sect. 4.4.6.

[288]This is proposed by, e.g., *Josef Drexl*, see Drexl (2006–2007), p. 539.

[289]*WTO* General Council, Trade Negotiations Committee, Council for Trade-Related Aspects of Intellectual Property Rights (2006).

[290]Regarding the opposition of the local generic industry in Central America, see Castro (2015), p. 89.

originates from a proposal by Brazil, Chile, Nicaragua and Uruguay for "Work related to Exceptions and Limitations" presented to the WIPO Standing Committee on Copyright and Related Rights (SCCR) in March 2008.[291] A further example in the copyright area is the Marrakesh Treaty to Facilitate Access to Published Works for Persons Who Are Blind, Visually Impaired or Otherwise Print Disabled, which entered into force on September 30, 2016. It facilitates the production and international transfer of books adapted for people with blindness or visual impairments by establishing a set of limitations and exceptions to copyright.[292] However, the concept of mandatory limitations collides with the structure of TRIPS, which focuses on minimum protection, as expressed in Article 1 TRIPS, which provides only for the right of the members to provide for *more* protection than required by TRIPS.[293] It is far from clear that mandatory ceilings will be broadly recognized, because of the "minimum protection" legal structure of TRIPS and the political ramifications.[294]

1.6.3.4 Transition Periods

Another policy option to draft IP provisions more flexible are transition periods.[295] They have the appeal of allowing the differentiation of obligations on a country-by-country basis, without fragmenting the overall legal structure of IP provisions. Article 66 TRIPS, for example, provides for longer transitional periods for least-developed countries than for other countries.

References

Abbott FM (1996) Commentary: the international intellectual property order enters the 21st century. Vand J Transnatl Law 29:471

Abbott FM (2007) The problems of intellectual property in Latin America and how to address them. United Nations, Santiago, Chile

Barton JH (2007) The future of the intellectual property system and consequent negotiation topics. In: Barton JH, Abbott FM, Correa CM, Drexl J, Foray D, Marchant R (eds) Views on the future of the intellectual property system. International Centre for Trade and Sustainable Development, Geneva, Switzerland

[291] WIPO (2008); on this proposal see Grosse Ruse-Khan (2009), section 3.A.

[292] On the current status of the agreement see the information available at https://www.wipo.int/marrakesh_treaty/en/ (accessed 2 Nov 2024).

[293] Lüers, Jan-Carl in Busche et al. (2013), Article 1, Nr 14-25.

[294] Drexl (2016), p. 61.

[295] See, e.g., MPI Principles (2013), Nr. 22.

Beattie P (2007) The (intellectual property law and) economics of innocent fraud - the IP and development debate. IIC 2007:6–30
Bendaña-Guerrero GJ (1999) *Curso de Derecho* de Propiedad Industrial. Hispamer, Managua, Nicaragua
Bennett P (1994) TRIPS — a victory for US Industry, Patent World, May 1994 62:31–35
Booth J, Wade Christine J, Walker Thomas W (2006) Understading Central America: global forces, rebellion and change, 4th edn. Westview Press, Bolder, Colorado
Böttger F (2008) Zwangslizenzen im Patentrecht - Eine systematische Bewertung der neueren Praxis insbesondere im Bereich der öffentlichen Gesundheit. GRUR Int 2008:881–891
Busche J, Stoll P-T, Wiebe A (eds) (2013) TRIPS - Internationales und europäisches Recht des geistigen Eigentums, 2nd edn. Verlag, Carl Heymanns
Castro A (2015) Intellectual property rights in CAFTA-DR and pharmaceuticals in Costa Rica. In: Koehler-Geib F, Sanchez SM (eds) Costa Rica five years after CAFTA-DR: assessing early results. Directions in development. World Bank, Washington
Colburn FD, Cruz AS (2007) Varieties of liberalism in Central America: Nation-States as works in progress. University of Texas Press, Austin
Collins-Chase CT (2008) The case against TRIPS-plus protection in developing countries facing aids epidemics. Univ Pa J Int Law 29:763
Collopy D et al. (2014) Measuring Infringement of Intellectual Property Rights. Available at https://assets.publishing.service.gov.uk/government/uploads/system/uploads/attachment_data/file/325020/IP_Measuring_Infringement.pdf. Accessed 2 Nov 2024
Comisión para el Esclarecimiento Histórico (1999) Guatemala - Memoria del Silencio, 1st edn. UNOPS, Guatemala
Cornish W, Liddell K (2016) The origins and structure of the TRIPS agreement. In: Ullrich H, Hilty RM, Lamping M, Drexl J (eds) TRIPS plus 20: from trade rules to market principles. Springer-Verlag, Berlin
Cornish W, Llewelyn D, Aplin T (2013) Intellectual property: patents, copyright, trade marks and allied rights, 8th edn. Sweet & Maxwell (cited as Cornish et al. (2013))
Correa CM (2006) Implications of bilateral Free Trade Agreements on access to medicines. Bull World Health Organ 84:399–404. Available at https://www.researchgate.net/publication/278153297_Implications_of_bilateral_free_trade_agreements_on_access_to_medicines. Accessed 2 Nov 2024
Davis MH, Neacsu D (2000–2001) Legitimacy, globally: the incoherence of free trade practice, global economics and their governing principles of political economy. UMKC Law Rev 69:733
Díaz Á (2008) América Latina y el Caribe: La propiedad intelectual después de los tratados de libre comercio. Comisión Económica para América Latina y el Caribe (CEPAL), Santiago de Chile
Dinwoodie GB (2006) The international intellectual property law system: new actors, new institutions, new sources. Marquette Intell Prop Rev 10:205
Drahos P (2003) The global ratchet for intellectual property rights: why it fails as policy and what should be done about it. Available at https://www0.anu.edu.au/fellows/pdrahos/reports/pdfs/2003globalipratchet.pdf. Accessed 2 Nov 2024
Drexl J (2004) Intellectual property and antitrust law. IMS Health and Trinko - Antitrust Placebo for Consumers Instead of Sound Economics in Refusal-to-Deal Cases, IIC 2004, 788–808
Drexl J (2006–2007) IP in bilateral trade agreements. some ideas on how they promote market power and distort international competition. In: Ghidini G, Genovesi LM (eds) Intellectual property and market power, ATRIP Papers 2006 – 2007. Universidad de Buenos Aires, Buenos Aires

Drexl J (2018) In: Beck CH (ed) Internationales Immaterialgüterrecht, Münchener Kommentar zum BGB, vol 12, 7th edn, Munich

Drexl J, Conde Gallego B, Enchelmaier S, Leistner M, Mackenrodt M-O (2006) Comments of the Max Planck Institute for Intellectual Property, Competition and Tax Law on the Directorate-General Competition Discussion Paper of December 2005 on the Application of Article 82 of the EC Treaty to Exclusionary Abuses, 37 IIC 2006, 558–572

Drexl J (2007) Responding to the challenges with a competition-oriented approach. In: Barton JH, Abbott FM, Correa CM, Drexl J, Foray D, Marchant R (eds) Views on the future of the intellectual property system. International Centre for Trade and Sustainable Development, Geneva, Switzerland

Drexl J (2016) The concept of trade-relatedness of intellectual property rights in times of post-TRIPS bilateralism. In: Ullrich H, Hilty RM, Lamping M, Drexl J (eds) TRIPS plus 20: from trade rules to market principles. Springer-Verlag, Berlin

European Parliament (2011) Honduras Country Briefing 2011. Available at http://www.europarl.europa.eu/meetdocs/2009_2014/documents/dcam/dv/cbhonduras_/cbhonduras_en.pdf. Accessed 2 Nov 2024

European Patent Office (2006) Scenarios for the future. European Patent Office, Munich

Finger JM (2000) The WTO's special burden on less developed countries. Cato J 19(3):425–437. Available at https://www.cato.org/sites/cato.org/files/serials/files/cato-journal/2000/1/cj19n3-9.pdf. Accessed 2 Nov 2024

Flanzbaum R (2005) VI Seminario de Propiedad Industrial e Intelectual en Iberoamérica. Clarke Modet, Mardid

Fleury S et al (2013) Right to health in Latin America: beyond universalization. CEPAL, ECLAC, United Nations, Santiago, Chile

Götting H-P (2004) Biodiversität und Patentrecht. GRUR Int 2004:731–736

Granados J, Cornejo R (2006) Convergence in the Americas: some lessons from the DR -CAFTA process. The World Economy, 2006. Available at http://idbdocs.iadb.org/wsdocs/getdocument.aspx?docnum=862038. Accessed 2 Nov 2024

Grave HG (2002) Gewerbliche Schutzrechte in Mexiko - Eine Untersuchung vor dem Hintergrund der maßgeblichen Bestimmungen der NAFTA- und TRIPS-Abkommen. Nomos, Baden-Baden

Grosse Ruse-Khan H (2009) Re-delineation of the role of stakeholders: IP enforcement beyond exclusive rights. In: Li X, Correa CM (eds) Intellectual property enforcement international perspectives

Hassemer M (2000) Gewerbliche Schutzrechte im Mercosur. Nomos, Baden-Baden

Heath C (2008) Harmonisation of International Patent Law? – A Reply to Straus and Klunker, IIC 2008, 210–216

Industry Functional Advisory Committee on IPR for Trade Policy Matters (IFAC-3) (2004) The U.S.-Central American Free Trade Agreement (FTA) - The Intellectual Property Provisions. Available at https://ustr.gov/archive/assets/Trade_Agreements/Regional/CAFTA/CAFTA_Reports/asset_upload_file571_5945.pdf. Accessed 2 Nov 2024

Institute of Policy Innovation (IPI) (2007) The true cost of sound recording piracy to the U.-S. economy. https://www.ipi.org/ipi_issues/detail/the-true-cost-of-sound-recording-piracy-to-the-us-economy

Jaramillo CF, Lederman D (2005) CAFTA-DR: challenges and opportunities for Central America. World Bank. Available at http://documents.worldbank.org/curated/en/249751468212969403/pdf/329530DR0CAFTA1Challenges.pdf. Accessed 2 Nov 2024

Kolstad O (2008) Competition law and intellectual property rights - outline of an economics-based approach. In: Drexl J (ed) Research handbook on intellectual property and competition law. Edward Elgar, Cheltenham

Koul AK (2006) Guide to the WTO and GATT – economics, law and politics. Springer Nature, Singapore

Kur A, Grosse Ruse-Khan H (2008) Enough is enough – the notion of binding ceilings in international intellectual property protection, Max Planck Institute for Intellectual Property, Competition & Tax Law Research Paper Series No. 09-01. Available at http://papers.ssrn.com/sol3/papers.cfm?abstract_id=1326429. Accessed 2 Nov 2024

Lederman D, Maloney WF (2003) R&D and development. World Bank Policy Research Working Paper N° 3024. Available at http://papers.ssrn.com/sol3/papers.cfm?abstract_id=402480. Accessed 2 Nov 2024

Liebig K (2005) Die internationale Regulierung geistiger Eigentumsrechte und ihr Einfluss auf den Wissenstransfer in Entwicklungsländern. Nomos, Baden-Baden

Liebig K (2007) Ensuring Development Friendly Economic Partnership Agreements (EPAs), study commissioned by BMZ and GTZ Germany. Available at https://www.idos-research.de/uploads/media/07-1380.pdf. Accessed 2 Nov 2024

Lobos Luna AJ (2012) Marca Sonora, Thesis, Universidad Rafael Landívar, Guatemala (on file with the author)

Maskus KE (2004) Encouraging International Technology Transfer, UNCTAD, ICTSD Project on Intellectual Property Rights and Sustainable Development, ICTSD, Geneva. Available at https://www.files.ethz.ch/isn/111411/2010_01_encouraging-international-technology-transfer.pdf. Accessed 2 Nov 2024

Matthews D (2011) Counterfeiting and public health. In: Geiger C (ed) Criminal enforcement of intellectual property: a handbook of contemporary research. Edward Elgar, Cheltenham

Menocal C (2005) Guatemala es paraíso de la falsificación, Prensa Libre, 7 August 2005 (on file with the author)

Musungu SF, Oh C (2005) The use of flexibilities in TRIPS by developing countries: can they promote access to medicines?, Commission on Intellectual Property Rights, Innovation and Public Health (CIPIH), South Centre, Geneva

Nadde-Phlix S (2014) IP protection in EU Free Trade Agreements vis-à-vis IP negotiations in the WTO. In: Drexl J, Grosse Ruse-Khan H, Nadde-Phlix S (eds) (2014) EU bilateral trade agreements and intellectual property: for better or worse?, MPI Studies on Intellectual Property and Competition Law 20. Springer-Verlag, Berlin

OECD (2007) The Economic Impact of Counterfeiting and Piracy, Executive Summary. Available at https://web-archive.oecd.org/2012-06-15/136568-38707619.pdf. Accessed 2 Nov 2024

OECD/EUIPO (2016) Trade in counterfeit and pirated goods: mapping the economic impact. OECD Publishing, Paris. Available at https://doi.org/10.1787/9789264252653-en. Accessed 2 Nov 2024

Olson M (1971) The logic of collective action: Public goods and the theory of groups. Harvard University Press, Cambridge

Ostry S (2000) Regional dominos and the WTO: building blocks or boomerang. In: Kreinin ME (ed) Building a partnership: the Canada-United States Free Trade Agreement. University of Calgary Press, Calgary

Pacón AM (1995) Was bringt TRIPS den Entwicklungsländern? GRUR Int 1995:875–886

Penrose E (1951) The economics of the international patent system. Johns Hopkins Press

Perez-Brignoli H (1989) A brief history of Central America. University of California Press, Berkeley

Petersmann E-U (1996–1997) Constitutionalism and International Organizations. Northwestern J Int Law Bus 17:398

Powell SJ (2005) Regional economic arrangements and the rule of law in the Americas: the human rights face of Free Trade Agreements. Florida J Int Law 17(1):59

Public Citizen's Global Trade Watch (2006) Dangerous CAFTA liaisons. Available at https://www.citizen.org/documents/CAFTA_Liaisons_Report1.pdf. Accessed 2 Nov 2024

Reid M (2007) Forgotten continent: the battle for Latin America's soul. Yale University Press, New Haven

Retana Chinchilla RJ (2007) Derecho Marcario en Centroamérica y Panama. Investigaciones Jurídicas, San José

Rodlauer M, Schipke A (2005) Central America: Global Integration and Regional Cooperation, International Monetary Fund Occasional Paper No. 243. Available at http://www.imf.org/external/pubs/ft/op/243/. Accessed 2 Nov 2024

Roffe P (2013) Free Trade Agreements and the Americas, IIC 2013, 932–943

Roffe P, Genovesi LM (2011) Implementación y Administración de los Capítulos de Propiedad Intelectual en los Acuerdos de Libre Comercio con los Estados Unidos: La Experiencia de Cuatro Países de América Latina", Inter-American Development Bank, Sector of Integration and Trade, Policy Brief (No. IDB-PB-129)

Shaikh OH (2016) Access to medicine versus test data exclusivity – safeguarding flexibilities under international law, Munich Studies on Innovation and Competition. Springer-Verlag, Berlin

Stevens C, Irfan I, Massa I, Kennan J (2015) The impact of Free Trade Agreements between developed and developing countries on economic development in developing countries: a rapid evidence assessment. Overseas Development Institute, London

Stiglitz J (2006) Making globalization work. Norton, New York

Stöbele P, Hacker F, Thiering F (2018) Markengesetz - Kommentar, 12th edn. Heymanns, Cologne

Straus J (2003), Patentschutz durch TRIPS-Abkommen - Ausnahmeregelungen und -praktiken und ihre Bedeutung, insbesondere hinsichtlich pharmazeutischer Produkte, Bitburger Gespräche, Yearbook. C. H. Beck, Munich

Straus J, Klunker N-S (2007) Harmonisation of International Patent Law IIC 2007, 907–936

Tharin M (2008) Dealing with a bad deal: two years of CAFTA-DR in Central America. Council on Hemispheric Affairs. Available at http://www.bilaterals.org/article.php3?id_article=13774. Accessed 2 Nov 2024

Thomas K (2009) Structural adjustment, spatial imaginaries, and "Piracy" in Guatemala's apparel industry. Anthropol Work Rev 30(1):1–10

Thomas, K (2011) An ethnography of brand piracy in Guatemala, Doctoral dissertation, Harvard University

Thomas K (2012) Intellectual property law and the ethics of imitation in Guatemala. Anthropol Quart 85(3):785–814

USTR, CAFTA Policy Brief (2005) Free Trade With Central America and the Dominican Republic, Highlights of the CAFTA. Available at https://ustr.gov/archive/assets/Trade_Agreements/Regional/CAFTA/Briefing_Book/asset_upload_file834_7179.pdf. Accessed 2 Nov 2024

USTR, Special 301 Report 2005. Available at https://ustr.gov/sites/default/files/2005%20Special%20301%20Report.pdf. Accessed 2 Nov 2024 (cited as USTR, Special 301 Report 2005)

USTR, Special 301 Report 2007. Available at https://ustr.gov/about-us/policy-offices/press-office/reports-and-publications/archives/2007/2007-special-301-report. Accessed 2 Nov 2024 (cited as USTR, Special 301 Report 2007)

USTR, Special 301 Report 2011. Available at https://ustr.gov/sites/default/files/uploads/gsp/speeches/reports/2011/301/2011%20Special%20301%20Report.pdf. Accessed 2 Nov 2024 (cited as USTR, Special 301 Report 2011)

USTR, Special 301 Report 2016. Available at https://ustr.gov/sites/default/files/USTR-2016-Special-301-Report.pdf. Accessed 2 Nov 2024 (cited as USTR, Special 301 Report 2016)

USTR, TPP Chapter Summary Intellectual Property. Available at https://ustr.gov/sites/default/files/TPP-Chapter-Summary-Intellectual-Property.pdf. Accessed 2 Nov 2024

Vargas V, Rama M, Singh R (2022) Pharmaceuticals in Latin America and the Caribbean: Players, Access, and Innovation Across Diverse Models, https://doi.org/10.1596/36871

von Lewinski S (2016) The WTO/TRIPS dispute settlement mechanism: experiences and perspectives. In: Ullrich H, Hilty RM, Lamping M, Drexl J (eds) TRIPS Plus 20: from trade rules to market principles. Springer-Verlag, Berlin

WIPO (2008) Proposal by Brazil, Chile, Nicaragua and Uruguay for Work Related to Exceptions and Limitations, WIPO Doc. SCCR/16/2, 17 July 2008. Available at www.wipo.int/edocs/mdocs/copyright/en/sccr_16/sccr_16_2.pdf. Accessed 2 Nov 2024

WTO General Council, Trade Negotiations Committee, Council for Trade-Related Aspects of Intellectual Property Rights (2006) Communication from Brazil, China, Colombia, Cuba, India, Pakistan, Peru, Thailand and Tanzania, Doha Working Programme - The Outstanding Implementation Issue on the Relationship between the TRIPS Agreement and the Convention on Biological Diversity, *WT/GC/W/564*/Rev. 2, TN/C/W/41/Rev. 2, IP/C/W/474, 5 July 2006. Available at https://docs.wto.org/dol2fe/Pages/SS/directdoc.aspx?filename=Q:/IP/C/W474.pdf&Open=True. Accessed 2 Nov 2024

Yu PK (2008) Teaching intellectual property law. St Louis Univ Law J 52:923

Chapter 2
Legal and Institutional Framework of IP Protection in Central America

2.1 The International Legal Framework

IP legislation in Central America today has become quite complex, and it is difficult to assemble a current and comprehensive list of the international treaties applicable in Central America, especially after the implementation of CAFTA-DR.[1] This section provides an overview over the applicable international, bilateral and regional agreements. CAFTA-DR, the EU-CARIFORUM-EPA and EU-C-AA are discussed in Sects. 2.2 and 2.3. Table 2.1 provides an overview of international agreements in the field of IP and their status in Central America and the USA.

2.1.1 Multilateral Agreements

2.1.1.1 Paris Convention

The first international agreement to regulate IP was the Paris Convention. Importantly, Article 2(1) Paris Convention, also adopted later by Article 3(1) TRIPS, requires national treatment with regard to the protection and use of IP rights. The Paris Convention had less impact in Central America than in other Latin American countries or regions, *e.g.*, in Brazil.[2] Only the Dominican Republic had become a party to the Paris Convention before TRIPS (in 1890). Costa Rica (1995), El

[1] In Central America, *Carlos Castillo* in El Salvador and *Guy Bendaña-Guerrero* in Nicaragua are among the few lawyers who tried to account for all international and national IP statutes and their applicability in their respective countries, see, in relation to Nicaragua, Bendaña-Guerrero (1999), pp. 28–34.

[2] See Böttger, Fabian / Quarch, Tilman, Brazil, in Henning-Bodewig (2013), p. 142.

F. Böttger, *CAFTA-DR, European Free Trade Agreements and the Industrial Property System in Central America*, Munich Studies on Innovation and Competition 21, https://doi.org/10.1007/978-3-031-93440-7_2

Table 2.1 Status of International IP Agreements in Central America

Agreement	Costa Rica	Dom. Rep.	El Salvador	Guatemala	Honduras	Nicaragua	USA
Beijing Treaty	In force	In force	In force	Signed	Signed	Signed	Signed
Berne Convention	In force	In force	In force	In force	In force	In force	In force
Brussels Convention	**In force**	–	**In force**	–	**In force**	**In force**	**In force**
Budapest Treaty	**In force**	**In force**	**In force**	**In force**	**In force**	**In force**	**In force**
Hague Agreement	–	–	–	–	–	–	In force
Lisbon Agreement	In force	In force	–	–	–	In force	
Madrid Agreement (Indications of Source)	–	In force	–	Signed	–	–	–
Madrid Agreement (Trademarks)	–	–	–	Signed	–	–	–
Marrakesh Treaty	In force	In force	In force	In force	In force	In force	In force
Nairobi Treaty	–	–	In force	In force	–	–	–
Nice Agreement	–	–	–	–	–	–	In force
Paris Convention	**In force**	**In force**	**In force**	**In force**	**In force**	**In force**	**In force**
PCT	**In force**	**In force**	**In force**	**In force**	**In force**	**In force**	**In force**
Phonograms Convention	In force	–	In force	In force	In force	In force	In force
PLT	–	–	–	–	–	–	In force
Rome Convention	In force	In force	In force	In force	In force	In force	–
Singapore Treaty	Signed	Signed	–	–	–	–	In force
Strasbourg Agreement	–	–	–	–	–	–	In force
TLT	**In force**	**In force**	**In force**	**In force**	**In force**	**In force**	**In force**
TRIPS	**In force**	**In force**	**In force**	**In force**	**In force**	**In force**	**In force**
UPOV Convention	**In force (1991)**	**In force (1991)**	–	–	–	**In force (1978)**	**In force (1991)**
WCT	**In force**	**In force**	**In force**	**In force**	**In force**	**In force**	**In force**
WIPO Convention	In force	In force	In force	In force	In force	In force	In force
WPPT	**In force**	**In force**	**In force**	**In force**	**In force**	**In force**	**In force**

Treaties which must be ratified under CAFTA-DR are highlighted in bold

Salvador (1994), Honduras (1994), Guatemala (1998) and Nicaragua (1996) became members of the Paris Convention during or after the negotiation and ratification process of TRIPS.[3]

2.1.1.2 TRIPS

Contemporary IP law in Central America, therefore, begins with TRIPS. All CAFTA-DR parties acceded to the WTO and TRIPS in the course of 1995, together with the USA and other developed countries. Costa Rica, Honduras and the USA joined on 1 January 1995, the Dominican Republic on 9 March 1995, El Salvador on 7 May 1995, Guatemala on 21 July 1995 and Nicaragua on 3 September 1995.[4]

Even though all Central American countries were already parties to TRIPS, its ratification was required by a regional trade agreement in the late 1990ies (the Central America—Dominican Republic Agreement of 1998).[5] The ratification of TRIPS is not stated as an obligation in CAFTA-DR, probably because of the existing obligations under this Central America—Dominican Republic Agreement and because all countries had already ratified TRIPS. Article 15.1(7) CAFTA-DR refers only to "existing rights and obligations under the TRIPS Agreement".

All Central American countries were allowed to utilize the transition periods for implementing certain provisions according to Article 65(2) and (4) TRIPS because of their status as developing countries. These periods expired on 31 December 2004 for requirements relating to product patents and otherwise on 31 December 1999.[6] The extensions for least developed countries do not apply to any CAFTA-DR country. TRIPS is, therefore, fully applicable within the CAFTA-DR region since 1 January 2005.[7]

TRIPS contains provisions on copyright and related rights, trademarks and geographical indications, industrial designs, patents, topographies and undisclosed information. By reference to the Paris Convention, trade name protection[8] and unfair competition[9] are also part of the scope of TRIPS.

---

[3] More detailed information on the ratification history of the Paris Convention in Central America is given in the Table of Legislation.

[4] See the information provided by the WTO at https://www.wto.org/english/thewto_e/whatis_e/tif_e/org6_e.htm (accessed 2 Nov 2024).

[5] Article 14.01 Central America – Dominican Republic Agreement, available at http://www.sice.oas.org/trade/camdrep/indice.asp (accessed 2 Nov 2024).

[6] The only Latin American country with an extended transition period until 2006, granted by Article 66(1) TRIPS, is Haiti (which is a neighboring country of the Dominican Republic).

[7] On the application of TRIPS during the transition period see Hassemer (2000), pp. 26–27.

[8] Report of the Appellate Body, United States – Section 211 Omnibus Appropriations Act of 1998, AB-2001-7, WT/DS176/AB/Rv of 2 January 2002, available at https://www.wto.org/english/tratop_e/dispu_e/176abr_e.doc (accessed 2 Nov 2024), see also Lüers, Jan-Carl in Busche et al. (2013), Article 1, Nr 30.

[9] The inclusion of unfair competition follows from the reference to Article 10bis Paris Convention, however, the inclusion is only partial because of the limited reference, see Lüers, Jan-Carl in Busche et al. (2013), Article 1, Nr 31.

Even after the ratification of the bilateral FTAs, TRIPS is still important as a reference, because these agreements build upon it. The provisions in CAFTA-DR, for instance, expand or specify TRIPS protection usually without restating it. Thus, only TRIPS and the respective bilateral FTAs read together provide the full picture of the legal framework established by international agreements. Also, several TRIPS areas are not regulated by CAFTA-DR, such as design and topography protection.[10]

2.1.1.3 Multilateral Agreements on Trademarks and Geographical Indications

In addition to the Paris Convention and TRIPS, IP law is regulated by specific international agreements. This and the following section address the treaties applicable in (at least some) Central American countries, mainly those treaties that the countries shall ratify or accede to according to Article 15.1(2) to 15.1 (5) CAFTA-DR.

In the field of trademark law, the Central American countries shall ratify the *Trademark Law Treaty* (TLT) of 1994.[11] Because CAFTA-DR was signed in 2005, the reformed TLT from 2006 could not be considered. The Dominican Republic shall "endeavor" to ratify the reformed TLT under the FTA with the EU.[12] The Central American countries on the other hand "shall make all reasonable efforts to [...] comply with the Trademark Law Treaty (Geneva, 1994)".[13] The TLT has meanwhile been ratified by all Central American countries.[14] Guatemala, the last country to ratify the TLT, became a member on 12 December 2016.[15] However, the impact of the ratification of the TLT in Central America is practically limited and, therefore, the agreement is not analyzed in detail in this study.[16]

Additionally, the countries are not required to ratify the Madrid Agreement Concerning the International Registration of Marks (Madrid Agreement (Trademarks)) itself, but "shall make *all reasonable efforts* to ratify or accede to" the Protocol Relating to the Madrid Agreement Concerning the International Registra-

[10] Design law is addressed, by comparison, in Article 146 EU-CARIFORUM-EPA and Articles 251 to 257 EU-CA-AA, see Sect. 5.1.

[11] Article 15.1.4(b) CAFTA.

[12] Article 144(E) EU-CARIFORUM-EPA.

[13] Article 238 EU-CA-AA.

[14] WIPO, TLT Contracting Parties, available at http://www.wipo.int/treaties/en/ShowResults.jsp?lang=en&treaty_id=5 (accessed 2 Nov 2024).

[15] Ibid.

[16] The effects are limited to procedural questions, because CAFTA-DR exceeds the substantive level of protection established by the Trademark Law Treaty (1994); for example, Article 2(1)(b) Trademark Law Treaty (1994) explicitly does not require the protection of sound and scent marks.

tion of Marks (Protocol relating to the Madrid Agreement (Trademarks)).[17] The strict obligation to ratify the protocol was strongly opposed by local attorneys, while it would be an important facilitation for international enterprises.[18] It is interesting to note that in this case the efforts of IP lawyers turned out to be more effective than that of international businesses. Likewise, under the subsequent EU-FTAs, the Central American countries must only "make all reasonable efforts to ratify or accede to"[19] or "endeavor to accede to"[20] the Protocol relating to the Madrid Agreement (Trademarks). However, until 2024, no Central American country has ratified the Protocol relating to the Madrid Agreement (Trademarks).[21]

WIPO developed several *joint recommendations* regarding the protection of trademarks, namely the WIPO Joint Recommendation Concerning Well-Known Marks, the WIPO Joint Recommendation Concerning Trademark Licenses and the WIPO Joint Recommendation Concerning the Protection of Marks on the Internet.[22] They have been incorporated differently into CAFTA-DR, the EU-CARIFORUM-EPA and the EU-CA-AA. Under the EU-CARIFORUM-EPA, the Central American countries "shall endeavor to apply" the WIPO Joint Recommendation Concerning Well-Known Marks[23] the WIPO Joint Recommendation Concerning the Protection of Marks on the Internet[24] and the WIPO Joint Recommendation Concerning Trademark Licenses.[25] CAFTA-DR instead incorporated their content into the text of the IP chapter.[26] The EU-CA-AA neither references the joint recommendations nor incorporates their content.

One focus of CAFTA-DR is to restrict the protection of geographical indications in relation to trademarks.[27] Therefore, CAFTA-DR does not require the ratification of the *Madrid Agreement for the Repression of False or Deceptive Indications of*

---

[17] Article 15.1(6) CAFTA-DR; the text of the protocol is available at http://www.wipo.int/treaties/en/ShowResults.jsp?lang=en&treaty_id=8 (accessed 2 Nov 2024).

[18] Officially, the Protocol relating to the Madrid Agreement (Trademarks) was criticized as "unconstitutional" because it allows international applications to be effective for Central America, see e.g. the discussion in Castegnaro Montealegre and Madrigal Azofeifa (2016) p. 131 et seq.; practically, attorneys loose trademark application business if international applications are nationalized automatically through WIPO, which in many countries resulted in opposition by trademark practitioners to the Protocol, see for various examples, such as Turkey and Vietnam, Bennett (2015).

[19] Article 238 EU-CA-AA.

[20] Article 144(E) EU-CARIFORUM-EPA.

[21] See the list of contracting parties available at http://www.wipo.int/treaties/en/ShowResults.jsp?lang=en&treaty_id=8 (accessed 2 Nov 2024).

[22] WIPO Joint Recommendation Concerning Provisions on the Protection of Marks, and Other Industrial Property Rights in Signs, on the Internet, adopted by the General Assembly of WIPO, 24 September to 3 October 2001.

[23] Article 144(B) EU-CARIFORUM-EPA.

[24] Article 144(C) EU-CARIFORUM-EPA.

[25] Article 144(D) EU-CARIFORUM-EPA.

[26] Article 15 CAFTA-DR.

[27] Article 15.3 CAFTA-DR, see Sect. 4.4.

Source on Goods (Madrid Agreement (Indications of Source)) or the *Lisbon Agreement*, which provide for stronger protection of geographical indications. Also the EU-CARIFORUM-EPA and the EU-CA-AA do not mandate the ratification of these agreements.[28] However, some Central American countries have ratified the Madrid Agreement (Indications of Source) or the Lisbon Agreement on an individual basis.

The Dominican Republic ratified the Madrid Agreement (Indications of Source) on 23 June 1950 and it entered into force on 6 April 1951. Guatemala signed the Madrid Agreement (Indications of Source) on 14 April 1891 as one of the original signatories, but never ratified it.[29]

Costa Rica ratified the Lisbon Agreement on 30 April 1997 and it entered into force on 30 July 1997; Nicaragua ratified it on 15 March 2006 and it entered into force on 15 June 2006. Both countries acceded to the Stockholm version of 1967. Both countries also signed the Geneva Act (2015), Costa Rica signed it on 13 October 2015 and Nicaragua on 21 May 2015. The Dominican Republic acceded to the Stockholm version of 1967 of the Lisbon Agreement effective as of 17 January 2020.

2.1.1.4 Multilateral Agreements on Patents, Designs and Related Areas

In the field of patent law, both CAFTA-DR[30] and the EU-CARIFORUM-EPA[31] require the ratification of the *Patent Cooperation Treaty* (PCT) harmonizing patent procedure and the *Budapest Treaty* on the International Recognition of the Deposit of Micro-organisms for the Purposes of Patent Procedure (Budapest Treaty). Additionally, under Article 15.1(6)(a) CAFTA-DR, the parties "shall make all reasonable efforts to ratify or accede to" the Patent Law Treaty (PLT). All CAFTA-DR members have ratified the PCT and the Budapest Treaty.

Interestingly, the EU-CA-AA provides that all "[p]arties shall comply with the Budapest Treaty",[32] but only Panama is required to "adhere to the Patent Cooperation Treaty (Washington 1970, last modified in 2001)".[33] At first glance, the differentiation between the agreements seems surprising, because Panama and the other Central American countries are required to ratify both agreements under CAFTA-DR and the US-Panama-TPA. However, when the EU and the Central American countries (including Panama) signed the EU-CA-AA on 29 June 2012, Panama had not yet ratified the PCT and was also not required to do so in relation to

[28] However, they do contain substantive requirements regarding the protection of geographical indications, see Sect. 4.4.

[29] See WIPO, List of Contracting Parties, available at http://www.wipo.int/treaties/en/ShowResults.jsp?lang=en&treaty_id=3 (accessed 2 Nov 2024).

[30] Article 15.1.6(a) CAFTA.

[31] Article 9 EU-CARIFORUM-EPA.

[32] Article 258.1 EU-CA-AA.

[33] Article 276.2 EU-CA-AA.

the USA, because the US-Panama-TPA was not yet in force.[34] All other Central American countries had already ratified the PCT (at the latest) as part of the implementation of CAFTA-DR.[35] Accordingly, it made sense to include in the EU-CA-AA the obligation to join the PCT system specifically for Panama. Panama became a PCT member less than three months after signing the EU-CA-AA, on 7 September 2012.[36] The PCT procedure is practically operable in the region, as evidenced by the statistics of WIPO showing nationalizations of PCT patent applications.[37]

The ratification of the *UPOV Convention* is also required by CAFTA-DR for all Central American countries, except for El Salvador,[38] but not by the EU-CARIFORUM-EPA and the EU-CA-AA.[39] The latter "flexibility" offered by the EU FTAs is practically ineffective, however, because of the mandatory obligation to accede to it by CAFTA-DR. Costa Rica, the Dominican Republic and Nicaragua are already members of the UPOV Convention. Guatemala and Honduras have requested membership, but have not yet been accepted as members.[40]

Under CAFTA-DR, the contracting parties shall also make an effort to ratify the *Hague Agreement (1999)* concerning the international registration of designs,[41] *i.e.*, the Hague Agreement as amended by the Geneva Act of 1999. The EU-FTAs contain similar provisions.[42] However, no Central American country has ratified the Hague Agreement (1999).[43]

2.1.1.5 Evaluation

Most of the specific multilateral agreements have been created or reformed after TRIPS to deal with "leftover" issues. Developing countries including Central America have been rather reluctant to ratify such agreements, because they focus primarily on the protection of right holders (who are mostly from developed countries) and

[34] The US-Panama-TPA entered into force on 31 October 2012, see https://ustr.gov/trade-agreements/free-trade-agreements/panama-tpa (accessed 2 Nov 2024).

[35] Available at http://www.wipo.int/pct/en/pct_contracting_states.html (accessed 2 Nov 2024).

[36] Ibid.

[37] See the statistics available at http://www.wipo.int/ipstats/en/statistics/country_profile/ (accessed 2 Nov 2024).

[38] Articles 15.1.3. and 15.1.5. CAFTA-DR.

[39] See Article 149(2) EU-CARIFORUM-EPA; Article 259 EU-CA-AA.

[40] UPOV, Press Release No. 82 (21 October 2010), available at http://www.upov.int/edocs/pressdocs/en/upov_pr_082.pdf (accessed 2 Nov 2024); upon review, UPOV found the Guatemalan legislation not to be in compliance with the requirements of the UPOV Convention; on the accession process of these two countries see in more detail Sect. 3.3.

[41] Article 15.1.6(b) CAFTA.

[42] Article 146(A) EU-CARIFORUM-EPA, Article 251 EU-CA-AA.

[43] WIPO, Contracting Parties of the Hague Agreement (Geneva Act (1999), available at http://www.wipo.int/treaties/en/ActResults.jsp?act_id=7 (accessed 2 Nov 2024).

their ratification was, therefore, not perceived as beneficial for these countries as such, and not connected with market access or other compensation.[44] Both the USA and the EU incorporated an obligation to ratify specific IP agreements into their bilateral FTAs, because the participation of developing countries in these agreements remained lackluster and because they intended to promote a right holder-friendly international IP agenda. While Article 2(1) TRIPS also incorporated parts of the Paris Convention,[45] the incorporation appears more problematic in the case of the specific IP agreements. When TRIPS was signed, the incorporated Paris Convention had already many members, including developing countries. There was, in other words, broad international support for the Paris Convention at the time TRIPS was concluded. The specific agreements incorporated by FTAs such as CAFTA-DR, however, had often only been ratified by developed countries and by no means represented an international consensus. The WIPO Copyright Treaty (WCT) had only 44 members (among them 15 European and also 15 Latin American countries) at the time it was included in CAFTA-DR, and the TLT a mere 31 (among them 20 European countries). This leads not only to the proliferation of controversial international IP treaties, but it actually increases the fragmentation of the multinational legal environment. First, these treaties are still not ratified by many countries not bound by FTAs, and second, each FTA requires the ratification of a different set of treaties. In addition to the differences between the EU-FTAs and the US-FTAs discussed above, the list of agreements to be adopted evolved over time, also within the set of US FTAs. While for instance, the ratification of the Trademark Law Treaty is mandatory in the US-Singapore-FTA,[46] CAFTA-DR only requires "reasonable efforts".[47]

2.1.2 Free Trade Agreements

2.1.2.1 Overview

This section provides a general overview of the evolution of FTAs, in particular in the western hemisphere.[48] The global role and number of FTAs has grown substantially over the past decades, and the total number of agreements is in the hundreds. The complexity is especially intense in Latin America, because when CAFTA-DR was concluded, on average, a country in this region belonged to eight different

[44] *Álvaro Díaz* provides a summary of the ratification history of these agreements in Central America following TRIPS and CAFTA-DR, see Díaz (2006), pp. 19–20.

[45] Article 1 through 12 and 19 Paris Convention.

[46] Article 16.1.2.b(ii) US-Singapore-FTA.

[47] Article 15.1(6) CAFTA-DR.

[48] CAFTA-DR, the EU-CARIFORUM-EPA and the EU-CA-AA are analyzed in detail in Sects. 2.2 and 2.3.

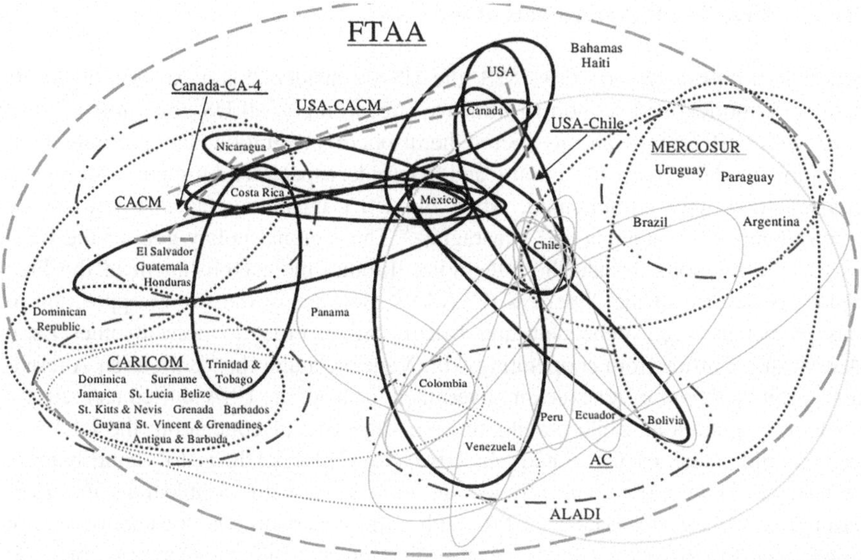

Fig. 2.1 The "Spaghetti Bowl" of Free Trade Agreements in the Americas (Pereira Goncalves/Stephanou (2006), p. 16)

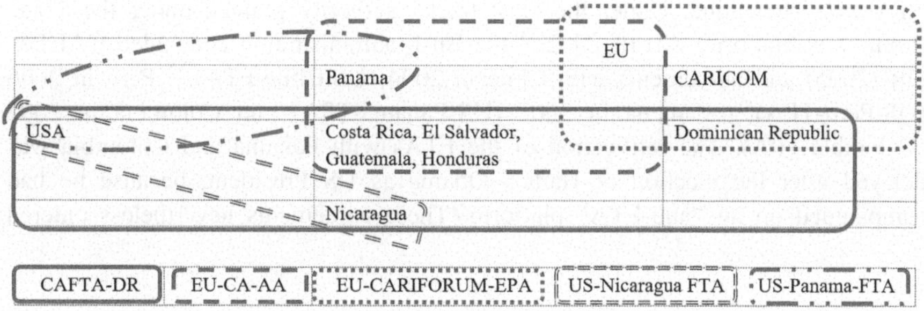

Fig. 2.2 The Central American FTA Bowl (prepared by the author)

FTAs, which is the highest number among developing countries.[49] Since then, the number has further increased. The situation regarding the trade agreements in the Americas (including those without rules on IP) has been compared to a "spaghetti bowl" (Fig. 2.1):

The focus on just bilateral FTAs of the USA and the EU with significant IP chapters in Central America shows that the various agreements even in this relatively small region create different layers of agreements (and corresponding IP obligations) for the respective counties (Fig. 2.2).

[49] Pereira Goncalves and Stephanou (2006), p. 16.

2.1.2.2 Free Trade Agreements of the USA

Since the *Monroe Doctrine* of 1823, the USA considers Latin America to be its sphere of political and economic influence. Accordingly, all US governments have tried with different means to secure hemisphere integration and promote their economic model of market economy and free trade, especially during the ideological confrontation with communism, when the USA intervened against left-leaning governments in Guatemala and Nicaragua.[50] The regional policy goal of the USA was in the previous decade the integration through the establishment of the Free Trade Agreement of the Americas (FTAA).[51] Because of the strong opposition to this project by, *e.g.*, Venezuela and Brazil, and in order to prevent other Latin American countries from cooperating with Venezuela and the "Bolivarian Alternative" promoted by the Venezuelan government instead, the USA shifted its focus on bilateral cooperation, while maintaining the objective of concluding the FTAA.[52] For example, one of the stated objectives of CAFTA-DR is to "contribute to hemispheric integration and provide an impetus toward establishing the *Free Trade Area of the Americas*".[53] FTAs with Latin American countries are of special importance to US foreign policy because they are not only of economic, but also geopolitical significance. The series of modern bilateral agreements in the region was initiated by the establishment of the North American Free Trade Agreement (NAFTA) with Canada and Mexico (1994). In 2001, the USA concluded a special FTA with Nicaragua. Under the "fast track" authority granted under the Trade Promotion Authority Act of 2002,[54] the Bush administration concluded CAFTA-DR (2005) and agreements with Chile in 2004 (US-Chile-FTA),[55] Peru in 2006 (US-Peru-TPA),[56] Panama in 2007 (US-Panama-TPA) and Colombia in 2007 (Colombia-TPA). The ratification of the FTAs with Panama and Colombia was delayed after the election of Barack Obama as US President, because he had campaigned on an "anti-FTA" platform. These agreements nevertheless entered

[50] See Sect. 1.3.3.

[51] See the FTAA website available at http://www.ftaa-alca.org/alca_e.asp (accessed 2 Nov 2024); the website is no longer updated.

[52] One of the objectives of the US-Peru-TPA is to "contribute to hemispheric integration and provide an impetus toward establishing the Free Trade Area of the Americas" (Preamble of the US-Peru-TPA).

[53] Preamble CAFTA-DR, emphasis in the original; this wording is identical to the Preamble of the US-Peru-TPA.

[54] Trade Promotion Authority Act, 19 U.S.C. Chapter 24, §§ 3803–3805.

[55] Information on this agreement is provided by the USTR, available at http://www.ustr.gov/trade-agreements/free-trade-agreements/chile-fta (accessed 2 Nov 2024).

[56] Information on this agreement is provided by the USTR, available at http://www.ustr.gov/trade-agreements/free-trade-agreements/peru-tpa (accessed 2 Nov 2024).

into force, in 2011[57] and 2012,[58] respectively. All of these agreements include (similar) chapters on IP protection. Nicaragua concluded the US-Nicaragua IP Agreement with the USA in 1999, which is still in force.[59] However, its requirements have been largely superseded by CAFTA-DR. In addition, the USA and Nicaragua concluded a BIT in 2001, which does not set specific standards of IP, but includes IP (including the licensing of IP rights) in its definition of investment.[60]

The USA has been also active outside the western hemisphere. Around the time CAFTA-DR was signed, the USA had concluded FTAs with Singapore (2003), Australia (2005), Bahrain (2006), Oman (2007), Israel (1985 and 2004), Jordan (implementation finalized in 2010) and Morocco (2007).[61] The FTA with Korea (signed in 2007) entered into force on 15 March 2012.[62] The USA also negotiated bilateral FTAs with Malaysia (from 2006 to 2008),[63] the Southern African Customs Union (suspended in 2006 due to divergent views on the scope and content of the FTA),[64] Thailand (from 2004 to 2006, suspended after a military coup)[65] and the United Arab Emirates (initiated in 2004).[66]

There are substantial differences between the IP rules of earlier FTAs concluded by the USA, namely NAFTA, and subsequent FTAs, because of the evolution of the content occurring over time. The "ever increasing" nature of protection is in fact a key element of the overall negotiation strategy of the USA.[67] The FTAs concluded by the USA with Australia, Chile and Peru, for example, each differ on such issues as trademark subject matter, compulsory licenses for patents and data exclusivity.

[57] Information on this agreement is provided by the USTR, available at http://www.ustr.gov/uspanamatpa (accessed 2 Nov 2024).

[58] Information on this agreement is provided by the USTR, available at http://www.ustr.gov/uscolombiatpa (accessed 2 Nov 2024).

[59] US-Nicaragua IP Agreement, signed on 7 January 1998, in force since 1 July 1999, available at https://www.wipo.int/wipolex/en/treaties/details/491 (accessed 2 Nov 2024).

[60] This agreement is discussed in more detail by Drahos (2001), pp. 5–8, in particular, the implications as an example for patterns of negotiation strategy.

[61] See the list provided by the USTR, available at https://ustr.gov/trade-agreements/free-trade-agreements (accessed 2 Nov 2024).

[62] Information on this agreement is provided by the USTR, available at http://www.ustr.gov/trade-agreements/free-trade-agreements/korus-fta (accessed 2 Nov 2024).

[63] Information on this agreement is provided by the USTR, available at https://ustr.gov/trade-agreements/other-agreements/malaysia-fta (accessed 2 Nov 2024).

[64] Information on this agreement is provided by the USTR, available at https://ustr.gov/countries-regions/africa/regional-economic-communities-rec/southern-african-customs-union-sacu (accessed 2 Nov 2024).

[65] Information on this agreement is provided by the USTR, available at https://ustr.gov/countries-regions/southeast-asia-pacific/thailand (accessed 2 Nov 2024).

[66] Information on this agreement is provided by the USTR, available at https://ustr.gov/archive/Trade_Agreements/Bilateral/UAE/Section_Index.html (accessed 2 Nov 2024).

[67] See Sect. 1.6.3.

However, the subsequent agreements, including CAFTA-DR and the agreements with Panama, Colombia and South Korea, are relatively coherent in structure and content. The IP chapter of the US-Panama-TPA is practically identical with Chapter 15 of CAFTA-DR.[68]

2.1.2.3 Free Trade Agreements of the EU

In addition to CAFTA-DR, the EU-CARIFORUM-EPA and the EU-CA-AA,[69] the EU has negotiated and partly concluded FTAs with a number of other regions and countries. Among these agreements are in particular

- In Asia, the Economic Partnership Agreement with Japan, which entered into force on 1 February 2019,[70] the FTA with South Korea, in force since 1 July 2016,[71] the FTA with Vietnam, where the negotiations were finalized in October 2018,[72] and the trade and investment agreements with Singapore, which was signed also in October 2018.[73]
- In the Americas, the Trade Agreement with several Andean countries (Colombia and Peru), provisionally applied since 2013,[74] and the Comprehensive Economic and Trade Agreement (CETA) between the EU and Canada, provisionally applied since 21 September 2017.[75]

[68] The US-Panama-TPA was signed on 28 June 2007 and entered into force on 31 October 2012; the text of the agreement is available at http://www.ustr.gov/trade-agreements/free-trade-agreements/panama-tpa (accessed 2 Nov 2024).

[69] These agreements are discussed in Sect. 2.3.

[70] Further information on the agreement is available at https://policy.trade.ec.europa.eu/eu-trade-relationships-country-and-region/countries-and-regions/japan/eu-japan-agreement_en (accessed 2 Nov 2024).

[71] Further information on the agreement is available at http://www.consilium.europa.eu/en/documents-publications/treaties-agreements/agreement/?id=2010036 (accessed 2 Nov 2024).

[72] Further information on the agreement is available at https://policy.trade.ec.europa.eu/eu-trade-relationships-country-and-region/countries-and-regions/vietnam/eu-vietnam-agreement_en (accessed 2 Nov 2024).

[73] Further information on the agreement is available at https://policy.trade.ec.europa.eu/eu-trade-relationships-country-and-region/countries-and-regions/singapore/eu-singapore-agreements_en#:~:text=The%20EU%2DSingapore%20trade%20and,force%20on%2021%20November%202019 (accessed 2 Nov 2024).

[74] The text of the agreement is available at http://www.consilium.europa.eu/en/documents-publications/treaties-agreements/agreement/?id=2011057 (accessed 2 Nov 2024).

[75] Further information on the agreement is available at https://policy.trade.ec.europa.eu/eu-trade-relationships-country-and-region/countries-and-regions/canada/eu-canada-agreement_en (accessed 2 Nov 2024).

- In Africa, the Economic Partnership Agreement with the Southern African Development Community[76] and the Interim Agreement establishing a framework for an Economic Partnership Agreement with certain Eastern and Southern Africa States.[77]

2.1.2.4 Free Trade Agreements of Central America

Overview

Central American countries have also concluded bilateral FTAs with third countries which include IP provisions, apart from CAFTA-DR, the EU-CARIFORUM-EPA and the EU-CA-AA.[78] Table 2.2 lists the main FTAs concluded by Central American countries. The significant number of these agreements is not surprising, because the Central American countries rely strongly on trade due to the small size of their individual markets and their developing economies. However, as Table 2.2 illustrates, for Central America trade with the rest of Latin America and Asia becomes increasingly important compared to trade with the USA and Europe, which led to the increasing number of FTAs concluded by Central American countries with countries other than the USA and Europe. Such agreements usually do not contain significant IP rules. The CARICOM-Dominican Republic-FTA (CARICOM-DR-FTA), for instance, contains only one article with two paragraphs on IP rights, referring only to the existing TRIPS rules and possible subsequent negotiations.[79]

Specific Agreements

Individual Central American states concluded agreements with Asian countries, in particular (mainland) China and Taiwan. Costa Rica and China have concluded an FTA which came into force on 1 August 2011.[80] The China-Costa Rica FTA contains a chapter on IP, but the text contains mainly general principles, such as the protection of public health and biodiversity in Articles 111 and 112, and some "ceilings", namely obligations of right holders regarding evidence and security payments when initiating border measures in Article 114.[81] The provisions are,

[76] The text of the agreement is available at https://trade.ec.europa.eu/access-to-markets/en/content/epa-sadc-southern-african-development-community (accessed 2 Nov 2024).

[77] Further information on the agreement is available at http://www.consilium.europa.eu/en/documents-publications/treaties-agreements/agreement/?id=2009014 (accessed 2 Nov 2024).

[78] These agreements are discussed in Sect. 2.3.

[79] Article 12 CARICOM-DR-FTA.

[80] The text of the Agreement is available at http://fta.mofcom.gov.cn/topic/encosta.shtml (accessed 2 Nov 2024).

[81] Ibid.

Table 2.2 Selected Free Trade Agreements in Central America including the Dominican Republic (see for further information and references the Table of Legislation)

Title	Date	Parties	Content
Americas			
CAFTA-DR	2006–2009	Central America, Dominican Rep., USA	Comprehensive IP chapter
CARICOM-DR-FTA	22 August 1998 (Signature)	CARICOM Dominican Rep.	Broad FTA Very limited IP chapter
Mexico-Northern Triangle-FTA	29 June 2000 (Signature) between 15 March 2000 and 1 June 2000 (Entry into force)	Mexico, El Salvador, Guatemala, Honduras	Broad FTA Comprehensive IP chapter (TRIPS-level of protection)
Chile-Central America-FTA	18 October 1999 (Signature) between 15 February 2002 and 19 October 2012 (Entry into force)	Chile, Costa Rica, El Salvador, Guatemala, Honduras, Nicaragua	Broad FTA No IP provisions except geographical indications (Article 3.12)
Colombia-Costa Rica-FTA	22 May 2013 (Signature) 1 August 2016 (Entry into force)	Colombia, Costa Rica	Comprehensive IP chapter
Europe			
EU-CA-AA	2012 with regard to IP	Central America, European Union, Panama	Comprehensive IP chapter
EU-CARIFORUM-EPA	2008 with regard to IP	Dominican Rep., CARICOM, European Union	Comprehensive IP chapter
EFTA-Central American States-FTA	19 August 2014/ 29 August 2014/ 5 September 2014 (Entry into force)	EFTA, Costa Rica, Panama (pending for Guatemala)	IP "Chapter" very short, refers mainly to TRIPS
Asia			
Taiwan-El Salvador-Honduras-FTA	07 May 2007 (Signature) between 1 January 2008 and 15 July 2008 (Entry into force)	El Salvador, Honduras, Taiwan	Broad FTA No IP provisions
China-Costa Rica-FTA	08 April 2010 01 August 2011	China, Costa Rica	IP chapter with general principles and "ceilings" (in particular, limitations on border measures)
Central America-Korea FTA	21 February 2018 (signature)	South Korea, Costa Rica, El Salvador, Honduras, Nicaragua, Panama	Comprehensive IP chapter

therefore, noticeably less strict than CAFTA-DR. Individual FTAs have also been concluded with Latin American neighbors. For example, an FTA has been concluded between Costa Rica and Colombia. The two countries launched negotiations on 5 June 2012 and concluded them on 6 March 2013. The Free Trade Agreement Colombia-Costa Rica (Colombia-Costa Rica-FTA) was approved on 8 April 2014 by the Colombian Senate and the Costa Rican National Assembly on 24 April 2014. The agreement entered into force on 1 August 2016.[82]

The Central American countries also concluded further regional agreements, notably an FTA with EFTA. The FTA was signed on 24 June 2013. The FTA entered into force on 19 August 2014 for Costa Rica, Panama and Norway, on 29 August 2014 for Liechtenstein and Switzerland and on 5 September 2014 for Iceland. Negotiations for the accession of Guatemala have been completed, but negotiations with Honduras have been put on hold.[83]

2.1.2.5 Current Developments

The process of concluding and implementing new FTAs between the USA and the EU on the one hand and developing countries on the other hand is still ongoing. In May 2016, the EU and Mexico started negotiations for a new (or "modernized") FTA; the negotiations were concluded in April 2020, but as of 2024, the internal processes were still ongoing.[84] Negotiations are also ongoing between the EU and the Mercosur countries, but after a political agreement on a text in 2019 the ratification process has (as of 2024) not progressed further.[85] In addition, several FTAs with a significantly broader geographical scope are (or were) being negotiated by the USA: The USA had been negotiating the Trans-Pacific Partnership (TPP), with Australia, Brunei, Canada, Chile, Japan, Malaysia, Mexico, New Zealand, Peru, Singapore and Vietnam from 2009 to 2016. On 30 January 2017, the USA officially withdrew from the ratification process and the TPP (after signature, but prior to ratification).[86] TPP was subsequently replaced by the Comprehensive and

[82] Information on the ratification timeline is available at https://investmentpolicy.unctad.org/international-investment-agreements/treaties/treaties-with-investment-provisions/3397/colombia%2D%2D-costa-rica-fta-2013- (accessed 2 Nov 2024).

[83] Further information on the agreement is available at https://www.efta.int/trade-relations/free-trade-network/central-american-states-costa-rica-guatemala-honduras-and-panama (accessed 2 Nov 2024).

[84] Further information on the negotiations is available at https://policy.trade.ec.europa.eu/eu-trade-relationships-country-and-region/countries-and-regions/mexico_en (accessed 2 Nov 2024).

[85] Further information on the negotiations is available at https://policy.trade.ec.europa.eu/eu-trade-relationships-country-and-region/countries-and-regions/mercosur/eu-mercosur-agreement_en (accessed 2 Nov 2024).

[86] See the withdrawal notice by the USTR available at https://ustr.gov/sites/default/files/files/Press/Releases/1-30-17%20USTR%20Letter%20to%20TPP%20Depositary.pdf (accessed 2 Nov 2024).

Progressive Agreement for Trans-Pacific Partnership (CPTPP) between the remaining countries. The agreement was signed by the remaining countries on 8 March 2018 and entered into force on 30 December 2018 for Australia, Canada, Japan, Mexico, New Zealand and Singapore and on 14 January 2019 for Vietnam.[87] The USA and the EU were conducting negotiations on the Transatlantic Trade and Investment Partnership (TTIP) since 2013; Negotiations were stopped without conclusion in late 2016, following the election of a new administration in the USA.[88] In February 2018, the Central American countries (excluding the Dominican Republic, but including Panama) signed an FTA with South Korea. The agreement is in the process of being ratified by the parties. Guatemala was part of the negotiations but did not sign the final agreement.[89]

2.1.3 *Economic Integration*

2.1.3.1 Latin America

The idea of Latin American integration emerged soon after the region achieved independence from Spanish rule in the early nineteenth century. But *Simon Bolivar's* "Treaty for perpetual union, league and confederation of the Latin American countries" from 1824, aiming for the politically and economically unity of the newly independent nations of Latin America, never entered into force.[90] Economic integration was again proposed at the First International Conference of the American States in 1889,[91] without success. Interestingly, one of the few lasting regional measures of the era was adoption of the Inter-American Trademark Convention of 1929.[92]

After World War II, plans for regional integration were intensified to supplement the import substitution industrialization (ISI) development policy favored by many developing countries.[93] In the 1960ies and 1970ies, the Central American countries, like their Latin American peers, focused on economic development by such an ISI

[87] Further information on the negotiations is available at https://www.dfat.gov.au/trade/agreements/in-force/cptpp/comprehensive-and-progressive-agreement-for-trans-pacific-partnership (accessed 2 Nov 2024).

[88] Further information on the negotiations is available at https://www.bmwk.de/Redaktion/DE/Artikel/Aussenwirtschaft/freihandelsabkommen-aktuelle-verhandlungen.html (accessed 2 Nov 2024).

[89] Further information on the negotiations is available at http://www.sice.oas.org/TPD/CACM_KOR/CACM_KOR_e.ASP (accessed 2 Nov 2024).

[90] Baquero-Herrera (2005), p. 140.

[91] Ibid.

[92] See Sect. 2.1.4.1.

[93] Hufbauer and Kotschwar (2000), p. 172.

policy.[94] This system was also known as the "New International Economic Order", and was promoted at the time by the influential *United Nations Economic Commission for Latin America and the Caribbean* (ECLAC, or CEPAL in Spanish).[95] This policy was aimed at the creation of domestic industrial production by restricting trade to keep off imports from developed countries. The complementary regional trade integration was to balance the scale limitations resulting from the closed ISI markets of small Latin American countries.[96] However, this policy had unintended consequences. While it did not significantly diminish the quantity of imports, together with the industries it protected, however, it created new special interest groups, which later opposed the creation of an integrated, free market in the hemisphere.[97]

The most ambitious plan, the Montevideo Treaty of 1960, which encompassed most South American countries, failed to achieve economic integration because of the differences in size, economic development and political concepts among the parties.[98] More successful was the focused, sub-regional approach in integration,[99] resulting in the establishment of the Mercosur, the Andean Community and the Central American Common Market. The failure to create a regional economic union in Latin America also caused several countries to turn to the USA for economic cooperation.

In opposition to the FTAA and the influence of the USA in Latin America, Venezuela started several initiatives for Latin American integration, mainly the "Bolivarian Alternative for the Americas" (*Alianza Bolivariana para los Pueblos de Nuestra América,* ALBA), which includes Venezuela, Cuba, Bolivia and since 11 January 2007 Nicaragua.[100] However, the cooperation did not affect the implementation of CAFTA-DR in Nicaragua or Honduras.

2.1.3.2 Central America

Central American integration was initiated with the creation of the Central American Bank for Economic Integration in 1959 and the Central American Common Market (CACM) in 1960. Because of the subsequent political and economic turmoil in several countries, these undertakings were of limited practical consequence.[101] After

---

[94] Hufbauer and Kotschwar (2000), p. 171.

[95] Baquero-Herrera (2005), p. 141.

[96] Hufbauer and Kotschwar (2000), p. 172.

[97] Baquero-Herrera (2005), p. 175.

[98] Baquero-Herrera (2005), p. 143.

[99] Baquero-Herrera (2005), p. 144.

[100] See the organization's website, https://www.albatcp.org/historia/ (accessed 2 Nov 2024).

[101] O'Keefe (2009), p. 5.

the "lost decade for integration"[102] of the 1980ies, integration efforts in Central America were renewed within the new open, market-based economic approach[103] under the slogan of "New Regionalism".[104] Substantial progress was made since the 1990ies with the establishment of the Central American Integration System (*Sistema de la Integración Centroamericana,* SICA) and the strengthening of the CACM[105] by the Tegucigalpa Protocol in 1991,[106] the regional free trade zone in 1993 and the common external tariff in 2001.[107] SICA includes Belize and Panama, while excluding the Dominican Republic.[108] The Central American Monetary Council on the other hand, composed of the Central Bank Presidents and the Central American Council of Bank Superintendents, also includes the Dominican Republic.[109] However, there are substantial obstacles for regional cooperation in Central America, such as social tensions, border disputes and also the "challenging geography" of rainforests and mountain ranges.[110] These factors contributed to the limited success prior projects for regional cooperation, including free trade and the creation of regional institutions. CAFTA-DR is expected to foster regional cooperation and trade. It is not only conceived as a tool for trade facilitation between Central America and the USA, but also an integration tool between the Central American members themselves. It is supposed to support the ongoing process of cooperation among these countries by harmonizing the economic and legal framework in the areas covered by the agreement. CAFTA-DR is, therefore, an instrument of regional integration, because it is also applicable between the Central American countries. Intra-regional trade is low in comparison with Mercosur, the NAFTA countries and the EU,[111] because of the similar structure of Central American economies and the lack of specialization. But as the economic specialization increases, so can regional trade and the importance of the applicability of the CAFTA-DR rules. For the Central American governments, CAFTA-DR might also have been an opportunity for integration beyond the level politically possible without US involvement. The EU, which concludes its FTAs preferably with trade blocks like the ASEAN

---

[102] Baquero-Herrera (2005), p. 176.

[103] Ibid.

[104] On this term see Devlin and Estevadeordal (2001), pp. 5–14; see also Hufbauer and Kotschwar (2000), p. 174.

[105] Even today, the term "common market" for CACM is technically incorrect. A common market includes an internal free trade zone, common external tariffs and the free movement of factors of production (such as labor and capital), however, the CACM does not provide for such free movement of factors of production, and has not fully established a common external tariff, see Rodlauer and Schipke (2005), Box 1.1, p. 4.

[106] Baquero-Herrera (2005), p. 161.

[107] Rodlauer and Schipke (2005), Box 1.1, p. 4.

[108] Baquero-Herrera (2005), p. 161.

[109] Rodlauer and Schipke (2005), Box 1.1, p. 4.

[110] See Sect. 1.3.2.

[111] Jaramillo and Lederman (2005), p. 10.

countries or Mercosur, rather than individual countries like Brazil or Thailand, also concluded its EU-CA-AA with the Central American countries as a group.

2.1.4 Regional Harmonization and Cooperation

2.1.4.1 Legislative Harmonization

There have been repeated attempts to regionally harmonize legislation in the Americas with regard to IP during the last century. However, none of the following agreements is practically relevant today. Against the backdrop of earlier international harmonization under the Paris Convention, the *Inter-American Trademark Convention* was signed on 20 February 1929 by many countries in the American hemisphere.[112] In Central America, it was ratified by Guatemala on 30 December 1929, by Honduras on 29 November 1935 and by Nicaragua on 7 June 1935.[113] It is still in force today and directly applicable.[114] However, the level of IP protection it mandates is lower than the TRIPS level of protection and, therefore, its practical effect is limited. On 1 June 1968, the *Central American Convention on Industrial Property (Trademarks and Trade Names)* (Central American Convention (Trademarks)) was adopted by the contracting parties (Costa Rica, El Salvador, Guatemala, Honduras and Nicaragua) as a follow-up to the economic integration through the CACM.[115] The convention implemented the new protectionist, independent economic strategy that was promoted in the 1960ies for Latin American countries by the United Nations' Latin American section CEPAL.[116] This strategy called for regional IP regimes, different from that of the USA and (supposedly) tailored to the needs of the developing countries. The Central American Convention (Trademarks) was directly applicable in the contracting parties and replaced the existing national trademark legislation.[117] It became the legal basis of trademark protection in Central America until it was revoked in 1999, when the parties adopted a *Protocol to the Central American Convention on Industrial Property (Trademarks and Trade Names)* which abolished the Convention and stated the expectation that the contracting parties would pass harmonized, more industrial-property-friendly legislation based on TRIPS by the year 2000.[118] Accordingly, the Convention was

[112] See https://www.wipo.int/wipolex/en/treaties/parties/353 (accessed 2 Nov 2024).

[113] Ibid.

[114] See, e.g., CSJ (GT), Civil Law Chamber, Case No. 73-93, 16 March 1994; CSJ (NI), 12 July 1996.

[115] The Convention was implemented in Costa Rica by Decree N.° 4543, on 18 March 1970, see Registro Nacional (Costa Rica), Propiedad Industrial, Background, available at http://www.registronacional.go.cr/industrial_property/background.htm (accessed 2 Nov 2024).

[116] Regarding CEPAL's development approach see also Sect. 3.1.1.2.

[117] Article 230 Central American Convention (Trademarks).

[118] This timeline was largely achieved, see Sect. 2.4.1.

replaced by national laws enacted between 1999 and 2001.[119] The implementation of the complementary *Project of the Central American Convention on Industrial Property (Inventions and Industrial Designs)* (Central American Convention (Patents)), which was signed in 1997, was subsequently considered inconsistent with the obligations under TRIPS and was, therefore, abandoned.[120] Nevertheless, many provisions of the Central American Convention (Patents) were incorporated into the subsequent national laws.

2.1.4.2 Institutional Cooperation

The regional harmonization and cooperation in Central America in the field of IP was quite deep prior to the implementation of TRIPS and the bilateral FTAs with the USA and Europe. It was based on the Central American Convention (Trademarks) and planned to be further deepened by a Central American Convention (Patents). These harmonization efforts were suspended following the ratification of TRIPS by the Central American countries, and the existing legislation was further fragmented by successive layers of statutory requirements of TRIPS and the bilateral FTAs. Even after the Central American Conventions were replaced by national laws, cooperation continued between the Central American countries.[121] The Central American IP Registers cooperate in particular with regard to patent examination procedures.[122]

The Central American countries also cooperate with neighboring countries, especially Mexico regarding IP. Mexico is involved in regional cooperation with Central America in several ways. Its patent legislation became the model for the Salvadoran law of 1993. Also, Mexico's patent office (IMPI) trains patent examiners and sometimes examines patent applications from Central America. While such projects often have only a limited scope, Mexico and Central America have much in common in terms of the legal cultural and the institutional system network and, therefore, cooperation could be particularly effective.

---

[119] See, e.g., in Costa Rica the Law No. 7982, Approving the Protocol of the Central American Agreement for the Protection of Industrial Property (Trademarks, Trade Names and Advertising Slogans or Signs), available at https://www.wipo.int/wipolex/en/legislation/details/890 (accessed 2 Nov 2024); on the specific national legislation in each Central American country see Sect. 2.4.

[120] This second convention is discussed in more detail by Bendaña-Guerrero (1999), p. 218.

[121] For example, in October 2008 the Administrative Register Tribunal (TRA) in Costa Rica and the University of Costa Rica hosted a 2-day conference in San José, where IP lawyers and other experts from all Central American CAFTA-DR contracting parties presented their experience with the implementation process, which was then still ongoing in Costa Rica. This allowed them to share experiences and best practices both regarding efficient protection and balancing of IP rights.

[122] This cooperation resulted in particular in the draft of the joint Patent Examiner Manual, see Sect. 2.5.2.

2.1.5 *National Application and Implementation of International Law*

2.1.5.1 National Application

With regard to geographical indications, Article 356 EU-CA-AA explicitly does not require direct application of the respective provisions in national laws, "unless otherwise provided in […] domestic legislation". CAFTA-DR does not contain provisions regarding the applicability of the IP provisions. The legislation implementing CAFTA-DR in the USA provides that USA domestic law prevails in case of conflict with the provisions of CAFTA-DR, unless explicitly stated otherwise.[123] In Central America, international agreements are directly applicable within each country, unlike, for example, in the Andean Community.[124] This principle has been established, *e.g.*, in Guatemala and Nicaragua with regard to the Central American Convention (Trademarks).[125] In addition, some Central American laws contain a provision stating that the respective law is subject to the requirements of "international law"[126] or "treaties".[127] In Guatemala, the Constitution of 1993 explicitly states that owners of IP rights enjoy the exclusive right in their work or invention in accordance with the law *and international agreements* (emphasis added).[128] However, these laws and precedents do not clarify whether such international agreements supersede conflicting national constitutional or ordinary laws. In Costa Rica, international treaties have a higher rank than ordinary laws.[129] Nevertheless, for clarification, the obligations imposed by international law are usually implemented through national legislation (as was the case with CAFTA-DR). It has been suggested by *Roffe* that the legislation implementing CAFTA-DR in the USA "makes the obligations assumed by [FTA] parties absolutely asymmetric".[130] This view is based on the position taken by the USTR that bilateral FTAs do not bind the

---

[123]"[N]o provision of [CAFTA-DR], nor the application of any such provision to any person or circumstance, which is inconsistent with any law of the United States shall have effect [and] nothing in [the implementation act] shall be construed (A) to amend or modify any law of the United States, or (B) to limit any authority conferred under any law of the United States, unless specifically provided for in [the implementation act]", section 101(a) Dominican Republic-Central America-United States Free Trade Agreement Implementation Act.

[124]Regarding the Andean Community, see the decision of the Court of Justice of the Andean Community (Tribunal de Justicia de la Comunidad Andina), 28 September 2001, Nr 89-AI-2000, reported by Markowski (2004), p. 44.

[125]See, e.g., CSJ (GT), Civil Law Chamber, Case No. 73-93, 16 March 1994; CSJ (NI), 12 July 1996.

[126]Article 9 Nr. 3 Biodiversity Law (CR).

[127]Article 2 IP Law (SV).

[128]Article 42 Constitution (GT); the text of the Constitution of Guatemala is available at www.wipo.int/wipolex/en/details.jsp?id=7526 (accessed 2 Nov 2024).

[129]See Sect. 6.1.3.2.

[130]Roffe (2013), p. 935.

US legislator: "Even if a dispute settlement panel found the US acted inconsistently with the FTA, it could not require Congress to amend the law".[131] However, as *Roffe* also points out, this view is inconsistent with the obligations, *e.g.*, under Article 15.9 (2) CAFTA-DR.[132] From a legal perspective, therefore, CAFTA-DR is not asymmetrical, because the agreement binds the USA and the Central American countries in the same way. Any asymmetry could only result from differences in the ability to ensure compliance with CAFTA-DR obligations politically and practically. However, the analysis of the implementation of CAFTA-DR shows that there are numerous cases of statutory or practical non-compliance with CAFTA-DR by the Central American countries, which had no measurable consequences.[133]

2.1.5.2 Implementation

Mostly, obligations under international agreements are implemented on the national level trough transformation, *i.e.*, the creation or modification of national laws.[134] These laws are then applied by the national legal institutions. The legal norm implementing international obligations has to provide legal certainty, including applicability in judicial procedures. Therefore, mere administrative directives are insufficient.[135] The transformation of international law in Central America generally follows the international practice of the signature of the international treaty by the executive branch and the subsequent parliamentary approval of the treaty together with the adoption of the implementing legislation. In Central America, the provisions of CAFTA-DR were mostly literally inserted into the national IP legislation. The countries probably wanted to avoid the risk of non-compliance with the CAFTA-DR requirements and, as a consequence, the delay of the trade benefits provided by the agreement.[136] In Costa Rica, laws ratifying international treaties are subject to prior approval by the Constitutional Chamber (*Sala IV*) of the Supreme Court of Justice (*Corte Suprema de Justica*, CSJ).[137] The CSJ also reviews the laws implementing the obligations of these treaties.[138]

---

[131] Statement of the USTR in relation to the US-Australia-FTA, cited by Roffe (2013), p. 936.

[132] Roffe (2013), p. 937.

[133] These cases are summarized in Sect. 8.7.

[134] Lüers, Jan-Carl in Busche et al. (2013), Article 1, Nr 11-13.

[135] Report of the Appellate Body, India – Patent Protection for Pharmaceutical and Agricultural Chemical Products, WT/DS50/AB/R, 19 December 1997, section 62.

[136] See Sect. 8.6.

[137] Article 96(a) Constitutional Jurisdiction Law (CR).

[138] Article 96(b) Constitutional Jurisdiction Law (CR).

2.1.5.3 Ordre Public

Article 1(1) TRIPS provides that the WTO members are free to determine the appropriate method of implementing TRIPS within their own legal system and practice. This leaves ample room for implementing the international obligations.[139] According to Article 15.11(1)(b) CAFTA-DR, enforcement procedures and remedies are established in accordance with the foundations of the respective national legal system. This provision can be interpreted as going beyond the TRIPS flexibility and enabling the parties not to implement CAFTA-DR obligations at all, if they violate fundamental legal principles. For this interpretation, in effect permitting non-compliance, one can systematically point to the fact that unlike Article 15.11 (2) CAFTA-DR, Article 15.11(1) CAFTA-DR does not contain an explicit compliance clause. Also, while TRIPS only allows the WTO members to choose *methods* appropriate within their own legal system, CAFTA-DR mandates that any implementation must be in accordance with the fundamental legal principles themselves. This interpretation would be at odds with the principles of minimum standards and harmonization, which are basic principles of international IP law.[140] However, it should be noted that the right of countries to safeguard their fundamental legal principles under the *ordre public* exception and protect public policy interest is also a basic principle of international law.[141] One example for non-compliance for reasons of a conflict with the foundations of the national legal system might be the CAFTA-DR provision on pre-established damages, which was not implemented in any country because it was considered to be an enforcement mechanism of common law incompatible with the civil law tradition of the Central American legal orders.[142] However, while the Central American countries may have been legally entitled not to implement certain provisions in their national legislation, practically the (more or less) full statutory implementation of the IP chapter of CAFTA-DR was a requirement for the entry into force of the agreement, and thus a requirement for obtaining the economic advantages of the trade rules under the agreement.[143] Article

[139] Lüers, Jan-Carl in Busche et al. (2013), Article 1, Nr 6 and 13, referring to the Report of the Appellate Body, India – Patent Protection for Pharmaceutical and Agricultural Chemical Products, WT/DS50/AB/R of 19 December 1997, section 59.

[140] Lüers, Jan-Carl in Busche et al. (2013), Article 1, Nr 14.

[141] For example, Article 8(1) TRIPS explicitly states that countries may "adopt measures necessary to protect public health and nutrition, and to promote the public interest in sectors of vital importance to their socio-economic and technological development".

[142] See Sect. 7.3.2.2.

[143] Possibly the most contentious issue in relation to the implementation of the IP provisions of CAFTA-DR and non-compliance was the change to Costa Rica's Biodiversity Law (CR) to clarify that inventions essentially derived from traditional knowledge can be patented, if they otherwise meet the patentability requirements, see Sect. 3.1.4.4. The USTR declined to confirm Costa Rica's compliance with CAFTA-DR until such change was made. While the protection of biodiversity and traditional knowledge in Costa Rica might well be a fundamental legal principle, this issue does not relate to the enforcement, but protection of patents and, therefore, in any case the exception under Article 15.11(1)(b) CAFTA-DR does not apply. However, even if it did, this may not have

139(4) EU-CARIFORUM-EPA is modeled after Article 1(1) TRIPS and provides that the "EC Party and the Signatory CARIFORUM States shall be free to determine the appropriate method of implementing the provisions of this Section within their own legal system and practice".

2.2 CAFTA-DR

2.2.1 The Negotiation and Implementation Process

2.2.1.1 Overview

The negotiations between the USA and the Central American countries (except the Dominican Republic) regarding a Central America-United States Free Trade Agreement (CAFTA) commenced in January 2003 and were concluded by January 2004. Also in January 2004, negotiations were initiated with the Dominican Republic, and concluded in March 2004. The title of the agreement was subsequently amended to Central America-Dominican Republic-United States Free Trade Agreement (CAFTA-DR).[144] CAFTA-DR was signed on 5 August 2004 and ratified by all parties except Costa Rica in 2005 and 2006. Because it is a bundle of agreements, it entered into force between the USA and each Central American country on different dates (see Table 2.3).[145] Despite the joint negotiations, CAFTA-DR is legally a bundle of bilateral agreements between the USA and each Central American country. However, the provisions also apply directly between the Central American countries.[146] CAFTA-DR is, therefore, expected to raise the level of economic integration within Central America further, because tariff measures and legal standards are harmonized across the region.[147]

practically helped Costa Rica. Not only would the USTR have had to agree with an assessment by the Costa Rican government that the local legal principle should prevail, but it would have had to do so prior to the expiration of the USTR's authority for concluding CAFTA-DR. The deadline set by the US legislator, in any case, precluded any further discussions or negotiations.

[144] The negotiation history is available at http://www.sice.oas.org/TPD/USA_CAFTA/USA_CAFTA_e.ASP (accessed 2 Nov 2024).

[145] Further information on the ratification process is provided on the CAFTA-DR webpage of SICA, available at http://www.sice.oas.org/TPD/USA_CAFTA/USA_CAFTA_e.ASP#EntryintoForce (accessed 2 Nov 2024).

[146] Jaramillo and Lederman (2005), p. 5.

[147] Rodlauer and Schipke (2005), p. 5.

Table 2.3 CAFTA-DR Timeline

Country	Signature	Ratification	Entry into force
Costa Rica	5 August 2004	14 November 2008	1 January 2009
Dominican Republic		9 September 2005[a]	1 March 2007
El Salvador		17 December 2004	1 March 2006
Guatemala		10 March 2005[b]	1 July 2006
Honduras		3 March 2005	1 April 2006
Nicaragua		10 October 2005[c]	1 April 2006
USA		2 August 2005	Different for each Central America country

[a]The parliament of the Dominican Republic ratified the agreement on 6 September 2005 and the government promulgated the respective resolution no. 357-05 on 9 September 2005
[b]Date of the legislative approval, provided on the CAFTA-DR webpage of SICA, available at http://www.sice.oas.org/TPD/USA_CAFTA/USA_CAFTA_s.ASP (accessed 2 Nov 2024)
[c]Ibid

2.2.1.2 Special Focus: Costa Rica

The deadline for the entry into force in Costa Rica had to be extended several times, because of the complications in the ratification and implementation process in this country. Although the agreement was highly controversial even in the USA,[148] only in Costa Rica the government of *Oscar Arias* initially failed to achieve legislative approval.[149]

A broad range of anti-CAFTA-DR stakeholders participated in the discussions regarding the ratification of CAFTA-DR and were able to prevent the ratification of the agreement by the Costa Rican parliament. Costa Rica's parliament decided not to ratify the agreement and instead to submit it to a referendum. This was the first referendum worldwide on an FTA,[150] and the second referendum in Costa Rican history, following the referendum on independence in 1821. The decision of the parliament to neither approve nor reject CAFTA-DR suggests that the respective political influence of the pro-CAFTA-DR businesses groups and the anti-CAFTA-DR coalition was about even. It may be seen as a sign of the strength of the civil society that the opposition to CAFTA-DR in Costa Rica, arguably the most developed country in the region, was able to force a referendum on CAFTA-DR. IP issues

[148]The treaty could be passed by a simple 54 to 45 majority in the US Senate, because of the President's Fast Track authority; the detailed vote is available at http://www.senate.gov/legislative/LIS/roll_call_lists/roll_call_vote_cfm.cfm?congress=109&session=1&vote=00170 (accessed 2 Nov 2024); the House of Representatives voted for the agreement with the smallest possible majority of 217 (202 Republicans and 15 Democrats) against 215 on 27 July 2005, available at https://clerk.house.gov/evs/2005/roll443.xml (accessed 2 Nov 2024).

[149]Díaz (2008), p. 17.

[150]Díaz (2008), p. 17.

were part of the public debate regarding the ratification of CAFTA-DR, but at its core it was an "ideological battle between supporters of the liberal capitalist world view [represented by the USA] and those who prefer a socialist path, as personified by Venezuelan President Hugo Chávez [and Cuban President Fidel Castro]".[151] The referendum was organized by the Supreme Electoral Tribunal and held on 7 October 2007, when a narrow majority of the people (51,5%) voted in favor of the agreement.[152] Support for CAFTA-DR was strongest in and around the capital city San José, while opposition was strongest in rural areas.[153] While the USA strongly advocated the agreement, this intervention in the referendum campaign might have had a negative impact, because of local sensitivity to "imperial diplomacy" by the USA.[154]

Like the ratification, the *implementation* of CAFTA-DR was highly controversial in Costa Rica. The opposition successfully challenged the first draft of the implementation law, because it exceeded the requirements of CAFTA-DR.[155] In particular, the conformity of the CAFTA-DR implementation with the national biodiversity legislation was questioned.[156] The *Sala IV* of the CSJ (CR) found the law unconstitutional in October 2008, considering that changes to the Biodiversity Law (CR) made during the implementation unduly affected the indigenous population.[157] With only weeks before the final (already extended) deadline for implementing the requirements of CAFTA-DR in Costa Rica, the legislative consultation process could not have been completed in time. Therefore, the Costa Rican government enacted a special executive "interpretation" of the Biodiversity Law (CR) in November 2008, which was considered compliant with CAFTA-DR by the USTR and allowed the agreement to enter into force. This executive decree was found unconstitutional by the *Sala IV* of the CSJ (CR) in 2012, on the same grounds as the implementation law of 2008.[158]

---

[151] Breuer (2009), p. 459.

[152] The political ramifications and the process of the referendum are discussed in detail by Breuer (2009), pp. 456–460.

[153] Breuer (2009), p. 461.

[154] Breuer (2009), p. 460, concludes that the "long history of US intervention in Central America has engendered lasting sensitivity to imperious diplomacy among the region's population" may have created a "backfiring effect of the warnings issued by Washington" against the rejection of CAFTA-DR during the referendum campaign in Costa Rica.

[155] Breuer (2009), p. 461.

[156] These challenges related in particular to the required changes to Article 78 Nr. 6 Biodiversity Law (CR), see Sect. 3.1.4.4.

[157] Specifically, the CSJ held that legislative changes that affected the indigenous communities required prior consultation of these communities, which had not happened in this case, see Sect. 3.1.4.4.

[158] These decisions are discussed in more detail in Sect. 3.1.4.4.

2.2.1.3 Evaluation

The negotiations of CAFTA-DR between the USA and the Central American countries (except the Dominican Republic) commenced in January 2003 and were concluded by January 2004. In other words, the negotiations were completed within 1 year. The agreement was soon afterwards ratified by all Central American countries except Costa Rica.[159]

There was only a limited possibility to negotiate all the aspects of the IP rules in detail (if that was at all a viable option given the respective bargaining power), because of the short period of 1 year for the negotiation of such a comprehensive agreement. The negotiation of the IP rules, like the agreement as a whole, was in reality largely a binary "yes/no" choice for the Central American countries, and accordingly local stakeholders could no in a meaningful way influence the negotiations.[160] Accordingly, local policy priorities were not considered during the negotiations or at least not implemented in the final version of the agreement, as is demonstrated by the fact that CAFTA-DR contains no IP provisions which were introduced into CAFTA-DR in the interest of the Central American countries.

For example, the protection of genetic resources and traditional knowledge in Costa Rica is comparatively well developed. A helpful mechanism to protect genetic resources both locally and abroad could have been to ensure that, during patent examination in the USA, the origin of genetic inventions must be disclosed and that foreign oral information must be considered as prior art by the examiner.[161] However, despite demands from the Central American public and interested third parties and despite the fact that this issue played a prominent role during the negotiation and the implementation of CAFTA-DR from Costa Rica's perspective, no provision on these issues was included in CAFTA-DR. Interestingly, the requirement to consider foreign oral information as prior during patent examination was incorporated into US patent law in 2011 in the America Invents Act, but not because of political pressure from developing countries or FTA partner countries, but to align US patent procedure with the EPO patent procedure.[162]

Even when input from the Central American stakeholders was possible, their position was not successfully introduced into the negotiations and ultimately not included in the agreement. CAFTA-DR contains a list of "distinctive products", for instance, but only several types of US products are protected. While the Central American countries have similar products with distinct characteristics, in particular

[159] See Sect. 2.2.1.

[160] Díaz (2006), p. 27, notes the almost identical structure and content of CAFTA-DR and other US-FTAs and concludes that the text was not subject to meaningful discussion.

[161] See Sect. 3.1.3.1.

[162] See 35 U.S.C. § 102 (a)(1); regarding the expansion of the scope of prior art under the AIA see Sect. 3.1.3.1.

coffee, which is protected by several trademarks and geographical indications, these products were not included in the list of "distinctive products".[163]

Notably, one restriction of IP protection, which was added in CAFTA-DR, compared to earlier agreements, is the explicit reference to the Doha Declaration. However, it resulted from demands by the US Congress and was not the consequence of successful negotiations by the Central American countries.[164]

This demonstrates the imbalance of the negotiation in favor of the USA, because, the IP chapter agreed upon in CAFTA-DR largely corresponds to similar FTAs concluded by the USA, *e.g.*, the FTAs with Colombia and Peru. Because of the overriding political interest in Central American countries to improve the access to the US market, the Central American countries accepted the IP chapter proposed by the USA "as is".

2.2.2 *Trade Liberalization*

Besides IP protection, CAFTA-DR covers mainly trade liberalization, the protection of foreign investment, labor and environmental issues and dispute settlement mechanisms. A summary of the agreement was published by the USTR.[165] The following two subsections (Sects. 2.2.2 and 2.2.3) discuss the rules of CAFTA-DR on trade and investment, while the provisions on IP are discussed in more detail in Sect. 2.2.4.

2.2.2.1 Background

The political change in Central America (and around the globe) and the shift in economic policy since the late 1980ies and early 1990ies opened a policy window for a new level of trade liberalization and economic integration in the region. Many countries, including the countries of Central America, became unable to pay their foreign debt. In response, the creditor countries assembled in the so-called "Paris Club" required the involvement of the IMF in the debt rescheduling process. The IMF elaborated structural adjustment programs, which included low-tariff

[163] As discussed in Sect. 4.3, during the time of the CAFTA-DR negotiations, several countries were in the process of selecting "brands" and establishing protection and, therefore, the absence of Central American distinctive products may also be attributable to the fact that the Central American countries had no distinctive products to put on the list. However, as the example of the ongoing negotiations regarding Established Geographical Indications under Article 247 EU-CA-AA ("Addition of New Geographical Indications") shows, it would have been possible to provide for the option of Central American countries to submit additions to the list of distinctive products after the finalization of CAFTA-DR.

[164] See Sect. 3.1.11.2.

[165] The summary is available at https://ustr.gov/archive/assets/Trade_Agreements/Regional/CAFTA/Briefing_Book/asset_upload_file74_7284.pdf (accessed 2 Nov 2024).

Table 2.4 Trade to GDP Ratio in Central America

	Average middle-income country	CR	DR	SV	GT	HN	NI
2005	61	102	66	70	66	136	72
2015	51	72 (2014)	54	68	51	109	93

The data was obtained from the World Bank database, available at http://data.worldbank.org/indicator/NE.TRD.GNFS.ZS?end=2015&start=2005. Accessed 2 Nov 2024)

components to curtail protectionism.[166] Accordingly, throughout the region, tariffs and non-tariff barriers were reduced.[167] The annual economic growth per capita in Central America had averaged 1.8% during the 1990ies, and poverty and extreme poverty rates were reduced by 10%.[168] This process was favorable to the conclusion of the CAFTA-DR agreement.

The integration of the Central American countries into the global economy can be measured based on the trade to GDP ratio, as shown in Table 2.4.[169] The data shows that the trade integration of Central America is higher than that of the average middle-income country.[170] This indicates a substantial dependency on trade, which is a strong incentive (at least for certain segments of the economy) to conclude FTAs.

The USA also had a strong economic incentive to conclude CAFTA-DR. In the USA, several years of experience with NAFTA and similar agreements had shown the positive effects of regional FTAs for the US economy in general. Even before CAFTA-DR entered into force, Central America had become a major export destination for US businesses. Central America and the Dominican Republic made up the second largest market for US exports in Latin America (after Mexico, and ahead of Brazil), and were a more important export market than India, Indonesia and Russia combined.[171]

However, CAFTA-DR did not lead to a steady growth of US exports into the region; during the period from 2011 to 2015 (after the effects of the financial crisis receded), exports remained constantly around 30 billion USD per annum.[172] This data suggests that the anticipated trade increase did not happen (while it is unclear whether CAFTA-DR did not have an effect or whether this effect was overcompensated by other factors). Between 2020 and 2022, exports from the USA to Central America increased significantly, but this corresponded with increases to the rest of the world and therefore seems not attributable to CAFTA-DR.[173]

[166] Baquero-Herrera (2005), p. 174.

[167] Jaramillo and Lederman (2005), p. 2.

[168] Rodlauer and Schipke (2005), pp. 2–3.

[169] The trade-to-GDP ratio is the average share of exports and imports of goods and services in GDP.

[170] See Table 2.4.

[171] USTR, CAFTA Policy Brief (2005).

[172] Data available at www.statista.com (accessed 2 Nov 2024).

[173] Data available at www.statista.com (accessed 2 Nov 2024).

Another reason from the perspective of Central America was the increasing competition from Asia and other Latin American countries.[174] The privileged access to the US market granted by prior FTAs to third countries, especially in Latin America, worsened the competitive position of countries without such an agreement, which created an economic "domino effect": In order to even out the preferential access of existing "FTA-countries", other countries feel economically obliged to engage in FTA negotiations as well.[175] These agreements can be, and generally are, notified as regional agreements under Article XXIV(5) GATT, so that the *most favored nation* (MFN) principle[176] does not apply and the preferential access is not extended to the other WTO members.[177] CAFTA-DR is a good example for this "domino effect": The effects of Mexico's privileged access under NAFTA incentivized the Central American countries to level the playing field by negotiating CAFTA-DR. In turn, Panama and Colombia became willing to negotiate similar agreements, even before CAFTA-DR went into effect.

In addition, Central America also intended to improve its competitive position in relation to Asian countries by creating its own privileged access to the US market. This was considered indispensable to respond to the increasing competition from Asian, especially Chinese exports to the US.[178] However, as the evidence from the implementation of NAFTA by Mexico shows, Central America will have to struggle to compete with China even in a privileged position, not least because China is performing better in terms of technological progress.[179]

The relocation of Intel's microprocessor manufacturing plant from Costa Rica to Malaysia and Vietnam in 2014[180] illustrates the challenges created by the trade "domino effect" and the competition with Asia.[181] Intel's decision was announced a year before the negotiations between the USA and several other Pacific nations, including Malaysia and Vietnam, in relation to the Trans-Pacific Partnership (TPP) were officially concluded.[182]

---

[174] In particular local businesses in Central America are concerned about the competition by, e.g., Vietnam, see https://ticotimes.net/2015/12/14/ex-trade-minister-anabel-gonzalez-tpp-like-cafta-will-help-costa-rica-in-long-run (accessed 2 Nov 2024).

[175] Correa (2004), p. 81.

[176] Article I(1) GATT.

[177] Importantly, the exception to the MFN principle under Article XXIV GATT only applies to trade in goods, whereas the MFN principle in Article 4 TRIPS allows for no similar exceptions. This is the basis for the "multilateralization" effect of bilateral FTAs, see Drahos (2001), p. 12.

[178] Jaramillo and Lederman (2005), p. 3.

[179] Stiglitz (2006), p. 66.

[180] See Sect. 1.3.4.

[181] *The Economist*, Intel Outside, 19 April 2014, available at http://www.economist.com/news/americas/21600985-chipmaker-shuts-factory-slicing-away-one-fifth-countrys-exports-intel-outside (accessed 2 Nov 2024).

[182] *BBC News*, Trans-Pacific free trade deal agreed creating vast partnership, 6 October 2015, available at http://www.bbc.com/news/business-34444799 (accessed 2 Nov 2024).

In short, both the governments of the Central American countries (in particular the agriculture and textile industries) identified the trade benefits offered by CAFTA-DR and the EU-FTAs as critically important for their national economies and there was strong political pressure to accept the proposed trade deals, including the IP chapter, because of the economic importance of the export-based business sectors. As a result, while there was strong criticism of the TRIPS-plus requirements in CAFTA-DR during the negotiation phase by both local stakeholders and international observers, this criticism had little practical impact on the negotiation and ratification of CAFTA-DR in Central America, except to some extent for the civil society in Costa Rica defending the particular national biodiversity system and the generic pharmaceutical industry.[183]

2.2.2.2 The "Caribbean Basin Initiative"

When Latin America adopted the new economic approach in the 1980ies, the USA opened its market to Central American and Caribbean imports by granting preferential access based on the "Caribbean Basin Initiative" (CBI), which unilaterally eliminated the tariffs on most imported goods. The CBI privileges could be terminated unilaterally by the USA and were scheduled to expire in 2008.[184] Such trade preferences gave significant power to the granting country by creating economic dependency on the side of the beneficiary, because politically, the fear of losing preferred access may compel the beneficiary to act in the interest of the granting country. Critics argue that "[p]references can be taken away if the developing country does not do what the granting country wants. Preferential treatment has become a political instrument, a tool for getting developing countries to "toe the line"."[185]

Economically, new industries and special interests could develop around the privileged access, which might pressure the government to protect their business model. This way, unilateral preferences granted in the first stage of economic cooperation can create domestic allies for the second stage of economic cooperation, the bilateral trade agreement. Permanent privileged access to the US market was a major reason for Central America to conclude the CAFTA-DR agreement (the so-called "safe haven"-rationale).[186] Chapter 3 Article G CAFTA-DR makes the privileged access of Central American textile producers to the USA permanent, which had been temporary under the CBI.[187]

[183] See Sect. 2.2.1.

[184] Sanchez and Koehler-Geib (2015), p. 1.

[185] Stiglitz (2006), p. 82.

[186] Ministry of Economy of Guatemala (2002), p. 29.

[187] Ibid.

2.2.2.3 Content of CAFTA-DR

Trade in Goods

The primary objectives of CAFTA-DR relating to free trade are to reduce barriers to trade[188] and to facilitate market access and to increase investment opportunities. Because of the economic interests of the parties, the regulation of trade in goods represents the central element of CAFTA-DR.[189] CAFTA-DR eliminates tariffs for most products. However, the reduction of tariffs is probably not the most significant element of CAFTA-DR for US businesses, because the Central American countries already apply a common external tariff, ranging from 5% up to 20% and averaging less than 10%. More important from the US perspective are probably the rules on non-tariff barriers and related issues. The parties must implement the WTO Agreement on Sanitary and Phytosanitary Measures.[190] Also, the parties apply WTO principles on technical barriers to trade, especially standards.[191] In addition, CAFTA-DR provides for rules on customs administration.[192] These shall "encourage transparency, predictability and efficiency".[193] To this end, the parties are, for instance, required to publish customs measures and regulations.

Rules of Origin

CAFTA-DR also contains elaborate rules of origin (Chapter 4 CAFTA-DR). While it is understandable that countries do not want to allow the tariff-free import of goods merely passing through the exporting FTA partner, the need to rely on domestic components restricts the possibility for specializing in processing. As a result of rules of origin, the affected country has to maintain a substantial production of primary goods. This could slow the industrial and technological development. These restrictions on the importation of primary material may be especially problematic for the Central American countries, because they are so small that they probably cannot efficiently maintain a broad economic base on each level of processing. In effect, these countries may become even more locked into a commodity- or primary goods-based economy. Especially with regard to the entry of textile products to the USA,

[188] Article 1.2(b) CAFTA-DR.

[189] Chapters 3 to 5 CAFTA-DR.

[190] Chapter 6 CAFTA-DR.

[191] Chapter 7 CAFTA-DR.

[192] Chapter 5 CAFTA-DR.

[193] USTR, The Dominican Republic – Central America – United States Free Trade Agreement, Summary of the Agreement, p. 8, available at https://ustr.gov/archive/assets/Trade_Agreements/Regional/CAFTA/Transmittal/asset_upload_file888_7818.pdf (accessed 2 Nov 2024).

the rules of origin in CAFTA-DR have, therefore, been labeled "excessively restrictive".[194]

Trade in Services

Trade in services is regulated by Chapter 11 CAFTA-DR. Chapters 12 and 13 CAFTA-DR provide for special rules on financial services and telecommunications regulations, which were the economically most critical service sectors. In particular in Costa Rica, the requirement to open the highly regulated telecommunications and insurance sectors to foreign private competition was one of the most controversial issues in the ratification process of CAFTA-DR. Eventually a special annex to Chapter 13 was included in CAFTA-DR to accommodate Costa Rica's concerns.[195] For US businesses, the opening of the financial sector was highly relevant. Allegedly, the insurance companies and banks were the biggest donors in relation to the CAFTA-DR vote in the US Congress.[196]

2.2.2.4 Escalating Tariffs

A particular effect of tariffs on the industrial and technological development of developing countries is "escalation". Lower tariffs make the import of goods containing IP into developing countries cheaper and can thus contribute to more technology transfer.[197] It also enables the creation and growth of technologically more advanced industries in developing countries, if processed products can be exported more easily. However, to protect domestic industries, developed countries often apply higher tariffs on manufactured, processed goods than on unprocessed commodities. As this tariff covers the value of the whole good, while only the lower tariff applies to the unprocessed commodity, the effective tariff on the process is even higher. This mechanism is often referred to as "escalation", as the tariffs involved increase with the level of processing (*i.e.*, industrial sophistication) involved. This mechanism discourages industrialization and automation, *i.e.*, technology-based economic activities in favor of producing (or growing) commodities. It also discourages the economic diversification necessary to become

---

[194] Jaramillo and Lederman (2005), p. 4; similarly, studies by CEPAL show that rules of origin restrict exports by Central American counties to the USA, see Hernández (2007), p. 117.

[195] Costa Rica had created public monopolies in these markets and was reluctant to allow competition, see Jaramillo and Lederman (2005), p. 4.

[196] Public Citizen, Dangerous CAFTA liaisons (2006), p. 30, available at https://www.citizen.org/documents/CAFTA_Liaisons_Report1.pdf (accessed 2 Nov 2024).

[197] The import of goods containing technology is an important factor in technology transfer, but the practical problem is that this technology often is not absorbed in the importing country because of other impediments to technology absorption, e.g., an underdeveloped technological base or low levels of education; UNCTAD (2014), pp. 3 and 16.

independent from volatile demand for any specific goods. This arguably results in less technological investment and inventive activity in the exporting country.[198]

In this respect, CAFTA-DR will probably help the Central American countries, as the tariffs on almost all processed goods are eliminated with the entry into force of the agreement.[199] Therefore, there are no tariff-specific economic obstacles to engage in technologically more complex processing and internalizing the corresponding economic benefits.

Similarly, the EU-CA-AA and EU-CARIFORUM-EPA reduce or eliminate tariffs on most products to enable Central America to "move up the value-added chain".[200] The EU-CARIFORUM-EPA also removes quotas on exports to the EU.[201] Both agreements also contain no escalation mechanism.

2.2.2.5 Evaluation

Before the entry into force of CAFTA-DR, the World Bank projected an additional 0.6% growth in GDP for Central America because of the establishment of CAFTA-DR.[202] This expectation was based on empirical studies showing the large effect on economic growth of free trade agreements concluded by small developing countries with large partners.[203] The European experience has also shown that a free trade area is especially beneficial for small countries.[204] The evidence of CAFTA-DR effects from the first years is inconclusive and experience of the Central American countries after CAFTA-DR with the "privileged" access to the US market and other specific trade benefits is mixed. Some observers point to the general increase of imports from and exports to the USA. The annual economic growth in the region was substantially higher than before CAFTA-DR and the overall volume of trade, also with the USA, increased significantly.[205] However, it is unclear to what extent this can be directly attributed to CAFTA-DR.[206]

---

[198] Stiglitz (2006), p. 87.

[199] Practically all goods are either already duty-free, Annex 3.3 Nr. 1(g) CAFTA-DR, or become duty-free on the date of the entry into force of CAFTA-DR, Annex 3.3 Nr. 1(a) CAFTA-DR; see Rivera and Rojas-Romagosa (2007), p. 10.

[200] European Commission (2018), p. 3.

[201] Ibid.

[202] Jaramillo and Lederman (2005), p. 158.

[203] Jaramillo and Lederman (2005), p. 6.

[204] Kotschwar (1999), p. 135.

[205] With regard to Costa Rica, see Sanchez and Koehler-Geib (2015), p. 1, who note that it is difficult to show a direct causal link between changes in trade volume and CAFTA-DR, because of the (general) development trajectory and economic policies of the country, multiple other trade agreements joined by Costa Rica before and after CAFTA-DR (e.g., China), and the impact of the financial crisis, but consider it "likely" that CAFTA-DR contributed to the growth.

[206] Koehler-Geib and Clavijo (2015), pp. 15-17.

In addition, the imports by the Central American countries from the USA increased much more than the exports to the USA in the first years after CAFTA-DR went into effect, and as a result, the trade deficit of the Central American with the USA also increased sharply.[207] Imports from the USA increased more than exports to the USA such that the US goods and services trade surplus with CAFTA-DR countries reached $8.1 billion in 2022.[208] Several factors may have contributed to this development. The decrease of exports from Central America to the USA may be due to the same reasons as the decrease of exports to the EU, *i.e.*, the "coffee rust" epidemic limiting the coffee production capacity in Central America and the closure of the Intel manufacturing plant in Costa Rica, which together caused a 20 % trade decrease.[209] Also, while CAFTA-DR reduces tariffs and other trade restrictions, regulatory requirements regarding quality, health and safety remain in place. Central American products sometimes do not comply with US requirements and, therefore, cannot be exported. For example, when CAFTA-DR entered into force, only one processing facility for dairy products complied with US requirements.[210] Finally, Central America faces competition from third countries. On the one hand, reduced tariff rates were extended by the USA, over time, to other countries which concluded FTAs with the USA as well, thereby neutralizing or "eroding" the FTA-based competitive advantage of the CAFTA-DR countries ("domino effect").[211] Specifically, the preferential access to the US market was eroded by FTAs concluded after CAFTA-DR by the USA with Peru (entry into force on 1 February 2009), South Korea (entry into force on 15 March 2012), Colombia (entry into force on 15 May 2012) and Panama (entry into force on 31 October 2012). On the other hand, the market access facilitation was not enough to compensate other competitive advantages of Asian competitors, as evidenced, *e.g.*, by the relocation of Intel's microprocessor plant from Costa Rica to Southeast Asia.[212] This development was not expected and contrasts with the development in Mexico, where from 1993 to 2007, Mexico's USD 1.7 billion trade deficit became a USD 75 billion

---

[207] The data shown by Koehler-Geib and Clavijo (2015), p. 18, indicates that imports by Costa Rica from the USA grew between 2004 and 2012 from 400 million USD to 1.4 billion USD, while exports increase from 200 million USD to 400 million USD. In other words, the benefits for the USA outpace the benefits for Costa Rica both in absolute numbers and relative to the initial level.

[208] See https://ustr.gov/trade-agreements/free-trade-agreements/cafta-dr-dominican-republic-central-america-fta (accessed 2 Nov 2024).

[209] European Commission (2015) Annual Report on the Implementation of Part IV of the Agreement establishing an Association between the European Union and its Member States, on the one hand, and Central America on the other, https://www.europarl.europa.eu/meetdocs/2014_2019/documents/dcam/dv/report_partiv_aa_/report_partiv_aa_en.pdf (accessed 2 Nov 2024).

[210] Tharin (2008).

[211] See Sect. 2.2.2.

[212] See Sect. 1.3.4.

surplus.[213] It shows that from an economic perspective the USA benefited more from CAFTA-DR than Central America.

The effects on Central American workers and consumers were also mixed. Supporters of CAFTA-DR argue that lower tariffs as provided by CAFTA-DR are economically beneficial for Central American consumers. In addition to better export opportunities, the World Bank submits that lower tariffs in the agricultural sector are generally beneficial, as about 80% of the households in Central America were net consumers of agricultural products and thus would benefit from lower tariffs.[214] Critics contest that CAFTA-DR will increase poverty because it prematurely opens the Central American markets to subsidized US agricultural goods with which local farmers cannot compete.[215] In Central America, economic benefits are realized primarily by large agro-business companies; in Nicaragua, for instance, 70 % of export earnings go to only fifty businesses, and only one plant processing dairy products in the entire country has the capacity to pasteurize milk according to United States Department of Agriculture (USDA) standards, and that plant is owned by a foreign dairy conglomerate, *Parmalat*.[216] This corresponds with the experience of Mexico, where after NAFTA was implemented the rural south of the country witnessed a decrease in the standard of living.[217] Finally, the protection of certain US agricultural sectors[218] resulted in special import restrictions in Chapter 3 Article F and in Annex 3.15 CAFTA-DR, containing Agricultural Safeguard Measures,[219] which protect primarily the US market.

The trade liberalization created by CAFTA-DR was expected to accelerate the technical specialization among the parties, which could mean that more advanced countries like Costa Rica focus on technology-based industries and less-developed countries like Nicaragua strengthen their primary sector. However, it is yet unclear whether technical specialization will increase because of CAFTA-DR. After CAFTA-DR, the share of primary sector exports *increased* notably in the region, which suggests that no country increased technical specialization.[220]

There are specific trade mechanisms which could limit the economic benefits of Central America under CAFTA-DR, especially with regard to technological development: Subsidies to US products harm the level playing field for Central American products that CAFTA-DR supposedly creates. The rules of origin limit the

[213] Congressional Research Service, The North American Free Trade Agreement (NAFTA), 2017, https://sgp.fas.org/crs/row/R42965.pdf (accessed 2 Nov 2024).

[214] Jaramillo and Lederman (2005), p. 8.

[215] Tharin (2008).

[216] Ibid.

[217] Schwanen (2004), p. 348.

[218] Especially corn, being an important staple crop for local farmers, Jaramillo/Lederman (2005), p. 7.

[219] E.g., corn in Central American countries, potatoes in Costa Rica and sugar in the USA, see Chapter 3, section F CAFTA-DR.

[220] See Sect. 1.3.4.

possibility of the small Central American countries to specialize in products and/or technologies.

On the other hand, the elimination of escalation tariffs is favorable to the development of more complex and technology-driven industries. Also, the trade chapter provides for another mechanism which may help technological development in Central America. Any party has the right to introduce safeguard tariffs in case of sudden surges in imports threatening domestic industries.[221] Since these safeguard tariffs are not limited to certain industries, this mechanism could also be invoked in case of a surge in IP-related imports in Central America. If the elimination of any tariff on copyright content, *e.g.*, of imported CDs and DVDs, threatens the domestic film or music industry, the Central American countries could re-introduce such a tariff. Likewise, if US imports threaten technologically more advanced industries, *e.g.*, the production of generic pharmaceuticals, safeguard tariffs could be imposed.

2.2.3 *Protection of Foreign Direct Investment*

The investment provisions of CAFTA-DR are not the focus of this study. However, this section briefly discusses the CAFTA-DR rules, because the increase in foreign direct investment (FDI) is one of the alleged benefits of FTAs and the protection of FDI can also cover IP.

2.2.3.1 FDI Protection in General

The protection of FDI is particularly important for Central American countries, where little capital is available because of small markets, little trust in banks and low savings rates. The low capitalization limits the possibility for technological development, because technological development often involves high financial risks and requires large investments.[222] There is evidence that the level of R&D is correlated with the depth of the credit market.[223] While in many developed countries there are (semi-)public savings institutions and private investors that provide capital for technology enterprises, such funds are scarcely available in Central America. In Guatemala, for example, because of the low level of tax revenues and public expenditure, public capital formation is very low and the government is not able to provide significant funding for R&D.[224] In such an environment it is very difficult to

[221] Chapter 8 CAFTA-DR.

[222] Stiglitz (2006), p. 57.

[223] Jaramillo and Lederman (2005), p. 19.

[224] See UNCTAD (2011), p. 19. In Guatemala, taxes and other revenues of the state account for 10.0% of GDP in 2020 (the last year for which data was available), which is among the lowest shares in the world; according to the CIA World Factbook, Guatemala ranks 197 out of 222, see https://www.cia.gov/the-world-factbook/countries/guatemala/#economy (accessed 2 Nov 2024).

finance innovation domestically and more foreign direct investment could alleviate such constraints.

Chapter 10 of CAFTA-DR protects foreign direct investment. The term investment comprises both financial capital and technology. This protection shall foster capital investment and technology transfer.[225] The agreement provides for the usual substantive protection of investment, including fair and non-discriminatory treatment and compensation for expropriations.[226] In addition to the substantive protection discussed above, Chapter 10 of CAFTA-DR also establishes special dispute settlement procedures for disputes related to FDI. These procedures are discussed together with the general dispute settlement procedures under CAFTA-DR below.[227]

The NAFTA experience suggests that FTAs can substantially increase foreign investment, especially in technology-based industries.[228] CAFTA-DR is likewise expected to increase the domestically available capital by creating new financial services, *e.g.*, venture capital and small and micro-scale finance because of additional protection for FDI.[229] This protection might also improve the investment climate relative to other countries that already have strong investment protection or offer other advantages such as bigger markets. Capital investments are also expected to modernize the internal productive structure by creating high tech and knowledge intensive businesses.[230]

Bearing in mind the difficulties in establishing causation, a clear correlation between the rise in FDI and the entry into force of CAFTA-DR can be observed in Guatemala. While prior to CAFTA-DR, FDI was almost non-existent, it rose to USD 500 million in 2005 and continued to increase to a level of more than USD 1 billion each year between 2011 and 2015.[231]

2.2.3.2 Protection of IP as Investment

The protection of IP as a type of FDI has given rise to concerns that this might undermine the limitations contained in the IP chapter. In particular, it is argued that a

[225] These goals are typical for trade agreements in Latin America; see the discussion on NAFTA in Grave (2002), p. 32.

[226] Chapter 10 CAFTA-DR.

[227] See Sect. 2.2.6.

[228] Since NAFTA came into effect, the share of high-technology products in Mexico's exports rose from 21% to 30%, see Schwanen (2004), p. 347 (Fn 2).

[229] Costa Rica, Conceptual Proposal for a National Action Plan, December 2002, p. 22, available at http://sice.oas.org/TPD/USA_CAFTA/Negotiations/Trade_Capacity/NAP_CRI_e.pdf (accessed 2 Nov 2024).

[230] Ministry of Economy of Guatemala (2002), pp. 29-30.

[231] World Bank, Foreign direct investment, net inflows (BoP, current USD), available at http://data.worldbank.org/indicator/BX.KLT.DINV.CD.WD?locations=GT (accessed 2 Nov 2024).

compulsory license might be considered an expropriation requiring compensation according to investment standards.[232] Also, while the protection of IP investments under CAFTA-DR was justified in part as increasing the incentive for foreigners to engage in technology transfer,[233] the evidence of other FTAs, namely NAFTA, suggests that stronger IP protection actually leads to an increase in technology transfer.[234]

In CAFTA-DR, IP rights and licenses are defined as one form of protected investment.[235] Therefore, certain types of non-compliance by Central American countries with the IP provisions of CAFTA-DR could theoretically be seen as violations of the investment provisions. However, a key question for the protection of an investment is whether the investor had a *legitimate* expectation the investment would be protected. An investor cannot expect, for example, that a granted patent or trademark would not be revoked or no compulsory license would be granted.[236] Accordingly, Article 10.2 CAFTA-DR expressly provides that the substantive rules of other chapters prevail in the case of inconsistencies. In particular, the investment chapter "*does not apply to the issuance of compulsory licenses (…) or to the revocation, limitation, or creation of intellectual property rights*" if the measure is consistent with TRIPS and the IP chapter.[237] This addresses the concerns that FDI protection could undermine the limitations contained in the IP chapter. Also, generally no party may require the transfer a particular technology, a production process, or other proprietary knowledge to a person in its territory in connection with the establishment, acquisition, expansion, management, conduct, operation, or sale or other disposition of an investment. However, this restriction does not apply when a Party authorizes use of an IP right in accordance with Article 31 TRIPS, or to measures requiring the disclosure of proprietary information that fall within the scope of, and are consistent with, Article 39 TRIPS.[238]

2.2.4 Intellectual Property

This section provides a summary of the IP chapter of CAFTA-DR and briefly discussed the basic "minimum protection" structure, transparency requirements and copyright and e-commerce provisions, that are not the focus of this study. The

[232] On this discussion see, e.g., Correa (2004–2005), pp. 331-352; Rutledge (2012), pp. 149–163, highlights the notable absence of any example of an arbitration filed by a patent owner under a BIT claiming that a compulsory license constituted an indirect expropriation.

[233] Ministry of Economy of Guatemala (2002), pp. 29–30.

[234] See Sect. 3.1.1.2.

[235] Article 10.28 CAFTA-DR.

[236] Grosse Ruse-Khan (2016), pp. 171–184.

[237] Article 10.7(5) CAFTA-DR.

[238] Article 10.9(3)(b) CAFTA-DR.

other IP provisions (i.e., on industrial property rights and enforcement) are discussed in detail in the following chapters of this study. IP is regulated in Chapter 15 CAFTA-DR. The general provisions are followed by the provisions on distinctive signs, *i.e.*, trademarks,[239] geographical indications[240] and domain names.[241] The following parts address obligations pertaining to copyright and related rights,[242] patents[243] and measures related to certain regulated products, *i.e.*, test data protection and patent linkage for pharmaceutical or agricultural chemical products[244] and the enforcement of IP rights,[245] including limitations on the liability of service providers.[246] Article 15.12 CAFTA-DR contains final provisions.

2.2.4.1 General and Procedural Issues

Minimum Protection

CAFTA-DR is essentially a contract between the USA and the Central American countries and primarily contains provisions important to the business interests of the USA in the other countries that are parties to the agreement, and considers principles important for public policy objectives much less.[247] It establishes additional "minimum protection" for the right holder compared to TRIPS (*i.e.*, TRIPS-plus protection). The focus on the right holder is also due to the fact that the IP chapters of FTAs like CAFTA-DR are mainly influenced by international companies (namely the entertainment and pharmaceutical industries) who own large global portfolios of IP rights.[248] Policy-making by the USTR is informed in particular by the Industry Functional Advisory Committee on Intellectual Property Rights for Trade Policy Matters (IFAC-3). IFAC-3 comprised, when CAFTA-DR was negotiated, fashion, entertainment and pharmaceutical companies etc., i.e., IP right holders.[249] The report of the IFAC-3 emphasizes the importance of ensuring that the model FTA IP text, which has been carefully developed through the course of negotiation of seven FTAs, continues to form the "base line" for these other agreements.[250] The intent of US business in promoting FTAs such as CAFTA-DR as templates of

[239] Article 15.2 CAFTA-DR.

[240] Article 15.3 CAFTA-DR.

[241] Article 15.4 CAFTA-DR.

[242] Articles 15.5 to 15.7 CAFTA-DR; see also Sect. 2.2.4.2.

[243] Article 15.9 CAFTA-DR.

[244] Article 15.10 CAFTA-DR.

[245] Article 15.11 CAFTA-DR.

[246] Article 15.11(27) CAFTA-DR.

[247] Díaz (2008), p. 21.

[248] See, e.g., Díaz (2006), p. 26; Barton (2007), p. 14.

[249] IFAC-3 (2004), p. 3.

[250] Ibid.

ever-increasing "minimum protection" for future agreements has also been expressed in the "Report of the Industry Sector Advisory Committee for Chemicals and Allied Products" on CAFTA-DR. The "level of intellectual property protection that [CAFTA-DR] contains should not be viewed as setting a *ceiling* for the intellectual property chapters for future FTA's. Rather, each individual FTA should be viewed as setting a new *base line* for future FTA's" (emphasis in the original).[251] CAFTA-DR makes clear that it is based on the concept of minimum protection in the very first paragraph of the IP chapter, by stating that the parties must "at a minimum, give effect to [the IP] Chapter [and] may [...] implement in its domestic law more extensive protection and enforcement of intellectual property rights than is required under [the IP] Chapter".[252]

National Treatment

According to Article 15.1(8) CAFTA-DR, the national treatment principle applies to the "*enjoyment* of (...) and any *benefits* derived from such rights". While not literally identical to Article 3(1) TRIPS, this wording arguably corresponds to the "use" of rights under TRIPS and does not create additional obligations for the parties. Article 15.1(9) CAFTA-DR, which restates Article 3(2) TRIPS, allows members to require a domestic address or agent for foreign right holders, if this does not constitute a disguised restriction on trade.[253] According to Article 15.1(10) CAFTA-DR, the national treatment does not apply to procedures provided in WIPO agreements relating to the acquisition or maintenance of IP rights.

Transparency

In addition to the substantive and procedural requirements for the national legislation, CAFTA-DR also provides for formal requirements, especially transparency. The issue is addressed generally by Chapters 9 and 18 CAFTA-DR.[254] To ensure

[251] USTR ISAC-3 (2004) Report of the Industry Sector Advisory Committee for Chemicals and Allied Products, 19 March 2004, https://ustr.gov/archive/assets/Trade_Agreements/Regional/CAFTA/DR_Reports/asset_upload_file602_3335.pdf (accessed 2 Nov 2024).

[252] Article 15.1(1) CAFTA-DR.

[253] As the exceptions of Article 2.2 and 2.3 Paris Convention have also been incorporated by Article 2(1) TRIPS, the novelty introduced by TRIPS is the requirement that these procedural exceptions "are not applied in a manner which would constitute a disguised restriction of trade" (Article 3(2) TRIPS).

[254] Chapter 9 CAFTA-DR contains obligations on fair and transparent public procurement, based on the WTO Agreement on Government Procurement, see USTR, The Dominican Republic – Central America – United States Free Trade Agreement, Summary of the Agreement, p. 11, available at https://ustr.gov/archive/assets/Trade_Agreements/Regional/CAFTA/Transmittal/asset_upload_file888_7818.pdf (accessed 2 Nov 2024); Chapter 18 CAFTA-DR addresses general questions of transparency.

legal transparency with regard to IP, Article 15.1(14) CAFTA-DR contains the obligation that the respective laws and regulations shall be in writing and published, or at least publicly available.[255] Article 15.1(14) CAFTA-DR requires this for the benefit of governments and right holders, but in practice this of course also benefits users and the general public. The Central American countries have generally complied with these transparency requirements through publication of their laws on the internet and/or in print.[256]

2.2.4.2 Substantive Provisions

Industrial Property Rights and Enforcement

The provisions on distinctive signs (trademarks, geographical indications and domain names) in Articles 15.2 to 15.4 CAFTA-DR, patents and test data in Articles 15.9 and 15.10 CAFTA-DR and enforcement in Article 15.11 CAFTA-DR are discussed in detail in the following chapters of this study and therefore are not separately summarized here.

Copyright, Related Rights and Digital Rights Management (DRM)

Articles 15.5 to 15.7 CAFTA-DR contain the obligations pertaining to copyright and related rights, dealing especially with technological (digital) rights management (DRM) and the protection of encrypted program-carrying satellite signals.[257] The term of copyright protection is extended in comparison with Article 12 TRIPS: The parties must provide protection for the life of the author plus 70 years (for works measured by a person's life), or 70 years after the authorized publication (for corporate works). The strict rules on DRM do not reflect the fact that the legal framework was controversial and the practical feasibility was questioned by some of the affected companies themselves while CAFTA-DR was negotiated. *Peter Yu* observed with regard to the DRM regime in CAFTA-DR that the level of protection is "stronger than what is required under the DMCA [and t]his type of DMCA-plus legislation is particularly troublesome because less developed countries actually need to have greater access to information and knowledge than their developed counterparts", and while CAFTA-DR "still includes many narrow exceptions

[255] According to Article 15.1(14) CAFTA-DR, "(e)ach party shall ensure that all laws, regulations and procedures concerning the protection or enforcement of intellectual property rights shall be in writing" and shall be publicly available, preferably through publication".

[256] At least the intellectual and industrial property, trademark and plant variety laws are available on the websites of national and international institutions such as WIPO or UPOV. Many Central American IP Registers also maintain legislative databases. It is more difficult to find amendments, such as the CAFTA-DR implementations or regulations online.

[257] Article 15.8 CAFTA-DR.

commonly found in the DMCA, it omits other important ones and has made it more difficult for the signatory countries to introduce new exceptions".[258] In this situation, the fixation of the current "state of the art" DRM protection is problematic, because the legal framework is "cast in stone" and future developments cannot be accompanied by legal reform on the national level.[259]

E-Commerce

Under Article 14.3(1) CAFTA-DR, no party may impose customs duties on or in connection with the importation or exportation of digital products (such as computer programs, text, video, images and sound recordings)[260] by electronic transmission. In the case of "physical transmission", *i.e.*, using a carrier medium bearing a digital product, when "determining applicable customs duties, each Party shall determine the customs value based on the cost or value of the carrier medium alone, without regard to the cost or value of the digital product stored on the carrier medium", Article 14.3(2) CAFTA-DR.[261] In plain terms, this means that digital (copyright) content is exempted from any tariff, because the value of the carrier medium (CD, DVD) is generally negligible. This clause reflects long-standing U.S. policy, where digital products are tariff-exempt, whether they are delivered digitally or on a CD, DVD or other physical medium.[262] It has to be seen in connection with the stronger protection of IP rights and especially stronger enforcement. Stronger protection strengthens US goods against domestic copies and ensures that royalties are paid to US firms, increasing the export revenues of the US. To counter the resulting trade imbalance, the country importing goods protected by IP rights might be tempted to increase tariffs on such goods. CAFTA-DR closes this "loophole" by excluding tariffs on imported goods, which means that no competitive advantage can be created for domestic competitors.

2.2.4.3 Review and Change Procedures

CAFTA-DR does not provide for any formal review and change procedure regarding the IP chapter. Accordingly, the implementation of the IP provisions is monitored and assessed by the parties, in case of the USA, the USTR. As the example of the implementation in Costa Rica highlights, this provides considerable leverage to the

---

[258] Yu (2006), p. 14.

[259] See Sect. 8.9.

[260] See the definition in Article 14.6 CAFTA-DR.

[261] The same substantial rule was included, e.g., in Article 16.3 US-Australia FTA and Article 14.3 US-Panama FTA.

[262] Congressional Research Service, Digital Trade and U.S. Trade Policy, 9 December 2021, p. 14, available at https://crsreports.congress.gov/product/pdf/R/R44565 (accessed 2 Nov 2024)

USA. Practically, the USTR had to approve the "successful" implementation of the IP obligations until a certain deadline (end of 2008). When the USTR determined that the CAFTA-DR Reform Law I (CR) was not fully compliant with CAFTA-DR after the decision of the CSJ invalidating the amendment of the Biodiversity Law (CR) relating to patentability requirements,[263] the only option of Costa Rica to avoid CAFTA-DR not entering into force (possibly permanently) was to implement an executive decree in contravention of constitutional requirements for the participation of indigenous peoples.[264] There is no ongoing review process of IP issues after CAFTA-DR entered into force. The CAFTA-DR Free Trade Commission (CAFTA-FTC) is the central oversight body for CAFTA-DR, composed of the USTR and the trade ministers of the Central American countries or their designees. However, in its annual statements the CAFTA-FTC has not reviewed IP issues.[265] Practically, the "performance" of Central America in relation to IP is addressed in the annual Special 301 Report issued by the USTR. Industry observers represented in IFAC-3 expressed the expectation that the USTR, "through a thorough and aggressive monitoring mechanism over agreement compliance" ensures that all the obligations of [CAFTA-DR] are promptly and fully implemented. In particular "the Dominican Republic must redeem [its] commitments immediately and effectively *or be made subject to prompt withdrawal of benefits afforded* under this agreement [and] the United States should be prepared to move quickly to dispute settlement should the Dominican Republic [...] fail to implement or enforce its patent and regulated product related obligations" (emphasis added).[266] Interestingly, however, while there are cases of non-compliance with CAFTA-DR obligations, in particular regarding the protection of patents and regulated products in the Dominican Republic,[267] some of which were raised in earlier Special 301 Reports of the USTR, none has resulted in any formal action being taken or sanctions being imposed by the USA, despite the request of IFAC-3. In subsequent reports (2016), the sections on Central American countries focused on practical enforcement activities and the protection of European geographical indications and only briefly mentioned test data protection.[268] Chapter 20 CAFTA-DR establishes a dispute settlement procedure between the parties, which has been rarely used by the USA so far (most prominently in a dispute relating to the labor chapter), and never in relation to the implementation of the IP chapter.[269]

[263] These amendments were provided for in Article 3 CAFTA-DR Reform Law I (CR).

[264] See Sect. 3.1.4.4.

[265] See the statements of the CAFTA-FTC available at https://ustr.gov/trade-agreements/free-trade-agreements/cafta-dr-dominican-republic-central-america-fta/free-trade (accessed 2 Nov 2024).

[266] IFAC-3 (2004), p. 3.

[267] See Sect. 8.6.

[268] USTR Special 301 Report (2016), pp. 58–60.

[269] See Sect. 2.2.6.

2.2.4.4 Retroactive Application of IP Protection

CAFTA-DR requires that the obligations of the IP chapter apply to all subject matter existing on the entry into force of the agreement.[270] Therefore, also the procedural provisions have to be applied to pending applications.[271] This retroactive application of the stronger IP protection under CAFTA-DR appears questionable from a policy perspective, at least with regard to the sections on patents and similar rights: The objectives of CAFTA-DR are the strengthening of the incentive to innovate (Preamble of CAFTA-DR) and stronger IP protection.[272] While stronger patent protection of future subject matter may increase the investment in research and development, it obviously cannot affect such investments in the past, which were made for existing subject matter. The retroactive application of stronger protection to existing patents, utility models and plant varieties, therefore, does not serve efficiency, because the resources have already been allocated to the technology development process and, therefore, seems unjustifiable in the light of the goal of IP protection to "foster creativity and innovation".[273] There are other objectives for the protection of IP rights, namely moral and social objectives, which could justify retroactive protection in certain cases. Even critics of IP protection in general support the creation of protection for (existing) genetic resources and traditional knowledge.[274] The reasons for retroactive protection in such cases are moral considerations and an incentive for protecting biodiversity as the basis of such resources and knowledge. However, these objectives are not the focus of CAFTA-DR, and seem not to justify the specific provisions contained in this agreement. The retroactive application, therefore, serves the interests of the existing right holders, but does not promote the objective of the IP system to strengthen the incentive to innovate.

2.2.5 *Labor and Environment*

CAFTA-DR also contains provisions regarding labor standards and the environment, but these do not appear to be the focus of the agreement. The parties reaffirm their obligations under the standards of the International Labor Organization (ILO) and commit themselves to due process in labor procedures.[275] This commitment is mitigated, however, because each party only "shall strive to ensure" their compliance and retains the right "to establish its own domestic labor standards".[276]

[270] Article 15.1(11) CAFTA-DR.

[271] PhRMA (2007), p. 2.

[272] Article 15 CAFTA-DR.

[273] Preamble of CAFTA-DR.

[274] See Sect. 6.

[275] Article 16.1(1) CAFTA-DR.

[276] Article 16.1(2) CAFTA-DR.

Furthermore, "decisions [...] shall not be subject to revision or be reopened under the provisions of this Chapter".[277] In sum, the wording seems to avoid carefully any binding effect of the numerous commitments included in the chapter on labor standards. Interestingly, the first state-state dispute under CAFTA-DR was initiated by the USA in relation to labor standards.[278] The protection of the environment is regulated in parallel with the labor chapter, *i.e.*, no substantial obligations are created.[279] Also, "the right of each Party to establish its own levels of domestic environmental protection" is recognized.[280]

2.2.6 *Enforcement and Dispute Settlement*

2.2.6.1 State-State Disputes

One important element of the WTO system in general and TRIPS and bilateral FTAs such as CAFTA-DR in particular are the strong dispute settlement mechanisms. They are the "teeth" for the substantive requirements. CAFTA-DR states that one of the main objectives of the agreement is to "create effective procedures for the implementation and application of this agreement ... and for the resolution of disputes".[281] The dispute settlement procedure between the parties of the agreement consists of two steps: Initially, consultations take place, and if these do not successfully resolve the issue, sanctions can be imposed.[282] This possibility of control and enforcement is supposed to force parties to exert more care in compliance and in legislative reforms.[283]

So far only few trade disputes have been conducted under the dispute settlement procedure of Chapter 20 CAFTA-DR between parties. Importantly, no disputes relating to IP have been initiated under CAFTA-DR by either the USA or Central American countries, even though the USTR has repeatedly identified non-compliance of Central American countries with IP obligations under CAFTA-DR. The USA brought one case against Guatemala in relation to labor rights. Discussions regarding the alleged violation of labor obligations under CAFTA-DR by Guatemala were initiated by the USTR in 2010, and after an unsatisfactory resolution, a formal dispute was initiated in 2014;[284] the case was

[277] Article 16.3(8) CAFTA-DR.

[278] See Sect. 2.2.6.

[279] Chapter 17 CAFTA-DR

[280] Article 17.1 CAFTA-DR.

[281] Article 1.2 CAFTA-DR.

[282] Chapter 20 CAFTA-DR.

[283] Dörmer (1998), p. 934.

[284] See USTR, In the Matter of Guatemala – Issues Relating to the Obligations Under Article 16.2.1 (a) of the CAFTA-DR, available at https://ustr.gov/issue-areas/labor/bilateral-and-regional-trade-agreements/guatemala-submission-under-cafta-dr (accessed 2 Nov 2024).

completed by a final report of the arbitration panel on 14 June 2017 which found one individual violation of labor rights, but that this did amount to a breach of CAFTA-DR obligations.[285] Another case was brought by Costa Rica against the Dominican Republic for violations of the trade chapter.[286]

The USTR has been monitoring the statutory implementation of CAFTA-DR closely, and its negative evaluation of the reforms in Costa Rica caused the significant delay in the entry into force of the agreement with regard to this country. Because IP protection is part of the CAFTA-DR dispute settlement system, one might expect that the USA also enforces its rights with regard to IP rights and impose sanctions if the practical implementation of the agreement appears insufficient.[287] However, as the analysis of the implementation of the IP chapter of CAFTA-DR will show, there are several cases of non-compliance.[288] It is, therefore, interesting that the USA has not used the dispute settlement mechanisms available under CAFTA-DR in relation to such IP issues. While enforcement and dispute settlement mechanism are often considered to benefit primarily the USA, which utilizes this mechanism more often under bilateral FTAs, these provisions also channel disputes and provide for a binding legal framework, which can also protect the politically and economically weaker parties.[289] This advantage may practically be limited by the fact that tariff-related sanctions affect developing countries much stronger than developed countries, which limits the effect of retaliation by developing countries in cases where the WTO dispute settlement bodies found a violation by developed countries. Therefore, cross-retaliation, *e.g.*, the suspension of protection of IP rights of foreign companies from developed countries, might be a more effective sanction than retaliation relating to the same products.[290] The right to cross-retaliation has been recognized by WTO arbitrators in two cases, in favor of Ecuador against the European Communities and in favor of Antigua against the United States.[291]

2.2.6.2 Investor-State Disputes

In addition to the substantive FDI protection discussed above, Articles 10.15 to Article 10.27 CAFTA-DR provide for (privately initiated) "Investor-State Disputes" under the International Centre for Settlement of Investment Disputes (ICSID)

---

[285] See https://ustr.gov/sites/default/files/files/agreements/FTA/CAFTA-DR/Guatemala%20Final%20Report%20of%20the%20Panel.pdf (accessed 2 Nov 2024).

[286] See summary available at www.centralamericadata.com/en/article/home/Costa_Rica_Files_Arbitration_against_Dominican_Republic (accessed 2 Nov 2024).

[287] The USA has initiated the majority of TRIPS related complaints submitted under the WTO dispute settlement mechanism, see Correa (2008), p. 64, fn 38, so a similar approach under CAFTA-DR could be considered.

[288] See Sect. 8.6.

[289] Grave (2002), p. 35.

[290] Abbott (2009), p. 38.

[291] On these cases see Abbott (2009), pp. 5–8 and von Lewinski (2016), pp. 613–618.

Convention and Rules of Procedure for Arbitration Proceedings or under the UNCITRAL Arbitration Rules. Foreign investors do not have to claim damages in national proceedings, but can initiate a binding international arbitration procedure against the respective country. This arbitration mechanism can be initiated privately without governmental involvement.[292] Since IP rights are defined as one form of investment,[293] IP right holders may also use this mechanism. Unlike the dispute settlement procedure between the parties, an investor-state dispute is a procedure that can be initiated against a state by a private entity without governmental involvement. So far, various disputes have been brought by investors under Chapter 10 of CAFTA-DR against Central American countries. However, as this topic is not the focus of this study, the investor-state disputes under CAFTA-DR are not analyzed in detail. This section briefly discusses in the following two typical cases to illustrate the practical relevance of this mechanism.[294]

The first dispute decided on the merits under the FDI rules of CAFTA-DR was the claim of a US railroad company against Guatemala.[295] In June, 2007, the company filed a claim under the investment chapter of CAFTA-DR with the ICSID, alleging that Guatemala indirectly expropriated the company's assets by not complying with a contract, and requested USD 65 million in damages.[296] The case was decided on 29 June 2012. The arbitration tribunal held Guatemala liable for violating "minimum standard of treatment" (MST) principles. Importantly, the arbitration tribunal found that the MST principles are "constantly in a process of development".[297] This means that acts of government considered in accordance with MST principles can, due to the development of these principles, in the future be found a violation of MST principles. This creates legal uncertainty and may result in a chilling effect on any government action affecting foreign investors (including in case of IP investments).[298]

Another dispute under the FDI rules of CAFTA-DR was brought in 2009 by the mining company Pac Rim Cayman against El Salvador, which had denied certain mining concessions. The arbitration tribunal denied its jurisdiction, because it concluded that Pac Rim Cayman, which had been formed as a Cayman Island company and had relocated its place of incorporation to Nevada, USA in 2007,

---

[292] See the provisions on Investor-State Disputes in Articles 10.15 to 10.27 CAFTA-DR.

[293] Article 10.28 CAFTA-DR.

[294] Another dispute was initiated by TCW Group, Inc., alleging the breach of certain concession agreements relating to electricity distribution. The case was settled prior to the final ruling; see Jennifer Thornton, Courts and Tribunals of Regional Economic Integration Agreements, in Giorgetti (2012), p. 504. Another example relates to the construction of a large hotel complex, Aven and others v. Costa Rica, ICSID Case No. UNCT/15/3; information on the case can be found at https://www.italaw.com/cases/2959 (accessed 2 Nov 2024).

[295] Railroad Development Corporation v Republic of Guatemala, ICSID Case No ARB/07/23, available at https://www.italaw.com/cases/887 (accessed 2 Nov 2024).

[296] Ibid.

[297] Ibid.

[298] See Sect. 2.2.3.

did not have any substantial business activities was "a passive actor both in the USA and the Cayman Islands".[299] The arbitration tribunal found that a shell company does not meet the conditions set out in CAFTA-DR.[300] However, the company also sued under local Salvadorian investments laws and the arbitration tribunal upheld this lawsuit. On the merits, the arbitration tribunal held on 14 October 2016 that the denial of the mining concession, and the criteria of the laws on which it was based, did not violate investment rules and dismissed Pac Rim Cayman's claim.[301]

Interestingly, despite various cases of non-compliance of Central American countries with CAFTA-DR obligations in relation to IP rights, to the author's knowledge no investor-state dispute has been initiated in the field of IP in the first 10 years of CAFTA-DR.

2.3 EU-CARIFORUM-EPA and EU-CA-AA

The Central American countries tried to reduce their economic dependence from the USA by diversifying their trade relations. One important part of this strategy was the cooperation with Europe. This strategy coincided with the approach of the EU to enter into FTAs with countries and regions of the Cotonou-System of trade preferences for former colonies in Africa and the Caribbean and Pacific (ACP) regions, including the Dominican Republic and other CARIFORUM states, but also with other regions such as Central America. The cooperation was formalized in the Association Agreement between the European Union and Central America (EU-CA-AA) and the Economic Partnership Agreement between the EU and certain Caribbean countries (EU-CARIFORUM-EPA).

2.3.1 The Negotiation and Implementation Process

The EU-CARIFORUM-EPA[302] was signed in October 2008 and both sides started to provisionally apply and implement the EPA since 29 December 2008.[303] The agreement was approved by the European Parliament in March 2009. It has not yet

[299] See Pac Rim Cayman LLC v. Republic of El Salvador, ICSID Case No. ARB/09/12, available at https://www.italaw.com/cases/783 (accessed 2 Nov 2024).

[300] Ibid.

[301] Ibid.

[302] The Agreement is published in the Official Journal of the European Union, Nr. L 289 of 30 October 2008, available at https://eur-lex.europa.eu/LexUriServ/LexUriServ.do?uri=OJ:L:2008:289:0003:1955:EN:PDF (accessed 2 Nov 2024).

[303] SICE, Provisional Application of the EPA, available at http://www.sice.oas.org/TPD/CAR_EU/Negotiations/provisional_application_e.pdf (accessed 2 Nov 2024).

formally entered into force, because not all EU member states have ratified it.[304] It includes the Caribbean Community (CARICOM) countries and the Dominican Republic, which is not a member of CARICOM, but has concluded a cooperation agreement with this group and engages in the Association of Caribbean States and other regional projects.[305]

The European Union concluded the EU-CA-AA with the Central American countries including Panama.[306] The EU expressly concluded the agreement with Central America as a region to promote regional integration.[307] The negotiations were finalized in May 2010.[308] One of the major obstacles during the negotiations was the section on geographical indications, which arguably conflicts with the trademark provisions in CAFTA-DR and was considered detrimental to local business interest.[309] The controversial issues were resolved and the agreement was signed on 29 June 2012 in Tegucigalpa, Honduras.[310] The provisions related to trade, including the IP chapters, have been provisionally applied since 1 August 2013 with Honduras, Nicaragua and Panama, since 1 October 2013 with Costa Rica and El Salvador, and since 1 December 2013 with Guatemala, in accordance with Article 353(4) EU-CA-AA.[311] The Agreement, as a whole, will enter into force after it is ratified by all signatory states. This process has not been completed.[312]

Like the CAFTA-DR negotiations, the negotiations of the EU-FTAs did not permit a meaningful discussion on the IP provisions. In particular, the Central

---

[304] See the status of the agreement on the "Caribbean" page of the European Commission, available at https://policy.trade.ec.europa.eu/eu-trade-relationships-country-and-region/countries-and-regions/caribbean_en (accessed 2 Nov 2024).

[305] The list of Association of Caribbean States members is available at http://www.acs-aec.org/index.php?q=content/members-and-associate-members (accessed 2 Nov 2024).

[306] See https://trade.ec.europa.eu/access-to-markets/en/content/eu-central-america-association-agreement (accessed 2 Nov 2024).

[307] See, e.g., European Commission (2011).

[308] Ibid.

[309] This issue is discussed in more detail in Sect. 4.4.

[310] European Commission, EU and Central America sign Association Agreement, press release, available at http://europa.eu/rapid/press-release_IP-12-713_en.htm (accessed 2 Nov 2024); information on the negotiations is available at http://www.sice.oas.org/TPD/CACM_EU/CACM_EU_e.ASP (accessed 2 Nov 2024).

[311] Available at https://trade.ec.europa.eu/access-to-markets/en/content/eu-central-america-association-agreement (accessed 2 Nov 2024).

[312] Available at http://europa.eu/rapid/press-release_IP-12-713_en.htm (accessed 2 Nov 2024). There have been no reports since the provisional application on the ratification process in the EU. However, at the time of writing of this study, this process has not been completed and the agreement is not in full force, see the information provided by the EU commission on the agreement, available at https://trade.ec.europa.eu/access-to-markets/en/content/eu-central-america-association-agreement (accessed 2 Nov 2024).

American countries accepted the requirement to register a long list of European geographical indications despite the opposition of some countries to strong protection in this field and foreseeable conflicts with existing local and foreign trademarks.[313]

2.3.2 *Trade Liberalization*

The EU-CA-AA largely eliminates tariffs for manufactured goods and fisheries subject to a tariff phase-out period of 10 to 15 years.[314] The agreement also addresses technical barriers to trade, e.g., by establishing cooperation in the areas of "standards" and market surveillance, simplifying labeling requirements and providing for transparency of sanitary and phytosanitary import requirements.[315] The EU-CARIFORUM-EPA also removes all tariffs on Caribbean exports to the EU, with tariffs on sugar and rice being phased out over short periods of time. In addition, the agreement promotes the progressive harmonization of the external tariffs of the CARIFORUM countries to create a regional market.[316]

2.3.3 *Protection of Foreign Investment*

There is no specific section on FDI in the EU-CA-AA. However, the agreement contains rules related to foreign investment, namely national treatment obligations.[317] The EU-CARIFORUM-EPA focuses on facilitating foreign investment by ensuring fair access of investors to the respective markets, but not on the protection of investors in these markets.[318]

---

[313] See Sect. 4.4.6.

[314] Part IV, title II, chapters 2 and 3 EU-CA-AA; see European Commission (2011), p. 2.

[315] Part IV, title II, chapters 4 and 5 EU-CA-AA.

[316] European Commission, The CARIFORUM-EC Economic Partnership Agreement (2008), available at http://europa.eu/rapid/press-release_MEMO-08-624_en.htm (accessed 2 Nov 2024).

[317] See part IV, title II, Article 163 EU-CE-AA, fn 12, including a reference to investor-state dispute settlement procedures that can be initiated by investors in case of alleged infringements of the national treatment obligations.

[318] Like the EU-CA-AA, the EU-CARIFORUM-EPA contains no specific section on FDI, but rules related to foreign investment, namely national treatment obligations, see Article 68 EU-CARIFORUM-EPA.

2.3.4 *Intellectual Property*

This section provides an overview of IP-related provisions of the two EU-FTAs and briefly discusses the basic "minimum protection" structure. The provisions on specific IP rights are discussed in detail in the following parts of this study.

2.3.4.1 Overview

In the EU-CA-AA, IP is regulated in Title VI, Articles 228 to 276 EU-CA-AA. Title VI is divided into objectives and Principles (chapter 1), standards concerning specific IP rights (chapter 2), enforcement (chapter 3) and institutional provisions (chapter 4). In contrast to CAFTA-DR, the EU-CA-AA focuses less on copyright issues and mainly refers to multilateral agreements, without creating additional obligations. Notably, the agreement does not include DRM rules. On the other hand, geographical indications are addressed in great detail. E-commerce rules are provided for in Articles 201 to 203 EU-CA-AA.

In the EU-CARIFORUM-EPA, IP is regulated in Title IV, Chapter 2, Section 2, which is divided into four Subsections: Subsection 1 on "Principles" (Articles 139 to 142), Subsection 2 on "Standards concerning intellectual property rights" (i.e., specific IP rights, Articles 143 to 150), Subsection 3 on the "Enforcement of intellectual property rights" (Articles 151 to 163) and Subsection 4 on "Cooperation" (Article 164).

Regarding IP protection, the EU-FTAs vary significantly among themselves.[319] In particular the EU-CARIFORUM-EPA and the EU-CA-AA differ in structure and content, which significantly reduces potential regional harmonization effects on IP law. Moreover, the EU-CARIFORUM-EPA and the EU-CA-AA establish IP rules reflecting different policy priorities than CAFTA-DR and contain partially conflicting requirements, which will be discussed in more detail in relation to specific IP rights below. Some of the most notable differences are the following:

- In CAFTA-DR, objectives are not explicitly included.[320] However, the goals can arguably be inferred from similar earlier agreements such as the US-Chile-FTA, which states that "[…] the protection and enforcement of intellectual property rights is a fundamental principle […] that helps promote technological innovation as well as the transfer and dissemination of technology to the mutual advantage of technology producers and users […]". The objective of the EU-FTAs is to create "adequate and effective protection of intellectual property rights […] taking into consideration the economical situation and the social or cultural need of each Party", Article 228(a) EU-CA-AA. By complementing the goal of IP protection

[319] For examples beyond the EU-CARIFORUM-EPA and the EU-CA-AA, see Drexl (2018) Nr 120.

[320] See Sect. 2.2.

with considerations of adequacy, namely the economic and social situation, these agreements aim and arrive at generally more balanced and "flexible" provisions than CAFTA-DR.[321]

- There are also significant substantive differences in relation to the balancing of trademarks and geographical indications. The Central American countries had to some extent to violate the terms of either CAFTA-DR or the EU-FTAs. The Central America legislation is aligned more closely with CAFTA-DR.[322]
- Finally, the EU-FTAs take institutional aspects of IP protection into consideration, while CAFTA-DR explicitly refrains from regulating this field.[323]

2.3.4.2 Substantive Provisions

Like CAFTA-DR, the EU-FTAs are based on the minimum protection principle. The EU-CARIFORUM-EPA explicitly states that "CARIFORUM States may [...] implement in their law more extensive protection than is required by [the IP] section",[324] similar to the minimum protection principle in Article 1 TRIPS. While requiring the implementation of international IP standards, it creates fewer TRIPS-plus obligations and contains more balancing or "maximum protection" provisions than US-FTAs such as CAFTA-DR.[325] However, the reference in Article 139(2) EU-CARIFORUM-EPA to public policy objectives, in particular public health, raises the same questions as the public policy provisions in Articles 7 and 8 TRIPS: How should the EU-CARIFORUM-EPA be interpreted specifically to be aligned with the policy needs of the Central American countries? The EU-CA-AA is structured more like a US-type FTA and contains more TRIPS-plus "minimum protection" components.

However, the EU-FTAs are generally more "flexible" than CAFTA-DR and include references to the Doha Declaration and Article 8 TRIPS and reflect the need to differentiate the level of IP protection based on the level of development. The Doha Declaration has been included in both EU-FTAs.[326] In addition, Article 139(2) EU-CARIFORUM-EPA provides that "the principles set out in Article 8 of the TRIPS Agreement apply to [the IP] section [and] that an adequate and effective enforcement of intellectual property rights should take account of the development needs [...], provide a balance of rights and obligations between right holders and users and allow the [parties] to protect public health and nutrition. Nothing in [the EU-CARIFORUM-EPA] shall be construed as to impair the capacity of the [parties] to promote access to medicines".

[321] See Sect. 2.3.4.2.

[322] See Sect. 4.4.

[323] See Sect. 2.5.2.2.

[324] Article 139(5) EU-CARIFORUM-EPA.

[325] Drexl (2018) Nr 50, 119.

[326] Article 229(2)(a) EU-CA-AA and Article 147.B EU-CARIFORUM-EPA.

In contrast to CAFTA-DR, the EU-CARIFORUM-EPA also reflects the need for differentiation between different levels of development by stating that "[the parties] recognize that the protection and enforcement of intellectual property plays a key role in fostering creativity, innovation and competitiveness, and are determined to ensure increasing levels of protection appropriate to their levels of development".[327] While this wording indicates that the level of IP protection should be raised, it clarifies that this increase must be "appropriate" and is, therefore, conditioned upon the achievement of a higher level of development. Also, it clarifies that the level of protection is not "ever increasing", but must be relative to the development status.[328]

Both EU-FTAs did not result in the adoption of broad TRIPS-plus implementation laws as CAFTA-DR. However, this is maybe not because of the fewer TRIPS-plus provisions or references to public policy goals, which are often vague, but because several TRIPS-plus obligations had at that time already been implemented (because of the CAFTA-DR reforms) and because, in relation to the EU-CA-AA, the EU focused more on institutional and practical aspects, e.g., the registration of the Established Geographical Indications, and less on statutory changes.

2.3.4.3 Institutional Provisions

The institutional provisions in the EU-CA-AA stand in noticeable contrast to CAFTA-DR, which is limited to substantive and procedural issues, but does not address institutional questions. An example or the bigger emphasis on institutional changes is the establishment of the "Sub-Committee on Intellectual Property" between the parties created by Article 274 EU-CA-AA.[329] Its purpose is mainly to follow-up on the implementation of the provisions relating to geographical indications, in particular recommending new geographical indications for protection[330] and to promoting technology transfer and keeping a registry of activities relating to the transfer of technology.[331] The EU-CARIFORUM-EPA does not create specific institutions in the field of IP to implement or monitor the provisions in the IP Chapter of the EU-CARIFORUM-EPA. In contrast to CAFTA-DR, the EU-FTAs also explicitly provide for training activities in the field of IP. Articles 133-138 EU-CARIFORUM-EPA contain several provisions regarding cooperation and training. Such measures have also been included in the EU-CA-AA, which not only provides for mutual cooperation and technical assistance initiatives on issues related to IP, but specifically identifies a number of cooperation activities which are set out in the agreement.[332] During the 3 year period from 2012 to 2014, *i.e.*, after the signing of

---

[327] Article 131(2) EU-CARIFORUM-EPA; on this issue see Roffe (2013), p. 937.

[328] Roffe (2013), p. 937.

[329] Article 274 EU-CA-AA.

[330] Article 274(2)(a) and (b) EU-CA-AA.

[331] Article 274(2)(c) and (d) EU-CA-AA.

[332] Article 275 EU-CA-AA.

the EU-CA-AA, the EU institutions (or institutions of its Member States) organized several trainings and meetings for representatives of Central American IP agencies on IP generally (in cooperation with WIPO) and two trainings on plant varieties and the UPOV Convention for Latin American countries, including several Central American countries.[333] The EU also organized a training by the EPO for the use of the Patent Examiner Manual in 2010.[334] However, no specific trainings in relation to the implementation of the EU-CA-AA were conducted.

2.3.5 Labor and Environment

Under the EU-CA-AA, the parties commit to international standards and multilateral agreements relating to labor and environmental law.[335] Similarly, under the EU-CARIFORUM-EPA, the parties commit to labor and environmental standards, *e.g.*, in relation to foreign investment, promotion of tourism and generally the implementation of the EU-CARIFORUM-EPA.[336] In addition, the agreement envisions cooperation activities relating to environmentally-friendly innovation and renewable sources of energy.[337]

2.3.6 Enforcement and Dispute Settlement

The dispute settlement mechanism of the EU-CA-AA includes in particular transparency rules, such as open hearings and *amicus curiae* briefs, a mediation mechanism for non-tariff barriers and excludes retaliation until non-compliance is verified.[338] The dispute settlement provisions of the EU-CARIFORUM-EPA provide for a two-step mechanism of mediation and arbitration that also includes transparency rules, such as open hearings.[339]

---

[333] These activities included one training for IP Register personnel and one training for judges and the Ministerio Público of several Central American countries in 2012, see WTO (2013), pp. 52–53, and two meetings of IP Register personnel of several Central American countries (at WIPO, organized by Portugal) in 2013–2014, see WTO (2015), p. 48.

[334] WTO (2011), p. 51.

[335] European Commission (2011), p. 4.

[336] Articles 3.2(a), 8, 72(c), 73, 116, 117.2(b) EU-CARIFORUM-EPA.

[337] Article 138 EU-CARIFORUM-EPA.

[338] European Commission (2011), p. 3.

[339] See in particular Article 116.2 EU-CARIFORUM-EPA.

2.4 The National Legal Framework in Central America

This section provides a regional picture on the development of the IP legislation and discusses the main IP laws on in each Central American CAFTA-DR country.

2.4.1 Introduction

2.4.1.1 Pre-TRIPS

The earliest trademark regulations applicable in Central America were issued by the Spanish Crown in the eighteenth century, more to control trade than to protect producers or consumers. The first patent legislation was passed by Spain in the early nineteenth century.[340] The first patent laws in Central America were passed in the late nineteenth century, e.g., in Nicaragua in 1899.[341]

Throughout the twentieth century, IP laws were repeatedly and substantially modified as a result of policy shifts. In the beginning of the century, the IP system was designed by the Paris Convention to restrict protectionist measures such as overly restrictive local working requirements for patents.[342] In the 1960ies, developing countries started to change their legal systems in order to become not only politically, but also economically more independent from the developed world.[343] The restriction of IP rights was an important element of this new approach. Latin American countries excluded the patentability of pharmaceuticals to reduce prices for medicines.[344] Restrictions on patent protection were also designed to facilitate the transfer of technology and reduce the technological dependency from developed countries, on the one hand,[345] and to improve the terms of trade by reducing license payments and trade deficits, on the other hand.[346]

In Central America, these considerations resulted in the (restrictive) Central American Convention (Trademarks) as the common regional legislation on

[340] According to Bendaña-Guerrero, the patent legislation was passed in 1826 after Central America and the Dominican Republic had become independent, see Bendaña-Guerrero (1999), p. 217; according to *Heinrich Grave*, the first Spanish Patent Law was adopted in 1811 and was also applicable in the colonies, including Central America, see Grave (2002), pp. 21–22, with further references.

[341] Bendaña-Guerrero (1999), p. 217.

[342] Grave (2002), p. 23.

[343] See Sect. 2.1.3.

[344] For the policy in Mexico see Grave (2002), p. 24.

[345] Beier and Kunz (1972), p. 385; Kunz-Hallstein (1976), p. 64.

[346] Correa (1981), pp. 381–409; Grave (2002), p. 27.

trademarks[347] and harmonized legislation the field of patent law.[348] Even though not accompanied by a regional court as in the case of Andean Community, this made case law and doctrine of all countries comparable. The only comprehensive textbook on patent and trademark law in Central America, the "Curso en Propiedad Industrial" of *Bendaña-Guerrero* from Nicaragua, published in 1998, regularly refers to the law of the other Central American countries, which was at the time very similar.

2.4.1.2 Post-TRIPS

In the 1980ies, the policy approach towards IP began to move back to stronger and broader protection. The respective developments in the developed countries also influenced the developing countries. The patentability of pharmaceuticals was reintroduced, *e.g.*, in Mexico in 1986.[349] Because the restrictions of patent protection had not helped to close the technology gap, the protection of foreign technology was also strengthened.[350] Legal certainty, transparency and strong protection of IP were perceived as corollaries of economic openness and investment promotion. The Central American countries became WTO members in 1995 and enjoyed the five-year transitional period of Article 65 TRIPS. Accordingly, all national laws in Central America implementing TRIPS were passed around the year 2000 and these laws still form the basis of the current structure of the IP legislation in Central America. Despite the global harmonization of IP law based on TRIPS, in Central America the agreement led to the abolition of the regional legislation, namely the Central American Convention (Trademarks), and to different systems of IP legislation in each country, as shown in Table 2.5. Since then, the implementation of international IP rules is a purely national matter. Notably, trademarks and geographical indications, patents and designs are regulated sometimes together in "IP Laws" and sometimes separately. This legislative structure was maintained by the laws implementing CAFTA-DR.

2.4.2 Costa Rica

In Costa Rica, Article 47 Constitution (CR) provides that "every author, inventor producer or trader shall enjoy temporarily the exclusive protection of his work,

[347] See Sect. 2.1.4.1.

[348] For references to the pre-TRIPS patent legislation in Central America, see Bendaña-Guerrero (1999), p. 219.

[349] Grave (2002), p. 30.

[350] Notably the socialist countries had special regimes, e.g., the "*Erfinderschein*" (inventor's certificate) in East Germany and the USSR, see Grave (2002), p. 26.

Table 2.5 Legislation in Central America to implement TRIPS

Country	Trademarks	Patents and Designs	Copyright
Costa Rica	Trademark Law (1999/2000)	Patent and Design Law (1983/2000)	Copyright Law (1982/2000)
Dom. Rep.	Industrial Property Law (2000)		Copyright Law (2000)
El Salvador	Trademark Law (2002)	Intellectual Property Law (1993)	
Guatemala	Industrial Property Law (2000)		Copyright Law (1998/2000)
Honduras	Industrial Property Law (1999)		Copyright Law (1999)
Nicaragua	Trademark Law (2001)	Patent and Design Law (2000)	Copyright Law (1999)

invention, trademark or trade name, as regulated by law".[351] The legal regulation of IP is contained in several specific laws, namely the Patent and Design Law (CR) (*Ley de Patentes de Invención, Dibujos, Modelos Industriales, Modelos de Utilidad*),[352] the Trademark Law (CR) (*Ley de marcas y otros signos distintivos*),[353] the Undisclosed Information Law (CR) (*Ley de información no divulgada*), which covers test data protection,[354] the Plant Variety Law (CR) (*Ley de Protección de las Obtenciones Vegetales*)[355] and the IP Enforcement Law (CR) (*Ley de Procedimientos de Observancia de Derechos de Propiedad Intelectual*).[356] As part of the implementation of CAFTA-DR, all these laws were amended by the Trademark Law, Patent and Design Law and Biodiversity Law Reform (*Modificación de Varios Artículos de la Ley de Marcas y Otros Signos Distintivos, de la Ley de Patentes de Invención, Dibujos y Modelos Industriales y Modelos de Utilidad, y de la Ley de Biodiversidad*) (CAFTA-DR Reform Law I (CR))[357] and the Law amending, adding or repealing various Rules on Matters pertaining to Intellectual Property (*Reforma, Adición y Derogación de varias normas que regulan materias relacionadas con Propiedad Intelectual*) (CAFTA-DR Reform Law II (CR)) in

[351] Constitución Política de la República de Costa Rica, enacted on 7 November 1949, entered into force on 8 November 1949, available at https://www.wipo.int/wipolex/es/legislation/details/15377 (accessed 2 Nov 2024).

[352] Law No. 6867, enacted on 25 April 1983, entered into force on 13 July 1983, available at https://www.wipo.int/wipolex/es/legislation/details/9125 (accessed 2 Nov 2024).

[353] Law No. 7978, enacted on 22 December 1999, entered into force on 1 February 2000, available at https://www.wipo.int/wipolex/es/legislation/details/9130 (accessed 2 Nov 2024).

[354] Law No. 7975, enacted on 4 January 2000, entered into force on 18 January 2000, available at https://www.wipo.int/wipolex/es/legislation/details/886 (accessed 2 Nov 2024).

[355] Law No. 8631, enacted on 6 March 2008, entered into force on 19 March 2008, available at https://www.wipo.int/wipolex/es/legislation/details/9018 (accessed 2 Nov 2024).

[356] Law Nr. 8039, enacted on 6 January 2000, entered into force on 31 January 2000, as amended last by Law Nr. 9524 enacted on 7 March 2018, available at https://www.wipo.int/wipolex/es/legislation/details/21459 (accessed 2 Nov 2024).

[357] Law No. 8632, enacted on 25 March 2008, entered into force on 25 April 2008, available at https://www.wipo.int/wipolex/es/legislation/details/8948 (accessed 2 Nov 2024).

2008.[358] Costa Rica did not pass a law to implement the IP provisions of EU-CA-AA.

2.4.3 Dominican Republic

In the Dominican Republic, trademark and patent law (and related fields of law) are regulated by the IP Law (DR) *(Ley Nr. 20-2000 de (sobre) Propiedad Industrial)* of 2000.[359] It was amended by the CAFTA-DR Reform Law I (DR) (*Ley No. 424-06 de Implementación del Tratado de Libre Comercio, entre la República Dominicana, Centroamérica y los Estados Unidos de América (CAFTA-DR)*) of 2006[360] and the CAFTA-DR Reform Law II (DR) (*Ley No. 493-06 que modifica los Artículos 6, 49, 58 y 62 de la Ley No. 424-06, de fecha 20 de noviembre de 2006, sobre la Implementación del Tratado de Libre Comercio, entre la República Dominicana, Centroamérica y los Estados Unidos de América*) of 2006.[361] Also part of the "CAFTA-DR package" was the Plant Variety Law (DR) (*Ley No. 450-06 sobre Protección de los Derechos del Obtentor de Variedades Vegetales*) of 2006.[362] The Dominican Republic did not pass a law to implement the IP provisions of the EU-CARIFORUM-EPA.

2.4.4 El Salvador

In El Salvador, it is "an obligation of the State to recognize and guarantee intellectual property" according to Article 103 Constitution (SV).[363] There existed IP legislation since the early twentieth century.[364] However, modern IP protection starts with the

---

[358] Law No. 8686, enacted on 21 November 2008, entered into force on 26 November 2008, available at https://www.wipo.int/wipolex/es/legislation/details/9019 (accessed 2 Nov 2024).

[359] Law No. 20-2000, enacted 8 May 2000, entered into force on 10 May 2000, available at https://www.wipo.int/wipolex/en/legislation/details/1190 (accessed 2 Nov 2024).

[360] Law No. 424-06, enacted on 20 November 2006, entered into force on 1 March 2007, available at https://www.wipo.int/wipolex/es/legislation/details/10145 (accessed 2 Nov 2024).

[361] Law No. 493-06, enacted on 22 December 2006, entered into force on 22 December 2006, available at https://www.wipo.int/wipolex/es/text/235437 (accessed 2 Nov 2024).

[362] Law No. 450-06, enacted on 6 December 2006, entered into force on 6 December 2006, available at https://www.wipo.int/wipolex/es/legislation/details/10139 (accessed 2 Nov 2024).

[363] Constitución de la República de El Salvador, enacted on 15 December 1983, entered into force on 20 December 1983, available at https://www.oas.org/dil/esp/constitucion_de_la_republica_del_salvador_1983.pdf (accessed 2 Nov 2024).

[364] See the list of Salvadorean IP legislation by WIPO, available at https://www.wipo.int/wipolex/en/members/profile/SV (accessed 2 Nov 2024).

IP Law (SV) of 1993 (*Ley de Fomento y Protección de la Propiedad Intelectual*),[365] which was based on the corresponding Mexican legislation of 1991 and covers patents and trademarks.[366] Distinctive signs are regulated by the Trademark Law (SV) of 2002 (*Ley de Marcas y otros Signos Distintivos*).[367] The IP Law (SV) was reformed by the CAFTA-DR IP Reform Law (SV), implementing the IP requirements of CAFTA-DR (*Reformas a la Ley de Fomento y Protection de la Propiedad Intelectual*)[368] and the Trademark Law (SV) by the CAFTA-DR Trademark Reform Law (SV) (*Reformas a la Ley de Marcas y otros Signos Distintivos*).[369] In 2013, to implement the EU-CA-AA, El Salvador passed the EU-CA-AA Trademark Reform Law (SV) (Restatement of the Trademark Law (SV)).[370] In 2017, El Salvador amended the IP Law (SV) again, but these changes relate almost exclusively to the exploitation of copyright and to collecting societies.[371]

2.4.5 Guatemala

The Guatemalan Constitution of 1993 recognizes the author's right and the inventor's right; the owners of these rights enjoy the exclusive right in their work or invention, "in accordance with the law and international agreements".[372] The first modern patent law in Guatemala, adopted in 1985, was still based on the restrictive IP policies originating in the 1960ies, but it allowed users to gain the first experience

[365] Law No. 604, enacted on 15 July 1993, entered into force on 15 October 1993, available at https://www.wipo.int/wipolex/es/legislation/details/3760 (accessed 2 Nov 2024).

[366] This origin is indicated clearly by the identical (and unusual) title; the Mexican law was renamed Ley de Propiedad Industrial in 1994, following amendments due to the implementation of TRIPS and NAFTA into national Mexican law, see Grave (2002), pp. 51–52; the legislator in El Salvador, by contrast, decided to keep the original title.

[367] Law No. 868, adopted on 6 June 2002, entered into force on 17 July 2002, available at https://www.wipo.int/wipolex/en/legislation/details/3779 (accessed 2 Nov 2024).

[368] Law No. 912, enacted on 14 December 2005, entered into force on 12 January 2006, available at https://www.wipo.int/wipolex/es/legislation/details/3785 (accessed 2 Nov 2024).

[369] Law No. 913, enacted on 14 December 2005, entered into force on 12 January 2006; the text of the law is available at https://www.wipo.int/wipolex/es/legislation/details/3786 (accessed 2 Nov 2024). For purposes of simplification, the term "CAFTA-DR Trademark Reform Law (SV)" is also used in relation to minor amendments made by Law No. 986, enacted on 17 March 2006, entered into force on 31 March 2006, available at https://www.wipo.int/wipolex/es/legislation/details/3786 (accessed 2 Nov 2024).

[370] Law No. 358, enacted on 19 April 2013, entered into force on 14 Mai 2013, available at https://www.wipo.int/wipolex/es/legislation/details/14764 (accessed 2 Nov 2024).

[371] Law No. 611, enacted on 15 February 2017, available at https://www.wipo.int/wipolex/en/text/455892 (accessed 2 Nov 2024).

[372] Article 42 Constitution (GT), emphasis added.

with patent registration and management.[373] The entire field of IP law was reorganized into the Copyright Law (GT) (*Ley de Derecho de Autor y Derechos Conexos*) in 1998[374] and the IP Law (GT), covering patents (Title I) and trademarks (Title II), in 2000.[375] Both laws were reformed by two simultaneous amendment laws in the same year to complete the TRIPS implementation. These laws were also substantially amended by the CAFTA-DR Reform Law (GT) in 2005.[376] To implement the obligations regarding geographical indications under the EU-CA-AA, Guatemala passed the EU-CA-AA Reform Law (GT) in 2013.[377]

2.4.6 Honduras

Honduras passed its legislation implementing TRIPS in 1999, the Copyright Law (HN) (*Ley del Derecho de Autor y de los Derechos Conexos*)[378] and the IP Law (HN) (*Ley de Propiedad Industrial*), covering patents (Title II) and trademarks (Title IV) (and neighboring fields of law).[379] The IP chapter of CAFTA-DR was implemented by Article 3 to 9 CAFTA-DR Reform Law (HN) (*Ley de Implementación del Tratado de Libre Comercio, República Dominicana, Centroamérica, Estados Unidos*) of 2006.[380] It must be noted that the CAFTA-DR Reform Law (HN) does not only modify the existing provisions of the IP Law (HN), but also introduces a separate set of provisions which complement the existing provisions in the IP Law (HN). Further reforms were necessary, because this

[373] The law excluded from patentability not only plant varieties, which are now protected by sui generis legislation, but also food and chemical compounds, i.e., pharmaceuticals; see presentation of Flor de María Gracia Díaz, Seminar on Intellectual Property, Industrial Property and New Technologies, San José, Costa Rica, 28 October 2008, on file with author).

[374] Law No. 33-98, enacted on 19 May 1998, entered into force on 21 June 1998, available at https://www.wipo.int/wipolex/es/legislation/details/2010 (accessed 2 Nov 2024), consolidated by the Copyright Reform Law (GT), the text of the law is available at https://www.wipo.int/edocs/lexdocs/laws/es/gt/gt002es.pdf (accessed 2 Nov 2024).

[375] Law No. 57-2000, enacted on 18 September 2000, entered into force on 1 November 2000, available at https://www.wipo.int/wipolex/es/legislation/details/2009 (accessed 2 Nov 2024).

[376] Law No. 30-2005, enacted on 18 March 2005, entered into force on 19 March 2005, available at https://www.wipo.int/wipolex/es/legislation/details/15425 (accessed 2 Nov 2024).

[377] Law No. 3-2013, enacted on 13 June 2013, entered into force on 26 June 2013, available at https://www.wipo.int/wipolex/es/legislation/details/15895 (accessed 2 Nov 2024).

[378] Law No. 4-99-E, enacted on 13 December 1999, entered into force on 15 January 2000, available at https://www.wipo.int/wipolex/es/legislation/details/10172 (accessed 2 Nov 2024); this version includes the amendments by the CAFTA-DR Reform Law (HN).

[379] Law No. 12-99-E, enacted on 30 December 1999 and entered into force on 28 February 2000, available at https://www.wipo.int/wipolex/es/legislation/details/2136 (accessed 2 Nov 2024).

[380] Law Nr. 16-2006, enacted on 21 March 2006, published in La Gazeta, El Diaro Oficial de la República de Honduras, on 24 March 2006, available at http://www.cerlalc.org/derechoenlinea/dar/leyes_reglamentos/Honduras/Ley_16.htm (accessed 2 Nov 2024).

implementation was considered incomplete. One reform law had been proposed in 2008, but not adopted.[381] Another reform law was passed in 2011, which in the field of IP is limited to specific questions of patent procedure.[382] In addition, to implement obligations regarding geographical indications under the EU-CA-AA, Honduras passed the EU-CA-AA Reform Law (HN) in 2013.[383]

2.4.7 *Nicaragua*

In Nicaragua, the Copyright Law (NI) (*Ley de Derecho de Autor y Derechos Conexos*) was passed in 1999,[384] the Patent and Design Law (NI) (*Ley de Patentes de Invención, Modelos de Utilidad y Diseños Industriales*) in 2000,[385] and the Trademark Law (NI) (*Ley de Marcas y otros Signos Distintivos*) in 2001.[386] Nicaragua passed several laws to implement the CAFTA-DR requirements regarding IP protection, in particular the CAFTA-DR Trademark Reform Law (NI) (*Ley de Reformas y Adiciones a la Ley N° 380 sobre de Marcas y Otros Signos Distintivos*) in 2006[387] and the CAFTA-DR IP Reform Law (NI) (*Ley de Reformas y Adiciones a la Ley N° 354, Ley de Patentes de Invención, Modelos de Utilidad y Diseños Industriales*) in 2006.[388] In 2007, Nicaragua added Article 38*bis* Patent and Design Law on patent term extension to the Patent and Design Law (NI).[389] For simplification, the reference to the CAFTA-DR IP Reform Law (NI) of 2006 in this thesis includes the reference to this amendment law of 2007, unless explicitly stated otherwise. Nicaragua passed the EU-CA-AA Trademark Reform Regulation (NI) (*Reformas y Adiciones al Decreto N° 83-2001, Reguladora de la Ley de Marcas*

[381] The text is on file with the author.

[382] Law No. 51-2011, adopted on 3 May 2011, entered into force on 15 July 2011, available at https://faolex.fao.org/docs/pdf/hon137904.pdf (accessed 2 Nov 2024).

[383] Law No. 219-2012, adopted on 18 January 2013, entered into force on 19 March 2013, available at https://www.wipo.int/wipolex/es/legislation/details/21421 (accessed 2 Nov 2024).

[384] Law No. 312-1999, enacted on July 6, 1999, entered into force on 31 August 1999, available at https://www.wipo.int/wipolex/en/legislation/details/3160 (accessed 2 Nov 2024).

[385] Law No. 354-2000, enacted on 1 June 2000, entered into force on 21 November 2000, available at https://www.wipo.int/wipolex/es/legislation/details/3170 (accessed 2 Nov 2024).

[386] Law No. 380-2001, enacted on 14 February 2001, entered into force on 16 April 2001, available at https://www.wipo.int/wipolex/es/legislation/details/3171 (accessed 2 Nov 2024).

[387] Law No. 580-2006, enacted on 21 March 2006, entered into force on 24 March 2006, available at http://www.wipo.int/wipolex/es/details.jsp?id=5094 (accessed 2 Nov 2024).

[388] Law No. 579-2006, enacted on 21 March 2006, entered into force on 24 March 2006, available at http://www.wipo.int/wipolex/es/details.jsp?id=5096 (accessed 2 Nov 2024).

[389] Law No. 634-2007, enacted on 13 September 2007, entered into force on 12 October 2007, available at https://www.wipo.int/wipolex/es/legislation/details/5097 (accessed 2 Nov 2024).

y Otros Signos Distintivos) in 2012 to implement the IP provisions of the EU-CARIFORUM-EPA.[390]

2.5 The Institutional Framework

2.5.1 Introduction

Most multilateral IP agreements and FTAs in the IP field contain mainly substantive or procedural legal requirements, but few if any provisions on institutional aspects of the IP system. To the contrary, many FTAs explicitly state that their rules shall not bind parties in relation to institutional decisions. CAFTA-DR contains very few institutional provisions, such as the obligation that the Central American IP Registers shall, to the maximum degree practical, establish an electronic registration system and shall work to establish a database for publishing registration of trademarks.[391] Therefore, if an IP Register does not or only in a very limited way grant patents, as the IP Register in the Dominican Republic did for several years, it does not violate the obligations under TRIPS and CAFTA-DR, which contain mainly legislative requirements.[392] Likewise, the provisions on competition law in CAFTA-DR do not create an obligation for Central American countries to establish a competition agency. Notable exceptions are the two FTAs of the EU which regulate competition law agencies.[393] However, to paraphrase a saying attributed to *Otto von Bismarck*, the best laws are not effective if they are not implemented by functioning institutions. Accordingly, the analysis of the implementation of CAFTA-DR in this study will not only address the legislative changes, but also discuss institutional and practical aspects. The institutional framework in Central America will be analyzed in this section for all IP rights jointly, because IP rights are typically handled by the same institutions, *e.g.*, WIPO on the international level and the IP Registers on the national level in Central America.

2.5.2 International and Regional Institutions

2.5.2.1 WIPO

The Central American countries are integrated into the international IP system through the inclusion into the registration procedure of international institutions established for the harmonization of application procedures, in particular the IP Registers, which are designated as Searching and Preliminary Examining

[390] Reguladora No. 25-2012, enacted and entered into force on 20 June 2012, available at https://www.wipo.int/wipolex/es/legislation/details/12906 (accessed 2 Nov 2024).

[391] Article 15.2.7. CAFTA-DR.

[392] This issue is further analyzed in Sect. 8.7.

[393] See above Sect. 2.3.

Authorities under the PCT system of WIPO[394] and the International Depositary Authorities (IDA) under Article 7 Budapest Treaty.[395] WIPO, together with several other international and foreign IP institutions, also informally influences the Central American IP system through cooperation and technical assistance.[396] However, until 2024 none of the Central American countries had ratified the Protocol Relating to the Madrid Agreement (Trademarks) to enable the processing of trademark applications filed in a third country.[397]

2.5.2.2 Institutions Established by Bilateral FTAs

CAFTA-DR

The implementation and operation of CAFTA-DR in general is supervised by the *Free Trade Commission* of the parties' trade ministers, established by Chapter 19 CAFTA-DR.[398] The Free Trade Commission meets annually. In addition, several chapters create committees and councils to address specific questions: the Committee on the Trade in Goods (Chapter 3), the Sanitary Measures (SPS) Committee (Chapter 6), the Committee on Technical Barriers to Trade (Chapter 7), the Labor Affairs Council (Chapter 16), the Environmental Affairs Council (Chapter 17) and the Committee on Trade Capacity Building (Chapter 19).[399] The purpose of these committees is merely consultation, cooperation and assistance, and they do not have dispute resolution authority.

The establishment of the *Committee on Trade Capacity Building* (TCB Committee) in CAFTA-DR is a novelty in bilateral FTAs concluded by the USA. This could suggest the recognition by the USA of the importance of such assistance in promoting economic growth, reducing poverty, and taking full opportunity of liberalized trade.[400] The USA and the Central American countries agreed to cooperate through the TCB Committee in the following capacity-building activities:[401]

- educational and dissemination projects on the use of IP as a research and innovation tool, as well as on the enforcement of IP rights;

[394] The list of offices is available at https://www.wipo.int/pct/en/quality/authorities.html (accessed 2 Nov 2024).

[395] Budapest Treaty on the International Recognition of the Deposit of Microorganisms for the Purposes of Patent Procedure, available at https://www.wipo.int/treaties/en/registration/budapest/ (accessed 2 Nov 2024).

[396] See Sect. 2.5.2.

[397] See Sect. 2.1.1.3.

[398] This system follows the example of NAFTA, see Grave (2002), p. 34.

[399] Interestingly, the abolition of Trade Capacity Building measures and the respective committee is the only change that was made in the US-Panama FTA.

[400] Available at https://ustr.gov/about-us/policy-offices/press-office/press-releases/archives/2005/april/us-and-cafta-dr-countries-hold-meetings-exp (accessed 2 Nov 2024).

[401] Article 15.1(16) CAFTA-DR.

- appropriate coordination, training, specialization courses, and exchange of information between the IP offices and other institutions of the USA and the Central American countries; and
- enhancing the knowledge, development, and implementation of the electronic systems used for the management of IP.

This - according to CAFTA-DR - shows the importance of assistance by the USA to the Central American countries.[402] The TCB Committee met once a year between 2006 and 2008.[403] No public information is available regarding activities or meetings of the TCB Committee in the IP field after 2008. This could suggest that the Committee did not produce any notable results. Practically, the limited effectiveness of this cooperation body is shown by the fact that, 10 years after its creation, one of its main objectives, the implementation of electronic systems for the management of IP in the Central American countries, remains incomplete.[404]

In the field of IP, there are also no specific institutions created by CAFTA-DR. The USTR and Central American trade ministries are responsible for monitoring the implementation of the agreement.[405]

EU-CARIFORUM-EPA

The EU-CARIFORUM-EPA does not create specific institutions in the field of IP to implement or monitor the provisions in the IP Chapter of the agreement. However, the IP chapter of the EU-CARIFORUM-EPA provides for cooperation specifically related to regional institutions in the field of IP, namely that

- "the parties agree to cooperate [in the area of] reinforcement of regional initiatives, organizations and offices in the field of IP rights, the training of personnel and the development of publicly available databases, with a view to improve regional regulatory capacity, regional laws and regulations, as well as regional implementation",[406]
- "[t]he EU-CARIFORUM States agree to increase action at the regional level"[407] and
- "the Signatory EU-CARIFORUM States undertake to continue to consider further steps towards deeper integration in their respective regions in the field of

[402] See Article 19.4(1) CAFTA-DR.

[403] Available at https://ustr.gov/issue-areas/trade-development/trade-capacity-building/cafta-dr-tcb (accessed 2 Nov 2024).

[404] See Sect. 2.5.3.3.

[405] The Free Trade Commission supervises the implementation of CAFTA-DR according to Article 19.1(2) CAFTA-DR; the Free Trade Commission is composed of the USTR and Central American trade ministries according to Annex 19.1 CAFTA-DR.

[406] Article 164 EU-CARIFORUM-EPA.

[407] Article 133 EU-CARIFORUM-EPA.

> intellectual property rights. This process shall cover further harmonization of intellectual property laws and regulations, further progress towards regional management and enforcement of national intellectual property rights, as well as the creation and management of regional intellectual property rights, as appropriate".[408]

While the EU-CARIFORUM-EPA, therefore, seems to provide for regional institutions in some detail, a closer look at the wording shows that the agreement does not create any regional institutions. Article 164 EU-CARIFORUM-EPA refers to the reinforcement and improvement of existing regional initiatives and in Article 133 EU-CARIFORUM-EPA the parties agree on regional "actions", which are not necessarily executed by regional institutions.

Article 141 EU-CARIFORUM-EPA, on the other hand, which refers to "regional management and enforcement of national intellectual property rights, as well as the creation and management of regional intellectual property rights" and, therefore, envisions regional institutions. However, the provision is worded extremely softly, because the parties only "undertake to continue to consider further steps", which does not require any specific measures by the CARIFORUM countries.

EU-CA-AA

The EU-CA-AA, on the other hand, contains no provisions related to regional institutions in the field of IP. However, unlike the EU-CARIFORUM-EPA, the agreement creates a specific institution to implement or monitor the provisions in the IP Chapter. Article 274 EU-CA-AA establishes the Sub-Committee on Intellectual Property, mainly to follow-up on the implementation of the provisions relating to geographical indications, in particular recommending new geographical indications for protection[409] and promoting technology transfer and keeping a registry of activities relating to transfer of technology.[410]

2.5.2.3 Regional Institutions

Overview

The Central American countries have established a free trade area with the Central American Common Market (CACM).[411] However, this regional economic integra-

---

[408] Article 141 EU-CARIFORUM-EPA.

[409] Article 274.2(a) and (b) of the EU-CA-AA.

[410] Article 274.2(c) and (c) of the EU-CA-AA.

[411] This CACM is a free trade area comparable in many respects to the Andean Community established by Colombia, Peru and Ecuador.

tion has not led to the creation of regional IP institutions.[412] In this respect, Central America resembles less the Andean Community, where the Court of the Andean Community has jurisdiction on IP matters[413] (in addition to the integration achieved by regional IP legislation through Decision 486)[414] and more the Mercosur, where also no regional IP institutions exist.[415] The same is true in the field of competition law, where in Central America no regional institutions exist, in contrast to CARICOM, which established a common "Competition Commission" based in Suriname.[416] The current absence of regional institutions is surprising at first glance. However, the IP Registers in Central America lack the necessary infrastructure because of the small size of the Central American countries and their generally small budgets. The administrative staff is small.[417] Therefore, there is little time to provide services to the business community and help small enterprises to make full use of the IP system or for a comprehensive examination of patent applications. To strengthen the system, the creation of regional IP institutions has been proposed, especially in the light of European developments, to avoid redundant work in IP Registers, *i.e.*, the establishment of a Central American IP Office.[418] But so far, any such proposals have not led to any tangible results in relation to institutional integration so far, in particular regarding the registration of IP rights.[419] The efficiency benefits that could be achieved by regional institutions and the example of successful institutional integration, in particular in Europe, raise the question why such regional integration has not been successful. It may be due to the unwillingness of national governments to relinquish their political and fiscal control over "their" IP Registers. As will be discussed in more detail later, the IP Registers generate revenues for the (national) government which could, at least partly, be lost if regional institutions were created.[420] In addition, national registrations of IP rights create more work for domestic IP law firms than regional registrations, which may be another incentive for national governments not to create regional systems.[421]

---

[412] Noticeably, while Articles 277 and 279 EU-CA-AA require the establishment of a regional competition agency (see Sect. 2.6), there is no comparable requirement in relation to IP rights; similarly, Article 133 CARIFORUM-EPA states the necessity of measures and policies to be taken at the regional level, but requires no specific action.

[413] Unterguggenberger (1999), p. 23.

[414] Namely the Decision 486 (Common Intellectual Property Regime), available at https://www.wipo.int/edocs/lexdocs/laws/es/can/can012es.pdf (accessed 2 Nov 2024).

[415] Hassemer (2000), p. 17.

[416] See Sect. 2.6.

[417] See Sect. 2.5.3.

[418] O'Regan and O'Regan (2015), p. 9.

[419] In a study published by WIPO in November 2017, the Patent Examiner Manual and Trademark Manual are still listed as the only specific regional integration measures in the IP field, see WIPO (2017), p. i.

[420] See Sect. 2.5.2.3.

[421] Regional registrations could reduce work in a way similar to the registration of trademarks under the Protocol Relating to the Madrid Agreement Concerning the International Registration of Marks B.II.1.b(1).

Regional Harmonization

The regional integration in Central America has so far been limited to procedural and legislative *harmonization*. The CAFTA-DR members and Panama envision "the constitution of a homogenous culture in the administration, management and use of the patent system".[422] Their effort was consolidated by the joint Manual for the Organization and Examination of Patent Applications (*Manual de Organización y Examen de Solicitudes de Patentes de Invención de las Oficinas de Propiedad Industrial de los paises del Istmo Centroamericano y la República Dominicana*) (Patent Examiner Manual) published in November 2006.[423] This Patent Examiner Manual shall strengthen the national IP system by complementing "modern access methods" and "empowering examiners".[424] It explicitly considers "the patent system a tool for the economic development" of the region.[425] Representatives of the IP Registers of Central America, the Dominican Republic and Panama and experts from the Secretariat for Central American Economic Integration (SIECA), WIPO and the European, Spanish and Mexican patent offices met in five sessions to develop this Patent Examiner Manual, not only to harmonize the procedure among the participating offices, but also to provide reliable practical guidance to local examiners, because there were no publications regarding patent applications and examination on the national level before. A case decided by the Administrative Register Tribunal (*Tribunal Registral Administrativo*) (TRA) in Costa Rica in 2013 underlines the legal relevance the Patent Examiner Manual has gained.[426] Although the Patent Examiner Manual is not legally binding for the IP Registers of the region, the TRA held that the Patent Examiner Manual has the force and effect of law, because the IP Register itself established these guidelines for use by patent examiners during the examination of patent applications.[427] After the completion of the Patent Examiner Manual, the Central American IP Registers prepared a Harmonized Manual regarding Trademark Criteria (*Manual armonizado en materia de criterios de marca*) (Trademark Manual), which was finalized in 2014.[428] A series of presentations and seminars were organized to familiarize the IP Register personnel and

[422]Patent Examiner Manual, p 8.

[423]The Patent Examiner Manual is available at http://www.rnp.go.cr/propiedad_industrial/Documentos/PI_Servicios_Formularios/PI_Manualpatentes.pdf (accessed 2 Nov 2024).

[424]Patent Examiner Manual, p. 8.

[425]Patent Examiner Manual, p. 8.

[426]The TRA is discussed in Sect. 2.5.4.

[427]See the report available at http://www.lexology.com/library/detail.aspx?g=e542b44f-32b2-478a-ba3d-c3f2ac937451 (accessed 2 Nov 2024) (no date or case number provided).

[428]The text of the Trademark Manual is available (in Spanish) at https://www.rnpdigital.com/propiedad_industrial/Documentos/Manual%20Armonizado%20Marcas.pdf (accessed 2 Nov 2024).

trademark practitioners with the Trademark Manual, *e.g.*, in the Dominican Republic in 2015.[429] Similarly, on 17 April 2023, the CARIFORUM Intellectual Property and Innovation Project (CarIPI) published a Trademark Manual developed by the CARIFORUM IP offices and the EUIPO that is envisioned to be generally applied by the CARIFORUM IP offices.[430]

There are also projects for stronger regional cooperation, *e.g.*, regarding IT projects of the IP Registers. Interestingly, however, while such projects result in harmonized procedures, the reforms in the examination process and the IT-infrastructure result from the cooperation of the Central American country with international and foreign institutions, and are not (only) a joint regional effort.

Legislative harmonization had been achieved by the Central American Convention (Trademarks), which, however, was abandoned in the course of implementing the modern international IP agreements.[431] From a legislative perspective, the Central American IP system appears to be continuing to disintegrate, not least due to the differences in implementing CAFTA-DR.[432]

Regional Cooperation

More relevant than regional integration may be the *cooperation* of the Central American countries with third countries. Given the limited resources, their small size and high turnover in staff, support from third countries is important for the Central American IP institutions, and both international and foreign institutions regularly engage in cooperation with Central American institutions. Especially the IP Registers rely on external support and training by international and foreign organizations such as WIPO, the EPO, the Mexican IMPI, the Spanish PTO and the USPTO.[433] The USA is especially active in this field. Article 15.1 (16) CAFTA-DR provides for the establishment of the Committee on Trade Capacity Building and for activities to be organized by the Committee, including education on the use of IP, training of staff and development of electronic systems for IP management.[434] In implementing CAFTA-DR, the agency USAID was given the

[429] See *El Nacional*, 27 April 2015, available at http://elnacional.com.do/onapi-capacita-su-personal-tecnico-para-fortalecer-sistema-marcario-del-pais/ (accessed 2 Nov 2024).

[430] See https://internationalipcooperation.eu/en/caripi/news/manual-types-marks-and-distinctiveness (accessed 2 Nov 2024).

[431] See Sect. 2.1.4.

[432] This issue will be analyzed further throughout this study, see in particular Sect. 8.4.

[433] See, e.g., WTO (2011), p. 51.

[434] This Committee on Trade Capacity Building is not a regular feature in the otherwise similar US-FTAs. It was not included, for example, in the US-Peru-TPA and the US-Panama-TPA.

task to provide IP rights workshops and outreach events and training on competition law and policy.[435] The IP Registers in the region cooperate with other patent offices for institutional development. For language and cultural reasons, offices who can provide assistance in Spanish are especially active, mainly the Mexican, Spanish and European Patent Offices. All of them helped developing the common *Patent Examiner Manual*.[436] Training for Central American examiners is regularly provided, e.g., by the Mexican IMPI and the EUIPO.[437] Moreover, the Mexican IMPI also examines patent applications referred to it from Central American IP Registers.[438] To a lesser extent, international organizations also provide support. The World Bank, for instance, was involved in projects concerning judicial modernization in El Salvador and Guatemala and public sector management in Nicaragua.[439]

2.5.3 *Industrial Property Registers*

2.5.3.1 Overview

The patent and trademark offices (IP Registers) play the central role within the IP system in Central America. In Central America (in the narrow sense) they are named "Industrial Property Registers" (*Registros de Propiedad Industrial*) or "Intellectual Property Registers" (*Registros de Propiedad Intelectual*) and in the Dominican Republic "National Industrial Property Office" (*Oficina Nacional de la Propiedad Industrial*). The name "register" is based on the traditional view of these agencies as part of the registration administration, including also the registration of real estate, businesses etc.,[440] and the IP Registers are usually a department within the national register agency. This had the notable consequence that often IP law was traditionally taught in legal education as part of registry law, *i.e.*, administrative law, contrary to, *e.g.*, Germany or the USA, where it is usually part of the business law curriculum, *i.e.*, private law.

The registers in Central America are not only responsible for the administration of IP rights, but they are arguably the most important institution for the IP system in

---

[435] See, for instance, the following material on implementation event: USAID/PROCAFTA, Cumplimiento de los compromisos del DR-CAFTA después de los 6 meses de la entrada en vigor, 2008, available at http://pdf.usaid.gov/pdf_docs/PA00HPR9.pdf (accessed 2 Nov 2024) and the report by Palacios (2012).

[436] See Sect. 3.1.6.

[437] See, for example, a training event in 2020 organized by the EUIPO with representatives of the RPIs, see https://ipkey.eu/es/latin-america/activities/capacitacion-en-marcas-para-examinadores-de-paises-centroamericanos-mexico (accessed 2 Nov 2024).

[438] See Sect. 2.5.3.

[439] See, regarding the project in Guatemala, World Bank (2005).

[440] In El Salvador, under the previous Article 109 IP Law (SV), the Commerce Registry (Registro de Comercio) was also responsible for the registration of IP rights.

general. As they often are the only specialized IP institution in the country, they are important for the development of IP policy (including participation in the negotiations of FTAs), the training of other public entities and users, the promotion of innovation and even in some cases the enforcement of IP rights,[441] by collaborating with the *Ministerio Público* and participating in criminal proceedings as experts.[442] Nevertheless, while the term "Industrial Property Office" would better reflect the institutions responsibilities, in this study the term "Industrial Property Register" or short "IP Register" is used in accordance with the regional terminology.

This section describes the organizational structure and the responsibilities of the IP Registers, focusing on the organization of the examination and registration of IP rights. The registration and examination procedures will be analyzed within the section on patent and trademark procedure (see Sect. 3.1.6 and Sect. 4.1.4).

2.5.3.2 Organization

Supervision and Infrastructure

In Central America, only the IP Register in the Dominican Republic (ONPI) has "technical autonomy and its own budget".[443] Maybe this technical and financial autonomy is part of the reason why the ONPI is considered one of the more developed IP Registers in the region.[444] All other IP Registers are governmental departments, usually under the supervision of the Ministry of Economy and, therefore, are not politically autonomous.[445] These IP Registers are also not autonomous financially. The application and especially renewal fees exceed the related administrative costs, so the IP Registers are profitable and can be used as profit centers by the government: In Costa Rica, for example, some of the revenues are allocated by law to special institutions. 40% of the revenues are earmarked for the public publishing enterprise, "Editorial CR", and 10% for the Technical University of Costa Rica; 20% are reserved for trainings and only 30% of the revenues become the actual budget of the IP Register.[446]

Costa Rica has started to strengthen its IP Register in several ways when CAFTA-Dr was concluded. In 2006, the IP Register in Costa Rica had 35 employees, and the number was intended to increase to around 90.[447] Until 2020, the patent department

[441] See Sect. 2.5.3.

[442] See Sect. 7.1.2.

[443] Article 138 IP Law (DR).

[444] Interview with *Ana Catalina Monge Rodríguez.*

[445] In Nicaragua, for example the IP Register, is part of the Ministry of Public Works, Industry and Trade (MIFIC), see https://www.wipo.int/directory/es/contact.jsp?country_code=NI&type=ADMIN (accessed 2 Nov 2024).

[446] Article 95 TM Law (CR).

[447] See Registro de la Propiedad Industrial de Costa Rica (2006), p. 22.

alone had more than doubled its staff from 7 to 16 persons.[448] The IP Register in El Salvador had, in 2020, 77 employees, out of which 26 had general responsibilities (11 for general administration, 5 for customer relations and 10 for other responsibilities), 29 worked in the trademarks department, six in the patents department, three in the copyright department and 13 in the archives and digitalization departments.[449] The IP Register in Guatemala had, in 2008, 80 employees, including the copyright department. In the patent department, there were four examiners in 2022.[450] All IP Registers experience high turnover of their personnel, because low salaries of the IP Registers are not competitive with the private sector. The technical staff is hired by private industries and the legally trained management sometimes moves into private practice to work for an IP law firm after some years.[451]

To improve services, some IP Registers have opened regional offices in other towns in the respective country. In the Dominican Republic, the law explicitly provides for the right of the ONPI to open offices in other towns.[452]

Patent Examination

Overview Patent applications in Central America are examined by internal examiners or, for lack of capacity, often by foreign patent offices or external experts (*peritos*). These three options for examination are sometimes explicitly specified in national laws.[453] The examination of local applications by foreign PTOs, especially the Mexican IMPI, is common in Central America, because many IP Registers do not have (enough) internal examiners.[454] The Mexican IMPI provides a special internet portal, CADOPAT, for Central American IP Registers and does not charge for the examinations.[455] If there is a parallel Mexican patent application, the Central American IP Register can also rely on the substantive examination of this application

[448] See the published work report by Karen Quesada (2020), available at https://www.rnpdigital.com/Institucion/Institucion/Informe%20Final%20de%20Gestion%20Karen%20Quesada%20Bermudez%202020.pdf (accessed 2 Nov 2024).

[449] The organizational chart is available at https://www.transparencia.gob.sv/institutions/cnr/documents/391710/download (accessed 2 Nov 2024).

[450] Based on the data provided by the WIPO IP Statistics Data Center for 2022 (the last yar for which data was available), there were 289 applications and 72,3 applications per examiner, according to the Intellectual property statistical country profile 2022 for Guatemala, see https://www.wipo.int/ipstats/en/statistics/country_profile/ (accessed 2 Nov 2024).

[451] See below Sect. 2.5.3.

[452] See, e.g., Article 138 IP Law (DR) and Article 152 IP Law (SV).

[453] See, e.g., Article 117(3) IP Law (GT) 2006.

[454] Regarding the cooperation by the Dominican Republic with a foreign patent office see USTR Special 301 Report (2018), p. 76.

[455] This service was established in 2007 and has since then been extended also to other Latin American countries, see the presentation of CADOPAT by the Mexican IMPI to WIPO in 2016, available at https://www.wipo.int/meetings/en/doc_details.jsp?doc_id=345737 (accessed 2 Nov 2024).

through CADOPAT.[456] The other option is to hire external examiners (*peritos*) from private companies or industry associations and universities.[457] However, this practice comes with several disadvantages: In any case, the respective *perito* requires training; in Costa Rica, the regulation establishing the use of peritos details the necessary qualifications and training requirements in detail.[458] Also, if the *peritos* are simply paid per examined patent, like in Costa Rica, there could the risk that the examination will be done too fast and superficial, resulting in low quality patents.[459] Finally, it also means that the IP Registers do not acquire practical and technical know-how internally. Finally, the IP Registers cannot make sure that the examination is done according to the procedural rules required by law. For these reasons, there is a general trend among Central American IP Registers to hire full-time internal examiners, as is already the case in the trademark departments. Following the implementation of the PCT process around 2005/2006, patent applications increased, which made it even more pressing to hire new examiners. However, the IP Registers compete with the private sector for these examiners, and private industries and law firms have a strong interest in lawyers, engineers or biochemists, in particular those with experience in the patent office and can "buy them out".[460]

Country-specific Analysis In Costa Rica, the IP Register had no internal examiners in 2008, and also in 2010 the IP Register relied on external examiners (*peritos*), and the IP Register's lawyers performed the formal exam.[461] Therefore, the IP Register (CR) signed a cooperation convention the University of Costa Rica (UCR), under which UCR scientists would work as external patent examiners. This mechanism was implemented within the UCR department "Proinnova". This department, in addition to being the technology transfer office of UCR, was in charge of conducting the substantive patent examination received by the IP Register (CR).[462] The Costa Rican IP Register also established a convention of cooperation with the *Instituto Technologico de Costa Rica*. In 2024, both the UCR and the Instituto Technologico de Costa Rica were identified as patent examination

[456] Ibid.; this procedure was, for example, formally established in El Salvador by an amendment to Article 152 IP Law (SV).

[457] Article 152 IP Law (SV); Cabrera Medaglia (2010), p. 10; in case of Costa Rica, pharmaceutical patents shall be examined by the College of Pharmacists.

[458] Article 7 Reglamento para la Contratación de Examinadores Externos para la Oficina de Patentes del Registro de Propiedad Industrial, available at https://www.wipo.int/edocs/lexdocs/laws/es/cr/cr093es.pdf (accessed 2 Nov 2024).

[459] According to Article 14 Reglamento para la Contratación de Examinadores Externos para la Oficina de Patentes del Registro de Propiedad Industrial, available at https://www.wipo.int/edocs/lexdocs/laws/es/cr/cr093es.pdf (accessed 2 Nov 2024), the external examiners receive USD 525 for each patent.

[460] In this context it is illuminating that the first examiner hired by the RPI in the Dominican Republic was from Cuba and not a local engineer, see Gil Abinader (2015), p. 11; also, the author personally met several former RPI staff members who had gone into private practice.

[461] Cabrera Medaglia (2010), p. 10.

[462] Registro de la Propiedad Industrial de Costa Rica (2006), p. 32.

institutions in Costa Rica by WIPO.[463] Finally, pharmaceutical patents could be examined by the College of Pharmacists.[464] However, these institutions were apparently not able to process a significant number of patent applications, as evidenced by the fact that no patents were examined or granted in Costa Rica for several years.[465] Therefore, the IP Register (CR) hired four full-time internal examiners for pharmaceutical patent applications alone, based on a 2010 regulation.[466]

In 2023, negotiations were underway between Costa Rica and the EPO regarding a validation agreement that would enable applicants to validate patents examined by the EPO also in Costa Rica without additional examination.[467] This could facilitate patent prosecution significantly, as applicants could opt for such an extension of a European patent instead of a local filing.

In the Dominican Republic, there were no patent examiners and accordingly no patents were examined and granted for several years after CAFTA-DR was signed. In 2016 and 2017, however, similar to other countries in the region, internal examiners were hired.[468] In El Salvador, according to WIPO data, as of 2022 there were two patent examiners.[469] In Guatemala, there were four specialized examiners in 2008, for biochemical, pharmaceutical, mechanical and chemical inventions.[470] According to WIPO data, there were still four internal examiners as of 2022.[471]

---

[463] See the information provided by WIPO, available at https://www.wipo.int/tisc/en/search/details.jsp?id=5557 and https://www.wipo.int/tisc/es/search/details.jsp?id=5558 (accessed 2 Nov 2024).

[464] Based on a special inter-institutional agreement between the RPI (CR) and the College of Pharmacists, see Article 7 Reglamento para la Contratación de Examinadores Externos para la Oficina de Patentes del Registro de Propiedad Industrial, available at https://www.wipo.int/edocs/lexdocs/laws/es/cr/cr093es.pdf (accessed 2 Nov 2024).

[465] Regarding the statistics on patent applications and grants, see Sect. 3.1.7.

[466] Regulation No. 12 of 18 March 2010, for Hiring of External Examiners for the Patent Office of the Industrial Property Registry; the Spanish text of the regulation is available at http://www.wipo.int/wipolex/en/details.jsp?id=11342 (accessed 2 Nov 2024).

[467] See https://www.epo.org/en/news-events/news/epo-and-costa-rica-continue-validation-agreement-talks (accessed 2 Nov 2024).

[468] USTR Special 301 Report (2018), p. 76.

[469] Based on the data provided by the WIPO IP Statistics Data Center for 2022 (the last yar for which data was available), there were 149 applications and 74,5 applications per examiner, according to the Intellectual property statistical country profile 2022 for El Salvador, see https://www.wipo.int/ipstats/en/statistics/country_profile/ (accessed 2 Nov 2024).

[470] Presentation of F. Gracia, Seminar on Intellectual Property, Industrial Property and New Technologies, San José, Costa Rica, 28 October 2008 (on file with the author).

[471] Based on the data provided by the WIPO IP Statistics Data Center for 2022 (the last year for which data was available), there were 289 applications and 72,3 applications per examiner, according to the Intellectual property statistical country profile 2022 for Guatemala, see https://www.wipo.int/ipstats/en/statistics/country_profile/ (accessed 2 Nov 2024).

2.5.3.3 Electronic Systems

The main responsibilities of the IP Register are the registration of trademarks and the examination of patents.[472] According to Article 15.2.7. CAFTA-DR, the Central American IP Registers shall, to the maximum degree practical, establish an electronic registration system and shall work to establish a database for publishing the registration of trademarks. CAFTA-DR does not contain rules on patent databases. The IP Register in Central America, as elsewhere, have started to establish electronic systems for these services. The creation of the appropriate electronic infrastructure has (officially) been prioritized within the IP system in several countries.[473]

Electronic Registration of IP Rights

In Costa Rica, for many years there was no possibility to submit electronic trademark registrations. However, on 20 August 2020, as per the Directive DRPI-00001-2020, the RPI in Costa Rica established the possibility to submit electronic trademark registrations via the "WIPO File" system.[474] Practically, Costa Rica created the possibility to file both trademark and patent applications electronically through WIPO's system.[475] The Dominican Republic introduced the "E-SERPI" electronic filing system for trademarks in 2019.[476] El Salvador accepts electronic patent applications through WIPO's "ePCT" system.[477] In 2024, the possibility to apply for trademarks online had been introduced as well.[478] In Guatemala, as late as August 2022, no electronic trademark applications were accepted, but the implementation of an electronic system seemed to be in progress.[479] Subsequently, this

[472] See Sect. 3.1.6 and Sect. 4.1.4.

[473] E.g., in its National Action Plan of 2002, Guatemala announced a regional "pilot project"; see Ministry of Economy of Guatemala (2002), p. 25. This project lead by Guatemala to develop a system in one country that could be adopted by the other offices seems not to have been seriously pursued. Instead, the systems are usually based on the "WIPO File" system provided by WIPO and specified within each country.

[474] The text of the directive is available at https://www.rnpdigital.com/DIRECTRIZ%20DRPI-001-2020%20SISTEMA%20DE%20RECEPCION%20EN%20LINEA%20DE%20SIGNOS%20DISTINTIVOS,%20WIPO%20FILE.pdf (accessed 2 Nov 2024).

[475] See the link at https://rpi.rnp.go.cr/wipofileindex/xhtml/sesion/index.xhtml (accessed 2 Nov 2024).

[476] See the service provided by the IP Register (DR) for applications available at https://www.onapi.gob.do/siteServices/Login.aspx?ReturnUrl=%2fsiteServices (accessed 2 Nov 2024).

[477] See the information provided by WIPO, available at https://www.wipo.int/export/sites/www/pct/guide/en/gdvol1/annexes/annexc/ax_c_sv.pdf (accessed 2 Nov 2024).

[478] See the link Salvadorean IP Register's website, https://www.e.cnr.gob.sv/ServiciosOL/portada/rpi.htm (accessed 2 Nov 2024); however, this link is accessible only for registered agents.

[479] See https://www.lexology.com/library/detail.aspx?g=2b75c9ea-cc9c-4dd1-af86-52aa3223ffe6 (accessed 2 Nov 2024).

electronic system has been put in place[480] In Honduras, the IP Register provides the option to register trademarks electronically via the "WIPO File" system.[481]

In Nicaragua, there is no option to register trademarks electronically.[482] Accordingly trademark applications have to be submitted in person.[483] However, an electronic filing system for patents is available.[484]

To summarize, the possibility for electronic filings has been introduced in all Central American countries, often via the "WIPO File" system.

Electronic Databases of Registered IP Rights

As far as could be ascertained, several (but not all) Central American IP Registers provide online search tools to access patent information, relying on international databases, especially *LATIPAT*, a database with patent information established by the EPO especially for Latin American countries[485] and "WIPO Publish" to enable trademark searches.

In Costa Rica, in 2008, current patent information could only be researched at two public computer stations in the IP Register.[486] Currently, there is neither an electronic patent database nor other online documentation of registered patents on the IP Register's website, but the IP Register (CR) integrated WIPO search tools ("WIPO Publish") into its website so that trademarks and designs can be searched in the respective WIPO databases via the IP Register.[487] The website of the IP Register in the Dominican Republic provides a link to the *LATIPAT* database for patent searches.[488] In Guatemala, the IP Register maintains a database for local trademarks, but apparently no database for patent searches.[489] In Honduras, like in Costa Rica,

[480] See https://portal.rpi.gob.gt/marcas/ (accessed 2 Nov 2024).

[481] See https://www.ip.gob.hn/direcciones/propiedad-intelectual/menu-propiedad-intelectual (accessed 2 Nov 2024).

[482] See European Commission, Executive Agency for Small and Medium-sized Enterprises (2024), p. 6.

[483] Ibid.

[484] See https://pctlegal.wipo.int/eGuide/view-doc.xhtml?doc-code=NI&doc-lang=en (accessed 2 Nov 2024).

[485] The LATIPAT project provides a search interface for the search of technical information in Spanish and Portuguese in patent documents of Latin American countries and Spain, available at https://lp.espacenet.com (accessed 2 Nov 2024).

[486] Observation by the author.

[487] As of 2024, see https://rpi.rnp.go.cr/wipofileindex/xhtml/sesion/index.xhtml (accessed 2 Nov 2024).

[488] See the link on the websites of the IP Register in the Dominican Republic, available at http://www.onapi.gob.do/index.php/cati/bases-datos-cati (accessed 2 Nov 2024).

[489] See https://portal.rpi.gob.gt/consulta-de-marcas/ (accessed 2 Nov 2024).

the IP Register integrated "WIPO Publish" into its website to provide access to a trademark database.[490] Honduras in addition provides for a *post-grant* opposition, which can be filed within three months after a summary of the granted patent is published.[491] In 2001, the legislation, Article 55 IP Law (HN), was reformed and now provides that the summaries are no longer published in the official gazette, but on the website of the IP Register. This publication requirement has meanwhile been implemented.[492] In Nicaragua, the IP Register's website does not provide access to a trademark or patent database.[493]

2.5.3.4 Training

Like the PTOs in other regions, the Central American IP Registers have started to provide services beyond the registration and management of IP rights, especially relating to the information and training of other public entities and users of the IP system: In Costa Rica, the IP Register engages in the training (*capacitación*) of the private sector (SMEs) and universities.[494] The situation is similar in Nicaragua, where the IP Register organizes training programs with the National Council of Universities (*consejo nacional de universidades*) for universities and with the Chamber of Commerce for SMEs; in addition, the IP Register trains judges on IP issues.[495] In El Salvador, the IP Register created the Intellectual Property Academy in 2022 to train enforcement bodies and SMEs to protect IP rights.[496]

2.5.3.5 Evaluation

The fact that the trademark department is usually several times larger than the patent department in IP Registers underlines the higher practical relevance of trademarks in Central America and the still small number of patent applications in the region. The small number of patent examiners in each IP Register (if they exist at all) is not enough to permit a sufficient technical specialization of these examiners to conduct a thorough and efficient examination. The lack of specialization, and sometimes the absence of examiners, explains why applications from Central America are often

[490] See https://www.ip.gob.hn/direcciones/propiedad-intelectual/menu-propiedad-intelectual (accessed 2 Nov 2024).

[491] Article 55 IP Law (HN).

[492] See https://www.ip.gob.hn/direcciones/propiedad-intelectual/menu-propiedad-intelectual/publicaciones-avisos-resoluciones-de-patentes (accessed 2 Nov 2024).

[493] See European Commission, Executive Agency for Small and Medium-sized Enterprises (2024), p. 6.

[494] Registro de la Propiedad Industrial de Costa Rica (2006), p. 67.

[495] Registro de la Propiedad Intelectual de Nicaragua (2006), p. 18.

[496] European Commission, Executive Agency for Small and Medium-sized Enterprises (2020), p. 1.

examined by the Mexican IMPI, or, even if applications are examined internally, the examiner often relies on the prior examination of the Mexican IMPI.[497]

The high staff fluctuation creates another significant problem. While staff fluctuation is not uncommon even in well-funded PTOs in developed countries, it poses specific problems in Central America. Because of the small size of the IP Registers, there are less internal experienced replacements available. Because information on projects, best practices and procedures are sometimes not well documented, "institutional knowledge" is lost when key staff members leave, successor often must start from scratch, and projects have to be started all over again or might be discontinued despite an existing legal and financial framework because of such changes in staff.[498] In short, the IP Registers in Central America lack the personnel, institutionalized know-how and resources to perform appropriately. These institutional deficits could limit the effective protection of IP rights more than the absence of specific statutory enforcement provisions, because the IP Registers are relevant not only for obtaining IP rights, but also for enforcing them.[499]

2.5.4 Courts

The role of the courts in the IP system in Central America is in practice not comparable to the IP Registers, mainly because they are not specialized in IP matters and, therefore, cannot act as a focal point from an institutional perspective, with the notable exception of the TRA in Costa Rica.[500] Nevertheless, their role in IP protection and enforcement, including safeguarding applicable limitations and balances, is crucial.

2.5.4.1 Organization

Overview

The court system in Central America in principle is similar to that of other civil-law countries in terms of institutional design and procedures, including the separation of civil and administrative courts. Within the civil court system, the Central American countries usually established courts or divisions responsible for "mercantile" or commercial cases.[501] Cases relating to the administration of IP rights emerging from the IP Register, *e.g.*, appeals against the refusal or grant of an application,

---

[497] See Sect. 2.5.3.

[498] Interview with *Ana Catalina Monge Rodríguez*.

[499] See Sect. 7.1.2.

[500] See Sect. 2.5.4.

[501] E.g., in El Salvador, Article 184 IP Law (SV).

fall under the jurisdiction of the administrative courts (*Contencioso Administrativo*).[502] In both the civil and administrative branch, there are appellate courts as a second instance.[503] The last instance is the respective supreme court (*Corte Suprema de Justicia*), which is also the constitutional court (unlike Germany and similar to the USA).[504]

Specialized Courts

Under TRIPS and CAFTA-DR, there is no "obligation to put in place a judicial system for the enforcement of IP rights distinct from that for the enforcement of law in general".[505] This provision only clarifies the national flexibility regarding the institutional framework. As both TRIPS and CAFTA-DR are generally extremely restrictive in creating institutional obligations, even without such an explicit provision the freedom to design the judicial system would probably have to be considered a national prerogative as a matter of principle. Unlike the USA and many European countries, no Central American country has established *formally* specialized IP courts (or specialized sections in the commercial courts).[506] In El Salvador, there has been a legislative proposal for a specialized IP court, but this court was not established.[507]

The only court practically specialized in IP matters in Central America is the Administrative Register Tribunal (*Tribunal Registral Administrativo*) (TRA) in Costa Rica. The TRA has jurisdiction for appeals against the administrative decisions by the National Centre of Registers (*Centro Nacional de Registros*, CNR), *i.e.*, on validity and registrability of IP rights, but not enforcement of IP rights.[508] While this includes also the registers for vehicles and real estate, more than 80% of the cases of the TRA relate to IP rights, and the majority of those to trademarks.[509] The TRA was established by the IP Enforcement Law (CR) the in the year 2000.[510] The judges within the tribunal are not *de jure* specialized, but *de facto* focus on IP

[502] See, e.g., in Costa Rica, Article 110 Judiciary Law (CR); the text of the law is available at https://www.pgrweb.go.cr/scij/Busqueda/Normativa/Normas/nrm_texto_completo.aspx?nValor1=1&nValor2=33635 (accessed 2 Nov 2024).

[503] See, e.g., in Costa Rica, Article 97 Nr. 4 Judiciary Law (CR).

[504] See, e.g., in Costa Rica, Article 54 Judiciary Law (CR).

[505] Article 41 TRIPS; Article 15.11.2(a) CAFTA-DR.

[506] Article 184 IP Law (SV), for example, provides that the general courts have jurisdiction also in IP matters.

[507] Interview with *Carlos Castillo*.

[508] Article 1(1) IP Enforcement Law (CR).

[509] The predominant role of IP cases is not least evidenced by the fact that the TRA was established by the IP Enforcement Law (CR), and not a general registral law. During the first ten years of operation, the TRA handled some 6500 cases, see the report by WIPO on the TRA, available at http://www.wipo.int/wipo_magazine/en/2012/05/article_0006.html (accessed 2 Nov 2024).

[510] Articles 19 et seq. IP Enforcement Law (CR).

because of the large share of IP cases in the overall caseload.[511] The court is also responsible for decisions relating to patentability, and in order to have access to the necessary technical know-how, the court can select ad-hoc technical judges.[512]

The TRA was established based on the procedural specialization of registration matters in general, rather than the substantive specialization of IP matters.[513] But even in the present form it has the advantage of accumulating know-how in the IP field, both with regard to the members of court and the library. This is no small advantage, because generally access to IP literature and online resources is limited in Central America. Moreover, the TRA actively engages in the development of the IP system through outreach activities.[514]

Even without an obligation to do so, therefore, the establishment of specialized IP courts might be good policy. In Central America, the judges in the generalized civil courts often lack experience in the area of IP, because of the little number of cases in this field.[515] This can be problematic for both the right holders and alleged infringers, because the appropriate application of statutory bars or limitations requires some understanding of this field of law. Under these circumstances, specialized courts might actually be more capable of securing the interests of users and the public.

2.5.4.2 Training

The problems experienced in relation to the IP enforcement highlight the necessity to educate judges in IP law.[516] A lack of knowledge and experience in relation to IP matters seems not to be the only issue, (at least some) judges traditionally seem to consider IP protection to be of little importance (in line with a widely shared view in the region).[517] As a result, training programs have been initiated, especially in cooperation with the USA, *e.g.*, in Guatemala, by the American Chamber of

---

[511] Article 25 IP Enforcement Law (CR).

[512] Article 24 IP Enforcement Law (CR).

[513] However, it is noteworthy that the court was established in Articles 19 et seq. IP Enforcement Law (CR), i.e., not a general registral law but an IP law; given that the TRA is composed of five judges and employs assistants, there would be the practical possibility for additional substantive specialization.

[514] In the other countries, only the IP Registers and law firms (especially those working for international right holders) have the knowledge and manpower to engage in such activities.

[515] For example, regarding trademark cases in Guatemala, see Castillo-Chacon, Francisco, Country report on Guatemala World Trademark Review, Yearbook 2005, p. 145, available at http://www.worldtrademarkreview.com/Intelligence/Yearbook/2005/Country-chapters/Guatemala (accessed 2 Nov 2024).

[516] Escoto (2004), p. 1.

[517] In 2004, Escoto (2004), p. 1, found social and cultural changes to be required so that the judiciary become aware of the importance of the protection of intellectual property rights; in other words, at least some judges considered IP protection to be irrelevant. In 2016, the USTR still observed a "lack of emphasis" of the judiciary, USTR Special 301 Report (2016), pp. 58–60.

Commerce (AmCham).[518] However, the lower court judges in most countries have less incentive to participate in national and international trainings than employees of specialized agencies, because the judges have no specific IP specialization or background.[519] By contrast, the TRA judges in Costa Rica regularly participate in national and international trainings regarding IP matters, because they are primarily occupied with such cases.[520]

2.5.4.3 Precedent

In Central America, courts often do not follow precedent, which is considered non-binding based on civil law principles.[521] This practice can create legal uncertainty.[522] Practitioners in Central America also face the additional problem that the parties and public institutions involved in a legal dispute prefer deals or "conciliation" to court decisions, and that, therefore, little case law is available, in particular in field like IP where not many cases are initiated.[523] In addition, case law is not comprehensively published, and, therefore, even the existing precedent is not easily available.[524] However, in this regard the emergence of the internet seems to improve the situation, as foreign legal sources become available, *e.g.*, sources from WIPO and legal literature from Spain.[525]

2.5.5 *Ministerio Público*

CAFTA-DR, like other US-FTAs, focuses on criminal enforcement to improve IP protection.[526] This gives special importance to work of the prosecutor's office (*Ministerio Público*) in the field of IP. Most Central American countries have established special IP units within their *Ministerio Público* after TRIPS to improve

---

[518] For this purpose, AmCham Guatemala has established the "Comité Propiedad Intelectual", see https://amchamguate.com/nuestros-comites/ (accessed 2 Nov 2024).

[519] European Commission, Executive Agency for Small and Medium-sized Enterprises (2019), p. 13.

[520] See Sect. 2.5.4.

[521] Malone (2012), p. 38.

[522] Interview with *Ninoshka Urrutia* and *Carlos Castillo*.

[523] This issue is discussed in more detail in Sect. 7.1.2.

[524] In Guatemala, the CSJ maintains an electronic database with its own decisions which can be researched by keyword at https://jurisprudencia.cc.gob.gt/sjc/, however, only a few of these decisions relate to IP law (accessed 2 Nov 2024).

[525] Regarding the work by WIPO see Sect. 2.5.2.1.

[526] The enforcement provisions of CAFTA-DR will be analyzed in Sect. 7.

their enforcement record.[527] The specialization was first introduced in El Salvador, where a dedicated unit for "private and intellectual property" crimes was established.[528] In Costa Rica, there is no specialized IP unit.[529] In Guatemala, while there has not been established a formal specialized "IP office", IP cases have been assigned to a distinct IP unit.[530] In Nicaragua, IP cases have been centralized in the special unit for organized crime (as shown by organizational information provided in 2016 and 2024).[531] Honduras re-established its specialized IP unit within the *Ministerio Público* in 2010, that also supports the application of border measures (with few cases reported e.g. in 2017 and 2018).[532]

In the Dominican Republic, a specialized IP prosecutor has been designated and trained in every province. As a result, the number of IP cases rose from 73 cases in 2018, to 217 cases in 2021, and 584 cases in 2022.[533]

The prosecutors of the *Ministerio Público* are often not trained in IP matters, because these specialized unites were formed not very long ago and because IP law is largely not part of the general legal education in Central America.[534] These specialized prosecutors, therefore, receive training from the IP Registers (*e.g.*, in Nicaragua)[535] or from foreign institutions, in particular from US and EU agencies and WIPO.[536] Despite the official claim by some governments to focus more on IP protection, most prosecutors have other priorities. In contrast to the other institutions, local observers mostly do not attribute this to a lack of resources at the *Ministerio Público*, but mainly to a lack of interest.[537] However, the *Ministerio Público* is also considered insufficiently equipped in most countries, because they lack resources and staff.[538] There seem to be several reasons which might explain

---

527 Ministry of Economy of Guatemala (2002), p. 23.

528 For further information on this special unit see European Commission, Executive Agency for Small and Medium-sized Enterprises (2020), p. 10.

529 This is shown in the organigram as of 2024, see https://ministeriopublico.poder-judicial.go.cr/index.php/organigrama (accessed 2 Nov 2024).

530 See European Commission, Executive Agency for Small and Medium-sized Enterprises (2019), p. 12; the unit is shown the organizational chart on file with the author.

531 See the reports of the Ministerio Público in 2016 (on file with the author) and in 2020 (on file with the author).

532 USTR, Honduras, 2013, available at https://ustr.gov/sites/default/files/2013%20NTE%20Honduras%20Final.pdf (accessed 2 Nov 2024); European Commission, Executive Agency for Small and Medium-sized Enterprises (2019), p. 12.

533 USTR Special 301 Report (2023), p. 75.

534 The role of IP law in the legal education is discussed below in Sect. 2.5.6.

535 Registro de la Propiedad Intelectual de Nicaragua (2006), p. 22.

536 Registro de la Propiedad Intelectual de Nicaragua (2006), p. 18; WTO (2011), p. 51.

537 E.g., US right holders reported that in Costa Rica, often there is a "lack of interest" to prosecute IP cases to the end, see https://www.state.gov/reports/2020-investment-climate-statements/costa-rica/ (accessed 2 Nov 2024).

538 Regarding, e.g., Costa Rica, see Escoto (2004), pp. 33–35 and regarding Honduras, see USTR, Honduras, 2013, available at https://ustr.gov/sites/default/files/2013%20NTE%20Honduras%20Final.pdf (accessed 2 Nov 2024).

this apparent lack of motivation: First, the Central American countries suffer from high overall crime rates, including organized crime and violent crimes related to youth gangs and/or drug trafficking, and the investigation of such crimes has a higher priority than IP enforcement.[539] In addition, the *Ministerio Público* is not immune to corruption and in some cases, it is also claimed that the police resells infringing goods for their own profit.[540]

Finally, IP infringements are often considered "petty crimes".[541] In particular the common trademark piracy (fake luxury apparel and the like) is hardly considered a crime at all.[542] This observation by local practitioners is also evidenced by the fact that such infringing goods have been sold on the streets within view of the *Ministerio Público's* office (*e.g.*, in Guatemala) and in shops in shopping malls.[543] In such cases prosecutors or the police could easily intervene, which demonstrates that the lack of criminal enforcement is not due to a lack of resources, but the absence of real intention to prosecute IP crimes.

However, it must be noted that a disinterested *Ministerio Público* is not unique to Central America (or developing countries in general). In Germany, prosecutors are also not keen to initiate criminal procedures against IP infringement, neither private copyright infringements nor commercial trademark counterfeiting or patent infringements. Practically, criminal procedures are often only initiated if the right holder supports the *Ministerio Público* "logistically". This seems to be the case especially with regard to international right holders, because they are considered to have enough own resources to enforce their rights.[544] First, the right holder must prepare the evidence, *e.g.*, by using private investigators, and present it to the *Ministerio Público*.[545] Second, the right holder must often also support the investigation and enforcement measures of the *Ministerio Público*. Generally, criminal enforcement in the IP field seems to have the character of a "public-private partnership".[546] In conclusion, while CAFTA-DR requires the possibility of *ex officio* actions, this possibility is rarely, if at all, used in practice in Central America. However, it must be noted that, *e.g.*, in Germany this possibility is also not often used.

539 OSAC (2019).

540 Thomas (2009), p. 5.

541 See, e.g., in relation to a previous policy in Costa Rica, https://ruizcamposlex.com/ing/news.php?idn=23 (accessed 2 Nov 2024).

542 See Sect. 4.1.1.2.

543 Observation by the author in 2008.

544 Escoto (2004), pp. 32–34.

545 Escoto (2004), pp. 32–34.

546 Escoto (2004), pp. 32–34.

2.5.6 *Legal Education and Private Practice*

IP has previously not only been outside the focus of the public legal institutions, but also that of private practitioners, and few attorneys specialized in the IP field. Also, there were few opportunities to study IP law in Central America.[547]

However, this situation is changing because more special courses are offered and more and more students specialize in IP law. Courses in IP law are offered in several Central American universities. In Guatemala, in the academic year 2023/2024, the public *University San Carlos* offers a specialized postgraduate Master's program and the private *University Francisco Marroquin* courses as an optional part of the pre-graduate curriculum.[548] In Costa Rica, the *National University for Distance Education* (Educación de Distancia, UNED) offers a specialized postgraduate Master's program since 2003/2004, which was still active in 2023/2024.[549] Because of the previously limited specialized legal education and the limited economic relevance of IP law, around the time CAFTA-DR was implemented, few lawyers or law firms were active in this field and in most countries just a few small law firms handled most of the business.[550] Today IP law firms are growing in numbers and size, and this specialization is presumably possible because there is more business in general.[551] This increase in specialized activities is exemplified by in-person and online events organized in 2023 by a regional group of AIPPI.[552] Specialized lawyers represent often international companies. This includes creating favorable publicity for their clients directly or through specialized associations and establishing constructive relationships with the responsible administration.[553] In this regard, the Central American law firms have become similar to those from the USA or Europe.

[547] Interview with *Néstor Morera*.

[548] The curriculum of the postgraduate Master's program of the University San Carlos is available at https://posgradosderecho.usac.edu.gt/propiedad-intelectual.php (accessed 2 Nov 2024); the curriculum of the University Francisco Marroquin for the year 2023/2024 as an example is available at https://derecho.ufm.edu/wp-content/uploads/2023/12/Prerrequisitos-Primer-Semestre-2024-UFM-FACULTAD-DE-DERECHO-.pdf (accessed 2 Nov 2024).

[549] The curriculum of the program is available at https://www.uned.ac.cr/ecsh/posgrado/maestria-profesional-en-propiedad-intelectual (accessed 2 Nov 2024).

[550] Observation by the author in 2008.

[551] For example, in late October 2008, the author attended a Seminar on IP law in San José, Costa Rica, with about 100 participating lawyers mostly from this country (but also many visitors from other Central American countries), which is considerable given its population of about 5 million.

[552] See https://www.aippi.org/news/first-central-american-and-caribbean-aippi-group-annual-congress-took-place-on-21st-july-in-san-salvador-el-salvador/ (accessed 2 Nov 2024).

[553] Arenales & Skinner-Klee (2010), p. 112-113; the establishment of good working relationships is facilitated by such law firms hiring IP Register personnel, see Sect. 2.5.3.

2.5.7 Other Stakeholders

Many stakeholders in society resist the new IP rules created by bilateral FTAs, which are perceived as "imposed" by the USA (and/or the EU) and not beneficial from a local policy perspective. Local businesses are traditionally not interested in actively using IP rights and, therefore, opposed any strengthening of the IP system.[554] The public often does not consider counterfeiting or piracy to be a crime, which may be partly due to the fact that some people make their living by selling pirated goods on street markets and partly due to a practically different understanding of what is "legal". In her anthropological studies into trademark piracy in the Guatemalan highlands, *Kendron Thomas* notes that the understanding of crimes and illegal acts especially among poor people is influenced by the widespread impunity (which is common in many Latin American countries) and the observation that sometimes the police resells apprehended pirated goods. Based on her observations, she cautions that the idea that criminalizing certain activities will automatically have a deterring effect and reduce illicit activities is "misguided".[555] The skepticism of local stakeholders is strongest with regard to patents. Traditionally, the Central American countries have not been very innovative (if measured by patent terms) and its universities and private companies have generated few patent applications. Local companies mainly obtained trademarks and subsequently collective marks and geographical indications.

It appears widely accepted that governments and publicly funded research institutions play an important role in the promotion of innovation and advancing technology,[556] and the key role of universities for innovation has been recognized in Central America.[557] Nevertheless, the universities in the region have not (yet) established a culture of legally protecting innovation and a positive attitude toward using the IP system.

Also, during the implementation of CAFTA-DR, several domestic business sectors strongly opposed the IP rules. In particular, the local producers and distributors of generic pharmaceuticals criticized the broader protection for pharmaceuticals based on test data protection and patent linkage as unbalanced and exerting "a particularly high cost on the health systems and agricultural sectors of the poor countries of Central America and the Dominican Republic".[558]

---

[554] As described by, e.g., Montero Sequeira (2003), many locals consider IP protection to be beneficial only for foreign right holders.

[555] Thomas (2012), p. 791.

[556] Stiglitz (2006), p. 32.

[557] Costa Rica, Conceptual Proposal for a National Action Plan, December 2002, p. 15, available at http://sice.oas.org/TPD/USA_CAFTA/Negotiations/Trade_Capacity/NAP_CRI_e.pdf (accessed 2 Nov 2024).

[558] Román Macaya in a briefing by the Costa Rican National Chamber of Generic Products, see Macaya (2005), p. 1; Díaz (2006), p. 50.

However, this negative attitude is starting to change. Central American governments officially declared that effective IP protection and administration are important.[559] Also, domestic entities increasingly make use of the IP system. Regarding patents, while the traditional approach of university scientists is to treat their research results as a public good, there seems to be an emerging interest at universities to start to file patent applications. One of the few examples of institutionalized IP management in Central America exists in the *University of Costa Rica* (UCR). The UCR maintains an IP department called *PROINNOVA*. But if at all, patent applications are often filed in the USA, because of the problems regarding expedient patent prosecution in Costa Rica itself.[560]

While from an economic perspective the lack of protection in the small domestic market might not seem important, the application in English and in a foreign country is nevertheless more difficult and costly, complicating protection and exploitation. Sometimes universities become part of the patent administration process in Central America, if they assume examination responsibilities for registries without internal examiners.[561] But generally they are users of the patent system. However, there is little cooperation between universities and the private sector in Latin America in general.[562] Therefore, the possibility of exploiting, and in turn protecting, inventions are often not relevant and universities file few patents. In addition, scientists often prefer not to privatize publicly funded inventions. As a result, few patent applications are filed by universities.

Practically, the most relevant area is the increased use of distinctive signs. Especially the powerful coffee industry is actively creating a portfolio of trademarks and geographical indications to position itself in the global marketplace in several countries.[563] This can create a stronger impulse for the respective government and administration to facilitate the utilization of the IP system than the obligations under bilateral FTAs regarding the legislative protection of (foreign) right holders.

Regarding counterfeit apparel, "for many producers, piracy remains a routine part of the manufacturing and marketing process. Some producers however have created their own brands, for instance, using indigenous symbols and signs from Classic Maya hieroglyphs to terms from their native *Kaqchikel*."[564] The garment manufacturers in highland Guatemala (and presumably in other Central American regions) use not only pirated foreign brands, but also self-created designs. These designs are often copied by local competitors, if they are successful.[565] As legal protection is

---

[559] Ministry of Economy of Guatemala (2002), p. 23.

[560] See Sect. 2.5.3.2.

[561] See Sect. 2.5.3.

[562] See Sect. 6.1.5.3.

[563] See Sect. 4.3.

[564] Thomas (2009), p. 6.

[565] A garment manufacturer in highland Guatemala can copy international fashion brands easily and without significant legal risk, but it is just as easy for local competitors to copy original design patterns created by this manufacturer, see Thomas (2012), p. 806.

practically not available, they must utilize other "evasive" action to keep their designs hidden from their competitors, e.g., by selling their products not openly on local markets, but during the night, in their shop or directly to customers.[566]

2.6 Competition Law and General Concepts Relating to IP

In order to comprehensively analyze the legal framework relating to IP, it is necessary to discuss the competition law framework as well, because of the complementarity of the two areas of law and their joint objective of protecting "dynamic competition".[567] In particular, it must be clarified how competition law is used to restrict abuses of IP rights. This becomes even more relevant when, as in the case of CAFTA-DR, the level of IP protection is raised. The concern is that too broad protection, as such, will overly restrict competition by conferring market dominance.[568]

Other issues of general relevance for the IP system are the concept of exhaustion and conflict of laws principles, which are analyzed in Sects. 2.6.2 and 2.6.3 below.

2.6.1 Competition Law

2.6.1.1 Policy Considerations

Generally speaking, the violation of competition law in the field of IP requires (1) a dominant market position based on IP protection and (2) the abuse of this position. Whether the protection of IP rights actually confers market dominance in a given case depends on the type of right, the respective market and the level of protection.[569] Trademarks and patents affect competition in different ways. Because of the basic objective of trademarks to distinguish products, without restricting the use of functional elements, they are less likely to negatively affect competition.[570] In the field of patent law, there are several constraints and exceptions limiting the actual market power of the right holder. One way to maintain competition is to allow the use of IP rights by third parties if compensation is paid, *e.g.*, the right to issue

[566] Thomas (2012), p. 806.

[567] See Sect. 1.6.2.

[568] Market dominance is the power to behave "to an appreciable extent" independently of its competitors or customers, see CJEU, United Brands v Commission 27/76, ECR 1978, 207; CJEU Hoffmann-La Roche 85/76, ECR 1979, 461.

[569] Drexl (2004), p. 793.

[570] On the contrary, they enable consumers to make informed choices and thus foster competition. This might be different in cases where the number of available forms is limited, e.g., in relation to color trademarks (see Sect. 4.1.2.3.

compulsory licenses to pharmaceutical patents to allow generic versions of a drug to enter the market.[571] In such cases the discretionary power of the right holder is limited to the amount of compensation that has to be paid.[572] Investigations of the competition agencies in the USA and Europe have analyzed several types of anti-competitive behavior in this area, including obtaining IP rights in a fraudulent way, anti-competitive license practices (including refusal-to-deal) and the abusive enforcement of IP rights.[573]

2.6.1.2 Legal Framework

International Law

In accordance with the complementary view of IP and competition law, TRIPS authorizes WTO members to apply national competition laws to IP-related cases.[574] Article 40 TRIPS relates to anti-competitive licensing practices and requires that they constitute an abuse of the IP rights and have an adverse effect on competition. In addition, Article 31(k) TRIPS allows the issuance of compulsory licenses in case of anti-competitive practices.[575] Article 8(2) TRIPS allows the prevention of the abuse of IP rights by right holders. Such abuse could represent anti-competitive behavior, *e.g.*, the refusal-to-deal by a dominant right holder.[576]

Because the WTO members are permitted under TRIPS to implement the control of IP law by competition law, an explicit clause to this effect is not necessary in bilateral FTAs. Nevertheless, the FTAs concluded by the USA generally provide for the restriction of anti-competitive behavior.[577] However, rules on anti-competitive

---

[571] This option was used with great effect by the Brazilian government. When the companies owning the patents for certain HIV drugs demand prices for their drugs in Brazil that inhibited the responsible agency to provide treatment to citizens, the Brazilian government threatened to issue compulsory licenses, if prices were not substantially lowered. Because of the risks of losing revenues completely and (maybe even more) of generic production facilities being built in a large developing country, the companies complied for years and significantly lowered the costs for HIV treatment in Brazil (and other Latin American countries). So far, only one compulsory license was issued in Brazil, in May 2007. President Lula signed Decree Nr. 6.108 on 24 May 2007, thereby issuing licenses for the patents protecting the drug Efavirenz, see Böttger (2008), pp. 887–888.

[572] Beyond the scope of this study, it can be noted that also copyright can convey market dominance, e.g., CJEU, Joined Cases C-241/91 P and 242/91 P, *Radio Telefis Eireann et al. v Commission ("Magill"), ECR* 1995 I-00743, see also IIC 1996, 78; this case is discussed by, e.g., Drexl (2004), pp. 792–793.

[573] For example, regarding practices in the pharmaceutical industry, see in particular CJEU, Case C-457/10 P, AstraZeneca v Commission [2012] EU:C:2012:770; see also European Commission (2008), p. 1.

[574] Articles 8.2 and 40 TRIPS.

[575] Compulsory licenses are analyzed in more detail in Sect. 3.1.11.2.

[576] Drexl (2014), p. 284.

[577] See Article 1501 NAFTA.

practices in relation to IP rights have been used inconsistently over time: Article 1704 NAFTA allows the parties to specify anti-competitive "licensing practices or conditions". There is no reference to competition law in the IP chapter of the Singapore FTA.[578] Article 15.1(15) CAFTA-DR contains the broadest rule, which allows the restriction of all types of anti-competitive practices, not just licensing. The reference to competition law was again omitted in the IP chapter of the Korean FTA (KORUS).[579] In contrast to this restrictive approach, the TPP contains commitments to adopt or maintain national competition laws that make anticompetitive business conduct illegal and to apply these competition laws to all commercial activities in their territories.[580]

The FTAs of the EU take a different approach in relation to competition law. Articles 125 to 130 EU-CARIFORUM-EPA provide a framework for competition policy, including obligations to pass competition laws, establish competition agencies and cooperate in the field of competition policy. Articles 277 to 282 EU-CA-AA contain similar provisions.[581] In addition, Articles 278 EU-CA-AA enumerates certain types of anti-competitive behavior "incompatible with" the EU-CA-AA.[582]

Central America

Most countries in Central America have enacted competition legislation. Costa Rica enacted the Competition Law (CR)[583] to "effectively protect the rights and legitimate interests of the consumer; monitor and promote the competitive process and free competition by preventing and prohibiting monopolies, monopolistic practices,

---

578 Singapore has adopted a competition law following the conclusion of the US Singapore FTA; Article 12.2 Singapore FTA required Singapore to adopt measures to "proscribe anticompetitive business conduct", establish an authority responsible for the enforcement of such measures and to enact a competition law.

579 The IP Chapter of KORUS (Chapter 18) does not contain such a rule, and there is also no reference in the Competition Chapter (16), which features in KORUS for the first time.

580 USTR, The Trans-Pacific Partnership - Detailed Summary of US Objectives (2015), p. 23, available at https://ustr.gov/sites/default/files/TPP-Detailed-Summary-of-US-Objectives.pdf (accessed 2 Nov 2024).

581 The provisions affecting regional integration are discussed in Sect. 2.6.1.3.

582 These are, in so far as they may affect trade between the Parties:

(a) agreements between undertakings, decisions by associations of undertakings and concerted practices between undertakings, which have as their object or effect the prevention, restriction or distortion of competition as specified in their respective competition laws;
(b) any abuse by one or more undertakings of a dominant position or a substantial market power or notable market participation, as specified in their respective competition laws; and
(c) concentrations between undertakings, which significantly impede effective competition, as specified in their respective competition laws (emphasis added).

583 Law for the promotion of competition and effective defense of the consumer (Ley de Promoción de la Competencia y Defensa Efectiva del Consumidor), Law No. 7472, adopted on 20 December 1994, entered into force on 19 January 1995.

and other restrictions on efficient market operation, and eliminate unnecessary regulations affecting economical activities".[584] In addition, Article 19 Patent and Design Law (CR) provides for compulsory licenses if the competition agency (*Comisión para Promover la Competencia*) determines that the right holder has used anti-competitive practices.[585]

In the Dominican Republic, the protection of competition is mandated by Article 50 Constitution (DR),[586] which (1) mandates the protection of the exercise of free enterprise, trade, and industry, (2) prohibits monopolies of private corporations and (3) authorizes the state to retain authority to exercise certain economic and strategic activities. Furthermore, penalties can be imposed in cases where competition is threatened by acts of price-fixing, rumor-spreading or collusion among business executives.[587]

In El Salvador, competition law is governed by the Competition Law (SV), which was amended in 2021.[588] Salvadorian law seems to follow the traditional view that competition law does not apply to the exercise of IP rights.[589]

Honduras enacted the Competition Law (HN) to "promote and protect the exercise of free competition to facilitate efficient market function and consumer welfare".[590]

Nicaragua passed the Competition Law (NI) in 2006 and a corresponding regulation in 2007 as the basis of its competition law.[591] Competition law shall "promote and monitor free competition among economic agents and guarantee the efficiency of the market and consumer welfare by encouraging the culture of competition, and by preventing, prohibiting or sanctioning anticompetitive practices".[592]

In Guatemala, there is no specific competition legislation. Like in the Dominican Republic, in Guatemala, the Constitution mandates the protection of free competition, in particular the prevention of the concentration of goods and means of production,[593] monopolies, privileged relationships and associations that tend to restrain the free market.[594] Also like in the Dominican Republic, anti-competitive behavior, *i.e.*, behavior that restricts free competition and involves monopolies, is

[584] Article 1 Competition Law (CR).

[585] Alvarez/Horna (2008), p. 100.

[586] The text of the Constitution is available at https://www.cijc.org/es/NuestrasConstituciones/REP%C3%9ABLICA-DOMINICANA-Constitucion.pdf (accessed 2 Nov 2024).

[587] Articles 419 and 420 Criminal Code (DR), the text of the law is available at https://www.wipo.int/wipolex/en/legislation/details/10813 (accessed 2 Nov 2024).

[588] The text of the law is available at https://www.sc.gob.sv/index.php/sala_multimedia/ley-de-competencia-reglamento-y-glosario/ (accessed 2 Nov 2024).

[589] Interview with *Carlos Castillo*.

[590] Article 1 Competition Law (HN); on this issue see also Alvarez/Horna (2008), p. 100.

[591] The text is available at https://www.wipo.int/wipolex/es/legislation/details/9854 (accessed 2 Nov 2024).

[592] Article 1 Competition Law (NI).

[593] Article 119(h) Constitution (GT).

[594] Article 130 Constitution (GT).

penalized.[595] However, despite the constitutional mandate, and even though the government officially recognized that competition policy requires the "appropriate legal frameworks to regulate anticompetitive practices",[596] no specific legislation has been passed. So far, there have been only law proposals which were discussed in parliament.[597]

On 11 May 2016, the Guatemalan Ministry of Economy presented a draft Competition Law to parliament, based on Articles 43, 119 and 130 Constitution (GT), to comply with the obligations under the EU-CA-AA.[598] However, the law has not yet been approved by the Guatemalan parliament.[599] The Guatemalan parliament has debated the draft once in 2018, but not subsequently and (as of September 2022) the law has not been approved.[600]

2.6.1.3 Institutional Framework

National Institutions

While most countries in Central America have enacted competition legislation, the institutional framework seems still insufficient. In Costa Rica, the responsible competition agency is the Competition Promotion Commission (*Comisión para Promover la Competencia, COPROCOM*). But the agency was considered not effective enough and law reforms aim at strengthening it.[601] The Dominican Republic created the National Competition Defense Commission (*Comisión Nacional de Defensa de la Competencia, PROCOMPETENCIA*) as the agency responsible for competition in 2011.[602] The agency in charge of executing the competition law in El Salvador is the Competition Superintendency (*Superintendencia de Competencia, SC*).[603] In Guatemala, there is no competition authority, which is not surprising, because there is also no competition legislation to establish such an agency.[604] In Honduras, the competition authority is the Competition Defense and Promotion

[595] Articles 340 and 341 Criminal Code (GT); Alvarez/Horna (2008), p. 100.

[596] Ministry of Economy of Guatemala (2002), p. 25.

[597] This includes, prior to 2016, an earlier competition law proposal, Law Nr. 4426, see AESA/EY (2022), p. 18.

[598] Aguilar Castillo Love (2020).

[599] Ibid.

[600] AESA/EY (2022), p. 18.

[601] Alvarez and Horna (2008), p. 102.

[602] Drexl (2014), p. 284.

[603] See OECD (2017), p. 2.

[604] The draft competition law proposes to establish a Competition Superintendency (*Superintendencia de Competencia, SC*), see Aguilar Castillo Love (2020).

Commission (*Comisión para la Defensa y Promoción de la Competencia, CDPC*).[605] The competition authority in Nicaragua is the National Competition Promotion Institute (*Instituto Nacional de Promoción de la Competencia, PROCOMPETENCIA*).[606]

Regional Integration

Article 125.1 EU-CARIFORUM-EPA references the CARICOM Competition Commission as a regional competition agency. However, the CARICOM Competition Commission has no jurisdiction in the Dominican Republic, which is only part of CARIFORUM, but not CARICOM.[607] Therefore, this institution is not analyzed further in this thesis.[608] The EU-CA-AA does not establish, but anticipates the establishment of regional competition legislation and institutions. Article 277.1 EU-CA-AA defines as the "competition law" of Central America

- "the Central American Competition Regulation (hereinafter referred to as "the Regulation") which shall be established according to Article 25 *Protocolo al Tratado General de Integración Económica Centroamericana (Protocolo de Guatemala)* and Article 21 *Convenio Marco para el Establecimiento de la Unión Aduanera Centroamericana* (Guatemala, 2007) and
- until such time as the Regulation is adopted [...] the national competition laws".

Similarly, 277.2 EU-CA-AA defines as "competition authority"

- a Central American Competition Body and
- until such time as the Central American Competition Body is established and becomes operational the national competition authorities.

Article 279.2 EU-CA-AA obliges the Central American countries to establish such regional competition legislation and institutions within a period of 7 years after the entry into force of the EU-CA-AA. Many substantive provisions of the agreement are provisionally applied, but the agreement is not yet in force.[609] Accordingly, the implementation period has not yet started.

The Central American countries initiated projects to create both regional competition legislation (*Norma Regional de la Competencia* (NRC)) and a joint competition authority (*Autoridad Centroamericana de la Competencia* (ARC)) within the Central American Network of Competition Authorities (*Red Centroamericana de Autoridades Nacionales Encargadas del Tema de Competencia*, RECAC), but progress is slow. A predecessor of RECAC was created in 2006, which was renamed

---

605 See OECD (2017), p. 2.

606 Ibid.

607 This distinction is expressed, e.g., in Article 125.1 EU-CARIFORUM-EPA.

608 On the CARICOM Competition Commission see Drexl (2012), p. 231.

609 Regarding the status of the ratification of the EU-CA-AA, see Sect. 2.3.1.

RECAC in 2012. El Salvador, Honduras, Nicaragua and Panama joined RECAC prior to or in 2012. However, also in 2012, Guatemala suspended its participation and, since 2014, the country has observer status.[610] At the end of 2016, Costa Rica was in the process of signing the underlying agreement and the Dominican Republic was considering the participation in the project[611] and by December 2017, both Costa Rica and the Dominican Republic have joined RECAC.[612]

2.6.1.4 Practical Relevance

Legal and factual monopolies play an important role in the Central American economy. While cartels and other anti-competitive behavior exist in all countries, both developed and developing, and the discovery of individual cases of anti-competitive behavior is no sign that competition is particularly weak, there are factors which make Central America particularly susceptible to restrictions of free competition.

First, state monopolies have a strong tradition in Central America, as in all Latin America, as a result of the development policy advocated by the UN and CEPAL for decades.[613] In Costa Rica, the telecom and insurance monopolies had to be abolished under CAFTA-DR rules, which was perhaps the most controversial part of the entire agreement in this country.[614]

Second, especially small economies, like the ones of the Central American countries, are often highly concentrated.[615] The protection of the free market is particularly important in Central America, because small countries face several socio-economic factors restricting competition and are more susceptible to market dominance than large markets.[616] Stronger protection of IP is more likely to create market dominance in small, developing economies like Central America than in large, developed economies like the USA or the EU. In large markets, there is a higher probability that alternative ways to meet a specific demand exist, in which case the market power of the right holder is limited to the efficiency or quality difference in relation to the alternative supply ("substitution competition").[617]

Another problem is a lack of political support for competition law enforcement. An OECD report notes with regard to Panama that the "lack of [political protection

---

[610] Olmedo (2015), pp. 7-8.

[611] Escolán and Schatan (2017), p. 25; as the reference to "network" in the title already implies, RECAC has no decision-making authority, but is mainly active in competition advocacy and technical cooperation, see Escolán and Schatan (2017), p. 26.

[612] See OECD (2017), p. 2.

[613] See Sect. 2.1.3.

[614] See Sect. 2.2.2.

[615] OECD/IDB (2010), p. 12.

[616] Alvarez and Horna (2008), p. 107.

[617] Drexl (2007), p. 20.

of the competition agency] against special interests who are threatened by the [a] gency's pro-competitive [...] work".[618] This assessment may apply similarly to other Central American countries.[619]

2.6.1.5 Evaluation

Because of the possibility of anti-competitive use of IP rights, any strengthening of these rights should be accompanied by an adaptation of competition law and policy.[620] TRIPS allows the WTO members to provide for competition policy complementing and balancing the stronger IP protection.[621] However, the lack of explicit competition safeguards in many FTAs seems to underline the bias of these agreements towards the interest of right holders, while disregarding the public interest in protecting competition. It is, therefore, a helpful clarification that Article 15.1(15) CAFTA-DR permits explicitly "measures necessary to prevent anticompetitive practices that may result from the abuse of the intellectual property rights". One could criticize that this provision does not explain how to distinguish between legal and anti-competitive use of IP rights. However, as *Josef Drexl* cautions, considerable divergence exists between different (developed) jurisdictions as to the most appropriate balancing rules, *e.g.*, regarding anti-competitive use of IP rights.[622] *Drexl* gives the example of anti-competitive use of licenses.[623] In such case, including specific flexibilities in the text of an agreement could preempt a discussion on the national level as to the appropriate scope of the limitation and ultimately restrict the use utilization of competition law tools to balance the extension of IP rights. Therefore, the more flexible approach used by CAFTA-DR actually leaves more policy space to the national legislators (whether they make use of this opportunity is another question). Likewise, the EU-CARIFORUM-EPA and the EU-CA-AA include substantial competition sections.[624] As has been shown in this section, the Central American countries have deficits on the institutional side in relation to the protection of competition and, therefore, competition law does not play a significant practical role. It is, therefore, important to build capable competition authorities. A joint competition authority in Central America, similar to the CARICOM Competition Commission created by the CARICOM parties as required by Articles 277 and 279 EU-CA-AA, could alleviate some of the concerns discussed above, because it could, to some extent, balance on the regional level the national

[618] OECD/IDB (2010), p. 66.

[619] As explained to the author by local practitioners in the CAFTA-DR countries, businesses often receive political protection for the market exclusivity enabling additional profit margins.

[620] Drexl (2007), p. 21.

[621] Drexl (2014), p. 284.

[622] Drexl (2007), p. 21.

[623] Ibid.

[624] See Sect. 2.6.1.2.

self-interest of individual states and the political influence of legal or factual monopolies existing on the national level.[625] Such integration is politically challenging in Central America, however, because of the power of state-owned monopolies and established economic players.[626] Not surprisingly, the activities in the region to this effect by RECAC have so far not led to any tangible results in terms of regional institutions.

2.6.2 Exhaustion of Rights

The term "exhaustion" refers to the limitation of IP rights by establishing that, once a product protected by an IP right has been sold by the owner of the right or by others with consent of the owner, the rights can no longer be exercised to prevent further use or sales of this product. The right has been "exhausted". Sometimes this limitation is also called the "first sale doctrine".[627] In the EU, the *Court of Justice of the European Union* (CJEU) applies the principle of international exhaustion for the internal market, thus creating a regional exhaustion regime, and the principle of national exhaustion for imports from third countries.[628] In the USA, the principle of national exhaustion was applied as a matter of legal practice. However, on 30 May 2017, the US Supreme Court reversed long-standing Federal Circuit precedent and held that, in relation to patents, the "first sale doctrine" applies globally, thereby establishing the principle of international exhaustion for the USA.[629] National (or regional) exhaustion could have the advantage of encouraging foreign direct investment and the transfer of technology, but leaves the country (or the region) unprotected against market segmentation and price discrimination. International exhaustion prevents such practices, but facilitates importation and could, therefore, discourage foreign investment and the transfer of technology.[630] As a compromise, *WIPO* proposes the concept of "controlled national exhaustion": In principle, exhaustion only occurs at the national level, unless IP rights are abused and/or the product is not made available in sufficient quantity or quality or at reasonable prices. In such cases, a competent national authority may, *ex officio* or upon request,

---

[625] Similarly, Drexl (2012), p. 242, who focuses on the role of "state-owned incumbents" in former socialist transition economies; however, as the examples of the telecom and insurance monopolies in Costa Rica have shown, this issue also exists in countries without any socialist history; regarding the CARICOM Competition Commission see Drexl (2014), p. 284.

[626] In this, Central America is no different from other developing regions. On the political dimension of regional competition policy-making see Geber (2012), pp. 259–262.

[627] WIPO, International Exhaustion and Parallel Importation, 2012 (on file with the author).

[628] The CJEU established this principle in Silhouette International Schmied GmbH & Co. KG v Hartlauer Handelsgesellschaft mbH, case C-355/96, ECR 1998, I-4799.

[629] *Impression Products, Inc. v. Lexmark, Int'l, Inc.*, 137 S. Ct. 1523 (2017).

[630] See WIPO, Public Policy-related Assistance - Flexibilities, available at https://www.wipo.int/ip-development/en/policy/flexibilities.html (accessed 2 Nov 2024).

consider that the sale of that product under a parallel IP right owned by the same IP owner (or someone under his/her control) has exhausted the respective IP right. According to WIPO, countries increasingly choose this third option (although WIPO provides very few examples).[631]

The regulation of the exhaustion of rights is, therefore, one of the most practically relevant elements in the IP system.[632] However, international agreements do not address this controversial issue. CAFTA-DR and the EU-CARIFORUM-EPA refrain entirely from referring to the topic. Article 6 TRIPS states explicitly that "nothing in this Agreement shall be used to address the issue of the exhaustion of intellectual property rights". It has been argued that the unconditional prohibition of parallel imports would constitute a restriction of trade liberalization and thus violate one of the TRIPS objectives. Under this view an "unconditional" national exhaustion regime would violate TRIPS. However, this interpretation is in conflict with the explicitly restrictive approach of Article 6 TRIPS.[633] The EU-CA-AA states that "(t)he Parties shall be free to establish their own regime for exhaustion of intellectual property rights, subject to the provisions of the TRIPS Agreement".[634] Article 273 EU-CA-AA states that "there shall be no obligation to apply [border measures] procedures to imports of goods put on the market in another country by or with the consent of the right holder". These provisions confuse more than they clarify, because, as just discussed, it is subject to debate whether TRIPS provides for any exhaustion requirements at all. Also, the explicit permission of international exhaustion in Article 273 EU-CA-AA raises the questions whether international exhaustion is considered by the EU-CA-AA not to be in line with the TRIPS requirements. If international exhaustion is considered permitted under TRIPS, the clause seems redundant.

In the absence of international regulation, the Central American countries can choose between national (or regional) and international exhaustion. They generally provide for international exhaustion for patents and trademarks.[635] For trademarks, this usually requires that the packaging of the product bearing the trademark was not modified.[636] While this system may, as just discussed, be detrimental to technology

[631] Ibid.; the document does not give examples, one country identified by WIPO elsewhere is Oman, see WIPO, Committee on Development and Intellectual Property (CDIP) (2012).

[632] Heath (2008), p. 216, emphasizes the importance of international exhaustion for unrestricted trade.

[633] There are two different interpretations of Article 6 TRIPS, the procedural approach, which considers Article 6 TRIPS to be limited to the exclusion of exhaustion from the dispute settlement process, and the substantive view, under which Article 6 TRIPS generally excludes the issue of exhaustion from the TRIPS agreement, see Schmidt-Pfitzner, Jan Hendrik / Schneider, Mathias in: Busche et al. (2013), Article 16, Nr 12-16 with further references.

[634] Article 232 EU-CA-AA.

[635] This principle is explicitly stated, e.g., in Nicaragua in Article 29 Trademark Law (NI) and Article 47 Patent and Design Law (NI) and in Costa Rica in Article 27 Trademark Law (CR).

[636] See, e.g., Article 37 IP Law (GT).

transfer, it prevents the abuse of rights and is probably beneficial for the consumers in Central America.

2.6.3 *Conflict of Laws*

The increase in IP-related trade and the new digital means to share and access knowledge raise the issue of cross-border IP disputes.[637] This issue is addressed by the principles of the conflict of laws. As there are no international agreements on this matter, several proposals have been put forward to provide guidance, for legal disputes in general the draft convention by the Hague Conference on Private International Law, and for IP-related cases, the drafts by the American Law Institute[638] and the Max Planck Group on the Conflict of Laws in Intellectual Property (CLIP).[639] However, despite the existing problems created by the principle of territoriality and the consequences of forum shopping, on the global level no rules have yet been adopted on the matter.[640] In the Central American Common Market, unlike in the European Union, there are no regional regulations of the conflict of laws.[641] This is not surprising given that the level of integration in the region is much lower. Because the integration or harmonization of IP law is even less than the economic integration, there are also no specific provisions on conflict of laws in this field.

References

Abbott FM (2009) Cross-Retaliation in TRIPS: Options for Developing Countries, ICTSD Programme on Dispute Settlement and Legal Aspects of International Trade Series, Issue paper No. 8, International Centre for Trade and Sustainable Development. Available at https://papers.ssrn.com/sol3/papers.cfm?abstract_id=1415802. Accessed 2 Nov 2024

AESA/EY (2022) Legal review of the Central American Competition framework. Available at https://trade.ec.europa.eu/access-to-markets/en/country-assets/Activity%20E-Competition%20Framework%20in%20Central%20America_fv.pdf. Accessed 2 Nov 2024

[637] Cornish et al. (2013), at Nr 2-71, 2-86.

[638] See Cornish et al. (2013), at Nr 2-71, fn 329.

[639] The CLIP principles are available at https://www.ip.mpg.de/fileadmin/ipmpg/content/clip/Final_Text_1_December_2011.pdf (accessed 2 Nov 2024).

[640] The Hague Conference of Private International Law proposed a draft convention relating to certain conflict of law issues in relation to IP, which was, however, not adopted, see Cornish et al. (2013), at Nr 2-86.

[641] In the EU, this topic is covered by the Brussels I Regulation; on the interpretation of the Brussels I Regulation see the decisions of the CJEU C-04/03 (GAT vs LUK) and C-539/03 (Roche) of 13 July 2006.

Aguilar Castillo Love (2020) In review: the legislative framework for private antitrust enforcement in Guatemala. Available at https://www.lexology.com/library/detail.aspx?g=a7f17dfd-d6b5-4d47-86a8-7f5465dc3778. Accessed 2 Nov 2024

Alvarez AM, Horna P (2008) Implementing competition law and policy in Latin America: the role of technical assistance. Chi-Kent Law Rev 83:91–127

Arenales & Skinner-Klee (2010) World Trademark Review, Anti-counterfeiting 2010 – A Global Guide – Guatemala, p. 111 (on file with the author)

Baquero-Herrera M (2005) Open regionalism in Latin America: an appraisal. Law Bus Rev Am 11: 139

Barton JH (2007) The future of the intellectual property system and consequent negotiation topics. In: Barton JH, Abbott FM, Correa CM, Drexl J, Foray D, Marchant R (eds) Views on the future of the intellectual property system. International Centre for Trade and Sustainable Development, Geneva, Switzerland

Beier F-K, Kunz HP (1972) Die Bedeutung des Patentrechts für den Transfer von Technologie in Entwicklungsländer. GRUR Int 1972:385–396

Bendaña-Guerrero GJ (1999) *Curso de Derecho* de Propiedad Industrial. Hispamer, Managua, Nicaragua

Bennett B (2015) Study on Accession to the Madrid system for the International Registration of Marks. Available at https://www.wipo.int/edocs/pubdocs/en/marks/954/wipo_pub_954.pdf. Accessed 2 Nov 2024

Böttger F (2008) Zwangslizenzen im Patentrecht - Eine systematische Bewertung der neueren Praxis insbesondere im Bereich der öffentlichen Gesundheit. GRUR Int 2008:881–891

Böttger F, Quarch T (2013) Brazil. In: Henning-Bodewig F (ed) International handbook on unfair competition. Nomos, Baden-Baden

Breuer A (2009) Costa Rica's 2007 Referendum on the Dominican Republic - Central American Free Trade Agreement (CAFTA-DR): citizen participation or manipulation? Representation 45(4):455–469. Available at http://papers.ssrn.com/sol3/papers.cfm?abstract_id=2179433. Accessed 2 Nov 2024

Busche J, Stoll P-T, Wiebe A (eds) (2013) TRIPS - Internationales und europäisches Recht des geistigen Eigentums, 2nd edn. Verlag, Carl Heymanns

Cabrera Medaglia JA (2010) The disclosure of origin requirement in Central America, ICTSD Programme on Natural Resources, International Trade and Sustainable Development, Issue Paper No.3. International Centre for Trade and Sustainable Development, Geneva, Switzerland

Castegnaro Montealegre M, Madrigal Azofeifa F (2016) La viabilidad de la implementación del protocol de Madrid en Costa Rica: Ventajas y desventajas, Tesis para optar por el grado de licenciatura en Derecho, Universidad de Costa Rica, San José

Cornish W, Llewelyn D, Aplin T (2013) Intellectual property: patents, copyright, trade marks and allied rights, 8th edn. Sweet & Maxwell (cited as Cornish et al. (2013))

Correa CM (1981) Transfer of technology in Latin America: a decade of control. J World Trade Law 15:388–409

Correa CM (2004) Bilateralism in intellectual property: defeating the WTO system for access to medicines. Case Western Reserv J Int Law 36:79

Correa CM (2004–2005) Investment protection in bilateral and Free Trade Agreements: implications for the granting of compulsory licenses. Mich J Int Law 26:331

Correa CM (2008) The push for stronger enforcement rules: implications for developing countries, ICTSD Programme on Intellectual Property Rights and Sustainable Development. ICTSD, Geneva

Devlin R, Estevadeordal A (2001) What's new in the new regionalism in the Americas?, Inter-American Development Bank, INTAL - ITD - STA, Working Paper No. 6. Available at https://publications.iadb.org/en/publication/whats-new-new-regionalism-americas. Accessed 2 Nov 2024

Díaz Á (2006) TLC y propiedad intelectual: Desafíos de Política Pública - en 9 países de América Latina y el Caribe, preliminary and unedited version, https://repositorio.cepal.org/server/api/core/bitstreams/44194f7d-0b13-41f0-be93-3553029996f6/content. Accessed 2 Nov 2024

Díaz Á (2008) América Latina y el Caribe: La propiedad intelectual después de los tratados de libre comercio, Comisión Económica para América Latina y el Caribe (CEPAL), Santiago de Chile

Dörmer S (1998) Streitbeilegung und neue Entwicklungen im Rahmen von TRIPS: eine Zwischenbilanz nach vier Jahren. GRUR Int 1998:919–934

Drahos P (2001) Bilateralism in Intellectual Property. Available at https://oxfamilibrary.openrepository.com/bitstream/handle/10546/111967/bilateralism-intellectual-property-041201-en.pdf?sequence=1&isAllowed=y. Accessed 2 Nov 2024

Drexl J (2004) Intellectual Property and Antitrust Law. IMS Health and Trinko - Antitrust Placebo for Consumers Instead of Sound Economics in Refusal-to-Deal Cases, IIC 2004, 788–808

Drexl J (2007) Responding to the challenges with a competition-oriented approach. In: Barton JH, Abbott FM, Correa CM, Drexl J, Foray D, Marchant R (eds) Views on the future of the intellectual property system. International Centre for Trade and Sustainable Development, Geneva, Switzerland

Drexl J (2012) Economic integration and competition law in developing countries. In: Drexl J, Bakhoum M, Fox EM, Gal MS, Gerber DJ (eds) Competition policy and regional integration in developing countries. Edward Elgar, Cheltenham

Drexl J (2014) Intellectual property and implementation of recent Bilateral Trade Agreement in the EU. In: Drexl J, Grosse Ruse-Khan H, Nadde-Phlix S (eds) EU Bilateral Trade Agreements and intellectual property: for better or worse?, MPI studies on intellectual property and competition law, vol. 20. Springer-Verlag, Berlin

Drexl J (2018) Internationales Immaterialgüterrecht, Münchener Kommentar zum BGB, Vol. 12, 7th edn. C. H. Beck, Munich

Escolán C, Schatan C (2017) Panorama y retos de la política de competencia en Centroamérica. Available at http://repositorio.cepal.org/bitstream/handle/11362/40014/4/S1700446_es.pdf. Accessed 2 Nov 2024

Escoto CM (2004) Intellectual Property Rights and Trade Enforcement Procedures in Costa Rica. Available at http://www.wipo.int/edocs/mdocs/enforcement/en/wipo_ace_2/wipo_ace_2_www_33725.doc. Accessed 2 Nov 2024

European Commission (2008) Pharmaceutical Sector Inquiry – Preliminary Report, Fact Sheet, Prices, time to generic entry and consumer savings. Available at https://competition-policy.ec.europa.eu/system/files/2022-05/pharmaceutical_sector_inquiry_factsheet_1_prices_time_to_generic_entry_and_consumer_savings.pdf. Accessed 2 Nov 2024

European Commission (2011) Highlights of the trade pillar of the Association Agreement between Central America and the European Union, 20 June 2011. Available at https://ec.europa.eu/commission/presscorner/detail/en/MEMO_11_429. Accessed 2 Nov 2024

European Commission (2015) Annual Report on the Implementation of Part IV of the EU-Central America Association Agreement, COM(2015) 131 final, 18 March 2015. Available at https://eur-lex.europa.eu/legal-content/EN/TXT/PDF/?uri=CELEX:52015DC0131. Accessed 2 Nov 2024

European Commission (2018) Factsheet: how the EU is putting the EPA into practice. Available at https://www.europarl.europa.eu/meetdocs/2014_2019/documents/dcar/dv/factsheet/factsheeten.pdf. Accessed 2 Nov 2024

European Commission, Executive Agency for Small and Medium-sized Enterprises (2019) Latin America IP SME Helpdesk – Central America IP country factsheet, Publications Office, 2019, https://data.europa.eu/doi/10.2826/267757. Accessed 2 Nov 2024

European Commission, Executive Agency for Small and Medium-sized Enterprises (2020) Latin America IP SME Helpdesk, El Salvador IP country factsheet, Publications Office of the European Union, 2023, https://data.europa.eu/doi/10.2826/422379. Accessed 2 Nov 2024

European Commission, Executive Agency for Small and Medium-sized Enterprises (2020) Latin America IP SME Helpdesk, Nicaragua IP country factsheet, Publications Office of the European

Union, 2024, https://intellectual-property-helpdesk.ec.europa.eu/publications/cfs-nicaragua_en#details. Accessed 2 Nov 2024
Geber DJ (2012) Regionalization, development and competition law: exploring the political dimension. In: Drexl J, Bakhoum M, Fox EM, Gal MS, Gerber DJ (eds) Competition policy and regional integration in developing countries. Edward Elgar, Cheltenham
Gil Abinader L (2015) Desempeño Institucional de la Oficina Dominicana de Patentes, Tesis de maestría, FLACSO, Buenos Aires
Grave HG (2002) Gewerbliche Schutzrechte in Mexiko - Eine Untersuchung vor dem Hintergrund der maßgeblichen Bestimmungen der NAFTA- und TRIPS-Abkommen. Nomos, Baden-Baden
Grosse Ruse-Khan H (2016) The protection of intellectual property in international law. Oxford University Press, Oxford
Hassemer M (2000) Gewerbliche Schutzrechte im Mercosur. Nomos, Baden-Baden
Heath C (2008) Harmonisation of international patent law? – A reply to Straus and Klunker. IIC 2008:210–216
Hernández RA (2007) Is the phasing out of the Agreement on Textiles and Clothing eroding competitiveness in Central America and the Dominican Republic?, CEPAL Review 93, December 2007. Available at https://repositorio.cepal.org/items/59565e72-af6c-4e55-b86e-8d1c4aaf2956. Accessed 2 Nov 2024
Hufbauer G, Kotschwar B (2000) The future of regional trading arrangements in the Western Hemisphere. In: Kreinin ME (ed) Building a partnership: the Canada-United States Free Trade Agreement. University of Calgary Press, Calgary
Industry Functional Advisory Committee on IPR for Trade Policy Matters (IFAC-3), The U.S.-Central American Free Trade Agreement (FTA) - The Intellectual Property Provisions (2004). Available at https://ustr.gov/archive/assets/Trade_Agreements/Regional/CAFTA/CAFTA_Reports/asset_upload_file571_5945.pdf. Accessed 2 Nov 2024
Jaramillo CF, Lederman D (2005) CAFTA-DR: challenges and opportunities for Central America. World Bank. Available at http://documents.worldbank.org/curated/en/249751468212969403/pdf/329530DR0CAFTA1Challenges.pdf. Accessed 2 Nov 2024
Koehler-Geib F, Clavijo M (2015) The context of CAFTA-DR in Costa Rica. In: Koehler-Geib F, Sanchez SM (eds) Costa Rica five years after CAFTA-DR: assessing early results. Directions in development. World Bank, Washington
Kotschwar B (1999) Small countries and the Free Trade Area of the Americas. In: Mendoza MR, Low P, Kotschwar B (eds) Trade rules in the making - challenges in regional and multilateral negotiations. Organization of American States, Washington
Kunz-Hallstein HP (1976) Revision der Pariser Verbandsübereinkunft zugunsten der Entwicklungsländer - neuere Entwicklungen und Vorschläge. GRUR Int 1976:64–75
Macaya R (2005) The economic and social consequences of an overprotection of intellectual property rights in CAFTA-DR, Briefing Paper, 2005
Malone MFT (2012) The rule of law in Central America: citizens' reactions to crime and punishment. Bloomsbury Academic
Markowski A (2004) Der gewerbliche Rechtsschutz in den Ländern der Andengemeinschaft. Nomos, Baden-Baden
Ministry of Economy of Guatemala (2002) National Action Plan for Trade Capacity Building in Guatemala, 12 December 2002. Available at http://www.sice.oas.org/TPD/USA_CAFTA/Negotiations/Trade_Capacity/NAP_GTM_e.pdf. Accessed 2 Nov 2024
Montero Sequeira A (2003) Propiedad intelectual: espina del Cafta, El Financiero, 24 March 2003 (on file with the author)
O'Regan CA, O'Regan PT (2015) Using GATT-TRIPs to improve development opportunities: a proposal for Central America. Hast Sci Technol Law J 7:1
OECD (2017) Global Forum on Competition, Challenges faced by Small Agencies and those in Developing Countries, Contribution from the RECAC, December 2017. Available at https://one.oecd.org/document/DAF/COMP/GF/WD(2017)27/en/pdf. Accessed 2 Nov 2024

OECD/IDB, Competition Law and Policy in Panama, A Peer Review (2010). Available at https://www.oecd.org/en/publications/2010/01/competition-law-and-policy-in-panama-a-peer-review-2010_d825288b.html. Accessed 2 Nov 2024

O'Keefe TA (2009) Latin American and Caribbean Trade Agreements, BRILL ACADEMIC PUB, Leiden

Olmedo E (2015) Hacia una Norma y Autoridad Regional de Competencia en Centroamérica. Available at http://www.sela.org/es/centro-de-documentacion/base-de-datos-documental/bdd/32638/hacia-una-norma-y-autoridad-regional-de-competencia-en-centroamerica. Accessed 2 Nov 2024

Overseas Security Advisory Council (OSAC) of the U.S. Department of State (2019) El Salvador 2019 Crime & Safety Report. Available at https://www.osac.gov/Content/Report/d1222be6-4e5d-461f-912c-15f4aec90b02. Accessed 2 Nov 2024

Palacios MA (2012) Datos de prueba y "patent linkage" en materia farmacéutica. Available at http://pdf.usaid.gov/pdf_docs/PA00HTM7.pdf. Accessed 2 Nov 2024

Pereira Goncalves M, Stephanou C (2006) Financial services and Trade Agreements in Latin America and the Caribbean: an overview. World Bank Paper, https://doi.org/10.1596/1813-9450-4181

PhRMA, Special 301 Submission 2007 (on file with the author)

Registro de la Propiedad Industrial de Costa Rica (2006) Situación actual de la Propiedad Industrial en Costa Rica, WIPO document OMPI/JPI/BUE/06/2 CR. Available at http://www.wipo.int/edocs/mdocs/lac/es/ompi_jpi_bue_06/ompi_jpi_bue_06_2_cr.doc. Accessed 2 Nov 2024

Registro de la Propiedad Intelectual de Nicaragua (2006) Situación Actual de la Propiedad Industrial en Nicaragua, OMPI/JPI/BUE/06/2 NI. Available at http://www.wipo.int/edocs/mdocs/lac/es/ompi_jpi_bue_06/ompi_jpi_bue_06_2_ni.doc. Accessed 2 Nov 2024

Rivera L, Rojas-Romagosa H (2007) Free Trade Agreements, Poverty and Inequality in Central America. Available at https://www.gtap.agecon.purdue.edu/resources/download/3458.pdf. Accessed 2 Nov 2024

Rodlauer M, Schipke A (2005) Central America: Global Integration and Regional Cooperation, International Monetary Fund Occasional Paper No. 243. Available at http://www.imf.org/external/pubs/ft/op/243/. Accessed 2 Nov 2024

Roffe P (2013) Free Trade Agreements and the Americas. IIC 2013:932–943

Rutledge PB (2012) TRIPS and BITs: an essay on compulsory licenses, expropriation, and international arbitration. North Carolina J Law Technol Online 13:149. Available at http://digitalcommons.law.uga.edu/fac_artchop/827. Accessed 2 Nov 2024)

Sanchez SM, Koehler-Geib F (2015) Overview. In: Koehler-Geib F, Sanchez SM (eds) Costa Rica Five Years after CAFTA-DR: assessing early results. Directions in Development. World Bank, Washington

Schwanen D (2004) Deeper, broader: a roadmap for a treaty with North America. In: Courchene TJ, Savoie DJ, Schwanen D (eds) The art of the state, vol. 2, Thinking North America, No. 4, 2004. Available at http://irpp.org/wp-content/uploads/2014/08/schwanen_roadmap.pdf. Accessed 2 Nov 2024

Stiglitz J (2006) Making globalization work. Norton, New York

Tharin M (2008) Dealing with a bad deal: two years of CAFTA-DR in Central America, Council on Hemispheric Affairs. Available at http://www.bilaterals.org/article.php3?id_article=13774. Accessed 2 Nov 2024

Thomas K (2009) Structural adjustment, spatial imaginaries, and "Piracy" in Guatemala's apparel industry. Anthropol Work Rev 30(1):1–10

Thomas K (2012) Intellectual property law and the ethics of imitation in Guatemala. Anthropol Quart 85(3):785–814

UNCTAD (2011) Investment Policy Review of Guatemala. Available at http://unctad.org/en/Docs/diaepcb201009_en.pdf. Accessed 2 Nov 2024

UNCTAD (2014) Transfer of technology and knowledge sharing for development - science technology and innovation issues for developing countries, UNCTAD Current Studies on

Science Technology and Innovation, No. 8. Available at http://unctad.org/en/PublicationsLibrary/dtlstict2013d8_en.pdf. Accessed 2 Nov 2024
Unterguggenberger T (1999) Das Urheberrecht in der Andengemeinschaft. Nomos, Baden-Baden
USTR, Special 301 Report 2016. Available at https://ustr.gov/sites/default/files/USTR-2016-Special-301-Report.pdf. Accessed 2 Nov 2024 (cited as USTR, Special 301 Report 2016)
USTR, Special 301 Report 2018. Available at https://ustr.gov/sites/default/files/files/Press/Reports/2018%20Special%20301.pdf. Accessed 2 Nov 2024 (cited as USTR, Special 301 Report 2018)
USTR, Special 301 Report 2023. Available at https://ustr.gov/sites/default/files/2023-04/2023%20Special%20301%20Report.pdf. Accessed 2 Nov 2024 (cited as USTR, Special 301 Report 2023)
USTR, CAFTA Policy Brief (2005) Free Trade With Central America and the Dominican Republic, Highlights of the CAFTA. Available at https://ustr.gov/archive/assets/Trade_Agreements/Regional/CAFTA/Briefing_Book/asset_upload_file834_7179.pdf. Accessed 2 Nov 2024
von Lewinski S (2016) The WTO/TRIPS dispute settlement mechanism: experiences and perspectives. In: Ullrich H, Hilty RM, Lamping M, Drexl J (eds) TRIPS Plus 20: from trade rules to market principles. Springer-Verlag, Berlin Heidelberg
WIPO (2017) Estudio de incidencia sobre la utilización del sistema de propiedad intelectual en Centroamérica y la República Dominicana. Available at https://www.wipo.int/export/sites/www/econ_stat/en/economics/docs/economics_studies_central_america.pdf. Accessed 2 Nov 2024
WIPO Committee on Development and Intellectual Property (CDIP) (2012) Interface between Exhaustion of Intellectual Rights and Competition Law, Eighth Session, Geneva, November 14 to 18, 2011, WIPO Doc. CDIP/8/INF/5 REV, 17 APRIL 2012. Available at https://www.wipo.int/edocs/mdocs/mdocs/en/cdip_8/cdip_8_inf_5_rev.doc. Accessed 2 Nov 2024
World Bank (2005) Guatemala - The Role of Judicial Modernization in Post Conflict Reconstruction and Social Reconciliation. Social Development Notes, No. 21, http://hdl.handle.net/10986/11233. Accessed 2 Nov 2024
WTO Council for Trade-Related Aspects of Intellectual Property Rights (2011) Technical Cooperation Activities: Information from Members, European Union, IP/C/W/550/Add.7, 1 June 2011. Available at https://docs.wto.org/dol2fe/Pages/SS/directdoc.aspx?filename=Q:/IP/C/W550A7.pdf. Accessed 2 Nov 2024
WTO Council for Trade-Related Aspects of Intellectual Property Rights (2013) Technical Cooperation Activities: Information from Members, European Union - Addendum, IP/C/W/593/Add.3, 4 October 2013. Available at https://docs.wto.org/dol2fe/Pages/FE_Search/DDFDocuments/119825/q/IP/C/W593A3.pdf. Accessed 2 Nov 2024
WTO Council for Trade-Related Aspects of Intellectual Property Rights (2015) Technical Cooperation Activities: Information from Members, European Union, IP/C/W/601/Add.7, 24/02/2015. Available at https://docs.wto.org/dol2fe/Pages/FE_Search/FE_S_S009-DP.aspx?language=E&CatalogueIdList=135144,135092,134874,134825,134826,134821,134669,134625,130538,128045&CurrentCatalogueIdIndex=8&FullTextHash. Accessed 2 Nov 2024
Yu PK (2006) Anticircumvention and anti-anticircumvention. Denv Univ Law Rev 84:13

Chapter 3
Inventions, Plant Varieties and Test Data

The patent, plant variety and test data provisions are probably the most controversial part of the IP chapter of CAFTA-DR. In particular, stronger patent protection, the extension of the exclusive right through data exclusivity and the patent linkage mechanism are considered to substantially increase the cost of, and thus limit the access to, medicines. The protection of plant varieties as provided for by the UPOV Convention (incorporated into CAFTA-DR) is criticized for creating a dependency of local farmers in Central America on multinational agrochemical corporations. In Costa Rica, for instance, the patent law requirements of CAFTA-DR were one of the two main reasons for the opposition against the ratification of the agreement, together with the liberalization of formerly monopolistic public services.

3.1 Patents

In Central America, the term "patent" (*patente*) is used in the broad sense of "permits", including also other publicly granted rights, especially the right to operate certain businesses, such as restaurants. These rights are referred to as *municipal patents* or *commerce patents*.[1]

Similar to the USA, the Central American laws use the term patent sometimes also for "related" rights, including utility models (sometimes referred to as *utility patents*) and designs (*design patents*). In this thesis, the term "patent" is used for patents in the narrow sense in accordance with the English terminology of international IP agreements.

[1] See for example "patents" granted for the establishment of companies in Guatemala according to Article 344 of the Commercial Code (*Codigo de Comercio*) of Guatemala.

F. Böttger, *CAFTA-DR, European Free Trade Agreements and the Industrial Property System in Central America*, Munich Studies on Innovation and Competition 21, https://doi.org/10.1007/978-3-031-93440-7_3

3.1.1 *Policy Considerations*

The evaluation of the patent system, in particular the level of protection established by CAFTA-DR, depends on the policy objectives patent protection is expected to achieve. In this section therefore, the main objectives underlying the patent system will be analyzed, *i.e.*, fostering innovation and facilitating the transfer of technology and moral and social objectives. TRIPS and CAFTA-DR emphasize innovation (in the narrow sense of inventive activity) and technology transfer, while critics of strong patent protection, and TRIPS-plus rules in particular, tend to emphasize moral and social objectives. Any patent system must balance these different objectives. However, it must be noted that there is little empirical guidance as to the ideal design of the patent system.[2]

3.1.1.1 Incentive to Innovate

General Considerations

Patent law should foster innovation and contribute to the transfer and dissemination of technology.[3] Inventions are global public goods that, once published, are available globally and can be used by anyone, including competitors.[4] The exclusive right conferred by the patent shall allow innovators to exclude competitors and recoup their research and development investment by charging higher prices and making higher profits, the so-called monopoly rent, thereby providing the incentive to innovate.[5] It is generally assumed that patent protection contributes to inventive activity if calibrated appropriately.[6]

To foster creativity and innovation is one of the purposes of CAFTA-DR, but not stated as one of the objectives included in the text of CAFTA-DR itself.[7] Objectives of the IP chapter are only the adequate and effective protection and enforcement of IP[8] and fair competition.[9] The assumption that (strong) patent protection has a

[2] See, e.g., the discussion of the public goods theory and the property rights theory by Drexl (2016), pp. 70–71; controversies regarding the determination of the right level of patent protection have been part of the patent system since its inception, see the historical analysis by Penrose (1951), who also identifies the difficulties in using economic models for such determination, see Penrose (1951), pp. 112–127, in particular 113, and 226–227.

[3] Article 7 TRIPS.

[4] See, e.g., Drexl (2016), p. 70.

[5] Ann (2022) § 3.II nr 10.

[6] See for a detailed analysis of the arguments see Ann (2022) § 3.VI nr 63.

[7] See the preamble of CAFTA-DR.

[8] Article 1.2(e) CAFTA-DR.

[9] Article 1.2(c) CAFTA-DR.

positive effect on innovation is usually referred to by multilateral and bilateral agreements containing patent law provisions.[10]

The analysis of the effects of patent protection on innovation requires a clear understanding of the scope of the term "innovation". In the narrow definition, "innovation" relates solely to the generation and industrial application of new technology, with "new" referring to a global perspective of novelty in the way it is used for inventions. This definition excludes the diffusion of existing technology to new users. It seems to underpin the wording of Article 7 TRIPS, which distinguishes between "technological innovation" and the "transfer and dissemination of technology". The same distinction is made by US-FTAs (though not explicitly by CAFTA-DR).[11]

The wider definition, which is used, e.g., by the United Nations (UNCTAD), argues that also the absorption of existing technology by new users should be considered to be innovation.[12] The same understanding is utilized in the Oslo Manual of the OECD.[13] Included into this concept of innovation are the adaptation of businesses to new methods of production and the dissemination of best practices, i.e., also the imitation by one company of new technology of another company qualifies as innovation.[14] This definition eliminates the terminological distinction between technology generation and technology transfer, which is made explicitly by Article 7 TRIPS. However, as it encompasses also the long-term social objective of making newly generated technology available to a broader user base (with the inherent effects on competition) it represents a more holistic view of the process of technological development. Therefore, and as it is more widely used, this wider definition is used in this thesis.

Irrespective of the terminology discussion, there is much debate about the validity of this rationale. Critics claim that patent protection makes future inventive activity more difficult and costly.[15] There might be other ways to permit sufficient monopoly rents, *e.g.*, through the first mover advantage only. However, this advantage is limited, if the costs of development are very high and the first mover advantage is only enjoyed for a short time, because the respective technology is easy to copy. This is the case, *e.g.*, with regard to pharmaceuticals.

Empirical research on this issue is inconclusive. Early studies by *Fritz Machlup* and *Edith Penrose* in the 1950s concluded that one could neither prove or disprove a positive effect of patent protection on innovation.[16] Several studies in subsequent

[10] See, e.g., Article 131.1 EU-CARIFORUM-EPA.

[11] See, e.g., the objectives stated in Chapter 17 of the US-Chile-FTA.

[12] UNCTAD (2006), pp. 127 and 155.

[13] OECD, Oslo Manual 2018, Sections 3.9 (on the definition of innovation) and 3.14 (on the inclusion of diffusion of technology).

[14] UNCTAD (2006), pp. 127 and 155.

[15] Stiglitz (2002), p. 245; Penrose (1951), pp. 112–127, in particular 113, and 226–227.

[16] Penrose (1951), p. 40, famously stated that "if national patent laws did not exist, it would be difficult to make a conclusive case for introducing them; but the fact that they do exist shifts the

decades also found no connection.[17] A study by *Lederman* and *Maloney*, however, found a significant connection between patent protection and R&D.[18] Such finding is in line with the underlying incentive framework: When a technology is patent protected, returns on investment will probably be significantly higher, and as a result, it will be easier for the patent owner to attract investment capital for the further development of the technology. If an invention is not patent protected, it can be easily copied by competitors and will not attract investors. Accordingly, there would be less incentive to further invent. It is widely acknowledged in legal literature that there is a positive effect of patent protection on inventive activity and that patent protection creates an incentive for inventions.[19]

However, the level of patent protection most conducive for inventive activity is disputed, not least because of the abovementioned empirical limitations. Also, from the general assessment that patent protection supports inventive activity it does not automatically follow that this is also true in countries without the technological and economic basis for inventive activity, or that the increased inventive activity adequately compensates the welfare loss from reduced competition. Already the analysis by *Edith Penrose* in the 1950s suggested that the global extension of patent protection incurs a heavy social cost by increasing prices and creating an inefficient use of resources.[20]

Innovation in Central America

This global assessment changes from the perspective of developing countries, especially small ones. Critics of strong patent protection argue that these countries are only consumers of innovative technology and would, therefore, be better off with low patent protection and easier and cheaper access to new technology. An economic analysis by *Klaus Liebig* concluded that the welfare loss due to the decrease in the incentive for innovation, because of weak patent protection in the respective country is clearly more than compensated by the welfare gain due to more competition and lower prices.[21] This corresponds to the earlier studies by *Edith Penrose*

---

burden of proof and it is equally difficult to make a really conclusive case for abolishing them"; similarly, Machlup (1958), p. 80, found that "[I]f we did not have a patent system, it would be irresponsible, on the basis of our present knowledge of its economic consequences, to recommend instituting one. But since we have had a patent system for a long time, it would be irresponsible, on the basis of our present knowledge, to recommend abolishing it."

[17] See Branstetter (2004), pp. 350–370, in particular the summary on pp. 369–370 and the references in Fn 51.

[18] Lederman and Maloney (2003), pp. 4, 13 and 18–19.

[19] Yu (2002), p. 635, cited by Helfer (2004), Fn 2; see also Heath (1996), pp. 1169–1185; Foray (2007), p. 4; Foray also points to the transactional efficiency patents provide by creating transferable rights and structuring technology transactions.

[20] Penrose (1951), pp. 112–127, in particular 113, and 226–227.

[21] Liebig (2005), pp. 95–100.

regarding the economic benefit of international patent protection for individual countries.[22] However, it must be noted that *Klaus Liebig's* analysis was limited to the effects in the respective country, if one considers also the effects in other countries, less patent protection could still result in a global welfare loss. In addition, critics argue that because of the low economic and technical development, developing countries lack the necessary resources and conditions for inventive activity. Therefore, the incentive created by patent law has no effect. Conversely, the (better) protection of patents benefits only foreign right holders and increases the costs for the domestic technological development. This is certainly the case in Central America. In particular, very few patents originate from local applicants. Internationally, only Costa Rican and Dominican entities filed successful patent applications (*i.e.*, which were later granted) prior to the implementation of CAFTA-DR.[23] In addition, the of local patents applications has not increased since CAFTA-DR entered into force, but rather remained constant or even slightly decreased (during the years 2010 and 2021, prior to this period only limited data was available).[24] This suggests that the level of local innovation has not changed, if measured by patent grants. In relation to the development of pharmaceuticals, the general considerations regarding the incentive to innovate are modified by specific industry and public health considerations discussed below.[25]

3.1.1.2 Technology Transfer

Types of Technology Transfer

Many international agreements like TRIPS and the EU-CARIFORUM-EPA expressly state that patent law should not only foster inventive activity, *i.e.*, generate new technology, but also enable technology transfer, especially with regard to developing countries.[26] Also some non-WIPO treaties recognize the importance of IP protection for technology transfer.[27] Behind the term "technology transfer" in the broad sense we find several different activities. The term usually refers to the explicit transfer of technology, but it also includes the implicit transfer of technology, the dissemination of technology and the absorption of technology. In the debate about technology transfer the term is mostly used in the narrow sense of *explicit technology transfer*. IP law influences the explicit technology transfer through the legal protection of technology and rules on licensing and other connected activities. *Implicit*

---

[22] Penrose (1951), pp. 112–127, in particular 113, and 226–227.

[23] According to the EPO statistics, the only patent granted to a Central American country between 2011 and 2016 was one granted to a patentee from the Dominican Republic.

[24] See Table 3.4.

[25] These will be discussed further in Sect. 3.1.1.4 and in relation to text data protection in Sect. 3.4.

[26] Article 132(e) EU-CARIFORUM-EPA.

[27] E.g., Article 16(2)(2), (3) CBD.

technology transfer occurs through the importation of products incorporating technology, *e.g.*, high-technology machinery. For many developing countries, it is the main form of technology transfer. But while it leads to higher productivity,[28] it does not increase the domestic knowledge base if the technology cannot be absorbed. The main policy measure to increase this type of technology transfer is lowering tariffs on high-technology imports. IP policy influences this effect by establishing a national or international exhaustion regime, prohibiting or allowing cheaper parallel imports. Both implicit and explicit technology transfer only serve the domestic knowledge base if the technology is disseminated to others. The patent system supports this *dissemination of technology* by the publication requirement for patent information, which facilitates the use and further development of innovation. This obviously depends on the accessibility of these publications.[29] The effective utilization and exploitation of transferred technology requires also the *absorption of technology* in the production and business processes. The understanding and incorporation of new technology is demonstrated by successful imitation or follow-on inventive activity.[30] The main obstacle in developing countries for absorption is the lack of technical education of the workforce. IP protection can support this process by creating an environment where contractual technical cooperation is possible that includes not only the transfer of technology but also enables effective absorption through training and the transfer of know-how.

General Considerations

Generally, the assumption is that patent protection creates legal certainty and thus establishes a market for technology, enabling contractual transfer. Empirical studies also conclude that stronger IP protection leads to more technology transfer.[31] The historical experience also suggests that patent protection is supportive of or even necessary for technology transfer. It should be remembered that the incentive for technology transfer was the reason for the first patent-like privileges granted in the Middle Ages, e.g., for the introduction of the printing press in the Republic of Venice,[32] and for the patent protection of foreign technology in the Soviet Union, which was introduced because the former lack of protection significantly impeded technology transfer. Interestingly, the Soviet Union did not provide similar patent

---

[28] Stiglitz (2006), pp. 30–31.

[29] The status and accessibility of the publication of patent literature by the Central American IP Registers is discussed in Sect. 2.5.3.

[30] It is probably in this sense that the UNCTAD considers imitation to be one form of innovation, see UNCTAD (2006), p. 68.

[31] Branstetter (2004), pp. 368–369, found that more patent protection leads to more technology transfer. His study was based on license revenues, but he found that not only the fees increased, but that there was "real deployment of new technology".

[32] See, e.g., Osterrieth (2015), Nr 75.

protection for domestic inventions, but had to grant exclusive protection to foreign technology in order to enable technology transfer.[33]

But there is also evidence from *Central America* showing the necessity of legal protection of technology to enable its transfer. Policies restricting patent protection were largely unsuccessful, maybe even counterproductive. For a long time, the attitude of the Central American countries toward IP protection was strongly influenced by its perceived negative impact on explicit technology transfer and the closing of the "knowledge gap" of developing countries. Since the 1960s, advised by CEPAL, Central and other Latin American countries wanted to restrict especially patent protection to facilitate access to foreign technology. Even during the 1980s and 1990s, when protection was extended in many regions, Central America continued with its restrictive IP policy, as reflected in the draft Central American Convention (Patents)[34] and the IP Law (GT) of 1985.

In Costa Rica, which is technologically more developed than the other Central American countries and, therefore, more capable of absorbing technology transfers, right holders try to protect their technology by means of confidentiality agreements, which permit more effective civil and criminal enforcement, because the protection provided by IP law is perceived as insufficient.[35] This behavior suggests that the legal protection of technology is necessary to enable or at least facilitate its transfer.

However, while patent protection can improve technology transfer, there is also evidence that too much patent protection can lead to welfare losses in developing countries with regard to technology transfer.[36] Several explanations are possible. First, protection in developing countries allows companies from developed countries to charge additional (or higher) license fees. These revenues were the major motivation for developed countries to include IP protection in TRIPS and bilateral trade agreements, and the empirical evidence strongly suggests that this strategy was successful. The additional technology transferred to developing countries because of the increased protection might not compensate the increase in license fees that these countries have to pay.[37] Second, some industries might engage less in technology transfer than others, irrespective of the level of protection, *e.g.*, the pharmaceutical industry.[38]

[33] See Beier (1998), p. 188.

[34] See Sect. 2.1.4.

[35] Interview with *Ana Catalina Monge Rodríguez*.

[36] Branstetter (2004), p. 369.

[37] The study by *Lee Branstetter* found that companies usually charge higher license fees if protection becomes stronger, see Branstetter (2004), p. 369.

[38] Beattie (2007), p. 20.

International Legal Framework

Because of the importance of technology transfer especially for developing countries and the risks connected with over-protection, TRIPS allows the members to protect technology transfer against abuses of rights in general[39] and restrictive licensing practices in particular.[40] CAFTA-DR does not specifically address abuses adversely affecting the transfer of technology. Article 15.1(15) CAFTA-DR only applies to abuses of rights which may constitute anti-competitive practices. The EU-CARIFORUM-EPA addresses the question more broadly within the context of innovation in general, not only IP protection. Article 142(2) EU-CARIFORUM-EPA requires the control of "licensing practices which may affect the *international* transfer of technology" not only in cases of "an abuse of intellectual property rights by right holders", but also in cases of "an abuse of obvious information asymmetries in the negotiation of licenses".[41]

Central America

With regard to Central America, there is no evidence to suggest that the stronger patent protection will improve the transfer of technology. The improvement of technology transfer in Central America can be impeded by several factors. The main restriction is the limited technical capacity of Central American countries to absorb new technologies, even if the increased patent protection provides the legal certainty for more technology transfer. In the region, Costa Rica received most of the transferred technology since the mid-1990s. Given that IP protection in Costa Rica was not substantially stronger than in the neighboring countries, the likely reason for this were the complementary factors like better infrastructure, political stability and an educated workforce.[42] In the other countries in the region, these complementary factors are still not conducive to technology transfer. The level of general and technical education is low.

---

[39] Article 8(2) TRIPS.

[40] Article 40 TRIPS.

[41] *Henning Grosse Ruse-Khan* notes that this clause could be interpreted as requiring the EU-CARIFORUM-EPA parties, more specifically, the EU competition authorities to also control the effect of license agreements on the Caribbean market, see Grosse Ruse-Khan (2009), p. 49; concurring Drexl (2018) Nr 49–50. This exceeds the competition law limitations in TRIPS, which only permits the application of competition law to protect the domestic market.

[42] The most notable example is the establishment of an Intel microprocessor factory in Costa Rica, see Sect. 1.3.4.

3.1.1.3 Moral Objectives

In addition to these utilitarian objectives, there are also other possible objectives for patent protection. According to the moral justifications, the inventor has a natural property right on its own idea and society is morally obligated to recognize and protect the right, and justice requires that a man receives a reward from society for useful services, and inventors render useful services.[43] Such moral considerations can also be found in Central America. The national legislation recognizes, *e.g.*, the right of the inventor to be named,[44] based on European concepts moral rights of inventors. But this view is in line with indigenous traditions: In Nicaragua, for instance, indigenous healers value their cures as private property.[45] However, while these moral objectives can justify protection as such, they do not provide guidance regarding the scope and length of such protection, and in particular regarding the feasibility of the level of protection provided for in CAFTA-DR.

3.1.1.4 Access to Medicines and Public Health

Introduction

With regard to developing countries, observers are concerned that (stronger) patent protection created by TRIPS-plus provisions prevents poor people from receiving life-saving medications, because public health systems are non-existent or insufficiently funded and people would not be able to pay the higher prices of patented medicine. In particular, critics consider the increased protection of test data to be harmful for developing countries.[46] As a result of pressure from NGOs and developing countries, especially from Latin America, the importance of safeguarding the social objectives of IP law against too much protection has been recognized by the international community, *e.g.*, in the *Declaration on the TRIPS Agreement and Public Health* (Doha Declaration) adopted by the WTO Ministerial Conference in Doha on 14 November 2001 and the Decision of the General Council of 30 August 2003 on the *Implementation of paragraph 6 of the Doha Declaration on the TRIPS Agreement and Public Health*.[47] Unlike CAFTA-DR, which makes no reference to social objectives related to IP, Article 3.2(a) EU-CARIFORUM-EPA echoes this concern by stating that the "agreement shall fully take into account the [...] social, health and environmental best interests of their respective population and future generations". This provision points to two dimensions of the relationship between IP and social objectives.

---

[43] Cornish et al. (2013) at 3-36.

[44] See, e.g., Article 102 IP Law (GT).

[45] Dutfield (2001), citing Dennis (1988), p. 16.

[46] See, e.g., Abbott (2007), p. 8.

[47] WTO General Council (2003).

Pharmaceutical Patents and the Incentive to Innovate

Decision-Making on the National Level The reference in Article 3.2(a) EU-CARIFORUM-EPA to the "best interests of *their* (emphasis added) respective population" makes clear that when taking social interests into account, the *national* view matters. Two policy aspects must be taken into account in this regard, first the question on which level the decisions regarding the appropriate level of patent protection should be made and second the national and global incentive to innovate. This increases the risk of national free-riding, because IP rights protect global public goods.[48] While the pursuit of social objectives is legitimate, because IP protection must serve public, including social, interests, including them into IP policy as an explicit limitations, combined with the discretion for national governments to implement such "social limitations", carries the risk of arbitrary national measures, and in particular the violation of the principle of national treatment through the back door, in the name of "public interest". The experience with the effects of the Doha Declaration in the area of compulsory licenses to pharmaceutical patents provides evidence of such abuse; some of the most prominent cases of compulsory licenses issued served fiscal and economic priorities of the issuing country, not only public health needs.[49] It is, therefore, necessary to take a closer look at the issue of patent protection and access to medicines. However, while abuse is possible, it seems nonetheless reasonable to enable a national assessment of social policy, because only on this level can it be made appropriately, given the significant differences between countries. The national view maintains policy space for national governments to balance goals in a flexible way. This is the case even within the region Central America, considering for example the different percentages of people living with HIV, the structure of the health care systems or environmental challenges in each country. This approach, in line with Article 3.2(a) EU-CARIFORUM-EPA, is also consistent with TRIPS. According to Appellate Body case-law, countries have some flexibility in interpreting their TRIPS obligations.[50]

Incentive to Innovate The second aspect is the effect of the national view on the incentive to innovate. *Forey* suggests that, in terms of IP policy, one must ask what "the right mechanism for a socially efficient solution to the problem" is, particularly "helping the market to invent a new vaccine for a global disease".[51] It is argued that the small size of the markets in developing countries do not affect the incentive of global companies to develop new drugs and that the large developed markets may be

[48] See Sect. 1.6.2 above.

[49] See in particular the case of the compulsory license issued in Brazil in 2007, on this case see Böttger (2008), pp. 887–888.

[50] In relation to enforcement obligations see WTO Dispute Settlement Body, Panel Report, China—Measures Affecting the Protection and Enforcement of Intellectual Property Rights, Decision of 26 January 2009, WT/DS362/R; on this decision Wallot (2016), p. 215.

[51] Foray (2007), p. 6.

sufficient to secure the necessary incentive.[52] Some economists point out that international companies, especially pharmaceutical companies, were never making substantial profit in developing countries, and that, therefore, the theoretical incentive resulting from patent protection did not exist in reality.[53] The lack of research on diseases existing almost exclusively in developing countries seems to support this assumption. In developing countries with small markets in terms of the number of consumers and their purchasing power, weak patent protection may not significantly decrease the global incentive for research. This view points to the observation that neither TRIPS nor TRIPS-plus protection for pharmaceuticals has so far led to a significant increase in research for medicines needed especially by developing countries[54] This raises the question whether the absence of research means that patent protection is superfluous (at least in Central America). However, this conclusion could create a vicious circle. Developing countries contribute little to global inventive activity, in particular innovative drugs, based on the concept that pharmaceutical companies do not research developing country-specific drugs. However, it must be considered that statutory patent protection for pharmaceuticals was introduced only between 2000 and 2005, and in many countries, practically, patent protection for pharmaceuticals still does not exist. This means that, so far, no effective incentive by means of patent protection has been created in relation to neglected diseases. This approach in turn could perpetuate the low level of development-country specific research, because the low level of patent protection signals to pharmaceutical companies that even if they developed developing country-specific drugs, they would not be able to recuperate their investment and the pharmaceutical countries prioritize their research activities accordingly.[55] Therefore, the fact that privately funded research has been done in this area is not conclusive evidence that patent protection is ineffective. It is unclear whether effective patent protection in Central America combined with a sizable health market would incentivize research.

Static Versus Dynamic Competition According to Article 3.2(a) EU-CARIFORUM-EPA, the interests of *future* generations have to be considered. This is a reminder of the balance between present *free* and future *dynamic* competition, which should be at the heart of IP protection. Taken literally, this would also mean that the EU-CARIFORUM-EPA cannot be interpreted in a way that only benefits present competition, *e.g.*, by restricting IP rights in a way that enables total competition at the risk of completely removing the incentive to innovate. A global decision to abolish patent protection for HIV drugs might serve the "best interests of

[52] This is the underlying assumption of the study of Klaus Liebig, who determined the impact of patent protection on innovation on the national level, but not globally, see the discussion in Section 1.6.2.2.

[53] Stiglitz (2002), p. 8.

[54] Drexl (2007), p. 18.

[55] Regarding the impact of patent policy of developing countries, especially Brazil, on global research in the pharmaceutical field, see Böttger (2008), pp. 887–888.

their respective population" today, but would ignore the interests of future generations that companies invest in continued pharmaceutical research.

Many critics claim that TRIPS-plus patent protection serves the rent-seeking strategies of pharmaceutical companies, suggesting that it does not contribute to innovation. However, while rent-seeking may well be a motivation behind the efforts for increased protection for pharmaceutical companies, it is necessary to take a differentiated look at this issue.

To the extent increased patent protection is awarded to existing inventions, it does not create an incentive to innovate and therefore is questionable from a policy perspective.[56] To the extent increased patent protection is awarded to future inventions, however, assuming the critics are correct and this will enable innovative companies to charge higher prices, this will increase the incentive to innovate. One must note that many pharmaceutical companies maintain significant research and development budgets and acquire innovative small biotechnology companies because their current patent portfolios are "aging" and many drugs loose patent protection. In other words, they invest in inventions to obtain new exclusive products, as the incentive theory of patent law would predict.[57]

With regard to patent protection for pharmaceuticals in Central America (and more broadly in developing countries), there is another aspect to consider. Even if one accepts the premise as true that developing countries cannot or need not contribute to the global incentive to invent new drugs, does the assessment change in relation to diseases which are endemic to developing countries? While sudden epidemic outbreaks create a global rush of research, these singularities do not sustain inventive activity in this field. With developed markets not (strongly) affected and middle-income markets in the region (like Costa Rica and Brazil) establishing a policy framework directed at helping generic companies and reducing public health care costs, where does the incentive for inventive activity come from?[58]

This is a concern in particular in relation to those diseases prevalent in some developing regions which are viral diseases, such as Malaria or HIV, because they require constantly new drugs, because the viruses become immune to existing drugs after some time.[59] However, while for some authors this justifies stronger patent protection to create a strong incentive for inventive activity, for others the rapid pace of obsolescence in this field requires less patent protection.[60]

---

[56] See Sect. 2.2.4.4 regarding the retroactive application of CAFTA-DR rules.

[57] See Sect. 3.1.1.1.

[58] On this question see Böttger (2008), pp. 881–891.

[59] See Böttger (2008), p. 884 for further references.

[60] For example, Joseph Straus recommends strong patent protection and argues in particular against compulsory licenses, Straus (2003), pp. 130–131; on this issue see also Böttger (2008), p. 884.

Procurement Practices and Price Controls

A specific policy problem related to pharmaceuticals is that, because pharmaceuticals satisfy such fundamental health needs, people have no choice regarding these goods and, therefore, demand for these products is relatively in-elastic, *i.e.*, the consumers are not price-sensitive. The maximization of the monopoly rent of the right holder can, therefore, be controlled by the consumer only to a limited extent. This means that the right holder might be capable of charging higher prices than the exclusive right would normally enable the right holder to do. In many countries, in which public health systems have been created, the public health agencies are able to control prices also of patent-protected pharmaceuticals by establishing reimbursement prices, at least to some extent. It is argued, for example by the US government, based on a study conducted in 2004, "that price controls and regulatory and other barriers diminish returns on pharmaceutical products, and reduce the amount of global pharmaceutical research and development compared to what it would otherwise be under market conditions, inhibiting the development of the next generation of lifesaving drugs".[61] This factual finding seems plausible, because under the incentive model one would expect that a decrease in the return of investment would decrease the investment itself. Other studies have shown that economic models indicate that lower monopoly rents on patented goods increase the distribution of these goods and increase the social benefit of innovation.[62] The problem is obviously to quantify the decrease in research caused by the lower prices due to price controls and relate it to the increase in availability of new and improved drugs. While the price setting by the government or public agencies under reimbursement regimes, therefore, is controversial, it is well established in many countries, including patent-friendly countries like Germany, and seems a reasonable approach enabling the balance between the necessary return of investment for innovative drugs and the availability of such drugs to the patients, taking into account the real added value of a drug on a case-by-case basis.

Procurement law in general, including price controls, is outside the scope of this analysis, but the practical experience shows that these tools can be extremely effective in balancing the effect of patent protection.[63]

3.1.1.5 Access to Medicines in Central America

Under CAFTA-DR, the level of patent protection itself is little more than TRIPS. However, the protection of pharmaceutical test data and the enforcement measures have become much stricter. To put the TRIPS-plus rules in CAFTA-DR and the

[61] USTR Special 301 Report (2008), p. 14.

[62] Liebig (2001), p. 17.

[63] Regarding policy options to mitigate the effect of patent protection during the public procurement process, see Kanavos (2017), pp. 10–11.

criticism regarding access to medicines in context, this section briefly describes the situation of public health and pharmaceutical patents in Central America.

Introduction

The public health situation in Central America generally is challenging and faces many issues common to developing countries. On the one hand, except for Costa Rica, there is no developed public health insurance system, and accordingly, people have to buy medicines themselves. On the other hand, the region suffers particularly from infectious diseases, mainly malaria and HIV, but also Dengue fever. In the Dominican Republic, the percentage of the population infected with HIV is significant.[64] To put this issue into perspective, it must also be noted that, many people are so poor that they probably cannot afford to buy any drugs (e.g., in Nicaragua *annual* health expenditure in 2019 per person was around 150 USD)[65] and face even more fundamental health problems, notably access to hospitals and clean water.[66]

Pharmaceutical Patents and the Incentive to Innovate

In this context, pharmaceutical patents play an important role. While the overall number of patents and patent applications is low in the region, patents from foreign pharmaceutical companies play a relatively big role. In Guatemala in 2022, for instance, around 33% of patent applications related to pharmaceuticals, and these originate mostly from abroad.[67] This underlines the role of foreign pharmaceutical companies in this country. The numbers for other countries in the region are similar.[68] On the other hand, in Central America, *e.g.*, Costa Rica, the Dominican

[64] See USAID statistics, available at http://pdf.usaid.gov/pdf_docs/pdacu642.pdf (accessed 2 Nov 2024).

[65] Based on WHO statistical data for the year 2019, the annual per capita total expenditure on health in Nicaragua in 2013 was around 150 USD, while it was around 900 USD in Costa Rica; the data can be obtained from the WHO database available at http://www.who.int/gho/countries/en/ (accessed 2 Nov 2024).

[66] See the overview over the Nicaraguan health system of PATH, available at https://www.path.org/publications/files/TS-nicaragua-health-system-rpt.pdf (accessed 2 Nov 2024).

[67] There are no exact data on the number of pharmaceutical patents applications, and the ratio of domestic and foreign applications is not broken down by industry. However, the data from WIPO shows that in Guatemala 33% of patent applications related to pharmaceuticals and the majority of patents applications came from foreign applicants, see the data for the year 2022 available at https://www.wipo.int/edocs/statistics-country-profile/en/gt.pdf (accessed 2 Nov 2024).

[68] In Costa Rica in 2022, 50% of patent applications relate to pharmaceuticals and almost all patent applications came from foreign applicants https://www.wipo.int/edocs/statistics-country-profile/en/cr.pdf (accessed 2 Nov 2024).

Republic and Guatemala have developed a domestic generic drug industry, which heavily opposed the ratification and implementation of CAFTA-DR.[69]

In the Dominican Republic and Costa Rica, because of the traditionally restrictive policy regarding pharmaceutical patents, the number of granted patents, including pharmaceutical patents, is much lower than in other countries in the region. This significantly reduces the effect of stronger patent protection on access to medicines.[70] The historically low rate of granting patents on pharmaceuticals also reduces the potential impact of the patent linkage mechanism.[71] In Guatemala, on the other hand, more patents have been granted for pharmaceuticals. In this case, stronger patent protection and an effective system of patent linkage may have a bigger impact.[72] Accordingly, there are concerns regarding the effects of the CAFTA-DR patent rules, including test data protection, on the access to medicines. According to a report by the "The Stop CAFTA Coalition", 6 months after CAFTA-DR was implemented, imported medicines in the Dominican Republic almost tripled in price.[73] However, according to another study, 5 years after CAFTA-DR no significant effects of the patent provisions on public health in Costa Rica were found.[74]

Procurement Practices and Price Controls

In Costa Rica, the public health insurance, the Costa Rican Social Security Fund [*Caja Costarricense de Seguro Social*, CCSS (CR)], maintains a list of (455 as of 2015) relevant medicines which are included as prescription drugs in the public health system. On average 1.6 new medicines are added each year.[75] This may be partly due to the fact that the CCSS (CR) for medical safety reasons implemented a policy of observing the effects of a new pharmaceutical for about 4 years after market entry, before including it in its reimbursement scheme.[76] Because of this slow, conservative approach of the CCSS (CR) of including new medicine on the list, it contains only very few drugs with test data or patent protection.[77] As a result,

---

[69] See, e.g. Shaffer and Brenner (2009), p. 957; in Costa Rica, critics argued that it would become economically and legally difficult for the public health agency CCSS (CR) to provide broad access to medicines, see Castro (2015), p. 89.

[70] The number of annual patent grants has increased, but the overall numbers are still low, see Sect. 3.1.7.

[71] See Sect. 3.1.7.

[72] See the data on registered patents in Sect. 3.1.7. The available data only provides aggregate numbers, however, the increase in registered patents generally represents with a high probability also an increase in registered pharmaceutical patents, because these represent by far the largest part of patents in the country, as in the entire region.

[73] Tharin (2008).

[74] Castro (2015), pp. 97–99.

[75] Castro (2015), pp. 96–97.

[76] Castro (2015), p. 96.

[77] Castro (2015), p. 98.

patent protection has a smaller impact on the price and availability of drugs, in addition to the restrictive policy of the IP Register in relation to pharmaceutical patents. While the number of patents granted by IP Register has increased, the management of the CCSS (CR) of the "basket" of reimbursable drugs in relation to patents and prices will probably continue to keep the impact of pharmaceutical patents on public health low. This assumption is supported by a study which, 5 years after CAFTA-DR, found no significant effects of the patent provisions on public health in Costa Rica.[78]

3.1.1.6 Environmental Protection

The relationship between IP and the environment has become another important social concern in the context of IP protection. Earlier, the focus was on the possibilities of using IP protection to support environmental protection, *e.g.*, by giving economic value to information derived from genetic resources by creating a proprietary right and thus creating an incentive for protection. Out of this development emerged in Costa Rica the privately organized National Institute for Biodiversity (*Instituto Nacional de Biodiversidad*, INBio).[79] However, subsequently the focus shifted to the exclusionary and price-increasing effects of patent protection for environmental technology which restrict the incentive of developing countries to use environmentally friendly equipment for energy production and consumption.[80] Therefore, a balanced approach is necessary, as exemplified EU-CARIFORUM-EPA, which contains sustainable development as an overriding principle and provides that the EU-CARIFORUM-EPA and the CBD shall be implemented in a mutually supportive way.[81]

3.1.2 Patentable Inventions

This and the following sections analyze the substantive law provisions of international agreements and national laws in Central America and their application in practice, as the basis for evaluating the effects of the changes introduced by CAFTA-DR.

[78] Castro (2015), pp. 97–99.

[79] On the organization and responsibilities of INBio see Sect. 6.1.7.1; on this institution see also in detail Bucher (2008), pp. 267–270.

[80] See Gupta (2012), pp. 54–55.

[81] Article 150(3) EU-CARIFORUM-EPA.

3.1.2.1 Problem-Solution

While "[p]atents shall be available for any invention",[82] international agreements do not define the term "invention".[83] This permits a flexible application by the national patent offices and courts.[84] However, it seems to be international consensus that an invention is the solution of an (industrial) problem with technical means.[85]

Several Central American countries had detailed definitions in their earlier national laws[86] and included a definition in the 1997 project for the Central American Convention (Patents).[87] After this project was abandoned,[88] different definitions were adopted in the new national statutes. Costa Rica and the Dominican Republic use a short version which briefly restates the requirements of novelty and industrial application: "every creation of the human intellect capable of being applied in the industry",[89] but does not provide guidance as to the nature of an invention. The definition used in Guatemala and Honduras refers to creations "transforming nature", which are useful because of the "immediate satisfaction of a specific need".[90] This definition points to the technical and problem-solving nature of inventions. Only the Nicaraguan and Salvadoran statutes clearly refer to the "technical solution of a specific problem"[91] or the "solution of a technical problem".[92]

The Central American literature also uses the technical "problem-solution" approach, based on the international legal opinion.[93] The Patent Examiner Manual drafted by the Central American IP Registers is also based on this approach.[94]

3.1.2.2 Field of Technology

Under Article 27(1) TRIPS, patents shall be available without discrimination as to the field of technology. Article 15.9(1) CAFTA-DR restates that the parties shall

---

[82] Article 27(1) TRIPS.

[83] E.g., Article 27 TRIPS, Article 15.9(1) CAFTA-DR.

[84] Moufang, Rainer, § 1 Nr 14, in: Schulte (2017).

[85] Götting (2014), p. 126 at nr 3.

[86] El Salvador in Article 106 IP Law (SV), Guatemala in Law Nr. 153-85 (1985) and Honduras in Article 4 IP Law (HN); see Bendaña-Guerrero (1999), p. 219.

[87] Bendaña-Guerrero (1999), p. 218.

[88] See Sect. 2.1.4.

[89] Article 1 Patent and Design Law (CR) and Article 1 IP Law (DR).

[90] Article 4 IP Law (GT) and Article 4 IP Law (HN).

[91] Article 3 Patent and Design Law (NI).

[92] Article 106 IP Law (SV).

[93] E.g., Bendaña-Guerrero (1999), p. 217, who quotes Breuer Moreno, Tratado de Patentes de invención, Buenos Aires, 1957, p. 69.

[94] Patent Examiner Manual, pp. 64–65.

make patents available in all fields of technology. The TRIPS provision required changes in the Central American legislation, because under old patent laws, patent protection was not available for pharmaceuticals.[95]

The Dominican Republic previously maintained a system of "*confirmation patents*" for inventions claimed by foreigners for pharmaceutical products, which could not be protected by normal (examination) patents. This reflected the restrictive attitude of many (developing) countries regarding patent protection for pharmaceuticals.[96] Confirmation patent applications were not examined and were not subject to a novelty requirement. The IP Register of the Dominican Republic invalidated two confirmation patents on the grounds that (1) the applications for these confirmation patents did not comply with the "right of priority" that would maintain the "novelty" of the invention in the application and (2) the applicants had not received approval to apply from the "Medical Board" as required by statute. These decisions were considered without merit by the right holders, not least because the "Medical Board" did not exist at the time of the application or later.[97] The system of *confirmation patents* was abolished with the extension of patentable subject matter to pharmaceutical inventions in the IP Law (DR) in 2000.

Under the new (post-TRIPS) legislation no fields of technology are excluded and no further amendment was necessary during the implementation of CAFTA-DR. From a policy perspective, the broad definition is generally useful, because, in order to encompass new fields of technology, the concept of technicality must be dynamic.[98] This is best achieved by a definition which does not enumerate specific fields of technology, but can incorporate technical progress in a flexible way.

It is argued that at least in developing countries like those in Central America, pharmaceutical patents have a negative impact on access to medicines and public health and, therefore, patents should not be available in this field. In Central America, Costa Rica and the Dominican Republic have found a practical solution to discriminate against certain fields of technology. For some time, there were no examiners in the IP Registers responsible for these fields, and, therefore, the respective patent applications were not processed. Despite the statutory possibility to obtain patent protection for pharmaceuticals, they were until a few years ago (almost) unavailable.[99]

---

[95] There is an ongoing discussion on the interpretation of Article 27 TRIPS. The interpretation underlying Article 15.9(1) CAFTA-DR is that the requirement that patents shall be available "without discrimination as to the field of technology" means that patents must be available "in all fields of technology". The opposing view considers differentiations in relation to requirements of patentability to be non-discriminatory if they are based on policy differences, see Lamping et al. (2014), p. 4.

[96] The exclusion of patent protection for pharmaceuticals was not limited to developing countries, however, such exclusion existed also in, e.g., Italy; see Bartling (1972), p. 401.

[97] PhRMA (2007), p. 3.

[98] Götting (2014), p. 126 at nr 6.

[99] See Sect. 3.1.7.

3.1.2.3 Process Patents

Article 27 TRIPS and 15.9(1) CAFTA-DR provide that both products and processes must be patentable.[100] Processes can be patented also under Central American law. The protection of process patents had already been included in Article 2 of the Project for the Central American Convention (Patents), and is now explicitly provided for in most national laws.[101] While the explicit protection of processes was not included in Guatemala,[102] it can be inferred systematically from the fact that several exceptions are created for certain (especially biological) products and processes in Articles 91 and 92 IP Law (GT). These exceptions would not be necessary if processes were not generally included. The exceptions regarding special products (*e.g.*, animals) and processes (*e.g.*, medical treatment) are further analyzed with the context of subject matter exceptions below.

3.1.3 Requirements

Inventions are patentable if "they are new, involve an inventive step and are capable of industrial application".[103] This harmonizes the patentability requirements for all WTO members.[104] These requirements were restated in Article 15.9(1) CAFTA-DR[105] and are included in the patent laws of all CAFTA-DR countries.[106]

3.1.3.1 Novelty

State of the Art

An invention is not new if the respective information has been publicly disclosed prior to the filing of the patent application, *i.e.*, if it is already *state of the art*. Unlike the state of the art of utility models, the state of the art relevant for patent applications is generally the *absolute* standard of novelty.[107] Earlier, foreign oral disclosures

---

[100] Internationally, most jurisdictions have introduced process patents explicitly, see, e.g., 35 U.S.C. § 100(b) and 101, Article 21 of the Spanish Patent Law and Decision 486 of the Andean Community.

[101] Article 3 Patent and Design Law (NI), Article 4.2 IP Law (HN) and Article 106 IP Law (SV).

[102] See Articles 91–93 IP Law (GT).

[103] Article 27(1) TRIPS.

[104] Gervais (1999), p. 159.

[105] The use of the singular ("invention") in Article 15.9(1) CAFTA-DR has no modifying effect.

[106] Article 1 IP Law (DR), Article 3 Patent and Design Law (CR), Article 111 IP Law (SV), Article 93 IP Law (GT), Article 6 IP Law (HN), Article 8 Patent and Design Law (NI).

[107] E.g., Article 54.1 EPC.

were not part of the state of the art in the USA, which relied on a *relative* standard of novelty. The exception of foreign oral disclosures in § 102(a) US Patent Act [35 U.S.C. § 102(a)] excluded especially traditional knowledge which exists usually only in oral form.[108] However, subsequently the courts have extended the state of the art to foreign oral sources, especially in cases relating to knowledge relating to plants.[109] This extension has been codified in 2011 by the so-called "America Invents Act" (AIA), which introduced the *absolute* standard of novelty also in the USA.[110]

Central American countries also use the *absolute* standard of novelty, *i.e.*, the disclosure may have occurred anywhere in the world and in any form.[111] Therefore, even an oral disclosure abroad would exclude novelty. In Nicaragua *relative* (*i.e.*, national) novelty used to be sufficient, if the invention was disclosed abroad but not known in the country.[112] Since the TRIPS implementation, however, the *absolute* standard of novelty applies.[113] This standard has been restated by the Patent Examiner Manual: "The state of the art (…) is everything which has been put at the disposition of the public by *written or oral* description, by use, commercialization or in any other way, *anywhere in the world* prior to the filing of the patent application".[114] For the determination of novelty, but not the inventive step, the examiner also takes into account the information contained in an application processed in the national patent office. The claims are not measured against the state of the art as a whole, but against each individual document.[115]

However, even though traditional knowledge which exists only orally in Central America is now part of the prior art both in the USA and Central America, this prior art might not be accessible for the patent examiner, even if it has to be considered during the examination. Therefore, traditional knowledge that contributed to the claimed invention may not be noticed. This problem could be solved by the establishment of a (preferably electronic) prior art database. Such a database has been established in Costa Rica by INBio.[116] Undocumented traditional knowledge will only become practically relevant during an opposition or nullity procedure. But even if the state of the art is accessible, the insufficient number of examiners or *peritos* complicates the practical review of novelty. In cases of PCT applications entering the national phase in the respective country, the examiner might simply adopt the prior substantive decision of the designated PCT office during the

[108] Bucher (2008), p. 92.

[109] Bucher (2008), p. 92.

[110] See 35 U.S.C. § 102 (a)(1); regarding the expansion of the scope of prior art under the AIA; see Merges (2012), p. 1027.

[111] See, e.g., Article 94(2) IP Law (GT); for the similar wording in pre-TRIPS statutes see Bendaña-Guerrero (1999), p. 220.

[112] Bendaña-Guerrero (1999), p. 221.

[113] Article 9 Patent and Design Law (NI).

[114] Patent Examiner Manual, p. 21.

[115] Patent Examiner Manual, p. 22.

[116] See Sect. 6.1.6.1.

international phase. In El Salvador, for example, most applications are successful, which suggests that the four examiners responsible for several hundred PCT applications each year rely on the prior examination of other patent offices.[117]

Prior Public Disclosure Made by the Applicant

Prior public disclosure can be disregarded if the patent is filed within a certain grace period after the disclosure has occurred *and* the disclosure was made or authorized by the applicant. This grace period is beneficial for scientists, who want to publish their discoveries early, and small enterprises, which depend on third parties for further developing, testing on manufacturing their inventions.[118] This possibility for prior public disclosure by the applicant is subject of an ongoing controversy especially between the USA (where it exists) and Europe. It was resolved neither in the Revision of the Paris Convention nor in TRIPS.[119] It is now mandated by Article 15.9(7) CAFTA-DR. The EU-CARIFORUM-EPA and EU-CA-AA contain no provision on this matter.

The Central American countries did not provide a grace period before the new legislation in 2000. But a 12 months grace period was subsequently included, *e.g.*, in the new Guatemalan law[120] and in Nicaragua.[121] Under the examination guidelines set by the Patent Examiner Manual, prior public disclosure is disregarded if the patent is filed within 12 months after the disclosure has occurred and the disclosure was made or authorized by the applicant.[122] Accordingly, Central American practice is in line with the CAFTA-DR requirements. In addition, the law of the Dominican Republic explicitly provides for a 12 months grace period.[123]

Prior Public Disclosure Made by Third Parties

Prior public disclosure can also be disregarded if it was made by a third party illegally, *e.g.*, through the breach of a confidentiality agreement, and if a patent application for the disclosed invention is filed within a certain time period. However, such a grace period is not mandated by international agreements or CAFTA-DR, and some countries provide that in such cases of prior disclosure novelty is destroyed as well. The reason for not providing for this kind of grace period is to promote the filing of patents. The inventor has to disclose the information to ensure protection

[117] Regarding the organization of the IP Registers and patent examination see Sect. 2.5.3.

[118] Götting (2014), p. 140 at nr 16.

[119] Likewise, the issue was not addressed in the US-Nicaragua IP Agreement of 1999.

[120] Article 94(3) IP Law (GT).

[121] Article 10 Patent and Design Law (NI).

[122] Patent Examiner Manual, p. 52.

[123] Article 5(3) IP Law (DR).

against illegal disclosure. However, in Central America, such grace period exists, *e.g.*, in Guatemala[124] and is foreseen also by the Patent Examiner Manual.[125]

Under the Guatemalan provision, if the inventor protects the invention by means of confidentiality agreements, the inventor is entitled to the grace period. This enables the protection of the invention even without disclosure. This, however, contravenes the idea to grant patent protection (also) as a compensation for disclosure. While theoretically such protection can foster the transfer of technology in cases where the inventor does not want to disclose the invention and normally would not provide it even to contractual partners because of the risk involved with illegal disclosure, in practice this is unlikely because even if the inventor is protected by the grace period in Guatemala, the invention would no longer be new in most other countries, which do not recognize this kind of grace period.

3.1.3.2 Inventive Step

The inventive step requirements shall exclude simple innovations which result from routine development work. The inventive step can result from several factors, namely

- identifying a new problem,
- finding a new solution for a known problem or
- transferring a known solution to a known, but unrelated problem.[126]

The inventive step is assessed from the perspective of a "reference person" (the "person skilled in the arts" or simply "skilled person"), who is an average technician.[127] This requirement, aims at safeguarding "a free space ... for continuous development" by excluding simple innovations from patent protection and thus preventing unjustified monopolization.[128] A footnote to Article 27 TRIPS, and Article 15.9(1) CAFTA-DR adds the option of using the term "non-obviousness" instead of "inventive step" and "useful" instead of "capable of industrial application" in national legislation. This option is relevant only with regard to US law, where 35 U.S.C. §§ 101 and 103 require a "useful" and not "obvious" invention. In Central America, the terms "inventive step" and "industrial application" were used in Article 8 of the (draft) Central American Convention (Patents).[129] These terms were later

[124] Article 94(4) IP Law (GT); similar provisions exist in Europe, e.g., § 3(4) Nr. 1 German Patent Law.

[125] Patent Examiner Manual, p. 52.

[126] Patent Examiner Manual, p. 66; in international doctrine Götting (2014), p. 143 at nr 28.

[127] Patent Examiner Manual, p. 23.

[128] Bendaña-Guerrero (1999), p. 222, citing Bercovitz, Los requisitos positivos de patentabilidad en el derecho alemán (1969), p. 305; Bercovitz appears to refer to a decision of the German *Reichsgericht* of 1941, see RG GRUR 1941, 468.

[129] See Bendaña-Guerrero (1999), p. 221; regarding the Central American Convention (Patents), see Sect. 2.1.4.

adopted by the post-TRIPS national laws.[130] The exact term used is "inventive level" (*nivel inventivo*), which corresponds to the German term "*Erfindungshöhe*".[131] However, sometimes the inventive step is defined as being "not obvious" and "not following evidently from the state of the art for a person skilled in the arts", thus combining both terms.[132]

The assessment of the inventive step is particularly difficult if the invention under consideration is derived from or connected to an existing invention. Relevant categories in this regard are combinations and especially new applications (second use) of prior inventions. In Central America, the *juxtaposition* or *combination* of known elements without technical relation can also be protected.[133] As the elements are known, the inventive step must be based on the result, which has to be "different"[134] or "not obvious".[135] However, the strict examination practice of many IP Registers makes it difficult to apply for inventive combinations. In Nicaragua, for example, while the legislation allows the patenting of combinations that are not obvious, the IP Register seems to considered only the novelty or inventiveness of the elements, not the non-obviousness of the combination and thus seems to miss the real question in establishing the patentability of this type of invention.[136] Especially controversial is the protection of the so-called "second use" patents, in particular the protection of a new medical application or second indication of a pharmaceutical. While new indications can be protected, *e.g.*, in Europe under Article 54(4) EPC, second use patents are not explicitly required under CAFTA-DR. The Central American IP Registers traditionally deny protection for such inventions.[137] However, the Patent Examiner Manual provides that they may be patented.[138]

3.1.3.3 Industrial Application

According to Article 1(2) of the Paris Convention, "industry" is to be understood in a broad sense, including industry in the narrow sense, *i.e.*, the secondary sector, but also natural products, especially food, *i.e.*, the primary sector. Article 15.9

[130] E.g., Article 93 IP Law (GT) and Article 12 Patent and Design Law (NI).

[131] This point is made also by Bendaña-Guerrero (1999), p. 221.

[132] See, e.g., Article 1(2)(d) Patent and Design Law (CR); Article 12 Patent and Design Law (NI); the term non-obviousness was also used as an equivalent to inventive step in Article 8 Central American Convention (Patents).

[133] Patent Examiner Manual, p. 66.

[134] Bendaña-Guerrero (1999), p. 239.

[135] See, e.g., Article 1(2)(d) Patent and Design Law (CR).

[136] Permanent Mission of the Republic of Nicaragua (WIPO) (2018), p. 3.

[137] E.g., regarding Costa Rica, see Martínez Piva and Tripo (2019), p. 62.

[138] Patent Examiner Manual, p. 31.

(11) CAFTA-DR provides that a claimed invention is industrially applicable if it has specific, substantial and credible utility.[139]

In Central America, all countries provide for a non-exhaustive list of positive examples including craft, agriculture, gardening, manufacturing, construction, mining, fishing and services.[140] This definition has also been included in the Patent Examiner Manual.[141]

3.1.4 Exceptions

3.1.4.1 Ordre Public

Under TRIPS, inventions can be excluded from patentability which are contrary to the *ordre public*.[142] This option would exist under international law also without specific provision in TRIPS, therefore, more important is the clarification of what does not constitute an *ordre public* exception. In particular, a patent cannot be denied because the exploitation of the patented invention is prohibited by domestic law.[143] Most Central American countries make use of the *ordre public* exception. According to the CSJ in Nicaragua, *ordre public* comprises "all positive norms absolutely obligatory (which) affect fundamental principles of society or preconditions of existence".[144] Examples might be devices to facilitate suicide and letter bombs.[145] *Bendaña-Guerrero* observes that such patent applications are rare, as it is hardly conceivable that someone would apply for a patent for such an invention.[146] Most CAFTA-DR members also explicitly provide for the clarification that the mere statutory prohibition of exploitation of a certain invention is not, in itself, sufficient grounds to consider an invention contrary to the *ordre public*.[147] Only in Costa Rica it is not explicitly included in the national statute.[148] The limitation of the exception in Costa Rica would, therefore, have to be achieved through restrictive interpretation.

[139] Patent Examiner Manual, p. 23.

[140] Article 3 IP Law (GT); Article 112 IP Law (SV); Article 8 IP Law (HN); Article 2 Nr 6 Patent and Design Law (CR); Article 13 Patent and Design Law (NI).

[141] Patent Examiner Manual, p. 23.

[142] Article 27(2) TRIPS.

[143] Article 27(2) TRIPS; this clause was first introduced on the international level as Article 4*quarter* of the Paris Convention by the Lisbon Revision and later included in Article 27(2) TRIPS.

[144] Supreme Court of Justice of Nicaragua, 9 January 1962, B.J. 7—Judicial Bulletin p. 7.

[145] Bendaña-Guerrero (1999), p. 240.

[146] Bendaña-Guerrero (1999), p. 242.

[147] Article 92(b) IP Law (GT); Article 7(d) Patent and Design Law (NI).

[148] This is the case in Costa Rica, see Article 1(4) Patent and Design Law (CR).

3.1.4.2 Software

One of the most controversial issues of patent law is the patenting of software or "computer-implemented inventions". The principle of non-patentability of computer programs has been established in Europe by the EPC (1973). Under Directive 91/250/EEC of 14 May 1991 on the legal protection of computer programs, protection was established according to copyright law.[149] Subsequently, Article 10 Annex 1(C) TRIPS adopted this system of protection only by copyright law, but not patent law. Patent protection is only available if the computer program is part of an industrial process (so-called "computer-implemented inventions"). In practice, it is often difficult to draw the line between software and such computer-implemented inventions.[150] All Central American laws generally exclude computer programs from patentability,[151] taking over the EPC system.[152] Patent protection is only available for computer-implemented inventions.[153]

3.1.4.3 Exceptions for Biological Subject Matter

Overview

Another controversial issue is the patenting of biological subject matter. Critics emphasize that biological material already existing in nature, or "life", should not be patentable.[154] This opinion is particularly strong in Latin America, where it is included in some legislation as well as expressed in the regional legal literature.[155]

In developed countries, the prevailing position is to allow the patenting, even if the biological subject matter occurred in nature.[156] It is argued that the novelty and the merit of an invention in the field of biotechnology lies not in the organism itself, but is the discovery of its utility and the isolation from its natural status; the invention is novel not because the subject matter did not exist before, but because the information about it is new, *i.e.*, because the process of isolating or extracting material or the type of use of biological material is new.[157] From a policy

---

[149] Directive 91/250 has subsequently been repealed and replaced by Directive 2009/24/EC of 23 April 2009 on the legal protection of computer programs.

[150] Götting (2014), p. 132 at nr 21.

[151] Patent Examiner Manual, p. 28; in Nicaragua, the patentability was established by the case-law of the CSJ, Bendaña-Guerrero (1999), pp. 227–228.

[152] Bendaña-Guerrero (1999), p. 228.

[153] Patent Examiner Manual, p. 28.

[154] This view argues that biological material should be classified as discoveries rather than inventions, see Lamping et al. (2014), p. 5.

[155] See, e.g., Article 6 of the Patent and Utility Models Law of Argentina.

[156] Article 3 Biotech Directive and § 1(2) German Patent Act; on this issue Götting (2014), p. 128 at nr 10.

[157] Götting (2014), p. 130 nr 18; Taubmann (2003), p. 231.

perspective, patentability of biological subject matter is considered beneficial as it allows patent protection for drugs based on biological material.[158]

Since the inventive element is limited to the discovery of the isolation or production process, in these cases only process patents should be available. To establish whether the invention is based not on the analysis of the existing biological subject matter and natural processes, but on the discovery of something novel, the relevant criterion is the application of a technical process.[159] In other words, the invention requires human (physical/chemical) intervention in the process.

The international agreements do not regulate this issue. The Central American countries are, therefore, free whether to grant protection for subject matter existing in nature. The national legislation in Central America does not explicitly provide for such cases, except in the Guatemalan and Nicaraguan legislation, which excludes from patentability "biological processes which occur in nature and *do not require human intervention*, except microbiological processes".[160] However, local literature has argued that, while micro-organisms as found in nature are not protected, the process to discover them should be patentable.[161] Reference was made to the *Chakrabarty* case in the USA[162] to argue for the protection of, *e.g.*, at least man-made bacteria.[163] This position has been accepted by the Patent Examiner Manual, which states that a complex biological process can still be patented if it includes a sufficient level of human intervention.[164]

Plants and Animals

Another controversial issue is patent protection for plants and animals. In Europe, for example, patent protection for plants and animals is permitted in principle, but it applies only to new elements, not discoveries, and requires that the technical feasibility of the invention is not confined to a *particular* plant or animal.[165] The reference to *particular* species bases the protection on the taxonomic level of the plant or animal the invention applies to. Excluded are, therefore, patents for individual species, while inventions relating to higher taxonomic levels can be protected. This distinction also helps separating patentable inventions relating to plants (higher

[158] Götting (2014), p. 129 nr 14; Ann (2022), § 14.III.f nr 240.

[159] Taubmann (2003), p. 231.

[160] Article 19(c) IP Law (GT), Article 6(c) Patent and Design Law (NI).

[161] Bendaña-Guerrero (1999), p. 234.

[162] U.S. Supreme Court, Diamond v. Chakrabarty, 447 U.S. 303 (309).

[163] Bendaña-Guerrero (1999), p. 235.

[164] Patent Examiner Manual, p. 29; however, the practical skepticism in the region against protection of any invention related to biology and/or pharmaceuticals and the strict interpretation of novelty suggests that applications for patents on biological subject matter existing in nature will probably be subject to particular scrutiny in Central America.

[165] Articles 52.2, 53 (b) EPC; Article 4(2) Biotech Directive.

taxonomic level) and plant varieties (species) in countries where *sui generis* plant variety protection exists. Under TRIPS, plants and animals can be excluded from patent protection, except for plant varieties.[166] Article 15.9(2) CAFTA-DR modifies the TRIPS framework by providing that the parties do not have to *introduce* patent protection for animals, but shall *maintain* such protection if it already exists. This flexibility reflects the ethical concerns that exist in many countries regarding the patentability of plants and animals.

In Central America, except for El Salvador, all CAFTA-DR members have used the flexibilities under TRIPS to exclude biological processes for plant or animal reproduction which do not require human intervention.[167] Some countries like Costa Rica also have excluded patent protection for plants,[168] while Guatemala allows protection.[169] The provisions in Nicaragua are not clear on this issue.[170] Because of the special requirements of CAFTA-DR, Nicaragua can keep animals excluded from patentability,[171] while Guatemala, that did not provide for such an exception in its new law, cannot now introduce such an exclusion.

This CAFTA-DR provision is, therefore, problematic. While on the one hand it affords some level of policy flexibility to Central American countries to maintain existing exceptions to patentability, on the other hand it perpetuates differences in the local patent laws and thus restricts the possibility to harmonize Central American IP laws in a certain way, if the countries chose to do so.

Micro-Organisms

Even if they are not themselves excluded from patentable subject matter, plants and animals can be controlled by patent rights, if they are a "product obtained" by a patented process or include a patented product, *e.g.*, microbiological processes or micro-organisms. Central American countries have to provide protection for microbiological processes and micro-organisms according to Article 27(3)(b) TRIPS. Article 15.9(2) CAFTA-DR restates Article 27(3)(b) TRIPS and, therefore, does not modify this requirement. Mostly, the corresponding Central American patent laws exclude biological processes from patentability, in accordance with Article 27.3 (a) TRIPS, and provide for a counter-exception for microbiological processes.[172]

---

[166] Article 27(3)(b) TRIPS; plant variety protection can be established also by a sui generis system, e.g., the UPOV Convention, see Bucher (2008), p. 83 with further references.

[167] Patent Examiner Manual, p. 26; see, e.g., Article 19(c) IP Law (GT); Article 6(c) Patent and Design Law (NI).

[168] Article 1(4) Patent and Design Law (CR).

[169] Article 97 IP Law (GT).

[170] Article 7(d) Patent and Design Law (NI) excludes "the protection of human, animal or plant health or life", while Article 7(a) Patent and Design Law (NI) excludes only "the registration of animals", which could be interpreted to mean that conversely the registration of plants is possible.

[171] Article 7 Patent and Design Law (NI).

[172] Article 91 IP Law (GT), Article 6 Patent and Design Law (NI).

However, the Costa Rican law excludes biological processes from patentability, but does not contain the counter-exception for microbiological processes.[173] Therefore, microbiological processes are also excluded, in violation of Article 27(3)(b) TRIPS and Article 15.9(2) CAFTA-DR.

Genes

The patentability of genes is particularly controversial.[174] In Europe, genes can be protected if they have been isolated and the industrial application of the gene or gene sequence is disclosed.[175] In Central America, genes are not excluded explicitly from protection in national statutes, but, as biological material, genes *as such* are not protectable. *Bendaña-Guerrero* refers to the exclusion in Argentinian law and proposes the same conclusion.[176]

General Health Exceptions

Apart from these explicit exceptions, no field of technology can be excluded. Generally patents have to be available "in all fields of technology" according to Articles 27(1) TRIPS and 15.9(1) CAFTA-DR.[177] This non-discrimination requirement applies also to the controversial fields of pharmaceuticals and agrochemicals.[178] This follows from the unequivocal wording of Article 27(1) TRIPS, which is reinforced systematically by the explicit mentioning of certain other exceptions and also by the fact that TRIPS created transitional periods especially for pharmaceutical patents, which would be unnecessary if this field could be excluded from patentability under Article 27(1) TRIPS. Also, the negotiating history shows clearly that pharmaceutical patents were subject of fierce debate, and one would expect that an exception for such a broad and important area would have been included expressly in the text, along with the other exceptions. Permitted are exceptions to protect public (human and animal) health.[179] However, this exception does not justify a general exception for pharmaceuticals, because this would contradict its inclusion in Article 27(1) TRIPS. CAFTA-DR does not provide for changes regarding the patentability of pharmaceuticals or the exception to protect public health.

---

[173] Article 1.4 Patent and Design Law (CR).

[174] See Ann (2022) § 14.III.d nr 134-178.

[175] Article 5.3 Biotech Directive.

[176] Bendaña-Guerrero (1999), p. 244.

[177] This reflects the broad scope of patent protection established by the U.S. Supreme Court in Diamond v. Chakrabarty, 447 U.S. 303 (309): "everything under the sun that is made by men".

[178] Bendaña-Guerrero (1999), p. 225.

[179] Article 27(2) TRIPS.

In the pre-TRIPS legislation, most Central American countries had special rules regarding these two areas. In Guatemala, chemical products (including pharmaceuticals) were excluded from patentability.[180] In Costa Rica, patent protection for medicines was conditional upon local working. In El Salvador and Honduras, the term of protection was restricted to 15 years and 17 years, respectively, for pharmaceuticals.[181]

The post-TRIPS legislations use the flexibility provided by TRIPS to provide for specific exceptions.[182] Methods for the treatment of humans or animals[183] and inventions necessary to protect the health of humans or animals are excluded from patentability. Not related to health and, therefore, patentable are cosmetic methods with merely aesthetic effects.[184]

The registration and protection practices regarding patents for pharmaceuticals and health-related patents in general differ from country to country. In the Dominican Republic and Costa Rica, the IP Register have for many years practically denied registration of patents for pharmaceuticals under the new post-TRIPS legislation, as shown by the low overall number of patent registrations. Between 2006 and 2011, Costa Rica granted patents on less than 5% of foreign patent applications,[185] which affected particularly the pharmaceutical industry which has a significant share in patent applications. In Guatemala and El Salvador, on the other hand, most patent applications (including for pharmaceuticals) have been granted.[186]

The picture regarding the protection of originator pharmaceuticals is also unclear. The Ministerio Público in at least some countries enforces IP rights against counterfeit drugs, but from the available data it is unclear whether this is restricted to SSFFC (falsified) medicines or also covers measures against generic drugs which only violate patent rights.[187]

One must note that, despite these apparent insufficiencies regarding patent registration or enforcement, the activities by the Central American countries constitute no

---

[180] Article 2 Patent Law (GT).

[181] Bendaña-Guerrero (1999), p. 225.

[182] See, e.g., Article 92 IP Law (GT); Article 7 Patent and Design Law (NI).

[183] According to Bendaña-Guerrero (1999), p. 240, these methods are applied directly to the human being or animal and accordingly have no industrial application. The purpose of the exception is, therefore, merely clarification. The products or machines used in the treatment are (usually) patentable, however, as are treatments not directly applied, such as methods of blood analysis, see Patent Examiner Manual, p. 30. As it might be doubtful in specific cases whether a method is "directly" applied, the Patent Examiner Manual provides a list of examples from the examination practice of the EPO, see Patent Examiner Manual, Annex IV-1.

[184] Patent Examiner Manual, p. 31; Annex IV-1 of the manual refers to examples from decisions of the EPO.

[185] See Table 3.4.

[186] See Table 3.4.

[187] The USTR reports measures against counterfeit medicines in Guatemala, USTR, Special 301 Report (2011), and in the Dominican Republic, see USTR Special 301 Report (2016), p. 59. However, these accounts to not specify whether "counterfeit" in these cases relate to SSFFC medicines or patent-infringing generics.

infringement of TRIPS or CAFTA-DR, because both agreements do not require specific protection performance in practice. There also is no violation of the national treatment principle, because there is no clear indication that national applicants are privileged. For example, between 2006 and 2011, Costa Rica granted patents on exactly 5% of patent applications from national applicants,[188] *i.e.*, a percentage similar to the percentage of patent grants on foreign applications.

3.1.4.4 Traditional Knowledge

In Costa Rica, in addition to the exceptions to patentability regulated in Article 1(4) Patent and Design Law (CR), as discussed above, Article 78 Nr. 6 Biodiversity Law (CR) excludes inventions *essentially derived from traditional knowledge.*[189] Insofar as Article 1(4) Patent and Design Law (CR) and Article 78 Nr. 6 Biodiversity Law (CR) both exclude plants, animals and mainly biological processes from patentability, they are not in conflict. However, Article 78 Nr. 6 Biodiversity Law (CR) excludes inventions essentially derived from traditional knowledge generally, even if they meet the patentability requirements under Article 1(4) Patent and Design Law (CR) and would, therefore, be protectable. *Bucher* argues that the Patent and Design Law (CR) should prevail for two reasons. First, it is the younger law and it was intended by the legislator to supersede the Biodiversity Law (CR). Second, there was no social consensus in Costa Rica regarding the treatment of traditional knowledge which would allow its inclusion in the general morality exception of Article 1(4)(a) Patent and Design Law (CR).[190] In addition, one can argue that the Biodiversity Law (CR) as an ordinary law must be interpreted restrictively in accordance with international law. In Costa Rica, international treaties have a higher rank than ordinary laws.[191] The special exception of Article 78 Nr. 6 Biodiversity Law (CR) is not covered by the exceptions provided for by Article 27(3) TRIPS.[192] While existing traditional knowledge is not patentable for lack of novelty, inventions derived from it are not necessarily excluded.[193] Therefore, one would have to interpret Article 78 Nr. 6 Biodiversity Law (CR) restrictively and only apply it to cases in which the invention lacks novelty or inventive step, because of the traditional knowledge which is part of the state of the art and, therefore, the invention

---

[188] See Table 3.4.

[189] The use of traditional knowledge as an exception to patentability and how these two articles relate to each other is analyzed in this section, while the protection of traditional knowledge as an exclusive right is discussed in Sect. 6.2; on this issue see in particular the analysis by Bucher (2008), p. 288.

[190] Bucher (2008), p. 288.

[191] See Sect. 6.1.3.2.

[192] Bucher (2008), p. 293.

[193] Taubman and Leistner (2003), p. 79, distinguish between "established components of the collective heritage of a community" in the public domain and "the inventive product of an individual TK practitioner".

cannot be patented for not meeting the general patentability requirements. Traditional knowledge can be state of the art, unless it was successfully kept secret from the public, because (with regard to patents) also foreign and/or oral sources can be novelty-destroying.[194] The legislative clarification of this issue resulted in one of the most complex and controversial CAFTA-DR implementation measures in Central America.[195] While the above interpretation complies with TRIPS, as analyzed above, it makes Article 78 Nr. 6 Biodiversity Law (CR) practically inapplicable. As the interpretation of a law should not practically eliminate the respective provision, it was important that this interpretation is mandated by statute. The implementation of CAFTA-DR was delayed significantly in Costa Rica because of the referendum held on the agreement.[196] During the summer of 2008, as part of the legislative CAFTA-DR implementation package adopted after the successful referendum (which had been held on 7 October 2007), the Costa Rican government intended to delete Article 78 Nr. 6 Biodiversity Law (CR) to remove the conflict with Article 1(4)(a) Patent and Design Law (CR).[197] However, in an effort to expedite the implementation of the CAFTA-DR requirements, the *Arias* government had prepared the draft law without consulting the indigenous population as required by the Costa Rican Constitution. On 11 September 2008, the CSJ (CR) invalidated this draft reform legislation, because it affected indigenous communities which had not been consulted as required by law.[198] However, the clarification of this issue was required by the USA. The final deadline set by the Bush Administration for the implementation was December 2008, because it was unclear whether the new (Obama) administration, taking office in January 2009, would grant another extension. After the decision of the CSJ (CR), with only weeks before the final (already extended) December 2008 deadline for implementing the requirements of CAFTA-DR, the consultation process could not have been completed in time and another legislative reform was, as a consequence, impossible. The CAFTA-DR Reform Law II (CR), which was passed on 21 November 2008 and published on 26 November 2008 (as law No. 8686), was restricted to other changes to the Biodiversity Law (CR) and the text modifying Article 78(6) Biodiversity Law (CR) was eliminated. The CSJ decided that this new law was constitutional.[199] In order to comply with US expectations, Article 78(6) Biodiversity Law (CR) was interpreted by an executive decree: On 11 December 2008, the Costa Rican government, to salvage the

[194] See Sect. 3.1.3.

[195] This process is discussed in detail by Cabrera Medaglia (2010), p. 14.

[196] The ratification and implementation process of CAFTA-DR in Costa Rica in general is discussed in detail in Sect. 2.2.1.

[197] This change had not been included in the CAFTA-DR Reform Law I (CR) adopted on 14 March 2008 (law Nr. 8632); it was part of draft law No. 16955, which became the basis for CAFTA-DR Reform Law II (CR) (law Nr. 8686).

[198] Sala IV of the CSJ (CR); Decision N° 2008-13832 of 11 September 2008; the consultation is required under Article 6 and 7 the Convention No. 169 on Indigenous Peoples and Tribes of the International Labor Organization (ILO).

[199] Cabrera Medaglia (2010), p. 14.

CAFTA-DR implementation process, enacted a special executive "interpretation" of Article 78 Nr. 6 Biodiversity Law (CR) by *Regulation 34959-MINAET-COMEX* issued by the president,[200] which provided that an invention is only essentially derived from traditional knowledge if it lacks inventive step (thereby making Article 78 Nr. 6 Biodiversity Law (CR) practically inapplicable). This was considered by the USA as compliant with CAFTA-DR, which entered into force on 1 January 2009. Similarly, the *Regulation 34958-MINAET-COMEX* had been enacted in late 2008 after the invalidation of the reform legislation amending the Biodiversity Law (CR) to modify Article 80 Biodiversity Law (CR), in line with CAFTA-DR requirements.[201] While politically expeditious, this process raises significant legal concerns. In addition to the methodological problem of amending an act of legislature by an executive decree, the enactment of the Regulation 34959-MINAET-COMEX without consultation of affected indigenous communities raised the same constitutionality issues as the previous law did. In 2009, the regulation was challenged soon after its enactment, but only after CAFTA-DR had entered into force.[202] On 14 December 2012, the *Sala IV* of the CJS (CR) invalidated the Regulation 34959-MINAET-COMEX for the same reason as the previous law, *i.e.*, the non-consultation of indigenous communities.[203] The *Regulation 34958-MINAET-COMEX* was also invalidated on 5 December 2012 by the *Sala IV* of the CJS (CR), for the same reason.[204]

3.1.4.5 Other Exceptions

Articles 27(2) and 27(3) TRIPS and 15.9(3) CAFTA-DR allow parties to provide for general exceptions to patentability. Most Central American countries explicitly enumerate non-exhaustive lists of non-patentable subject matter.[205] These examples are no exceptions in the strict sense, because they cover subject matter which is not an invention with industrial application and thus could be considered excluded from protection because it does not meet the patentability requirements. Explicit examples are listed in the legislations of Guatemala and Nicaragua.[206] Such exceptions include:

[200] The text of the law is available at http://www.pgrweb.go.cr/DOCS/NORMAS/1/NOVIGEN/D/2000-2009/2005-2009/2008/FC3E/C1D0D.HTML (accessed 2 Nov 2024).

[201] The text of the law is available at http://www.pgrweb.go.cr/DOCS/NORMAS/1/VIGENTE/D/2000-2009/2005-2009/2008/FC3D/F19AB.HTML (accessed 2 Nov 2024).

[202] Sala IV, Unconstitutionality action No. 09-09870-0007-CO, Boletín Judicial N° 137 of 17 July 2013, available at https://www.imprentanacional.go.cr/pub-boletin/2013/07/bol_17_07_2013.html (accessed 2 Nov 2024).

[203] Ibid.

[204] Boletín Judicial N° 111 of 11 June 2013, available at https://www.imprentanacional.go.cr/pub-boletin/2013/06/bol_11_06_2013.html (accessed 2 Nov 2024).

[205] Bendaña-Guerrero (1999), p. 226.

[206] See Article 91 IP Law (GT), Article 6 Patent and Design Law (NI).

- simple discoveries,[207]
- scientific methods,[208]
- aesthetic and artistic creations,[209] and
- business methods.[210]

3.1.5 *Ownership and Employee Inventions*

International agreements contain few rules regarding the ownership of patents. The Central American countries, therefore, have much leeway to regulate the related legal issues.

The *right of the inventor to be identified* in the patent is protected internationally[211] and nationally.[212] In Central America, the inventor's name must, therefore, be indicated in the patent application.[213]

3.1.5.1 Ownership

The *right to the invention* in Central America always belongs to the inventor, who must be a natural person.[214] Most Central American countries provide for joint inventions (*en común*), *e.g.*, Article 99(1) IP Law (GT).[215] Joint inventors must be identified in the patent application. The *right to the patent* can be owned by natural persons or legal entities, the latter especially if an employee invention is assigned to or claimed by an employer.[216] Ownership is transferable.[217] In Central America, the right to the patent belongs to the first inventor to apply for the patent.[218] This "first to

[207] Discoveries are "the revelation of something pre-existing" in nature, while inventions require "human intervention" in nature; this criterion is especially important in the field of biotechnology, see Patent Examiner Manual, p. 26.

[208] These are abstract principles that lack practical industrial application, Patent Examiner Manual, p. 27.

[209] These are protected by design rights and copyrights, see Bendaña-Guerrero (1999), p. 227 and Patent Examiner Manual, pp. 28–29.

[210] Patent Examiner Manual, p. 28; according to Bendaña-Guerrero (1999), p. 227, they "lack industrial applicability". This exclusion could indicate more generally that "industry" does not extend to the service sector or to processes related to public administration and liberal professions.

[211] Article 4*ter* Paris Convention.

[212] E.g., Article 102 IP Law (GT).

[213] Patent Examiner Manual, p. 10.

[214] Patent Examiner Manual, p. 12.

[215] The Patent Examiner Manual, p. 12 refers to "co-inventors" (*con-inventores*).

[216] See, e.g., Article 103 IP Law (GT); Article 11 (1) IP Law (DR).

[217] Article 99 (2) IP Law (DR).

[218] See, e.g., Article 99 (3) IP Law (GT).

file" principle follows the traditional European system, in contrast to the "first to invent" principle, which applied in the USA, until the country adopted also the "first to file" principle under the "Leahy-Smith America Invents Act".[219] The "first to file" principle means that, in case several inventors made the invention independently from each other, the first inventor to file a patent application (i.e., the person "first to file") is entitled to the patent for that invention. Conversely, the "first to invent" principle means that the first person who made the invention is entitled to the patent (i.e., the person "first to invent"), even if the other inventor (one could say the "second to invent") filed for a patent before the first inventor.[220] This principle shall create an incentive to apply for the patent quickly and thereby disclose the invention at an early stage.[221] It shall also create legal certainty, as the formal question of the filing date is easier to prove than the substantive question who was the first person to make the invention.

3.1.5.2 Employee Inventions

The *law on employee inventions* is not regulated by international agreements. This is not surprising, since it only applies to inventions made in the country where the invention was made. Therefore, the Central American law on employee inventions does not affect US or other foreign patents. Nevertheless, it is of significant practical importance and will, therefore, be briefly discussed, taking the Guatemalan legislation as an example.

The Guatemalan law differentiates between research service contracts and research employment contracts on the one hand and ordinary employment contracts on the other hand. Inventions made under research service contracts or research employment contracts are regulated similarly to the US "work made for hire" system and the Austrian system. The right to the invention is automatically assigned to the person who commissioned the research or to the employer. The inventor receives no financial compensation.[222] If an employee, who is not required to perform an inventive activity, makes an invention in the field of business of the employer or by means of data or equipment the employee had access to because of the employment, the employee must notify the employer in writing about the invention and provide to the employer the information necessary to understand it.[223] The employer can claim the invention in writing within 2 months after receiving the notification or after becoming aware of the invention by other means.[224] If the invention is claimed,

[219]The text of the act is available at https://www.uspto.gov/sites/default/files/aia_implementation/20110916-pub-l112-29.pdf (accessed 2 Nov 2024).

[220]On these two principles see, e.g., the OECD Patent Statistics Manual 2009, p. 154.

[221]Cornish et al. (2013) at 4-10.

[222]Article 100 IP Law (GT).

[223]See, e.g., Article 101 (1) IP Law (GT).

[224]See, e.g., Article 101 (2) IP Law (GT).

the employer must pay an *equitable* remuneration based on the economic value of the invention. The parties must conclude a separate contract regarding the remuneration,[225] and if they cannot agree, the remuneration will be fixed by the courts competent for labor law disputes.[226] The differentiation between research and other contracts makes sense. If the inventor was specifically employed or otherwise contracted to perform research, which ideally results in inventions being made, the invention can be considered part of the required job performance and as such already compensated by the contractual remuneration or salary. Problematic from a practical point of view, based on the experience of the German law of employee inventions, is first the requirement that the employer must claim the invention of an ordinary employee in writing and within 2 months. If the employer fails to fulfil either of these two formal requirements, the employer will not acquire the right to the invention and eventually the patent. This is a rather drastic sanction, since small and medium-sized enterprises as well as their employees often are unaware of these requirements. Therefore, in Germany companies often applied for the patent and used the invention, even though legally it still belonged to the employee. This mechanism was reversed by a legislative reform in 2009. Now the law provides that an invention is automatically claimed by the employer unless the employer explicitly waives the rights to the invention within 4 months.[227] Second, the law does not clarify whether the employee can claim that the remuneration agreed upon between the parties subsequently turned out to be too low because of an unforeseen commercial success and, therefore, is not *equitable*. However, these issues are probably not practically relevant, because the available data on patent applications suggests that very few patentable inventions are generated in Guatemala.[228]

Costa Rican law also distinguishes between research employment contracts ("aimed at the production of invention") and other employment contracts. The right to patent inventions made under research employment contracts are co-owned by the employer and the employee, inventions made under other employment contracts are solely owned by the employee.[229]

3.1.6 Procedure

TRIPS and CAFTA-DR do not contain procedural requirements regarding patents, in contrast to trademarks, neither for the pre-grant procedure, *e.g.*, the electronic

[225] See, e.g., Article 101 (3) IP Law (GT).

[226] See, e.g., Article 101 (4) IP Law (GT); this mechanism is similar to the German system established under the Employee Inventions Act (*Gesetz über Arbeitnehmererfindungen, ArbEG*).

[227] Article 6(2) German Employee Inventions Act.

[228] As shown in Table 3.4, based on the available data, very few patents based on local inventions were filed in Guatemala during the last decades.

[229] Article 4 (3) and (4) Patent and Design Law (CR).

application, nor for post-grant judicial review options. The Central American countries are, therefore, relatively free in the design of their procedural rules.

3.1.6.1 Application

Overview

Practical harmonization of the patent application and examination procedure in Central America was achieved by the Patent Examiner Manual for patent applications and examination for the IP Registers in Costa Rica, the Dominican Republic, El Salvador, Guatemala, Honduras and Nicaragua.[230] The patent application must provide information about the applicant, the inventor and the legal representative.[231] In El Salvador and the Dominican Republic, the representative of the applicant has to submit a domestic address[232] and in Costa Rica and the Dominican Republic, the representative must be a resident. In Costa Rica, foreign right holders are required to be represented by a local agent.[233] While the participation of a local patent attorney facilitates the procedures, their participation is not mandatory.[234] If applicable, the application has to include the certificate of the depository institution for biological material.[235] In Guatemala, Honduras and Nicaragua, the patent offices provide application forms on paper.[236] The application can consist of one or more claims, provided these are related.[237] Furthermore, it has to be submitted in Spanish or with a translation into Spanish.[238]

PCT Applications

Prior to the introduction of the PCT system in Central America, patent applications were national applications filed by the local subsidiaries of international companies.[239] Under the Central American Convention (Patents), the declaration of

[230] See Sect. 2.5.2.3.

[231] Patent Examiner Manual, p. 10.

[232] See Article 137 IP Law (SV) and Article 12 (a) IP Law (DR).

[233] IP Helpdesk, Latin America—Frequently Asked Questions (FAQ), available at https://intellectual-property-helpdesk.ec.europa.eu/regional-helpdesks/latin-america-ip-sme-helpdesk/frequently-asked-questions-faq_en (accessed 2 Nov 2024).

[234] Ibid.

[235] Patent Examiner Manual, p. 10.

[236] These forms have been included into the Patent Examiner Manual.

[237] Patent Examiner Manual, p. 10.

[238] Patent Examiner Manual, p. 16.

[239] Interview with *Diana Hasbún*.

nationality was required.[240] Today, all Central American countries participate in the PCT system. The accession to the PCT system is mandated by CAFTA-DR. However, Costa Rica and Nicaragua had already ratified the treaty prior to the conclusion of CAFTA-DR.[241] The other countries, however, only joined as a result of CAFTA-DR:

- Costa Rica: 3 August 1999;
- Nicaragua: 6 March 2003;
- Honduras: 20 June 2006;
- El Salvador: 17 August 2006;
- Guatemala: 14 October 2006;
- Dominican Republic: 28 May 2007.[242]

The PCT system has not only been implemented on the legislative level, but the patent offices also have been sufficiently trained to handle PCT applications in practice.[243] Initially, there was a temporary reduction in applications after PCT was introduced, *e.g.*, in Guatemala, where applications fell from 528 in 2006 to 108 in 2007.[244] This can probably be attributed to the fact that it takes some time for international applications to be processed by the receiving patent office and forwarded to other offices. While local practitioners observed that in the medium term the PCT system led to an increase in patent applications, such a trend did not last; to the contrary, the number of patent applications decreased in all Central American countries after 2010.[245] However, this decrease is not specific to Central America but occurred globally, as evidenced by the fact that the Central American countries maintained or even improved their "patent application" ranking, *i.e.*, the decrease in other countries was even larger.[246] Therefore, the decrease is probably not related to the introduction of the PCT system.

Most patent applications in Central America are international PCT applications that already underwent examination by the USPTO or the EPO, and the Central American examiners often accept the result of the prior examination.[247]

---

[240] Interview with *Diana Hasbún*.

[241] Nicaragua had joined the PCT system because of the respective obligation under the US-Nicaragua IP Agreement.

[242] Available at http://www.wipo.int/pct/en/pct_contracting_states.html (accessed 2 Nov 2024).

[243] This is evidenced by the fact that most patent applications and granted patents are based on the PCT procedure.

[244] See Table 3.4.

[245] See statistical data in Table 3.4.

[246] See the ranking shown on the WIPO country profiles, available at http://www.wipo.int/ipstats/en/statistics/country_profile/ (accessed 2 Nov 2024).

[247] This procedure was, for example, formally established in El Salvador by an amendment to Article 152 IP Law (SV); see also the presentation of CADOPAT by the Mexican IMPI to WIPO in 2016, available at https://www.wipo.int/meetings/en/doc_details.jsp?doc_id=345737 (accessed 2 Nov 2024).

Table 3.1 Deadlines for claiming priority

Country	Beginning of period	Period (months)	Source
Costa Rica	–	–	Article 12 Patent Regulation (CR)[a]
Dom. Rep.	Date of filing	2	Article 135 Law IP Law (DR)
El Salvador	Date of filing	6	Article 77(a) IP Reform Law (SV)
Guatemala	End of priority period	3	Article 104(4) IP Law (GT)
Honduras	Date of filing	1	Article 141 IP Law (HN)
Nicaragua	End of priority period	4	Article 90 Patent and Design Law (NI)

[a]The text of the regulation is available at http://www.wipo.int/wipolex/es/details.jsp?id=9331 (accessed 2 Nov 2024)

Priority

The date of the patent application is the basis for the evaluation of the novelty of the invention and from this date onward, the disclosed information becomes part of the state of the art for other patent applications. The possibility to claim an earlier application date in a third country as the relevant date for subsequent applications (priority), therefore, helps protecting the novelty of the invention.[248] Article 4 (C) Paris Convention introduced the possibility to apply for a patent in third countries based on the date of the original application for at least 1 year following the original application. The priority period is generally restricted to the minimum of 1 year in Central America.[249] The deadline to claim the priority can be set by the parties according to Article 4(D) Paris Convention. It varies substantially among the Central American countries.[250] In Costa Rica, the priority must be claimed in the application, which corresponds to the European system.[251] In all other countries, the priority can also be claimed later. In the Dominican Republic, El Salvador and Honduras, the deadline is calculated based on the filing date, with a minimum period to claim the priority of 3 or 4 months after the date of filing. In Guatemala and Nicaragua, the deadline to claim the priority is based on the end of the priority period. Practically, this means that the period to claim priority is extended if the patent application is filed some time before the end of the priority period. In Nicaragua, if the application is filed 6 months after the priority application, the priority can be claimed 10 months later. Compared to the European system, these flexibilities, as shown in Table 3.1, create legal uncertainty. While the EPC allows the applicant to supply documentary evidence of the priority after the application, the declaration regarding the priority must be made with the application. Especially in

[248]Cornish et al. (2013) at 4-11.

[249]E.g., Article 104(3) IP Law (GT).

[250]See the overview in Table 3.1.

[251]See R 26(2)(g) EPC.

Guatemala and Nicaragua, the priority and thus the relevant date for the state of the art remain uncertain up to possibly 15–16 months.[252]

Modifications to the Invention

The strict rules on novelty and priority in combination with the first-to-file principle pressure inventors to apply for a patent at an early stage, maybe even before the invention is fully understood or equivalent technology can be tested.[253] Therefore, through the possibility to modify the initial application without losing the priority, applicants are given "room for maneuver".[254] However, the disclosure of the earlier application cannot be amended, *e.g.*, in Europe.[255] As the claims must be supported by the disclosure, overreaching claims cannot be "healed" by subsequent amendments. CAFTA-DR requires "at least one opportunity to submit amendments, corrections, and observations",[256] without specifying limitations regarding the scope of such amendments. Nevertheless, national laws in Central America, in accordance with the international practice described above, while permitting modifications, exclude "amplifications" of the disclosed invention.[257]

Enabling Disclosure

The claims of the patent application define the scope of legal protection, but the disclosure section provides the information about the essential working of the invention to competitors and others.[258] For the disclosure to be useful and a contribution to technology dissemination, it must be so clear and complete that it "enables" a person skilled in the art to use the invention.[259] While the competitors have an interest in being informed fully about the invention, the inventor will try to maintain a competitive edge by only providing the necessary basic information. The protection of fair competition might call for strict disclosure requirements, including the obligation to reveal the "best mode" of using the invention.[260] However, the difficulties in proving an insufficient disclosure and the goal of rewarding innovative

---

[252] Under Rule 53 of the EPC (2000) the documentary evidence of the priority can be submitted until 16 months after the priority date. This corresponds with the period provided for in Nicaragua, but there the claim of the priority itself can be made until such date.

[253] Cornish et al. (2013) at 4-10.

[254] Cornish et al. (2013) at 4-11.

[255] Article 87 EPC; see Cornish et al. (2013) at 4-12.

[256] Article 15.9.8. CAFTA-DR.

[257] E.g., Article 29 Patent and Design Law (NI), Article 8(1) Patent and Design Law (CR).

[258] Cornish et al. (2013) at 5-82.

[259] See, e.g., Article 29 TRIPS, Article 15.9(9) CAFTA-DR, Article 83 EPC.

[260] On this issue see Cornish et al. (2013) at 5-83–5-86 with further references.

"technological leaders" caused, *e.g.*, the European system to shift toward lower standards, where an "acceptable, but not necessarily optimal" disclosure is sufficient.[261]

The Budapest Treaty creates a special procedure for the deposition of micro-organisms, if an invention relating to biological material cannot be fully explained by the disclosure without access to the material itself.[262] The ratification of the Budapest Treaty is mandated by Article 15.1.3 (b) CAFTA-DR. This deposition procedure is foreseen also in Central America by the national laws and referred to in the Patent Examiner Manual.[263] Under TRIPS, WTO members have several possibilities to implement the requirement of "enabling disclosure" in a way that could increase the technological accessibility of the patent application, thus increasing the potential for technology transfer and absorption:

- the *best mode* requirement,
- the definition of the *skilled person* and
- the disclosure of the *manufacturing process* of product patents.

Article 29 TRIPS permits countries to require *best mode* disclosures so as to not prejudice a decision on this issue. Article 15.9(9) CAFTA-DR, however, provides that a disclosure permitting the invention to be made and used by a person skilled in the art, *without undue experimentation*, shall be considered sufficiently "clear and complete". Central American countries are not permitted under CAFTA-DR to require the disclosure of the "best mode" of using the invention and, accordingly, in Central America there is no best mode requirement. The Patent Examiner Manual similarly requires only that the "description must allow the invention to be understood and applied by a person skilled in the arts".[264]

However, international agreements do not specify the *skilled person.*[265] To promote effective technology dissemination,[266] the Central American countries could provide for a *local content disclosure* requirement.[267] Under this approach, the person skilled in the art to whom the description of the invention is addressed is a person who has studied and acquired the technical skills in the country that receives the application, and not, if the application has a foreign origin, in the country of origin. With this requirement, it is ensured that local experts are able to understand

[261] Cornish et al. (2013) at 5-88.

[262] It should be noted that the system is criticized not only for being a danger to local genetic resources, but also for the risk of giving competitors access to the respective biological material. Regarding the latter controversy see Cornish et al. (2013) at 5-87.

[263] Patent Examiner Manual, p. 34.

[264] Patent Examiner Manual, p. 32.

[265] See, e.g., Article 29 TRIPS; Article 15.9(9) CAFTA-DR.

[266] Article 7 TRIPS.

[267] See WIPO, Public Policy-related Assistance—Flexibilities, available at http://www.wipo.int/ip-development/en/policy/flexibilities.html (accessed 2 Nov 2024).

the technical contents of patent applications filed in their country.[268] In other words, if a PCT application has been examined by the EPO and has been considered sufficiently clear for the skilled person (by European standards) by the European examiner, a Central American examiner could still reject the application if it is not clear to a Central American skilled person with a different level of education, practice and specialization. Such an approach would be compatible with CAFTA-DR. However, it would require a re-examination of PCT applications by local examiners, which due to the staffing constraints in all IP Registers probably would not be feasible.

Another approach that could contribute to the dissemination of technology is the obligation to disclose the *manufacturing process* of a product (or part thereof), if the patent application claims a product or part of a product. Such an approach could reduce the necessity of the competitors of the patentee to engage in costly and time-consuming reverse engineering if the process of making the product is not disclosed.[269]

3.1.6.2 Disclosure of Origin

Technical Background

A very controversial issue in the field of patent procedure is the requirement to disclose the origin of material used for the invention, in particular, genetic sources for pharmaceuticals. While this is not traditionally required, supporters argue that it is necessary to restrict "bio-piracy", *i.e.*, to prevent companies from developed countries to exploit knowledge developed in and belonging to developing countries and obtained by the companies from developed countries without consent (hence the term "piracy").[270] In addition, some companies have managed or tried not only to exploit such knowledge in developed countries, but even to enforce patents based on such "piracy" against firms in the country of origin that used to provide products based on such knowledge.[271] Therefore, the disclosure of origin shall not only prevent abusive exploitation abroad, but also give domestic producers a defense against an abusive patent application in their own market.[272]

---

[268] Ibid.

[269] Ibid.

[270] Stiglitz (2002), p. 246.

[271] For examples regarding such access to biodiversity see Sect. 6.1.5.4.

[272] Stiglitz (2002), p. 246.

Legal Background

The main legal argument against such disclosure, known as the "stolen microscope" argument, was developed in the US case *Moore v. Regents of University of California*.[273] Under the stolen microscope concept, patent law protects only information and can, therefore, disregard the origin of the physical material or equipment used. Patent law requires an invention, not that the material or procedure used was legal or ethical; these issues might be addressed by civil or criminal law. It is, therefore, irrelevant for attributing the patent right whether the biological material from which the genetic information was taken was obtained illegally or without consent. Even if biological material were obtained illegally, the inventor would be entitled to the patent, as the inventor made the inventive steps (in the *Moore* case, the isolation and use of the genetic sequence).[274] In other words, if the microscope with which the invention was made had been stolen, it would still be an invention of the thief. Similarly, it is an invention if the material which was analyzed had been stolen. However, the biological sources of an invention cannot be simply qualified as physical material. The physical organism embodies and contains the genetic information, which is the relevant source for the research. If the biological source was obtained through illegal bio-prospecting, it is not (only) a stolen physical organism (and comparable to the microscope), but also stolen *genetic information*. As such, proponents argue that it should be considered in the application process.[275] The "stolen microscope" argument is misleading for another reason in this case: Most jurisdictions grant the inventor a grace period for filing a patent application after the invention was disclosed illegally, *e.g.*, by breach of a contractual confidentiality obligation. Even though the invention is not technically novel at the time the patent application is filed, it is legally novel because the prior illegal disclosure is disregarded. Conversely, one could argue that, if the invention includes and/or is based on information obtained illegally, the patentability could be denied. Most importantly, without comparing the claimed invention with the biological sources as found in nature, it is impossible to examine novelty and inventive step.[276] The disclosure of origin can, therefore, in the respective cases be relevant for examining prior art and patentability. Moreover, if disclosure is not required at this stage, the review of patentability is shifted to cancellation or nullity procedures, and "competitors" (possibly small domestic producers) would have to invest financial resources to pursue litigation and may lose access to the market for a significant period up to the final decision.[277] Finally, the disclosure of origin is considered by many WTO members and scholars to be necessary to ensure that TRIPS is compatible with the

[273] Supreme Court of California, Decision of 9 July 1990, 51 Cal. 3d 120.

[274] See also Pires de Carvalho (2000), p. 390.

[275] On this issue see Hassemer (2003), pp. 209–210.

[276] Bucher (2008), p. 106 with further references.

[277] Stiglitz (2002), p. 246.

access and benefit sharing (ABS) rules of the Convention on Biological Diversity.[278]

International Law

It is disputed whether the current wording of TRIPS permits members to require the disclosure of origin. Opponents claim that TRIPS provides for an exhaustive list of permissible substantive requirements and exceptions[279] and disclosure requirements.[280] Supporters point out that additional procedural requirements are permitted under Article 62(1) TRIPS.[281] Many developing countries, based on the latter view, have included disclosure requirements, at least regarding domestic genetic resources.[282] However, the protection of genetic resources can only become truly effective if also the "major markets" in the developed countries have a similar requirement in their patent system.[283] Accordingly, several developing countries have started an initiative to include the disclosure of origin requirement in TRIPS, as a new Article 29*bis* TRIPS. When the TRIPS amendment was first proposed in 2006, the wording required WTO members to "ensure that administrative and/or judicial authorities have the authority to prevent the further processing of an application or the grant of a patent and to revoke [...] a patent" if the applicant has not complied with disclosure of origin requirements (as well as PIC/ABS obligations).[284] The mandatory authority to not grant or revoke a patent is such cases rejects the "stolen microscope" concept of *Moore* and would require WTO members to treat the misappropriation of biological material and the failure to disclose the appropriation process as grounds for rejecting patents. In 2011, a similar group of countries has presented a draft decision for the WTO with a modified wording, according to which "members shall impose sanctions, which may include administrative sanctions, criminal sanctions, fines and adequate compensation for damages (and) may take other measures and sanctions, including revocation".[285] This wording permits members to keep their national laws requiring the disclosure of origin, but allows other countries to grant patents even in case of misappropriation of biological resources and/or misrepresentation to the patent office and only impose other sanctions, *e.g.*,

---

[278] WTO General Council, Trade Negotiations Committee, Council for Trade-Related Aspects of Intellectual Property Rights (2006); WTO Trade Negotiations Committee (2011); see also Sarnoff and Correa (2006), p. iv.

[279] Article 27 TRIPS, see Hassemer (2003), p. 209.

[280] Article 29 TRIPS.

[281] Bucher (2008), p. 106 with further references.

[282] Bucher (2008), p. 344.

[283] Ibid.

[284] WTO General Council, Trade Negotiations Committee, Council for Trade-Related Aspects of Intellectual Property Rights (2006).

[285] WTO Trade Negotiations Committee (2011).

damages or fines. This wording, therefore, is a compromise, because it allows, *e.g.*, the USA to continue applying the *Moore* concept.

CAFTA-DR and the EU-FTAs

Article 15.9(10) CAFTA-DR does not refer to this issue directly, but provides that the parties "shall provide that a claimed invention is sufficiently supported by its disclosure if the disclosure reasonably conveys to a person skilled in the art that the applicant *was* in possession of the claimed invention as of the filing date". This could be interpreted to exclude the requirement to disclosure *how* the applicant obtained possession. Thus, CAFTA-DR would limit the possibility to require proof that biological material was legally obtained.[286]

The EU-CARIFORUM-EPA provides that the "parties may require as part of the administrative requirements for a patent application concerning an invention which uses biological material as a necessary aspect of the invention, that the applicant identifies the sources of the biological material used".[287] This optional wording falls short of the abovementioned proposal, as it is not only optional with regards to sanctions, but also with regard to the "disclosure of origin" requirement. Interestingly, an earlier draft of the EU-CARIFORUM-EPA included the additional requirement that the biological material was "described as part of the invention". However, this section was deleted during the negotiations.[288] The deletion of this section is an improvement, because the simple omission of a reference to the biological material in the description of the invention does not relieve the applicant from identifying the sources of the biological material. The only criterion is, therefore, whether the biological material constitutes a *material* aspect of the invention. This gives countries the possibility to interpret this clause in a way that biological material used during the development of the invention is *material*, even if the invention itself, as protected by the patent claims, does not include properties of such biological material as found in nature.

Under Article 229.4 EU-CA-AA, the parties may adopt or maintain measures to promote the conservation of biological diversity, the sustainable utilization of its components and the fair and equitable participation in the benefits arising from the utilization of genetic resources, in conformity with what is established in the CBD. This wording neither requires the parties to introduce a disclosure of origin provision, nor prevents them from doing so.

[286] Bucher (2008), p. 309.

[287] Article 150.4 EU-CARIFORUM-EPA.

[288] However, it is nevertheless included in some literature on the topic, e.g., Roffe (2013), p. 35.

Central America

In Central America, disclosure of origin is neither required as part of the patent application process nor apparently is there any political initiative to introduce it.[289] The only exception is Nicaragua, which requires the disclosure of origin in Article 84 Biodiversity Law (NI) since 2012.[290]

3.1.6.3 Examination

The examination is conducted in two steps, the formal examination (*examinación de forma*) and the substantive examination (*examinación de fondo*). The formal examination has to be completed within the time specified by patent or general administrative law, ranging from 1 week in El Salvador and 2 weeks in Costa Rica and Nicaragua to 1 month in Guatemala and Honduras and 2 months in the Dominican Republic.[291] The substantive examination includes the assessment of the patentability and the evaluation of the description, the claims (*reivindicaciones*) and drawings with regard to novelty, inventive step and industrial application, and the unity and clarity of the invention.[292] In Guatemala, the period for requesting the substantive examination after publication was extended from 2 to 3 months by the legislation implementing CAFTA-DR.[293]

3.1.6.4 Registration of Licenses

Under international law, countries may require patent licenses to be registered, unlike trademark licenses.[294] Several Central American laws provide for this registration.[295] The registration is usually inexpensive, *e.g.*, 20 USD in Guatemala.[296] This registration requirement, even though the fee is low, may complicate the grant

[289] In Costa Rica, if a patent is considered by the IP Register to contain genetic material of Costa Rican origin, CONAGEBIO participates in the patent examination process by confirming whether to applicable local access and benefit sharing (ABS) rules have been complied with, on this mechanism see Sect. 6.1.6.1; however, this does not constitute an obligation of the patent applicant to disclose the origin of the genetic material, see Cabrera Medaglia (2010), pp. 7–8.

[290] See Sect. 6.1.6.2.

[291] Patent Examiner Manual, p. 12.

[292] Patent Examiner Manual, p. 19.

[293] Article 117(1) IP Law (GT), as modified in 2006.

[294] See Sect. 3.1.6.4.

[295] See, e.g., in Costa Rica, Article 27 Patent and Design Law (CR) and in Guatemala, Article 132 IP Law (GT).

[296] Article 2 (b) Nr. 14 of the Acuredo Gubernativo No. 862-2000 of 21 December 2000, as amended by Acuerdo Gubernativo No 148-2014, available at https://portal.rpi.gob.gt/wp-content/uploads/2020/12/Acuerdo148-2014v2.pdf (accessed 2 Nov 2024).

of licenses and, therefore, the transfer of technology, because in Central America, the typical case would be the grant of a license by a foreign right holder for a local licensee. However, if the formal registration requirement is accompanied by substantive requirements regarding license agreements, in particular to protect local licensees against certain anti-competitive licensing practices, a formal registration requirement could be useful.[297]

3.1.6.5 Publication and Accessibility of Patent Information

The publication of the patent information is one of the core principles of patent law.[298] In practice, the positive effect on technology diffusion depends on the convenient accessibility of the patent information. Companies often review patent information as part of their business strategy. CAFTA-DR contains no provisions on the issue.[299]

The electronic patent databases of the Central American IP Registers provide only limited access to patent information, mostly by reference to the LATIPAT database of the European Patent Office.[300] Therefore, the objective of diffusion of technology is not (fully) reached in Central America; however, patent information is still accessible through international patent databases.

3.1.6.6 Legal Review

The establishment of mechanisms to review the rejection or grant of patent applications is critical to ensure the quality of granted patents and ensure that exclusivity is obtained only in relation to inventions that meet the patentability criteria.

Observations and Oppositions Procedures

The section on patents in CAFTA-DR requires no opposition procedure, which may seem surprising at first. However, as shortcomings in the opposition procedure tend to favor the right holder, it is consistent with the goal of CAFTA-DR to improve the

---

[297] On the relationship between IP law and competition law and the practical relevance of competition law in Central America see Sect. 2.6.1.

[298] The underlying idea of this principle is that patent protection is a reward for the inventor's public disclosure of the invention, instead of keeping the invention as a trade secret. In doing so, the inventor facilitates the diffusion of knowledge and enables the public to take the invention into account in further research, see Ann (2022) § 3 nr 11.

[299] This is not surprising because the publication of patents per se is global standard. In addition, requirements to ensure effective and easy access to patent information is the interest primarily of users and not a policy objective of right holders, which influenced the IP chapter of the US-FTAs.

[300] See Sect. 2.5.3.

Table 3.2 Time limits for the submission of pre-grant observations (Patent Examiner Manual, p. 17)

Country	Period in months	Source
Costa Rica	1	Article 12 Patent and Design Law (CR)
Dom Rep	2	Article 21 Law IP Law (DR)
El Salvador	2	Article 149 IP Reform Law (SV)
Guatemala	3	Article 116 IP Law (GT)
Honduras	No limit	Article 40 IP Law (HN)
Nicaragua	No limit[a]	Article 33 Patent and Design Law (NI)

[a]In Nicaragua observations can be submitted any time "before the final resolution of the application", i.e., the conclusion of the substantive examination, Article 33 Patent and Design Law (NI)

position of the right holder that there are no rules on the issue in the agreement. However, improving the opposition procedures can be an efficient way to prevent patents without merit being granted and thus to prevent overprotection. In Central America, the examiners can make observations during both formal and substantive examination, which the applicant must address within a certain period.[301] Observations (in Costa Rica called *oppositions*)[302] can be submitted also by third parties after formal examination is completed and the patent application has been published.[303] These observations are analyzed during the substantive examination. As they are designed as a contribution to the substantive examination, Costa Rica restricts oppositions to substantive issues, whereas formal questions must be raised in nullification procedures.[304] The period during which the observations must be made varies between 1 and 3 months in most countries, and is unlimited in Honduras and Nicaragua (see the overview in Table 3.2). In Nicaragua, the examination process is not suspended, because there is no time limit to file observations.[305] In Costa Rica, the examination process begins only after the time limit for the filing of an opposition has lapsed.

Honduras in addition provides for a *post-grant* opposition, which can be filed within 3 months after a summary of the granted patent is published.[306] In 2001, the legislation, Article 55 IP Law (HN), was reformed and now provides that the summaries are no longer published in the official gazette, but on the website of the IP Register.

[301] See, e.g., Article 113 IP Law (GT).

[302] Patent Examiner Manual, pp. 102–104.

[303] Patent Examiner Manual, p. 9.

[304] See Article 12(1) Patent and Design Law (CR).

[305] Article 33 (4) Patent and Design Law (NI).

[306] Article 55 IP Law (HN).

Judicial Review of Administrative Decisions

CAFTA-DR does not provide for the legal review of administrative decisions. While this could theoretically be problematic for the right holder, if a patent application is denied, in Central America judicial review of administrative decisions was generally available before CAFTA-DR and therefore this "omission" had no practical effect for patent applicants and right holders. Decisions during the application procedure can be brought before an appellate body of the IP Register. While these cases are pending, the patents are nonetheless granted. This is very beneficial for the applicant, while it creates the risk that patents are active and block competition even though legitimate objections were raised. These appellate decisions can generally be appealed to the administrative courts, in Costa Rica to the specialized Administrative Register Tribunal (TRA).[307] In Central America, the administrative legal review has the important advantage over civil proceedings that the respective administrative bodies are more specialized in patent matters, because a significant share of the proceedings coming from the national registries originate in the IP Registers, whereas civil courts, responsible for nullification cases, usually hear few IP cases.[308] However, in Nicaragua many administrative cases are pending for several years before they are abandoned, probably because they have become practically obsolete.[309]

CAFTA-DR also does not require the publication of final administrative decisions on individual cases. Only final *judicial* decisions or administrative rulings *of general applicability* have to be published.[310] As opposition procedures are not initiated by the right holder, transparency in this field was of no concern for CAFTA-DR. However, the lack of publication in administrative cases is detrimental, because there are more administrative than judicial decisions in the area of patents. Making the existing administrative decisions more easily available to IP lawyers and the interested public would facilitate the development of this area of law, which today suffers greatly from the lack of (available) case-law.

Judicial Nullity Procedures

After the patent is granted, its validity can be challenged in nullification proceedings. The nullification of a patent can be based on substantive or formal grounds. Article 15.9.4. CAFTA-DR provides that patents may be cancelled only in two cases:

[307] The TRA is discussed in detail in Sect. 2.5.4.

[308] The most prominent example for the expertise and specialization an administrative court can acquire is the TRA in Costa Rica, see Sect. 2.5.4.

[309] The author analyzed IP decisions in Nicaragua covering a period of several years, which are available electronically; the analysis revealed that a large number of cases are terminated by a desist declaration by one party after the respective case had been pending for many (often about 5) years.

[310] Article 15.11(3) CAFTA-DR.

Substantively on "grounds that would have justified a refusal to grant the patent", *i.e.*, the invention did not fulfill the patentability or procedural requirements. Formally nullification may be based on "fraud, misrepresentation or inequitable conduct". This can only specifically affect cases where the ground is unrelated to the patentability requirements. It is an extension compared to prior FTAs, which only provided for fraud as possible grounds to revoke or cancel a patent.[311] Central American laws also provide for nullification of a patent on both grounds, substantively for contraventions of patentability,[312] and formally for contraventions of application requirements.[313] While these provision does not literally implement CAFTA-DR, it legally appears to have the same scope, because it broadly covers contraventions of formal requirements, and while CAFTA-DR is not literally limited to the application procedure, it can reasonably only apply to conduct during the application procedure.

3.1.6.7 Fees

Several observations can be made with regard to the fee policy in Central America, as shown in Table 3.3. Both the costs of obtaining and of maintaining patents are significantly lower than in the USA or Europe. While this may be justified with regard to local inventors, it seems less necessary for international applicants. In order to create an incentive for applications and technology transfer as well as for relinquishing patents after they have lost their economic value, steeply increasing annual fees like in Nicaragua seems appropriate from a policy perspective. Such progressive fees are used in most developed countries, and, *e.g.*, in Germany they cause the right holders to abandon patents on average after about 8 years, not even half the maximum term.[314] Constant annual fees like in Costa Rica and in Honduras by contrast do little to incentivize right holders to evaluate their patent portfolios and possibly abandon patents earlier.

In Costa Rica this situation is especially complicated. The annual fees had to be determined by a regulation under the pre-CAFTA-DR legislation.[315] The regulation was invalidated by the *Sala IV* of the CSJ (CR), which held that it is unconstitutional to establish fees by regulation and not by law. This decision can be questioned for several reasons. First, the *Sala IV* of the CSJ (CR) could have granted a transitional period for the government to pass a law, while the regulatory fees would still apply. This would have prevented right holders from maintaining their exclusive right for free and secured much needed funding for the IP Register and the educational

[311] Fn 24 to Article 17.9.5 US-Chile-FTA.

[312] E.g., Articles 57 in connection with 5–10 IP Law (HN), which corresponds to Article 15.9.4. CAFTA-DR.

[313] E.g., Article 57 with Article 50–52 IP Law (HN).

[314] Cooter and Ulen (2000), p. 134.

[315] Based on Article 33 Patent and Design Law (CR) of 2000.

Table 3.3 Fees for patent prosecution charged by the Central American IP Registers

Country	Currency	Application & examination	Renewal 3rd year	Renewal last year	Other fees
CR[a]	Colón	The fees are specified in USD in Article 33 Patent and Design Law (CR)			
	USD	500	500	500	
DR[b]	Peso	28,995 plus 3965 for publications	6610	15,870	
	USD	561 (total)	112	270	
SV[c]	EUR	292	95	836	
GT[c]	EUR	644	64 (total until year 5)	946 (total until year 20)	
HN[d]	Lempira	2200.00	200.00	200.00	300.00 (license)
	USD	29	8	8	12
NI[c]	Pesos	The fees in Nicaragua are calculated in Central American Pesos, an artificial currency used for easier conversion and corresponding always to one USD			
	EUR	425	83 (total until year 5)	3325 (total until year 20)	

[a]Article 33 Patent and Design Law (CR); local currency converted as of Jan 2024
[b]Available at https://www.wipo.int/export/sites/www/pct/guide/en/gdvol2/annexes/do.pdf (accessed 2 Nov 2024); local currency converted as of 2024
[c]Fee structure available at https://intellectual-property-helpdesk.ec.europa.eu/patent-protection-cost-country-latin-america_en (accessed 2 Nov 2024)
[d]See https://pctlegal.wipo.int/eGuide/view-doc.xhtml?doc-code=HN&doc-lang=en#GENERAL%20INFO (accessed 2 Nov 2024), the fees are specified in Article 174 IP Law (HN); local currency converted as of Jan 2024

institutions funded by the IP Register fees.[316] But the decision also seems impractical. Fees require regular adjustment for inflation and in case new services are introduced, *e.g.*, reduced fees for online registration. It is overly burdensome to oblige the parliament to deal with this question, which obviously does not draw its attention, as evidenced by the fact that annual fees were introduced only as part of the CAFTA-DR Reform Law I (CR). Even under the new framework, no annual fees are payable for patents filed before 25 April 2008.[317] As part of the implementation of CAFTA-DR, a list of fees was introduced in Article 33 Patent and Design Law (CR), including a constant 500 USD annual fee.[318] However, the annual fee only applies to patents filed after the introduction of this fee.[319]

[316]See Sect. 2.5.3.
[317]Luis Diego Castro, Costa Rica—Payment of patent annuities (2016) (on file with the author).
[318]Article 33(f) Patent and Design Law (CR); the specifics of the payments were further clarified in 2014, however, the constant annual fee as such was kept, see https://intellectual-property-helpdesk.ec.europa.eu/patent-protection-cost-country-latin-america_en (accessed 2 Nov 2024).
[319]Luis Diego Castro, Costa Rica—Payment of patent annuities (2016) (on file with the author).

Like other patent offices around the world, some IP Registers in Central America, such as El Salvador and the Dominican Republic, offer significant fee reductions for individual inventors and/or small and medium enterprises (SMEs).[320] This provides a competitive advantage to smaller local businesses, but also allows them to more easily obtain a patent which can then be used in negotiations with international partners.

3.1.7 Statistical Data

The data available regarding patent applications and grants is incomplete. This makes it difficult to perform a detailed analysis. However, some trends are noticeable (see Table 3.4).

3.1.7.1 Patent Applications

In the years after CAFTA-DR entered into force (2010–2014), the number of patent applications actually decreased in all Central American countries. However, this decrease in patent applications is not specific to Central America, but occurred globally. CAFTA-DR, therefore, had probably no negative effect on patent application: To the contrary, it may have contributed to the "relatively" slow decrease of patent applications, which may have been more pronounced without CAFTA-DR. In absolute numbers, patent applications fell from around 750 to around 600 in Costa Rica and from around 350 to around 250 in the Dominican Republic and Guatemala, and even lower in the case of Honduras and Nicaragua. Between 2014 and 2018, the decrease in patent applications continued. In absolute numbers, patent applications fell to less than 500 in Costa Rica and to around 150–200 in other countries. No numbers have been reported for Nicaragua. During the same time, the number of patent applications rose globally, meaning that during this period the decrease happened against global trends. The long-term development suggests that CAFTA-DR had no positive effect on patent applications, even though the possibility of PCT filings makes patent applications now easier. As regards local inventions, until 2010, very few patent applications originated from Central America (mainly from Costa Rica). Since 2011, the region started to see more patent applications originating from residents in Central American countries, also from the Dominican Republic and Honduras. It is not clear whether this trend was based on the changes in patent policy due to CAFTA-DR and represented a fundamental shift in the regional approach to patent rights, or is simply a short-term spike. The data basis was too small for a solid assessment. Importantly, the number of patent applications from local applicants fell as well during the period of 2014–2018 in most countries. This

[320] See, e.g., Article 10 IP Law (DR), Article 33 Patent and Design Law (CR).

Table 3.4 Patent statistics for Central America

		2003	2004	2005	2006	2007	2008	2009	2010	2011	2012	2013	2014	2015	2016	2017	2018	2019	2020	2021
Costa Rica	Resident applications	33	26	17	22	20	24	16	8	13	9	18	15	17	9	19	8	16	12	15
	Non-res. applications	238	294	423	571	647	774	507	606	610	578	580	529	582	497	504	490	483	524	566
	Grants	6	14	13	6	13	46	35	34	35	66	100	111	125	68	18968	165	191	170	130
	Patents in force								239	245	309	413	515	629	677	830	629	1068	1175	1188
Dom Republic	Resident applications	18	24	8	15	34	8	17	15	15	19	12	16	25	28	20	17	23	10	7
	Non-res. applications	184	181	217	280	111	45	238	328	318	265	256	244	227	242	251	211	220	207	220
	Grants						94	273	91	71	114	68	129	155	100	127	95	158	138	227
	Patents in force										201	229	294	311	265	282	635	758	861	938
El Salvador	Resident applications													7	4	4	3	1	4	2
	Non-res. applications										217	183	187	196	171	178	136	147	143	144
	Grants										33	48	77	35	40	24	36	117	67	58
	Patents in force													85						
Guatemala	Resident applications	6	9	17	28	9	5	7	7	4	7	4	10	7	3	3	6	7	7	9
	Non-res. applications	296	266	388	500	99	306	322	374	327	337	319	288	341	266	275	228	231	205	249
	Grants	75	124	104		110	96	191	104	39	86	65	105	51	52	50	30	50	40	38
	Patents in force			1030		433	523	521	590	636	681	746	840	867	883	908	914	235	257	224

Honduras	Resident applications								2	8	6		4	10	4	8				
	Non-res. applications								253	233	211		224	185	189	148	187		188	
	Grants	173	16	85	11	30	31	46	81	151	136	132	94	69	53	54	88	85	40	92
	Patents in force									965					82	1654	1765	267	252	349
Nicaragua	Resident applications								2	4	3	1								
	Non-res. applications								208	172	124	145								
	Grants									61	68	72	62							
	Patents in force									219	250	328	387							

Data provided by the WIPO IP Statistics Data Center [https://www3.wipo.int/ipstats/ips-search/patent (accessed 2 Nov 2024)], based on input from the national IP Registers. Empty boxes represent data not reported suggests that, at least as measured by patent applications, that innovative activity in the region decreased in absolute terms and that the region lost ground compared to the rest of the world. However, the numbers fluctuate significantly from year to year, possibly due to the small overall numbers. Nevertheless, on average, the local filings are slightly decreasing in all countries that reported figures over this period. Between 2019 and 2021, the last years for which data was available, the number of patent applications from both local and foreign applicants continued to decline slowly. This suggest that neither the level of local innovative activity nor the international perception of the value of patent protection in the region improved.

3.1.7.2 Patent Grants and Active Patents

The statistics regarding patent grants provide a more complex picture, with strong differences between Costa Rica and the Dominican Republic and the other Central American countries.

Prior to 2006, in Costa Rica, very few patents had been granted for several years (which especially affects those regarding pharmaceutical inventions as they represent the majority of applications).[321] In addition, the IP Register refused many pharmaceutical patents based on very strict criteria regarding second use and medical treatment.[322] Because of this practical denial of patent protection, Costa Rica was repeatedly criticized by the USTR.[323] Since 2006 the number of patent grants in Costa Rica has increased steadily, from around 10 in 2006 and 2007 to around 40 between 2008 and 2011 to more than 100 in 2013 and 2014. However, it must be noted that this still represents less than 20% of patent applications received. This practice of Costa Rica was consistent with TRIPS rules until the transition period with regard to the registration of patents in all fields expired.[324] However, even after the end of the transition period and the entry into force of CAFTA-DR, the registration practice apparently did not immediately change. In the Dominican Republic, prior to the implementation of CAFTA-DR, no patents were granted on applications filed after the entry into force of the new patent law in 2000. Based on the WIPO data, one can estimate that only around 15 patents were granted annually from 2006 until 2011.[325] Affected US businesses, therefore, considered pharmaceutical products not protectable by patents in the Dominican Republic as a practical

[321] See the data reported by Registro de la Propiedad Industrial de Costa Rica (2006), p. 39 and Annex I; see also PhRMA (2007), p. 153.

[322] Regarding the restriction on second medical use patents see, e.g., European Commission, Executive Agency for Small and Medium-sized Enterprises (2019), p. 5.

[323] USTR Special 301 Report (2016), pp. 58–60; USTR Special 301 Report (2017), p. 64.

[324] Article 65 TRIPS.

[325] See Table 3.4, based on the number of active patents and assuming an average patent life of 8 years.

Table 3.5 Number of active patents in Central America and other countries between 2010 and 2014 [based on data provided by WIPO, available at https://www3.wipo.int/ipstats/ips-search/patent/ (accessed 2 Nov 2024)]

Country	Active patents	Year	Active patents	Year	Annual increase	Active patents	Year	Annual increase
Central America								
CR	239	2010	515	2014	21.3%	629	2018	15.6%
DR	201	2012	294	2014	20.9%	635	2018	20.8%
SV	n/a	2010	n/a	2014	n/a	n/a	2018	n/a
GT	590	2010	840	2014	9.2%	914	2018	2.1%
HN	n/a	2011	n/a	2014	n/a	1765	2018	n/a
NI	219	2011	387	2014	20.9%	n/a	2018	n/a
Other countries								
MX	82,017	2010	106,340	2014	6.7%	113,286	2018	1.6%
US	2,017,318	2010	2,527,750	2014	5.8%	3,063,494	2018	4.9%
DE	514,046	2010	576,273	2014	2.9%	703,606	2018	5.1%

matter.[326] This delay in granting patents has been repeatedly criticized by the USTR.[327] Between 2012 and 2014, around 100 patents were granted on average, representing about 35% of patent applications. In other countries, (foreign) patent applications had a higher success rate. There is apparently no (or at least less) bias against foreign applications, as evidenced, *e.g.*, by the fact that Honduras and Nicaragua grant more than 50% of all patent applications. The absolute number of granted patents decreased significantly in Honduras and Nicaragua from 2011 to 2014, however, this development is aligned with the decrease in patent applications. The development of patent grants between 2014 and 2018 presents a very diverse picture. While the numbers in the Dominican Republic and Honduras are relatively constant, the numbers fell by more than half in Guatemala and El Salvador (even when factoring in the decrease in applications). In Costa Rica, more patents were granted even though less patents were filed. As shown in Table 3.5, the number of active patents increased substantially in most Central American countries between 2010/2011 and 2014, although it must be noted that despite the significant increase the absolute number of active patents is still extremely low. The increase in active patents continued between 2014 and 2018, but at a slower relative rate (partly because the absolute numbers were higher in 2014 as in 2010/2011).[328]

[326] PhRMA (2007), pp. 26, 157–158.

[327] USTR Special 301 Report (2016), pp. 58–60; USTR Special 301 Report (2017), p. 64.

[328] However, as noted already these numbers are not always reliable and consequently their interpretation must be viewed with caution. For example, for Honduras and Nicaragua, for many years no data is available. Also, the Dominican Republic reported an increase in active patents between 2017 and 2018 from 282 to 635 (plus 353), but only 127 and 95 patents were granted in 2017 and 2018, respectively.

3.1.8 Term of Protection

3.1.8.1 Basic Term

With regard to the patent term, the question whether "one size fits all" types of subject matter and technology has been repeatedly raised. Economically, one term for all patents may not be optimal, because of different industry frameworks and research costs, and as a consequence, different incentive structures.[329] However, even if term differentiation would make sense economically, it would also have to be politically feasible. The discussions about differentiation of protection according to subject matter, which concerned in particular medicines, agro-chemicals (additional test data protection)[330] and plant varieties (longer *sui generis* protection),[331] however, have shown the political difficulties of term differentiations.

Article 33 TRIPS introduced a minimum term of protection of 20 years from the filing date for all patents. Therefore, it applies also to patents for *TRIPS-plus* subject matter introduced by bilateral FTAs and CAFTA-DR did not have to restate this term. This term extension was controversial in Latin America.[332] Some countries delayed its implementation as long as possible under TRIPS, which granted a transitional period of 5 years generally for developing countries and additional 5 years for subject matter which had been excluded from patent protection before TRIPS.[333]

El Salvador restricted the term of protection for patents on medicines to 15 years[334] prior to 2005, when the country implemented CAFTA-DR.[335] In other Central American countries the uniform patent term was already implemented in the post-TRIPS legislation.

In Costa Rica, the term of protection for PCT patents begins on the date of filing of the patent application in the country of origin, rather than from the filing date of the application in Costa Rica.[336] This provision has been challenged as contrary to Article 33 TRIPS and Article 4*bis* of the Paris Convention, which allegedly require a 20 year patent term from the filing date of the application in the respective country.[337] However, Article 33 TRIPS refers only generally to the filing date, not the *domestic* filing date. While a WTO dispute resolution panel Appellate Body clarified some issues regarding Article 33 TRIPS in the *Canada—Term of patent protection* decision, this decision did not address the questions when the term starts (priority or

[329] See Zhang (2013), p. 64 with references to further studies.

[330] See Sect. 3.4.

[331] See Sect. 3.3.

[332] Hassemer (2000), p. 25.

[333] Article 65(2) and (4) TRIPS.

[334] Article 109(2) IP Law (SV).

[335] This exception was removed by Article 56 CAFTA-DR IP Reform Law (SV).

[336] Article 17(1) Patent and Design Law (CR).

[337] PhRMA (2007), p. 153.

national filing date).[338] Therefore, it is not clear whether the Costa Rican provision contradicts the TRIPS requirement.

3.1.8.2 Patent Term Extension for Delays During Examination

Background

After the formal term of patent protection had been established by TRIPS, CAFTA-DR focused on expanding the effective term by providing for extensions for procedural delays during the patent application and marketing approval processes, which will be analyzed in the following two sections. Test data protection will be analyzed separately, as it legally constitutes a distinct right and only practically can function as an extension of the effective patent term.

The adjustment or restoration of the term for procedural delays ensures that the right holder is not deprived of the effective period of protection because of administrative activities (or lack thereof). From a policy perspective, the extension improves legal certainty for the right holder, as protection does not depend on internal factors of the administration, which it can hardly foresee and cannot influence.

CAFTA-DR

With regard to term extension for such procedural delays, CAFTA-DR requires a term *compensation* (*i.e.*, extension) for *unreasonable* delays.[339] Delays in the granting of a patent of more than 5 years from the date of filing or 3 years after a request for examination shall always be considered unreasonable and, therefore, shall always be compensated, unless the delay is attributable to actions of the patent applicant.[340] This mandatory extension does not exclude the possibility to define other circumstances in which delays are considered *unreasonable* and entitle the right holder to compensation. The *Bipartisan Trade Deal* of May 2007 provides for flexibility of developing country FTA partners in relation to restoring patent terms to compensate for processing delays.[341] However, this flexibility was not explicitly granted retroactively to existing FTAs such as CAFTA-DR.

[338] WTO Appellate Body, Decision of 18 September 2000, WT/DS170/AB/R.

[339] Article 15.9.6(a)(1) CAFTA-DR.

[340] Article 15.9.6(a)(2) CAFTA-DR.

[341] USTR (2007), p. 3; see also Roffe (2013), p. 937.

National Legislation

Most Central American countries provide for compensation of the patent term only in the two cases explicitly specified in CAFTA-DR, *i.e.*, delays of more than 5 years from the date of filing or 3 years after a request for examination, but (except for Guatemala) omitting the reference to the broader concept of *unreasonableness*.[342] This limitation in the national laws is narrower than the wording in CAFTA-DR, but it cannot be considered an insufficient implementation. As the two aforementioned cases are the only ones explicitly mandated, conversely all other cases are not mandatory. Therefore, the parties are permitted to provide that no other cases are considered unreasonable. While the mandatory clause in CAFTA-DR is unequivocal, several Central American countries included restrictions of the calculation of the term of such extensions in their implementation laws.

- First, most countries provide for a *maximum extension term*, even if the delay by the IP Register exceeds this maximum. The maximum extension term differs from country to country and ranges from 550 days, *i.e.*, approx. 16½ months in El Salvador and Nicaragua,[343] and 18 months in Costa Rica[344] to 3 years in the Dominican Republic.[345] Only Guatemala does not provide for a maximum term.[346] This restriction evidently violates CAFTA-DR, as its wording clearly does not provide for such a limitation.[347]
- Second, in El Salvador and Nicaragua, the extension period is calculated based only on the delay *caused by the IP Register*, not by third parties.[348] These provisions also conflict with CAFTA-DR, which only excludes actions attributable to the *patent applicant*, but not those of third parties from the calculation.[349] It also changes the burden of proof, as under CAFTA-DR the extension is excluded only if the delay can be attributed to the right holder, while the national laws only grant the extension if the delay can be attributed to the IP Register.

Honduras did not implement the term extension required by CAFTA-DR in the CAFTA-DR Reform Law (HN) of 2006. Subsequently, a reform law proposal was introduced in 2008 to provide for the extension in an amended Article 15 (3) IP Law

[342] See, e.g., Article 27 IP Law (DR); Article 109-A IP Law (SV) [as amended by Article 57 CAFTA-DR IP Reform Law (SV)], Article 38bis Patent and Design Law (NI); Article 126 bis (a) IP Law (GT) in Guatemala limits the extension to "unjustified" delays.

[343] Article 109-A IP Law (SV), introduced by Article 57 IP Law (SV); Article 38bis Patent and Design Law (NI).

[344] Article 17(3) Patent and Design Law (CR).

[345] Article 27 para I sec 1 IP Law (DR).

[346] Article 126 bis (a) IP Law (GT).

[347] Article 15.9.6(a)(2) CAFTA-DR.

[348] Article 109-A IP Law (SV), Article 38bis Patent and Design Law (NI).

[349] CAFTA-DR was correctly implemented in this respect in the other countries, see, e.g., Article 17 Patent and Design Law (CR); Article 126bis(a) IP Law (GT).

(HN).[350] Notably, this amendment was not included in the reform law of 2011, which modified other aspects of patent law.[351]

Evaluation

The maximum limitations on the extension term created in Central American legislation, being one of the few cases in which they deviated from CAFTA-DR requirements, suggest that the Central American countries had serious concerns regarding this requirement. They are especially noteworthy, because they are one of the very few balancing provisions included in the implementation laws that do not have some basis in flexible TRIPS or CAFTA-DR provisions or prior national laws. It must also be noted that these maximum limitations were included in the legislation before the Bipartisan Trade Deal was adopted by the US Congress. Whether the extension for procedural delays is practically relevant in Central America is unclear. As its application depends on the expediency of the national examination process, one has to consider the work of the respective IP Register. In El Salvador, for instance, patents are granted relatively easy and fast, examinations do not take more than 5 years and, therefore, this extension may rarely be applied. In countries with a slower examination process, such as Costa Rica and the Dominican Republic, some examinations can take longer than 5 years.[352] In such cases, the extensions can become relevant. In the Dominican Republic, the IP Register does not grant applications for patent term adjustments according to information provided to the USTR.[353]

Apart from the direct effect of extending the patent term, one can imagine another indirect effect of this mechanism. Because there is political interest in not prolonging protection and because examinations longer than 5 years are legally considered "delays", examiners may feel they are expected to conclude the examination within this period, that the "examination must be done within five years".[354] This may motivate examiners to grant patents prematurely to avoid the risk of delaying the procedure and causing the compensation mechanism.[355] As a result, the quality of the examination may suffer.[356] To safeguard the quality and thoroughness of the

[350] The draft law proposal is on file with the author.

[351] See Sect. 2.4.6.

[352] Regarding the Dominican Republic, see USTR Special 301 Report (2017), p. 64.

[353] In addition, the IP Register maintains that adjustments do not apply to applications submitted before March 2008, see USTR Special 301 Report (2017), p. 64 and USTR Special 301 Report (2018), p. 77. This position is legally incompatible with the retroactive effect of the IP provisions in CAFTA-DR, required by Article 15.1(11) CAFTA-DR. On the retroactive effect of the IP provisions see Sect. 2.2.4.2.

[354] This concern has been suggested to the author by local practitioners.

[355] Castro (2015), p. 94.

[356] A similar concern has been raised with regard to other formal examination requirements such as the fixed number of cases that have to be concluded by examiners at the EPO.

examinations, it might, therefore, be helpful to include an exception to the automatic extension in cases where because of special circumstances an excess of the 5 year term is not *unreasonable*. This could be due to, *e.g.*, the technical complexity of an invention or delays caused by third parties. However, such an exception is not permitted under CAFTA-DR and does not exist under current Central American legislation, with the possible exception of third-party delays in El Salvador and Honduras.

3.1.8.3 Patent Term Extension for Delays During Marketing Approval

Background

Patent term extensions can be granted not only for delays in the patent examination process, but also for delays during the marketing approval of pharmaceutical products. The rationale for term extensions for delays during marketing approval is similar to the extension for delays in the patent examination process. It shall provide legal certainty with regard to the expectation of exclusivity for the period of protection "promised" by the patent term, in order to maintain the incentive to innovate.[357]

CAFTA-DR

Under Article 15.9.6(b) CAFTA-DR, the "restoration" of the patent term is required (1) with respect to any *pharmaceutical product* that is covered by a patent (2) for *unreasonable curtailment* of the effective patent term resulting from the marketing approval process related to the first commercial marketing of the product. The "restoration" of the effective patent term is practically achieved by extending the patent term. This extension of the patent term meets two main concerns: On the *legal* level, Article 27(1) TRIPS provides that "patents shall be available and patent rights enjoyable without discrimination as to … the field of technology". The "restoration" or extension of the term only for pharmaceutical products under Article 15.9.6 (b) CAFTA-DR represents a positive discrimination of patent rights in the field of pharmaceuticals. On the *policy* level, the clause links two typically unrelated areas, the regulatory sphere and the patent sphere. In the end, the patent office when deciding about an extension may have to assess whether the examination of the health authorities which caused a delay was unreasonable. Conversely, the health authorities may be tempted to grant marketing authorization more quickly to avoid the extension of the patent term.

[357] Cornish and Liddell (2016), p. 37.

National Legislation

Most Central American provisions refer for the extension to a *pharmaceutical product* covered or protected by a (valid) patent.[358] Only the Salvadoran legislation seems to be limited to registered product patents (*patente del producto registrada*).[359] This would exclude all process patents, which are practically important also for pharmaceutical products. Given their importance, one cannot assume that CAFTA-DR uses the term "patent" in the restricted sense of "product patent". Therefore, the Salvadoran limitation would violate the requirement of Article 15.9.6 (b) CAFTA-DR if interpreted that way; a compliant interpretation would be to construe the phrase as referring to "product-related" patents.

The extension under CAFTA-DR is limited to the first commercial marketing of the product.[360] On the national level, it is granted only for new entities or compounds, *i.e.*, not second indications.[361]

While CAFTA-DR specifies cases in which the delay is automatically considered unreasonable with regard to *examination* delays,[362] there are no criteria for unreasonable delays during *marketing approval*. Nevertheless, several countries limit the marketing approval procedure to a certain maximum period after which it is automatically considered unreasonably delayed. The respective period ranges from 2 years and 6 months in the Dominican Republic[363] and 3 years in Costa Rica[364] to 5 years in El Salvador[365] after the application for the marketing authorization. Some countries limit the term restoration for marketing approval delays in correspondence with the limit for the compensation of delays during patent examination, even though such limits are not provided for under CAFTA-DR.[366] The limits are set at 18 months in Costa Rica,[367] 550 days in El Salvador[368] or 3 years in the Dominican Republic.[369]

---

[358] Article 17(4) Patent and Design Law (CR), Article 27(2) IP Law (DR) 2006.

[359] Article 109-A IP Law (SV), introduced by Article 57 CAFTA-DR Reform Law; Article 10 Test Data Regulation (SV).

[360] Article 15.9.6(b) CAFTA-DR.

[361] In El Salvador see Article 1 Test Data Regulation (SV).

[362] Article 15.9.6(b) CAFTA-DR.

[363] Article 27 para I sec 2 IP Law (DR).

[364] Article 17(4) Patent and Design Law (CR).

[365] Article 109-A IP Law (SV), introduced by Article 57 CAFTA-DR IP Reform Law (SV), Article 10 Test Data Regulation (SV).

[366] See also above Sect. 3.1.8.3.

[367] Article 17 (5) Patent and Design Law (CR).

[368] Article 109-A IP Law (SV) (introduced by Article 57 CAFTA-DR IP Reform Law (SV) and also Article 10 Test Data Regulation (SV).

[369] Article 27 para I sec 2 IP Law (DR).

Honduras did not implement the term extension required by CAFTA-DR in the CAFTA-DR Reform Law (HN) of 2006.[370]

Special Focus: Guatemala

In Guatemala, the extension was unlimited and had to be equivalent to the delay according to Article 126*bis*(b) IP Law (GT), introduced by the CAFTA-DR Reform Law (GT). This enabled the right holder to apply for an "adjustment" if the marketing approval was granted more than 3 months after the patent application was filed. This surprising provision raised two important questions: First, why is the extension linked to the patent application? Delays in the patent examination are regulated separately.[371] Also, the patent application is typically filed several years before the application for the marketing authorization for the drug covered by the patent, because clinical trials, which typically take several years to complete, are typically performed after the patent application is filed, but are required for the marketing authorization. If Article 126*bis*(b) IP Law (GT) would be applied literally, it would probably apply to most pharmaceutical patents, and the extension would be enormous, because it would be calculated based on the earlier event of the patent application and, therefore, include the entire period of clinical trials, and it would be unlimited in time. In the other countries, the extension is limited to the marketing approval process from the submission of the application for marketing approval (after the completion of the clinical trials) until grant of the marketing approval. Second, why is the term of the delay so short (3 months)? This term is not only much shorter than in all other Central American countries, but also shorter than, *e.g.*, in Europe.

While no public information is available on the background or legislative intent behind this provision, it appears that these questions have been discussed also locally and the wording been amended in the meantime. In 2013, the existing Article 126*bis*(b) IP Law (GT) was replaced with a clause granting a term extension if the marketing approval is granted more than *one year* after the *marketing approval* application was filed.[372]

Evaluation

As there is the possibility that the term extension will become practically more relevant in the long term, it is important to evaluate its policy justification and legal implementation. The term extension for delays during marketing approval has been strongly criticized, mainly for the same reasons patent protection in developing

[370] See Sect. 3.1.8.2.

[371] In Guatemala, in Article 126*bis* (a) IP Law (GT).

[372] Article 126*bis* (b) IP Law (GT) as amended by the EU-CA-AA Reform Law (GT).

countries is criticized generally.[373] The extension is viewed as a rent-seeking strategy of the pharmaceutical companies, designed to longer exploit existing products, because these companies have less and less innovative products. There is some foundation for this view, because CAFTA-DR also applies to existing products, where the incentive rationale of patent protection does not apply. The fact that international pharmaceutical companies have specifically monitored whether the laws implementing CAFTA-DR are retroactive, as shown by their submission to the USTR in 2007, further supports this view that rent-seeking was part of the reason of obtaining stronger patent protection.[374]

On the other hand, one must acknowledge that it has become more and more difficult and time-consuming to conduct the clinical trials necessary to obtain marketing approval, because for public safety and health reasons the requirements for these trials are becoming more demanding. While these demanding requirements are reasonable from a public policy perspective, they affect the return of investment for pharmaceutical in two ways: It increases the investment required for launching a product by increasing the costs of the clinical trials. Second, it reduces the time period from marketing authorization to patent expiry during which the investment can be recovered through monopoly prices. For this dilemma, some economic solution is necessary. The extension on a case-by-case basis represents a feasible solution, because the alternative would be a patent extension for pharmaceutical patents generally, which is politically unlikely and could also benefit drugs with a sufficiently long period of exclusive exploitation. However, the extension could create an incentive for the health authorities to grant marketing authorization more quickly to avoid the extension of the patent term and compromise scientific scrutiny.[375]

Regarding the implementation of the CAFTA-DR requirements in Central America, it is noteworthy that this issue is one of the few cases where the implementation has been more restrictive than the CAFTA-DR rules. While the limitation to product patents in El Salvador (depending on the interpretation of the clause) and the maximum term extension in several countries are not compatible with the wording of Article 15.9.6(b) CAFTA-DR, the specification of the term "delay" and clarification that the delay is computed from the date of submission of the marketing authorization (except *for some time* in Guatemala) use the existing vagueness of the agreement. This is not only beneficial potential generic competition, but also increases legal certainty, which may be helpful to all parties involved.

---

[373] See Sect. 3.1.1.

[374] PhRMA (2007), p. 2.

[375] See also Sect. 3.1.8.

3.1.9 Patent Linkage

3.1.9.1 Background and CAFTA-DR

As discussed above, CAFTA-DR linked the patent sphere and the regulatory sphere by providing for a term extension of the patent term for delays during the (regulatory) marketing approval. But CAFTA-DR also makes the reverse link by making the marketing approval subject to patent law requirements. Specifically, marketing approval cannot be granted for a pharmaceutical product if:

- the application for marketing approval is based on undisclosed information used without authorization,[376]
- the product was developed under a research exemption[377] and
- the product is a generic version of a drug still protected by patents.[378]

The third case will be analyzed in this section. This "patent linkage" extends the rights of the right holder by enabling the exclusion of generic competitors from obtaining marketing approval. This patent linkage is based on an equivalent mechanism under US law introduced by the Hatch-Waxman Act in 1984. Under this patent linkage mechanism, the originator company provides, together with the new drug application (NDA), a list of the patents which claim the drug, which the FDA publishes in the Orange Book.[379]

If a generic company files an abbreviated new *drug application* (*ANDA*) for the same drug, it must file a statement regarding these patents. In particular, it can submit a "paragraph IV certification" if it believes the patents to be invalid or unenforceable. The first generic company to submit an ANDA that contains a "paragraph IV certification" is eligible for the exclusive right to market the generic drug for 180 days. The patent owner is notified of the "paragraph IV certification" and can file a patent infringement action, while the generic company can file a nullity action against the patent. If an infringement action is filed, the FDA approval for the generic drug is stayed for 30 months unless the patent expires or is judged to be invalid or not infringed before that time.[380]

Article 15.10(2) CAFTA-DR provides for an equivalent *patent linkage* mechanism between the regulatory process and patent law. It requires (1) measures in the drug marketing approval process to prevent other persons from marketing a product covered by a patent claiming the product or its approved use during the term of that

[376] Article 15.10(1) CAFTA-DR; this provision extends the patent linkage protection to the protection of test data; on this issue, see Sect. 3.4.

[377] Article 15.9.5. CAFTA-DR; see Sect. 3.1.11.4.

[378] Article 15.10(2) CAFTA-DR.

[379] See 21 U.S.C. 355(b)(1).

[380] This process is described in more detail on the FDA's website, see https://www.fda.gov/drugs/abbreviated-new-drug-application-anda/patent-certifications-and-suitability-petitions (accessed 2 Nov 2024).

patent to third parties during the patent term and (2) providing information to the patent owner about applications by third parties for marketing approval. CAFTA-DR states that the duration of this link is limited to the patent term.[381]

The *Bipartisan Trade Deal* of the US Congress provides flexibility for FTA partners in relation to "the types of procedures that developing country partners may implement to prevent the marketing of patent-infringing products" (*i.e.*, patent linkage).[382] However, this flexibility was not explicitly granted retroactively to existing FTAs such as CAFTA-DR.

3.1.9.2 Central America

This linkage between patent law and the marketing authorization can be implemented in two (cumulative) ways:

First, the applicant for the marketing authorization can be required to provide a declaration about the patent protection of the product for which it wishes to obtain marketing authorization. This mechanism is used in El Salvador, where the legislation provides how this system will be practically implemented: The patent owner applying for marketing approval for a certain pharmaceutical product must provide a list of the patents covering this product together with the application for marketing approval.[383] This list is later published to enable third parties to inform themselves about possible patent protection. Subsequent applicants then must provide a sworn statement that no patent protection exists in relation to the pharmaceutical product for which they seek approval.[384] The patent owner is in the respective cases informed about applications by third parties.[385] This mechanism mirrors the procedure established by the Hatch-Waxman Act in the USA discussed above, including the statement submitted by the generic applicant, which is analogous to the "paragraph IV certification". Similarly, in Guatemala, subsequent applicants must provide a sworn statement that either (a) they are owner or licensee of the respective patents or (b) no patent protection exists in relation to the pharmaceutical product for which they seek approval.[386]

Second, the IP Register and the regulatory agencies can exchange information regarding patent applications and applications for marketing authorization. This mechanism is used in Guatemala, where information about the patent status of pharmaceuticals is provided to the health administration by the IP Register and the

[381] Article 15.10(2) CAFTA-DR.

[382] USTR (2007), p. 3.

[383] Article 181-A(4) IP LAW (SV).

[384] Article 5 Test Data Regulation (SV).

[385] Article 9 Test Data Regulation (SV).

[386] Article 13.1.18 Reglamento para el Control Sanitario de los Medicamentos y Produtos Afines, as amended by Acuerdo Gubernativo 351-2006.

health administration informs the IP Register and the right holder about generic drug applications.[387]

The implementation in El Salvador requires applications for marketing approval of a "new product" to include information about any patents that cover the product for which approval is requested.[388] This wording has been criticized by *PhRMA*, because it could be interpreted to mean that information on patent status will be required and linkage will be provided only on newly filed applications for marketing approval, not on applications granted or pending, while Article 15.1(11) CAFTA-DR requires that the obligations in the Agreement apply retroactively, and thus also to all marketing approvals in force or pending on the date of entry into force of CAFTA-DR.[389] However, this criticism is unjustified, since the linkage provisions in CAFTA-DR themselves refer to "new products" and have simply been implemented literally. According to Article 15.10.1(c) CAFTA-DR, a new product is one that does not contain a chemical entity that has been previously approved in the territory of the respective country.

However, the statement required under Salvadoran law differs from the "paragraph IV certification" in the USA in an interesting detail: As noted above, under US law the generic company can submit a certification claiming that the patent in question is invalid. Under Article 181-E IP Law (SV), this option was not included. If a patent has been listed by the original applicant, the subsequent applicant must declare that it will not market its (generic) drug before the patent has expired. CAFTA-DR does not specify that a "paragraph IV certification"-type statement must be submitted, so it seems plausible that the Salvadoran law was modelled directly based on the Hatch-Waxman rules. Nevertheless, the Salvadoran legislator included this modification, which practically means that the patent owner does not have to file an infringement action (as in the US), but can "wait" for the nullity action of the subsequent applicant.

In Guatemala, Article 13(1) of the Regulation for the Sanitary Control of Medicines, as modified by the CAFTA-DR reform legislation, is even more restrictive. The statement by applicants can only state that the applicant is the patent owner, has a license or that no patent exists.[390] While in EL Salvador a generic company can file an application while a patent is pending but has to wait until expiry to market the drug, the wording of the Guatemalan regulation suggests that no application can be filed.

In Costa Rica, the Ministry of Health and other competent authorities shall take steps during the marketing approval process for drugs to prevent any person other than the patent owner from marketing a product covered by the patent.[391]

[387] Martínez Piva and Tripo (2019), p. 67.

[388] Article 181-E IP LAW (SV), as amended by the CAFTA-DR Reform Law.

[389] PhRMA (2007), p. 2.

[390] Article 13.1.18 Reglamento para el Control Sanitario de los Medicamentos y Produtos Afines, as amended by Acuerdo Gubernativo 351-2006.

[391] Article 16(4) Patent and Design Law (CR), as amended by the CAFTA-DR Reform Law I (CR).

3.1.9.3 Administrative Implementation

The implementation of this mechanism depends on the cooperation between the IP Registers and the Ministries of Health or related agencies, which requires a regulation establishing the procedure. However, some Central American countries after passing the necessary legislation to implement Article 15.10(2) CAFTA-DR did not pass complementary administrative regulations, in effect making the system inapplicable.

In Costa Rica, Article 23 of the Patent and Design Regulation (CR) provides that the IP Register *may* grant the Ministry of Health access to the national patent database.[392] In addition, Article 24.2.3 of Regulation No. 28466-S for the Inscription, Control, Import and Publicity of Pharmaceuticals specified that marketing authorization requires that the applicant submits an affidavit indicating that it is the patent owner or is authorized to use the patent.[393] However, while four active ingredients have been put on a "patent linkage" list, it is unclear whether a generic approval procedure has been denied based on patent linkage.[394]

In the Dominican Republic, there seems to be no patent linkage mechanism in practice because the legislative provision had not been practically implemented by the health authorities.[395]

In Nicaragua, the Ministry of Health, which is responsible for granting marketing authorization, adopted Resolution 115-2006 establishing a 5-year patent linkage period;[396] until 2014 Nicaragua had apparently not practically implemented an effective system for patent linkage.[397] However, by 2024 such system was available and (very few) drugs had been included in a "patent linkage list" published by the health authorities.[398]

In Honduras, there also was not yet a patent linkage system in 2014; draft regulations were published in 2008, but the regulations for enforcement mechanisms were not adopted.[399] In El Salvador, the Superior Council for Health Security

---

[392] The text of the regulation is available at https://www.wipo.int/wipolex/en/legislation/details/9350 (accessed 2 Nov 2024), amended by regulation 38308-JP, adopted on 12 February 2014 and entered into force on 24 April 2014, the text of the regulation is available at https://www.wipo.int/wipolex/en/legislation/details/16553 (accessed 2 Nov 2024).

[393] Reglamento de Inscripción, Control, Importación y Publicidad de Medicamentos, N° 28466-S.

[394] Castro (2015), p. 91.

[395] Palacios (2012), p. 12, no more current information could be obtained.

[396] Resolución Ministerial Nr. 115-2006, adopted on 22 March 2006 and published on 22 March 2006; the text of the law is available at http://legislacion.asamblea.gob.ni/normaweb.nsf/($All)/FA3A49786444B6C10625755A0055D260?OpenDocument (accessed 2 Nov 2024).

[397] PhRMA (2014), p. 190, no more current information could be obtained.

[398] The list contained no active pharmaceutical ingredients with valid patent protection, but six where protection had expired; see the data from the health authorities available at https://latinalliance.co/en/2024/03/13/listado-de-productos-con-proteccion-de-datos-y-patentes-actualizados-nicaragua/ (accessed 2 Nov 2024).

[399] PhRMA (2014), p. 190, no more current information could be obtained.

(*Consejo Superior de Salud Pública*) is the competent authority for the authorization of pharmaceutical products;[400] a regulation has been created, but the respective agencies had not yet established an operating system based on the regulation.[401]

3.1.9.4 Evaluation

The introduction of patent linkage mechanisms through FTAs has been the subject of an intense and often very critical discussion. The main concern is that such mechanisms could unduly delay generic competition and thereby negatively impact public health.[402] However, in Central America, to the extent the patent linkage system becomes operational, it might have little practical effect, and thereby impact on public health, in the short and medium term.

In Costa Rica, for instance, because of the slow, conservative approach of CCSS of including new (patented) medicines on its list of relevant drugs,[403] the effect of patent linkage will probably be limited, because the respective patents will already have expired. More importantly, in Costa Rica and the Dominican Republic, very few pharmaceutical patent applications have been granted in the past and, therefore, the patent linkage mechanism applies to very few medicines. However, the system may become practically more important in the longer term and patent linkage may apply to more cases, because the number of pharmaceutical patents may increase under the PCT system and because of better practical patent protection. As statistical data shows,[404] in particular in Costa Rica and the Dominican Republic, the number of granted patents increased significantly. In other countries, the number of granted patents decreased, in line with global developments, but the number of pharmaceutical patents remained significant.[405]

This type of patent linkage provides significant benefits for the right holder. First, the competitor is obliged to submit a statement regarding the nonexistence of patent protection, which is then reviewed by the regulatory (and possibly patent) agencies, which can (temporarily) withhold the marketing authorization for the generic drug. This means that, unlike in countries without such linkage, the competitor cannot simply "risk" the introduction of generic drugs if it concludes that the patent is weak and will probably be nullified in a judicial proceeding. The competitor must seek and obtain a nullity decision before being able to obtain marketing approval. The mechanisms in El Salvador and Guatemala, unlike the "paragraph IV certificate" process in the USA, furthermore does not require the patent owner to first file a

[400] Article 68 Constitution (SV).

[401] PhRMA (2014), p. 190.

[402] See, e.g., Raju (2021), pp. 329–363.

[403] See Sect. 3.1.1.4.

[404] See Table 3.4.

[405] The data for, e.g., Nicaragua is available at the WIPO IP Statistics Data Center, https://www3.wipo.int/ipstats/ips-search/patent (accessed 2 Nov 2024).

patent infringement action. Second, the mechanism generally does not rely solely on IP enforcement to prevent generic drugs from entering the market, but utilizes public health agencies to protect the right holder from generic competition.[406] In this way, it relieves the patent owner from monitoring competitors and enforcing the rights by itself (and at its own cost) and shifts effort and risk to the public administration and the competitors.

Conversely, the "paragraph IV certificate"-style mechanisms introduced in El Salvador and Guatemala show that the implementation of the CAFTA-DR requirements also took into account the underlying rules of the Hatch-Waxman Act. CAFTA-DR does not preclude the adoption of additional Hatch-Waxman elements not included in the CAFTA-DR text. However, it seems that, for example, the 180-day exclusivity period for the first generic applicant was not adopted, despite the potential incentive it could create for generic competition. In the case of El Salvador and Guatemala, this is probably consistent, because the respective mechanism does not foresee a statement by the subsequent applicant "challenging" the invalidity of listed patents and therefore the incentive rationale underlying the Hatch-Waxman rule does not apply.

However, the empirical evidence regarding the actual impact of these rules on public health in Central America is (yet) inconclusive. While it shows that to some, but very small, extent they enabled pharmaceutical companies to keep generic competitors off the market, they did not show that this practically affected treatment options or the public healthcare budget.[407]

3.1.10 Rights

3.1.10.1 Right to Use

The *right to use* the invention is generally not specified in international law. Article 28 Nr. 2 TRIPS refers to positive rights of the owner only with respect to the right to license or transfer the right. The right to use can be conditional upon administrative permission with regard to certain products, *e.g.*, marketing approval for pharmaceuticals by the health administration. However, in Central America such an approval does not affect the validity of the patent (unlike in Brazil).[408] There are no provisions on the subject in CAFTA-DR.

---

[406] Armouti (2020), p. 3.

[407] See Shaffer and Brenner (2009), p. 963; Castro (2015), p. 98; these studies are discussed in more detail in Sect. 3.4.7.

[408] In Brazil, the grant of a patent for pharmaceuticals depends on the approval by the Ministry of Health, see Article 229-C of the Brazilian Patent Law. This linkage does not exist in Central America.

3.1.10.2 Right to Exclude

Article 28 Nr. 1 TRIPS specifies the right of the patent owner to *exclude* others from the use of the invention. Product patents exclude others from making, using or trading the product, while process patents exclude others from using the process and using or trading the product obtained directly by that process. This still allows making the product with another process and using or trading a product obtained by another process. In most cases, the exclusion right is relevant to prevent *importation*. Only with regard to the generic pharmaceuticals industry in some Central American countries the prohibition of *production* is also relevant.[409]

It is practically much more difficult to prove the infringement of a process patent than of a product patent, because the process used by the alleged infringer can usually not be observed by the right holder. Because the evidence of the alleged infringement is in the sphere of the infringer, international law shifts the burden of proof to him. According to Article 34 TRIPS, members shall provide, in at least one of the following circumstances, that any identical product, in the absence of proof to the contrary, shall be deemed to have been obtained by the patented process (1) if the product obtained by the patented process is new or (2) if there is a substantial likelihood that the identical product was made by the process and the owner of the patent has been unable through reasonable efforts to determine the process actually used. Therefore, under TRIPS, the members are only required to provide for the shift of the burden of proof in one of the two options. CAFTA-DR does not contain any obligations with regard to process patents.

The Central American generally have chosen to implement the first option, often literally. The laws in Costa Rica and El Salvador, for instance, provide that "with regard to process patents, in the absence of proof to the contrary, any identical product (…) shall be deemed to have been obtained by the patented process, if the product obtained by the patented process is new".[410] The Nicaraguan law contains similar wording,[411] but it also provides that with regard to the presentation of any proof to the contrary by the defendant, the legitimate interests to protect its business secrets must be taken into account.[412] Article 109(2) Patent and Design Law (NI) enables the courts to establish procedures to protect the defendant.[413]

---

[409] See Sect. 1.3.4.

[410] Article 39(3) IP Enforcement Law (CR); Article 171 IP Law (SV).

[411] Article 109(1) Patent and Design Law (NI).

[412] Article 109(2) Patent and Design Law (NI).

[413] This is practically an important balance to the rights of the patent owner, to prevent the "fishing for evidence" or even industrial espionage. Unlike the USA, where the rules of civil procedure require the defendant to produce evidence during discovery, the civil law countries are more restrictive. In Europe for example, where the right holder has the possibility to obtain a search order by the court if the infringement of a process patent is likely, the legislature and courts had to develop solutions to protect the business secrets of the defendant. Special procedures are used in several major jurisdictions, including France (*saisie contrefacon*), the UK (*Anton Pillar Order*) and

Table 3.6 Possible restrictions of abusive licensing activities

Activity	Effect	TRIPS	CAFTA-DR	EU-CARIFORUM-EPA	EU-CA-AA
Abuse of IP Rights	Anti-competitive	Optional (Article 40)	Optional[a] [Article 15.1 (15)]	–	–
	Anti-tech transfer	Optional (Article 8)	–	Mandatory (Article 142.2)	Mandatory (Article 231.3)

[a]Article 15.1(15) CAFTA-DR states that the parties are not prevented from preventing an abuse that may result in anti-competitive practices, thus following the optional Article 40(2) TRIPS

The exclusivity right of the patent owner is broadened under Article 15.10 (2) CAFTA-DR, which provides for a *patent linkage* mechanism excluding third parties from obtaining marketing authorization for a drug which is protected by a patent.[414]

3.1.11 Limitations

International law provides for certain categories of limitations of the rights of the patent owner. In accordance with TRIPS, this section differentiates between four types of limitations, the restriction of abusive licensing practices,[415] compulsory licenses,[416] forfeiture[417] and other limitations and exceptions to patent rights.[418]

3.1.11.1 Restriction of Abusive Licensing Practices

The patent right can be abused through certain licensing practices. The abuse can result from the content of a licensing agreement or from the refusal to conclude such an agreement (*refusal to deal*).[419] TRIPS, CAFTA-DR and the EU-CARIFORUM-EPA consider this problem, reflecting its relevance for countries with a developed IP system. However, as Table 3.6 shows, the issue is not regulated systematically, even though both FTAs are generally based on TRIPS.

Germany (*Besichtigungsverfahren*); the protection of the alleged infringers confidential information was codified in Germany in § 140(c) Patent Act.

[414]On patent linkage see Sect. 3.1.9 above.

[415]Articles 8 and 40 TRIPS.

[416]Article 31 TRIPS.

[417]Article 32 TRIPS.

[418]Article 30 TRIPS.

[419]Bakhoum and Conde Gallego (2014), pp. 552–553.

The different rules can be explained by the different approaches of the agreements:

- TRIPS establishes primarily *minimum protection for IP rights* and their use, including some mostly optional limitations;
- CAFTA-DR establishes a *higher level of minimum protection* and is more restrictive regarding the limitation of IP rights;
- The EU-CARIFORUM-EPA and the EU-CA-AA regulate IP rights within a broader *system based on IP objectives* such as competition, innovation, development and technology transfer.

While the abusive licensing practices can theoretically affect all objectives of patent protection, international law is limited to the protection of competition and technology transfer with regard to abusive licensing practices, excluding innovation and social objectives such as public health. As discussed below, by contrast, compulsory licenses can be based on any ground, as clarified by the adoption of the Doha Declaration, in particular on grounds of public health.[420]

The potential restriction of competition caused by patent licenses is of little practical concern in Central America, because in the region competition law (with the exception of unfair competition law) plays a small practical role.[421] Accordingly, most countries have no specific legislative provisions against anti-competitive abuses of patent rights. Apparently, only Guatemala used the option to regulate the "abuse of intellectual property rights having an adverse effect on competition" under Article 40(2) TRIPS. Article 133 IP Law (GT) nullifies "clauses of license agreements having the purpose or effect of *restricting competition or implying an abuse of the patent*" (emphasis added). This provision appears to be partly too broad and partly to narrow in relation to TRIPS. It is too broad with regard to the requirements "abusive licensing practice" and "anti-competitive effect". They are *cumulative* under Article 40(2) TRIPS, but *alternatives* according to the Guatemalan provision.[422] Since the limitation must not be extended beyond TRIPS, the alternative "or" should in accordance with international law be restricted to a cumulative "and". On the other hand, the provision only covers "clauses" of an existing license agreement having an anti-competitive effect. Literally, this excludes cases where the abuse consists especially in the fact that no license is granted (*refusal to deal*).

In Europe and the USA, the control of abusive licensing practices by competition law is highly relevant. Several investigations by competition agencies have been conducted, notably the sector inquiry of the European Commission regarding the pharmaceutical industry. These investigations found, among other results, abuses with regard to abusive licensing in the form of *refusals to deal* cases relating

[420] See Sect. 3.1.1.4.

[421] On competition law and practice in Central America see Sect. 2.6.1.

[422] The historic interpretation reinforces the view that the "and" in Article 40(2) TRIPS signals the cumulative application of both requirements, see Brand, Oliver in Busche et al. (2013), Article 40, Nr 27.

industrial standards covered by patents and "pay for delay" schemes with licenses granted as part of a dispute settlement.[423] There also exist specific regulations regarding illegal anti-competitive clauses in license and research agreements, see the Regulation (EU) No 316/2014 of 21 March 2014 on the application of Article 101(3) TFEU to categories of technology transfer agreements and the (Block Exemption) Regulation (EU) No 1217/2010 of 14 December 2010 on the application of Article 101(3) TFEU to certain categories of research and development agreements.[424]

In Central America, this issue might practically also be relevant. Given that in many industries in the region market power is highly concentrated, and the usual practice of foreign companies to grant exclusive licenses, license agreements, if they exist, could be abusive and anti-competitive by European or US standards. In Central America, however, even if the respective competition legislation exists, as in Guatemala, there are no strong competition agencies to enforce the law.[425]

3.1.11.2 Compulsory Licenses

Compulsory licenses can be granted based on patent law rules, but also based on competition law to remedy anti-competitive behavior. In Central America, however, competition legislation has not yet been utilized to enable compulsory licenses. Therefore, the following section focuses on compulsory licenses that can be granted based on patent law, which are explicitly provided for in local legislation. Even though they are part of the patent legislation, they may still have a competition policy objective (see, e.g., compulsory license to remedy abusive licensing practices).

Background

Multilateral Legal Framework Article 31 TRIPS gives countries the right to provide for compulsory licenses subject to certain substantive and formal requirements.

Compulsory licenses came into the focus of the international IP debate after the year 2000, because (effective) patent protection became available in many developing countries, including Central America, only under the new TRIPS legislations enacted at the end of the transition period around the year 2000.[426] Without a

---

[423] On the sector inquiry of the pharmaceutical industry of the European Commission see European Commission (2008), p. 1.

[424] Even before the introduction of these regulations, the CJEU had held that the licensing of IP rights can be anti-competitive, depending on the circumstances, see Case 258/78 [1982] ECR 2015 *Nungesser v Commission* (aka "*Maize Seed*").

[425] See Sect. 2.6.1.

[426] Even though most countries became members of TRIPS in 1995, developing countries benefited from the 5 year transition period.

significant number of granted patents, compulsory licenses were not a practical issue before.[427]

Many developing countries were concerned about the effects of the "new" patent protection. In addition, because Article 31(f) TRIPS prohibited export/import compulsory licenses schemes, the system established by TRIPS was of little use for countries without domestic production capacity. The concern focused on public health and especially drugs against HIV, the high prices of which were attributed mainly to patent protection and which were unaffordable for many countries, especially in sub-Sahara Africa. In 2001 South Africa issued the first and highly publicized compulsory license for an HIV drug. Also many academics advocated broader use of compulsory licenses to balance the increased level of patent protection seen as detrimental, especially to developing countries. The South African compulsory license legislation and the licensing arrangement between the South African competition agency and several international pharmaceutical companies triggered counter-activities, including international legal disputes, from the affected companies and business associations and developed countries, which in turn galvanized the support by NGOs for the increased use of compulsory licenses.[428]

Developing countries used the new foreign policy objectives of the USA after 11 September 2001 to push for the adoption of the Doha Declaration to modify TRIPS in relation to compulsory licenses. The new system was formalized later by the Decision of the General Council of 30 August 2003 on the *Implementation of paragraph 6 of the Doha Declaration on the TRIPS Agreement and public health*[429] and the Decision of 6 December 2005 on the *Amendment of the TRIPS Agreement*.[430]

Bilateral FTAs Evidence for the new trend is that the restrictions of compulsory licenses in FTAs especially of the USA were abolished completely after the Doha Declaration, even though it was not legally necessary. It would also have been possible for the USA to try to use the post-Doha FTAs such as CAFTA-DR to re-introduce stricter provisions on compulsory licenses. This might be the effect of stronger international opposition by developing countries and NGOs or the fact that after using compulsory licenses domestically, the USA found it more difficult to prohibit them internationally, or both.[431]

---

[427] In the literature on the global patent system, however, the use of compulsory licenses had been advocated earlier, e.g., by *Edith Penrose*, who stated that countries should be encouraged to use compulsory licenses more, see Penrose (1951), pp. 231–232.

[428] For background on the licensing arrangement between the South African competition agency and several international pharmaceutical companies and the development of international compulsory licensing law in general see Böttger (2008), pp. 881–885.

[429] WTO General Council (2003).

[430] WTO General Council (2005).

[431] On the compulsory license issues by the USA see Böttger (2008), p. 885.

Earlier post-TRIPS FTAs concluded by the USA contained restrictions on compulsory licenses beyond TRIPS, *e.g.*, Article 17.9(7) US-Australia FTA.[432] CAFTA-DR reflects the changed international development after the Doha Declaration. Provisions restricting compulsory licenses were not included any more. But the provisions of the Doha Declaration were also not explicitly included in the text. In addition, unlike the exception under Article 30 TRIPS, the possibility of compulsory licenses under Article 31 TRIPS was not restated. One might argue that this omission shows the parties' intent to exclude the option of Article 31 TRIPS.

However, under Article 15.1(7) CAFTA-DR, the parties affirm their rights under TRIPS and, therefore, any limitation of the amendments by the Doha Declaration would have to be clearly stated. Furthermore, as all parties had committed themselves to the possibility of compulsory licenses in the Doha Declaration, one would expect any policy reversal on this issue to be explicitly mentioned. Moreover, the parties agreed on maintaining all Doha Declaration flexibilities, including the waiver on Article 31(f) TRIPS for pharmaceuticals, in a side-letter to the agreement (*Side Letter to CAFTA-DR*).[433]

National Legal Framework The post-TRIPS legislation in Central America includes the possibility of compulsory licenses according to the conditions set out in Article 31 TRIPS. However, while TRIPS provides for a set of procedural requirements, the members are free to determine the grounds upon which compulsory licenses can be issued.[434]

Substantive Requirements

This section analyzes the four main grounds, which safeguard different policy objectives and which are of very different practical relevance: Lack of domestic (local) working, dependent patents, abusive licensing practices, and "national emergency" or "public interest".

Local Working To protect and foster local industries, many countries allowed (and sometimes issued) compulsory licenses in cases where the right holder did not produce the protected product in the country where it had validated the patent.

The Paris Convention permitted the parties to grant such compulsory licenses, subject to the requirement that the grant was only possible after *three years* of

[432] The text of the IP chapter of the US-Australia FTA is available at https://www.ustr.gov/sites/default/files/uploads/agreements/fta/australia/asset_upload_file469_5141.pdf (accessed 2 Nov 2024).

[433] The text of the "Understanding regarding certain public health measures" is available at http://www.ustr.gov/sites/default/files/uploads/agreements/cafta/asset_upload_file697_3975.pdf (accessed 2 Nov 2024).

[434] Lamping et al. (2014), p. 9; only for patents on semiconductor technology are grounds for compulsory licenses restricted, Article 31 (c) TRIPS.

non-working.[435] Article 27(1)(2) TRIPS now states that "patent rights (shall be) enjoyable without discrimination as to [...] whether products are imported or locally produced". This is interpreted by some scholars to prohibit local-working compulsory licenses, as these are based on the fact that the patented product is imported,[436] but this view is disputed.[437] There is no WTO panel decision on this subject, as the only related case has been withdrawn before the final decision.[438]

From a policy perspective, many scholars support local working requirements and compulsory licenses as a sanction to foster technology transfer and economic development. Under this view, the refusal of the patent holder to grant a license may prejudice the establishment or development of domestic industries is prejudiced.[439] However, this technology transfer reasoning is not convincing in Central America, because the region has limited capacity to absorb new technology. In effect, the license would probably benefit importers, not local innovators. Also, as already indicated, the mere production itself does not necessarily lead to the dissemination of the technology in the country. Also, the local working requirement can have negative effects on trade and economics of scale, and might, in turn, make products more expensive for consumers. As *Bendaña-Guerrero* puts it, it would "impose a heavy burden on the inventors, a higher price on the consumer and a barrier on trade in goods and services".[440]

The Central American countries do not provide for compulsory licenses in such cases.[441] The dominant view is that local working requirements are incompatible with Article 27(1)(2) TRIPS.[442] Article 18(3) Patent and Design Law (CR), for example, states that the legal importation of products constitutes sufficient exploitation and excludes the possibility to issue compulsory licenses for the lack of working.

Dependent Patents According to Article 31(l) TRIPS, compulsory licenses can be provided also for controlling patents to enable the use of a dependent patent. In Central America, this possibility has been implemented, *e.g.*, in Costa Rica in Article 19(a) Patent and Design Law (CR) and in Guatemala in Article 137 IP Law (GT).

Abusive Licensing Practices More important may be the possibility to issue compulsory licenses to remedy anti-competitive practices to protect dynamic competition. This mechanism can help ensure that the economic benefit the right holder derives from the patent is limited to the function of this right and not extended, *e.g.*,

[435] Article 5(A) Paris Convention.

[436] Neef in Busche et al. (2013), Article 27, Nr 57.

[437] See, e.g., Lamping et al. (2014), p. 9; this issue is discussed in more detail by Böttger (2008), p. 883.

[438] Höhne, Focke in Busche et al. (2013), Article 31, Nr 8.

[439] Lamping et al. (2014), p. 9.

[440] Bendaña-Guerrero (1999), p. 225 (translation by the author).

[441] See, e.g., Article 137 IP Law (GT).

[442] Bendaña-Guerrero (1999), p. 225.

into related or derivative markets and that the licensing terms on balance foster and not limit dynamic competition.[443] This view is underlined by the special provisions in Article 31(k) TRIPS relating thereto and the fact that compulsory licenses on these grounds are not excluded even by the most restrictive US-FTAs.[444] The fact that Article 31(k) TRIPS limits the position of the right holder to the right to be remunerated for the issuance of such a compulsory license and exempts the grant of the compulsory license from the prior negotiations and the restriction to supply only the local market (Article 31(b) and (f) TRIPS) suggest that, in cases of anti-competitive behavior, there are no legitimate interests of the right holder affected which would merit compensation or the application of the procedural safeguards. Given these restrictions that the clause enables, it should not be interpreted too broadly, or the respective safeguards could be easily circumvented.[445] For example, if "excessive pricing" as such, determined locally, were used as a basis for a compulsory license, it would provide the respective country with considerable policy discretion to issue compulsory licenses for purely financial reasons and, as a consequence, significant leverage in negotiations with the patent owner.[446] To be clear, however, while relying on purely financial reasons, without additional functional considerations, seems questionable based on a functional approach to balancing IP rights and competition law, it is not necessarily a breach of the TRIPS requirements. Article 31 TRIPS focuses on procedural requirements for issuing compulsory licenses and leaves significant flexibility regarding substantive requirements.[447]

Practically, in Central America, compulsory licenses in cases of abusive licensing practices can be issued, *e.g.*, under the legislation of Guatemala and Costa Rica.[448] According to Article 19(b)(1) Patent and Design Law (CR), they are issued by the antitrust agency (*Comisión para Promover la Competencia*) if it is determined that

[443] The relationship between IP law and competition law is discussed in more detail in Sect. 2.6.1 above.

[444] E.g., Article 17.9(7) US-Australia FTA; the text of the IP chapter of the US-Australia FTA is available at http://www.ustr.gov/sites/default/files/uploads/agreements/fta/australia/asset_upload_file469_5141.pdf (accessed 2 Nov 2024).

[445] Lamping et al. (2014), p. 10, argue that any illegitimate exploitation of a patent should justify the application of Article 31(k) TRIPS, because it is, by definition, anti-competitive. Such illegitimate exploitation should include discrimination, restrictions of output and excessive pricing. In other words, if the patentee does not supply the patent product locally (1) to everybody, (2) in the amounts requested and (3) at a fair price, each as determined locally, a compulsory license under Article 31 (k) TRIPS could be issued. If all these conditions are met by the patentee, there would typically be no reason to issue a compulsory license. In effect, under this view, all compulsory licenses could be subsumed under Article 31(k) TRIPS. This could render Article 31(b) and (f) TRIPS practically meaningless.

[446] An instructive example in this regard is the approach taken by the Brazilian authorities and in particular the compulsory license issued for the HIV drug efavirenz, see Böttger (2008), pp. 887–888.

[447] Böttger (2008), p. 888.

[448] Article 134 IP Law (GT).

the patent owner engaged in anti-competitive behavior. This category may be of special relevance to the Central American countries, as small countries are more likely to experience monopolies, as their markets are less attractive for new competitors to enter.[449]

Public Interest The Doha Declaration reaffirms the right of WTO members under TRIPS to use compulsory licenses on grounds of public interest, especially to address urgent health needs. While earlier FTA concluded by the USA, *e.g.*, Article 17.9(7) US-Australia FTA, limited compulsory licenses to mainly competition-related grounds, such limitations were no longer used by USA in its FTAs after the adoption of the Doha Declaration, including CAFTA-DR.[450] This possibility has been implemented, *e.g.*, in Costa Rica in Article 20 Patent and Design Law (CR) and in Guatemala in Article 134 IP Law (GT).

Procedural Requirements

Article 31 TRIPS provides for a number of procedural requirements for the issuance of compulsory licenses, *e.g.*, prior negotiations with and compensation of the right holder. These requirements in Central America are modeled based on TRIPS.[451] These procedural requirements are considered by some to be the reason that compulsory licenses are issued relatively rarely in practice and are, therefore, a controversial issue. However, as they were not affected by either CAFTA-DR, the EU-FTAs or the implementing legislation in Central America, this issue is not analyzed here.[452]

Practical Relevance and Evaluation

So far, no compulsory licenses have been granted by any Central American country.[453]

FTAs concluded subsequently to CAFTA-DR, *e.g.*, Article 16.13 US-Peru-TPA,[454] Article 16.13 US-Colombia-TPA[455] and Article 15.12(2) US-Panama-

[449] The practical ramifications of competition law and policy issues in Central America are discussed in more detail in Sect. 2.6.1 above.

[450] In CAFTA-DR, it was included by way of the Side Letter to CAFTA-DR.

[451] Articles 43 and 44 IP Law (DR).

[452] On the procedural aspects see Böttger (2008), pp. 881–882 and 888.

[453] Correa (2013).

[454] The text of the agreement is available at https://www.ustr.gov/trade-agreements/free-trade-agreements/peru-tpa (accessed 2 Nov 2024).

[455] The text of the agreement is available at http://www.ustr.gov/uscolombiatpa (accessed 2 Nov 2024).

TPA[456] include explicit references to the Doha Declaration in the text of the IP chapter, based on the Bipartisan Trade Deal of May 2007.[457] The growing acceptance of compulsory licenses for public health reasons led observers to state that "going forward, the most adverse consequences (regarding the effects of patents on public health) will be circumscribed".[458] However, even though there were several compulsory licenses issued worldwide following the Doha Declaration, the use of compulsory licenses has not significantly increased and has been limited to cases based on the public interest.[459]

That there have not been practical cases of compulsory licenses in Central America is not unusual for developing countries, because there have been generally few practical cases in which compulsory licenses have been issued.[460] Some observers have interpreted the lack of widespread use of compulsory licenses as a sign that the formal requirements are too strict or complicated.[461] However, at least in Central America the absence of compulsory licenses has probably other reasons. It has been said provocatively that in Central America "there are no compulsory licenses, because there are *no patents*".[462] This corresponds with the abovementioned observation that generally compulsory licenses became only an issue after the protection of pharmaceutical patents had become stronger in some developing countries. As the statistical analysis has shown, in the past this was correct, as especially in Costa Rica and the Dominican Republic few patents had been granted.[463] However, the number of granted patents is increasing, and if the number of granted patents in Central America continues to increase, the attractiveness of compulsory licenses could also increase.

However, the empirical evidence shows that compulsory licenses are used primarily in countries with *public health systems*, because only in these cases the government has a strong economic incentive to issue compulsory licenses to reduce public health costs.[464] In Central America, only Costa Rica maintains a strong public health system, which also includes IP considerations in its health policy.[465] But especially in Costa Rica the practical protection of pharmaceutical patents is still

[456] The text of the agreement is available at http://www.ustr.gov/trade-agreements/free-trade-agreements/panama-tpa (accessed 2 Nov 2024).

[457] USTR (2007), p. 3.

[458] Stiglitz (2002), p. 245.

[459] See Böttger (2008), pp. 885–888; in Germany, the Federal Patent Court granted a compulsory license in a preliminary decision to Merck for an HIV drug of Shionogi in 2016, see the report on the decision in GRUR-Prax 2017, 105.

[460] In Latin America only Brazil and Ecuador, see Böttger (2008), pp. 885–888; Correa (2013).

[461] See Sect. 3.1.11.2.

[462] Comment by local practitioner in Costa Rica, where traditionally few pharmaceutical patents were granted.

[463] See Sect. 3.1.7.

[464] Böttger (2008), pp. 885–888.

[465] See in particular the procurement activities by the CCSS (CR), Sect. 3.1.1.4.

relatively weak, which makes it unlikely that compulsory licenses will be used in this country.

Even if compulsory licenses are not used, the possibility of governments to issue compulsory licenses under the respective national legislations might still have some deterring effect on the pricing schemes of pharmaceutical companies and, therefore, mitigate the increase in prices for medicines, even if this effect is hard to measure in practice.[466]

3.1.11.3 Forfeiture

According to Article 5(A)(3) Paris Convention, parties can provide for the forfeiture of a patent in cases where the grant of compulsory licenses would not be sufficient to prevent abuses of the patent which are grounds for granting a compulsory license. CAFTA-DR explicitly does not limit the possibility to allow the forfeiture.[467]

In Central America, forfeiture is foreseen in Honduras. Article 44(3) IP Law (HN) provides a non-exhaustive list of grounds for forfeiture, including (1) unjustified or abusive conditions imposed in a license or sublicense agreement, (2) unjustifiably high prices and (3) if the patent is used to restrict commercial activities related to products or processes not covered by the patent, in other words, if the patentee interferes in secondary markets.[468] The procedure established for forfeiture corresponds literally to Article 5(A)(3) Paris Convention. In particular, forfeiture can only be declared if (1) a compulsory license has been granted, (2) this license has been insufficient to end the abuse and (3) the request for forfeiture is made at least 2 years after the grant of the (first) compulsory license.[469] As this issue is not regulated by CAFTA-DR, it is compliant with CAFTA-DR that Honduras has not amended Article 44 IP Law (HN) as part of the implementation process.

3.1.11.4 Other Limitations and Exceptions

Limitations and exceptions to patents rights are subject to the *three-step test* under Article 30 TRIPS.[470] This mechanism was adopted also in Article 15.9 (3) CAFTA-DR. Especially problematic in this context was the question which acts of competitors in relation to patented pharmaceuticals “conflict with a normal

[466] See Beier (1998), p. 186; Böttger (2008), p. 884.

[467] Article 15.9(4) CAFTA-DR.

[468] Article 31(k) TRIPS.

[469] Article 44(1) and (2) IP Law (HN).

[470] The three-step test originated in the Berne Convention in relation to copyright and was transferred to the area of industrial property in TRIPS, see Kur and Grosse Ruse-Khan (2008), p. 7; on the interpretation of the three-step test see Lamping et al. (2014), p. 8.

exploitation" or "unreasonably prejudice the legitimate interests of the patent owner".

Under WTO case-law, the *Bolar* exception, *i.e.*, the rule that the performance of research to generate information for marketing approval, especially to establish bio-equivalence, and clinical trials for generic drugs, but not the production and stockpiling of generic drugs, are permitted during the term of patent protection and do not constitute a patent infringement.[471] Article 15.9(5) CAFTA-DR, while not prohibiting the *Bolar* exception itself, provides that no marketing approval based on this research exemption may be granted during the term of the patent. The national legislation in Central America is similar to this international system. Some laws explicitly include the *Bolar* exception.[472]

3.2 Utility Models

3.2.1 Legal Framework

Inventions can also be protected by utility models. Because of the traditionally lower substantive and formal requirements and the shorter period of protection utility models (or "utility patents") are also considered "petty patents" or "small patents".[473] Utility models were of less importance than patents during the negotiations of modern international agreements. Accordingly, these agreements do not provide for their protection, *e.g.*, TRIPS, CAFTA-DR and the EU-CA-AA, or make their protection optional, *e.g.*, Article 148 EU-CARIFORUM-EPA.[474] The Paris Convention only includes utility models in the definition of IP, thus requiring members to provide national treatment under their utility model systems; also, the provisions on compulsory licenses for patents apply accordingly (Article 5(A) Paris Convention).[475] In Central America, all countries have established statutory protection for utility models.[476]

[471] WTO Dispute Settlement Body, Canada—Patent Protection for Pharmaceutical Products, Decision on 17 March 2000, WT/DS114/R.

[472] E.g., Article 130(d) IP Law (GT).

[473] Francois Dessemontet, Protection of Undisclosed Information, in Correa and Yusuf (2008), p. 276.

[474] On this issue see also Grosse Ruse-Khan (2012), p. 6.

[475] On the international legal framework for utility models see in particular Grosse Ruse-Khan (2012), pp. 1–2.

[476] Articles 25–31 Patent and Design Law (CR), Articles 120–122 IP Law (SV), Articles 142–146 IP Law (GT), Articles 23–27 IP Law (HN), Articles 62–66 Patent and Design Law (NI).

3.2.2 Subject Matter and Requirements

The legislation on utility models is very similar in all Central American countries. The patentability requirements of novelty and industrial application also apply to utility models. Therefore, *absolute novelty* is necessary also for utility models, and even foreign and/or oral state of the art is novelty-destroying.[477] In some countries like Germany, the *inventive step* requirement is similar to patent law.[478] However, no inventive step is required under Central American law. Only utility models which do not "contain any useful improvement to the state of the art" (or do not "add any discernible utilitarian characteristic to the state of the art" or "better function") are not considered novel and cannot be registered.[479]

3.2.3 Procedure and Fees

Unlike in Germany, where utility models are only formally examined before the registration,[480] in Central America a substantive examination is always performed, e.g., in Costa Rica and Guatemala.[481]

From a policy perspective, it is interesting to compare the fees for utility models with those for patents. Generally, because of the shorter term of protection, the economic value of utility models is lower than that of patent, and the fees should reflect this. In developing countries like Central America, given that utility models may be the first step for inventors on the path of technological progress, lower fees may improve the access of local companies to the IP system and strengthen their competitive position and help endogenous technological development. However, the fees in Central America do not always reflect such policy considerations. In Guatemala, the fees for examination and application of utility models are about 25% lower than the patent fees, and the annual fees in the first years are even higher than the fees payable for patents.[482] Therefore, the fees create little economic incentive to choose utility model protection. In El Salvador and Honduras, the application and examination fees are the same for patents and utility models; in these particular cases,

[477] In the Salvadoran legislation, the utility models provisions [Article 122 IP Law (SV)] explicitly refer to the novelty requirement of the patent chapter [Article 113 IP Law (SV)]; the other laws refer generally to the patent law provisions, including the novelty requirement [see, e.g., Article 142 IP Law (GT), Article 23 IP Law (HN), Article 66 Patent and Design Law (NI)].

[478] § 1(1) German Utility Model Law.

[479] See, e.g., Article 25(1) Patent and Design Law (CR), Article 122 IP Law (SV), Article 144 IP Law (GT), Article 25(2) IP Law (HN), Article 66 Patent and Design Law (NI).

[480] §§ 4–4b German Utility Model Law.

[481] Article 142 IP Law (GT), Article 29(1) Patent and Design Law (CR).

[482] European Commission, Executive Agency for Small and Medium-sized Enterprises (2019), p. 6; European Commission, Executive Agency for Small and Medium-sized Enterprises (2023), pp. 3–4.

however, the fees are generally low.[483] Therefore, the fees could facilitate the participation of local inventors even without differentiating between patent and utility model fees. Only in Nicaragua, the application and examination fees are about half of the patent fees and thus significantly lower than those for patents.[484] But it is noteworthy that even these reduced fees are still much higher than the fees in Honduras or even Costa Rica, a country with a much stronger economy and higher per capita GDP where inventors probably could afford higher fees more easily.

3.2.4 Term of Protection

The term of protection of utility models is 10 years in all Central American countries except Honduras, where the term is 15 years.[485]

3.2.5 Evaluation

Utility models could be of importance for local companies in Central America, because they are easier to obtain, *e.g.*, because the requirements are lower compared to patents, they are not examined substantively and the fees are lower. Therefore, they have the potential to improve local technological capacity in developing countries by protecting incremental innovation.[486] Utility models are practically relevant in Central America, because national inventors seem to prefer utility models over patents.[487] They are less relevant for international companies from developed countries.[488] This is suggested by the fact that utility models are not regulated by CAFTA-DR (and other international agreements). Because the national utility model legislation is not limited by CAFTA-DR requirements, policy space remains for the Central American countries to establish a framework in accordance with local needs.[489] However, this policy space has not been exploited fully. For example, the fee structure could be better adapted to local needs, e.g., by reducing fees generally or at least for local SMEs or individual inventors.[490]

[483] European Commission, Executive Agency for Small and Medium-sized Enterprises (2019), p. 6.
[484] Ibid.
[485] Article 27 IP Law (HN).
[486] Punchi Hewage (2015), p. 285.
[487] WIPO (2017), pp. 27–31.
[488] WIPO (2017), pp. 27–31.
[489] Similarly, regarding developing countries in general under international law, Grosse Ruse-Khan (2012), p. 1.
[490] Punchi Hewage (2015), p. 293.

3.3 Plant Varieties

The protection of plant varieties by an IP right is one of the most controversial issues in the international IP debate and the obligation to accede to the UPOV Convention was one the most heavily criticized provisions of CAFTA-DR in Central America.[491]

3.3.1 *Policy Considerations*

The criticism concerns several issues: *Culturally*, many people, *e.g.*, indigenous Mayan people living mainly in the northern Central American countries of Guatemala, El Salvador and Honduras and their advocates, find exclusive legal protection for life and nature immoral.[492] Plants, in particular corn, play an important role in Mayan religion and society. With this view, the privatization of plant varieties can hardly be reconciled.[493] The most vocal opposition against the introduction of plant variety protection through the implementation of the UPOV Convention existed in Costa Rica. While the percentage of indigenous people there is not larger than in other Central American countries, Costa Rica has a very developed and active civil society.[494] The *socio-economic* concerns relate to the fundamental importance of agriculture for many developing societies. In Central America, it is still the most important economic sector and constitutes the bulk of exports in most countries (except Costa Rica, where agricultural products are second after electronic and medical devices).[495] As previous food crises have highlighted, safe and steady supply of foodstuff is important for domestic consumption. The danger of a foreign and private monopoly on seeds is thus seen as a threat to economic and nutrition autonomy.[496] *Ecologically*, it is argued that the extensive use of new genetically modified organisms (GMO) or hybrid plants could lead to monocultures and ultimately harm *biodiversity*, as the use of traditional and diverse types of crops is discontinued.[497]

---

[491] See, e.g., Díaz (2006), p. 75.

[492] However, sometimes protection as traditional knowledge for the benefit of the indigenous communities is considered appropriate, see Sect. 6.2.1.

[493] According to traditional Mayan beliefs, the "god of corn" created the Mayan people out of corn, see, e.g., Keppeler and Romero (2017).

[494] Silvia Rodríguez Cervantes (interview conducted by GRAIN), Resistance to UPOV and the privatization of life in Costa Rica, 29 March 2008, available at https://grain.org/article/entries/2235-resistance-to-upov-in-costa-rica (accessed 2 Nov 2024).

[495] See Sects. 1.3.3 and 1.3.4.

[496] For further references see Bucher (2008), p. 310.

[497] See Sect. 6.1.2.3; see further references in Bucher (2008), p. 310; on the effect of hybrid (including transgenic) plants on increased reliance on monocultures by farmers, see Kochupillai (2016), p. 232.

However, this criticism must be put in perspective. The UPOV Convention merely provides the legal basis for the development and exploitation of new plant varieties. The farmers can continue to use traditional crops—even though critics can point to several cases where companies tried to appropriate traditional plants.[498] If farmers choose to buy and use new plant varieties instead of traditional crops, this could indicate that the farmers find that these new plant varieties have superior properties, because they are willing to pay a higher price. Also, the UPOV Convention and CAFTA-DR leave room for balancing the protection of users and the economic interests of agro-business through the establishment of "farmer's rights". Likewise, Article 259.3 EU-CA-AA states that "(t)he Parties shall have the right to provide for exceptions to exclusive rights granted to plant breeders to allow farmers to save, use and exchange protected farm-saved seed or propagating material.

However, using protected new plant varieties could lead to a practical economic dependency of local farmers, because the farmers may not be sufficiently informed about the legal and practical constraints related to the use of such plant varieties, in particular the necessity to buy new seeds each year.[499] However, such problems indicate that it is necessary to raise awareness and educate farmers, but they do not mean that the protection of new plant varieties, as such, is bad policy.

The UPOV Convention and CAFTA-DR also permit the parties to provide for conditions of GMO use to protect biodiversity. In Costa Rica, Article 1 Plant Variety Law (CR) states that the protection granted by that law shall not include the authorization for commercial exploitation of the variety, thus subjecting the use of, *e.g.*, GMO plant varieties to administrative control.[500] Similarly, administrative restrictions are explicitly provided for in the Dominican Republic.[501]

3.3.2 Legal Framework

3.3.2.1 International Legal Framework

The legal basis for the international protection of plant varieties is the UPOV Convention. The original convention from 1962 was replaced by new conventions in 1978 and ultimately in 1991. The latter convention entered into force in 1998,[502] but has not been ratified by all members.[503] It offers broader protection almost

[498] See for the case of the *neem* tree and other examples Sect. 6.1.4.

[499] Regarding El Salvador, for example, see, e.g., Keppeler and Romero (2017).

[500] The footnote to Article 15.1. CAFTA-DR states that "the Parties understand that there is no conflict between the UPOV Convention and a Party's ability to protect and conserve its genetic resources."

[501] Article 23 Plant Variety Law (DR).

[502] Bucher (2008), p. 84.

[503] The list of current members and the respective convention in force is available at https://www.upov.int/edocs/pubdocs/en/upov_pub_423.pdf (accessed 2 Nov 2024).

resembling patent protection.[504] Article 15.1(5) CAFTA-DR requires the accession to the UPOV Convention (1991) by the year 2010 for Nicaragua, 2007 for Costa Rica and 2006 for all other parties. Under the EU-CARIFORUM-EPA accession is optional[505] and the EU-CA-AA does not make reference to the UPOV Convention at all, but as the Central American countries are obliged to become members of UPOV under CAFTA-DR, this flexibility is not practically relevant. Following the implementation of CAFTA-DR, Costa Rica and the Dominican Republic have acceded to the UPOV Convention (1991). A country is not required to ratify the UPOV Convention and provide for *sui generis* protection if patent protection for plant varieties is available.[506] This is the case in El Salvador. Guatemala, Honduras and Nicaragua have neither become members of the UPOV Convention (1991) nor a working system of patent protection.

3.3.2.2 Central America

Because of the political controversies and the diverging legal obligations, the national legislations in Central America offer a complex picture:

In Costa Rica, protection of plant varieties was, before CAFTA-DR, envisaged under a Plant Variety Law (*Ley de Protección de las Obtenciones Vegetales*) and a Plant Breeders Law, that were under discussion in parliament for several years, but after the ratification of CAFTA-DR and subsequently the UPOV Convention (1991), the latter project was abandoned because it did not comply with the UPOV Convention (1991) or TRIPS.[507] The UPOV Convention (1991) entered into force for Costa Rica on 12 January 2009.[508] The first version of the Plant Variety Law was passed in March 2008, and an amended version was passed in November 2008, weeks before the final deadline for the full CAFTA-DR implementation.[509] The amended version introduced changes to three provisions of the Plant Variety Law (CR) considered incompatible with CAFTA-DR.[510]

The Dominican Republic had ratified the UPOV Convention. It entered in force on 16 June 2007.[511] The Dominican Republic passed its first Plant Variety

---

[504] Bucher (2008), p. 84.

[505] The parties "shall consider acceding to" UPOV Convention (version of 1991), Article 11 EU-CARIFORUM-EPA.

[506] Article 15.1(5) CAFTA-DR.

[507] The project is discussed in some detail by Bucher (2008), p. 311.

[508] Available at https://www.upov.int/edocs/pubdocs/en/upov_pub_423.pdf (accessed 2 Nov 2024).

[509] Law No 8631 (promulgated on March 6, 2008 and published on March 19, 2008), as amended by Article 7 Law No 8686 (promulgated on November 21, 2008 and published on November 26, 2008), see the English translation, p. 1, available at https://www.wipo.int/wipolex/es/legislation/details/9018 (accessed 2 Nov 2024).

[510] Articles 2, 3 and 8 Plant Variety Law (CR).

[511] Available at https://www.upov.int/edocs/pubdocs/en/upov_pub_423.pdf (accessed 2 Nov 2024).

Protection Law in 2006 as part of the implementation of CAFTA-DR.[512] El Salvador provides for patent protection of plant varieties. Several patents have been applied for regarding a plant variety of *vetiver,* a grass used against soil erosion and for perfume production, and for one variety, the patent was granted.[513] This patent is considered practical evidence for the effectiveness of plant variety protection based on patents in the country, and, accordingly, El Salvador is not required to ratify the UPOV Convention under Article 15.1(5) CAFTA-DR.[514]

Guatemala provides for special patent protection for plant varieties in Article 97 IP Law (GT) (novelty requirement) and Article 98 IP Law (GT) (other requirements). Legally, therefore, plant varieties can be patented in Guatemala. Nevertheless, the Ministry of Agriculture has initiated the procedure for becoming member of UPOV and had proposed a *sui generis* national plant variety law.[515] Guatemala had submitted an application to become an UPOV member and a draft plant variety law, but UPOV required changes to the law before admitting Guatemala.[516] This procedure became obsolete, when the Guatemalan parliament, in September 2014, following massive popular protests, repealed the plant variety law.[517] Interestingly, this evident violation of the CAFTA-DR obligations has apparently not led to any reaction from the other CAFTA-DR members, in particular the USA. The 2015 or 2016 Special 301 Reports would have provided an opportunity for the business community or the USTR to address this issue. However, while the reports address various issues in relation to Guatemala, namely the allegedly broad protection of geographical indications, the lack of coordination by different agencies regarding enforcement activities, the sale of counterfeit pharmaceuticals and use of illegal software by government entities, the repeal of the plant variety law was not mentioned.[518]

Honduras has submitted a plant variety law proposal to the UPOV secretariat, which was reviewed favorably already in the year 2000.[519] However, Honduras has not yet become a member of the UPOV Convention.[520]

---

[512] Plant Variety Law (DR) (Ley No. 450-06 sobre Protección de los Derechos del Obtentor de Variedades Vegetales).

[513] Cabrera Medaglia (2006), p. 89; Cabrera Medaglia (2009), p. 13.

[514] Cabrera Medaglia (2010), p. 21 refers to the "reasonable efforts" requirements under Article 15.1 (5)(b) CAFTA-DR, which applies only to countries with patent protection for plant varieties.

[515] Available at https://www.upov.int/export/sites/upov/about/en/pdf/pub437.pdf (accessed 2 Nov 2024).

[516] A description of the process and the required changes can be found at https://www.upov.int/edocs/mdocs/upov/en/c/43/c_43_15.pdf (accessed 2 Nov 2024).

[517] See https://www.bilaterals.org/?guatemala-repeals-plant-breeder&lang=en (accessed 2 Nov 2024).

[518] See USTR Special 301 Report (2015) and USTR Special 301 Report (2016).

[519] UPOV, Press Release, available at https://www.upov.int/edocs/pressdocs/en/upov_pr_042.pdf (accessed 2 Nov 2024).

[520] Available at https://www.upov.int/export/sites/upov/members/es/pdf/pub423.pdf (accessed 2 Nov 2024).

Nicaragua has ratified the UPOV Convention in its 1978 version.[521] The country created the Plant Variety Law (NI) and a corresponding regulation following the ratification of the UPOV Convention in 2000, establishing patent protection for plant varieties.[522] Under CAFTA-DR, Nicaragua must also accede to the UPOV Convention (1991) until 1 January 2010. However, there were no projects initiated for the ratification of the UPOV Convention (1991) after the entry into force of CAFTA-DR and Nicaragua is still no party to the UPOV Convention (1991).[523] Also, while the Plant Variety Law (NI) of 2000 complies largely with the UPOV Convention, the term of protection is generally 20 years, while 25 years are required by the UPOV Convention (1991) for trees and vines.[524]

Therefore, Guatemala, Honduras and Nicaragua are in breach of CAFTA-DR for the failure to ratify the UPOV Convention (1991).

3.3.3 Patent and Sui Generis *Protection*

Unlike under Article 2 (1) UPOV Convention (1978), under the UPOV Convention (1991), double protection by specific plant variety law and patent law is no longer prohibited. Therefore, national legislations are not required to determine the relationship between *sui generis* and patent protection with regard to plant varieties.[525]

Nevertheless, Costa Rica explicitly excludes plants generally from patent protection.[526] For plants only plant variety protection is available.

El Salvador is exempted from ratifying and implementing the UPOV Convention, as plant varieties are eligible for patent protection, and has not passed specific plant variety legislation.[527]

In Nicaragua, where plants are not excluded from patentability, the question arises whether double protection by patent and *sui generis* rights is possible. *Bendaña-Guerrero* supports such double protection, because patent law does not explicitly exclude plants and patent protection should, therefore, be available, if the

---

[521] The Convention entered into force for Nicaragua on 6 September 2001, available at https://www.upov.int/export/sites/upov/members/es/pdf/pub423.pdf (accessed 2 Nov 2024).

[522] The Plant Variety Law (NI) (Ley de Protección para las Obtenciones Vegetales), available at https://upovlex.upov.int/es/legislation/text/224452 (accessed 2 Nov 2024), was approved on 20 October 1999 and entered into force on 27 February 2000; see also Reglamento de la Ley de Protección para las Obtenciones Vegetales, available at available at https://www.wipo.int/wipolex/es/legislation/details/3174 (accessed 2 Nov 2024).

[523] Available at http://www.upov.int/export/sites/upov/members/es/pdf/pub423.pdf (accessed 2 Nov 2024).

[524] Article 19(2) UPOV Convention (version of 1991).

[525] Bucher (2008), p. 84.

[526] Article 1.4 Patent Law CR.

[527] See Sect. 3.3.2.2.

requirements are fulfilled.[528] This argument implies that the UPOV Convention does not constitute a special regime. It is argued that patent protection should be available, in accordance with Article 1(iv) of the UPOV Convention, in cases where the plant variety does not meet the special requirements of plant variety protection, *e.g.*, of homogeneity or stability, to avoid gaps in legal protection.[529] However, the requirements and limitations of plant variety law could be practically undermined, if patent protection is automatically available, as a residual type of protection, in case the plant variety law requirements are not fulfilled, especially because of the generally similar scope and term of protection. A solution could be that only in cases where a plant does not meet the subject matter criteria for plant variety protection, *e.g.*, because the inventions affects a higher botanical taxon rank, it should be patentable to ensure comprehensive legal protection, but not if the requirements are not met.[530] The UPOV system could, therefore, be considered a special regime and, therefore, if protection for plant varieties is *available* under a special law, this would exclude additional patent protection for plant varieties in case these do not meet the requirements. Article 27(3)(b) TRIPS provides flexibility to the contracting states in this regard. While protection for plant varieties must be available, each country may choose to grant *alternatively* patent or *sui generis* plant variety protection or cumulative protection.[531] Therefore, the double protection interpretation proposed by *Bendaña-Guerrero* is in line with the international legal framework.

3.3.4 Subject Matter and Requirements

The term "plant variety" is defined by Article 1(vi) UPOV Convention and means a plant grouping within a single botanical taxon of the lowest known rank. The plant must have at least one hereditary characteristic distinguishing it from other plants.

According to Articles 5 and 20 UPOV Convention, the breeder's right shall be granted if the variety is new, distinct, uniform and stable and it is designated by a denomination. No further conditions for the grant may be imposed.[532] The novelty requirement with regard to plant varieties is broader than with regard to patents, as it permits also discoveries[533] and is destroyed not by any prior disclosure, but only by

[528] Bendaña-Guerrero (1999), p. 236.

[529] On this issue see Götting (2014), p. 154 Nr 9.

[530] The structure established by European law in this respect is discussed by v. Saint-André, Susanne/Taşdelen, Alper in Busche et al. (2013), Article 27 Nr 97.

[531] The combination option was included in Article 27 TRIPS to accommodate US law, see v. Saint-André, Susanne/Taşdelen, Alper in Busche et al. (2013), Article 27 Nr 97.

[532] Except for formal requirements for the grant procedure, such as fees, see Article 5(2) UPOV Convention (1991).

[533] See, e.g., Article 1 Plant Variety Law (NI).

prior commercial exploitation.[534] This would permit also the protection of plant varieties which have been traditionally, but not commercially used by indigenous people.[535] However, the protection of such traditional plant varieties is complicated if they lack uniformity and stability, which is frequent.[536] The uniformity and stability requirements are also problematic because they favor monocultures and, therefore, might endanger biological diversity.[537] Nevertheless, these requirements have been included in the Central American statutes.[538]

3.3.5 *Ownership*

According to Article 4(1) UPOV Convention, the parties have to grant protection only to nationals of all other parties. This could create a problem with regard to El Salvador, which did not ratify the UPOV Convention and, therefore, Salvadoran nationals and companies could be excluded from protection in third countries.[539] However, at least the other Central American countries do not restrict protection as far as possible under the UPOV Convention. In Nicaragua, Article 5 Article 1 Plant Variety Law (NI) grants protection for nationals of "any State, irrespective of whether they are members of UPOV, granting effective protection", which includes patent protection as provided by El Salvador. In Costa Rica, according to Article 6(1) Plant Variety Law (CR), foreigners can also apply for plant variety protection irrespective of reciprocity.

3.3.6 *Procedure*

3.3.6.1 Institutions

There are three possible institutional arrangements for the protection and administration of plant varieties, which all exist in Central America. First, in countries where plant varieties are protected by patent law, like El Salvador, the administration of plant variety protection automatically falls within the jurisdiction of the IP Register. Second, plant varieties can be administered by existing agencies in countries with *sui generis* protection. This is the case in Nicaragua, where the patent department of the

---

534 See, e.g., Article 17 Plant Variety Law (NI).

535 Taubman and Leistner (2003), p. 73.

536 Bucher (2008), p. 85 with further references.

537 Hassemer (2003), p. 85.

538 See, e.g., Article 7 Plant Variety Law (DR); Article 93 sentence 2 IP Law (GT).

539 However, as discussed above in Sect. 3.3.2.2, El Salvador is not required to accede to the UPOV Convention under Article 15.1(5) CAFTA-DR, because it provides patent protection for plant varieties.

IP Register is responsible for the registration and the Ministry of Agriculture is responsible for the substantive examination.[540] Finally, it is also possible to create special agencies for the *sui generis* system. In Costa Rica, the Plant Variety Law (CR) establishes the National Seeds Office (*Oficina Nacional de Semillas,* "Ofinase"), which is part of the Environment and Energy Ministry as the office in charge of administration and examination.[541] Interestingly, micro-organisms submitted in connection with a patent application are not managed by the IP Register or another national agency, but an international depositary authority in accordance with the system established under the Budapest Treaty.[542] In the Dominican Republic, the Variety Registration and Breeder's Rights Protection Office (*Oficina de Registro de Variedades y de Protección de los Derechos de Obtentor*) of the Secretariat of Agriculture (*Secretaría de Estado de Agricultura*) is responsible for plant variety applications.[543]

3.3.6.2 Registration

The registration procedure is similar to patent law, including the international priority right based on the first application[544] and the examination and publication procedure.[545] Specific procedural provisions are necessary due to the requirements of uniformity and stability. The examination is not necessarily based solely on the applicant's documentation, but the examining office may itself make growing trials or other tests.[546]

3.3.6.3 Cancellation

The variety can be nullified or cancelled for substantive or formal reasons. It is cancelled if it lacks at least one substantive requirement of protection:

[540] Articles 24 and 43 Plant Variety Law (NI).

[541] Article 5 Plant Variety Law (CR).

[542] See, e.g., Article 109 IP Law (GT); regarding the Budapest Treaty, see Sect. 3.1.6.1.

[543] Articles 2 and 12 Plant Variety Law (DR).

[544] Article 11 UPOV Convention; Article 10 Plant Variety Law (CR); Article 37–40 Plant Variety Law (NI); Article 13 Plant Variety Law (DR).

[545] Article 12 UPOV Convention; Article 7 and 8 Plant Variety Law (CR); Article 42–47 Plant Variety Law (NI); Article 14 Plant Variety Law (DR); also similar to patent law is the nullification in case of a lack of requirements for protection, Article 21 UPOV Convention; Article 26 Plant Variety Law (CR); Article 73 Plant Variety Law (NI); Article 3 Plant Variety Law (DR).

[546] E.g., Article 8 (a) Plant Variety Law (CR).

- novelty or distinctiveness, as mandated by Article 21 UPOV Convention;[547]
- uniformity and stability if, the examination was based on the applicant's documentation, as mandated by Article 21 UPOV Convention;[548]
- uniformity and stability, if their lack was not found during the office's examination, as permitted by Article 22 UPOV Convention.[549]

The Central American countries also provide for cancellation for formal reasons:

- non-compliance with requests for information regarding uniformity and stability or samples of the propagating material;[550]
- inadmissible denomination;[551]
- no payment of the annual fee after notification.[552]

3.3.7 *Term of Protection*

The breeder's right shall be granted for at least 20 years and for trees and vines for 25 years, Article 19 UPOV Convention. This has been implemented, e.g., in the Dominican Republic in Article 24 Plant Variety Law (DR) 2006. As discussed above, in Nicaragua the term of protection under the Plant Variety Law (NI) of 2000 is generally 20 years (see Sect. 3.3.2.2). It is, therefore, not in compliance with the UPOV Convention (1991).

3.3.8 *Rights*

The breeder's (unrestricted) right to use plant varieties is not protected by Article 14 UPOV Convention and may thus be limited by administrative restrictions, as is explicitly provided for in the Dominican Republic.[553] These might serve, *e.g.*,

---

[547] Article 26(b)(1) Plant Variety Law (CR); Article 33(a) Plant Variety Law (DR).

[548] Article 26(b)(2) Plant Variety Law (CR); Article 33(b) Plant Variety Law (DR).

[549] Article 27(a)(1) Plant Variety Law (CR); Article 34(a) Plant Variety Law (DR); Article 75 (a) Plant Variety Law (NI).

[550] Article 27(a)(2) Plant Variety Law (CR); Article 34(b)(i) Plant Variety Law (DR); Article 75(c), (d) Plant Variety Law (NI).

[551] Article 27(a)(3) Plant Variety Law (CR); Article 34(b)(iii) Plant Variety Law (DR), Article 75 (e) Plant Variety Law (NI).

[552] Article 27(a)(4) Plant Variety Law (CR); Article 34(b)(ii) Plant Variety Law (DR); Article 75 (b) Plant Variety Law (NI); the respective provisions lack clarity. The Nicaraguan law requires an "express", but not "written" notification, as does the Plant Variety Law (CR). The Costa Rican law does not provide for the specific period after notification during which the fee must be paid, as does the Plant Variety Law (NI).

[553] Article 23 Plant Variety Law (DR), Article 1 Plant Variety Law (CR).

environmental purposes such as the precautionary principle included in the Convention on Biological Diversity.

According to Article 14(1) UPOV Convention and the respective national laws, the following acts in respect of the propagating material of the protected variety shall require the authorization of the breeder: The production or reproduction (multiplication), conditioning for the purpose of propagation, offering for sale, selling or other marketing, exporting, importing and stocking for any of the purposes mentioned above. Article 14(1) UPOV Convention, therefore, only protects the negative right to exclude third parties from using the protected subject matter. The breeder's right extends not only to propagating material, but also the harvest, if it was illegally obtained.[554]

3.3.9 Limitations

3.3.9.1 Farmer's Privilege

Traditionally, farmers use part of their harvest as propagating material for the next season for themselves and often also sell part of this material.[555] This practice, known as the "farmer's privilege", was included in the UPOV Convention (1978), but was restricted by the prohibition of reproduction under Article 14(1) UPOV Convention (1991).[556] However, Article 15(2) UPOV Convention provides for an optional exception to "restrict the breeder's right in relation to any variety in order to permit farmers to use for propagating purposes, on their own holdings, the product of the harvest which they have obtained by planting, *on their own holdings*" (emphasis added).

Whereas CAFTA-DR only makes reference to this limitation allowed under the UPOV Convention, the EU-CARIFORUM-EPA states that parties may also permit—as part of the farmer's privilege—the exchange of their harvest. Such an exception might jeopardize the business model especially of GMO businesses. However, such an exception would exceed the clear wording of Article 15(2) UPOV Convention, which restricts the use of the harvest to the farmer's *own holdings*, thus excluding the exchange with other farmers. Therefore, any country using the exception provided for in the EU-CARIFORUM-EPA would be in breach of its UPOV Convention obligations and, as a consequence, its CAFTA-DR obligations.

---

[554] Article 14(2) UPOV Convention.

[555] Bucher (2008), p. 294.

[556] This interpretation is not only supported by the wording of Article 14 UPOV Convention, but also systematically by the fact that Article 15(2) UPOV Convention creates an optional exception for this practice, which would not be necessary if it were not basically prohibited; on this issue see Taubman and Leistner (2003), p. 117.

This raises the interesting question whether the Dominican Republic could introduce a statutory limitation restricted to European breeders. The exception provided for in the EU-CARIFORUM-EPA could exclude European breeders from assessing their rights under the UPOV Convention, because the EU waived the respective right bilaterally. Similarly, they may not be able to invoke a violation of the MFN principle under TRIPS because of the waiver. European breeders could also be precluded from asserting a breach of CAFTA-DR as they are not nationals of a CAFTA-DR party. Practically, however, it seems unlikely that the Dominican Republic would introduce legislation in which rights or limitations apply only to persons or entities of certain countries. Such a distinction would be an anomaly in Central American IP legislation.

The technical restrictions of the re-use of the harvest in non-reproductive crops are of practical importance. Many crops are genetically altered to prevent propagation and, therefore, practically circumvent the farmer's privilege.[557] While this practice has been criticized, it does not violate the UPOV Convention or national laws.

But there are also legal limitations of the privilege, *e.g.*, the exclusion of fruits, flowers and forest plants (*florestales*) from the farmer's privilege in the Dominican Republic.[558]

3.3.9.2 Other Exceptions and Limitations

Article 15(1) UPOV Convention and the national laws also provide for the limitation of the breeder's right with regard to acts done (1) privately and for non-commercial purposes, (2) for experimental purposes and (3) for the purpose of breeding other varieties, provided these are not essentially derived varieties according to Article 14(5) UPOV Convention. Especially the latter exception, known as the breeder's privilege, is important for developing countries in order to develop new plant varieties to ensure food security.[559] According to Article 17 UPOV Convention, the free exercise of a breeder's right may also be restricted for reasons of public interest. CAFTA-DR requires for such restrictions the payment of equitable remuneration of the breeder (footnote to Article 15.1. CAFTA-DR).

3.3.10 Evaluation

Around the time CAFTA-DR was concluded, the use of protected plant varieties in Central America, and, therefore, the impact of the legal regime, varied. In Nicaragua,

[557] See, regarding the seeds sold by Monsanto in El Salvador, Keppeler and Romero (2017).

[558] Article 18 Plant Variety Law (DR).

[559] Hassemer (2000), p. 135.

the level of use was low; this might be due to the abundant availability of traditional crops and especially the limited purchasing power of many small farmers.[560] In El Salvador, on the other hand, protected seeds have been widely used for decades, and lead to significant economic dependency.[561] To reduce this dependency, and ensure food security for the poor who cannot afford to buy such seeds, the government initiated a seed distribution program, which included buying seeds only from local production. This program was challenged by Monsanto, previously the main supplier of seeds in the country, and the US government, as a violation of the public procurement rules under CAFTA-DR in 2013. The Salvadoran government agreed to initiate a public tender process, which ultimately was won by the local producers.[562] This case shows that at its core, the practical economic and food supply problems were not caused by the system of plant variety protection as such. In particular, the Monsanto seeds used previously were biologically incapable of propagation.[563] The legal restrictions, therefore, did not come into play. The main factor was an economic and political environment that made self-sufficiency and small farming difficult. This example suggests that, in the Central American countries, the system of plant variety protection could also be beneficial to local farmers and breeders, because of their own experience in the field. However, when CAFTA-DR was concluded, there were few plant varieties legally protected, the one granted as a patent in El Salvador[564] and several in Nicaragua for tobacco and rice.[565]

Subsequently, the most interesting development from a TRIPS-plus perspective was the repeal of the plant variety law in Guatemala.[566] While an evident violation of CAFTA-DR obligations, it triggered no official response, let alone sanction, from the US government. Therefore, it is a good example for both the insufficient implementation of CAFTA-DR obligations on the national level in Central America and the lack of consequences from the other CAFTA-DR parties, notably the USA.

In Costa Rica, where the respective law and procedures were created only in 2008, the relevance of system is slowly developing. As shown by statistical data provided by UPOV, between 2016 and 2020, a total of 20 plant varieties were granted protection, of which six were granted to residents (30%).[567] Regarding the Dominican Republic, the reported data is incomplete, but in 2021, five plant varieties were granted protection, of which three were granted to residents (60%), and 18 varieties were protected in total.[568] In Nicaragua, between 2016 and 2020, a

[560] Aguilar Espinoza (2007), p. 20.

[561] On the historical background, see Keppeler and Romero (2017).

[562] This controversy is explained in more detail by Keppeler and Romero (2017).

[563] Keppeler and Romero (2017).

[564] See Sect. 3.3.2.2.

[565] Ruiz Muller (2006), p. 34.

[566] See Sect. 3.3.2.2.

[567] UPOV, Plant Variety Protection Statistics for the period 2016–2020, C/55/INF/7, 2021, available at https://www.upov.int/edocs/mdocs/upov/en/c_55/c_55_inf_7.pdf (accessed 2 Nov 2024).

[568] Ibid.

total of nine plant varieties were granted protection, of which six were granted to residents (66%), and 17 varieties were protected in total.[569] In Honduras there are no plant varieties protected, as the legislative basis has not been put in place; this is also the case in El Salvador, where no *sui generis* protection is available.

After the ratification of the UPOV Convention in almost all countries, which excludes reciprocity, this lack of protection in Guatemala and Honduras and the low level of utilization in other Central American countries, is no longer a problem for protection abroad as such. But the practical underdevelopment of the system and the reservations of the local breeders against protection have been in the past and might still be an obstacle for economic exploitation of their varieties. The significant share of plant varieties registered to residents (30–66%) are evidence of the activities of local breeders and research institutions and suggest at least in this area there exists the possibility of leveraging domestic technological development.

3.4 Test Data Protection

Test data are generated during the development of a pharmaceutical or agricultural chemical product, especially its testing stages. It must be submitted to obtain the marketing approval for the product by the health and safety authorities. Test data are protected in Article 39(3) TRIPS "against unfair commercial use". Following TRIPS, originator pharmaceutical companies argued strongly for exclusive protection. Exclusive protection of such test data for a limited period of time, prevents competitors from using such test data to obtain approval for their own products, *i.e.*, generic drugs.[570] Increasing the protection of test data is one of the core elements, and one of the most controversial provisions, of the IP chapter in US-FTAs.[571] For example, Article 15.10 CAFTA-DR provides that such test data must be protected by an exclusive IP right. On the other hand, neither the EU-CARIFORUM-EPA nor the EU-CA-AA contain rules regarding test data.[572]

3.4.1 Policy Considerations

Pharmaceutical companies have to submit test data to a regulatory agency to prove that a new drug is safe and effective. Proponents of test data protection argue that the necessary testing constitutes the bulk of the financial investment for developing a drug and the exclusion of competition for certain period of time allows the company

[569] Ibid.

[570] Brenes (2005), section 2.

[571] Drexl (2006–2007), p. 528.

[572] See Sect. 3.4.2.1.

to recoup this investment. Without protection, the competition by generic drugs will preclude the company from charging the premium necessary to provide the incentive to invest in the development of the product.[573]

However, this view is disputed, at least the necessity of protection in developing countries. While the substantial investment necessary to obtain these data is often recognized, there is a widespread concern that CAFTA-DR (and other FTAs) grant too much protection and, therefore, are detrimental to public health. It is argued that the extension of exclusive protection is without justification and also detrimental to competition.[574] Also, it could result in monopoly rents which mean higher prices for medicines. From a consumer and public health perspective it is an important policy objective to safeguard the early entry of generics competition.[575] In a study concluded in 2009, the European Commission found that the entry of a generic version reduces the price of the drug significantly. Within 18 months after the entry of generic drugs, the price of the originator drug is about 85% of pre-entry price of the originator drug and the price of the generic drug is about 60% of the pre-entry price of the originator drug.[576]

Test data protection can also serve to *substitute* patent protection in cases where patent protection is not available or effective.[577] In Central America, many drugs were and remain free of patent protection. First, in several Central American countries, such as Costa Rica and the Dominican Republic, pharmaceutical products could practically not be patented or did not meet the strict patentability requirements, *e.g.*, because the drug was based on a combination of known substances and, therefore, not considered inventive.[578] Second, some companies choose not to apply for patents because of the enforcement problems. Test data protection could therefore have a significant practical effect because of these limitations to patent protection in Central America.[579]

3.4.2 Legal and Administrative Framework

3.4.2.1 International Legal Framework

Article 39(3) TRIPS introduced the protection of test data on the international level based on unfair competition, as indicated by the reference to Article 10*bis* Paris

[573] See Díaz (2006), p. 103; see also references in Andanda (2013), p. 142.

[574] Drexl (2007), p. 19.

[575] See UNCTAD-ICTSD (2005), p. 538.

[576] European Commission (2008), p. 1.

[577] Fackelmann (2009), p. 478, notes that in addition test data protection is easier to obtain because it does not require novelty or inventive step, making it a possibly "cheap" alternative to patent protection.

[578] See Sect. 3.1.3.2; see also PhRMA (2007), pp. 26, 157–158; Brenes (2005), section 2.

[579] Correa (2004), p. 84.

Convention in Article 39(1) TRIPS and the protection against "unfair commercial practices" in Article 39(3) TRIPS. As already noted, it does not require either an unfair competition- or (exclusive) IP right-based system. In particular, it does not indicate a minimum term of protection. The United States applies an exclusivity approach.[580] Other Latin American countries have adopted the unfair competition model in their laws implementing TRIPS, for example Argentina.[581] Also in Central America, TRIPS did not give an impulse to create exclusive protection, except for the legislation in Guatemala (which is analyzed below in detail).[582]

Therefore, the requirement to introduce exclusive protection for test data into the national legislation was included in Article 15.10 CAFTA-DR, creating a special IP right for test data relating to pharmaceutical and agrochemical products. This protection of test data was and is one of the most controversial elements of CAFTA-DR. The implementation of the CAFTA-DR obligations was heavily opposed by international NGOs and local social movements, who were (partly) influenced by interest groups such as the generic industry.[583]

As discussed in more detail below, this opposition caused the Central American countries to implement the CAFTA-DR requirements in a narrow way, which has been criticized as insufficient by US industries with regard to several Central American countries.[584]

The *Bipartisan Trade Deal* provides for flexibility of developing country FTA partners of the USA in relation to the protection of test data.[585] However, this flexibility was not explicitly granted retroactively to existing FTAs such as CAFTA-DR.

Also the European Union applies an exclusivity approach.[586] In the EU, new pharmaceutical products are entitled to 8 years of data exclusively, 2 years of marketing exclusively and an additional year of protection for new indications of existing products.[587] Nevertheless, neither the EU-CARIFORUM-EPA nor the EU-CA-AA contain requirements regarding the protection of test data. However, this may not be due to policy concerns of the European negotiators, but due to the fact that, at least with regard to the Dominican Republic and the Central American countries, European pharmaceutical companies benefit from the protection of test data required by CAFTA-DR based on the MFN principle.[588]

---

[580] See UNCTAD-ICTSD (2005), p. 535.

[581] See UNCTAD-ICTSD (2005), p. 533.

[582] See Sect. 3.4.2.2 below.

[583] Castro (2015), p. 89.

[584] See USTR Special 301 Report (2015), pp. 68–69.

[585] USTR (2007), p. 3.

[586] See UNCTAD-ICTSD (2005), p. 535.

[587] Ibid.

[588] See also Drexl (2018) Nr 120, who notes the difference between the EU-CA-AA and the almost concurrent EU-Colombia/Peru-FTA in this regard. Drexl suggests that the differences between some of the EU-FTAs appear "almost random". However, at least the omission of the protection of

3.4.2.2 Central America

Costa Rica provides for protection of test data in the Undisclosed Information Law (CR) (*Ley de Información No Divulgada*) of 2000.[589] Protection is limited to cases of unfair commercial use.[590] The reform of Article 8 Undisclosed Information Law (CR) in 2008 did not rectify this situation, because it only affected the requirements of protection, but did not replace the unfair competition protection with an exclusive right.[591] In the light of the discussion above, it seems questionable whether this complies with Article 15.10 CAFTA-DR. Costa Rica has subsequently created the possibility for the Ministry of Health to grant test data protection for active pharmaceutical ingredients, as evidenced by the fact that such protection was granted to several drugs between 2013 and 2023.[592] However, it is unclear what practical protection the grant of test data protection by the Ministry of Health actually conveys.[593]

In the Dominican Republic, test data protection was introduced by the CAFTA-DR Reform Law I (DR).[594] However, the regulation necessary to implement this law has not yet been passed.[595]

In El Salvador, Article 15.10 CAFTA-DR was implemented by Article 103 CAFTA-DR IP Reform Law (SV). The new Articles 181-A–181-E IP LAW (SV) form a separate chapter in the title on undisclosed information and follow closely the structure of Article 15.10 CAFTA-DR in that Articles 181-A–181-D IP LAW (SV) correspond with Article 15.10(1)(a) to (d) CAFTA-DR and Article 181-E IP LAW (SV) corresponds with Article 15.10(2) CAFTA-DR. The complementary regulation was enacted in 2008 [Test Data Regulation (SV)].[596] Article 2(1) of this regulation only protects test data "against any unfair commercial use", which raised the question how this restriction relates to the exclusive protection of Articles 181-A–181-D IP LAW (SV). This provision should be interpreted in a way compliant with CAFTA-DR and, accordingly, any application for marketing approval by third parties should be considered "unfair commercial use", because

test data in the EU-CA-AA may well not be random, but due to the pre-existing CAFTA-DR requirements.

[589] Law No. 7975, enacted 4 January 2000, entered into force 18 January 2000, available at http://www.wipo.int/wipolex/es/details.jsp?id=886 (accessed 2 Nov 2024).

[590] Articles 2 *caput* and 8 Undisclosed Information Law (CR).

[591] Article 8 Undisclosed Information Law (CR), as amended by Article 6 CAFTA-DR Reform Law II (CR).

[592] See Castro (2015), p. 93; see also https://www.ministeriodesalud.go.cr/index.php/biblioteca-de-archivos-left/documentos-ministerio-de-salud/tramites/registros/productos-registrados/5105-vinculacion-de-patentes-y-proteccion-de-datos-de-prueba-3/file (accessed 2 Nov 2024).

[593] According to Castro (2015), p. 93, the test data protection had no measurable effect on Costa Rica's healthcare system.

[594] Article 181 IP Law (DR), as amended by Article 32 CAFTA-DR Reform Law I (DR).

[595] USTR Special 301 Report (2016), p. 59 (no later data could be obtained).

[596] The text is available at www.wipo.int/wipolex/en/details.jsp?id=10285 (accessed 2 Nov 2024).

according to Salvadoran law, in case of conflict between the provisions of the IP LAW (SV) and those of international agreements, the latter prevail.[597]

The legislative history in Guatemala is an example for the difficulties of implementing legal concepts which are entirely new to a legal system, and doing so under international or foreign pressure. Test data protection was first introduced in 2003 with a term of protection of 15 years. This long term, which does not correspond to any term in other jurisdictions, indicates that the legislature chose this term without evaluating it and was probably unaware of the consequences. In 2004, a new government abolished the protection entirely, before reintroducing it in March 2005 (long before the general reform laws implementing CAFTA-DR of May 2006) to comply with Article 15.10 CAFTA-DR. As a result of these changes, some products protected by the test data regime enjoy 15 years of protection, some none, and the majority (since 2005) 5 years.[598]

In Honduras, like in the Dominican Republic, no regulatory framework was created to implement the obligations under CAFTA-DR for several years.[599] Honduras had drafted a corresponding regulation in 2008, but it was never enacted.[600] However, in 2018 a regulation was passed to establish test data protection.[601] By March 2022, 15 drugs were protected.[602]

In Nicaragua, test data protection was introduced in 2006 during the initial implementation of CAFTA-DR requirements.[603]

3.4.3 Subject Matter and Requirements

3.4.3.1 Products

Article 39(3) TRIPS, Article 15.10 CAFTA-DR and the national implementation legislation[604] protect test data relating to pharmaceutical and agricultural chemical products. CAFTA-DR regulates both types of products together and only differentiates with regard to the term of protection (5 and 10 years), unlike the US-Peru-TPA, where both types are separated.[605]

---

[597] Article 2 IP LAW (SV).

[598] The legislative history is described by Shaffer and Brenner (2009), p. 959.

[599] PhRMA (2014), p. 190 (no later data could be obtained).

[600] Ibid.

[601] Reglamento de Protección de Datos de Prueba (Acuerdo No. 024-2018).

[602] See https://arsateca.arsa.hn/index.php/2022/03/28/listado-oficial-de-medicamentos-con-proteccion-de-datos-de-prueba-version-02/ (accessed 2 Nov 2024).

[603] Resolución Ministerial 115-2006, "Protección de datos de prueba o información no divulgada de productos farmacéuticos".

[604] E.g., Article 8 Undisclosed Information Law (CR).

[605] Article 16.10 US-Peru-TPA.

The respective product must be new. Under Article 39(3) TRIPS, new are "products which utilize new chemical entities". This requirement excludes the protection of second indications, *i.e.*, new uses of the same drug. This exclusion is explicitly stated in the Salvadoran legislation.[606]

Under Article 15.10(1) CAFTA-DR, "a new product is one that does not contain a chemical entity that has been previously approved" nationally.[607] This clarifies novelty in two ways: First, if a product utilizes some old and some new chemical entities, it could qualify for protection under TRIPS, but not CAFTA-DR, which requires the utilization of only new entities. Second, it provides for *relative* novelty, as products which have been approved in other countries are not taken into account.[608]

The implementation of the novelty requirement in the Dominican Republic has been criticized as excluding from the new protection "old" products, where the respective test data were submitted before CAFTA-DR went into force.[609] Such an exclusion allegedly violates the retroactive effect of CAFTA-DR.[610] However, the criticism ignores that (a) the novelty requirement in Article 15.10 CAFTA-DR clearly relates substantively to the content of the product itself, and not procedurally to the date of submission, and (b) the national provision is literally identical to CAFTA-DR, so that the claim of non-compliance with CAFTA-DR is clearly not substantiated.

Costa Rican legislation contains also the specification that products must be new.[611] The considerations regarding the Salvadoran provision, therefore, apply accordingly.

3.4.3.2 Test Data

Protected test data is data which must be submitted to obtain marketing approval,[612] *i.e.*, test data required by the regulatory agency responsible for public health, e.g., in El Salvador, the Superior Council for Health Security (*Consejo Superior de Salud Pública*),[613] and in most other countries the health ministry.[614] These institutions are

[606] Article 1 Test Data Regulation (SV).

[607] See also, e.g., Article 8 Undisclosed Information Law (CR) and the Test Data Regulation (SV); the novelty of pharmaceutical products is phrased similarly in Article 16.10 US-Peru-TPA.

[608] Regarding relative and absolute novelty in relation to patents see Sect. 3.1.3.1.

[609] PhRMA (2007), p. 157; the criticism concerned Article 181(1)(1) IP Law (DR), as amended by Article 32 CAFTA-DR Reform Law I (DR), regulating the patent linkage, but it applies to novelty in general.

[610] PhRMA (2007), p. 157.

[611] Article 8 Undisclosed Information Law (CR).

[612] Article 39(3) TRIPS; Article 15.10(1) CAFTA-DR.

[613] Article 68 Constitution (SV).

[614] The competent authorities will not be discussed here, for more detail see Sect. 3.4.2.2.

responsible for protecting the test data they receive and for the cooperation with the IP Register with regard to patent linkage.

Article 15.10(1) CAFTA-DR requires protection of test data concerning safety or efficacy. This means that test data required for other purposes does not have to be protected. But CAFTA-DR does not provide that proof of efficiency and safety must be required for all approvals of pharmaceuticals.[615] Accordingly, the Central American countries may require for the marketing approval of generic drugs only bio-equivalence tests without separate proof of efficiency and safety. As such proof would significantly increase the necessary testing efforts of generic companies and, therefore, delay the introduction of generic competition and increase the price of such products, the permission of bio-equivalence tests is an important facilitation.

The protected data are further specified in El Salvador [Test Data Regulation (SV)]. The regulation provides that only information from the second and third phase of the clinical trials is considered test data, while information from other tests and studies is considered (general) undisclosed information. However, the regulation subsequently provides for the same protection for both types, so the distinction does not seem to have legal consequences.

3.4.3.3 Effort in Generating Test Data

According to Article 39(3) TRIPS, test data must be the result of *considerable effort*, a requirement still included in some Central American legislations as well [*e.g.*, Article 8 Undisclosed Information Law (CR), Test Data Regulation (SV)]. It was not included in Article 15.10 CAFTA-DR, which raises the question whether this limitation is still admissible. Protection of test data which required no "considerable effort" is questionable from the policy perspective, because the protection is awarded to compensate for this effort.

However, the legal analysis suggests that test data generated without considerable effort is protected under CAFTA-DR. Systematically, the comparison of Article 39(3) TRIPS and Article 15.10 CAFTA-DR show that other limitations provided for in TRIPS have been copied into CAFTA-DR, such as the disclosure to protect the public.[616] Therefore, one must assume that a limitation not copied in CAFTA-DR was intentionally excluded. In addition, Article 15.10 CAFTA-DR generally intends to replace the flexible TRIPS provision with strict rules.[617] The possibility of an (unspecified) evaluation of the respective effort would reintroduce legal uncertainty. The limitation of protection to test data generated with considerable effort is, by comparison, explicitly provided for in the subsequent Article 16.10 US-Peru-TPA.

---

[615] However, this is recommended by Brenes (2005), section 2.

[616] See Sect. 3.4.5.1.

[617] This is shown by the creation of an exclusive right as opposed to unfair competition protection and the establishment of fixed terms as opposed to flexible terms as in Article 16.10 US-Peru-TPA.

The parties of the US-Peru-TPA apparently considered the inclusion of the limitation necessary.[618]

Accordingly, CAFTA-DR should be interpreted to require protection of all test data, irrespective of the amount of effort required for generating the data. However, this differentiation probably is of little practical consequence. First, testing of pharmaceuticals requires significant effort on all stages, so it is unlikely that any test data could be practically considered to be generated without "considerable effort". Also, if test data can be generated without considerable effort, it can be generated again by competitors easily. Therefore, it does not create a meaningful barrier for the market entry of generics. Nevertheless, both the Costa Rican and Salvadoran law still contain the "considerable effort" requirement.[619]

3.4.4 Term of Protection

3.4.4.1 Basic Term

Test data must be protected 5 years for pharmaceutical products and 10 years for agricultural chemical products from the date of approval in the respective country.[620]

3.4.4.2 Exclusion Period

There are concerns that exclusive test data protection could be used to practically extend patent protection. If the marketing approval is applied for soon after the grant of the patent, the test data protection will normally expire before the patent term expires.[621] But, if the marketing approval is applied for less than 5 years before the end of the patent term (in case of pharmaceutical products), the term of test data protection will expire after the patent term. If one takes into account the grace period of 1 year for filing patents in third countries under the PCT, the respective product could be protected in third countries until almost 6 years after the protection ends in the country where the initial patent application was filed.[622] Since without marketing

[618] In Article 16.10 US-Peru-TPA, considerable effort is required for protection against disclosure, while the term of protection against marketing approval takes into account the efforts and expenditures of producing the respective data. This suggests that the protection against marketing approval might also be available if the effort was not considerable, but that in such cases the term of protection can be restricted.

[619] Article 8 Undisclosed Information Law (CR), Article 181-A IP LAW (SV).

[620] Article 15.10(1)(a) CAFTA-DR.

[621] Brenes (2005), section 2.

[622] If the patent grace period if fully used, the patent in the third country expires 1 year after the initial patent. If in addition the marketing approval is applied for shortly before the end of the later patent term, the total delay is 6 years.

authorization the right holder cannot sell the product in the respective country, this scenario might seem unlikely. However, it may also be part of a global marketing strategy to sell the new drug only in developed countries for some years before introducing the drug in the small markets of developing countries. This reduces the risk of parallel importation while the drug is patent protected and the price, therefore, is still high in developed countries; the right holder may during this period sell older drugs for the same indication in developing countries.

In order to prevent such delays, Article 15.10(1)(b) CAFTA-DR gives the possibility to provide for an exclusion period for the application for the marketing authorization and the submission of test data: "*(A) Party may require that the person providing the information in the other territory seek approval in the territory of the Party within five years after obtaining marketing approval in the other territory*" (emphasis added). In Central America, this exclusion period is provided for, *e.g.*, in El Salvador.[623]

However, while this ensures that eventually the right holder applies for marketing approval in Central America, the local application can nevertheless be delayed for 5 years after market introduction in the first country.

In addition, unlike the grace period for patent applications (which is calculated from the date of filing), the exclusion period for test data is not calculated from the date of the submission of the test data in the country where the test data were first submitted, but from the date of the grant of the marketing authorization, which creates an extension of the period for the duration of the granting process in the respective country in favor of the applicant. For example, if the right holder applies for marketing authorization in the USA in 2010 and it is granted in 2011, the right holder must apply for marketing authorization in Costa Rica in 2016 at the latest. If the application for marketing authorization is submitted there in 2016 and is granted in 2017, the term of protection extends until 2022.

Taken together, the exclusion period, the granting process and the term of test data protection allow a period of protection of about 12 years (in relation to pharmaceuticals) after the date of the initial marketing approval (assuming that the granting of marketing approval takes 1 year in each country). If the initial approval occurred less than 12 years before the initial patent expired, test data protection results in a practical extension of patent protection. In such cases, test data provides additional protection. In cases without patents claiming the pharmaceutical, the test data mechanism provides a stand-alone protection of about 12 years. Even with the introduction of the exclusion period, the test data mechanism can therefore be an attractive substitute for patent protection.

By calculating the exclusion period and therefore market exclusivity based on the local application for market authorization and allowing a delay of up to 5 years, the mechanism also does not create an incentive for an early market entry of the respective drug locally.[624]

---

[623] Article 181-B(2) IP LAW (SV); Article 2(2) Test Data Regulation (SV).

[624] Fackelmann (2009), pp. 376–377.

3.4.5 *Rights*

3.4.5.1 Protection Against Disclosure

Such test data are protected against disclosure, except if disclosure is *necessary* to protect the public.[625] In El Salvador, this requirement has been implemented literally.[626] Unlike TRIPS and CAFTA-DR, the Costa Rican legislation specifies cases of such necessity.[627] Under CAFTA-DR, if the test data is disclosed (because of necessity or otherwise), it must still be protected against unfair commercial use. This provision does not create an additional obligation for the Central American countries, because Article 39(3)(1) TRIPS also contains this requirement.[628]

3.4.5.2 Protection Against Marketing Approval of Generics

CAFTA-DR Requirements

The exclusion of marketing approval for third parties is the main element of the additional protection under CAFTA-DR.

Article 39(3)(1) TRIPS provides for protection against "unfair commercial use" generally, which based on the legislative history is predominantly understood to not necessarily include test data protection.[629]

Article 15.10.1(a) and (b) CAFTA-DR, however, specifically requires exclusive protection against use by third parties to obtain marketing approval for their products. Under CAFTA-DR, the right holder does not have to prove that unfair commercial practices were used by the competitor.[630] This mechanism creates absolute protection of test data in relation to the marketing approval process.

The protection under Article 15.10.1(a) and (b) CAFTA-DR excludes granting marketing approval to third parties if their submission is based on (1) the *information* submitted by another person or (2) the *approval* granted to the person who submitted the information, without the consent of that person.

Article 15.10.1(a) CAFTA-DR protects test data submitted in *domestic marketing approval procedures* against use by third parties. Therefore, competitors cannot rely on the test data submitted by the originator company to obtain marketing approval

[625] Article 39(3)(2) TRIPS, Article 15.10.1(d) CAFTA-DR.

[626] Article 181-D(1) IP LAW (SV).

[627] Article 8 para. 2 Undisclosed Information Law (CR), as amended by Article 6 CAFTA-DR Reform Law II (CR).

[628] Article 15.10(1)(d) CAFTA-DR; for the implementation in Central America, see, e.g., Article 181-D(2) IP LAW (SV).

[629] Fackelmann (2009), p. 375; Shaikh (2016), p. 91, who note that especially representatives of the US government support the contrary view that effective protection against "unfair commercial use" under Article 39(3)(1) TRIPS requires exclusivity.

[630] See UNCTAD-ICTSD (2005), p. 536.

for generic drugs. The protection of domestic test data enables pharmaceutical firms to delay the introduction of new drugs in secondary markets especially in developing countries.

Many developing countries and their health administrations reacted to this practice in the past by granting marketing approval for generic drugs based on the approval for the original drug in third countries, especially the primary markets of the USA and Europe. Instead of relying on information previously submitted to the domestic health authority, third parties could provide as evidence for the safety or efficacy information from the marketing approval process of another country, especially if the foreign information was not or no longer protected. In Central America, health laws sometimes refer to a list of foreign health agencies, whose approval of a drug can be used as evidence of product safety.[631]

To prevent this practice, Article 15.10.1(b) CAFTA-DR provides for the protection of *foreign test data* submitted in third countries. If the domestic health authority admits foreign evidence in the marketing authorization procedure, authorization shall not be granted on the basis of (1) evidence of prior (foreign) marketing approval or (2) information concerning safety or efficacy submitted to obtain marketing approval abroad. Foreign undisclosed information is protected if it was submitted by the same person who obtained domestic approval, for a period of 5 years after this domestic approval, irrespective of whether this information is protected abroad or not. The originator company could, therefore, prevent competitors from obtaining marketing approval in a certain country indefinitely by not applying for domestic marketing approval, because the term of protection of foreign test data in the domestic approval procedure is based on the submission by the originator company. The protection of foreign test data enables the patent owner to prevent the marketing of generics even if the original drug is not marketed domestically by the patent owner.

To ensure that an application is submitted at some point domestically and, consequently, the 5-year term of protection commences, under CAFTA-DR countries can require the person who submitted the test data abroad to seek domestic marketing approval and submit the test data domestically within 5 years after obtaining marketing approval in the foreign territory.[632] This exclusion period is analyzed in detail above.[633]

[631] See, for Costa Rica as an example, the Executive Decree No. 39433-S, published on 28 November 2023 together with the Administrative Resolution MS-DRPIS-9043-2023 listing the Regulatory Authorities of Reference.

[632] See Article 15.10.1(b) CAFTA-DR.

[633] See Sect. 3.4.4.

Implementation in Central America

The implementation of exclusive test data protection in Central America varies significantly in each country.

The (original) Costa Rican law provided for only unfair competition protection of test data according to general standards.[634] Those provisions limiting protection to unfair commercial use had to be reformed to comply with CAFTA-DR, which seemed to have been done subsequently.[635]

Statutory test data protection in the Dominican Republic was introduced by the CAFTA-DR Reform Law I (DR).[636] However, the regulation necessary to implement this law has not yet been passed.[637] In addition, allegedly, according to the legislation in the Dominican Republic the submission of undisclosed information to the national sanitary authority is not a condition of granting marketing approval and the public health administration, therefore, considers test data protection not applicable, even though in practice the submission of such information is nevertheless required.[638]

In El Salvador, Article 181-A IP Law (SV) provides for the protection of domestic test data. It combines both types of protection by providing protection against unfair commercial use generally (paragraph 1) and excluding especially the use by third parties for obtaining marketing approval (paragraph 2). The corresponding regulation requires the third-party applicant to provide written approval by the original applicant.[639] Article 181-B IP Law (SV) extends the same protection to test data submitted in a foreign country.

Guatemala has introduced the CAFTA-DR requirements in its legislation as part of the CAFTA-DR Reform Law (GT), but according to PhRMA, did not immediately create the procedural framework for effective protection.[640] However, as PhRMA removed this issue from subsequent submissions (while maintaining references to the lack of implementation of test data protection in other Central American countries), Guatemala seems to have effective implemented test data protection now.[641]

In Honduras and Nicaragua, the health authorities maintain list of active pharmaceutical ingredients subject to test data protection, but the exact scope of protection under local regulations could not be ascertained.[642]

---

[634] Articles 2 caput and 8 Undisclosed Information Law (CR).

[635] See Sect. 3.4.2.

[636] Article 181 IP Law (CR), as amended by Article 32 CAFTA-DR Reform Law I (DR).

[637] USTR Special 301 Report (2016), p. 59 (no later data could be obtained).

[638] PhRMA (2007), pp. 28, 157–158; however, the author could not confirm that the regulation 366-04 referred to by PhRMA is (still) in force.

[639] Article 4 Test Data Regulation (SV).

[640] PhRMA (2007), p. 38.

[641] PhRMA (2014), p. 190.

[642] See Sect. 3.4.2.

3.4.6 Limitations

3.4.6.1 Access to Test Data and Compulsory Licenses

The protection of test data against marketing approval under Article 15.10(1)(a) and (b) CAFTA-DR has been criticized because it does not provide for limitations. The question is whether the regime of compulsory licenses for patents is practically circumvented because even after the issuance of a compulsory license for the patent covering a drug, the respective generic drug cannot be approved for marketing based on the test data submitted domestically for the original drug without consent of the owner, and the generation of new test data would be prohibitively expensive for the generic manufacturer.[643]

However, in the *Side Letter to CAFTA-DR* the parties agreed to permit not only compulsory licenses to patents as specified in the Doha Declaration, but necessary public health measures generally.[644] This seems to reflect an understanding of the CAFTA-DR parties that while compulsory license can be an important tool in public health policy, other measures can be necessary as well. Therefore, it should be permitted to provide for measures to enable marketing approval of generic drugs to complement compulsory licenses. Still, the explicit reference in Article 16.10(2)(e) US-Peru-TPA to the Doha Declaration and the corresponding waiver provide more legal certainty in this regard and seems preferable in comparison to the *Side Letter to CAFTA-DR.*

In Costa Rica, the provision on *public utility* (compulsory) *licenses* was amended to address this issue and authorizes the use of protected test data to register generic products in the country, without disclosing the test data and while maintaining protection against unfair commercial use.[645] This provision does not differentiate between access to domestic and foreign test data. However, in practice, it is necessary to distinguish the two scenarios:

The originator company could try to prevent the entrance of a competitor under a compulsory license by withdrawing the domestic marketing authorization, thus preventing generic companies to rely on the marketing authorization of the originator company. This method was used, *e.g.*, by *Merck* in Thailand after a compulsory license was issued for the HIV drug *efavirenz.*[646] This could prevent generic companies from relying on the test data submitted domestically by the originator company. This raised the question whether in such cases generic companies could be allowed to rely on test data of foreign test data submissions to complement compulsory licenses.

[643] See UNCTAD-ICTSD (2005), p. 537.

[644] See Sect. 3.1.11.2.

[645] Article 20(4) Patent and Design Law (CR).

[646] Böttger (2008), p. 891, fn 179.

3.4.6.2 Other Limitations

Under Article 15.10 CAFTA-DR, countries may provide for exceptions to test data protection to protect the public, *i.e.*, permit disclosure of such data.

However, while this limitation is included in some laws in Central America, it is often itself restricted to special cases.[647] In Costa Rica, Article 8 para. 2 Undisclosed Information Law (CR) contains the possibility of the competent authorities to use the test data in the public interest, if the information is not disclosed in the process. Especially permitted is the use for studies conducted to prevent practices misleading the consumer or to protect human life and health, animal or plant life or the environment. However, this provision does not constitute a limitation, but rather a clarification of the test data rights, because it excludes disclosure and the information is used only for studies relating to the respective product and not to obtain marketing approval of another product and, therefore, does not fall within the scope of protection as established by TRIPS and CAFTA-DR.

As the protection only covers disclosure and the marketing approval itself, third parties (including competitors) may engage in research and testing in relation to the protected pharmaceutical product (*Bolar Exception*) and even initiate the marketing approval process.[648] The latter option is provided for explicitly in El Salvador.[649] In other words, generic competitors do not have to wait for the test data protection period to expire before submitting their own applications, but can start the process early to enable the health authority to examine their application during the protection period and only issue the marketing authorization on the date the test data protection period expires.

3.4.7 Evaluation

3.4.7.1 Summary of the Findings

The relevance of test data protection immediately after CAFTA-DR was implemented was limited. However, the limited effect may have been due to the fact that the necessary legislation and regulations have been passed not long ago, as in El Salvador and Honduras, or if legislation has been created, the necessary administrative procedures were not put in place for several years after the ratification of CAFTA-DR and existing laws were not properly applied, as in the Dominican

---

[647] This was also the case with regard to the implementation of the US-Peru-TPA, see the Peruvian Legislative Decree 1072 of 2008, which introduced test data protection and allowed in Article 4.1 to grant the right to third parties to use test data based on any exceptions provided for under the TRIPS system.

[648] Regarding the application of the Bolar Exception (research exemption) in the context of patent protection see Sect. 3.1.11.4.

[649] Article 8 Test Data Regulation (SV).

Republic.[650] Several years after CAFTA-DR entered into force, procedures have become operable, at least in some countries:

- In Guatemala, where test data protection has been introduced early, the marketing authorization for several generic drugs, relating to various diseases such as arthritis, hepatitis B and epilepsy, have been denied or revoked following the implementation of test data protection.[651]
- Also in Costa Rica, test data protection is granted by the Ministry of Health.[652] 30 active pharmaceutical ingredients received such protection between 2009 and 2012.[653] According to data published by the Costa Rican Ministry of Health in 2024, between 2013 and 2023, five drugs were granted test data protection.[654]
- In Nicaragua five products were protected as of May 2008.[655] The number of active pharmaceutical ingredients with test data protection increased to 15 by 2024, but the practical impact of this increase could not be ascertained.[656]
- In Honduras, protection was introduced much later and even though 15 drugs were protected as of March 2022, there is no data on the practical impact of this protection.[657]

Still, the evidence regarding the *practical* impact of test data protection on public health is limited.

The Guatemalan example shows that test data protection can be effective in keeping generic competition of the market, but it is difficult to determine the actual impact on public health. An early study in 2009 analyzing the practical scope of test data protection in Guatemala, which identified several generic drugs for which the marketing authorization was denied or revoked, also compared the prices of patent- and test data-protected drugs and in Guatemala compared them to the prices of generic drugs with other active ingredients for the same indication (disease), each based on the reference price of the Ministry of Health. It is of course not possible to compare the price for generic drugs with the same active ingredient, because those are the ones excluded by patent and test data protection. Not surprisingly, the generic drugs are much cheaper.[658] As this comparison shows, many diseases can be treated

[650] See Sect. 3.4.2.

[651] Shaffer and Brenner (2009), p. 961.

[652] See Castro (2015), p. 93.

[653] Castro (2015), p. 93.

[654] See https://www.ministeriodesalud.go.cr/index.php/biblioteca-de-archivos-left/documentos-ministerio-de-salud/tramites/registros/productos-registrados/5105-vinculacion-de-patentes-y-proteccion-de-datos-de-prueba-3/file (accessed 2 Nov 2024).

[655] Snodgrass Godoy and Cerón (2011), p. 1188.

[656] See the data from the health authorities available at https://latinalliance.co/en/2024/03/13/listado-de-productos-con-proteccion-de-datos-y-patentes-actualizados-nicaragua/ (accessed 2 Nov 2024).

[657] See https://arsateca.arsa.hn/index.php/2022/03/28/listado-oficial-de-medicamentos-con-proteccion-de-datos-de-prueba-version-02/ (accessed 2 Nov 2024).

[658] Shaffer and Brenner (2009), p. 963.

with different active ingredients, and the medical needs can be met by substituting the protected active ingredient with another active ingredient for which a generic version is available. Unfortunately, the study does not discuss if and to what extent, in the practical cases identified in Guatemala, the alternative treatment options were medically equal or what effect the exclusion of the generics had on the Ministry of Health's budget and, therefore, how the test data protection affected public health.

Another study published in 2019 by *Martínez Piva* and *Tripo* analyzed an HIV drug covered by test data protection in Guatemala, but showed that while the government procured the original and more expensive version instead of one of several available generic versions, the procurement decision could not be clearly attributed to test data protection, an unclear patent situation or other factors.[659]

Conversely, a *World Bank* study regarding the effect of the test data, patent linkage and term extension rules of CAFTA-DR on healthcare in Costa Rica showed that between 2009 and 2013 only one drug that received test data protection was included on the list of reimbursed drugs (the HIV drug Tenofovir).[660] The study finds that the share of costs for medicines of the CCSS (CR) budget remained constantly around 8–9% and concluded that this shows that these rules of CAFTA-DR had no impact on healthcare.[661]

The study by *Martínez Piva* and *Tripo* found significant impact of the test data protection of Tenofovir on pricing. For some years, the Costa Rican government purchased the drug for about 0.03 USD per pack of 100 tablets. After the originator company successfully invoked test data protection to block generic competition, the price rose ten times to about 0.30 USD. After test data protection expired, the price returned to about 0.03 USD.[662]

There are two factors limiting the reliability of this analysis. First, the study disregards the fact that in Costa Rica the protection required by CAFTA-DR had not been (fully) established prior to the study, which would limit the immediate impact of protection over the analyzed period. Also, it does not analyze how the budget on medicines was spent, e.g., whether the CCSS (CR) had to buy less drugs or inferior generics because of the existing legal protection of the new originator drugs. However, as noted above, the CCSS (CR) implemented a policy of including new pharmaceuticals in its reimbursement scheme about 4 years after market entry, which reduces the effective term of exclusivity to about 1 year.[663] It is important to note that this policy was not introduced because of the new test data rules, but is standard procedure of the Ministry of Health. It should therefore not be seen as a negative impact on the healthcare system due to the fact that the availability of new drugs is delayed. This is in line with the study's finding that only one drug was included on the list of reimbursed drugs that still enjoyed test data protection. This

[659] Martínez Piva and Tripo (2019), pp. 71–72.

[660] Castro (2015), p. 98.

[661] Ibid.

[662] Martínez Piva and Tripo (2019), pp. 66–67.

[663] See Sect. 3.1.1.4.

makes the conclusion of the study, i.e., that that the test data rules of CAFTA-DR had no impact on healthcare, plausible.

For the other countries, very little data could be found.[664] Test data protection is available also in El Salvador and Nicaragua, as evidenced by the (small) number of products for which test data protection has been registered.[665] However, a meta-study by *Snodgrass Godoy* and *Cerón* found that for many essential medicines there were significant price differences among the Central American countries even among drugs where competition was not restricted by patent or test data restrictions.[666] After reviewing procurement decisions by local governments and the possible impact of IP protection, especially test data protection, on it, the authors conclude that "IP laws are best understood as just another instrument in a varied, and locally determined, tool kit" for pharmaceutical companies. In other words, other instruments such as marketing efforts may have a bigger impact on the procurement of medicines.[667]

3.4.7.2 Evaluation and Recommendations

Some defend the introduction of test data protection in general, because it allegedly has little practical effect, because normally the patent term exceeds the term of test data protection and by the time generic products are developed, the test data protection has expired.[668] Generic drug producers could also legally do their own testing, however, it is unclear whether this is economically feasible.[669] These considerations raise the question why so much political and administrative effort was invested to create such protection, if the mechanism is considered of little importance in the first place. To the contrary, test data protection has the potential to create significant additional protection, not least because it can serve as a *substitute* protection in cases where patent protection is not available or effective.[670] In Central America the impact of the test data rules introduced by CAFTA-DR has so

[664] Because test data protection was introduced late or so far is granted in a small scope in several countries, no effects can be measured yet. In addition, the respective healthcare markets are significantly smaller (with the exception of the Dominican Republic), therefore they may also be less interesting "targets" for empirical research.

[665] Snodgrass Godoy and Cerón (2011), p. 1188, found five products in Nicaragua and 19 in El Salvador as of May 2008.

[666] Ibid., p. 1189.

[667] Snodgrass Godoy and Cerón (2011), p. 1190.

[668] Brenes (2005), section 2.

[669] Drexl (2006–2007), p. 528 fn 17, argues that (additional) clinical trials will be too expensive and generic manufacturers will therefore wait until the expiry of the test data protection to enter the market. The economic problems for the generic manufacturers are not only the high costs of the clinical trials, but also the significantly lower profit margin on drugs sold in a competitive market situation.

[670] See Sect. 3.4.1.

far been limited. The fact that the system was not effectively implemented locally and that, apart from Special 301 Report comments on this issue, no tangible consequences or sanctions by the USA followed, suggests that both sides considered the introduction not to be the highest priority from a policy perspective. This raises the question why it was included in the CAFTA-DR text and why so much effort was put into the creation of the system. It seems not an unexpected outcome that some Central American countries would not put a lot of effort into the creation of an effective system of test data protection. Test data protection so far had practical effect in a few cases in Central America, but it remains to be seen how the test data system evolves in the long term. In any case it established an alternative legal basis for protecting pharmaceuticals in addition to or as a substitute for patents, and now is a tool available to pharmaceutical companies. Given the limited evidence available for the region, it's worth looking beyond the borders of Central America for further experience. In Jordan, where an FTA with the USA and test data rules have been in place longer than in Central America, one analysis suggests that test data protection had a noticeable impact on the availability of generic drugs.[671]

References

Abbott FM (2007) The political economy of the WIPO development agenda. In: Barton JH, Abbott FM, Correa CM, Drexl J, Foray D, Marchant R (eds) Views on the future of the intellectual property system. International Centre for Trade and Sustainable Development, Geneva

Aguilar Espinoza E (2007) Evaluating a participatory plant breeding approach in a local seed system of Northern Nicaragua: challenges for upscaling technologies and institutions. Master's thesis. http://www.programafpma.com/PDF/capacitaciones/evaluandoFP.pdf. Accessed 2 Nov 2024

Andanda P (2013) Managing intellectual property rights over clinical trial data to promote access and benefit sharing in public health. IIC 2013:140

Ann C (2022) Patentrecht, 8th edn. C. H. Beck, Munich

Armouti W (2020) Evolution of data exclusivity for pharmaceuticals in free trade agreements. South Centre policy brief no. 76, April 2020. https://www.southcentre.int/wp-content/uploads/2020/04/PB-76.pdf. Accessed 2 Nov 2024

Bakhoum M, Conde Gallego B (2014) TRIPS and competition rules: from transfer of technology to innovation policy. In: Drexl J, Grosse Ruse-Khan H, Nadde-Phlix S (eds) EU bilateral trade agreements and intellectual property: for better or worse? MPI studies on intellectual property and competition law, vol 20. Springer, Heidelberg

Bartling D (1972) Die Rolle der Patente bei der Übertragung von Technologie auf Entwicklungsländer aus der Sicht der pharmazeutischen Industrie. GRUR Int 1972:396

Beattie P (2007) The (intellectual property law and) economics of innocent fraud - the IP and development debate. IIC 2007:6–30

Beier F-K (1998) Ausschließlichkeit, gesetzliche Lizenzen und Zwangslizenzen im Patent- und Musterrecht. GRUR 1998:185–195

Bendaña-Guerrero GJ (1999) Curso de Derecho de Propiedad Industrial. Hispamer, Managua

[671] See Shaikh (2016), pp. 31–32.

Böttger F (2008) Zwangslizenzen im Patentrecht - Eine systematische Bewertung der neueren Praxis insbesondere im Bereich der öffentlichen Gesundheit. GRUR Int 2008:881–891

Branstetter LG (2004) Do stronger patents induce more local innovation? J Int Econ Law 7:359–370

Brenes JP (2005) CAFTA and intellectual property rights, Business Costa Rica. AmCham Costa Rica 13(1) (on file with the author)

Bucher S (2008) Der Schutz von genetischen Ressourcen und indigenem Wissen in Lateinamerika – Eine Untersuchung am Beispiel der Andengemeinschaft, Brasiliens und Costa Ricas. Nomos, Baden-Baden

Busche J, Stoll P-T, Wiebe A (eds) (2013) TRIPS - Internationales und europäisches Recht des geistigen Eigentums, 2nd edn. Carl Heymanns Verlag

Cabrera Medaglia J (2006) El Salvador. In: Lewis-Lettington RJ, Mwanyiki S (eds) Case studies on access and benefit-sharing. International Plant Genetic Resources Institute. https://www.cbd.int/financial/bensharing/several-case-IPGRI.pdf. Accessed 2 Nov 2024

Cabrera Medaglia JA (2009) Propuesta de Contenidos de una Ley de Acceso a Recursos Genéticos y Bioquímicos para El Salvador. http://biblioteca.ribei.org/1592/4/MC-001-A3.pdf (on file with the author)

Cabrera Medaglia JA (2010) The disclosure of origin requirement in Central America. ICTSD Programme on Natural Resources, International Trade and Sustainable Development, Issue Paper No. 3. International Centre for Trade and Sustainable Development, Geneva

Castro A (2015) Intellectual property rights in CAFTA-DR and pharmaceuticals in Costa Rica. In: Koehler-Geib F, Sanchez SM (eds) Costa Rica five years after CAFTA-DR: assessing early results. Directions in development. World Bank, Washington

Cooter R, Ulen T (2000) Thomas, law and economics, 3rd edn. Longman, London

Cornish W, Liddell K (2016) The origins and structure of the TRIPS Agreement. In: Ullrich H, Hilty RM, Lamping M, Drexl J (eds) TRIPS Plus 20: from trade rules to market principles. Springer, Heidelberg

Cornish W, Llewelyn D, Aplin T (2013) Intellectual property: patents, copyright, trade marks and allied rights, 8th edn. Sweet & Maxwell

Correa CM (2004) Bilateralism in intellectual property: defeating the WTO system for access to medicines. Case West Reserv J Int Law 36:79

Correa CM (2013) Compulsory licenses in Latin America, southviews no. 60, April 2013. https://www.alainet.org/en/active/63292. Accessed 2 Nov 2024

Correa CM, Yusuf AA (2008) Intellectual property and international trade: the TRIPS Agreement, 2nd edn. Kluwer Law International

Dennis PA (1988) Herbal medicine among the Miskito of Eastern Nicaragua. Econ Bot 42:16

Díaz Á (2006) TLC y propiedad intelectual: Desafíos de Política Pública - en 9 países de América Latina y el Caribe, preliminary and unedited version. https://repositorio.cepal.org/server/api/core/bitstreams/44194f7d-0b13-41f0-be93-3553029996f6/content. Accessed 2 Nov 2024

Drexl J (2006–2007) IP in bilateral trade agreements. Some ideas on how they promote market power and distort international competition. In: Ghidini G, Genovesi LM (eds) Intellectual property and market power, ATRIP papers 2006–2007. Universidad de Buenos Aires, Buenos Aires

Drexl J (2007) Responding to the challenges with a competition-oriented approach. In: Barton JH, Abbott FM, Correa CM, Drexl J, Foray D, Marchant R (eds) Views on the future of the intellectual property system. International Centre for Trade and Sustainable Development, Geneva

Drexl J (2016) The concept of trade-relatedness of intellectual property rights in times of post-TRIPS bilateralism. In: Ullrich H, Hilty RM, Lamping M, Drexl J (eds) TRIPS Plus 20: from trade rules to market principles. Springer, Heidelberg

Drexl J (2018) Internationales Immaterialgüterrecht, Münchener Kommentar zum BGB, vol 12, 7th edn. C. H. Beck, Munich

Dutfield G (2001) TRIPS-related aspects of traditional knowledge. Case West Reserv J Int Law 33: 239

European Commission (2008) Pharmaceutical sector inquiry – preliminary report, fact sheet, prices, time to generic entry and consumer savings. https://competition-policy.ec.europa.eu/system/files/2022-05/pharmaceutical_sector_inquiry_factsheet_1_prices_time_to_generic_entry_and_consumer_savings.pdf. Accessed 2 Nov 2024

European Commission, Executive Agency for Small and Medium-sized Enterprises (2019) Latin America IP SME Helpdesk – Central America IP country factsheet, Publications Office, 2019. https://data.europa.eu/doi/10.2826/267757. Accessed 2 Nov 2024

European Commission, Executive Agency for Small and Medium-sized Enterprises (2023) Latin America IP SME Helpdesk – Guatemala IP country factsheet, Publications Office, 2023. https://data.europa.eu/doi/10.2826/085548. Accessed 2 Nov 2024

Fackelmann CR (2009) Patentschutz und ergänzende Schutzinstrumente für Arzneimittel im Spannungsfeld von Wettbewerb und Innovation. Heymann, Cologne

Foray D (2007) Patents and development in the knowledge economy. In: Barton JH, Abbott FM, Correa CM, Drexl J, Foray D, Marchant R (eds) Views on the future of the intellectual property system. International Centre for Trade and Sustainable Development, Geneva

Gervais DJ (1999) The TRIPS Agreement: interpretation and implementation. E.I.P.R. 21(3): 156–162

Götting H-P (2014) Gewerblicher Rechtsschutz: Patent-, Gebrauchsmuster-, Design- und Markenrecht, 10th edn. C. H. Beck, Munich

Grosse Ruse-Khan H (2009) Re-delineation of the role of stakeholders: IP enforcement beyond exclusive rights. In: Li X, Correa CM (eds) Intellectual property enforcement international perspectives

Grosse Ruse-Khan H (2012) The International Legal Framework for the protection of utility models. Paper prepared for the WIPO Regional Seminar on the Legislative, Economic and Policy Aspects of the Utility Model System, Kuala Lumpur

Gupta RR (2012) Compulsory licensing in TRIPS: Chinese and Indian comparative advantage in the manufacture and exportation of green technologies. Sustain Dev Law Policy 12(3):21

Hassemer M (2000) Gewerbliche Schutzrechte im Mercosur. Nomos, Baden-Baden

Hassemer M (2003) Genetic resources. In: von Lewinski S, von Hahn A (eds) Indigenous heritage and intellectual property: genetic resources, traditional knowledge and folklore. Wolters Kluwer Law

Heath C (1996) Bedeutet TRIPS wirklich eine Schlechterstellung von Entwicklungsländern? GRUR Int 1996:1169–1185

Helfer LR (2004) Regime shifting: the TRIPS Agreement and new dynamics of international intellectual property lawmaking. Yale J Int Law 29:1

Kanavos P (2017) Procurement policies for pharmaceuticals: the international experience. https://publications.iadb.org/bitstream/handle/11319/8407/Breve-18-Procurement-Policies-for-Pharmaceuticals-The-International-Experience.PDF?sequence=3&isAllowed=y. Accessed 2 Nov 2024

Keppeler T, Romero C (2017) Monsanto ein Schnippchen geschlagen, Frankfurter Rundschau, 11 May 2017. http://www.fr.de/panorama/el-salvador-monsanto-ein-schnippchen-geschlagen-a-1276946. Accessed 2 Nov 2024

Kochupillai M (2016) Promoting sustainable innovations in plant varieties, Munich studies on innovation and competition, vol 5. Springer, Heidelberg

Kur A, Grosse Ruse-Khan H (2008) Enough is enough – the notion of binding ceilings in international intellectual property protection. Max Planck Institute for Intellectual Property, Competition & Tax Law research paper series no. 09-01. https://doi.org/10.2139/ssrn.1326429

Lamping M et al (2014) Declaration on patent protection - regulatory sovereignty under TRIPS. IIC 45:679

Lederman D, Maloney WF (2003) R&D and development. World Bank policy research working paper N° 3024. http://papers.ssrn.com/sol3/papers.cfm?abstract_id=402480. Accessed 2 Nov 2024
Liebig K (2001) Geistige Eigentumsrechte: Motor oder Bremse wirtschaftlicher Entwicklung? Entwicklungsländer und das TRIPS-Abkommen, Deutsches Institut für Entwicklungspolitik, Bonn. http://edoc.vifapol.de/opus/volltexte/2013/4029/pdf/BuG_1_2001_DE.pdf. Accessed 2 Nov 2024
Liebig K (2005) Die internationale Regulierung geistiger Eigentumsrechte und ihr Einfluss auf den Wissenstransfer in Entwicklungsländern. Nomos, Baden-Baden
Machlup F (1958) An economic review of the patent system. https://mises.org/library/economic-review-patent-system. Accessed 2 Nov 2024
Martínez Piva JM, Tripo F (2019) Inovación y propiedad intellectual: el caso de las patented y el acceso a medicamentos, (LC/MEX/TS.2019/13), Comisión Económica para América Latina y el Caribe (CEPAL)
Merges RP (2012) Priority and novelty under the AIA. Berkeley Technol Law J 27:1023
OECD, Oslo Manual, 4th edition (2018). http://www.oecd.org/sti/oslo-manual-2018-9789264304604-en.htm. Accessed 2 Nov 2024 (cited as Oslo Manual 2018)
OECD, Patent Statistics Manual (2009). https://www.oecd-ilibrary.org/science-and-technology/oecd-patent-statistics-manual_9789264056442-en. Accessed 2 Nov 2024
Osterrieth C (2015) Patentrecht, 5th edn. C. H. Beck, Munich
Palacios MA (2012) Datos de prueba y "patent linkage" en materia farmacéutica. http://pdf.usaid.gov/pdf_docs/PA00HTM7.pdf. Accessed 2 Nov 2024
Penrose E (1951) The economics of the international patent system. Johns Hopkins Press
Permanent Mission of the Republic of Nicaragua (WIPO) (2018) Information Letter sent on 30 July 2018. https://www.wipo.int/export/sites/www/scp/en/meetings/session_29/comments_received/nicaragua_es.pdf. Accessed 2 Nov 2024
PhRMA (2007) Special 301 Submission 2007 (on file with the author)
PhRMA (2014) Special 301 Submission 2014 (on file with the author)
Pires de Carvalho N (2000) Requiring disclosure of the origin of genetic resources and prior informed consent in patent applications without infringing the TRIPS Agreement: the problem and the solution. Wash Univ J Law Policy 2:371
Punchi Hewage NS (2015) Promoting a second-tier protection regime for innovation of small and medium-sized enterprises in South Asia - the case of Sri Lanka, MIPLC studies, vol 26. Nomos, Baden-Baden
Raju KD (2021) Patent linkages and its impact on access to medicines: challenges, opportunities for developing countries. In: Correa CM, Hilty RM (eds) Access to medicines and vaccines. Springer Nature, Cham. https://doi.org/10.1007/978-3-030-83114-1
Registro de la Propiedad Industrial de Costa Rica (2006) Situación actual de la Propiedad Industrial en Costa Rica, WIPO document OMPI/JPI/BUE/06/2 CR. http://www.wipo.int/edocs/mdocs/lac/es/ompi_jpi_bue_06/ompi_jpi_bue_06_2_cr.doc. Accessed 2 Nov 2024
Roffe P (2013) Free trade agreements and the Americas. IIC 2013:932–943
Ruiz Muller M (2006) Central America. In: Lewis-Lettington RJ, Mwanyiki S (eds) Case studies on access and benefit-sharing. International Plant Genetic Resources Institute. https://www.cbd.int/financial/bensharing/several-case-IPGRI.pdf. Accessed 2 Nov 2024
Sarnoff JD, Correa CM (2006) Analysis of options for implementing disclosure of origin requirements in intellectual property applications, UNCTAD/DITC/TED/2005/14 (2006). http://unctad.org/en/docs/ditcted200514_en.pdf. Accessed 2 Nov 2024
Schulte R (ed) (2017) Patentgesetz mit Europäischem Patentübereinkommen – Kommentar auf der Grundlage der deutschen und europäischen Rechtsprechung, 10th edn. Heymanns, Cologne
Shaffer ER, Brenner JE (2009) A trade agreement's impact on access to generic drugs. Health affairs no. 5 (2009). https://www.researchgate.net/publication/26766700_A_Trade_Agreement%27s_Impact_On_Access_To_Generic_Drugs. Accessed 2 Nov 2024

Shaikh OH (2016) Access to medicine versus test data exclusivity – safeguarding flexibilities under international law, Munich studies on innovation and competition. Springer, Heidelberg

Snodgrass Godoy A, Cerón A (2011) Changing drug markets under new intellectual property regimes: the view from Central America. Am J Public Health 101(7):1186–1191

Stiglitz J (2002) Globalization and its discontents. Norton, New York

Stiglitz J (2006) Making globalization work. Norton, New York

Straus J (2003) Patentschutz durch TRIPS-Abkommen - Ausnahmeregelungen und -praktiken und ihre Bedeutung, insbesondere hinsichtlich pharmazeutischer Produkte, Bitburger Gespräche, Yearbook. C. H, Beck, Munich

Taubman A, Leistner M (2003) Traditional knowledge. In: von Lewinski S, von Hahn A (eds) Indigenous heritage and intellectual property: genetic resources, traditional knowledge and folklore. Wolters Kluwer Law

Taubmann A (2003) Genetic resources. In: von Lewinski S, von Hahn A (eds) Indigenous heritage and intellectual property: genetic resources, traditional knowledge and folklore. Wolters Kluwer Law

Tharin M (2008) Dealing with a bad deal: two years of CAFTA-DR in Central America, Council on Hemispheric Affairs. http://www.bilaterals.org/article.php3?id_article=13774. Accessed 2 Nov 2024

UNCTAD (2006) Least-Developed Country Report 2006. http://unctad.org/en/Docs/ldc2006_en.pdf. Accessed 2 Nov 2024

UNCTAD-ICTSD (2005) Resource Book on TRIPS and Development. https://unctad.org/system/files/official-document/ictsd2005d1_en.pdf. Accessed 2 Nov 2024

USTR (2007) Bipartisan Agreement on Trade Policy, May 2007, p 3. https://ustr.gov/sites/default/files/uploads/factsheets/2007/asset_upload_file127_11319.pdf. Accessed 2 Nov 2024

USTR, Special 301 Report 2008. https://ustr.gov/about-us/policy-offices/press-office/reports-and-publications/archives/2008/2008-special-301-report. Accessed 2 Nov 2024 (cited as USTR, Special 301 Report 2008)

USTR, Special 301 Report 2011. https://ustr.gov/sites/default/files/uploads/gsp/speeches/reports/2011/301/2011%20Special%20301%20Report.pdf. Accessed 2 Nov 2024 (cited as USTR, Special 301 Report 2011)

USTR, Special 301 Report 2015. https://ustr.gov/sites/default/files/2015-Special-301-Report-FINAL.pdf. Accessed 2 Nov 2024 (cited as USTR, Special 301 Report 2015)

USTR, Special 301 Report 2016. https://ustr.gov/sites/default/files/USTR-2016-Special-301-Report.pdf. Accessed 2 Nov 2024 (cited as USTR, Special 301 Report 2016)

USTR, Special 301 Report 2017. https://ustr.gov/sites/default/files/301/2017%20Special%20301%20Report%20FINAL.PDF. Accessed 2 Nov 2024 (cited as USTR, Special 301 Report 2017)

USTR, Special 301 Report 2018. https://ustr.gov/sites/default/files/files/Press/Reports/2018%20Special%20301.pdf. Accessed 2 Nov 2024 (cited as USTR, Special 301 Report 2018)

Wallot M (2016) The proportionality principle in the TRIPS Agreement. In: Ullrich H, Hilty RM, Lamping M, Drexl J (eds) TRIPS Plus 20: from trade rules to market principles. Springer, Heidelberg

WIPO (2017) Estudio de incidencia sobre la utilización del sistema de propiedad intelectual en Centroamérica y la República Dominicana. https://www.wipo.int/export/sites/www/econ_stat/en/economics/docs/economics_studies_central_america.pdf. Accessed 2 Nov 2024

WTO General Council (2003) Implementation of paragraph 6 of the Doha Declaration on the TRIPS Agreement and public health, Decision of 30 August 2003, WT/L/540 and Corr.1. https://www.wto.org/english/tratop_e/trips_e/implem_para6_e.htm. Accessed 2 Nov 2024

WTO General Council (2005) Amendment of the TRIPS Agreement, Decision of 6 December 2005, WT/L/641. https://www.wto.org/english/tratop_e/trips_e/wtl641_e.htm. Accessed 2 Nov 2024

WTO General Council, Trade Negotiations Committee, Council for Trade-Related Aspects of Intellectual Property Rights (2006) Communication from Brazil, China, Colombia, Cuba, India, Pakistan, Peru, Thailand and Tanzania, Doha Working Programme - The Outstanding

Implementation Issue on the Relationship between the TRIPS Agreement and the Convention on Biological Diversity, WT/GC/W/564/Rev. 2, TN/C/W/41/Rev. 2, IP/C/W/474, 5 July 2006. https://docs.wto.org/dol2fe/Pages/SS/directdoc.aspx?filename=Q:/IP/C/W474.pdf&Open=True. Accessed 2 Nov 2024

WTO Trade Negotiations Committee (2011) Draft decision to enhance mutual supportiveness between the TRIPS Agreement and the Convention on Biological Diversity, Communication from Brazil, China, Colombia, Ecuador, India, Indonesia, Peru, Thailand, the ACP Group, and the African Group, TN/C/W/59, 19 April 2011. https://docsonline.wto.org/dol2fe/Pages/SS/DirectDoc.aspx?filename=t%3A%2Ftn%2Fc%2Fw59.doc&. Accessed 2 Nov 2024

Yu PK (2002) Toward a nonzero-sum approach to resolving global intellectual property disputes: what we can learn from the mediators, business strategists, and international relation theorists Univ Cincinnati Law Rev 70:569. http://papers.ssrn.com/sol3/papers.cfm?abstract_id=309859. Accessed 2 Nov 2024

Zhang H (2013) Rethinking the patent system from the perspective of economics. In: Abbott FM, Correa CM, Drahos P (eds) Emerging markets and the world patent order. Edward Elgar, Cheltenham

Chapter 4
Distinctive Signs

This part analyzes distinctive signs, in particular the two categories most relevant in international agreements, *i.e.*, *trademarks*, including slogans, well-known, collective and certification marks and *geographical indications*. In addition, it briefly addresses other types of distinctive signs, namely domain names, distinctive products and trade names.

While the bilateral FTAs of the USA, such as CAFTA-DR, prioritize trademark protection, EU-CARIFORUM-EPA and CA-AA require strong protection for geographical indications. The Central American countries, therefore, face the challenge of implementing two sets of rules which are difficult to reconcile with each other.

Distinctive signs can be divided into different categories. They can identify the producer, like trademarks, well-known marks and trade names. Collective and certification marks, geographical indications and distinctive products identify characteristics of the product itself. Therefore, every producer offering products with the respective geographical or quality characteristics is entitled to use the sign, also in combination with a trademark.[1]

4.1 Trademarks

Trademark law has an intermediate position in the IP system, as it shares elements not only with IP law, but also unfair competition law. Many trademark law principles stem from unfair competition.[2] In contrast to patent or design law, trademarks do not require a creative (design) or technical (patent) novelty.[3]

[1] Correa (2002), p. 15.

[2] MML (2010), p. 735.

[3] Ibid.

F. Böttger, *CAFTA-DR, European Free Trade Agreements and the Industrial Property System in Central America*, Munich Studies on Innovation and Competition 21, https://doi.org/10.1007/978-3-031-93440-7_4

But other substantive and procedural elements are similar to other IP rights. Trademarks enable the producer to distinguish the products and to develop goodwill as an intangible asset, which is protected from appropriation by third parties. On the procedural level, trademarks are registered rights, administered by the same offices as patents and designs in all Central American countries, and almost everywhere else in the world.[4] This intermediate position is legally reflected by the fact that some countries in Central America include trademark law in the IP statutes, and others in separate trademarks laws. Also, under Central American law, some types of trademark infringements also constitute acts of unfair competition. Practitioners often prefer litigating trademark cases under unfair competition law, because it is considered more expeditious and judges are usually more familiar with this area of law.[5]

4.1.1 *Policy Considerations*

4.1.1.1 Identification

The protection of trademarks affects competition and trade probably more directly than other IP rights.[6] This is shown on the statutory level, *e.g.*, by the protection of well-known marks through unfair competition law and on the practical level in Central America by using the procedural framework of unfair competition to litigate substantive trademark cases.

Distinctive signs identify the origin of a product or service and enable producers to create distinguishable products.[7] They serve to overcome the information asymmetry regarding unobservable attributes of goods by evaluating the quality of the product based on the reputation of the producer.[8] This enables the consumers to make informed choices and reduces transaction costs.

Based on this rationale, one can distinguish information relevant for searching for the object ("search characteristics") and information on the object itself ("experience characteristics"). If consumers do not have the possibility or time to inspect the object, information on experience characteristics is relevant, and distinctive signs protect consumers against being misled.[9] On the other hand, trademarks for search

[4]The main exception is in Europe the separation of the EUIPO in Alicante for trademarks and designs and the EPO in Munich for patents, which is due to unique historic circumstances during the European integration.

[5]The Guatemalan CSJ held that trademark infringement generally constitutes an act of unfair competition, which would allow plaintiffs to base their claims on the general unfair competition clause, even in cases covered by special trademark provisions, see Decision No. 157-2000 of 20 February 2001.

[6]Hassemer (2000), p. 167.

[7]E.g., Correa (2007), p. 174.

[8]Correa (2002), p. 15.

[9]MML (2010), p. 737.

characteristics would exclude competition and should be avoided. Accordingly, generic terms can typically not be used for trademarks.[10]

As a result, distinctive signs exclude the danger that competitors benefit from the reputation of others by using confusingly similar signs. Thus, they enable the recuperation of investments in quality and/or innovation by charging a "quality premium". The magnitude of the quality premium depends on competition:

- supply competition by substitute products, and
- demand competition, *i.e.*, the elasticity of the demand.

Thus, they create an incentive for producers and service providers to maintain quality and to increase it through product innovations or more efficient production methods. This indirect protection of development investments is particularly relevant in cases where there is no patent protection for innovations.

While the law of trademarks and other distinctive signs helps the consumer by enabling informed choices, it affords protection only to the right holder, not the consumer, because the owner can enforce the law more effectively: "The legitimate trademark user's lower transaction costs in policing the mark are harnessed to the [...] consumer protection rationale".[11]

4.1.1.2 Reputation

Sometimes distinctive signs are used to induce consumption irrespective of quality. The product is not (only) bought because of its characteristics, but because of the prestige and appeal of the trademark (or "brand").[12] This prestige is an added "value", which reduces "consumer price sensitivity",[13] meaning that customers will pay a price above market level or "reputation premium". This is not only the case with luxury consumer products, also pharmaceutical companies advertise their drugs.[14] While trademark law enables these methods, their protection is not part of the underlying dynamic competition objective.

Brand names are under pressure from two sides: In developed countries, supermarket chains started to sell goods produced by brand manufacturers under their own trademarks (*i.e.*, the trademark belongs to the trader, not the producer). While they do not advertise these products, many consumers choose the cheaper generic version of the same quality. In many developing countries, including Central America, consumers do not demand no-name original products, but counterfeit brand name products. Interestingly, most consumers are aware of the fact that the *Louis Vitton* bags and *Puma* shoes they buy from street vendors are counterfeit, despite the fact

[10] MML (2010), p. 754.

[11] MML (2010), p. 736.

[12] Rangnekar (2002), p. 12.

[13] MML (2010), p. 737.

[14] MML (2010), p. 736.

that they carry the trademarks. They accept the inferior quality because they want the brand.[15]

In the strict sense there is, therefore, no problem with the identification of the product and consumer protection. But there remains the problem of deluding the reputation of the brand, and the risk that the pirated goods are sold not only on the black—and parallel—market, but in the ordinary shops as well.[16]

It is argued that "brands are powerful social symbols" permitting the creation and consumption of fashion styles. It has been argued that the "narrow understanding of property rights" in CAFTA-DR, therefore, privatizes fashion.[17] In other words, brands are considered important for social communication, and exclusive rights would privatize it to the benefit only of (international) corporations.[18] This argument suggests that trademark counterfeiting could be (at least socially) accepted as a means to be fashionable.

In these cases, the use of the trademark is clearly supposed to confuse the public about the origin, because otherwise the intended appropriation of the brand's fashionable reputation would not work. Therefore, they have to be distinguished from the use of a trademark in a free speech context, *e.g.*, the use of trademarks in critical media coverage regarding the trademark owner or as part of parody or satire by competitors or others. This is a complex topic which cannot be analyzed in detail in this thesis.[19]

4.1.2 Subject Matter

4.1.2.1 General Scope

Trademarks can be formed by any *sign* capable of distinguishing goods or services of one undertaking from those of another undertaking.[20] In contrast to the more general definition in 15 U.S.C. § 1127 ("word, name, symbol, or device, or any

[15]The observation by the author in 2008 that consumers are often aware that products are not original brand-name products is confirmed, for Guatemala, by Kedron Thomas, who distinguishes between deceptive "counterfeit" products and non-deceptive "pirated" products, see Thomas (2011), p. 3 (fn 4). Such non-deceptive "pirated" products are not considered particularly criminal or illegal.

[16]In Central America there is the additional problem of a large "gray" market area between the "black" street vendors and the "white" shopping malls.

[17]Thomas (2009), p. 5.

[18]Ibid.

[19]The relationship between trademark protection and free speech has become an intensely discussed issue in Europe in the wake of the "L'Oréal v Bellure" decision of the CJEU, case C-487/07 – L'Oréal/Bellure, decision of 18 June 2009; on this case see Kur et al. (2009).

[20]Article 15(1) TRIPS has been incorporated literally in all Central American statutes, see Article 3(1) Trademark Law (CR), Article 70 (a) IP Law (DR), Article 2 Trademark Law (SV), Article 16 (1) IP Law (GT), Article 79 IP Law (HN), Article 2 Trademark Law (NI).

combination thereof"), Central American countries provide a long, specific list of typical signs capable of serving as trademarks including *always* words, letters, monograms, portraits, labels, codes-of-arms, graphics, logos, frames, lines or bars (stripes) and *sometimes* word combinations, personal names, numerals,[21] slogans, abbreviations, (fictional) characters and, only in the Dominican Republic, fantasy names and pseudonyms.[22]

As these lists are non-exclusive, the inclusion or omission of a certain type of subject matter in the list is without legal consequence. As long as the other requirements (especially distinctiveness) are met, any type of sign may constitute a trademark. Therefore, the omission of "personal names and numerals" in Nicaragua is no breach of Article 5.1 US-Nicaragua IP Agreement or Article 15(1) TRIPS, which both mention these types of subject matter.

The Honduran reform law proposed in 2008 (which was not adopted) would have introduced a second more general list providing for denominative, figurative, three-dimensional, scent, sound and mixed signs, thus stating not examples, but the possible categories similar to US law.[23] However, this change was subsequently abandoned and not included in the laws passed in 2011 and 2013 following the implementation of the FTA with the EU.[24]

Under international law, the *nature of the goods or services* to which a trademark is to be applied shall not be an obstacle to its registration. Most countries included this provision explicitly in their domestic legislation.[25] In the Dominican Republic and Guatemala, this rule does not exist explicitly, but because, in principle, any sign may be registered for any goods or services, an exception would have to be stated in the law. In addition, one can argue that as international agreements have direct effect in Central America, Article 15(4) TRIPS applies at least in cases without any special provision to the contrary.

4.1.2.2 Service Marks

The protection of service marks is required by Article 6*sexies* Paris Convention and, because of the incorporation of Article 6sexies Paris Convention in Article 2 TRIPS, also by TRIPS, and has been restated in Article 5.1 of the US-Nicaragua IP

[21] E.g. the label "12939" for a local soft drink, which reads "PEPSI" if mirrored, see Guatemalan CSJ, Case No. 128-1997 of 19 May 1998.

[22] Article 3 (1) Trademark Law (CR); Article 72 (1) IP Law (DR); Article 4 (1) Trademark Law (SV); Article 16 (1) IP Law (GT); Article 82 IP Law (HN); Article 3 (1) Trademark Law (NI).

[23] Article 1 of the proposed reform IP Law.

[24] On the implementation legislation see Sect. 2.4.6.

[25] Article 7 Paris Convention; Article 15(4) TRIPS, Article 3(3) Trademark Law (CR), Article 4(3) Trademark Law (SV), Article 16(3) IP Law (GT), Article 4 Trademark Law (NI).

Agreement of 1999. Because the Central American countries were already required to provide such protection under TRIPS, it was not included in CAFTA-DR. The protection of service marks had also previously been included in all national legislations in Central America.[26]

4.1.2.3 Colors

"Combinations of colors" shall be eligible for registration as trademarks according to Article 15.1(2) TRIPS. Article 5.1 US-Nicaragua IP Agreement speaks more vaguely of "colors", which could also include individual colors.

Most Central American countries (except Honduras) include "combinations and *dispositions* of colors".[27] Systematically, the term "dispositions" appears to refer to individual colors, as a sign composed of several colors would probably be considered to be a combination. However, Costa Rica and Honduras explicitly exclude individual colors,[28] which would contradict the inclusion of "dispositions of (individual) colors". Therefore, at least in Costa Rica the term "dispositions" has to refer to a special kind of combination of colors. This problem does not exist in Honduras, because the law does not specifically list combinations and *dispositions* of colors as protected subject matter. In the other countries, individual colors can also be protected, if they meet the other requirements, namely distinctiveness, because the respective lists of eligible signs are non-exhaustive and individual colors are not explicitly excluded. While individual colors will usually not be distinctive, if the color acquires "secondary meaning" and the consumers associate the color with the respective product, the trademark could be registered. In this way, several individual colors have been registered in the European Union.[29]

Against such extension of protection there exist policy concerns. First, it has a negative effect on competition, because there is only a limited number of distinguishable colors. Second, in creates the risk of the protection of functionality. Third, it is practically difficult in Central America to conduct database searches for colors which are already protected.[30]

---

[26] Article 2, 3(1) Trademark Law (CR), Article 70 (a) IP Law (DR); Article 2 Trademark Law (SV), Article 16 (1) IP Law (GT); Article 79 IP Law (HN), Article 2 Trademark Law (NI), see also 15 U.S. C. § 1053.

[27] Article 3(1) Trademark Law (CR), Article 72 (1) IP Law (DR), Article 4 (1) Trademark Law (SV), Article 16 (1) IP Law (GT), Article 3 (1) Trademark Law (NI).

[28] Article 7(e) Trademark Law (CR), Article 83(5) IP Law (HN).

[29] See references in Fezer (2009), § 8 Nr. 173.

[30] Viefhues and Klauer (2004), p. 585.

4.1.2.4 Figurative Signs and Three-Dimensional Signs

According to Article 15.1(2) TRIPS, figurative elements shall also be eligible for registration as trademarks. The protection of figurative signs has been included in all Central American countries.[31]

The protection of figurative signs was expanded to three-dimensional signs in Article 5.1 US-Nicaragua IP Agreement, which provides the eligibility of *figurative elements* and the *form* of a product. No corresponding provision has been included in CAFTA-DR. Such a provision may have been considered unnecessary, because the Central American countries subsequently broadened their legislation and specified that three-dimensional signs are eligible for protection. Costa Rica, for example, includes in its list of eligible subject matter "the *form*, the presentation (and) its packaging or wrapping".[32] Also, Article 82(1)(2) IP Law (HN) contains an explicit reference to "the *form* of products".

Such protection of three-dimensional signs raises several policy questions. While the *trade dress* or packaging will usually be inherently distinctive, the product configuration requires secondary meaning.[33] The protection of the product design under trademark law may also undermine the limited term of protection under design law.

It is also important to exclude protection of functional elements of the product's form from trademark protection. Such functional elements can only be protected by patents and thus for a limited time. If novel functionalities could be protected by trademarks, they could be monopolized forever and competition would perpetually be restricted.[34]

4.1.2.5 Generic and Descriptive Terms

Multilateral agreements do not require the exclusion of generic terms from protection. This exclusion was provided for in NAFTA for descriptive terms in all three languages (therefore, *e.g.*, terms which are descriptive in French cannot be registered in Mexico),[35] but not in CAFTA-DR. It might have been omitted in CAFTA-DR because it provides for a mandatory limitation (*maximum* protection), which conflicts with the agreement's general objective of *minimum* protection.

In any case, such terms cannot be protected under Central American legislations. For example, in Honduras and Guatemala, trademarks that consist of terms that are "common descriptions" are explicitly excluded from registration.[36] Based on this

[31] See, e.g., Article 3 Trademark Law (CR), Article 82 (1) (2) IP Law (HN).

[32] Article 3 Trademark Law (CR).

[33] See Fezer (2009), § 8 Nr. 249.

[34] Cornish et al. (2013) at 18-40 to 18-45.

[35] Article 1708(13) NAFTA.

[36] See Article 83 (4) IP Law (HN) and Article 20(d) IP Law (GT).

exclusion, *e.g.*, the registrations of the trademark "Fried Cheeses" ("*Quesi Fritos*") for fried cheese sticks[37] was refused in Guatemala as being descriptive.

4.1.2.6 Geographical Names and Indications

Protection of geographical names is not specifically provided for in Article 15(1) TRIPS. Article 15.2(1) CAFTA-DR states that trademarks "may" include geographical indications, indicating the geographical origin and a characteristic attributable to it. In other words, unlike collective marks and sound marks, the protection of geographical indications as trademarks in not mandatory.

In the USA such signs can be protected as trademarks if they do not mislead the public.[38] Several Central American countries explicitly include geographical names as trademarks, *e.g.*, Costa Rica[39] and El Salvador.[40]

4.1.2.7 Sound and Scent Marks

Another type of trademark subject matter are sound and scent marks, which are discussed in more detail in this section. The development of sound and scent mark protection is a good example for the ever-increasing protection established by subsequent multinational agreements and bilateral FTAs.

Legal Framework

While under TRIPS neither sound nor scent marks had to be protected, under CAFTA-DR sound mark protection has become mandatory, while scent mark protection is optional.[41] By comparison, under the US-Peru-TPA, scent mark protection has also become mandatory.[42] The EU-CARIFORUM-EPA and EU-CA-AA do not require the protection of sound or scent marks.[43] However, this does not provide any practical flexibility regarding sound marks to those parties which are also parties of CAFTA-DR, because they are required to protect these sound marks under Article 15.2(1) CAFTA-DR.

[37] Decision by the CSJ (GT), Case No. 13-94, 11 October 1994 - QUESIFRITOS.

[38] See 15 U.S.C. § 1052.

[39] Article 3(2) Trademark Law (CR).

[40] Article 4(2) Trademark Law (SV).

[41] Article 15.2(1) CAFTA-DR.

[42] Article 16.2(1) US-Peru-TPA.

[43] See, e.g., Article 144 EU-CARIFORUM-EPA,

Most Central American countries have implemented the CAFTA-DR requirement.[44]

In Honduras, the provision on trademark subject matter[45] requires that (only) any *visible* sign can constitute a trademark.[46] The reform law proposed in 2008 would have removed this requirement, but the proposal was not adopted.[47] Most countries also provide for scent mark protection in their CAFTA-DR implementation legislation.[48]

The Costa Rican law provides for an open list of subject matter and scent marks are not explicitly excluded.[49] However, the CAFTA-DR Reform Law I (CR) of 2008 added only *sound* marks to the list, which considering the context of CAFTA-DR is a notable omission, suggesting that the legislator did not intend to also protect scent marks. Nevertheless, some local observers consider scent marks can be registered in Costa Rica, because of the broad and non-exhaustive list of subject matter.[50]

While earlier international agreements[51] and FTAs like NAFTA[52] permitted the requirement of *visual perception* of the mark for protection, it cannot be maintained under CAFTA-DR, which provides for at least sound mark protection. The requirement was, therefore, removed from the national legislations in Central America with the implementation of CAFTA-DR.

Registration of Sound and Scent Marks

One procedural problem of sound and scent mark protection is the (graphic) representation of trademarks, which affects the registration procedure and especially the publication.

One of the most prominent sound marks is the "MGM lion roar", which in Europe led to the decision *R 781/1999-4* of the Fourth Board of Appeal of the EUIPO of 25 August 2003, in which the board of appeal permitted only graphically represented

[44] Article 3(1) Trademark Law (CR), as amended by the CAFTA-DR Reform Law I (CR); Article 72(1) IP Law (DR) as amended by the CAFTA-DR Reform Law I (DR); Article 16 (1) IP Law (GT).

[45] Article 82 IP Law (HN).

[46] Article 79 (2) IP Law (HN)) was not changed by the CAFTA-DR Reform Law (HN).

[47] The reform law would also have added a second sentence to Article 82 IP Law (HN) providing explicitly that trademarks "can also consist of sound and scent marks".

[48] Article 72 (1) CAFTA-DR Reform Law I (DR); Article 16 (1) IP Law (GT), as amended by the CAFTA-DR Reform Law (GT).

[49] Article 3 TM Law (CR).

[50] Lizano Soto and Pal Antillón (2013), p. 229.

[51] Article 15.1. TRIPS, Article 2(1)(a) TLT.

[52] NAFTA preceded TRIPS and provides for a similar level of protection. Accordingly, Article 88 Mexican Industrial Property Law, which entered into force on 28 June 1991, as amended on 9 April 2012, still only permits visible signs.

sound marks and excluded written descriptions and musical notes (staves).[53] Similarly, in case C-273/00 the CJEU decided that the requirements of graphic representability set out in European law are not satisfied where a scent is reproduced by a chemical formula, a written description, an odor sample or a combination of these elements.[54] The WIPO Standing Committee on the Law of Trademarks, Industrial Designs and Geographical Indications (SCT) on the other hand expressed the opinion that registration offices may require the representation of the sound by musical staves or the recording of the sound. The EUIPO in 2005 permitted sound files.[55]

CAFTA-DR does not explicitly permit or exclude the requirement of visual or graphic representation of the trademark; in the absence of an explicit rule, CAFTA-DR should be interpreted to allow for such a requirement, because such a requirement is *per se* compatible with sound and scent marks and therefore should be considered permissible under CAFTA-DR. In general issues not addressed remain a national prerogative. Furthermore, this problem was well known and discussed at the time CAFTA-DR was concluded and one would therefore have expected the parties to also include it in Article 15.2 CAFTA-DR when introducing sound (and scent) marks.

Given the kaleidoscope of options discussed on the international level, it is not surprising that the Central American countries also permit a variety of options for the registration of sound and scent marks, as shown in Table 4.1, which mainly rely on some form of visual or graphic representation.

Central American countries offer different solutions, namely the graphical representation (sound and scent marks), the magnetic reproduction (sound marks), the chemical formula (scent marks), a textual description (sound and scent marks) and musical staves (sound marks).[56] Other options like sonographic representations or the deposition of an MP3 file have apparently not been considered.[57]

Notably, the first sound mark in Costa Rica (eagle's cry for *Imperial* beer) was registered on 8 September 2004, prior to the enactment of the CAFTA-DR Reform Law I (CR), based on the open list of trademark subject matter in Article 3(1) Trademark Law (CR).[58] In Nicaragua, a few sound marks have been registered.[59] In Guatemala, between 2009 and 2015, 21 sound mark applications have

[53] EUIPO, Fourth Board of Appeal, *R 781/1999-4*, 25 August 2003 - *Roar of a lion*; see also the case report in GRUR 2003, 1054.

[54] CJEU, Case C-273/00, 12 December 2002 - Sieckmann.

[55] WIPO, Smell, Sound and Taste – Getting a Sense of Non-Traditional Marks, WIPO Magazine, February 2009, available at http://www.wipo.int/wipo_magazine/en/2009/01/article_0003.html (accessed 2 Nov 2024).

[56] However, in practice musical staves can only be used for musical notes, not other sounds like the eagle cry protected for Imperial beer in Costa Rica.

[57] Regarding these options see Hoffrichter-Daunicht (2007), p. 935.

[58] Lobos Luna (2012), p. 32.

[59] del Carmen Romero Pérez and Tercero Garcia (2021), p. 109 report two cases until 2021.

Table 4.1 Representation of sound and scent marks in Central America

Representation	Costa Rica[a]	Dominican Republic[b]	El Salvador[c]	Guatemala[d]	Honduras[e]	Nicaragua[f]
Graphical representation		x	x	x	(x)	(x)
Magnetic reproduction			x	x		
Chemical formula			x	x		
Textual description						(x)
Compact Disc	x			x		
Musical staves	x			x		

[a]Lizano Soto and Pal Antillón (2013), p. 166
[b]Article 70 lit. a) CAFTA-DR Reform Law I (DR)
[c]Interview with *Diana Hasbún*
[d]Article 22(g) and (h) IP Law (GT), as amended by the CAFTA-DR Reform Law (GT); see also Gonzalez (2020)
[e]According to Article 85 IP Law (HN) as amended by the reform law of 2008 (which was not passed)
[f]Nicaragua provides for a description, but not representation for the application and publication of the trademark; therefore, the term description probably refers to the textual and the term representation to the graphical elements of the application; in practice, it seems also an audio sample is required by the IP Register, see del Carmen Romero Pérez and Tercero Garcia (2021), p. 109

been submitted.[60] The reform legislation in Guatemala only requires a "sufficiently clear description" of sound and scent marks.[61] Practically, however, the IP Register (GT) requires musical notes or the chemical composition of the trademark, which provides an exact representation of the trademark.[62] In the Dominican Republic, sound marks can also be represented by musical notes. To examine their distinctiveness, the IP Register created a cooperation with the National Music Conservatory.[63]

Evaluation

In Central America, there are no registered scent marks and only few registered sound marks, based on the available information, as shown in Table 4.2. The small number of sound and scent marks is not surprising, because these types of marks

[60] See Gonzalez (2020).
[61] Article 22 lit. (c) IP Law (GT).
[62] See Gonzalez (2020).
[63] Franco (2020).

Table 4.2 Sound marks in Central America

Country	Sound mark
Costa Rica[a]	11 registrations until 2013, including: – Eagle's cry for *Imperial* beer (Productora La Florida, S. A., Costa Rica) (two registrations) – Intel jingle (three registrations)
Dominican Republic[b]	Two registrations in January 2010: – Texaco whistle (*Silbido de Texaco*) (Chevron Intellectual Property LLC, USA) – Texaco chords (*Acordes Texaco*) (Chevron Intellectual Property LLC, USA) By 2020, ten sound marks have been registered, including the Texaco whistle[c]
El Salvador[d]	15 sound mark have been registered in 2018.
Guatemala[e]	Several applications until 2010, but by 2010, none of these (including the earliest, Eagle's cry for *Imperial* beer) had been granted: – Eagle's cry for *Imperial* beer (Productora La Florida, S. A., Costa Rica) – Texaco whistle (*Silbido de Texaco*) (Chevron Intellectual Property LLC, USA) – Texaco melody (*Tonadilla de Texaco*) (Chevron Intellectual Property LLC, USA) – Campana Deportiva (Emisoras Unidas S. A., Guatemala) By 2015, the number of applications had increased to 21[f]
Nicaragua[g]	Two applications and one registration for a cookie crunch in 2008 Two cases until 2021

[a]Lizano Soto and Pal Antillón (2013), p. 160
[b]El Día, Onapi con certificado de primeras marcas sonoras, 26 January 2010, available at http://eldia.com.do/onapi-con-certificado-de-primeras-marcas-sonoras/ (accessed 2 Nov 2024)
[c]Franco (2020)
[d]Martínez (2020)
[e]Registro de la Propiedad Intelectual de Guatemala (2010), p. 6
[f]See Gonzalez (2020)
[g]del Carmen Romero Pérez and Tercero Garcia (2021), p. 109

were only relatively recently introduced and because of the specific procedural problems regarding these marks.[64] In order to be fully developed, the system requires practical implementation, mainly training and information for both the administrators and the users.[65] However, some progress was made. The number of seven sound mark applications in Guatemala until 2013 and 21 until 2015 suggests that the system has been well accepted by the users, because the number is high in relation to other trademark applications, in comparison with the globally small number of sound mark applications/sound marks in relation to other trademark applications/trademarks. Also, practitioners and academic researchers have published several studies and gave presentations on this topic.[66] Nevertheless, the

[64] See the analysis of the registration aspects earlier in this section.

[65] Interview with *Carlos Castillo.*

[66] This study cannot list all such studies and presentations, for further references, see, e.g., Lobos Luna (2012).

small absolute number of international registrations suggests that, even if the registration system would function perfectly from a technical perspective, there may not be significantly more sound and scent marks in Central America. In Europe between 1996–2016, just 0.5% of Community trademark applications were for non-traditional marks, and of these most were 3D marks and only 2.5% sound marks, i.e., 0.01% of all applications.[67] This ratio is similar to Central America, where, depending on the country and year, between 8.000 and 11.000 trademarks have been applied for each year between 2005 and 2010, and (with the exception of Guatemala and Costa Rica) only few sound marks in total were applied for during this time.[68] Regarding scent marks, in Europe between 1996–2016, only nine Community trademark applications were related to these, representing 0.0005% of all applications.[69]

It is, therefore, questionable whether the introduction of these new types of subject matter was beneficial for Central America from a policy perspective, including the interests of foreign right holders. American industry used the flexibility in CAFTA-DR regarding scent marks to argue for their inclusion in the national laws.[70] But for the Central American IP Registers, protection of sound and scent marks requires significant administrative efforts and technical resources, while affecting about 0.01% of all trademark applications and, therefore, being practically of little significance. Compared to other changes to the trademark systems required by CAFTA-DR, such as the establishment of electronic filing systems and other procedural improvements, it is questionable whether it is the appropriate priority to require the IP Registers to use their resources for this purpose.

Beyond the practical relevance, sound and scent marks raise further policy questions in relation to the graphical representation and distinctiveness. As discussed, in Central America a variety of option for graphical representation are used, but they all have in common that these representations are not easily understandable for ordinary users and therefore create uncertainty as to the scope of protection. This is exemplified by the situation in the Dominican Republic, where the IP Register cooperates with the National Music Conservatory to examine the distinctiveness of sound marks.[71] This raises the question whether competitors can (or should) also be expected to consult the National Music Conservatory to determine the scope of protection of the trademark.

The issues regarding the distinctiveness of sound marks have so far been less relevant in Central America, because the legal discussion has been dominated by the issue of graphical representation.[72] Interestingly, in El Salvador a sound mark

---

[67] Adams and Scardamaglia (2018).

[68] See above Table 4.2.

[69] Adams and Scardamaglia (2018).

[70] Interview with *Carlos Castillo*.

[71] Franco (2020).

[72] Martínez (2020).

application for a "cookie crunch" was rejected for lack of distinctiveness, because "the sound was totally ordinary for a cookie".[73]

4.1.3 Requirements and Statutory Bars

4.1.3.1 Requirements

Trademarks in Central America require distinctiveness, use in commerce and registration.

Article 15(1) TRIPS requires *distinctiveness* of a sign as a condition for trademark protection. Accordingly, this requirement was not restated or modified by CAFTA-DR. In Central America, the lack of distinctiveness constitutes a statutory bar.[74]

Distinctiveness can be acquired through use (secondary meaning), which was the case for the otherwise generic terms "Telefonica" and "Supercola" in Guatemala, while in Costa Rica, the TRA rejected the registration of "Supercola" for lack of distinctiveness.[75] In Costa Rica, while the term "secondary meaning" is not used, under TRA case-law trademarks can be protected which have *acquired* distinctiveness, *e.g.*, in the case of "Rich Dough" ("*Masa Rica*").[76] In cases of notorious trademarks, the statutory bar does not apply, because these trademarks by definition have acquired distinctiveness through use.[77]

Article 15.3(1) TRIPS permits countries to require that the trademark is *used in commerce*. The applicant shall be given a grace period of three years from the date of application to start using the trademark, which shall give the applicant time to prepare the commercialization.[78] The Central American countries provide for such a requirement. The burden of proof rests with the right holder, who can submit evidence either of the commercialization (receipts and accounting documentation) or of the advertising of the branded product.[79] In Guatemala, the grace period was extended to five years, the implementation of TRIPS, therefore, exceeds the TRIPS requirement.[80] In practice, trademarks are often challenged for lack of use.[81] However, the requirement of use *in commerce* sometimes is interpreted

---

[73] Ibid.

[74] E.g., Article 7(g) Trademark Law (CR).

[75] TRA, VOTO No. 698-2011 – Super Cola, 4 November 2011; interestingly, while the applicant had argued that in several other Central American countries the trademark had been registered and was considered distinctive, the TRA did not consider this argument.

[76] TRA, VOTO N° 058-2006 – MASATICA CORONA, 15 March 2006.

[77] Ibid.

[78] Article 15.3(2) TRIPS.

[79] Article 41-D CAFTA-DR Trademark Reform Law (SV).

[80] Article 66 IP Law (GT).

[81] Interview with *Gabriela Contreras Aguilera*.

broadly. Practitioners in Guatemala report at least one case in which the judge accepted the payment of the renewal fee to the IP Register as *use in commerce*.[82] In another case, a lower court in Guatemala held that the grace period starts again with every renewal of a trademark (*i.e.*, every ten years); however, this decision was reversed by the Supreme Court (CSJ (GT)).[83]

Article 8 of the Central American Convention (Trademarks), that was repealed in 1999 during the TRIPS implementation process,[84] also provided for protection of *unregistered trademarks* that have acquired a certain reputation through their use in commerce. This is similar to common law jurisdictions such as the USA[85] or the UK.[86] Under the current legislation, only registered trademarks are protected in Central America, with the exception of well-known marks.[87]

4.1.3.2 Statutory Bars

Generic terms cannot be registered because they lack distinctiveness, unless they have acquired secondary meaning.[88] For example, in Guatemala the trademark application "Pulpifruta" (meaning "fruit pulp") for class 32 (covering beers and beverages, including fruit juice) was rejected as being generic.[89] In the case of three-dimensional marks, functional elements of the product are barred from protection.[90] Prior geographical indications can also constitute a bar to the registration of a trademark.[91]

4.1.4 Procedure

4.1.4.1 Overview

CAFTA-DR aims at the facilitation of trademark prosecution, especially for foreign applicant. First, the parties shall make all reasonable efforts to ratify or accede to the Protocol relating to the Madrid Agreement (Trademarks).[92] However, no Central

[82] Interview with *Gabriela Contreras Aguilera*.
[83] CSJ (GT), Case No. 3155-2009, 3 March 2010 - Canel's.
[84] See Sect. 2.4.
[85] In the USA, the mark can be protected under 15 U.S.C. § 1125(a) (Lanham Act).
[86] See, e.g., Cornish et al. (2013) at 17.01 et seq.
[87] See Sect. 4.2.
[88] See Sect. 4.1.2.5.
[89] Registro de la Propiedad Intelectual de Guatemala (2010), p. 3.
[90] Article 7(a) Trademark Law (CR); see also 15 U.S.C. § 1052(e)(5).
[91] This issue is analyzed in Sect. 4.4.6.
[92] See Sect. 2.1.1.

American country has so far ratified the Protocol relating to the Madrid Agreement (Trademarks). Second, the CAFTA-DR parties "shall work to provide" an electronic database of trademark applications and registrations, which shall also be available online. In practice, several (but not all) Central American IP Registers provide online trademark search tools to access trademark information, especially through "WIPO Publish" to enable trademark searches.[93] The Central American IP Registers harmonized the process of registering trademarks in the Trademark Manual of 2014.[94]

4.1.4.2 Electronic Application and Registration

Under CAFTA-DR, parties "shall work to provide" an electronic database of trademark applications and registrations, which shall also be available online,[95] and shall enable the electronic application, processing, registration, and maintenance of trademarks.[96] Under the EU-CARIFORUM-EPA, however, the parties *shall* create publicly available electronic databases of trademark applications and trademark registrations.[97] Therefore, while CAFTA-DR only requires activities towards the establishment of an electronic system, the EU-CARIFORUM-EPA creates a binding obligation. The EU-CA-AA, on the other hand, does not create a comparable obligation.

While creating a fully electronic application and examination process for trademarks requires significant efforts and resources for implementation, among other things, significant investments in the IT infrastructure of IP Registers and training of examiners, according to practitioners they could produce benefits in the long term for all stakeholders. *Electronic applications* would make the application procedure easier, faster and cheaper. Up-to-date databases and internet-based access to such databases would enable companies to monitor trademark prosecution activities of competitors more easily and facilitate oppositions, which will improve the quality of the registered trademarks. This would benefit not only the right holders, but also competitors and the public. An electronic database would facilitate the research of existing trademarks and reduce the number of futile trademark applications.

Despite these benefits, however, some countries in Central America introduced systems of electronic trademark applications and trademark databases relatively late. By now, however, the possibility for electronic filings (at least of trademarks) has been introduced in all Central American countries, often via the "WIPO File" system.[98] In Nicaragua, however, trademark applications have to be submitted in

[93] See Sect. 2.5.3.3.

[94] See Sect. 2.5.2.

[95] Article 15.2(7) CAFTA-DR.

[96] Article 15.2(6) CAFTA-DR.

[97] Article 144.A EU-CARIFORUM-EPA.

[98] See Sect. 2.5.3.3.

person and not electronically.[99] Also, several (but not all) Central American IP Registers provide access to "WIPO Publish" to enable trademark searches.[100]

4.1.4.3 Other Registrational Issues

Applications concerning trademarks shall be grouped according to the Nice Classification.[101] The international priority, applicable under TRIPS also to service marks,[102] usually must be claimed in the initial application and cannot be submitted later.

Article 15(5) TRIPS requires the *publication* of applications. In Central America the application is published after examination, at the expense of the applicant,[103] except for Nicaragua, where the examination starts only after publication.[104]

Usually the trademark is published three times in the Official Bulletin (*Diario Oficial*) and a newspaper with national circulation.[105] While the Official Bulletin is often made available online as a PDF scan (sometimes researchable, sometimes not), the applications (as well as the registrations) are not researchable in a database.[106]

In El Salvador, the IP Register delays the *registration* until the period of 6 months for the international priority has lapsed.[107] In all countries, the refusal of registration shall be in writing (or electronically) and has to be reasoned.

4.1.4.4 Opposition and Cancellation

Article 15(5) TRIPS requires that members provide for cancellation procedures in relation to trademarks, but not opposition procedures. Under Article 15.2(6)(c) CAFTA-DR, also opposition procedures are mandatory, and opposition decisions shall be in writing and reasoned.

These obligations did not require changes to the Central American legislation, which had already in place an elaborate system for opposition and cancellation

---

[99] See European Commission, Executive Agency for Small and Medium-sized Enterprises (2024), p. 6.

[100] See Sect. 2.5.3.3.

[101] Article 15.2(8) CAFTA-DR; the Nice Classification is based on the Nice Agreement Concerning the International Classification of Goods and Services for the Purposes of the Registration of Marks (1979); Article 11(1) CAFTA-DR Reform Law (HN), in conformity with Article 156 IP Law (HN).

[102] Article 62(3) TRIPS.

[103] E.g., Article 26(1) IP Law (GT).

[104] Interview with *Ricardo Bendaña*.

[105] Interview with *Diana Hasbún*.

[106] Interview with *Diana Hasbún*.

[107] Interview with *Diana Hasbún*.

procedures based on international and foreign legislative models.[108] These systems differentiate between procedures initiated by third parties and procedures initiated by the IP Registers: In Costa Rica and El Salvador, for example, third parties may file an opposition within two months after the first publication of the trademark application.[109] The opposition can be based on substantive grounds (requirements and statutory bars).[110] Oppositions initiated by the *IP Register* are called objections[111] or observations.[112] They can be based on formal or substantive grounds.[113]

Cancellation procedures apply after the registration of the trademark. They are required by TRIPS and CAFTA-DR. Cancellation decisions shall be in writing and reasoned.[114] In Central America there exist basically two systems: In Costa Rica, the IP Register is initially responsible for cancellation procedures.[115] As final administrative decisions, its cancellation decisions are subject to appeal to the specialized TRA.[116] Cancellation procedures can only be initiated within four years after the grant of the registration.[117] The provision does not state whether this statutory limitation also requires knowledge of the registration of the third party petitioning the cancellation. However, as the registration of the trademark is published, it does not seem necessary to protect third parties, while an objective date for the statutory limitation provides legal certainty for the trademark owner as well as third parties. Also, as any knowledge by a third party necessarily occurs after publication, if such knowledge were relevant, it would be more reasonable to only link the statutory limitation to such knowledge, without reference to the registration.

In Guatemala, only the courts are responsible for cancellation procedures.[118] The nullification based on grounds existing already at the time of registration falls within the jurisdiction of the civil courts.[119] There are three ground for nullification, (i) absolute grounds,[120] (ii) relative grounds, if the applicant acted in bad faith[121]

[108] The current legislation still has much similarity with the Central American Convention (Trademarks). In addition, the legislative development in Spain and WIPO materials are influential, not least because of the institutional cooperation.

[109] Article 16(1) Trademark Law (CR); Article 16(1) Trademark Law (SV).

[110] E.g., Article 16(1) Trademark Law (SV).

[111] E.g., Article 116 IP Law (GT).

[112] E.g., Article 14 Trademark Law (SV).

[113] E.g., Article 13 Trademark Law (SV).

[114] Article 15(5) TRIPS; Article 15.2(6) CAFTA-DR.

[115] Articles 37(1), 38(1) and 39(1) Trademark Law (CR).

[116] For further details on the TRA, see Sect. 2.5.4.

[117] Article 37(3) Trademark Law (CR).

[118] Articles 65 and 66 IP Law (GT).

[119] Article 67(1) IP Law (GT).

[120] Articles 67(2) and 20 IP Law (GT).

[121] Articles 67(2) and 21 IP Law (GT).

and (3) relative grounds, if the applicant acted in good faith, in which case the nullity proceeding must be initiated within five years.[122]

4.1.4.5 Legal Review

According to Article 41(4) TRIPS final administrative decisions are subject to *judicial review*, which applies to (i) the refusal to register a trademark, (ii) the registration and (iii) final opposition decisions, because they are also administrative (unlike cancellations decisions, *e.g.*, in Guatemala).

Surprisingly, Article 15.2(6) CAFTA-DR restates only the requirement of judicial review of the refusal to register a trademark, which is the type of decision negatively affecting the right holder, but not against the registration and final opposition decisions. This limitation practically meaningless, because of the broader requirements under Article 41(4) TRIPS.

The national laws provide for judicial review of administrative decisions in general, including decisions in favor of the right holder. In Costa Rica, administrative decisions are appealed to the TRA. The processing judge (*juéz tramitatora*) at the TRA holds a hearing and decides about the admission of the appeal within one month.[123]

4.1.4.6 Statistics

The registration process for trademarks in Central America takes a little more than half a year,[124] which is comparable to the registration of trademarks at trademark offices in Europe.[125] Interestingly, the number of trademark applications in the region did not increase but stagnated after the implementation of CAFTA-DR, *i.e.*, between 2006 and 2014.[126] In comparison, the number of trademark applications in the European Union increased by about 50%.[127] This suggests that registering trademarks in Central America has not become more attractive for right holders.

---

[122] Articles 67(2) and 21 IP Law (GT).

[123] This period can be extended by one month in complicated cases, see Article 24 IP Enforcement Law (CR).

[124] In Guatemala, it takes about 6–8 months, see https://shop.liesegang-partner.com/trademark-registration-guatemala.html (accessed 2 Nov 2024).

[125] In Germany it takes up to six months, see https://www.dpma.de/english/trade_marks/faq/index.html#a8 (accessed 2 Nov 2024).

[126] According to Worldbank data available at https://data.worldbank.org/indicator/IP.TMK.NRCT?locations=CR-GT-SV-DO-NI-HN (accessed 2 Nov 2024).

[127] Available at http://ec.europa.eu/eurostat/statistics-explained/index.php/File:Figure1_Total_number_EUTM_applications.png (accessed 2 Nov 2024).

4.1.5 Term of Protection

Article 15.2(9) CAFTA-DR extends the minimum renewable term of protection from seven (as required under Article 18 TRIPS) to ten years.[128] The Central American countries already provided for the renewable ten year term in their legislation implementing TRIPS and, therefore, were not required to amend their legislations following CAFTA-DR.[129] If the registration is not renewed, the right is lost.[130]

4.1.6 Rights

4.1.6.1 Introduction

Overview

The right holder can use the trademark itself or transfer or license it to a third party.

In Central America, the trademark can be *transferred* without the respective business. This is not always explicitly stated in the national laws. However, it follows from the principle of interpreting national laws according to the international obligations, in this case the respective requirement under Article 21 TRIPS. In addition, it can be inferred systematically from the fact that Central American *trade name laws* explicitly provide for the transfer jointly with the business, which shows that this is an exception to the general principle of trademark law permitting the transfer without the respective business.[131] While the transfer of the trademark without the business could be misleading with regard to the producer, in Central America, many countries provide for special labeling requirements to protect the consumer in such cases.[132]

Registration of a Contractual License

The main issue in *international agreements* in relation to the licensing is the *registration of the license*. TRIPS and the WIPO Joint Recommendation Concerning

[128] This requirement was not yet part of the US-Chile-FTA.

[129] See, e.g., Article 20 Trademark Law (CR).

[130] See, e.g., Article 62(a) IP Law (GT); if the trademark expires because the owner failed to extend the registration, the owner can also not rely on the trademark to oppose the registration of the trademark by a third party, see CSJ (GT), Case No. 112-96, Decision of 30 January 1997 - DETECTO.

[131] See Sect. 4.9 on trade names.

[132] See Sect. 4.1.7.

Trademark Licenses permit some restrictions on the licensee if the license is not registered (recorded) with the IP Register.[133] Article 15.2(10) CAFTA-DR, however, excludes the possibility of requiring the registration to establish the validity of the license or to assert any rights in a trademark. According to Article 15.2 (10) CAFTA-DR, parties may only "allow" the registration for the purpose of notification.

The incorporation of the TLT as well as of the WIPO Joint Recommendation Concerning Trademark Licenses into the EU-CARIFORUM-EPA leads to conflicting rules for the parties, including the Dominican Republic. While the WIPO Joint Recommendation Concerning Trademark Licenses allows licensees to be excluded from (any) proceedings concerning the trademark if the license is not registered, Article 19(2) of the TLT requires that licensees must be able to, at least, join infringement proceedings initiates by the licensor. As the exclusion in the WIPO Joint Recommendation Concerning Trademark Licenses is merely optional and the inclusion in the TLT mandatory, the latter provision should prevail. This is the case in the Dominican Republic, where, in addition to the provisions of the EU-CARIFORUM-EPA, the exclusion provided for in Article 15.2(10) CAFTA-DR applies. Such conflict does not exist in relation to the other Central American countries. According to Article 238(b) EU-CA-AA, the Central American countries shall make all reasonable efforts to comply with the Trademark Law Treaty, but the EU-CA-AA does not make reference to the WIPO Joint Recommendation Concerning Trademark Licenses. Accordingly, the requirements under CAFTA-DR and the EU-CA-AA are substantively the same.

In Central America, licenses had to be registered to be effective before the CAFTA-DR reforms.[134] Since the implementation of CAFTA-DR, all national laws state that the registration is no requirement for the validity of the license or for the assertion of any rights,[135] or for the legal effects of the license.[136] But the national laws still permit registration for the notification of the public.[137]

Practically, in at least some Central American countries licenses are registered, for a variety of reasons: In El Salvador and Guatemala most users still register licenses, because the courts often require it as proof of the existence of the license.[138] This contravenes CAFTA-DR, which excludes requiring the registration for asserting any rights.

---

[133] See Article 21 TRIPS.

[134] See, e.g., Article 46 (1) IP Law (GT).

[135] Article 35 Trademark Law (CR), as amended by the CAFTA-DR Reform Law I (CR); Article 46(1) IP Law (GT), as amended by the CAFTA-DR Reform Law (GT); Article 12 CAFTA-DR Reform Law (HN).

[136] Article 35 Trademark Law (SV).

[137] Article 35 Trademark Law (CR), as amended by the CAFTA-DR Reform Law I (CR); Article 35 Trademark Law (SV); Article 12 CAFTA-DR Reform Law (HN).

[138] Lopez-Davis (2011), section IV.

Also, in Guatemala, the tax administration requires the registration of trademark licenses.[139] Such requirement does not fall into the categories "validity", "assertion of rights" or "notification to the public". The registration is only relevant with regard to the fiscal treatment of the license fees, not for enabling the licensee to establish the validity of the license or to assert rights. Therefore, this requirement should be in conformity with CAFTA-DR. Another reason for registering a license is the fact that it enables the right holder to establish the use of the trademark and, therefore, its validity.[140] Some countries have *specific formal provisions* for license agreements. In Guatemala, the license agreement must be written in Spanish or accompanied with a certified translation, even if the agreement is not registered.[141] El Salvador provides separately for franchise and other license agreements.[142]

Practically, the relevance of trademark licensing in Central America varies. In Guatemala and El Salvador, large domestic franchise businesses have emerged, such as the *Pollo Campero* franchise, which rely on trademark licenses.[143]

Use in Commerce

The trademark is protected against use "in commerce" which causes confusion or dilution. Article 15.2(3) CAFTA-DR prohibits the act of using infringing trademarks "in the course of trade". This corresponds to the broad definition of use in Europe, where specific types of uses such as trading, packaging, importing and exporting or advertising are included only as a non-exclusive list.[144] In some Central American laws, however, the scope is not limited to "course of trade" or "commerce", because these countries reduce product piracy also by sanctioning the possession to provide separately for the infringing situations and the infringing acts. The Guatemalan trademark provisions are structured according to the remedies and leave out the specific acts, while the provisions on unfair competition cover generally "all acts and omissions".[145]

---

[139] Lopez-Davis (2011), section IV.

[140] In Costa Rica, however, registration is not necessary to establish validity, the actual use by the licensee is considered sufficient, see ALPILAW, Basics of Trademark Licensing in Costa Rica, https://alpilaw.com/trademark-license-costa-rica/ (accessed 2 Nov 2024).

[141] Article 45(1) IP Law (GT).

[142] Articles 36 and 35 Trademark Law (SV).

[143] The "Pollo Campero" brand has been so successful commercially that third parties tried to copy the brand, see USPTO, Trademark Trial and Appeal Board, 8 July 2015, Campero International Limited and Campero Inc. v. Marcelo Paolo Dicunta Servellon and Giovanna Lucrecia Dicunta Servellon, Opposition No. 91199515 - Pollo Campesino.

[144] Article 10(3) Trademark Directive and Article 9(2) Trademark Regulation.

[145] Article 173 IP Law (GT).

4.1.6.2 Relationship Between the Goods and Services

Three elements have to be considered for the infringement of a trademark, (i) the identity or similarity of the trademarks, (ii) the identity or similarity of the goods or services and (iii) the likelihood of confusion.

Identity

Originally, trademarks were protected only against intentional infringement by the use of an *identical sign* for an *identical product*. The Paris Convention limited protection to cases of identity and to well-known marks and the seizure of other marks at importation (*i.e.*, border measures), Articles 6*bis*(1) and 9(1) Paris Convention. Under Article 16(1) TRIPS, in cases of identical signs for identical products or services, the likelihood of confusion is presumed and does not have to be proven for an infringement.[146] This provision was not restated in the US-Peru-TPA, presumably because it was considered unnecessary given the TRIPS requirement.

A similar provision was included in Article 15.2(3) CAFTA-DR. However, this provision is not only a restatement, because it contains the clarification that the term "identical sign" includes geographical indications. In other words, trademarks must not only be protected against identical trademarks, but also against identical geographical indications. This is an example of the objective of the trademark provisions in CAFTA-DR to strengthen trademarks in relation to geographical indications.

Similarity and "Related" Goods and Services

However, trademark law quickly evolved to include also protection against *similarity* of the trademarks and/or products. In the USA, trademarks were protected in the case of similarity when there existed likelihood of confusion since 1905.[147]

Protection against similarity has also become a standard in international agreements. However, with regard to the similarity between the goods or services, while Article 16(1) TRIPS refers to *identical or similar* goods or services, Article 15.2 (3) CAFTA-DR provides that the trademark owner shall have the right to prohibit the use of an identical or similar sign for *related* goods or services, which is a broader term derived from US law.[148] A competitive *relationship* might exist also in cases of substitution, where no identity or similarity between the products or services

[146] See also Cornish et al. (2013) at 18–86.

[147] Beebe et al. (2016), p. 31.

[148] This extension had already been used in Article 17.2.4. of the US-Chile-FTA.

exists.[149] In other words, CAFTA-DR provides that the use of a trademark for substitute products must be considered a trademark infringement.

Article 15.2.8(b) CAFTA-DR provides that similarity cannot be assumed based only on the fact that goods or services are in the same class (first sentence) or be denied based only on the fact that they belong to different classes (second sentence). This provision reverses the contrary provision in Article 10(p) Central American Convention (Trademarks), which was included in some Central American national laws passed after the Central American Convention (Trademarks) was repealed.

Most national laws in Central America adopted the new CAFTA-DR requirements regarding similarity literally in the laws implementing CAFTA-DR.[150] In several countries, however, this literal implementation was not aligned with the existing structure of the national laws. In particular in Guatemala, the implementation of CAFTA-DR greatly complicates the trademark legislation.[151]

Also in Honduras, the reform law was drafted not in a practical way. Article 11 (second paragraph) CAFTA-DR Reform Law (HN) included the CAFTA-DR provision regarding confusion of trademarks based on the Nice Classification,[152] not in the section on infringement of trademarks, but in the section on procedural requirements regarding the Nice Classification,[153] because both provisions are combined in one section in CAFTA-DR.[154] To complicate matters even further, the provision in the CAFTA-DR Reform Law (HN) that contains these provisions in its title refers only to the section in the main law[155] dealing with the Nice Classification, which is part of the procedural section on the registration of trademarks, but does not refer to the infringement section of the main law, and the new provision on infringement by trademarks based on the Nice Classification forms the second sentence and the second paragraph of the new article (as in CAFTA-DR). Therefore, a user might not find this provision while reviewing the IP Law (HN) or the CAFTA-DR Reform Law (HN) for substantive provisions on trademark infringement without knowing the structure of the IP chapter of CAFTA-DR. It must be noted once more that the CAFTA-DR Reform Law (HN) does not modify the existing provisions of the IP Law (HN), but introduces a separate set of provisions which only make reference to the existing provisions in the IP Law (HN).

The Costa Rican law, after the CAFTA-DR reforms, contains different specifications of similarity of products or services: According to Article 8(a) Trademark Law (CR), a sign identical or similar to an existing trademark cannot be registered if the products or services are "related", which corresponds to the broader wording of

[149] However, while this wording in itself could cover a broader range of goods and services, the relationship would still have to be close enough to create a likelihood of confusion.

[150] See, e.g., Article 11 para. 2 CAFTA-DR Reform Law (HN).

[151] See Sect. 4.1.8.

[152] Article 15.2(8)(b) CAFTA-DR.

[153] Article 15.2(8)(a) CAFTA-DR.

[154] Article 15.2(8) CAFTA-DR.

[155] Article 156 IP Law (HN).

CAFTA-DR. According to Article 8(b) Trademark Law (CR), a sign which may cause confusion with an existing trademark cannot be registered if the products or services are "susceptible of being associated". However, Article 25 (*chapeau*) Trademark Law (CR) only gives the trademark owner the right to prohibit the use of an identical or similar sign for *identical or similar* (*parecido*) goods or services, in accordance with the TRIPS level of protection. Therefore, the Costa Rican legislation is not compliant with CAFTA-DR in this regard, as it only protects trademarks against the *registration*, but not the *use* of identical or similar signs for related goods.

Article 15.2 CAFTA-DR explicitly provides that the signs whose use can be prevented in case of confusion must include geographical indications. This again is an example of the objective of CAFTA-DR to strengthen trademarks in relation to geographical indications. In Central America, all laws provide explicitly that geographical indications can infringe trademarks. As in all Central American laws geographical indications are regulated as a special type or subgroup of distinctive signs, they are included anyway, so this modification is only a clarification.[156]

In all Central American national laws, similarity between the signs can be based on appearance, sound and meaning.[157]

4.1.6.3 Scope of Protection

Protection Against Confusion

Trademark infringement usually requires *likelihood of confusion* except in cases relating to *dilution*.[158]

Confusion in Central America is generally based on both the similarity between the signs and between the goods or services.[159] All Central American laws protect the trademark against the likelihood of confusion, and include the presumption of confusion in cases of identity of signs and products or services, see, *e.g.*, the provisions in Costa Rica[160] and Guatemala.[161]

Article 105 of the Central American Convention (Trademarks) provided that in case of doubt, the judge should decide in favor of the registered trademark and assume confusion. This means that confusion is a question of fact and not of law, and

[156] E.g., Article 13 CAFTA-DR Reform Law (HN).

[157] These criteria were adopted from Article 10 Central American Convention (Trademarks).

[158] See Sect. 4.1.6.

[159] Article 25 caput Trademark Law (CR).

[160] Article 8 Trademark Law (CR).

[161] Article 35(c)(1) IP Law (GT), as amended by the EU-CA-AA Reform Law (GT).

while the provision has not been incorporated explicitly in the subsequent national laws, confusion is still considered a question of fact in Central America.[162] Accordingly, to establish confusion, the right holder can submit market studies in the judicial proceeding.[163]

It is not the focus of this study to analyze in detail how confusion cases are handled in practice in Central America. This section is, therefore, limited to general remarks and examples mainly from Guatemalan case-law.

Even though trademark infringement cases are probably the most common ones in Central America in the area of IP, there are nonetheless few cases in absolute numbers, so it is difficult to determine the exact yardstick for the evaluation of the likelihood of confusion. However, the cases decided in Guatemala indicate a restrictive approach. Only few decisions by the Guatemalan CSJ found likelihood of confusion, *e.g.*, between the trademarks ZAMACORT and SANACORT.[164] On the other hand, the acoustic similarity of LA VIDA and FLORIDA was considered insufficient, given that in this case the words have a clear and distinct meaning.[165] Adding an additional word to the name of a product is considered to always exclude the likelihood of confusion.[166] This principle should be noted especially because it can also be applied to geographical indications.[167]

In the case of pharmaceuticals, the CSJ (GT) uses an especially restrictive interpretation. The court focuses more on the differences than the similarities. Based on the consumer's perspective, the court held that "pharmaceuticals require by nature special attention of the consumer". From the policy perspective, this restrictive approach has the advantage of maintaining more free space for competing products. Based on these considerations, the Guatemalan CSJ for example denied likelihood of confusion between NATALIN and NATALAC.[168]

By comparison, the CSJ in Honduras applies a lower bar for the likelihood of confusion. For example, it considered the trademarks SINCRIS and STIMRIS (both for pharmaceuticals) to be confusingly similar, and also SANSUI and SAMSUNG.[169]

---

[162] Regarding Honduras, see Mejia (2016), p. 98; this differs from the legal opinion in, e.g., Germany, see Fezer (2009), § 14 Nr. 230.

[163] Interview with *Ninoshka Urrutia*.

[164] CSJ (GT), Decision of 17 November 1998, Case No. 135-98 - ZAMACORT / SANACORT; the court stated that the sounds of the only two different letters Z and S, and M and N respectively, are confusingly similar.

[165] CSJ (GT), Decision of 17 November 1998, Case No. 135-98 - ZAMACORT / SANACORT.

[166] E.g., CSJ (GT), Decision of 5 September 1995 - CHOW CRUNCHIS and CRUNCH; CSJ (GT), Decision of 3 October 1995 - BONBOM BUM and BUM.

[167] See the case of PISCO and PISCO Chileno in Sect. 4.4.9.

[168] CSJ (GT), Decision from 23 August 1995, Case No. 40-95 - NATALIN and NATALAC.

[169] Mejia (2011), pp. 1035–1036.

Protection Against Association

In many jurisdictions, trademarks are not only protected against confusion, but also association. For example,[170] however, under TRIPS only well-known marks have to be protected against association, as shown by the explicit reference only to well-known marks in Article 16(3) TRIPS.[171]

This raises the question whether the term *confusion* in CAFTA-DR also includes *association*. The agreement does not contain an explicit extension of the term similar to, e.g., the European and German law.[172] CAFTA-DR also does not contain the explicit provision of Article 17.2.4 US-Chile-FTA that the definition of confusion was a question of national law. However, if CAFTA-DR is interpreted objectively, one has to assume that the parties understood the term confusion in accordance with TRIPS and not some third-party legislation. Therefore, the Central American countries are not required to grant protection against association for trademarks other than well-known marks, because "likelihood of confusion" under TRIPS does not necessarily include association.

In Costa Rica,[173] Guatemala[174] and El Salvador,[175] all trademarks are protected against association. In the other Central American countries, only well-known marks are protected against use which creates an association.[176]

Protection Against Dilution

Trademarks may also be protected against the *dilution* of their distinctive character or reputation. A trademark can be diluted, *e.g.*, in cases where the special reputation of a trademark is abused by association with the original trademark, *blurring* or *tarnishment* and which, therefore, can be considered unfair competition practices.[177] The protection of trademarks against dilution is generally not required by

[170] Article 10(2)(b) Trademark Directive; § 14 (2) Nr. 2 German Trademark Law.

[171] See also Schmidt-Pfitzner, Jan Hendrik/Schneider, Mathias, in Busche et al. (2013) Article 16 Rn 4.

[172] Under European and German law, "the likelihood of confusion includes the likelihood of *association* between the sign and the trademark", see Article 10(2)(b) Trademark Directive and § 14 (2) Nr. 2 German Trademark Law.

[173] According to Article 8(b) Trademark Law (CR), a sign "susceptible of being associated" with a trademark cannot be registered.

[174] As discussed in more detail in Sect. 4.1.8.

[175] According to Article 26(e) Trademark Law (SV), use of a sign "which can cause confusion or a risk of association" is infringing a trademark.

[176] See Sect. 4.2.4.

[177] Cornish et al. (2013) at 18-99 to 102.

international agreements, including CAFTA-DR, except in cases of famous or other well-known marks.[178]

In Central America, protection against dilution generally exists. In El Salvador, for example, all trademarks are protected against the use of a sign which is identical or similar to the trademark *and* which can cause the dilution of the distinctiveness or commercial or advertising value of the trademark or the unjust appropriation of its prestige.[179] Similarly, in Honduras, Article 96(6) IP Law (HN) protects all trademarks against dilution, provided that they have commercial value and/or prestige.

4.1.7 Exceptions and Limitations

4.1.7.1 Fair Use Exceptions

Article 17 TRIPS provides that parties "may provide limited exceptions to the rights conferred by a trademark, such as *fair use of descriptive terms*, provided that such exceptions take account of the legitimate interest of the owner of the trademark and of third parties". Article 15.2(4) CAFTA-DR merely restates this possibility, even though this already follows from the incorporation of TRIPS in Article 15.1 (7) CAFTA-DR.

The possibility to use descriptive terms is generally provided for in the legislation of the Central American countries.[180]

With regard to the *fair use of geographical indications*, the coexistence of CAFTA-DR and the EU-CARIFORUM-EPA in the Dominican Republic and the coexistence in the other countries of CAFTA-DR with the EU legal framework after the ratification of EU-CA-AA, leads to a specific problem: The EU-CARIFORUM-EPA, which is mandatory for the Dominican Republic, requires the possibility of "fair use of descriptive terms, including *geographical indications*".[181] Such *maximum* protection (or *minimum* limitation) for trademarks is rare in bilateral agreements. The reason why this limitation was mandated by the EU-CARIFORUM-EPA is indicated by the inclusion of the clause "including geographical indications", which does not exist in TRIPS and CAFTA-DR. The purpose is probably not limiting trademark protection as such, but strengthening the protection of geographical indications in relation to trademarks. In TRIPS and CAFTA-DR, the fair use exception for geographical indications does not exist. Moreover, Article 15.2 (3) CAFTA-DR provides that "the trademark-holder has the right to *prevent* the use of identical or similar signs, including explicitly *geographical indications*". The

[178] See Sect. 4.2.4; similarly, under European law, only trademarks which have a reputation are protected against use which "takes unfair advantage of, or is detrimental to, the distinctive character or the repute of the trade mark", Article 10.2(c) Trademark Directive.

[179] Article 26(f) Trademark Law (SV).

[180] E.g., Article 73.1(d) IP Law (DR), Article 8(c) Trademark Law (SV).

[181] Article 14(F) EU-CARIFORUM-EPA).

two provisions seem mutually exclusive. This conflict cannot be solved by distinguishing between geographical indications as rights and as signs, because the category "descriptive terms" in this context shows that only geographical indications as signs are regulated.

This conflict between CAFTA-DR and EU-FTA was avoided in the other Central American countries. Article 241 EU-CA-AA states that the "Parties *may* establish limited exceptions to the rights conferred by a trademark, such as the fair use of descriptive terms", without reference to geographical indications. Accordingly, the Central American countries have the possibility to exclude geographical indications from the scope of their fair use exceptions, which they are required to do under Article 15.2(3) CAFTA-DR.

In the Dominican Republic, the trademark owner has no rights against the use of indications or information regarding (among others) the *geographical origin*.[182] This exception was not amended by the CAFTA Reform Law (DR) in 2006. Also, in El Salvador, the indication of the *geographical origin* of a product constitutes an exception to the rights of the trademark owner.[183] This exception was not amended by the CAFTA Reform Law (SV) or the reforms in 2013. In both countries, the clause could be used to enable the use of geographical indications which infringe existing trademarks, in violation of the obligations under Article 15.2 (3) CAFTA-DR. However, this potential conflict has apparently not become practically relevant.

4.1.7.2 Labeling Requirements

Article 20 TRIPS permits labeling requirements to identify the origin of the product, *i.e.*, the producer. This does not exclude the possibility to also provide for other labeling requirements. In Central America most countries provide for *labeling requirements identifying the place (or country) of production*, the name of the producer and the owner of the trademark.[184] The requirement in the Central American Convention (Trademarks) to label specifically products from Central American countries has not been incorporated into the subsequent national laws and thus no longer applies,[185] except to some extent in Costa Rica where the Banana Law (CR) contains the obligation that all bananas exported from Costa Rica must be labeled "Banana of Costa Rica".[186] The requirement in the Central American

[182] Article 87.1(b) IP Law (DR).

[183] Article 27(b) Trademark Law (SV).

[184] E.g., Article 40 IP Law (GT); Article 99 IP Law (HN).

[185] On this requirement under the regime of the Central American Convention (Trademarks) see Bendaña-Guerrero (1999), p. 149.

[186] The text of the law is available at https://faolex.fao.org/docs/pdf/cos136105.pdf (accessed 2 Nov 2024).

Convention (Trademarks) to identify trademarks as "registered" or with an ®, which conflicted with Article 5(D) Paris Convention, was also abolished.[187]

Other labeling requirements are restricted by international agreements. Article 20 TRIPS prohibits unjustifiable requirements for the use of the trademark together with another trademark. This was a reaction to a strategy employed by some developing countries, which required the use of a domestic trademark together with a foreign one. This strategy was designed to establish the national trademark in the domestic market and to later substitute the foreign product with a national one using the same national trademark meanwhile known to the consumer.[188]

CAFTA-DR addresses a similar problem potentially affecting the trademark:[189] The requirement in national law to use the *common name* for a good or service shall not impair (*menoscabar*) the use or effectiveness of trademarks. This excludes only those labeling requirements which (a) mandate the use of the common name and (b) limit the use or effectiveness. The restriction of labeling requirements to other trademarks and the common name was implemented in Honduras, where any labeling requirement must be "justified"[190] and the right holder is not obliged to comply with requirements limiting the use or effectiveness of trademarks, *such as* those that relate to the common name of the good or service.[191] Literally, the last section of the sentence is an example for the entire prior section ("such as"). Accordingly, common name labeling requirements would by definition be a limitation to the use or effectiveness of trademarks and thus would not have to be complied with by the right holder. Such a broad restriction is not required by CAFTA-DR, which only refers to common name labeling requirements where a limitation to the use or effectiveness of trademarks can specifically be found. There is no apparent policy reason for excluding the possibility of the legislator to impose any common name labeling requirements, and such an exclusion is not mandated by CAFTA-DR. Therefore, an interpretation of Article 10(2) CAFTA-DR Reform Law (HN) restricting the scope of the provision to the scope of CAFTA-DR by linking the common name example only to the word "requirement", without its limitation qualification, is preferable. The sentence should then be read as follows: "[...] requirements, *such as* those that relate to the common name of the good or service, which limit the use or effectiveness of trademarks". However, the fact that this issue was not addressed in the reform law proposal of 2008 or the reform law passed in 2011 suggests that it has not yet led to practical problems.

In Guatemala, Article 16(6) IP Law (GT), as revised in 2006, protects the distinctive capacity (*capacidad distintiva*) of trademarks against labeling requirements, and thus only the primary purposes of trademarks. Article 15.2(2) CAFTA-DR protects the use and *effectiveness*, which in a broad sense would also include the

[187] See Bendaña-Guerrero (1999), p. 149.

[188] This strategy was used, e.g., in Mexico, see Grave (2002), p. 216, fn 223.

[189] Article 15.2(2) CAFTA-DR.

[190] Article 10(1) CAFTA-DR Reform Law (HN).

[191] Article 10(2) CAFTA-DR Reform Law (HN), emphasis added.

effectiveness in relation to reputation. However, these are effects exceeding the purpose of trademarks to identify origin, and, therefore, the protection of the effectiveness should be limited to this purpose. Based on this narrow interpretation of Article 15.2(2) CAFTA-DR, the wording of Article 16(6) GT 2006 is a correct clarification.

4.1.7.3 Compulsory Licenses

According to Article 21 TRIPS, compulsory licenses can no longer be issued for trademarks. This makes sense, because the use of the trademark by the state or a third party under the compulsory license would create the possibility of misleading the consumer with regard to the producer, since the trademark is separated from the original producer.[192] In any case, compulsory licenses for trademarks are not practically relevant.[193] This is different from compulsory licenses for patents and expropriations of businesses, which have occurred several times in Latin America.[194]

4.1.8 Special Focus: Guatemala

The Guatemalan provisions regarding the rights of the trademark owner, as modified by the CAFTA-DR Reform Law (GT), exemplify the confusing impact that the implementation of several layers of multilateral and bilateral agreements can have on an existing law, especially if such law has a different structure. The implementation in Guatemala is, therefore, analyzed in more detail.

The central provision, Article 35 IP Law (GT), is basically structured according to the remedies available in relation to certain individually designed infringements. Each subsection provides for the remedies depending on the relationship of the marks and products and the effect on the consumer. The CAFTA-DR Reform Law (GT) introduced the new Article 35 subsection (a) IP Law (GT), which broadly provides for the right to prevent infringing uses in commerce in case of confusion. The conflict of this new subsection with the existing subsections is the meaning of "confusion", which, as just discussed, may include "association". The pre-existing subsections (b) and (c)(1) of Article 35 IP Law (GT) differentiate between confusion and association, which means that the term "confusion" does not include the term "association" according to the traditional Guatemalan terminology. This would systematically require interpreting "confusion" in subsection (a) also as excluding association. However, there is no reason to enable the right holder, if there is a risk of

---

192 Abbott and Reichman (2007), p. 961.

193 Correa (1999), p. 6.

194 See Sect. 3.1.11.2.

association, to prevent a third party from *registering* a sign (subsection (b)) or from *identifying* a product with a sign (subsection (c)), but not from *commercializing* a product with such sign (subsection (a)). Therefore, it seems that the Guatemalan legislator did not intentionally exclude the risk of association in subsection (a), but only omitted it, because the respective CAFTA-DR provision (just referring to "confusion") was implemented literally.

The implementation of the presumption of confusion in the case of identical signs and products[195] also creates new frictions in the legislation. This presumption was not only included in subsection (a), which implements Article 15.2(3) CAFTA-DR, but also in subsection (c). However, this pre-existing subsection (c) provides that right holder can always prohibit the use of an identical or similar sign for identical or similar product, and requires confusion only if the respective products are different. Accordingly, the presumption of confusion introduced by the legislation implementing CAFTA-DR in subsection (c) is, therefore, inapplicable in all cases of identical signs and products, because subsection (c) explicitly does not require confusion.

Another issue relates to the remedies. The IP Law (GT) contains an enforcement section providing for civil remedies applicable to all infringements of IP rights.[196] However, Article 35 IP Law (GT) provides for specific remedies for each type of trademark infringement specified in the subsections. The remedies provided for trademark infringement in Article 35 IP Law (GT) should be considered special in relation to the general enforcement provisions in Article 186 *et. seq.* IP Law (GT). However, the new subsection (a), unlike the other subsections, does not specify any remedy. This raises the questions whether in this case, without a special regime, the general enforcement provisions apply. A referral to the general provisions would give the right holder much broader enforcement options under subsection (a) than any other subsection. As this new subsection also applies to a broad range of infringement cases, this referral would probably turn subsection (a) into a catch-all clause, which would make the differentiated structure of the subsequent subsections superfluous.

Probably easier to solve is the new terminological disparity between the terms "notoriously known" and "well-known" mark. The old subsections (a) and (b) of Article 35 IP Law (GT) used the term "notoriously known" trademarks, which is legally defined in Article 4 IP Law (GT). Subsection (b) was modified to comply with CAFTA-DR and became subsection (c)(3), which now refers to "well-known" marks. Given that this term is not legally defined and corresponds to the respective CAFTA-DR provision, the new term should mean the same as the old one.

Another surprise is the substitution of the term "distinctive sign" with "distinctive mark" in subsection (c), which literally would exclude all other distinctive signs, including slogans or registered geographical indications. This term "distinctive mark" does not exist elsewhere in the law. Also, the restriction of infringements to

---

[195] Articles 186 et seq. IP Law (GT).

[196] Articles 186 et seq. IP Law (GT).

the use of only *trademarks* would not correspond with the other provisions of Article 35 IP Law (GT) and the explicit extension of subsection (c) to geographical indications. Accordingly, it is unclear if the legislative intent behind this change was indeed to exclude distinctive signs other than trademarks.

While these issues do not affect the most relevant trademark infringement problems in practice, *i.e.*, trademark counterfeiting and the factual determination of confusion, Article 35 IP Law (GT) could be clarified and simplified in a future legislative reform. It would be both practical and corresponding to the structure of the international agreements to separate at least the remedies from the substantive provisions.

The Guatemalan legislature in the IP Reform Law 2013 not only implemented the requirements of the EU-CA-AA regarding geographical indications, but also made some "corrections" to the IP Law (GT). However, the amendments to the provisions addressing the rights of the trademark owner[197] that were made in this reform law did not substantially change the structure.

Table 4.3 illustrates the complexity of the legislation in Guatemala.

4.1.9 *Evaluation*

4.1.9.1 Relevance of the Trademark System After CAFTA-DR

Prior to the implementation of CAFTA-DR, there have been only few local brands and trademark protection was relevant mainly for foreign right holders. Brands require a marketing effort[198] and often companies in Central America lacked the necessary know-how and money. However, there are more and more successful local brands, especially in the food industry (*e.g.*, fast-food chains, dairy products and, of course, coffee). The fact that these companies start to experience local infringements of their brands might affect the general perception of trademark protection in the long term.

In Costa Rica, trademark applications from domestic applicants have increased by about 30% between 2010 and 2017, from about 5800 to 7900.[199] This suggests a growing importance of trademarks in the domestic economy and a growing awareness of domestic companies thereof. Improvements of the trademark registration infrastructure can, therefore, support domestic businesses as well as international companies. Such improvements include the creation of electronic and de-centralized trademark filing and search options, which facilitate access of local businesses and legal practitioners to the trademark system.

[197] In particular Article 35 IP Law (GT).

[198] Correa (2002), p. 21.

[199] See the data provided by the WIPO IP Statistics Data Center, https://www3.wipo.int/ipstats/ips-search/trademark (accessed 2 Nov 2024).

Table 4.3 Guatemalan legislation relating to trademark infringement

Article		Type of marks/signs and products covered	Type of use	Remedy
Article 35 and 35*bis* IP Law (GT)				
(a)		Identical/similar distinctive signs, including geographical indications and related products/services and likelihood of confusion (presumed for "double" identity)	Commercialization	*not specified*
(b)		Identical/similar distinctive signs, including geographical indications and identical/similar/different products/services and confusion, association, abuse of notoriety	Registration	Cancellation
(c)	(1)	Identical/similar distinctive *mark*, including geographical indications and identical/similar *products* or different products/services *if likelihood of confusion* (presumed confusion for "double" identity)	Identification	Injunction
	(2)	Identical/similar distinctive *mark*, including geographical indications and these products (*i.e.*, 35(c)(1)) and confusion, association, dilution	Packaging	
	(3)	Not registered well-known mark and identical/similar products if likelihood of confusion or different products/services indicating connection and harm to owner	*not specified*	
(d)		Products included in the cases of 35(c)	Importation	Border measures
(e) with *bis*		Products/services included in the cases of 35(c) or (g)	Commercialization Importation Marketing	Damages or criminal penalties
(f)		Violation of rights constituting a criminal act	*not specified*	Criminal penalties
(g)	*caput*	Cases of 35(c)	Use Importation	Provisional measures
	(1)-(4)	Cases of 35(c)	Modification Packaging Commercial Re-use	
(h)		Infringement of rights or dilution or abuse of prestige of the mark or of the right holder	*not specified*	*not specified*
(i)		Domain name obtained in bad faith and Imitation of notorious trademark and confusion, association, dilution	*not specified*	Cancellation
Article 275 Criminal Code (GT)				
(a)-(d)		Counterfeit registered distinctive sign for identical/similar products or services or modified registered distinctive sign or trademark whose disuse has been ordered because of confusion	Commercialization	Criminal penalties
(e)-(f)		Packaging displaying/containing registered distinctive sign or imitation	Commercialization Production Re-use	

However, the number of trademark applications from domestic applicants stagnated from a regional perspective; in Costa Rica, in the period of 2019 to 2022 around 4500.[200] This trend, which goes against the global trend of increasing numbers of trademark applications,[201] suggests that the trademark system in Central America could be further developed to be more useful to (potential) users.

4.1.9.2 Criticism of the Extension of Trademark Protection

The TRIPS-plus extension of trademark protection, which is required by CAFTA-DR, has been criticized from different angles: First, some critics fear the potential appropriation of cultural content[202] and the limitation of free speech, *e.g.*, if the use of trademarks by the media to critically report on the respective right holder and products could be prohibited by this right holder to suppress the criticism.[203] However, in Central America these issues have apparently not (yet) become practically relevant. Second, the extension of the subject matter of trademarks raises further policy questions, e.g., the protection of geographical names as trademarks potentially creates conflicts with the system of protecting geographical indications.[204] Finally, it is argued that in the practically most important cases of apparel counterfeiting, *e.g.*, in Guatemala, the quality of the trademark-carriers and products is so poor and the prices are so low that consumers cannot be confused about the origin.[205] Based on the author's experience, this observation in true in many cases. However, one must note that, first, neither the market for counterfeit apparel nor the legal protection in relation to such clear-cut cases of infringement changed and, second, in such cases there is by definition an identity of signs and products and likelihood of confusion is presumed, therefore, it does not matter from a legal perspective whether actual confusion exists.[206]

4.1.9.3 Practical Effect of the CAFTA-DR Trademark Rules

Regarding trademark infringement and enforcement in practice, the introduction of TRIPS-plus trademark protection had little impact. For foreign right

[200] Ibid.

[201] See Sect. 4.1.4.6.

[202] Assaf (2008), p. 82.

[203] Geiger (2007), pp. 317–327.

[204] See Sect. 4.4.6.

[205] Thomas (2009), p. 5.

[206] Generally, the likelihood of confusion is sufficient, in accordance with Article 15.2.3 (2) CAFTA-DR, this likelihood shall be presumed if an identical sign is used for identical goods or services.

holders, trademark counterfeiting is still one of the major issues, *e.g.*, in Guatemala.[207] However, pirated and counterfeit goods are still widely available. As *Thomas* notes, "brand piracy is a public and well-accepted practice in Guatemala".[208]

It is not surprising that the statutory changes were largely ineffective. Local consumers are often aware that, in particular, apparel bought cheaply on a street market are not original brand-name products but "pirated" products. In other words, they do not cause confusion and enforcement would not serve consumer protection purposes.[209] Therefore, there is little public pressure to increase enforcement activities, which is what CAFTA-DR focused on in relation to trademarks. In addition, in Guatemala, such goods are often produced locally in remote areas far away from the IP unit of the *Ministerio Público* in Guatemala City.[210]

This applies even to activities against counterfeit pharmaceutical products, which are a focus of criminal law enforcement. The sale of falsified pharmaceuticals constitutes a significant practical problem from a public health perspective.[211] However, related activities are generally still low.[212] The analysis suggests that previous institutional reforms, such as the creation of specialized IP units by the *Ministerio Público* and trainings by various international and foreign institutions, did not have a strong impact. This may be attributable to the limited resources of the enforcement agencies, who must deal with other areas of very serious crime and face budget constraints and the still skeptical view of the public regarding the enforcement of trademark rights.[213] The current economic and social context in Central America makes it unlikely that the capability and incentive to perform enforcement activities in Central America will significantly increase. Therefore, the creation of the "Intellectual Property Registry" to facilitate border measures against IP infringements in the Dominican Republic could well have a bigger practical impact on trademark counterfeiting than the respective statutory requirements in CAFTA-DR.[214]

---

[207] USTR Special 301 Report (2016), p. 59.

[208] Thomas (2011), p. 50.

[209] Thomas (2011), p. 3 (fn 4).

[210] The socioeconomic aspects of the apparel counterfeiting "industry" in Guatemala are analyzed in detail by Thomas (2011).

[211] USTR Special 301 Report (2016), p. 59.

[212] USTR Special 301 Report (2016), pp. 58–60.

[213] See Sect. 1.3.4.

[214] Regarding the creation of the "Intellectual Property Registry" and border measures under CAFTA-DR, see Sect. 7.6.

4.2 Well-Known Marks

4.2.1 Introduction

Trademarks with a high reputation enjoy special protection, but traditionally there was no uniform system for such protection. Instead, under the concept of *notoriety* (*well-known* marks), trademarks enjoyed protection even if they were not registered, while *famous* marks were not only protected against confusion, but also against association and dilution. However, the international trademark system has expanded the protection of notorious or well-known marks significantly, also with regard to association and dilution, and thus aligned their protection with the protection of famous marks.

On the *international level*, well-known marks are regulated in Article 16 TRIPS. Soon after TRIPS, the WIPO adopted the WIPO Joint Recommendation Concerning Well-Known Marks in 1999, which is not binding as such, but has been integrated into some FTAs. The US-Chile-FTA stresses the "importance of the WIPO Joint Recommendation",[215] while Article 6.2 EU-CARIFORUM-EPA explicitly incorporates Article 4 of the WIPO Joint Recommendation Concerning Well-Known Marks. CAFTA-DR, on the other hand, makes no reference to it and, instead, restates some (but not all) of its substantive provisions.

4.2.2 Subject Matter and Requirements

Article 16 (2) TRIPS extends the protection of well-known marks under Article 6*bis* Paris Convention to *service marks*, provided the other conditions for protection (notoriety, similarity and likelihood of confusion) are met.[216] This extension has been restated in Article 15.2(5) CAFTA-DR and has generally been included into the national legislation in Central America.[217]

Article 16(2) TRIPS provides that in order to determine whether a trademark is well-known, the reputation in the *relevant sector* must be assessed. According to CAFTA-DR, the relevant sector "need not extend beyond the sector of the public that normally deals with the relevant goods or services".[218] This is a literal restatement of Article 2(1)(b) of the WIPO Joint Recommendation Concerning Well-Known Marks.

Article 15.2.7 US-Peru-TPA, adopted after CAFTA-DR, states that "for greater certainty, the sector of the public that normally deals with the relevant goods or services is determined according to each Party's domestic law". This provision was

[215] Article 17.2.9 US-Chile-FTA.

[216] Schmidt-Pfitzner, Jan Hendrik / Schneider, Mathias in Busche et al. (2013), Article 16, Nr 26.

[217] See, e.g., Article 3 Trademark Law (CR).

[218] The footnote to Article 15.2(5) CAFTA-DR reads: "In determining whether a trademark is well-known, the reputation of the trademark need not extend beyond the sector of the public that normally deals with the relevant goods or services."

not included in CAFTA-DR, which raises the question whether in the case of CAFTA-DR, the term "relevant sector" has a specific meaning binding on the CAFTA-DR parties. However, the sector of the public that normally deals with the certain goods can only be established on case-by-case basis, as the sector will depend on the respective good and, therefore, a general definition would be difficult. Also, CAFTA-DR does not contain any more specific definition of the term. Therefore, one should assume that also under CAFTA-DR the term is determined according to each Party's domestic law (or rather by the national courts).

This finding is supported by the fact that Article 15.2.7 US-Peru-TPA states that the provision is included "for greater certainty", suggesting that even without this clarification, the parties assumed that each Party's domestic law would apply.

4.2.3 *Procedure*

Well-known marks do not legally have to be registered in order to be protected by law. While according to Article 16(3) TRIPS, the protection against association and dilution can be limited to registered well-known marks,[219] Article 15.2(5) CAFTA-DR provides for the protection of well-known marks according to Article 6*bis* of the Paris Convention against dilution applies whether the marks are "registered or not".

Also, on the national level in Central America, well-known marks enjoy protection without registration.[220] However, registration is often practically advisable. The enforcement of well-known marks may be difficult without registration in Central America.[221] Also, well-known marks are often important as grounds for opposition to a trademark application of a third party.[222] If well-known marks are registered, the trademark procedural provisions for trademarks in general apply.

4.2.4 *Rights and Limitations*

4.2.4.1 Overview

Table 4.4 shows the layers of protection provided for well-known marks under international law with regard to Central America (and Chile by comparison):

Table 4.4 shows in particular that the WIPO Joint Recommendation Concerning Well-Known Marks offers broader protection than CAFTA-DR, which only

[219] See Schmidt-Pfitzner, Jan Hendrik / Schneider, Mathias in Busche et al. (2013), Article 16, Nr 39.

[220] See, e.g., Article 44 TM Law (CR), Article 21(b) IP Law (GT).

[221] Lopez-Davis (2014), section X.

[222] See, e.g., Articles 8(e), 16 TM Law (CR); Article 35(c) IP Law (GT).

Table 4.4 Protection of well-known marks

Article/Agreement	6bis Paris Conv.	16 TRIPS	4 WIPO Joint Re-commend.	17.2 US-Chile-FTA	15.2 CAFTA-DR	144.B CARI-FORUM-EPA	240 EU-CA-AA
Protection of service marks	No	Yes					
Protection against related Goods and Services	No	Yes[a]	Yes				Yes[b]
Protection against Transliteration	No		Yes[c]		No	Endeavor	No
Protection against Association	No	Yes					Yes[d]
Protection against Dilution	No		Yes[e]		No	Endeavor	No

[a]The protection is subject to the requirement that the use of that trademark in relation to those goods or services would indicate a connection between those goods or services and the owner of the registered trademark and provided that the interests of the owner of the registered trademark are likely to be damaged by such use (Article 16(3) TRIPS)

[b]Article 240 EU-CA-AA restates Article 16(3) TRIPS, but in a way that the EU-CA-AA parties "may" extend the protection also to unregistered well-known trademarks. Article 240 EU-CA-AA reads: "Article 6bis of the Paris Convention shall apply, mutatis mutandis, to goods or services that are not identical or similar to those identified by a well-known trademark, provided that the use of that trademark in relation to those goods or services would indicate a connection between those goods or services and the owner of the trademark, and provided that the interests of the owner of the trademark are likely to be damaged by such use. For greater certainty, the Parties may also apply this protection to unregistered well-known trademarks". Article 16(3) TRIPS reads: Article 6bis of the Paris Convention (1967) shall apply, mutatis mutandis, to goods or services which are not similar to those in respect of which a trademark is registered, provided that use of that trademark in relation to those goods or services would indicate a connection between those goods or services and the owner of the registered trademark and provided that the interests of the owner of the registered trademark are likely to be damaged by such use."

[c]The protection is granted only against similar goods and services, but not other (related) goods and services

[d]The protection "may" be extended to unregistered well-known trademarks, see the definition in Article 240 EU-CA-AA, see fn 1851

[e]Protection against dilution can be restricted to trademarks known to general public, see Article 4(1)(c) WIPO Joint Recommendation Concerning Well-Known Marks

provides selected additional protection, but does not include protection against dilution. In this regard the EU-CARIFORUM-EPA offers more TRIPS-plus protection by incorporating the WIPO Joint Recommendation Concerning Well-Known Marks.

4.2.4.2 Protection Against Confusion and Association

Like normal trademarks, well-known marks are protected against confusion, even without registration. But well-known marks are also protected against association. Article 16(3) TRIPS requires protection against association only for *registered* well-known marks, but subsequent trade agreements extended this protection also to *unregistered* well-known marks. Apart from Article 15.2(5) CAFTA-DR these are, *e.g.*, Article 6.2 EU-CARIFORUM-EPA and Article 17.2 US-Chile-FTA, which refer to Article 4 WIPO Joint Recommendation Concerning Well-Known Marks. This protection against association for well-known marks might have been caused by the (erroneous) connection between the concept of well-known marks (protected against confusion) and famous marks (protected against dilution).[223]

As provided for by Article 15.2(5) CAFTA-DR, in Central America well-known marks are also protected against use that is not confusing, irrespective of registration, if such use indicates a connection between the goods or services and if the interests of the owner of the trademark are likely to be damaged by such use.[224]

The expression "use of that trademark" in Article 16(3) TRIPS (and similarly in Article 15.2(5) CAFTA-DR) has been interpreted as restricting the protection of the well-known mark to cases of *actual* use, excluding the consideration of the well-known mark during the registration procedure.[225] This restrictive interpretation would mean that the infringing mark would be registered, even if it is evident that the mark could subsequently not be used.

But this interpretation is not required by the wording of Article 16(3) TRIPS, because the section refers to Article 6*bis* Paris Convention, which covers both the registration and the use of the trademark. The term "use" in Article 16(3) TRIPS also does not restrict the provision to *actual* use, but to cases where the use *would* indicate a connection. This seems reasonable, because the examiner should consider hypothetically the use of the trademark during the registration process.

The Costa Rican law, therefore, appropriately excludes already the *registration* of another trademark if it is susceptible of causing confusion or association with another trademark, including well-known mark.[226]

---

[223] Schmidt-Pfitzner, Jan Hendrik / Schneider, Mathias in Busche et al. (2013), Article 16, Nr 44 with further references.

[224] See, e.g., Article 35(c)(3) IP Law (GT).

[225] Kur (1994), p. 994; concurring Schmidt-Pfitzner, Jan Hendrik / Schneider, Mathias in Busche et al. (2013), Article 16, Nr 37.

[226] Article 8(c) Trademark Law (CR).

4.2.4.3 Protection Against Dilution

The protection of well-known marks against the dilution of their distinctive character or reputation goes beyond the purpose of identifying origin. It applies when the special reputation of a well-known mark is abused and the use can, therefore, be considered *unfair competition*. Under European law, for example, protection against dilution is required only for registered trademarks[227] and the terminological reference to "unfair advantages" and "honest practices" underlines the connection with unfair competition law.[228] Infringement is then possible even in cases of non-trademark use, because the dilution can be seen as anti-competitive.[229]

Under international law, well-known marks to not have to be protected against dilution. The WIPO Joint Recommendation Concerning Well-Known Marks, referred to by Article 6.2 EU-CARIFORUM-EPA and Article 17.2 US-Chile-FTA, provides for protection against dilution only for those marks which are well-known to the general public (and, therefore, also are famous trademarks). Article 15.2 CAFTA-DR requires protection only against association, but not dilution.

In Central America, trademark dilution is often provided for as an act of unfair competition.[230] Examples of the dilution of famous trademarks are the following cases:

– in Guatemala, the conflict between the trademark "Arizona Tea" and the (locally) well-known mark "Arizona" used for teas,[231]
– in Costa Rica, the *Juan Valdez* case, in which the Costa Rican coffee company Café Britt used the well-known mark "Juan Valdez" for Colombian coffee on its own merchandise products ("Juan Valdez drinks Costa Rican coffee!"), which can be considered a dilution issue on the merits.[232]

4.3 Collective and Certification Marks

Collective and certification marks constitute special types of marks conveying specific information relating to the geographical origin and the quality of the product. In contrast to trademarks, collective and certifications marks do not identify the producer, but certain characteristic of the product. Collective marks usually belong to an association of producers; such association has the right to use the mark itself and manage the use by third parties. Certification marks indicate certain

[227] Article 10.2(c) Trademark Directive.
[228] Cornish et al. (2013) at 18-99.
[229] Ibid.
[230] In Guatemala, Article 173 (a) IP Law (GT); regarding Costa Rica, see Sect. 5.4.
[231] Barragan Rivas (2017), pp. 75–77.
[232] See Sect. 5.4.

characteristics of the products, and the right holder may not use the mark, but only certify its use to others.[233]

In Central America, collective and certification marks are probably as relevant in practice as geographical indications. However, they will be more briefly discussed in this thesis, because their protection is less affected by the implementation of CAFTA-DR and there is no conflict between CAFTA-DR and the EU-FTAs in relation to collective and certification marks as in relation to geographical indications.

4.3.1 Collective Marks

4.3.1.1 Introduction

On the *international* level, Article 2(1) TRIPS in connection with Article 7*bis* Paris Convention requires parties to provide protection for foreign collective marks, while leaving the protection of domestic collective trademarks at the member state's discretion. This requirement was included as well in Article 5.1 US-Nicaragua Agreement. Article 15.2(1) CAFTA-DR exceeds this obligation by providing that "trademarks shall include collective (and) certification (…) marks". The protection of collective marks has been included in the legislation of all *Central American* countries since the TRIPS reform laws, without differentiation between national and international right holders.[234] The procedural provisions on trademark law apply also to collective marks.[235]

4.3.1.2 Right Holder

The right holder of a collective mark must be a collective legal entity, usually an association, which establishes the characteristics of the respective product or service and authorizes the use of the mark by its members.[236] In Central America the right holder may use collective marks.[237]

[233] Geographical indications on the other hand also indicate the geographical origin, similar to collective marks, but offer broader protection against other distinctive signs. In Central America there are similarities, for example that the state is the right holder both of geographical indications and in some countries of certifications marks relating to products of domestic origin.

[234] Title IV Trademark Law (CR); Title II, Chapter III IP Law (DR); Title III Trademark Law (SV); Title II, Chapter II IP Law (GT); Title IV, Chapter III IP Law (HN); Chapter VIII Trademark Law (NI); see also 15 U.S.C. § 1054.

[235] Article 43 Trademark Law (SV); Article 48 IP Law (GT).

[236] E.g., Article 4 IP Law (GT); see also 15 U.S.C. § 1127(1).

[237] E.g., Article 54 IP Law (GT); Article 104(1) IP Law (DR); Article 49(1) Trademark Law (SV); see also 15 U.S.C. § 1127(2).

4.3.1.3 Procedure

For the registration, the applicant for a collective mark must submit both the mark and the regulation.[238] The latter must set out the characteristics that products or service with the respective mark must have, the conditions and control of its use and the potential users[239] While the registration with the IP Register is apparently not particularly difficult,[240] it is complicated to establish the regulation governing the use of the mark because it requires the coordination of a large number of often small producers.[241]

4.3.1.4 Practical Relevance

There were only very few collective marks registered in Central America, especially for national right holders, when CAFTA-DR was implemented. However, the number of applications for collective marks has increased.

In Costa Rica, there were a few collective marks in force as of 2021 (the last year for which data could be obtained), including marks for medical supply, beans and most notably "pura vida" for sustainable seefood.[242] The "pura vida" mark was created in a project supported by UNCTAD.[243]

Similarly, in El Salvador there were only few registrations when CAFTA-DR was implemented. Until 2011, there were several registrations for collective marks in El Salvador regarding coffee, namely "Cerro Amatepec" and "Cacahuatique".[244] In addition, the *Asociación Nacional de Fabricantes de Alcoholes y Licores* of Guatemala applied for the collective mark "Rones de Guatemala" in El Salvador in 2006.[245] As already discussed, it is difficult to perform online searches of collective marks, because, there seems to be no electronic database for trademarks in El Salvador.[246] However, based on a review of the Official Bulletin, there was at least one application in 2013.[247]

---

[238] Article 44(1) Trademark Law (SV); Article 49(1) IP Law (GT).

[239] E.g., Article 49(2) IP Law (GT), Article 44(2) Trademark Law (SV).

[240] Interview with *Ricardo Bendaña.*

[241] Interviews with *Ricardo Bendaña* and *Carlos Castillo.*

[242] See https://www.rnpdigital.com/bibl_virtual/Revista%20digital%20abril%202018.pdf and https://unctad.org/es/meeting/lanzamiento-de-pura-vida-la-marca-colectiva-de-mariscos-y-acuicultura-sostenibles-de-costa (both accessed 2 Nov 2024).

[243] See https://unctad.org/es/meeting/lanzamiento-de-pura-vida-la-marca-colectiva-de-mariscos-y-acuicultura-sostenibles-de-costa (accessed 2 Nov 2024).

[244] Gómez Linares et al. (2011), p. 183.

[245] Official Bulletin (El Salvador), 3 May 2006, p. 83.

[246] See Sect. 2.5.3.3.

[247] Official Bulletin (El Salvador), 9 September 2013, p. 188.

In Guatemala, a few collective marks had been registered when CAFTA-DR was implemented. There are different reports regarding the number of collective marks and the products for which they have been registered. In 2007, around ten collective marks were reported.[248] In 2011, according to one study, based on reports by local practitioners, already collective marks were in force, mainly for coffees and artisan products.[249] However, this seems a very high number considering the number of collective marks four years previously.

In Nicaragua, the only existing national collective mark application before CAFTA-DR was for a popular tourist destination, "San Juan del Sur - Bahías de Atardecer y Aventura".[250]

Collective marks have not yet been much used, despite the fact that there is a considerable number of products, especially of unprocessed and processed agricultural products, which could be marketed more effectively by using collective marks. One of the main reasons observed by practitioners is a lack of awareness of local business and business associations with the available legal protection.[251]

However, there are increased efforts to promote collective marks. Pilot projects initiated by important business associations, such as the national association of coffee-producers (*Asociacíon National del Café*, ANACAFE) in Guatemala, will probably increase the visibility of this type of right, as will trainings organized by national and international institutions for local businesses. Eight collective marks had been identified by ANACAFE in 2006:[252]

- Acatenango Valley
- Antigua Coffee
- Traditional Atitlán
- Rainforest Cobán
- Fraijanes Plateau
- Highland Huehue
- New Oriente
- Volcanic San Marcos

However, Anacafé later abandoned the process to obtain certification marks and instead opted to apply for geographical indications (denominations of origin).[253] The first denomination of origin registered in Guatemala was "Acatenango Valley" in 2012, six years after the initiation of the process.[254]

[248] Contreras Aguilera (2007), p. 10.

[249] See Valdés Samayoa (2012), p. 86.

[250] Official Bulletin (Nicaragua), 16 August 2004, p. 4243.

[251] Valdés Samayoa (2012), p. 86, based on interviews with local practitioners.

[252] Contreras Aguilera (2007), pp. 27–28.

[253] The use of the terms "geographical indications" and "denominations of origin" in Central America is discussed in Sect. 4.4.1.

[254] Available at http://www.centralamericadata.com/en/article/home/Guatemala_Tax_Calendar_for_October_2012 (accessed 2 Nov 2024).

Collective marks could also be a way to protect traditional knowledge at least indirectly. The collective ownership is particularly suitable for indigenous communities, because unlike geographical indications these rights are not necessarily owned by the state, but can belong directly to these communities.[255] The regulations would include the particular traditional techniques.[256] While the products and techniques as such are not protected, the collective mark permits the communication of the origin, which would appeal to fair-trade conscious consumers.

The example of an agricultural cooperative in El Salvador may serve as an example: While this mark is apparently used only domestically, it could be the basis the financial and organizational structure necessary for the commercialization in third countries.[257]

As *Annette Kur* rightly observed, the investment required for these structures will often be a practical obstacle for businesses based on distinctive signs.[258] The existence of these obstacles can be inferred from the fact that commodities from Central America are mostly commercialized internationally by foreign companies and merchants.

4.3.2 Certification Marks

4.3.2.1 Introduction

The purpose of certification marks is to certify[259] and control[260] the quality of the respective product. Unlike collective marks and geographical indications, certification marks are not used for quality related to geographical origin.[261] The policy reason behind this restriction is to ensure impartial control. Unlike trademarks and collective marks, whose quality is controlled by the users themselves for reasons of reputation and ultimately economic self-interest, certification marks are created for

---

[255] Regarding the ownership of geographical indications and the practical problems see Sect. 4.4.5.

[256] See Bucher (2008), p. 87.

[257] The collective mark "El Castano" has been registered for tomato sauce of an agricultural cooperative in the district of the same name, on this cooperative see Flores Zelada et al. (2005), p. 56.

[258] Kur (2008), pp. 127–129.

[259] In Central American legislation, see, e.g., Article 56 IP Law (GT); Article 51 Trademark Law (NI); Article 55 Trademark Law (CR).

[260] Article 57 IP Law (GT); Article 52 Trademark Law (NI); Article 56 Trademark Law (CR).

[261] Whereas in the USA certification marks may refer to the "regional origin", 15 U.S.C. § 1127, the existence of special protection in Central America for geographical indications, which is also based on the certification by a public entity, suggests that for those cases the more general system of certification marks is excluded.

reasons of consumer protection. Certification is necessary if the costs for one-time bad product choice are too high, *e.g.*, if health or safety is concerned.[262]

There was no certification mark protection included in earlier international agreements such as the Paris Convention, TRIPS or the US-Nicaragua IP Agreement.[263] Article 15.2(1) CAFTA-DR for the first time mandates the protection of certification marks, without specifying substantive or procedural rules.

Although they were not required to do so under international law, most Central American countries introduced protection for certification marks in the TRIPS reform laws.[264] Only El Salvador and Honduras did not provide for protection until the CAFTA-DR reform laws were adopted.[265]

4.3.2.2 Right Holder

To ensure impartial quality certification, there are special requirements with regard to right holders. In Central America there exist mainly two systems. The "public only" system in Costa Rica and Nicaragua, where the right holder must be a governmental agency,[266] and the "mixed public or private" system in El Salvador, Guatemala and Honduras (*i.e.,* the "Northern Triangle"), where any private or public company or institution, domestic or foreign individuals or regional, national or international governmental agencies can be the owner.[267]

In both systems, the certification mark cannot be used by the right holder[268] and the mark can only be transferred together with the right holder, the regulating entity.[269] Certification marks can be used for products or services whose characteristics or quality has been controlled and certified by the right holder.[270] The right holder must authorize the use of the certification mark for all who comply with the conditions set out in the certification regulation.[271]

---

[262] Regarding the policy functions of certification marks, which provide solely information about quality, and the differences to trademarks and collective marks, which identify and distinguish the origin of products and services, see Fezer (2009), § 97 no 9.

[263] Article 7bis Paris Convention only regulates collective marks.

[264] Title V Trademark Law (CR); Title II Chapter IV IP Law (DR); Title II Chapter III IP Law (GT); Chapter IX Trademark Law (NI); see also 15 U.S.C. § 1054.

[265] In Honduras, certification marks were provided for in Article 3 to 9 CAFTA-DR Reform Law (HN); in El Salvador, Article 13 CAFTA-DR Trademark Reform Law (SV) as Title III*bis* and Articles 51-A to 51-G Trademark Law (SV).

[266] Article 53 Trademark Law (NI); Article 57 (1) Trademark Law (CR).

[267] Article 51-B Trademark Law (SV); Article 56 IP Law (GT); Article 4 CAFTA-DR Reform Law (HN).

[268] Article 51-E Trademark Law (SV); Article 59 IP Law (GT); Article 54 (2) Trademark Law (NI); Article 58 (2) Trademark Law (CR); see also 15 U.S.C. § 1127 (1).

[269] Article 8(2) CAFTA-DR Reform Law (HN).

[270] E.g., Article 4 IP Law (GT).

[271] E.g., Article 7 CAFTA-DR Reform Law (HN).

4.3.2.3 Procedure

For the *registration*, the applicant for a certification mark must submit both the certification mark and the regulation, which sets out the conditions for and control of its use and specifies the guaranteed characteristics.[272] In addition to the examination of the certification mark by the IP register,[273] the regulations for the users have to be approved by the administrative authorities responsible for the respective product or service, at least in countries where the right holder does not have to be a governmental institution.[274] In addition to the special provisions regarding certifications marks, the general procedural provisions regarding trademarks apply.[275]

4.3.2.4 Term of Protection

Certification marks owned by national public entities are protected indefinitely without renewal, those owned by other entities are protected for 10 years with the possibility for renewal every 10 years.[276] If the certification of the relevant products is discontinued, the mark cannot be used again for 10 years.[277]

4.3.2.5 Practical Relevance

In Central America, few certification marks have been registered. In Guatemala, for example, one certification mark was registered for the Guatemalan Tourism Institute (Inguat) to certify the hygiene of hotels.[278]

4.4 Geographical Indications

While CAFTA-DR seeks to strengthen trademark protection, the EU-CARIFORUM-EPA and the EU-CA-AA require stronger protection for geographical indications. The Central American countries, therefore, face the challenge of

---

[272] E.g., Article 51-C Trademark Law (SV), Article 5 CAFTA-DR Reform Law (HN).

[273] E.g., Article 5 (1) CAFTA-DR Reform Law (HN).

[274] See, e.g., Article 51-C Trademark Law (SV); Article 57 IP Law (GT), Article 5 (2) 2 CAFTA-DR Reform Law (HN).

[275] See, e.g., Article 51-A Trademark Law (SV).

[276] See, e.g., Article 51-D Trademark Law (SV), Article 58 IP Law (GT), Article 6 CAFTA-DR Reform Law (HN).

[277] See, e.g., Article 51-G Trademark Law (SV), Article 61 IP Law (GT), Article 9 CAFTA-DR Reform Law (HN).

[278] Ramírez Argueta (2007), p. 106.

implementing two sets of rules which are sometimes difficult to reconcile with each other. This section analyzes the requirements regarding geographical indications in the different bilateral FTAs and the approach of the Central American countries regarding the balancing of the diverging systems in their national legislation.

4.4.1 Introduction

4.4.1.1 Conceptualizing the Protection of Geographical Names or References

Signs consisting of geographical names or references are protected under a wide range of concepts, also cumulatively.[279] These concepts include protection under:

- special *sui generis* laws for the protection of geographical indications against other signs capable of confusing the consumer[280] and in some cases against other signs even without the possibility of confusion,[281]
- trademark laws in the form of collective marks or certification marks, if the sign indicates a certain origin and if the quality of the product is attributable to it,[282]
- as (part of) a trademark, even if the name does not indicate the real origin, as long as the use does not confuse the public,
- laws against unfair competition and consumer protection laws, and
- specific laws or decrees that regulate individual geographical indications.[283]

This section covers the protection of geographical indications as an IP right under the *sui generis* legislation.

4.4.1.2 Terminology

Geographical indications are, according to Article 24(1) TRIPS, Article 15.3 (1) CAFTA-DR and Article 242(2) EU-CA-AA, "indications that identify a good as originating in the territory of a Party, or a region or locality in that territory, where a given quality, reputation, or other characteristic of the good is essentially attributable to its geographical origin". The TRIPS definition applies in relation to the EU-CARIFORUM-EPA, because this agreement does not contain any definition of

[279] See at https://www.wipo.int/geo_indications/en/faq_geographicalindications.html#what (accessed 2 Nov 2024).

[280] Article 22 TRIPS.

[281] Article 23 TRIPS.

[282] See Sect. 4.3.

[283] E.g., "balsam" in El Salvador and "bananas" in Costa Rica (see Sect. 4.4.2.2) and the protection of "distinctive products" in accordance with Article 3.12(1) CAFTA-DR, see Sect. 4.7.

geographical indications. This definition combines elements of *geography* and *quality*.

Appellations of origin or *denominations of origin* are a special type of geographical indication.[284] They are specified in the Lisbon Agreement (1958) and largely correspond to geographical indications as in Article 24(1) TRIPS.[285] The basic difference to geographical indications is that the link with the place of origin must be stronger in the case of an appellation or denomination of origin. The quality or characteristics of a product must result *exclusively* or *essentially* from its geographical origin.[286]

Indications of source are regulated in the Madrid Agreement (Indications of Source). They only refer to the geographical origin, but are *quality-neutral.*[287] Indications of source can (but do not have to be under TRIPS) be protected by unfair competition or trademark law.[288]

The term *geographical indication* is also used in NAFTA. It has been suggested that the term refers to *indications of source* as regulated in the Madrid Agreement (Indications of Source), *i.e.*, quality-neutral indications.[289] As CAFTA-DR builds upon NAFTA, this could suggest a different meaning of the term in this agreement as well. However, this view seems incorrect, because Article 1721 NAFTA defines the term in the same way as TRIPS, explicitly referring to "*quality* [...] attributable to its geographical origin". As explained above, Article 15.3(1) CAFTA-DR likewise refers to quality.

Denominations of origin are also a special type of geographical indication also in Central America. This structure is particularly visible in the Dominican Republic, where denominations of origin are expressly a type of geographical indication.[290]

However, traditionally, national Central American laws distinguish between geographical indications and denominations of origin in a different way than international law. Geographical indications are *not registered* and enjoy only relative protection. Denominations of origin are *registered*[291] and receive absolute protection. This system still applies in the Dominican Republic and Nicaragua.[292]

---

[284] Paz Cafferata and Pomareda (2009), p. 4.

[285] Correa (2002), p. 2.

[286] WIPO, Frequently Asked Questions: Geographical Indications, available at http://www.wipo.int/geo_indications/en/faq_geographicalindications.html (accessed 2 Nov 2024); see also the definition in Article 5.1 of the Regulation (EU) No 1151/2012 of 21 November 2012 on quality schemes for agricultural products and foodstuffs.

[287] Correa (2002), pp. 3 and 6.

[288] Correa (2002), p. 2.

[289] Correa (2002), p. 3, citing Gevers, The Conflict between Trademarks and Geographical Indications, 1995, pp. 147–148.

[290] Article 70(i) IP Law (DR).

[291] See Sect. 4.4.2.2.

[292] Articles 124 to 126 IP Law (DR) regarding denominations of origin and Articles 127 to 134 IP Law (DR) regarding geographical indications; Articles 71 to 78 Trademark Law (NI) regarding geographical indications and Articles 68 to 70 Trademark Law (NI) regarding denominations of origin.

The reform laws passed in Costa Rica in 2008 to adapt the trademark legislation to CAFTA-DR and the reform laws passed in El Salvador, Guatemala and Honduras in 2013 to implement the EU-CA-AA abolished this distinction, by replacing the formerly separate section on *denominations of origin* with a new section providing for more detailed procedural and substantive rules on both geographical indications and denominations of origin. While the laws still maintain two different definitions for geographical indications and denominations of origin,[293] both types of rights must be registered and the procedural and substantive rules apply to both rights in the same way.[294]

In this study, the term *geographical indication* is used as the general term, in accordance with TRIPS and CAFTA-DR terminology. Unless stated otherwise, it also refers to and includes the *denominations of origin* of the Central American legislation. In Costa Rica, El Salvador, Guatemala and Honduras, the two terms can be used synonymously, because under the reform laws both rights are procedurally and substantively identical. For simplification, the term *geographical indication* is also used in relation to the registered *denominations of origin* in the Dominican Republic and Nicaragua, to avoid terminological differentiations which do not affect the focus of the legal analysis.

4.4.2 Legal Framework

4.4.2.1 International Legal Framework

With regard to geographical indications, Article 22 to 24 TRIPS represent a compromise between the positions of the USA and the EU.[295] It allows the members to choose between a *sui generis* and a *trademark* regime. It also includes a compromise on the scope of protection by requiring *absolute* protection, *i.e.*, even against use not misleading the consumer, for wines and spirits.[296] For other subject matter, only *relative* protection against confusion is mandatory.[297] Article 24 TRIPS mandates further negotiations in the field of geographical indications. The scope and goals of these negotiations are disputed and, so far, they have not resulted in any additional binding multilateral commitments.[298] In addition, some Central American countries

---

[293] See Table 4.5.

[294] See Articles 67 to 74 Trademark Law 2013 (SV); Articles 78 to 89 IP Law (GT), as amended by the IP Reform Law 2013 (GT); Articles 126 to 133 IP Law (HN), as amended by the EU-CA-AA Reform Law (HN).

[295] McGuire, Mary-*Rose* / Strauch, Severin, in Busche et al. (2013), Introduction to Articles 22 - 24 Nr 131.

[296] Article 23 TRIPS.

[297] Article 22 TRIPS.

[298] The members have only concluded bilateral agreements on this issue, see McGuire, Mary-*Rose* / Strauch, Severin, in Busche et al. (2013), Article 24 Nr 3.

signed specific international agreements relating to geographical indications. The Dominican Republic signed the Madrid Agreement (Indications of Source) and the Dominican Republic, Costa Rica and Nicaragua signed the Lisbon Agreement.[299]

Both the USA and the EU have subsequently tried to require third countries to (at least partially) adopt their system by including corresponding obligations in their bilateral FTAs. The *USA* opposes the extension of absolute protection for geographical indications and proposes to limit the system to wine and spirits as already established by TRIPS.[300] Under CAFTA-DR, the parties are obliged to protect geographical indications according to Article 15.3 CAFTA-DR, but do not have to extend the subject matter in relation to TRIPS. Article 15.2(6)(c) CAFTA-DR requires the possibility for third parties to initiate opposition procedures against geographical indications, in order to restrict the registration of geographical indications which possibly conflict with trademarks.

The *European* model was included in the EU-CARIFORUM-EPA and the EU-CA-AA. Articles 145.B.3(a) EU-CARIFORUM-EPA and Article 246.1 (a) EU-CA-AA restate the *relative* protection of Article 22 TRIPS and Articles 145.B.3(b) EU-CARIFORUM-EPA and Article 246.1(b) of the EU-CA-AA extend the *absolute* protection of Article 23 TRIPS to all products, not just wines and spirits. To restrict the registration of trademarks possibly conflicting with geographical indications, Articles 144.A EU-CARIFORUM-EPA and Article 239 EU-CA-AA require the establishment of opposition procedures against trademarks, reflecting the contrasting CAFTA-DR provision. Importantly, however, neither the EU-CARIFORUM-EPA nor the EU-CA-AA require the ratification of the Lisbon Agreement.

These systematic differences have been a problem for the negotiation and implementation of the FTAs in Central America.[301] The Dominican Republic accepted the obligations regarding geographical indications under the EU-CARIFORUM-EPA and, therefore, the obligation to implement conflicting provisions into their law relatively quickly. Possibly as a consequence of this development, the Dominican Republic acceded to the Stockholm version of 1967 of the Lisbon Agreement effective as of 17 January 2020.

The other Central American countries requested to exclude any rules on geographical indications from the negotiations regarding the EU-CA-AA and to refer this topic to multilateral negotiations.[302] On the other hand, the European negotiators

---

[299] See Sect. 2.1.1; Costa Rica became a signatory of the Lisbon Agreement in 1997, Nicaragua in 2006 and the Dominican Republic in 2020, each to the Stockholm version of 1967, see list of parties available at https://www.wipo.int/export/sites/www/treaties/en/docs/pdf/lisbon.pdf (accessed 2 Nov 2024).

[300] USTR, Doha Development Agenda Policy Brief –Protecting Geographical Indications for Wine and Spirits, 2005, p. 1, available at https://ustr.gov/archive/assets/Document_Library/Fact_Sheets/2005/asset_upload_file850_8542.pdf (accessed 2 Nov 2024).

[301] Interview with *Diana Hasbún*.

[302] SICE, Avances en la negociación con UE, 16 April 2008, available at http://www.sice.oas.org/TPD/CACM_EU/Negotiations/round3_s.pdf (accessed 2 Nov 2024).

proposed to include, in addition to the statutory requirements, a list of geographical indications which should be protected in Central America irrespective of existing rights, a list which has been included also in other FTAs.[303] However, this list in Central America conflicted with existing rights, *e.g.*, in particular regarding certain cheeses.[304] Another point of criticism from the Central American side was that the system of geographical indications is less developed in Central America and, therefore, the stronger protection would be much more in the European interest than in the Central American interest.[305] However, the final text of the EU-CA-AA reflects largely the negotiation objectives of the EU. It not only included a detailed section on geographical indications, but also an extensive list of geographical indications which had to be registered in Central America before the EU-CA-AA went into effect.

4.4.2.2 Central America

The *Central American* countries traditionally supported strong protection of geographical indications on the legislative level, and already had introduced a *sui generis* legislation with absolute protection prior to CAFTA-DR within the respective law on distinctive signs. Several Central American countries have also promoted broader protection on the international level, especially with regard to the expansion of absolute protection according to Article 23 TRIPS to products other than wines and spirits. This concerns mainly important export commodities of the region, like coffee and bananas, which are protected in their countries of origin by special laws or administrative decrees that regulate individual geographical indications. For example, in Costa Rica, the Banana Law (CR) specifically addresses the labelling of bananas, but does not, however, create geographical indication protection.[306] It only contains the obligation to label any bananas exported from Costa Rica to be labeled "Banana of Costa Rica", but does not provide for special quality requirements or protection against use by third parties.[307] Similarly, in El Salvador, "balsam" is protected by special legislation.[308]

---

[303] These are the EU-South Korea FTA, the EU-Colombia/Peru FTA and the EU-Georgia-AA, see Engelhardt (2015), p. 793.

[304] During the implementation of the EU-CA-AA, the Central American countries were required to register a list of European geographical indications. When Costa Rica delayed the registration of certain cheeses, namely Emmental, Provolone Valpadana, Manchego, Parmigiano Reggiano, Gorgonzola and Fontina, Italy temporarily blocked the provisional application of the trade chapter of the EU-CA-AA, see Sect. 4.4.5.

[305] Interview with *Gabriela Contreras Aguilera*.

[306] Therefore, the information on the WIPO website is somewhat misleading. The title of the statute in the WIPO list on Costa Rican IP laws is "Geographical Protection for Bananas".

[307] See Sect. 4.4.2.2.

[308] See Sect. 4.4.2.2.

The post-TRIPS legislation in Central America was based on the distinction between general *geographical indications* that are not registered and enjoy only relative protection and *denominations of origin* that are registered and receive absolute protection. This system is still in place in the Dominican Republic. In Costa Rica, the latest revisions of the Trademark Law (CR) in 2008 occurred before the conclusion of the EU-CA-AA, but nevertheless provided for significant changes to the system of protection of geographical indications.

The national laws in El Salvador, Guatemala, Honduras and Nicaragua were substantially revised by the legislation implementing the EU-FTAs in 2013.[309] Nicaragua passed the EU-CA-AA Trademark Reform Regulation (NI) (*Reformas y Adiciones al Decreto N° 83-2001, Reguladora de la Ley de Marcas y Otros Signos Distintivos*) in 2012 to implement the IP provisions of the EU-CARIFORUM-EPA.[310]

The variety of multilateral agreements and bilateral FTAs applicable in Central America and the differences in the implementation of these agreements result in a complex matrix of definitions of geographical indications and denominations of origin in the various national laws, as shown in Table 4.5.

4.4.3 Subject Matter

Article 22 TRIPS does not define which signs can constitute a geographical indication. Under CAFTA-DR, any sign or combination of signs is eligible to be a geographical indication.[311] From the definition follows that any sign identifying the geographical origin of a product can constitute a geographical indication, both the use of the geographical name (*direct* indications) or other names or symbols (*indirect* indications).[312] With regard to the eligible goods, not only food and beverages, but also merchandise and other products can be protected.[313] The restriction to "wines and spirits" only relates to the scope of protection (absolute or relative protection). *Sui generis* protection as geographical indication is not required under international agreements.[314] However, services can be protected as trademarks or

[309] See the references to the national legislation above in Sect. 2.5.

[310] Reguladora No. 25-2012, enacted and entered into force on 20 June 2012, available at http://www.wipo.int/wipolex/es/details.jsp?id=12906 (accessed 2 Nov 2024); unlike in the other Central American countries, in Nicaragua the registration procedure regarding trademarks and geographical indications is not included in the Trademark Law, but in a separate regulation.

[311] Article 15.2, 15.3(1) CAFTA-DR.

[312] E.g., "Mozart" for Salzburg/Austria or the Eiffel-Tower for Paris/France, Correa (2002), p. 2; Article 23(1) TRIPS is an extension compared to Article 2 (1) of the Lisbon Agreement, which defined appellations of origin as (only) the geographical name, thereby excluding indirect indications, Correa (2002), pp. 8 and 10.

[313] Correa (2002), p. 10.

[314] Articles 22, 23 TRIPS; Article 15.3 CAFTA-DR; Article 242.2 EU-CA-AA.

Table 4.5 Definition of geographical indications (and denominations of origin)

Agreement/Law	Definition of geographical indications (or denominations of origin)		
TRIPS and TRIPS-based Definitions			
Article 22 TRIPS	Indications	Which identify a good as originating in the territory of a country, or a region or locality in that territory	Where a given quality, reputation or other characteristic of the good is essentially attributable to its geographical origin
Article 15.3 CAFTA-DR			
Article 145 EU-CARIFORUM-EPA; Article 242.2 EU-CA-AA[a]			
Article 2 Trademark Law (CR)			
Article 14 CAFTA-DR Reform Law (HN)[b]			
Lisbon Agreement and Lisbon Agreement-based Definitions			
Article 2 (ii) Lisbon Agreement (Geneva Act 2015)	Any indication/ indication […] consisting of or containing the name of a geographical area, or another indication known as referring to such area	Which identifies a good as originating in that geographical area	Where the quality or characteristics of the good are due exclusively or essentially to the geographical environment, including natural and human factors
Article 2 Trademark Law (SV) (*denomination of origin*)	Denomination of a country, region or determined area	Used to designate a product originating in them	
(Semi-)Autonomous Definitions			
Article 1 Trademark Law (NI) (*denomination of origin*)	Any geographical name, designation, image or sign	Which identifies or invokes a good originating in a given country, group of countries, region, locality or determined area	Where a given quality, reputation or other characteristic of the good is essentially attributable to its geographical origin
Article 2 Trademark Law (SV)			
Article 70(h) IP Law (DR)	Any name, denomination, expression, image or sign	Which indicates directly or indirectly that a product or service originates in a country, group of countries, region, locality or determined area	n/a
Article 79 IP Law (HN)			

(continued)

Table 4.5 (continued)

Agreement/Law	Definition of geographical indications (or denominations of origin)		
Article 4 IP Law (GT)	Any name, expression, image or sign or combination of these	Which identifies a good as originating in the territory of a country, or region or locality in that territory	Where a given quality, reputation or other characteristic of the good is essentially attributable to its geographical origin and the connection [...] is present in at least one stage of production or transformation

[a]The EU-CARIFORUM-EPA and EU-CA-AA does not contain a definition of geographical indications, therefore, the TRIPS definition applies

[b]According to Article 127 IP Law (HN), as amended by the EU-CA-AA Reform Law (HN), the definitions of Article 79 IP Law (HN) and Article 14 CAFTA-DR Reform Law (HN) apply cumulatively

collective marks. Some Central American laws refer in their definition of geographical indication simply to "indications" or denominations,[315] others enumerate categories of subject matter, such as names, denominations, expressions, images or signs.[316] According to Article 70(h) IP Law (DR) and Article 79 IP Law (HN), geographical indications can designate products *or services* and, therefore, seem to exceed the international requirements; however, under both laws geographical indications can only be registered by groups of *producers*.[317] Therefore, absolute protection is practically only available for geographical indications relating to products.

4.4.4 *Requirements and Statutory Bars*

4.4.4.1 Requirements

Geographical Scope

From the definition of geographical indications follows that they must have a *geographical* and *quality* component. As the definitions in Articles 22(1) TRIPS and 15(3)(1) CAFTA-DR make clear, there are no conditions with regard to the *geographical scope* of the indication. The entire territory of a country, a region or a "locality", *e.g.*, just one town or district, can be identified. The laws in Central America, despite the differences in the definitions of geographical indications, all

[315] Article 2 Trademark Law (CR).

[316] Article 70(h) IP Law (DR), Article 79 IP Law (HN).

[317] Article 127 IP Law (DR); Article 126 IP Law (HN), as amended by the EU-CA-AA Reform Law (HN).

provide for the same broad geographical scope.[318] Therefore, in Guatemala eight different coffee districts could be identified and protected separately. It is always necessary that the specified quality is related to the respective territory, which is more difficult the larger the respective geographic scope is. In cases such as "Café de Colombia", where the entire country is the respective territory, the common characteristic is naturally smaller than in Guatemala, where for example volcanic and other highland regions are protected separately.[319]

Characteristics

The geographical indication must have *quality, reputation, or other characteristics*, which are essentially attributable to the geographical origin.[320] With regard to coffee, for example, this could be the respective soil which affects the taste (volcanic/highland).[321] TRIPS and CAFTA-DR do not require that these characteristics are specified in a separate regulation or specification submitted together with the application for the geographical indication.

However, Article 244.2(d) and (e) EU-CA-AA obliges the parties to require applicants to establish specifications for the production of the respective goods and a system of controls to monitor that the product conforms with the respective specifications. The EU-CARIFORUM-EPA does not contain corresponding requirements.

Costa Rica and the Dominican Republic do not require the establishment of production specifications, including quality control, however, the application must state the respective quality characteristics.[322]

In El Salvador and Honduras, the application must contain in particular a regulation of use (*reglamento de uso*), specifying in particular the characteristics of the geographical indication and the procedure to control quality *before and after registration* (in Honduras) or the *proper use* (in El Salvador).[323] The IP Register (HN) performs a substantive review of the regulation of use and may solicit expert opinions on it from agencies responsible for the agricultural or industry sector to which the geographical indication pertains.[324] The Honduran law contains a peculiarity in this regard. As already noted, the CAFTA-DR Reform Law (HN) adopted

---

318 See above Table 4.5.

319 See Sect. 4.3 on the different collective marks for coffee regions in Guatemala; on the other hand, a broader geographical scope is more inclusive and reduces the risk that producers are unduly excluded, see Evans (2010), pp. 652–654.

320 Article 22(1) TRIPS and Article 15.3(1) CAFTA-DR.

321 Contreras Aguilera (2007), p. 27.

322 Article 76(e) Trademark Law (CR); Article 129.1(e) IP Law (DR).

323 Article 73-A Trademark Law (SV), as amended by the EU-CA-AA Trademark Reform Law (SV), Article 128(2) IP Law (HN), as amended by the EU-CA-AA Reform Law (HN) in 2013.

324 Article 128 IP Law (HN), as amended by the EU-CA-AA Reform Law (HN).

in 2006 did not amend the existing IP Law (HN) of 1999, but established a separate, additional set of rules.[325] In particular, Article 79 IP Law (HN) contains a definition of geographical indications and Article 14 CAFTA-DR Reform Law (HN) introduced a second definition, without clarifying the relationship between the two. According to Article 127 IP Law (HN), as amended by the EU-CA-AA Reform Law (HN), the definitions of Article 79 IP Law (HN) and Article 14 CAFTA-DR Reform Law (HN) apply cumulatively. The main difference between the two definitions is that the "old" definition under Article 79 IP Law (HN) did not include a quality component, while Article 14 CAFTA-DR Reform Law (HN), which is modelled after Article 22 TRIPS, introduced this component.

In Guatemala, the regulation of use (*normativa de uso*) can be submitted within a period of six months (extendable to nine months) after the registration of the geographical indication.[326]

Protection of Foreign Geographical Indications in the Country of Origin

According to Article 24(9) TRIPS, geographical indications do not have to be protected if they (i) are not or cease to be protected in their country of origin or (ii) have fallen into disuse in that country.

Under the EU-CARIFORUM-EPA, geographical indications do not have to be protected if they are not protected in their country of origin.[327] This provision omits the limitation of protection in case of *disuse* in the country of origin. The agreement does not explicitly state whether geographical indications which have fallen into disuse have to be protected, but the fact that the wording of Article 145.1 EU-CARIFORUM-EPA otherwise restates Article 24(9) TRIPS suggests that this was an intentional omission; this interpretation is further supported by the fact that, e.g., the FTA between the EU and South Korea explicitly states that the parties are not required "to protect a geographical indication which is not or ceases to be protected in its country of origin *or which has fallen into disuse in that country*" (emphasis added).[328] Under this interpretation, Article 145(1) EU-CARIFORUM-EPA provides for stronger protection than Article 24(9) TRIPS, which is permissible under Article 1(1) TRIPS.

The EU-CA-AA contains no provisions mirroring Article 24(9) TRIPS.[329] According to Article 243 EU-CA-AA, the "[p]arties reaffirm the rights and obligations established in Part II, section 3, of the TRIPS Agreement" (*i.e.*, the section on geographical indications) and "geographical indications [...] shall only be subject to

---

[325] See Sect. 2.4.6.

[326] Article 86 IP Law (GT), as amended by the EU-CA-AA Reform Law (GT).

[327] Article 145.1 EU-CARIFORUM-EPA.

[328] Article 10.21(4) of the agreement; the text is available at http://eur-lex.europa.eu/legal-content/EN/TXT/PDF/?uri=OJ:L:2011:127:FULL&from=EN (accessed 2 Nov 2024).

[329] Engelhardt (2015), p. 795.

this Article if they are recognized and declared as such in their country of origin. This wording differs from Article 24(9) TRIPS in two ways: First, Article 243.2 EU-CA-AA applies to geographical indications "not recognized and declared as [a geographical indication]", not geographical indications "not protected". As *Engelhardt* points out, Article 24(9) TRIPS does not require a formal act of recognition or declaration of protection in the country of origin,[330] therefore, geographical indications can also be protected as unregistered rights. The different wording is relevant if, and only if, a geographical indication is not registered, but is protected as an *unregistered* geographical indication in the country of origin. This can affect geographical indications in the Dominican Republic and Nicaragua, because these countries, as already noted, still distinguish between *unregistered* geographical indications and *registered* denominations of origin.[331] Any unregistered geographical indications could, therefore, be excluded from protection abroad. Second, however, Article 243.2 EU-CA-AA does not exclude such *unregistered* geographical indication from protection generally, but only from the (requirement of the) application of the protection under TRIPS provided for in Article 243.1 EU-CA-AA. The protection provided for in the other articles of the section in the EU-CA-AA, therefore, continue to apply. Article 243.2 EU-CA-AA has, therefore, no apparent effect. The (optional) exclusion of the protection of unregistered geographical indications provided by TRIPS would be compliant with the EU-CA-AA, but violate Article 1(1) TRIPS by reducing the level of protection provided by TRIPS.[332]

Engelhardt further notes that in the interest of legal certainty, the country of origin should notify the other parties of the bilateral FTA if it ceases to protect a particular geographical indication.[333] Unlike other bilateral FTAs concluded by the EU, the EU-CA-AA contains no such notification mechanism.[334] However, from a practical perspective this omission is unlikely to create problems. If a geographical indication ceases to be protected in the country of origin, this would most likely indicate that it is no longer used in commerce by any producer and, therefore, nobody would have an interest to enforce it.

In Central America, traditionally, protection did not require that the geographical indication is protected in the country of origin. In El Salvador, Guatemala and Nicaragua, however, under the legislation implementing CAFTA-DR, the registration of foreign geographical indication requires that the geographical indication is

[330] Engelhardt (2015), p. 809.

[331] See Sect. 4.4.2.2.

[332] Engelhardt (2015), p. 795, considers Article 243(2) EU-CA-AA to be TRIPS-compliant, because "it only extends the scope of the exception, but does not limit the protection [geographical indications] may enjoy in each Party"; however, in the author's view the provision limits the protection unregistered geographical indications enjoy.

[333] Engelhardt (2015), p. 796.

[334] Such a mechanism is provided for in Articles 210(3) and 212(2) EU-Colombia/Peru/Ecuador-FTA, Article 172(4) EU-Georgia-AA and Article 20.19.7 CETA; on this topic see Engelhardt (2015), p. 796.

protected in its country of origin.[335] This requirement was not included in the revised Honduran legislation.

4.4.4.2 Statutory Bars

Generic Terms

Under Article 24(6) TRIPS, countries are not required to protect geographical indications that are "identical with the term customary in common language as the common name for such good", *i.e.*, have become generic. However, under Article 24(6) TRIPS countries may also choose not to exclude generic terms from protection.

The TRIPS provision was not included in CAFTA-DR, which seems surprising, because CAFTA-DR generally is drafted in a way that limits the protection of geographical indications in favor of trademarks. However, if a certain name has become a generic term, any trademark conflicting with the geographical indication (*i.e.*, using the same name) would also lose its protection.[336] In this specific case, therefore, less protection for geographical indications would practically not mean more protection for trademarks.

Article 145.C.1 EU-CARIFORUM-EPA restates the TRIPS provision. Article 246.3 EU-CA-AA provides that, "[w]here a geographical indication contains within it a name which is considered generic […], the use of that generic name on the appropriate good […] shall not be considered to be [an infringement of geographical indications]. While this wording is different from Article 24(6) TRIPS, in effect it also permits countries not to protect geographical indications that are generic against the use of the generic term.

In Costa Rica and Guatemala, under the legislation implementing the EU-CA-AA, a geographical indication cannot be registered if it is considered to be the common or generic term of a product.[337] Honduran and Salvadoran legislation specifies that this is determined based on either by the relevant sector of the public (*conocedores*) or the public at large.[338]

---

[335] Article 67(4) Trademark Law (SV); Article 83(1) IP Law (GT), as amended by the EU-CA-AA Reform Law (GT); Article 58*bis* Trademark Regulation (NI), as amended by the EU-CA-AA Trademark Reform Regulation (NI).

[336] See Sect. 4.1.2.5.

[337] Article 75(c) Trademark Law (CR), Article 80(c) IP Law (GT), as amended by the EU-CA-AA Reform Law (GT).

[338] Article 68(c) Trademark Law (SV), Article 127(3) IP Law (HN), as amended by the EU-CA-AA Reform Law (HN).

"Exception from the Exception" for Established Geographical Indications and Protected Geographical Indications

Under Article 24(6) TRIPS, members are not required, but permitted to protect generic geographical indications. This enables countries to implement Article 6 Lisbon Agreement, which provides that geographical indications protected as appellations of origin *based on the international registration* cannot be deemed to have become generic as long as the protection in the country of origin persists. Among the members obliged in this way are Costa Rica and Nicaragua. The policy goal behind this exception from the exception is to enable the registration and protection of such geographical indications in third countries and "phase out prior use" of European geographical indications which have become generic.[339]

Similarly, Article 246.2 EU-CA-AA restricts the exception by stating that an *Established Geographical Indication*[340] cannot "be deemed to have become generic, as long as it is protected as a geographical indication in the country of origin".[341] This counter-exception to the exclusion of generic terms could violate the MFN principle of Article 4 TRIPS, because it grants better protection to Established Geographical Indications (all of which are European) than to other geographical indications. However, if the national legislation implementing this provision extends the protection to all geographical indications, a conflict with Article 4 TRIPS does not arise.[342]

This is the case in Central America, where, to the extent Article 246.2 EU-CA-AA was implemented, the "exception from the exception" for geographical indication protected in the country of origin was extended to all geographical indications: In Guatemala and El Salvador, "[g]eographical indications protected in accordance with [this law] are not considered common or generic [...] if protection in the country of origin exists".[343]

Article 246.2 EU-CA-AA was not implemented in other countries, where the trademark laws were not reformed after the conclusion of the EU-CA-AA. In particular, this rule does not exist in the legislation in Costa Rica and Nicaragua, even though these countries are required to implement it not only under the EU-CA-

[339] Engelhardt (2015), p. 785; this concept is worded differently in Article 13(2) of the Regulation (EU) No 1151/2012 of 21 November 2012 on quality schemes for agricultural products and foodstuffs, which states that "[p]rotected designations of origin and protected geographical indications shall not become generic", thereby protecting also geographical indications not protected in the country of origin, but in a third country.

[340] See Sect. 4.4.4.2.

[341] This provision corresponds to Article 13.2 of the Regulation (EU) No 1151/2012 of 21 November 2012 on quality schemes for agricultural products and foodstuffs.

[342] Engelhardt (2015), p. 793.

[343] Article 73-E Trademark Law (SV); Article 80(b) IP Law (GT), as amended by the EU-CA-AA Reform Law (GT).

AA, but also under the Lisbon Agreement. Nicaragua amended the Trademark Regulation (NI) in 2012 to implement certain TRIPS and EU-CA-AA obligations, however, it did not change the general exclusion of generic distinctive signs (including by reference geographical indications) from protection and registration.[344]

Homonymous Geographical Indications

According to Article 23(3) TRIPS, *homonymous* geographical indications relating to wines and spirits shall be registered, provided that the registration ensures the differentiation of geographical indications, equitable treatment of the producers and avoids confusion of the consumers. Article 145.C.3 EU-CARIFORUM-EPA extends this rule to all goods. The EU-CA-AA, on the other hand, contains no reference to homonymous geographical indications.

This rule has explicitly been incorporated into national law in Costa Rica and Nicaragua. In Costa Rica, it does apply to all goods.[345] Nicaragua also addressed *homonymous* geographical indications in its 2012 revision of the Trademark Regulation (NI), however, the clause is restricted to *homonymous* geographical indications relating to wines and spirits.[346] This is no breach of the country's obligations under the EU-CA-AA, which does not require the application to all goods. In other words, Nicaragua simply used the opportunity of the revision of the Trademark Regulation (NI) to clarify the TRIPS obligations, but refrained from expanding the protection of geographical indications beyond these minimum requirements, in contrast to Costa Rica.

Other Statutory Bars

Several Central American countries explicitly exclude the registration of a geographical indication contrary to morality or the *ordre public*.[347] Also, trademarks can constitute a bar to the registration of a geographical indication.[348]

---

[344] Articles 58(1) and 47 of the Trademark Regulation (NI); the text of the regulation is available at https://www.wipo.int/wipolex/es/legislation/details/5093 (accessed 2 Nov 2024).

[345] Article 74(2) Trademark Law (CR).

[346] Article 58*ter* of the Trademark Regulation (NI), as amended by the EU-CA-AA Trademark Reform Regulation (NI).

[347] Article 75(b) Trademark Law (CR); Article 68(b) Trademark Law (SV); Article 80(b) IP Law (GT), as amended by the EU-CA-AA Reform Law (GT); Article 127(2) IP Law (HN), as amended by the EU-CA-AA Reform Law (HN); Articles 58 and 7(b) Trademark Law (NI).

[348] This issue is analyzed in detail in Sect. 4.4.6.

4.4.5 *Right Holder and Procedure*

4.4.5.1 Right Holder and Applicant

Articles 22 to 24 TRIPS require the legal means for interested parties to prevent the infringement of geographical indications, but do not establish a proprietary right for a specific right holder and do not provide for the registration of geographical indications. Therefore, TRIPS provides no framework on this issue.

Article 15.3(2) CAFTA-DR provides that each Party shall enable persons from another Party to apply for geographical indications and accept foreign applications without the requirement for intercession by that Party, *i.e.*, the government, on behalf of its persons. This clarifies that private foreign entities can obtain geographical indications directly, and that geographical indications are not necessarily owned or obtained by the state and governments or states do not have to be involved in the process, as was often the case in Central America (see below in this subsection).

The EU-FTAs contain detailed procedural requirements, but do not state who can obtain geographical indications.

In Central American law, the right holder of *domestic* geographical indications was the state in several countries.[349] This rule complicated the registration and management of geographical indications for the respective users and is one of the reasons why practitioners prefer the system of collective marks, where associations of the producers can own the right.[350] These laws were amended by the legislation implementing the EU-CA-AA and no longer explicitly regulate ownership of *domestic* geographical indications. Accordingly, the applicant should also be the owner.

In Costa Rica, Article 76(2) Trademark Law (CR) implies that private entities may apply for domestic geographical indications and should, therefore, also be able to own such geographical indications. In El Salvador, Article 67(3) Trademark Law (SV) clarifies that producers can submit applications individually or by means of an association. The new Guatemalan legislation provides that *associations of producers* can apply for domestic geographical indications.[351] Under the new legislation enacted in Honduras in 2013, applications for domestic geographical indications can be submitted by one or more of the producers who are located in the territory to which the geographical indication relates or by the competent public authority.[352] In

[349] E.g., prior to the 2013 amendment of the laws, Article 67(2) Trademark Law (SV), Article 81 IP Law (GT).

[350] Contreras Aguilera (2007), p. 53.

[351] Article 81(caput) IP Law (GT), as amended by the EU-CA-AA Reform Law (GT); this clause does not explicitly state that these associations also are the right holder of such geographical indications. However, the fact that the reform law deleted the prior statement that the right holder is the state strongly suggests that the legislator intended to change this situation and, accordingly, these associations should be considered as the right holders.

[352] Article 126 IP Law (HN).

Nicaragua, any domestic entity representing producers or craftsmen as well as "competent authority" can submit applications.[353]

The only exception is El Salvador, where the state is still the owner of all *domestic* geographical indications.[354]

There are no restrictions regarding ownership of *foreign* geographical indications. Foreign geographical indications can be submitted by foreign producers or competent public authorities.[355] For example, in El Salvador, Article 67-(2) Trademark Law (SV) refers to the rules of the country of origin. In Guatemala, Article 83(5) IP Law (GT), as amended by the EU-CA-AA Reform Law (GT), permits any "natural or legal person" to apply for a foreign geographical indication. In Nicaragua, "foreign producers or craftsmen and competent authorities" can submit applications.[356]

Governmental *intercession* is not necessary under Central American law in relation to foreign applications, because private associations can submit their own applications. In Nicaragua, while foreign "competent authorities" can submit applications, intercession is not required, because "producers or craftsmen" also able to submit applications.[357]

4.4.5.2 Registration Procedure

According to Article 15.3(5) CAFTA-DR, the application including the geographical indication and the regulation has to be published. Interestingly, CAFTA-DR explicitly only requires that the application for a geographical indication, but not for a trademark, is published for opposition.[358] This wording permits the Central American countries to privilege trademarks during the registration proceeding. Article 244.2(d) and (e) EU-CA-AA require that the *application* has to include the description of the geographical indication and the regulation of the quality specifications. In addition, Article 244.2(b) EU-CA-AA requires an administrative process to verify the requirements. These publication and description requirements have been implemented in the Central American laws and regulations.[359]

[353] Article 71(1) Trademark Law (NI).

[354] Article 67(2) Trademark Law (SV).

[355] Article 67(3) Trademark Law (SV), as amended by the EU-CA-AA Trademark Reform Law (SV); Article 126 IP Law (HN), as amended by the EU-CA-AA Reform Law (HN); Article 59 of the Trademark Regulation (NI), as amended by the EU-CA-AA Trademark Reform Regulation (NI).

[356] Article 71(2) Trademark Law (NI).

[357] Article 71(2) Trademark Law (NI).

[358] Articles 15.2(6)(c), 15.3(5) CAFTA-DR.

[359] Typically, these procedural requirements have been elaborated in some details and numerous articles or sections. For the sake of brevity, therefore, individual references are omitted.

4.4.5.3 Established Geographical Indications Under the EU-CA-AA

One of the policy goals of the EU in its FTAs has become the immediate or automatic protection of comprehensive lists of geographical indications, because individual applications in another jurisdiction can be difficult, time-consuming and costly. Besides, local (or third party) trademark owners may be in an advantageous position to oppose such applications.[360] However, neither the EU-CA-AA nor the EU-CARIFORUM-EPA provide for such automatic protection.[361] Article 145.E EU-CARIFORUM-EPA envisages further negotiations between the parties in relation to geographical indications, similar to Article 24(1) TRIPS, no later than 1 January 2014. By September 2014, however, no negotiations had been initiated.[362] On 2 October 2017, the European Commission issued a Recommendation for a Council Decision authorizing the European Commission to negotiate an Agreement with the EU-CARIFORUM States to protect geographic indications based on Article 145 of the EU-CARIFORUM - EU Economic Partnership Agreement.[363]

While Article 245 EU-CA-AA provides for a list of "Established Geographical Indications", this clause does not create automatic protection.[364] Article 245 EU-CA-AA only outlines the process for registering Established Geographical Indications. It states that "[b]y the *entry into force of this Agreement*, [...] the Parties shall (a) have finalized the opposition and examination procedures at least with respect to those geographical indication applications [...] that were not opposed [...] and (b) have initiated the procedures [...] with respect to those geographical indication applications [...] that were opposed [...]". Article 353(5) EU-CA-AA restates that the requirements under Article 245 EU-CA-AA must be fulfilled before the entry into force of the EU-CA-AA.

The list of Established Geographical Indications encompasses several hundred European geographical indications and 10 from Central America (mostly relating to coffees). These numbers according to critics show a "dramatic imbalance" and a particular negotiation success of the EU.[365] However, considering the respective size of the two regions and the fact that there were very few domestic geographical

[360] Engelhardt (2015), p. 786.

[361] This "omission" may be due to the fact that the EU-CARIFORUM-EPA was drafted earlier than the EU-CA-AA and other comparable FTAs of the EU and, therefore, is less strict. As the example of the US-FTAs shows, the level of protection in FTAs increases over time; this "ever-increasing" nature of TRIPS-plus protection will be further analyzed in Sect. 8.9.

[362] Singh (2014), p. 53.

[363] The text of the recommendation is available at http://eur-lex.europa.eu/legal-content/EN/TXT/?uri=COM:2017:557:FIN (accessed 2 Nov 2024).

[364] Engelhardt (2015), p. 816 considers the list to provide automatic protection, however, this may be due to a different understanding of "automatic". Established Geographical Indications are only applied for automatically under the EU-CA-AA, but protection requires approval by the local IP Register.

[365] Engelhardt (2015), p. 794.

indications established in Central America when the EU-CA-AA was negotiated, the lists appear less one-sided.

This list was a major obstacle in the negotiations between the EU and Central America. The Central American countries initially rejected the list, because some of the geographical indications conflict with existing trademarks from local and US-American right holders.[366] However, the final text shows that the EU succeeded in the negotiations on this matter.

The linkage between the registration of the geographical indications and entry into force of the EU-CA-AA gave the EU significant leverage with regard to the applications for geographical indications. *Engelhardt* estimates that it enabled the EU to pressure Central American countries to grant protection to specific geographical indications, potentially even against legitimate concerns by the respective country or third parties.[367] While such an assumption is often hard to verify, in this case it is clearly documented by the public announcement of Italy to request the suspension of the entry into force of the Agreement in El Salvador and Costa Rica if these countries failed to expeditiously register the geographical indication applications.[368]

Not surprisingly, the applications were noticeably swift and successful: 114 geographical indication applications were filed in August 2012 and 108 were registered by October 2013 in Costa Rica (*i.e.*, a 95% registration rate within a year), a country with a "problematic" registration procedure.[369] In other words, the success rate in countries such as Honduras and Nicaragua with a more "convenient" registration procedure was most likely even higher. The speed and success is even more remarkable considering that the registration period can also be much longer. Around the same time (in November 2012), a local geographical indication was registered for "Turrialba" cheese, six years after the application had been filed.[370] One must also consider that oppositions were filed by Central American and North American companies against several of the geographical indications.[371] Nevertheless, the registration process was completed within about one year.

The six applications against which oppositions were initiated were all related to cheeses, namely *Parmigiano Reggiano, Gorgonzola, Provolone Valpadana, Fontina, Manchego* and *Emmental de Savoie*.[372] The protection of (especially single name) cheeses by geographical indications is seen by the USA as particularly problematic for US businesses.[373] Following the oppositions and the delay in the

366 Interview with *Carlos Castillo*.

367 Engelhardt (2015), p. 810.

368 Consortium Centro América Abogados (2013).

369 Ibid.

370 See the report available at http://www.centralamericadata.com/en/article/home/Designation_of_Origin_in_Costa_Rica (accessed 2 Nov 2024) and El Financiero (2019).

371 Consortium Centro América Abogados (2013).

372 Ibid.; see also El Financiero (2019).

373 USTR Special 301 Report (2015), p. 69.

registration of the geographical indications, Italy temporarily blocked the provisional application of the trade chapter of the EU-CA-AA.[374] The opposition against *Provolone Valpadana* was reversed on appeal.[375] The opposition against *Fontina* was reversed by the TRA in 2014.[376] No information on the opposition proceedings against *Gorgonzola* and *Manchego* could be obtained, but these names were still used as generic terms for non-European cheeses in Costa Rica in 2019.[377] Regarding *Parmigiano Reggiano* and *Emmental de Savoie*, no further information could be obtained.

The list of Established Geographical Indications covers several hundred geographical indications, but only a part of these are registered in the EU. Most of the European geographical indications are not included in the list and must, therefore, be registered according to the "normal" domestic procedure in each country to obtain protection.[378]

In 2022, as part of the celebration of the 10th anniversary of the signature of the EU-CA-AA, the EU agreed to protect 11 new geographical indications from Central America, mainly coffees from El Salvador.[379]

4.4.5.4 Costs

In Central America, the registration fees for geographical indications are traditionally higher than those for collective marks.[380] Also, the costs for establishing the characteristics and drafting the regulation containing the specifications of the geographical indication are significant.[381] These additional costs could be a deterrent for local companies to choose geographical indications instead of collective marks.

---

[374] See the report available at http://www.centralamericadata.com/es/article/home/Solicitan_prrroga_en_registro_de_marcas_de_quesos (accessed 2 Nov 2024).

[375] https://www.latincounsel.com/?Noticias=Defensa_a_oposiciin_de_registro_de_Indicaciin_Geogrifica_Provolone_Valpadana (accessed 2 Nov 2024).

[376] TRA, 10 November 2014, VOTO N°0773-2014 – "Fontina".

[377] See El Financiero (2019).

[378] This selective approach has been considered problematic from an internal European equality perspective, see Engelhardt (2015), p. 794. However, this issue will not be further analyzed here, because this study focuses on the international aspects of the bilateral FTAs and the effects in Central America.

[379] See the report available at https://agriculture.ec.europa.eu/news/eu-protects-11-new-geographical-indications-central-america-2022-06-23_en (accessed 2 Nov 2024).

[380] For example, in Guatemala the fee for filing a geographical indication is three times higher than the fee for filing a collective mark, about 300 Euro and 100 Euro respectively, see Article 2 (a) Nr. 6 and 14 of the Acuredo Gubernativo No. 862-2000 of 21 December 2000, as amended by Acuerdo Gubernativo No 148-2014, available at https://portal.rpi.gob.gt/wp-content/uploads/2020/12/Acuerdo148-2014v2.pdf (accessed 2 Nov 2024); in Costa Rica, by contrast, the fee for filing a geographical indication is the same as the fee for filing a collective mark, for each case 50 USD, see Art. 94 Trademark Law (CR).

[381] Regarding these requirements, see Sect. 4.4.4.

4.4.5.5 Legal Review

Article 15.3(5) CAFTA-DR requires procedures for the *opposition* and *cancellation* of registrations of geographical indication. This enables in particular trademark owners to oppose conflicting geographical indications. This exemplifies the overall approach of CAFTA-DR to strengthen trademarks in relation to geographical indications. TRIPS and CAFTA-DR do not provide for specific terms for such procedures.

In Central America, all national laws provide for *opposition* and *cancellation* procedures.[382]

4.4.5.6 International Registration Procedure

The Lisbon Agreement, which is in force in Costa Rica and Nicaragua, provides for a three-phase international registration procedure: First, the national registration procedure is initiated by the application to the competent authority in the country of origin. Second, the international registration procedure consists of the notification of the application by the competent authority in the country of origin to the other parties.[383] Third, other members can refuse registration within a year after receipt of the application.[384] The EU has proposed to create an international notification system with a similar procedure within the WTO structure.[385] However, the EU-FTAs have not introduced the system in Central America, because the ratification of the Lisbon Agreement is not mandatory under the EU-FTAs. Practically, in Costa Rica, as a party to the Lisbon Agreement, most foreign geographical indications (apart from the Established Geographical Indications), are registered under the international registration procedure.[386]

[382] Articles 77(2) (in connection with 17) and 81 Trademark Law (CR); Articles 130.1 (c) (in connection with 80(2)) and 134 IP Law (DR); Articles 70(2) (in connection with 16) and 74 Trademark Law (SV), as amended by the EU-CA-AA Trademark Reform Law (SV); Articles 84 (c) and 90 IP Law (GT), as amended by the EU-CA-AA Reform Law (GT); Articles 129-(3) (in connection with 89) and 133 IP Law (HN), as amended by the EU-CA-AA Reform Law (HN); Articles 58(1) and 27 Trademark Regulation (NI) in connection with Article 16 Trademark Law (NI), Articles 58(1) and 47–49 Trademark Regulation (NI) in connection with Article 34 Trademark Law (NI); the inclusion of opposition and cancellation procedures is, however, not a consequence of the implementation of CAFTA-DR, because such procedures are foreseen for all IP rights and have been part of the registrations procedure for geographical indication before the implementation of CAFTA-DR.

[383] Article 5(2) Lisbon Agreement.

[384] Article 5(3) to (5) Lisbon Agreement.

[385] Correa (2002), p. 33.

[386] Available at http://www.centralamericadata.com/en/article/home/Designation_of_Origin_in_Costa_Rica (accessed 2 Nov 2024).

4.4.6 Relationship Between Trademarks and Geographical Indications

4.4.6.1 Introduction

The relationship between trademarks and geographical indications poses raises specific issues, in particular in the context of TRIPS-plus and bilateral FTAs. In the case of, *e.g.*, patents, stronger protection of the rights and the right holders conflicts with the interests of the users and restricts the public domain, often leading to problems between developed nations, where right holders are dominant, and developing countries, which are predominantly users of IP rights. With regard to the relationship between trademarks and geographical indications, however, stronger protection of one system conflicts with the protection of the other system. The special nature of this conflict is also demonstrated by the fact that all bilateral FTAs analyzed here include a sub-section on the "relationship between trademarks and geographical indications".[387] This shows that both the USA and the EU were aware of the necessity to create some balance between these rights instead of simply requiring minimum protection.

At its core, the conflict is between two opposing concepts, "first in time, first in right" protection and strong *sui generis* system for geographical indications.[388] The *USA* favors equal, "first in time, first in right" or "first to file" protection of trademarks and geographical indications. Geographical indications should be protected like collective marks, which are restricted to relative protection against confusion and are limited by the existence or emergence of generic terms.

The European Union, from where most registered geographical indications originate, uses and promotes a *sui generis* system which provides protection against the use of other signs which do not mislead the consumer (absolute protection) and against generic terms.[389]

The Central American legislation, prior to the changes brought about by the implementation of the EU-FTAs, also applied the "first to file" principle. This became one of the key obstacles in the negotiation of the EU-CA-AA.[390]

---

[387] Article 15.11.7. CAFTA-DR, Article 248 EU-CA-AA and Article 145.D EU-CARIFORUM-EPA.

[388] See Correa (2002), p. 1; see also the INTA Resolution on the "Protection of Geographical Indications and Trademarks" of September 1997, as discussed and further developed by the subsequent Resolution "Protection of Geographical Indications" of November 2019, available at https://www.inta.org/wp-content/uploads/public-files/advocacy/board-resolutions/Protection-of-Geographical-Indications-11.2019.pdf (accessed 2 Nov 2024).

[389] On this issue see Grosse Ruse-Khan (2016), p. 299; the list of Established Geographical Indications included in the EU-CA-AA (see Article 245 EU-CA-AA) encompasses several hundred European geographical indications, and this list covers only a (small) part of the GIs protected in Europe, see Engelhardt (2015), p. 794.

[390] Instituto Interamericano de Cooperación para la Agricultura, Progress in Latin America in the application of geographical indications and appellations of origin, Technical Bulletin July 2011, available at http://repositorio.iica.int/bitstream/11324/4137/2/BVE17089198i.pdf (accessed 2 Nov 2024).

4.4.6.2 TRIPS and CAFTA-DR

Registration of Trademarks

According to Article 23(3) TRIPS, the registration of a trademark for wines or spirits which contains or consists of a geographical indication identifying wines or spirits shall be refused or invalidated with respect to such wines or spirits not having this origin.

The registration of a geographical indication shall, according to Article 24.5(b) TRIPS, not affect the registration of a trademark, which is identical with or similar to a geographical indication, (in particular) if the trademark, at the priority date of the geographical indication, has been (i) applied for or registered in good faith or (ii) acquired through use according to domestic law[391] before the geographical indication is *protected* in its country of origin.[392] According to Article 24.5(b) TRIPS, the priority date of the geographical indication may be not the application date in the country of protection or the country of origin, but the date of the *registration in the country of origin*. This does not represent a deviation from the "first in time, first in right" principle, even though regarding the trademark, the application date is relevant. Most countries require, based on Article 24(9) TRIPS, that geographical indications must be protected in their country of origin to be registerable in third countries. The date of the *registration* in the country of origin, which is relevant for the priority of the geographical indication, therefore, necessarily precedes the date of application in the country concerned, which would be the date analogous to the date relevant for the priority of the trademark.

Irrespective of the existence of a registered geographical indication, Article 22(3) TRIPS requires the refusal or invalidation of the registration of a trademark which contains or consists of a geographical indication with respect to goods not originating in the territory indicated, if use of the indication in the trademark for such goods in that Member is of such a nature as to mislead the public as to the true place of origin.[393]

Article 24(7) TRIPS provides for an optional limitation of oppositions to trademarks based on geographical indications to a period of five years after registration or use of the trademark.[394]

---

[391] This alternative applies to unregistered marks, which can be protected as well-known (or notoriously known) trademarks.

[392] The trademark must have been applied for and registered in good faith Article 24.5(b) TRIPS and 15.3.7(b) CAFTA-DR).

[393] See McGuire, Mary-*Rose* / Strauch, Severin, in Busche et al. (2013), Article 22 no 43-53.

[394] On this issue see Correa (2002), p. 11.

Registration of Geographical Indications

Under TRIPS and CAFTA-DR, if a trademark or trademark application does not fulfil the requirements for priority, it is revoked or rejected. However, in case of a conflict between a priority trademark and a subsequent geographical indication, TRIPS and CAFTA-DR provide for different consequences regarding the registration or application of the geographical indication.

Under Article 24(5) TRIPS, in case of a priority trademark, the registration of a geographical indication "shall not prejudice eligibility for or the validity of the registration of a trademark, or the right to *use* a trademark". This implies that even in case a prior trademark exists, a geographical indication can be registered. TRIPS allows cumulative protection of prior trademarks and subsequent geographical indications. Therefore, the geographical indication can be registered in case of conflict with a prior trademark, but prior trademarks may still be used and enjoys protection according to its scope. This protects the interest of the right holder of the prior trademark who maintains the trademark, but the effect of the trademark remains limited to its scope of protection. The geographical indication can be registered and is protected, to the extent it exceeds the scope of prior trademark (*e.g.*, translation of the indication, other classes of goods). Both rights can *co-exist*, which represents a compromise between the "first in time, first in right" approach advocated by proponents of trademarks and an absolute approach according to which geographical indications exclude valid, pre-existing trademark.[395]

Article 24(5) TRIPS provides that prior trademarks are protected against geographical indications which are identical or *similar.*

Article 15.3(7) CAFTA-DR requires that grounds for refusing protection of a geographical indication shall be the likelihood of confusion between the geographical indication and a trademark which has been (i) applied for or registered in good faith or (ii) acquired through use according to domestic law. The wording could be interpreted so that the registration of a geographical indication must be refused, if the trademark was applied for in the in the country of protection before the geographical indication is registered in the country of protection. This interpretation raises two concerns.

First, it could conflict with Article 24.5(b) TRIPS, which states that, even in case of similarity, a trademark only has to be registered if it has been applied for or registered (in the country of protection) before the geographical indication is protected in its country of origin. While under Article 24.5(b) TRIPS, the relevant "priority date" for the geographical indication is the protection in the *country of origin*, under Article 15.3(7) CAFTA-DR the registration in the *country of protection* is relevant. This potential conflict could be resolved if, based on Article 24.5 (b) TRIPS, trademark applications can be rejected or nullified if a corresponding geographical indication is (or was) protected in its country of origin at the time the trademark was filed in the respective country of protection, in which case they would

[395] McGuire, Mary-Rose/Strauch, Severin in Busche et al. (2013), Article 24 Nr 19.

not prevent any subsequent geographical indication being registered. However, local laws do not seem to provide for such a mechanism. For example, neither Costa Rica nor Guatemala created a statutory basis for a priority of a geographical indication based on the registration in the country of origin, as will be discussed further in the analysis of local laws below.

Whether the absence of such mechanism in Central America constitute a violation of Article 24.5 TRIPS depends on the question if this clause implies a mandatory protection of a geographical indication after it has been registered in the country of origin, and as a consequence whether a conflicting trademark application must be refused in a third country. According to WTO case law, however, Article 24.5 TRIPS "does not provide for the conferral of new rights on trademark owners *or GI holders*, but provides that the specifically mentioned rights shall not be affected by the measures that are the subject of the provision. If the drafters had intended to grant a positive right, they would have used positive language." (emphasis added)[396] In other words, the clause requires that trademarks cannot be rejected based on a corresponding geographical indication before it has been registered in the country of origin, but not that a trademark must be rejected after the corresponding geographical indication has been registered in the country of origin.

Second, it could violate the "first to file" principle, by stating that a geographical indication shall not be registered if the application of a confusingly similar trademark is pending, irrespective of whether the application for the geographical indication was filed before the application of the confusingly similar trademark or not.[397]

Also, under Article 15.3(7) CAFTA-DR, geographical indications cannot be registered, if they are *likely to be confusingly similar* to a prior trademark or trademark application. The CAFTA-DR clause seems narrower than the TRIPS provisions, because it protects prior trademarks only if there is a *likelihood of confusion*. However, in practice the same principles should apply as in the case of conflict between an existing trademark and the registration of a similar trademark, which is also barred only in case of a likelihood of confusion. The "likelihood of confusion" requirement would, therefore, probably be applied in practice also if it were not specifically included in CAFTA-DR.

The CAFTA-DR clause is, however, broader than the corresponding provision in the US-Chile-FTA,[398] according to which the protection or registration of a geographical indication must be refused if it "*is confusingly similar* to a pre-existing trademark", omitting the qualification "likelihood". Therefore, the US-Chile-FTA

[396] WTO Dispute Settlement Body, Decision WT/DS174/R, European Communities — Protection of Trademarks and Geographical Indications for Agricultural Products and Foodstuffs (2005) (complaint by the USA), section 7.610.

[397] *Handler* and *Mercurio* observe that "it may be the case that a first-used GI will be denied recognition if the application for protection of the GI post-dated the application for registration of a confusingly similar trademark. In either situation, coexistence of conflicting GIs and trademarks is not contemplated, and trademarks are given primacy over GIs", see Handler and Mercurio (2015), p. 343.

[398] Article 17.4.10(a) US-Chile-FTA.

only requires protection of prior trademarks if confusion is proven to exist, but under CAFTA-DR, confusion must only be possible.

4.4.6.3 EU-FTAs

Registration of Trademarks

According to the EU-FTAs, a trademark identical with, or similar to, a geographical indication in the same class of products shall not be registered if the geographical indication is registered or applied for and subsequently protected in the country of protection before the trademark is *applied for* in the country of protection.[399]

Notably, these clauses do not utilize the possibility under Article 24.5(b) TRIPS to require the rejection of trademarks that were applied for after the registration of the conflicting geographical indication in its country of *origin*, but before its application in the country of protection. Therefore, Central American countries can determine the priority of a geographical indication in relation to a trademark application sole based on the local application dates (as do Costa Rica and Guatemala, for example).

Registration of Geographical Indications

According to the EU-FTAs, in case the trademark does not have priority, an application shall not be granted and a registered trademark shall be invalidated. However, in case of a conflict between a priority trademark and a subsequent geographical indication, under the EU-FTAs, a geographical indication can co-exist with a prior trademark.

Article 145.D.4 EU-CARIFORUM establishes co-existence by providing that "[…] a trade mark […] which has been applied for, registered or established by use […] in good faith […] before the date of application for protection of the geographical indication in the respective territories, may continue to be used notwithstanding the registration of the geographical indication […]. In such case, the use of the geographical indication shall be permitted alongside the relevant trade mark."

Both the EU-CA-AA and the EU-CARIFORUM-EPA restrict the refusal of the registration and protection of a geographical indication to cases in which the use of the geographical indication, in the light of "a reputed or well-known trademark" (under the EU-CARIFORUM-EPA, "the reputation and renown and the length of time it has been used"), is liable to mislead consumers as to the true identity of the product. This limitation of protection is optional under Article 248.2 EU-CA-AA, but mandatory under Article 145.D.1 EU-CARIFORUM-EPA. The latter provision

[399] Article 145.D.2 EU-CARIFORUM-EPA and ARTICLE 248.1 EU-CA-AA.

corresponds to domestic European law.[400] These provisions conflict with Article 15.3(7) CAFTA-DR, which excludes the registration and protection of a geographical indication *confusingly similar* to a prior trademark, irrespective of the reputation and renown of the trademark.

4.4.6.4 Central America

Registration of Trademarks

The international legal framework, therefore, requires the refusal of trademark applications and the invalidation of trademarks (i) on *relative* grounds in case of confusion, irrespective of the registration of a geographical indication[401] and (ii) on *absolute* grounds in case of a prior registered geographical indication.[402]

The new legislation in Guatemala provides for two grounds of refusal of trademark applications, (i) on *relative* grounds if the trademark is identical or similar to or constitutes the translation of a geographical indication registered in Guatemala and may cause confusion or a risk of association[403] and (ii) on *absolute* grounds if the trademark is *applied for* in Guatemala after the geographical indication is applied for in Guatemala, for identical or related products.[404] While the refusal on absolute grounds reflects the requirements under Article 248.1 EU-CA-AA, the refusal on relative grounds requires in addition to confusion also the *registration in* Guatemala. This requirement is not included in Article 22(3) TRIPS, which does not require the registration of the geographical indication in the country where the trademark is applied for. It is also not supported by Article 24.5(b) TRIPS, which refers to the registration of the geographical indication, but only to establish the relevant priority date.[405]

---

[400] This limitation is based on European law. Article 6(4) of the Regulation (EU) No 1151/2012 of 21 November 2012 on quality schemes for agricultural products and foodstuffs, replacing the identical provision of Article 3(4) Regulation (EC) No 510/2006 of 20 March 2006 on the protection of geographical indications and designations of origin for agricultural products and foodstuffs, states that the likelihood of confusion must be based on the reputation, fame and duration of use of the trademark. These requirements were affirmed by the CJEU in the case Bavaria N.V. and Bavaria Italia Srl v. Bayerischer Brauerbund, Case C-343/07, CJEU, 2 July 2009, where the designation "Bavaria" had been used since 1925, had become part of the company name in 1930 and had been registered as a trademark first in 1947; see Evans (2010), pp. 645, 671.

[401] Article 22(3) TRIPS.

[402] Articles 23.2 regarding wines and spirits and Article 145.D EU-CARIFORUM-EPA and ARTICLE 248(1) EU-CA-AA regarding all products.

[403] Article 21(g) IP Law (GT) after the amendment by the CAFTA-DR Reform Law (GT).

[404] Article 88 IP Law (GT) after the amendment by the CAFTA-DR Reform Law (GT).

[405] In addition, Article 24.5(b) TRIPS refers to the registration of the geographical indication in the country of origin, not the country in the country where the trademark is applied for.

In Nicaragua, the registration of any distinctive sign is excluded (only) in case of confusion.[406] In other words, the refusal of trademark applications and the invalidation of trademarks on *absolute* grounds is not foreseen.

Priority of a Geographical Indication Based on the Country of Origin

As discussed, under Article 24.5(b) TRIPS the Central American countries can, but do not have to provide for the rejection of trademarks that were applied for after the registration of the conflicting geographical indication in its country of origin, but before its application in the country of protection. CAFTA-DR does not explicitly exclude this mechanism, while the EU-FTAs also do not explicitly require it.

Local laws do not seem to provide for such mechanism. For example, under Costa Rican law, trademarks are inadmissible in case of conflict with a geographical indication applied for earlier in Costa Rica, and conversely a geographical indication is rejected if there is a likelihood of confusion with a registered trademark or a pending trademark application. In other words, the priority of trademarks and geographical indications is determined simply based on the date of application in Costa Rica.[407] Also in Guatemala, trademarks are rejected if a geographical indication was applied for earlier in the country.[408]

Registration of Geographical Indications

The Central American countries literally implemented Article 15.3(7) CAFTA-DR, providing that grounds for refusing protection of a geographical indication shall be the likelihood of confusion between the geographical indication and a trademark which has been (i) applied for or registered in good faith[409] or (ii) acquired through use according to domestic law.[410] Therefore, the national legislation raises the same issues regarding compliance with TRIPS as Article 15.3(7) CAFTA-DR itself.[411]

---

[406] Article 58(2) of the Trademark Regulation (NI), as amended by the EU-CA-AA Trademark Reform Regulation (NI).

[407] See Articles 8(1) and 75(d) TM Law (CR).

[408] See Articles 3(g), 88 IP Law (GT) after the amendment by the CAFTA-DR Reform Law (GT).

[409] Article 75(d) Trademark Law (CR), Article 68(d) in connection with Article 9(a) Trademark Law (SV), Article 80(e) IP Law (GT), as amended by the EU-CA-AA Reform Law (GT); Article 82 (f) IP Law (GT), before the amendment by the CAFTA-DR Reform Law (GT), contained the same provision; the clause was published as a "second" Article 82 (d) IP Law (GT), even though it follows Article 82 (d) and (e) IP Law (GT), which appears to be a simple drafting error.

[410] Article 75(e) Trademark Law (CR), Article 82 (f) IP Law (GT), as amended by the EU-CA-AA Reform Law (GT).

[411] See Sect. 4.4.6.2.

The Honduran reform legislation creates a particular problem, because the law implementing the IP provisions of CAFTA-DR created a separate set of rules relating to IP, which did not amend, but apply *in addition* to the IP Law (HN).[412] In particular, Article 15.3(7) CAFTA-DR was implemented in CAFTA-DR Reform Law (HN). Simply put, following the implementation of CAFTA-DR, there are formally two IP laws in Honduras, the IP Law (HN) and the IP provisions in the CAFTA-DR Reform Law (HN). By contrast, the EU-CA-AA Reform Law (HN) only *amends* the existing provisions in the IP Law (HN). In particular, the EU-CA-AA Reform Law (HN) revised the requirements for the protection of geographical indications in Article 127(1) IP Law (HN) and definition of geographical indications in Article 14 CAFTA-DR Reform Law (HN). However, it does not refer to the rules on prior trademarks in Article 15(a) CAFTA-DR Reform Law (HN).

It is, therefore, unclear whether Article 15(a) CAFTA-DR Reform Law (HN) still applies. One the one hand, Article 127(1) IP Law (HN) only explicitly refers to Article 14, but not Article 15(a) CAFTA-DR Reform Law (HN), which could be an intentional omission. On the other hand, Article 15(a) CAFTA-DR Reform Law (HN) was not explicitly derogated. In addition, there is no policy or legal reason to allow a geographical indication, if it is confusing similar to a prior trademark.[413] Therefore, Article 15(a) CAFTA-DR Reform Law (HN) should still apply.

4.4.7 Term of Protection

TRIPS and CAFTA-DR do not require minimum terms of protection for geographical indications. According to Article 145.B.1 EU-CARIFORUM-EPA, the term of protection shall be indefinite; this term limit can also be implemented into national law by providing for an unlimited number of renewable periods of not less than 10 years. In Central America, geographical indications are protected indefinitely, without renewal.[414]

---

[412] As explained in Sect. 2.5.6, the CAFTA-DR Reform Law partially amends the existing provisions in the IP Law (HN), but also contains provisions on a variety of IP rights which do not modify the IP Law (HN), but apply separately. Article 15(a) CAFTA-DR Reform Law (HN) literally implements CAFTA-DR and, therefore, refers also to "domestic law" and does not specify the applicable provisions on well-known marks.

[413] In such a case, the protection of geographical indications is optional even under Article 248.2 EU-CA-AA.

[414] Article 75(b) Trademark Law (CR); Article 72(1) IP Law (SV); Article 85(3) IP Law (GT), as amended by the EU-CA-AA Reform Law (GT); Article 128 IP Law (HN), as amended by EU-CA-AA Reform Law (HN) in 2013).

4.4.8 Rights

4.4.8.1 Absolute Protection Against Third Party Use

International Agreements

Article 23 TRIPS requires protection for geographical indications identifying wines and spirits against any use for wines or spirits not originating in the place indicated by the geographical indication in question, even where the true origin of the goods is indicated or the geographical indication is used in translation or accompanied by expressions such as "kind", "type", "style", "imitation" or the like.

Such absolute protection, *i.e.*, protection against use by third parties irrespective of confusion, is mandated by Article 23 TRIPS only for wines and spirits.[415] The extension to other products is highly controversial among the WTO members. Several Central American countries explicitly supported international proposals to expand protection, namely the Dominican Republic, Honduras and Nicaragua.[416] However, the USA and other countries have strongly opposed such an expansion.[417]

Based on absolute protection, the use of a geographical indication by third parties can be prohibited for the same class of goods, even if it is not misleading the consumer. This not only substantially broadens the scope of protection, but also procedurally lifts the burden of proof from the producer with regard to misleading effect of the use.

Consequently, the geographical indication cannot be used even if the third party additionally indicates the true origin or adds clarifying elements such as "kind", "type" etc., which excludes or at least minimizes confusion.[418] However, the use of such delocalizing terms poses a risk to the sustainability of a geographical indication, because they increase the danger that the geographical indication in the long term becomes generic.[419] The broader scope of protection, therefore, has some policy justification.

CAFTA-DR does not provide for absolute protection. The EU-FTAs, on the other hand, extend absolute protection to all types of goods, which shall be protected against any use for goods which do not originate in the geographical area indicated, as further shown in Table 4.6.

---

[415] Such protection through a sui generis system was introduced in France in 1919, see Correa (2002), p. 4.

[416] WTO General Council (1999).

[417] See, e.g., USTR, Doha Development Agenda Policy Brief – Protecting Geographical Indications for Wine and Spirits, 2005, p. 1, available at https://ustr.gov/archive/assets/Document_Library/Fact_Sheets/2005/asset_upload_file850_8542.pdf (accessed 2 Nov 2024).

[418] Correa (2002), p. 12.

[419] Engelhardt (2015), p. 784.

Table 4.6 Protection of geographical indications in EU-FTAs

Article 145.B.3(b) EU-CARIFORUM-EPA	Article 246.1(b) EU-CA-AA
Any use of the protected names for goods in the same class of product as the geographical indication	The use of a protected geographical indication for the same products
Which do not originate in the geographical area indicated	That are not originating from the designated place of the geographical indication in question
Even where: (i) the true origin of the good is indicated;	Even if the true origin of the product is indicated or
(ii) the geographical indication in question is used in translation;	If the protected name is translated or
(iii) the name is accompanied by terms such as 'kind', 'type', 'style', 'imitation', 'method' or other expressions of the sort.	Accompanied by an expression such as 'style', 'type', 'imitation', 'like' or similar.

Despite the differences in the wording, both provisions have the same legal scope. In particular, they both limit protection to the same (class of) products.[420]

The protection under Article 246.1(b) EU-CA-AA is only required for Established Geographical Indications, *i.e.*, the list of geographical indications submitted by the parties. This provision, therefore, again raises issues in relation to the MFN principle of Article 4 TRIPS.[421] However, Article 4 TRIPS does not exclude granting advantages with regard to the protection of IP to other countries, as the EU-CA-AA parties did in relation to Established Geographical Indications under Article 246.1(b) EU-CA-AA, but only requires that such advantages "shall be accorded immediately and unconditionally to the nationals of all other countries". When (and to the extent) the Central American countries introduced absolute protection, it was established for all registered geographical indications. The implementation is, therefore, in compliance with Article 4 TRIPS.

Central American Legislation

The post-TRIPS legislation in most Central America did not provide for such absolute protection even for wines and spirits as required by TRIPS. Actionable were only the registration or use of other distinctive signs if they may cause confusion[422] or mislead the public.[423]

[420] The limitation of protection to a use in the "same" (class of) product is considered narrower than that, e.g., under Article 10.21(1)(b) EU-South Korea FTA, which refers to "like goods", see Engelhardt (2015), p. 810.

[421] See Sect. 4.4.4.2.

[422] In Costa Rica, Article 71 and 72 Trademark Law (CR); in Guatemala, prior to the amendment by the EU-CA-AA Reform Law (GT), Article 81 (2) IP Law (GT).

[423] In Costa Rica, Article 48 IP Enforcement Law (CR).

The two exceptions are Nicaragua and the Dominican Republic. In Nicaragua, Article 8(g) of the post-TRIPS TM Law (NI) provided that a trademark must be rejected based on third party rights "if the trademark contains a protected geographical indication [denomination of origin] *or* creates a risk of confusion or association" with such geographical indication [denomination of origin]. This alternative wording suggests that in case the trademark and geographical indication are identical, no confusion is required. Similarly, Article 77 TM Law (NI) provides that only producers operating in the respective geographical area may use the geographical indication, without requiring a likelihood of confusion. The scope of protection was not affected by the reform of the trademark regulation passed in 2012 to implement the EU-CA-AA.

Similarly, in the Dominican Republic, under Article 73(1)(j) IP Law (DR) a trademark is inadmissible if the trademark contains or imitates a protected geographical indication [denomination of origin] in relation to identical products *or* creates a risk of confusion or association in relation to similar products. This alternative wording again suggests that in case of identical products, no confusion is required and therefore the clause provides for absolute protection. Article 133 IP Law (DR) provides that only producers operating in the respective geographical area may use the geographical indication, without requiring a likelihood of confusion. These rules were not changed as part of the CAFTA-DR implementation legislation (and as noted the Dominican Republic did not pass legislation to implement the IP clauses of the CARIFORUM-EPA.

Absolute protection for all geographical indications was introduced in the legislation implementing the EU-CA-AA in Guatemala and Honduras. In Honduras, registered geographical indications may only be used for commercial purposes (i) for the products identified in the registration and (ii) by the producers operating in the geographical area indicated in the registration irrespective of confusion.[424] The legislation in Guatemala also explicitly state that the use of geographical indications is excluded "even where the true origin of the goods is indicated or the geographical indication is used in translation or accompanied by expressions such as "class", "kind", "type", "style", "imitation" or the like.[425]

Of particular interest is the legislation in El Salvador and Costa Rica, which both do not provide for absolute protection. It is worth remembering that both countries did not support the expansion of absolute protection on the international level, even though Costa Rica is a member of the Lisbon Agreement. Both countries do not grant absolute protection, even though both amended their laws in a similar way as

[424] Article 132 IP Law (HN), as amended by EU-CA-AA Reform Law (HN) in 2013.

[425] Article 87(c) IP Law (GT), as amended by the EU-CA-AA Reform Law (GT). This clause is also included in the Salvadoran legislation. However, Article 64(2) Trademark Law (SV), as amended by the EU-CA-AA Trademark Reform Law (SV), is part of the "old" section on relative protection. This raises the question whether the exclusion of the use of the geographical indication together with a translation or delocalizing term is always excluded (as suggested by the wording of Article 64(2) Trademark Law (SV)), or only then if such use does not prevent confusion, which is a requirement for the application of Article 64(1) Trademark Law (SV).

Guatemala and Honduras. However, both countries carefully avoided the inclusion of absolute protection.

In Costa Rica, the relevant clause is Article 80 Trademark Law (CR), which has not been modified by the CAFTA-DR implementation legislation (and Costa Rica did not pass legislation to implement the IP clauses of the EU-CA-AA).[426] Article 80 Trademark Law (CR)is entitled "right to use a geographical indication" and systematically placed at the location where absolute protection is regulated in other Central American laws, states that "only the authorized producers [...] may use *the term* "geographical indication" together with the respective geographical indication ". In other words, the geographical indication, as such, can also be used by third parties, unless such use infringes the relative protection of the geographical indication. This law clearly does not comply with Article 23 TRIPS and Article 246 EU-CA-AA requiring absolute protection of geographical indication. The legislation was not changes following the ratification of the EU-CA-AA.

El Salvador, like the other Central American countries, did not create absolute protection in the Trademark Law (SV) implementing TRIPS in 2002. It modified the clause establishing a requirement for users to obtain authorization from the right holder for use of a geographical indication and certain clauses regarding the registration procedure in the CAFTA-DR implementation legislation.[427] The EU-CA-AA implementation legislation also modified clauses regarding the registration procedure, but did not introduce absolute protection. The changes are limited to the process of obtaining authorization for (legitimate) users, but are silent on the scope of protection. As a consequence, the scope of protection remains limited to the relative protection against confusion granted by Article 64 Trademark Law (SV). Therefore, the new Salvadoran law also does not comply with Article 249 EU-CA-AA.

4.4.8.2 Grandfather Clause

The absolute protection established by Article 23 TRIPS also grants protection against pre-existing rights of third parties. In order to protect acquired rights (the so-called "grandfathering"), Article 24(4) TRIPS provides that members shall not be required "to prevent continued and similar use of a particular geographical indication of another Member identifying wines or spirits in connection with goods or services by any of its nationals or domiciliaries who have used that geographical indication in a continuous manner with regard to the same or related goods or services in the territory of that Member either (*a*) for at least 10 years preceding 15 April 1994 or (*b*) in good faith preceding that date".

The EU-FTAs extend absolute protection of geographical indications from wine and spirits also to all other products. Accordingly, Article 246.4. EU-CA-AA

[426] See Sect. 2.5.2.

[427] See, e.g., Article 73 Trademark Law (SV).

extends the protection of acquired rights to "geographical indications other than wines and spirit drinks", if a particular geographical indication was used "in good faith and in a continuous manner with regard to the same or related goods or services before the entry into force of the EU-CA-AA". This extension of the grandfather clause of Article 24(4) TRIPS may limit the success of the "phasing out" goal of the EU.[428] However, it must be remembered that under WTO case-law, the extension of the co-existence of trademarks and geographical indications beyond wines and spirits, and, therefore, the limitation of the prior trademark right, is only TRIPS-compliant as a limited exception to the rights of trademark owners under Article 17 TRIPS.[429] Without the grandfather clause, the trademark could no longer be used at all, which could be viewed as exceeding (and violating) Article 17 TRIPS.[430]

This broad grandfather clause was implemented by Guatemala in Article 89 IP Law (GT), as amended by the EU-CA-AA Reform Law (GT).

It was also adopted by El Salvador in Article 64(3) Trademark Law (SV), as amended by the EU-CA-AA Trademark Reform Law (SV). However, the applicability of this provision is unclear, because, as already noted, Article 64 Trademark Law (SV) does not establish absolute protection. This new clause is notable for another reason. Article 23 TRIPS and Article 246.4. EU-CA-AA provide for different dates to determine acquired rights, because each agreement refers to the respective date of entry into force of the agreement. Article 64 Trademark Law (SV) references "the date set by international agreements", because it attempts to combine both provisions. However, the clause does not clarify which date is relevant. This solution avoids any openly conflicting wording between the implementation law and the international regimes, but obviously creates legal uncertainty.

4.4.8.3 Relative Protection Against Confusion

Under TRIPS, all types of geographical indications are protected against certain misleading, deceptive or otherwise unfair activities of third parties. In these cases of

---

[428] Engelhardt (2015), p. 811.

[429] WTO Dispute Settlement Body, Decision WT/DS174/R, European Communities — Protection of Trademarks and Geographical Indications for Agricultural Products and Foodstuffs (2005) (complaint by the USA), WTO Dispute Settlement Body, Decision WT/DS290/R, European Communities — Protection of Trademarks and Geographical Indications for Agricultural Products and Foodstuffs (2005) (complaint by Australia).

[430] Article 246.4 EU-CA-AA is in contrast to Annex V, Article 7(2) EU-Chile-AA, that provides that certain Chilean trademarks conflicting with European geographical indications shall be cancelled within 12 years (after the conclusion of the FTA) for use on the internal market and five years for use for export from the date of entry into force of this Agreement. Appendix VI contains a list of Chilean trademarks relating to wine and champagne, such as "Baden", "Champagne Rabat", "La Rioja" and "Oro del Rhin" (Rhinegold). It must be noted that this "phase out" of domestic trademarks is not in line with the official EU policy of "co-existence with prior trademarks" (see Sect. 4.4.10). Also, this "European" approach is contrary to the US-approach of giving exclusivity to prior trademarks, as expressed by CAFTA-DR (see Sect. 4.4.10).

relative protection, the burden of proof with regard to the deceptive or misleading effect is placed on the producer, which can be difficult and costly.[431] Such activities are:

- the use of any means in the designation or presentation of a good that indicates or suggests that the good in question originates in a geographical area other than the true place of origin in a manner which misleads the public as to the geographical origin of the good;[432]
- use which constitutes an act of unfair competition within the meaning of Article 10*bis* of the Paris Convention (1967);[433]
- registration of a misleading trademark;
- use of a deceptive geographical indication, *i.e.*, a geographical indication which, although literally true as to the territory, region or locality in which the goods originate, falsely represents to the public that the goods originate in another territory.[434]

CAFTA-DR does not contain provisions relating to the scope of protection of geographical indications, but addresses primarily procedural aspects and the relationship between trademarks and geographical indications. The EU-FTAs restate Article 22.2(a) and (b) TRIPS.[435] In addition, the EU-CA-AA requires protection of geographical indications against "any other practice that misleads the consumer as to the true origin of the product".[436]

Such relative protection is granted under all Central American laws. The laws typically differentiate between the use of a geographical indication which is misleading regarding the geographic origin of the product and the use which may cause confusion regarding the geographic origin, quality or other characteristics of the product.[437]

4.4.8.4 Right to Use

Some jurisdictions can require users of geographical indication to become a member of an entity or to obtain a license for making use of the geographical indication or to apply for authorization by a government agency or a producer association, which could make the use significantly more cumbersome. One policy objective of the EU,

[431] Correa (2002), p. 31; Engelhardt (2015), p. 784.

[432] Article 22.2(a) TRIPS.

[433] Article 22.2(b) TRIPS.

[434] Article 22(4) TRIPS.

[435] Article 145.B.3(a) and (b) EU-CARIFORUM-EPA and Article 246.1(a) and (c)(second part) EU-CA-AA.

[436] Article 246.1(a) and (c)(first part) EU-CA-AA.

[437] E.g., Article 71 Trademark Law (CR); Article 64(1) Trademark Law (SV), as amended by the EU-CA-AA Trademark Reform Law (SV).

therefore, is to avoid such obligations.[438] Accordingly, Article 244.2(e) EU-CA-AA mandates "a right for any operator established in the area and who submits to the system of controls to use the protected name" and Article 249 EU-CA-AA provides that "the use of [a protected geographical indication] shall not be subject to any registration of users".

Most Central American laws do not require the users of geographical indications to obtain authorization from the right holder.[439] Only El Salvador requires an authorization from the right holder for use of a geographical indication.[440]

In addition, geographical indications can be used by those and only those persons or entities selling products with the respective specifications, because they indicate properties of the product and not the producer. Therefore, they cannot be licensed to a third party not meeting the specifications.[441]

4.4.9 Practical Relevance

In Central America, geographical indications have traditionally been perceived to be of interest mainly for foreign producers, but of little relevance for local businesses.[442] Often commodity products (coffee, cocoa, bananas etc.) were exported and a foreign trademark was used. For example, Central American coffee was advertised and sold in Germany using not the country (or region) of origin as an identifier, but the name of the importing coffee company. This has been an obstacle for the requirement of stronger protection for geographical indications in the EU-FTAs concluded by Central America and may have been the reason why some countries, particularly Costa Rica and El Salvador, were traditionally restrictive regarding geographical indications.[443]

However, the situation has changed. The prominent conflict between Peru and Chile regarding the brandy "Pisco" has been noted also by practitioners in Central America.[444] The success of the Colombian designation "Café de Colombia" was of

---

[438] Engelhardt (2015), p. 787.

[439] E.g., Article 79(4) IP Law (GT), as amended by the EU-CA-AA Reform Law (GT).

[440] Article 73 Trademark Law (SV); as noted above in Sect. 4.4.8.1, this clause does not comply with Article 249 EU-CA-AA.

[441] This is explicitly stated by Article 79(4) IP Law (GT), as amended by the EU-CA-AA Reform Law (GT).

[442] As Teuber (2010), Table 1, shows, as of August 2007 Colombia and Jamaica had registered geographical indications for coffee, but no Central American country, despite the relevance of this product for several Central American economies.

[443] This is not only shown by their restrictive legislation (see Sect. 4.4.8.2), but also by their slower registration of European geographical indication applications, see Consortium Centro América Abogados (2013).

[444] In this case, the geographical indication "Pisco" was registered as appellation of origin no. 865 by WIPO on 19 May 2005 for the state of Peru, but was also claimed by Chile. The

particular interest in Central America, because it was probably the first major project to protect and market coffee based on the geographic origin and related to one of the main export commodity products of Central America. At first, the Colombian coffee producers had relied on trademarks (including certification marks) for protection. In 2004, they decided to also apply for the registration of the term as a geographical indication, first in Colombia itself and subsequently in the European Union, where in September 2007 it became the first non-EU geographical indication to be registered.[445] It is generally assumed that geographical indications allows the producers to charge a premium above the average market price. While there is little economic research on the economics of single-origin coffee, the existing data and analysis strongly support this assumption.[446]

It is, therefore, not surprising that the coffee associations spearheaded initiatives to register domestic geographical indications in Central America. This is clearly demonstrated by the fact that 5 of the 10 geographical indications from Central America included in the list of Established Geographical Indications in Annex XVII EU-CA-AA designate coffee regions.

In Costa Rica, the national coffee association initiated the registration of geographical indications early on, as exemplified by the list of potential Costa Rican geographical indications included in the FTA concluded between Costa Rica and China in April 2010, which encompasses seven coffee regions plus the general term "Café de Costa Rica", and only two other geographical indications.[447] Only the general term "Café de Costa Rica" was included in the EU-CA-AA .[448] Costa Rica is the only Central American country to have applied for a geographical indication under the Lisbon System administered by WIPO. The country has applied for protection of "Banano de Costa Rica" on 1 August 2011.[449] Despite the previous efforts regarding coffee designations, the only geographical indication included in

conflict was resolved by the distinction between the terms "Pisco" for brandy from Peru and "Pisco Chileno" for brandy from Chile in the USA (see Article 3.15 of the US-Chile-FTA, where "Pisco Chileno" is protected as a "distinctive product", on this type of distinctive sign see Sect. 4.7) and the co-use of the designation "Pisco" for brandy from Peru and Chile in the European Union (see Regulation (EU) 2016/1067 of 1 July 2016 amending Annex III to Regulation (EC) No 110/2008 on the definition, description, presentation, labelling and the protection of geographical indications of spirit drinks).

[445] WIPO (2007), available at http://www.wipo.int/wipo_magazine/en/2007/05/article_0001.html (accessed 2 Nov 2024).

[446] Teuber (2010), pp. 277–298.

[447] The ten geographical indications are: Banano de Costa Rica, Café de Costa Rica, Guanacaste Madera (i.e., wood), Orosi (café), Tres Ríos (café), Turrialba (café), West Valley (café), Brunca (café), Central Valley (café) and Guanacaste (café), see Costa Rica-China-FTA, Annex 10.

[448] See Decision No 5/2014 OF THE EU-CENTRAL AMERICA ASSOCIATION COUNCIL of 7 November 2014 on the geographical indications to be included in Annex XVIII of the Agreement, available at https://eur-lex.europa.eu/legal-content/EN/TXT/PDF/?uri=CELEX:22015D1219 (accessed 2 Nov 2024).

[449] See the report by WIPO, https://www.wipo.int/wipo_magazine/en/ip-at-work/2021/banano.html (accessed 2 Nov 2024).

the list in Annex XVII EU-CA-AA was "Banano de Costa Rica". In November 2012, a local geographical indication was registered for "Turrialba" cheese.[450] However, by this time the list in Annex XVII EU-CA-AA had already been completed, which could explain why this geographical indication was not included.

In the Dominican Republic, there were six registered geographical indications in June 2007.[451]

For a long time, the only geographical indication in El Salvador has been "Balsamo de Salvador", established in 1935 by Decree 162-1935.[452] The pilot project for another domestic geographical indication was initiated by the national coffee association "Procafe".[453] As a result of this initiative, "Café Apaneca-Ilamapetec" was included in the list in Annex XVII EU-CA-AA together with "Balsamo de Salvador". Previously, geographical indications could not be registered by the IP Register because the procedural provisions were overly restrictive in practice. However, the EU-CA-AA Trademark Reform Law (SV) was expected to facilitate the registration of geographical indications for a broader range of products, and thereby also provide the basis for registrations abroad, an expectation that seems to some extent justified by the application in 2021 for protection in the Europen Union of six additional geographical indications from El Salvador.[454]

The fact that the famous Guatemalan "Café de Antigua" has been registered in the USA by a foreign company may also have underlined the necessity to actively build a portfolio of exclusive rights, even though the US trademark has meanwhile been abandoned.[455] Accordingly, "Café de Antigua" has become the pilot project for a domestic geographical indication in Guatemala.[456] As a practical matter it is interesting to note that in Guatemala not the entire country is covered by one geographical indication for coffee, as Colombia with "Café de Colombia", but that eight special regions are designated with distinct designations. Because of this focus, each coffee has distinct properties and there are fewer producers, which makes the administration easier to handle.[457] Of these regions, "Café Antigua" (probably the

---

[450] See reports available at http://www.centralamericadata.com/en/article/home/Designation_of_Origin_in_Costa_Rica (accessed 2 Nov 2024) and El Financiero (2019).

[451] O'Connor and Company (2007), pp. 380–381.

[452] The text of the law is available at https://www.wipo.int/edocs/lexdocs/laws/es/sv/sv007es.pdf (accessed 2 Nov 2024); similar requirements are stipulated by earlier legislation, see the Law regarding the use and registration of coffee and balm, available at www.wipo.int/wipolex/es/details.jsp?id=3764 (accessed 2 Nov 2024).

[453] Interview with *Diana Hasbún*.

[454] See the report from September 2021 by the Salvadorean ministr of Agriculture, available at https://www.mag.gob.sv/2021/09/25/cafe-de-el-salvador-aumentara-su-comercializacion-en-la-union-europea/ (accessed 2 Nov 2024).

[455] The trademark "CAFE ANTIGUA FRESH BREWED COFFEE", No. 76636078, has been filed on 15 April 2005 and abandoned on 21 May 2006, according to the USPTO online database TESS (accessed 2 Nov 2024).

[456] UNCTAD (2014), p. 139.

[457] Interview with *Ninoshka Urrutia*.

most famous region) was the first geographical indication granted in Guatemala, on 28 October 2011[458] and the only geographical indication for coffee of Guatemala included in Annex XVII EU-CA-AA. The other Guatemalan geographical indication in Annex XVII EU-CA-AA is "Ron de Guatemala".

In Honduras, the first geographical indication registered, "Café de Marcala", also relates to coffee.[459] Together with this geographical indication, "Cafés del Occidente Hondureño" was included in the list in Annex XVII EU-CA-AA.

In Nicaragua, protection for the geographical indication "Queso Chontaleño" cheese was granted in 2003.[460] It was included in the list of geographical indication in Annex XVII EU-CA-AA together with "Café de Nicaragua".

Prior to the EU-CA-AA, no Central American country has applied for or obtained protection for a geographical indication in the European Union, according to the "DOOR" database of the European Commission. Since then, two Central American geographical indication were registered in the EU, "Café de Valdesia"[461] of the Dominican Republic in 2014 and "Ron de Guatemala" in 2016,[462] in addition to the geographical indication protected directly under the EU-CA-AA.

4.4.10 Evaluation

4.4.10.1 Protection of Geographical Indications as Such

The active use of geographical indications could be beneficial for Central America, because it enables producers to charge an additional quality premium price, especially for agricultural products, beverages and foodstuff, which are the basis of the Central American economy. The practical cases, namely the coffee projects, underline that the system has become appealing to local producers. The higher prices that can be obtained on the market create higher incomes and enable the population to remain in rural areas.[463] It is estimated that in the USA and in Europe consumers pay between 10% and 30% more for authentic products, which corresponds to the observations made in relation to "Café de Colombia".[464]

---

[458] Case / registration No. 2006-01485, available at https://asipi.org/wp-content/uploads/2018/09/CAFE-ANTIGUA-RESOLUCION.pdf (accessed 2 Nov 2024).

[459] Paz Cafferata and Pomareda (2009), p. 10.

[460] Ayala Durán and Radomsky (2020), Table 1.

[461] See "GIView" database of the European Commission, available at https://www.tmdn.org/giview/gi/search (accessed 2 Nov 2024).

[462] See Regulation (EU) 2016/1067 of 1 July 2016 amending Annex III to Regulation (EC) No 110/2008 on the definition, description, presentation, labelling and the protection of geographical indications of spirit drinks.

[463] Correa (2002), p. 16.

[464] Correa (2002), p. 18, citing Vital, Protection of Geographic Indications (1999), p. 52.

While domestic producers from Central America have, therefore, much to gain in Europe, the corresponding benefit for foreign producers will probably not be significant. While some commentators are concerned about increased domestic activities based on foreign geographical indications,[465] one may also consider that the purchasing power in Central America is low and people may be more price-sensitive and less willing to pay an authenticity premium.

Geographical indications can also protect *manufactured* products.[466] This may include products based on traditional growth and production methods. In connection with the indication and protection of the geographical component, such protection could in the long term be an opportunity to support biodiversity and traditional knowledge.

The system of collective rights for geographical indications also has specific procedural advantages. The registration process can (or must) be managed by professional associations, which integrate the collective interests of small and local businesses and help balance the strong position of large international competitors. In addition, the enforcement costs are distributed among the participating producers, which on their own might be deterred from enforcement abroad. Protection and enforcement abroad is especially important, because the US and European markets promise high premiums and, therefore, the exclusion of foreign geographical indications from these markets by local trademarks—as was the case in the USA regarding a Starbucks trademark for "Sidamo" coffee from Ethiopia—should be avoided.[467] In order to achieve this, the generation and use of geographical indications and the registration in the domestic markets are necessary first steps.

Some criticism addresses more specific issues of the current system. For example, the maintenance of the system and the quality control are costly.[468] To alleviate these costs, public funding of the system has been proposed.[469]

4.4.10.2 Absolute Protection and Established Geographical Indications

The abovementioned potential benefits of geographical indications for local businesses in Central America, however, do not necessarily require a system of protection as mandated by the EU-FTAs. Especially the extension of absolute protection to all classes of goods is controversial.

In Article 24(1) TRIPS, the members "agree to enter into negotiations aimed at increasing the [absolute] protection of *individual* geographical indications under Article 23. The provisions [...] below shall not be used by a Member to refuse to conduct negotiations or to conclude *bilateral* or multilateral agreements" (emphasis

[465] Correa (2002), p. 22.

[466] Interview with *Gabriela Contreras Aguilera*.

[467] Heath and Marie-Vivien (2015), p. 826.

[468] Correa (2002), p. 22.

[469] Correa (2002), p. 37.

added). Article 24(1) TRIPS could be seen as supporting the EU approach of negotiating and entering into bilateral FTAs to strengthen the protection of geographical indications and in particular the inclusion of lists of Established Geographical Indications. This approach specifically enhances the protection of individual geographical indications.[470] However, this view is based on the understanding that Article 24(1) TRIPS relates to a stronger absolute level of protection, not stronger protection of wines and spirits.[471]

However, the Central American example shows the problems created by expanding absolute protection. Looking at CAFTA-DR and the EU-FTAs, it seems that any further expansion of absolute protection of geographical indications will encroach upon the protection already established for trademarks. The implementation of the FTAs in Central America shows the difficulties in balancing the respective requirements. Costa Rica and El Salvador chose to omit absolute protection altogether.[472]

The mechanism of Established Geographical Indications appears as the acknowledgement by the EU that further "gains" in protection are increasingly difficult to achieve on the local statutory level and therefore, geographical indications need to be strengthened in relation to trademarks on the administrative level, as discussed in the following subsection.

4.4.10.3 Relationship Between Trademarks and Geographical Indications

CAFTA-DR and the EU-FTAs try to develop the protection of geographical indications established by TRIPS into different directions.[473] This issue concerns, in particular, the co-existence of geographical indications and trademarks. CAFTA-DR determines protection based on the "first in time, first in right" principle. In contrast to TRIPS and the EU-FTAs, CAFTA-DR does not foresee the co-existence of any posterior geographical indication but requires exclusivity for the prior trademark. This pre-empts the approach pursued by the EU of a "co-existence of geographical indications with prior trademarks".[474] The principle of co-existence is recognized under WTO case-law, which found that the registration of a geographical indication is possible even when it conflicts with a prior trademark, because it was sufficiently

---

[470] Engelhardt (2015), p. 793.

[471] Ibid.

[472] See Sect. 4.4.8.1.

[473] This conflict is discussed in detail also by Handler and Mercurio (2015), in particular pp. 332–343.

[474] This principle is discussed, e.g., by Curzi and Huysmans (2021), p. 368.

constrained to qualify as a "limited exception" to trademark rights according to Article 17 TRIPS.[475]

This conflict could not be resolved by the USA and the EU on the multilateral level and has been transferred to third countries through bilateral FTAs, *e.g.*, CAFTA-DR and the EU-FTAs. The combination of restrictive rules in CAFTA-DR and expansive rules in the EU-CARIFORUM-EPA and EU-CA-AA regarding geographical indications significantly reduces the remaining policy space left to Central America. As the analysis in this section has shown, the Central American countries were not able to establish a system of protection of geographical indications that fully complies with TRIPS, CAFTA-DR and the EU-FTAs.

There exist a number of brands and products protected by trademarks in the USA and third countries identical or similar to European geographical indications. Any legal system must find a solution with regard to these cases. The classic example is the case of "Budweiser" beer, protected by a US company in the USA and other countries, and for beer from the Czech town of *Budweis* in Europe. In Nicaragua, the conflict was resolved in favor of the US company, and the application for the Czech geographical indication was rejected.[476] Another example in Central America for this issue is the *Bavaria* beer in Costa Rica. While it of course evokes an association with the quality and fame of beer from Bavaria, it nevertheless clearly communicates its Costa Rican origin, *e.g.*, in advertising, and, therefore, minimizes the practical likelihood of confusion with Bavarian beers.[477] So far, there has been no dispute between Bavaria's trademark and the European geographical indication. A final example in Central America is "Mozzarella Cheese", registered in Costa Rica as a trademark by the Dos Pinos Dairy Producers Cooperative.[478]

But this issue not only arises in relation to European geographical indications in Central America, but also in relation to Central American geographical indications abroad. For example, the prototype geographical indications in Guatemala, "Café de Antigua", has already (at least temporarily) been protected in the USA by the trademark of a US company.[479] In combination with the exclusion of geographical indications from use under fair use rules for descriptive terms, this trademark

[475] WTO Dispute Settlement Body, Decision WT/DS174/R, European Communities — Protection of Trademarks and Geographical Indications for Agricultural Products and Foodstuffs (2005) (complaint by the USA), WTO Dispute Settlement Body, Decision WT/DS290/R, European Communities — Protection of Trademarks and Geographical Indications for Agricultural Products and Foodstuffs (2005) (complaint by Australia); regarding these disputes Curzi and Huysmans (2021), p. 368.

[476] Interview with *Ricardo Bendaña.*

[477] See the advertisement of the beer on the company's website https://bavaria.cr/inicio/ (accessed 2 Nov 2024).

[478] Instituto Interamericano de Cooperación para la Agricultura, Progress in Latin America in the application of geographical indications and appellations of origin, Technical Bulletin July 2011, available at http://repositorio.iica.int/bitstream/11324/4137/2/BVE17089198i.pdf (accessed 2 Nov 2024).

[479] See Sect. 4.4.9.

prevented the Guatemalan producers from selling their coffee under this geographical indication.

The solution pursued by the EU is to "remove prior trademarks conflicting with geographical indications", *i.e.*, "phase out" such trademarks.[480] However, this approach faces statutory restrictions due to the common "first to file" approach and challenges involved in the registration of individual geographical indications in third countries. To avoid these issues, the EU included in bilateral FTAs such as the EU-CA-AA the protection of a list of "Established Geographical Indications" attached to the agreement which have to be protected irrespective of possibly prior trademarks. Article 145.E EU-CARIFORUM-EPA does not include such a list, but foresees further negotiations between the parties in relation to geographical indications, similar to Article 24(1) TRIPS. As the registration of the European geographical indications in Central America shows, this approach has been quite successful from an EU perspective, but put significant pressure on the Central American countries to quickly adapt their statutory framework and more importantly ensure that the IP Registers "fast track" the registration.

The USTR has repeatedly expressed concern regarding the possible negative effects of the protection of geographical indications on US businesses.[481] However, two years after the registration of the European geographical indications, the US Department of State (USDOS) observed no adverse effects on US businesses because of the implementation of geographical indication obligations under the EU-CA-AA.[482]

4.5 Brands

A particular and very region-specific element of the Central American system of distinctive signs is the protection of *brands*. Brands (*marcas de ganado*) protect marks of cattle ranchers burned on the skin of cattle, *i.e.*, serve as brands in the original sense of cattle markings. These brands are of great practical relevance in the region, because of the large cattle industry and several thousand of these brands are registered at the IP Registers in the region.

However, brands are only analyzed briefly here, because this type of distinctive sign is not governed by CAFTA-DR and does not create significant legal issues relating to other distinctive signs, in particular those covered by bilateral FTAs. By way of example, this section briefly describes the protection in Costa Rica.

---

480 Engelhardt (2015), p. 793.

481 See, e.g., USTR Special 301 Report (2015), p. 69.

482 USDOS, Nicaragua Investment Climate Statement 2015, May 2015, available at https://2009-2017.state.gov/documents/organization/241895.pdf (accessed 2 Nov 2024).

Costa Rica protects brands in a specific "Brand Law"[483] and established a Brand Office (*Oficina de Marcas de Ganado*) to process brand applications, which is part of the IP Register.[484] The IP Register provides application forms which are distinct from the forms for other trademarks.[485] As of 2006 (the last year for which such specific information could be obtained), four employees out of a total of 35 employees of the IP Register worked in the Brand Office, one more than in the patent department (three employees).[486] These numbers do not fully reflect the workload of the respective departments, because Costa Rica (in particular at that time) used external examiners for patent examinations. They nevertheless underline the practical relevance of these brands.

4.6 Slogans

4.6.1 Introduction

In Central America, slogans (*expresiones o señales de publicidad*) receive protection as *special distinctive signs*.[487] In Guatemala, for example, slogans and trademarks are mutually exclusive, but complementary.[488] Practically the slogan protection has two advantages compared to trademark protection. It is indefinite without the requirement of renewal and in some countries it is also cheaper.[489]

Regarding the applicable substantive and procedural law applicable to slogans, Central American laws generally refer to the trademark provisions.[490] Only in Nicaragua, Article 57 Trademark Law (NI) explicitly refers to Chapter II Trademark Law (NI) regarding just trademark subject matter. However, given that the section on slogans does not contain any special provisions regarding rights conferred to the

[483] Ley de Marcas de Ganado, Ley No. 2247, adopted on 7 August 1958, entered into force on 1 January 1959.

[484] Article 1 Brand Law (CR), the text of the law is available at http://www.rnpdigital.com/propiedad_industrial/documentos/pi_normativa/leyes/Ley%20de%20Marcas%20de%20Ganado.pdf (accessed 2 Nov 2024); Registro de la Propiedad Industrial de Costa Rica (2006), p. 21.

[485] These forms are available at http://www.registronacional.go.cr/propiedad_industrial/propiedad_industrial_guia_servicios_formularios.htm (accessed 2 Nov 2024).

[486] Registro de la Propiedad Industrial de Costa Rica (2006), p. 22.

[487] See, e.g., Article 68 IP Law (GT).

[488] The CSJ (GT) held in its decision from 7 December 2001 that the description of a coffee as "the smoothest American" ("el Americano más suave") was not a trademark and thus had to be protected as a slogan.

[489] For example, in El Salvador, for trademark protection a renewal fee of USD 100 must be paid every ten years, for slogan protection only a one-time registration fee of USD 75, interview with *Diana Hasbún*.

[490] Article 61 Trademark Law (CR), Article 52 Trademark Law (SV), Article 68 IP Law (GT), Article 57 Trademark Law (NI).

right holder or the registration procedure, other trademark provisions should apply by analogy.[491]

4.6.2 Subject Matter and Requirements

The *subject matter* of slogans is provided for by their respective legal definition[492] and includes explanations (*leyendas*), announcements, mottos, phrases, combination of words, images and engravings. The subject matter has to be categorized on a case-by-case basis, because there is no statutory differentiation from trademarks and no definition of slogans.[493] In correspondence with the distinctiveness requirement of trademarks, a slogan has to be original or characteristic.[494]

The absolute *statutory bars* of trademarks apply also for slogans.[495] Relative bars against the registration of slogans are namely the similarity to other protected slogans and trademarks,[496] the susceptibility to cause confusion[497] and the constitution of unfair competition.[498]

Moreover, slogans are only protected in their entirety, not in their elements, if considered separately.[499] This limitation seems logical as far as the individual words or combinations of words of the slogan are not distinctive, because these should belong to the public domain.

4.6.3 Procedure

The rules of trademark law apply for the registration procedure of slogans as well.[500]

[491] It is also possible that this limitation is simply due to the direct transfer of the provision from a prior version of the text or a foreign law, in which the law was structured differently; in El Salvador for example, Chapter II Trademark Law (SV) covers the entire trademark law.

[492] E.g., Article 2 Trademark Law (CR); Article 4 IP Law (GT).

[493] CSJ (GT), Decision from 7 December 2001.

[494] E.g., Article 2 Trademark Law (CR) and Article 4 IP Law (GT); the decision of the Guatemalan CSJ from 9 November 1993 considered the slogan "the proper nutrition for the new generation" ("la adequada alimentación para la nueva generación") to be distinctive.

[495] Article 62 (a) Trademark Law (CR), Article 53 (a) Trademark Law (SV), Article 69 (a) IP Law (GT), Article 58 (a) Trademark Law (NI).

[496] Article 62 (b), (c) and (e) Trademark Law (CR), Article 53 (c) and (d) Trademark Law (SV), Article 69 (b) and (c) IP Law (GT), Article 58 (b) and (c) Trademark Law (NI).

[497] Article 62 (d) Trademark Law (CR), Article 53 (b) Trademark Law (SV), Article 69 (d) IP Law (GT), Article 58 (d) Trademark Law (NI).

[498] Article 62 (f) Trademark Law (CR), Article 58 (e) Trademark Law (NI).

[499] Article 63 (1) Trademark Law (CR), Article 54 (1) Trademark Law (SV), Article 70 IP Law (GT); Article 59 (1) Trademark Law (NI).

[500] Article 61 Trademark Law (CR), Article 68 IP Law (GT).

4.6.4 *Term of Protection*

Like trademarks, slogans can be protected indefinitely.[501] However, with regard to the renovation of the registration, Nicaraguan law provides that the indefinite protection of the slogan depends on the trademark or trade name it refers to.[502] *I. e.*, the law distinguishes between slogans connected to a product protected by a trademark and slogans connected to the business itself and its trade name.

4.7 Distinctive Products

"Distinctive products" are protected by a special right regulated by CAFTA-DR, which applies to only two distinctive signs and which exists only in certain US-FTAs. The right falls outside of the usual categories of IP protection and it requires separate consideration.

4.7.1 *Introduction*

Under CAFTA-DR, "[t]he Parties shall not permit the sale of any product as Bourbon Whiskey or Tennessee Whiskey, unless it has been manufactured in the United States in accordance with the laws and regulations of the United States governing the manufacture of Bourbon Whiskey and Tennessee Whiskey."[503] This clause establishes a special kind of distinctive right. This protection of "Bourbon Whiskey" and "Tennessee Whiskey", which is Bourbon Whiskey produced in the State of Tennessee, as "distinctive products" of the United States is included in Chapter 3 (National Treatment and Market Access for Goods), Article E ("Other Measures"). Despite the title, the section only contains the provisions on distinctive products. The systematic position of this provision is surprising. It appears in Article 3 CAFTA-DR, which deals with trade in goods, not in Article 15 CAFTA-DR, which contains the provisions on IP (including, *e.g.*, geographical indications, which represent a comparable concept). However, the reason for this location was probably not to hide the provision, but the historical origin of it. The first FTA to provide for the protection of distinctive products was NAFTA, where it was included in an annex to the chapter on commerce. The respective provisions have remained in the

---

[501] Article 63 (2) Trademark Law (CR), Article 54 (3) Trademark Law (SV), Articles 68 with 31 IP Law (GT), Article 59 (2) Trademark Law (NI).

[502] Article 59(2) Trademark Law (NI).

[503] Article 3.12(1) CAFTA-DR.

commerce sections in subsequent FTAs, including CAFTA-DR, despite its systematic connection with IP rights.[504]

4.7.2 *Subject Matter*

The subject matter of distinctive products is similar to that of geographical indications or collective marks, because it protects distinctive signs relating to products with are associated with a certain region. Like geographical indications, distinctive products do not have to contain a literal geographical reference as long as the name is generally associated with one region, in this case Bourbon Whiskey or Tennessee Whiskey from the USA.

4.7.3 *Procedure*

There are two important procedural differences between distinctive products and geographical indications:

The distinctive products are protected directly under CAFTA-DR and no *registration* of these rights is foreseen as a requirement for protection. Nevertheless, registration as, *e.g.*, a geographical indication or collective mark might be helpful in judicial proceedings to prove such protection and not to rely on the direct application of the international agreement.

Also, no formal *regulations* are foreseen for the use of distinctive products, which are one condition for the protection of geographical indications and collective marks. These differences give the companies selling such distinctive products a stronger legal position than that of companies using geographical indications or collective marks.

4.7.4 *Practical Relevance*

In CAFTA-DR, the only protected distinctive products are from the USA, there are no corresponding distinctive products from Central America. This is notable, because earlier FTAs included distinctive products from all parties. NAFTA included products from Canada and Mexico. The US-Chile-FTA includes also

[504]The protection of distinctive products is also regulated outside the IP chapter in the KORUS FTA. Under Article 2.13.2 KORUS Agreement, the USA is required to protect "Andong Soju" and "Gyeongju Beopju" as distinctive products of Korea, and under Article 2.13.2 Korea is required to protect "Bourbon Whiskey" and "Tennessee Whiskey" as "distinctive products" of the United States.

Chilean products.[505] The absence of Central American products in CAFTA-DR is probably not due to the weaker negotiating power of the Central American countries, but the fact that the region had, at the time of negotiation, not yet fully developed brands for distinctive local products. The Guatemalan coffee producers only subsequently developed a portfolio of trademarks and geographical indications.[506]

The only exception at the time was the already known "Café de Antigua" from Guatemala, but this name had been registered as a trademark in the USA for a US company at the time CAFTA-DR was negotiated and the inclusion in CAFTA-DR would, therefore, have conflicted with existing trademark rights.[507]

4.7.5 Evaluation

The protection of distinctive products is noteworthy, because the protection and, even more, its implementation in national law is similar to the approach used by the EU regarding the absolute protection of geographical indications, which has been strongly opposed by the USA. In particular, distinctive products must be protected and enforced irrespective of existing local trademark or other rights and are not limited if the protected distinctive sign has become generic. The use of the concept of distinctive products suggests that the opposition of the USA against geographical indications is based less on legal considerations regarding the balance of IP law and more on business interests.

The strong interest of the USA in establishing special protection for "Bourbon Whiskey" is shown by the fact that the USA started to conclude special agreements providing for its protection with third countries outside of the system of bilateral FTAs. For example, on 9 April 2012, the USA and Brazil concluded an agreement which requires Brazil to grant distinctive product protection to Bourbon Whiskey and Tennessee Whiskey and the USA to grant distinctive product protection to the Brazilian sugarcane spirit *cachaça*.[508]

However, from a legal perspective, this approach is problematic. In support of it, one could argue that Article 24 TRIPS envisions negotiations aimed at increasing the [absolute] protection of individual geographical indications in bilateral or multilateral agreements[509] and that distinctive products have a different name, but a similar legal effect as geographical indications. But the creation of yet another category of protection could further complicate the development of a balanced system of

[505] Article 3.15(2) US-Chile-FTA.

[506] See Sect. 4.3.

[507] See Sect. 4.4.9.

[508] Distinctive Products Agreement effected by exchange of letters at Washington, on 9 April 2012, available at https://www.state.gov/wp-content/uploads/2019/02/12-409-Brazil-Trade-Distinc-Products-Letters.pdf (accessed 2 Nov 2024).

[509] See Sect. 4.4.10.

distinctive sign regulation on a global level. The distinctive products category is now implemented in—and for products of—the USA and countries with which the USA concluded bilateral FTAs and granted reciprocal protection for distinctive products, including Brazil. The more this category spreads in terms of countries and products covered, the more difficult it could be to balance it with other categories of protective rights.

4.8 Domain Names and Trademark Protection

After TRIPS, the issue of trademark infringements on the internet, especially through the registration of domain names (cyber-squatting) has become an important issue for right holders and has been addressed on the international and national level.

4.8.1 Procedure

4.8.1.1 Registration of a Domain Name

Traditionally, the prevention of cyber-squatting based on trademark protection has been difficult.[510] Article 15.4 CAFTA-DR does not contain substantive rules regarding the protection of trademarks against cyber-squatting, but the WIPO Joint Recommendation Concerning the Protection of Marks on the Internet provides some substantive guidance: The registration of a conflicting domain name as such does not constitute *use in commerce*.[511] Therefore, it is argued that the registration of a domain name cannot constitute a trademark infringement.[512] On the other hand, many countries permit already the refusal of the registration of conflicting trademarks, and correspondingly the registration of such domain names could be rejected as well. In addition, it seems impractical to register a domain name which could not legally be used.

Guatemala provides for the cancellation of a domain name registrations conflicting with well-known marks only if it has been obtained in bad faith.[513] This provision is potentially highly relevant, because in Guatemala cyber-squatting

[510] Beebe, Barton / Cotter, Thomas / Lemley, Mark / Menell, Peter / Merges, Robert, Trademarks, Unfair Competition, and Business Torts (2016), pp. 276–303, provide a detailed account of the development under US law.

[511] Article 2 of the WIPO Joint Recommendation Concerning the Protection of Marks on the Internet states that use on the Internet constitutes use in commerce relevant for trademark law, but registration with the respective authority does not amount to use on the Internet.

[512] Cornish et al. (2013) at 18-85.

[513] Article 35(h) IP Law (GT).

has been a problem for brands, as local businesses registered well-known international (*Heineken, Corona beer*)[514] and national (*Pollo Campero*)[515] trademarks.

In Nicaragua the right holder can also claim the cancellation of registrations of domain names and e-mail addresses which have been obtained in good faith, if they conflict with well-known marks. However, this claim is barred five years after the registration or use in electronic media of the respective domain name or e-mail address, whichever is the later.[516]

4.8.1.2 Other Procedural Issues

According to Article 15.4(2) CAFTA-DR, the managing entity of a country's top level domains (ccTLD) shall provide online public access to a reliable and accurate database of contact information for domain name registrants. The provision that "in determining the appropriate contact information, the management of a Party's ccTLD *may* give due regard to the Party's laws protecting the privacy of its nationals" is surprising. First, data privacy laws are typically mandatory and the parties, therefore, have no discretion whether to apply them. This sentence seems, therefore, to be simply a clarification without specific legal consequences. Second, such a clause is unusual for US-FTAs, because it provides protection for domestic citizens in the FTA partner county of the USA. These might have been reasons why the provision was not used again in subsequent FTAs concluded by the USA.[517]

Also, the parties shall provide dispute resolution procedures based on the *Uniform Domain-Name Dispute-Resolution Policy* (UDRP). The UDRP was established by the Internet Corporation for Assigned Names and Numbers (ICANN) and creates a procedure for the resolution of disputes regarding the registration of internet domain names, but also substantive rules for these disputes.[518]

---

[514] Interview with *Gabriela Contreras Aguilera*.

[515] The large Guatemalan fast-food chain "Pollo Campero" filed a complaint against Jordan Data Communication Services Company regarding the registration of the domain "cambolero.com" with the WIPO Arbitration and Mediation Center on 29 December 2004. On 31 March 2005, the WIPO Arbitration and Mediation Center decided that the "Pollo Campero" group had the rights to the trademark "campero" because of the longstanding use and registration of the trademark in various countries, and that the term "cambolero" was confusingly similar; WIPO Arbitration and Mediation Center, Administrative Panel Decision, Campero International, Corp., Campero International Limited, Campero International, S.A., Campero USA Corp., Pollo Campero, S.A., Pollo Campero, S.A. de C.V., Pollo Campero de Honduras, S.A. de C.V. v. Jordan Data Communication Services Company, Case No. D2004-1105, available at https://www.wipo.int/amc/en/domains/decisions/html/2004/d2004-1105.html (accessed 2 Nov 2024).

[516] Article 85 Trademark Law (NI); technically, domains and e-mails can only be used after their registration. But use can precede registration, for example, if references to it are made, e.g., on an existing website.

[517] E.g., Article 16.4(2) US-Peru-TPA.

[518] See Voegeli-Wenzel (2007), p. 807; Voegeli (2006).

In Central America, as exemplified by Guatemala, Costa Rica and Nicaragua, the entity responsible for the administration of the domains under the respective country's top level domain (ccTLD) is typically a university.[519] They maintain standard WHOIS databases, providing at least the following information: domain name, name of the applicant, name and contact information of the domain administrator. The dispute resolution procedure in both Guatemala and Nicaragua is also based on the UDRP model established by ICANN.[520]

4.8.2 Practical Relevance

Practically, even though cyber-squatting is legally prohibited in Central America, often right holders decide that it is not worth it to litigate the matter and instead buy the domain.[521] This is similar to the situation in Europe, at least the practice in the early stages of the development of information technology law.

4.9 Trade Names and Emblems (*Emblemas* and *Rotulos*)

4.9.1 Trade Names

4.9.1.1 Introduction

Article 8 Paris Convention contains some basic provisions on trade names. The fact that subsequent agreements like TRIPS and CAFTA-DR do not regulate this right at all suggests that for the developed countries, its protection was no longer considered important, either specifically with regard to developing countries or generally because of the economic and legal development of trademark law.

However, in Central America, trade names (*nombres comerciales*) still play an important practical role. Under Central American legislation, the general provisions on trademarks apply to trade names, subject to the special requirements of the respective trade name chapters.[522]

---

[519] In Guatemala, for example, the responsible entity is the Universidad del Valle de Guatemala, see https://www.gt/sitio/us.php (accessed 2 Nov 2024), in Nicaragua, the National University of Engineering (Universidad Nacional de Ingeniería), see https://www.nic.ni/Historia (accessed 2 Nov 2024) and in Costa Rica the National Academy of Science, see https://nic.cr/historia/ (accessed 2 Nov 2024).

[520] Regarding Guatemala see https://www.gt/sitio/dispute_policy.php (accessed 2 Nov 2024); regarding Costa Rica see https://nic.cr/capitulo-14-de-la-politica-de-solucion-de-controversias-en-materia-de-nombres-de-dominio-para-cr-vigente/ (accessed 2 Nov 2024).

[521] Observation by a local practitioner in 2008.

[522] E.g., Article 56 Trademark Law (SV); Article 120 IP Law (DR).

4.9.1.2 Subject Matter and Requirements

Because of the general reference to trademark law, the same subject matter is, therefore, admissible for trade names. Some laws nevertheless define trade names, *e.g.*, Guatemala: A trade name is a name or mixed sign, with which an enterprise or entity is identified and distinguished.[523]

In Central America, a trade name can be rejected on absolute grounds[524] or relative grounds.[525] However, most current laws in Central America only list *absolute* grounds of rejection, in particular if the trade name would be contrary to "moral or the public order" or would mislead the public with regard to the identity or activities of the enterprise or with regard to the respective products or services.[526] *Relative* grounds of rejection are generally not listed, as the respective provisions for trademarks on relative grounds apply accordingly.

This new legislation deviates from Article 49 *Central American* Convention (Trademarks), which is no longer in force, which listed also several relative grounds, in particular the conflict with the trade name or trademark of a third party. The only exception is Honduras, where the legislation resembles the *Central American* Convention (Trademarks) to a larger extent, and which explicitly excludes trade names identical to the well-known mark of a third party or to a trade name which has expired less than one year before.[527]

4.9.1.3 Right Holder

In contrast to trademarks, trade names are not separable from the enterprise using the trade name, and can only be transferred together with the entity to which it belongs.[528] Also, the exclusive right to the trade name terminates if the entity using it ceases to exist.[529] The provision in Guatemala on *right holders* was extended by the CAFTA-DR Reform Law (GT) and, in addition to "enterprises and businesses", includes now also "entities".[530] Whereas the "enterprises and businesses" refers to *private* entities, the latter term encompasses also *public* entities.

[523] Article 4 IP Law (GT).

[524] Article 58 Trademark Law (SV); Article 72(b) IP Law (GT); Article 63(a) Trademark Law (NI).

[525] E.g., Article 72(a) IP Law (GT).

[526] Article 113(1) IP Law (DR), Article 58 Trademark Law (SV), Article 72(b) IP Law (GT), Article 63(a) Trademark Law (NI).

[527] Article 119 Patent Law (HN).

[528] Article 62 (1) Trademark Law (SV); Article 76 IP Law (GT); Article 65 Trademark Law (NI).

[529] Article 57(2) Trademark Law (SV); Article 62 (2) Trademark Law (NI).

[530] Article 71(1) IP Law (GT).

4.9.1.4 Procedure

Article 8 Paris Convention provides that a trade name shall be protected without the requirement of filing or registration.[531] Contrary to this requirement, Article 50 of the *Central American* Convention (Trademarks) provided that "ownership of a trade name shall be acquired by its registration". Most current laws in Central America do not require registration and permit registration only for declaratory purposes, with the exception of Honduras, that, in line with the *Central American* Convention (Trademarks), still requires registration for use and protection against third parties.[532]

However, the right holder can request the *declaratory* registration of the trade name by the IP Register.[533] In Costa Rica, only a registered trade name can be used in a lawsuit against an unauthorized distributor.[534] In addition, even though the law clearly provides that the registration is declaratory, the First Civil Court of San José, Costa Rica, held that the registration of a trade name gave an enterprise the right to use "its name since it is protected by its registration, and a decision may not be taken (by the civil court) regarding the invalidity of its registration" and such use could, therefore, not constitute unfair competition, even if the name was identical to that of a competitor.[535] In the Dominican Republic, the registration also creates the legal presumption that the trade name is used in commerce and, therefore, prevents the expiration of the trade name for lack of use.[536]

4.9.1.5 Rights and Limitations

The Paris Convention provided only that "all goods unlawfully bearing a trademark or trade name shall be seized on importation"[537] and thus only protected the use of *identical* signs. In Central America today the trade name is protected against all other distinctive signs, including trademarks and slogans, which are (1) identical or (2) *similar* and capable of causing confusion or association.[538]

4.9.1.6 Term of Protection

The exclusive right to the trade name is acquired by its first public use in commerce.[539]

---

[531] Article 71(3) IP Law (GT).

[532] Article 118 IP Law (HN).

[533] Article 74 IP Law (GT), Article 60 Trademark Law (SV), Article 62 Trademark Law (NI).

[534] Article 47 IP Enforcement Law (CR).

[535] First Civil Court of San José, Decision No. 831-R, 6 July 2001.

[536] Article 116 (1) IP Law (DR).

[537] Article 9 Paris Convention.

[538] Article 73(1) IP Law (GT); Article 59(1) Trademark Law (SV), Article 60 Trademark Law (NI).

[539] Article 57 (1) Trademark Law (SV); Article 71(1) IP Law (GT); Article 60 Trademark Law (NI); Article 113 (1) IP Law (DR).

Like trademarks, trade names can be *protected* indefinitely and the protection expires only when the entity it applies to ceases to exist[540] or if the enterprise ceases to use the trade name.[541] If the trade name is *registered*, the registration period is also usually indefinite.[542] In the Dominican Republic, however, the registration must be renewed after ten years.[543] This provision aligns trade names more closely with the procedural rules on trademarks. In Honduras, the owner of the trade name must document to the IP Register every five years that the enterprise is still in existence.[544]

*4.9.2 Emblems (***Emblemas** *and* **Rotulos***)*

Emblems are a particular category of trade names. They are composed of figurative signs used to identify commercial or other entities.[545] The emblems of the *Red Cross* and the *United Nations* are protected by special legislative decrees, *e.g.*, in El Salvador.[546] To the registration and protection of emblems, the provisions regarding trade names apply accordingly.[547] Therefore, emblems are protected without registration in most countries,[548] except in Honduras.[549] If emblems have been used to distinguish different entities in different locations within the country, the protection only applies to the respective location.[550]

References

Abbott FM, Reichman JH (2007) The Doha round's public health legacy: strategies for the production and diffusion of patented medicines under the amended TRIPS provisions. J Int Econ Law 10(4):921–987

Adams M, Scardamaglia A (2018) Non-traditional trade marks in Europe: an historical snapshot of applications and registrations. Eur Intellect Prop Rev 40:623–629, available at SSRN: https://ssrn.com/abstract=3264994. Accessed 2 Nov 2024

Assaf K (2008) The dilution of culture and the law of trademarks. IDEA: J Law Technol 49(1)

---

[540] Article 57 (2) Trademark Law (SV); Article 60 Trademark Law (NI).

[541] Article 116(1) IP Law (DR).

[542] Article 62 (2) Trademark Law (NI).

[543] Article 116 (2) IP Law (DR).

[544] Article 120 (1) IP Law (HN).

[545] Article 77 IP Law (GT), Article 63 Trademark Law (SV).

[546] Law No. 789 of 26 January 1994 and Law No. 1105 of 14 July 1953.

[547] Article 77 IP Law (GT); Articles 66 (rotulos) and 67 (emblems) Trademark Law (NI); Article 63 Trademark Law (SV).

[548] E.g., Article 67 Trademark Law (NI).

[549] Articles 122 with 118 IP Law (HN).

[550] Article 66 Trademark Law (NI).

Ayala Durán C, Radomsky GFW (2020) Indicaciones Geográficas en Centroamérica: un crecimiento poco diversificado. Revista RIVAR 7(20):1–21, available at https://www.researchgate.net/publication/342104707_Indicaciones_Geograficas_en_Centroamerica_un_crecimiento_poco_diversificado. Accessed 2 Nov 2024

Barragan Rivas AA (2017) Las Marcas Notorias como una Excepción a la Naturaleza Registral de los Derechos Marcarios, Thesis, Universidad Rafael Landívar, Guatemala, available at http://recursosbiblio.url.edu.gt/tesisjrcd/2017/07/01/Barragan-Astrid.pdf. Accessed 2 Nov 2024

Beebe B, Cotter T, Lemley, M, Menell P, Merges R (2016) Trademarks, Unfair Competition, and Business Torts

Bendaña-Guerrero GJ (1999) *Curso de Derecho* de Propiedad Industrial. Hispamer, Managua, Nicaragua

Bucher S (2008) Der Schutz von genetischen Ressourcen und indigenem Wissen in Lateinamerika – Eine Untersuchung am Beispiel der Andengemeinschaft, Brasiliens und Costa Ricas. Nomos, Baden-Baden

Busche J, Stoll P-T, Wiebe A (eds) (2013) TRIPS - Internationales und europäisches Recht des geistigen Eigentums, 2nd edn. Carl Heymanns Verlag

Consortium Centro América Abogados (2013) Consortium Centro América Abogados is giving advice on matters of legal protection of Geographical Indications and Designations of Origin for the EU, Newsletter October 2013 (on file with the author)

Contreras Aguilera MG (2007) How collective marks can help protect the products of Guatemalan Artisans' small businesses in the local and international market?, available at http://lup.lub.lu.se/luur/download?func=downloadFile&recordOId=1555222&fileOId=1563587. Accessed 2 Nov 2024

Cornish W, Llewelyn D, Aplin T (2013) Intellectual property: patents, copyright, trade marks and allied rights, 8th edn. Sweet & Maxwell (cited as Cornish et al. (2013))

Correa CM (1999) Intellectual property rights and the use of compulsory licenses: options for developing countries. South Centre Working Paper

Correa CM (2002) Protection of Geographical Indications in CARICOM Countries, available at https://www.researchgate.net/publication/265104739_Protection_of_Geographical_Indications_in_Caricom_Countries. Accessed 2 Nov 2024

Correa CM (2007) Trade related aspects of intellectual property rights, a commentary on the TRIPS Agreement. Oxford University Press

Curzi, Huysmans (2021) The impact of protecting EU geographical indications in trade agreements. Am J Agr Econ 104(1):364–384. https://doi.org/10.1111/ajae.12226

del Carmen Romero Pérez A, Tercero Garcia CA (2021) Análisis Comparativo de la Marca Sonora Según la Ley 380 "Ley de Marcas y Otros Signos Distintivos" y la Ley de Marcas y Otros Signos Distintivos de Costa Rica, Ley N° 7978", available at https://repositorio.unan.edu.ni/16103/1/16103.pdf. Accessed 2 Nov 2024

El Financiero (2019) Queso Turrialba, un camino lleno de retos, 30 Aug 2019, available at https://www.elfinancierocr.com/opinion/queso-turrialba-un-camino-lleno-de-retos/2MPDPMVN4BDA7PAQFDV6UTU3SY/story/. Accessed 2 Nov 2024

Engelhardt T (2015) Geographical indications under recent EU trade agreements. IIC 2015:781–817

Evans GE (2010) The comparative advantages of geographical indications and community trade marks for the marketing of agricultural products in the European Union. IIC 2010:645–671

Fezer K-H (2009) Markenrecht, 4th edn. C. H. Beck, Munich

Flores Zelada WF, Morán Cañas PA, Santos Méndez AC (2005) Efectos socio jurídicos de la aplicación de los Decretos Legislativos No. 747 y 719 en tres asociaciones cooperativas de la reforma agraria de la zona central en El Salvador durante el período comprendido: 1997 – 2004, Universidad de El Salvador, San Salvador

Franco L (IP Register (DR)) (2020) Marcas no tradicionales RD (presentation), available at https://ipkey.eu/sites/default/files/ipkey-docs/2020/IPKeyLA_jul2020_Lesly%20Franco-Marcas%20no%20tradicionales%20RD-presentacion.pdf. Accessed 2 Nov 2024

Geiger C (2007) Trade marks and freedom of expression - the proportionality of criticism. IIC 2007: 317–327

Gómez Linares JE, Ponce Acosta SA, Salamanca Vasconcelos AM (2011) El Derecho de Marcas y su Incidencia an la Protección de las Pequeñas y Medianas Empresas, Graduation Thesis, University of El Salvador

Gonzalez D (IP Register (GT)) (2020) Marcas no tradicionales (presentation), available at https://ipkey.eu/sites/default/files/ipkey-docs/2020/IPKeyLA_jul2020_Debora%20Gonz%C3%A1lez-Ley%20de%20propiedad%20industrial%20y%20su%20reglamento-presentacion.pdf. Accessed 2 Nov 2024

Grave HG (2002) Gewerbliche Schutzrechte in Mexiko - Eine Untersuchung vor dem Hintergrund der maßgeblichen Bestimmungen der NAFTA- und TRIPS-Abkommen. Nomos, Baden-Baden

Grosse Ruse-Khan H (2016) The protection of intellectual property in international law. Oxford University Press, Oxford

Handler, Mercurio (2015) Intellectual property. In: Lester S, Mercurio B, Bartels L (eds) Bilateral and regional trade agreements: volume 1: commentary and analysis, 2nd edn. Cambridge University Press

Hassemer M (2000) Gewerbliche Schutzrechte im Mercosur. Nomos, Baden-Baden

Heath C, Marie-Vivien D (2015) Geographical indications and the principles of trade mark law – a distinctly European perspective. IIC 2015:819–842

Hoffrichter-Daunicht C (2007) Grafische Darstellbarkeit von Hörmarken: Wo ist das Problem? GRUR 2007:935–936

Kur A (1994) TRIPS und das Markenrecht. GRUR Int 1994:987–997

Kur A (2008) Collective marks and certification marks. In: von Lewinski S (ed) Indigenous heritage and intellectual property: genetic resources, traditional knowledge and folklore, 2nd edn. Wolters Kluwer Law

Kur A, Bently L, Ohly A (2009) Sweet Smells and a Sour Taste –The ECJ's L'Oreal Decision, Max Planck Institute for Intellectual Property, Competition & Tax Law Research Paper Series No. 09-12, University of Cambridge Faculty of Law Research Paper No. 10/01. https://doi.org/10.2139/ssrn.1492032

Lizano Soto A, Pal Antillón A (2013) Nuevas modalidades de marcas: olfativas, táctiles y gustativas. Viabilidad, utilidad y efectos jurídicos en Costa Rica, Thesis, Universidad de Costa Rica

Lobos Luna AJ (2012) Marca Sonora, Thesis, Universidad Rafael Landívar, Guatemala (on file with the author)

Lopez-Davis G (2011) General overview of renewals, assignments, changes of name and trademark licences in Guatemala, available at https://www.hg.org/legal-articles/general-overview-of-renewals-assignments-changes-of-name-and-trademark-licences-in-guatemala-21129. Accessed 2 Nov 2024

Lopez-Davis G (2014) General Overview of Trademark Protection and Enforcement in Guatemala (updated June 2014), available at https://www.hg.org/legal-articles/general-overview-of-trademark-protection-and-enforcement-in-guatemala-updated-june-2014-6802. Accessed 2 Nov 2024

Martínez KM (IP Register (SV)) (2020) Taller virtual sobre marcas no tradicionales y registros de mala fe (presentation), available at https://ipkey.eu/sites/default/files/ipkey-docs/2020/IPKeyLA_jul2020_Katya%20Mart%C3%ADnez-Taller%20marcas%20no%20tradicionales-presentacion.pdf. Accessed 2 Nov 2024

Mejia RA (2011) Honduras, The Trademark Reporter, Vol. 101 No. 3, 2011 (on file with the author)

Mejia RA (2016) Honduras. In: Eckhartt C (ed) Trademarks 2016 (on file with the author)

Merges RP, Menell PS, Lemley MA (2010) Intellectual property in the new technological age, 5th edn. Aspen Law & Business (cited as "MML (2010)")

O'Connor and Company (2007) Geographical indications and TRIPs: 10 Years Later… A roadmap for EU GI holders to get protection in other WTO Members, Report prepared for the European Commission, DG Trade, 22 June 2007, available at https://www.mapa.gob.es/es/alimentacion/

temas/calidad-diferenciada/iiggandtripsguideforgiholders_tcm30-520448.pdf. Accessed 2 Nov 2024
Paz Cafferata J, Pomareda C (2009) Indicaciones Geográficas y Denominaciones de Origen en Centroamérica: Situación y perspectivas, ICTSD, available at https://www.fao.org/fileadmin/templates/olq/documents/costarica/ppp/Martes/Pomaredadoc.pdf. Accessed 2 Nov 2024
Ramírez Argueta MP (2007) Titularidad y uso de Marcas de Certificación en Guatemala, Thesis, Universidad San Carlos (Guatemala), available at http://biblioteca.usac.edu.gt/tesis/04/04_6847.pdf. Accessed 2 Nov 2024
Rangnekar D (2002) Geographical Indications - A Review of Proposals at the TRIPS Council: Extending Article 23 to Products other than Wines and Spirits, UNCTAD-ICTSD Project on IPRS and Sustainable Development, Issue Paper N° 4, Geneva
Registro de la Propiedad Industrial de Costa Rica (2006) Situación actual de la Propiedad Industrial en Costa Rica, WIPO document OMPI/JPI/BUE/06/2 CR, available at http://www.wipo.int/edocs/mdocs/lac/es/ompi_jpi_bue_06/ompi_jpi_bue_06_2_cr.doc. Accessed 2 Nov 2024
Registro de la Propiedad Intelectual de Guatemala (2010) Comentarios relacionados con temas tratados en el documento SCT/22/2, en particular, con la práctica de las oficinas de marcas en relación con casos específicos y sus ejemplos, available at http://www.wipo.int/export/sites/www/sct/en/comments/pdf/sct23/ref_guatemala_3.pdf. Accessed 2 Nov 2024
Singh RH et al (2014) Monitoring the implementation & results of the CARIFORUM – EU EPA Agreement, Final Report, September 2014
Teuber R (2010) Geographical indications of origin as a tool of product differentiation – the case of coffee. J Int Food Agribus Market 22(3&4):277–298
Thomas K (2009) Structural Adjustment, Spatial Imaginaries, and "Piracy" in Guatemala's Apparel Industry. Anthropol Work Rev 30(1):1–10
Thomas K (2011) An ethnography of brand piracy in Guatemala. Doctoral dissertation, Harvard University
UNCTAD (2014) The Convention on Biological Diversity and the Nagoya Protocol: Intellectual Property Implications, available at https://unctad.org/system/files/official-document/diaepcb2014d3_en.pdf. Accessed 2 Nov 2024
USTR, Special 301 Report 2015., available at https://ustr.gov/sites/default/files/2015-Special-301-Report-FINAL.pdf. Accessed 2 Nov 2024 (cited as USTR, Special 301 Report 2015)
USTR, Special 301 Report 2016., available at https://ustr.gov/sites/default/files/USTR-2016-Special-301-Report.pdf. Accessed 2 Nov 2024 (cited as USTR, Special 301 Report 2016)
Valdés Samayoa RA (2012) Analisis de la Utilización de Marcas Colectivas en Guatemala y sus centajas económicas para las comunidades, Tesis, Universidad Rafael Landívar, Guatemala
Viefhues M, Klauer I (2004) Farbmarken nach der Libertel-Entscheidung des EuGH aus. deutscher und aus schweizerischer Sicht. GRUR Int 2004:584–596
Voegeli J (2006) Die Regulierung des Domainnamensystems durch die Internet Cooperation für Assigned Names and Numbers (ICANN). Heymanns, Cologne
Voegeli-Wenzel J (2007) Internet Governance am Beispiel der Internet Cooperation of Assigned Names and Numbers (ICANN). GRUR Int 2007:807–816
WTO General Council (1999) Agreement on TRIPS – Proposal Regarding Extension of Protection of Geographical Indications under Paragraph 9(a)(i) of the Geneva Ministerial Declaration – Communication from Cuba, Dominican Republic, Egypt, Honduras, India, Indonesia, Nicaragua and Pakistan, WT/GC/W/208, available at https://wtocentre.iift.ac.in/General%20Council/WT-GC-W-208.doc. Accessed 2 Nov 2024

Chapter 5
Designs, Topographies and Unfair Competition

5.1 Registered Industrial Design

5.1.1 Introduction

Design protection receives much less international attention in the TRIPS-plus discussion than patent or trademark protection. There are only few rules on this subject in TRIPS, and designs are not regulated at all in CAFTA-DR, except for the requirement to make *reasonable efforts* to ratify the Hague Agreement Concerning the Registration of Industrial Designs (1999) (Hague Agreement).[1] The reference to "1999" indicates the revision of the Hague Agreement under the Geneva Act adopted in 1999. Interestingly, at the time CAFTA-DR was drafted and negotiated, the USA had only signed, but not ratified the Geneva Act. The USA ratified the Geneva Act on 13 May 2015.[2] Until 2024, no Central American country has signed any version of the Hague Agreement.[3] The requirement to make *reasonable efforts* was included in the same way in similar bilateral FTAs concluded by the USA.[4] On the other hand, both the EU-CARIFORUM-EPA and the EU-CA-AA contain

[1] See Article 15.1.6(b) CAFTA-DR; the Geneva Revision of 1999 of the Hague Agreement has been ratified by only 21 countries as of 2008, but the number has increased to 52 in late 2017 and 73 in 2024.

[2] The list of contracting parties is available at http://www.wipo.int/treaties/en/ActResults.jsp?act_id=7 (accessed 2 Nov 2024).

[3] See https://www.wipo.int/treaties/en/ShowResults.jsp?lang=en&treaty_id=9 (accessed 2 Nov 2024); the simplification of the registration procedure of designs by an international application could have a similar impact on the business model of local law firms as the facilitation of international trademark registrations under the Protocol relating to the Madrid Agreement (Trademarks), see Sect. 4.1.4. Accordingly, there may be little incentive for any Central American country to adopt the Hague Agreement in the near future.

[4] Article 16.1(4)(b) US-Peru-TPA and Article 16.1(4)(b) US-Colombia-TPA.

F. Böttger, *CAFTA-DR, European Free Trade Agreements and the Industrial Property System in Central America*, Munich Studies on Innovation and Competition 21, https://doi.org/10.1007/978-3-031-93440-7_5

detailed provisions on designs, including the requirement to *endeavor to accede* to the Hague Agreement.[5] The fact that the Special 301 Reports of the *USTR* annually lists a variety of complaints regarding patent, copyright and trademark protection, but do not mention the inactivity regarding the ratification of the Hague Agreement, suggests a limited relevance of design protection from the US perspective, that could also explain why the issue is not addressed in CAFTA-DR.[6]

Design protection can be useful in developing countries, including local indigenous artisans. Indigenous people produce a wealth of traditional textile and artisan goods with characteristic patterns. The products, but also the patterns themselves are not only used by locals but have become increasingly popular for tourists in the region.[7] Therefore, better use of the design protection system at home and abroad could be important for domestic creators, to protect themselves against appropriation by third parties.

In Central America, design law used to play a minor practical role. There were only few designs registered when CAFTA-DR was implemented, mostly for foreigners. However, the awareness of local producers of design protection and economic challenges posed by copying has increased.[8] Also, after the implementation of CAFTA-DR the number of both applications and registrations had increased; however, beginning in 2016-2018 the number of design applications by local applicants began to decrease again.[9]

5.1.2 *Subject Matter*

The protection of industrial designs is traditionally divided in Central America into two-dimensional designs (*dibujos*) and three-dimensional designs (*modelos*).[10] This distinction is similar to the distinction between *Muster* and *Modelle* under the German *Geschmacksmustergesetz*, which was in force until 2004.[11] Designs are of aesthetic, not functional nature. There is a clear distinction between functional patents and aesthetic designs.[12] In other words, designs do not affect the utility of

[5] Article 146 EU-CARIFORUM-EPA; Articles 251 - 257 EU-CA-AA.

[6] See for example USTR Special 301 Report (2008), p. 48.

[7] Thomas described the local controversy about "copión" (copying other designer's patterns) in highland Guatemala and notes that this reinforces some of the same goals as intellectual property laws that cover trademarks and fashion design, see Thomas (2012), p. 806.

[8] See Thomas (2012), p. 806.

[9] See data provided by the World Bank at https://data.worldbank.org/ (accessed 2 Nov 2024).

[10] See, e.g., Article 25(1) Patent and Design Law (CR) and Article 123(1) IP Law (SV); see also Bendaña-Guerrero (1999), p. 295.

[11] The law was replaced by the *Designgesetz*, which entered into force on 1 June 2004.

[12] See Patent Examiner Manual (2006), p. 29.

the product, but appeal to the taste of the consumer.[13] But the aesthetic subject matter may in some cases also be protected by trademark and/or copyright law,[14] and usually the Central American statutes provide for the possibility of double or triple protection.[15] The critique expressed by some practitioners in Central America with regard to the "superposition" of several IP rights and the broad scope of design protection shows similarities with the discussions in Europe, *e.g.*, about design protection for spare parts.[16]

5.1.3 Requirements

According to TRIPS, designs must be *new* or *original.*[17] The *originality* requirement, referring to designs identical to an existing design, but independently created[18] (*i.e.*, not copied) is traditionally sufficient for unregistered designs.[19] But protection can also be restricted to *new* designs, *i.e.*, significantly different from known designs.[20] Today the requirement is often *novelty* instead of independent creation and *originality* in the sense that it has individual character. This is the case, *e.g.*, in European design law.[21]

European design law was the basis for Article 146(B)1 EU-CARIFORUM-EPA, providing that the parties "shall provide for the protection of independently created industrial designs that are new or original, and that have *individual character*". A "design shall be considered to have individual character if the overall impression it produces on the informed user differs from the overall impression produced on such a user by any design which has been made available to the public".[22] Under Article 252 EU-CA-AA, the parties "shall provide for the protection of independently created designs that are new or original. A design shall be considered to be new if it significantly differs from known designs or combinations of known design features".

The requirements in the *Central American* legislation regarding designs are in effect the same, despite the fact that the laws usually only refer to novelty.

---

[13] See Bendaña-Guerrero (1999), p. 295.

[14] Article 25(2) TRIPS gives the members the right to protect designs through a special design right or just by copyright.

[15] Article 148 IP Law (GT); Article 54(2) IP Law (DR); Articles 54, 67 Patent and Design Law (NI); Article 25(3) Patent and Design Law (CR).

[16] Regarding the discussion in Europe, see Beldiman and Blanke-Roeser (2015), pp. 915–919.

[17] Article 25(1)1 TRIPS.

[18] Article 25(1)1 TRIPS.

[19] Cornish et al. (2013) at 15–39.

[20] Article 25(1)2 TRIPS.

[21] See Articles 5 and 6 of the Regulation (EC) 6/2002 of 12 December 2001 on Community designs.

[22] Article 146(B)(1) EU-CARIFORUM-EPA.

The design must be *new*, defined as being significantly different from known designs.[23] The law does not address the question whether novelty is considered nationally or internationally.[24] Only Costa Rica also protects independently created, original designs similar to existing ones, based on the flexibility provided by Article 25(1)1 TRIPS.[25] The design is considered to be not new if it does not convey a "distinct overall impression" (*impresión de conjunto distinta*) which is different from existing designs.[26] This element of novelty corresponds to the individual character requirement in European law.[27]

In the Dominican Republic, the CAFTA-DR reform legislation explicitly introduced the individual character (*carácter singular*) as a new requirement, that is defined as producing a different overall impression.[28] It is interesting that this requirement was introduced by the CAFTA-DR Reform Law I (DR), despite the fact that CAFTA-DR does not contain any provisions on designs and only the EU-FTAs do.[29] However, because of this legislative amendment, the Dominican Republic was not required to update its design law as part of implementing the EU-CARIFORUM-EPA.

To distinguish between patents and designs, functional elements are excluded from design protection[30] and aesthetic elements from patent protection.[31]

[23] Article 152(1) IP Law (GT), Article 58 IP Law (DR), Article 72 Patent and Design Law (NI).

[24] In Europe, an existing design is only "deemed to have been made available to the public" (and, therefore, exclude novelty) "if it has been published [...] or exhibited, used in trade or otherwise disclosed [...], except where these events could not reasonably have become known [...] to the circles specialized in the sector concerned, operating within the Community", Article 7-(1) Regulation (EC) 6/2002 of 12 December 2001 on Community designs. Practically, this could be a problem for traditional indigenous designs in Central America which are not represented in publications or international exhibitions. For international scenarios, see also Cornish et al. (2013), para. 15-17 to 15-18.

[25] Article 25(1) Patent and Design Law (CR).

[26] Article 152 (3) IP Law (GT), Article 73 (2) Patent and Design Law (NI).

[27] This is similar to the European legislation on community designs, see Article 6 Regulation (EC) 6/2002 of 12 December 2001 on Community designs.

[28] Article 7 CAFTA-DR Reform Law I (DR), amending Article 58 IP Law (DR).

[29] This provision may have been inspired by European legislation.

[30] Article 25(1) TRIPS; Article 149(a) IP Law (GT); Article 68 Patent and Design Law (NI); Article 25(1) Patent and Design Law (CR).

[31] Patent Examiner Manual (2006), p. 29.

5.1.4 Procedure

The registration of the design is required for protection.[32] The responsible entity for the registrations is the IP Register in all Central American countries.[33] The registration procedure does not contain any particular requirements, especially no requirements that could be considered to "unreasonably impair the opportunity to seek and obtain protection".[34] The procedure is, therefore, compliant with the international obligations. Most countries in Central America provide for a grace period of six (Guatemala)[35] or 12 (Dominican Republic)[36] months after the first public display for registering a design. Only Nicaraguan law does not foresee a grace period, therefore, after the first public display, protection is restricted to that of unregistered designs. For the protection and administration of registered industrial designs in Central America, the provisions of patent law are applicable.[37]

5.1.5 Statistics

For Central America, the data on design applications since the implementation of CAFTA-DR is not complete. However, the available numbers from 2010 to 2021 (the last reported year) indicate that design applications both by residents and non-residents remained constant or slightly decreased in the region, between 30 and 100 per country.[38] These numbers contrast with the global trend of significant increases in design applications, suggesting that the practical relevance design protection in the region has not increased.

[32] Article 152 IP Law (GT); Article 58 IP Law (DR); the registration requirement was first introduced by the French design law of 1806, which also established the term "industrial design" (dessin de fabricants), see Bendaña-Guerrero (1999), p. 297.

[33] Article 28 Patent and Design Law (CR); Article 63 IP Law (DR); Articles 155–161 IP Law (GT); Article 84 Patent and Design Law (NI).

[34] Article 25(2) TRIPS.

[35] Article 152 IP Law (GT).

[36] Article 58(3) IP Law (DR).

[37] Article 147 IP Law (GT); Article 68 IP Law (DR); Article 88 Patent and Design Law (NI).

[38] These numbers are based on World Bank statistical data obtained in 2024, available at https://data.worldbank.org/ (also on file with the author).

Table 5.1 Term of protection of registered designs in Central America

Country	Initial protection	Renewal	Total maximum	Source
Costa Rica	10 years	Not renewable	10 years	Article 30 Patent and Design Law (CR)
Dominican Republic	5 years	Two renewals for 5 years each	15 years	Article 67 IP Law (DR)
El Salvador	5 years	One renewal for 5 years	10 years	Articles 130, 131 IP Law (SV)
Guatemala	10 years	One renewal for 5 years	15 years	Articles 159, 160 IP Law (GT)
Honduras	5 years	Two renewals for 5 years each	15 years	Articles 33, 34 IP (HN)
Nicaragua	5 years	Two renewals for 5 years each	15 years	Articles 85, 86 Patent and Design Law (NI)

5.1.6 *Term of Protection*

Article 26(4) TRIPS requires protection for at least 10 years for registered designs. In Central America, the term of protection for registered designs in all countries complies with this requirement, as shown in Table 5.1.

5.1.7 *Rights and Limitations*

Article 26 TRIPS provides for protection against a design which is a copy, or substantially a copy, without differentiating between registered and unregistered designs. Likewise, Article 146(D)1 EU-CARIFORUM-EPA and Article 254(1) EU-CA-AA require protection against "articles bearing, or embodying the protected design", *i.e.*, copies. In Central America, there are basically two systems:

The protection in Costa Rica is narrow in relation to the scope and term of protection and excludes unregistered designs. Costa Rica included the TRIPS provision literally in its legislation and thereby restricts protection to (substantially) copies.[39] Designs are protected in Costa Rica against the making, selling or importing of articles bearing or embodying a (protected) design for commercial purposes.[40]

The protection in other countries is broader and goes slightly beyond the provisions of TRIPS. In Guatemala, registered designs are protected not only against (substantially) identical reproductions or copies, but also similar reproductions and

[39] Article 25(4) Patent and Design Law (CR).

[40] Article 26(1) TRIPS, Article 25(4) Patent and Design Law (CR).

against "any form of commercial exploitation".[41] In Nicaragua, registered designs are also protected against products incorporating a design offering the same overall *impression*.[42] In Honduras, designs are protected against "products that reproduce the same general impression as the protected design".[43] In El Salvador, the right holder can act against someone manufacturing or commercializing a product which (a) reproduces or embodies a (protected) design or (b) offers the same general impression.[44]

Central American legislation does not explicitly provide for limitations of the design right, even though Article 26(2) TRIPS permits such limitations.

5.2 Unregistered Industrial Design

5.2.1 Introduction

The protection of industrial design originated in England as an unregistered right, and was only later complemented by the registered design.[45]

Article 26 TRIPS provides for protection against a design which is a copy, or substantially a copy, without differentiating between registered and unregistered designs. Under the EU-FTAs, unregistered designs *may* be protected according to Article 252.3 EU-CA-AA and *shall* be protected according to Article 146(b)4 EU-CARIFORUM-EPA, and shall be protected only against *copying* the protected design.[46]

In Central America, unregistered designs are protected in El Salvador, Nicaragua and Guatemala. In Costa Rica,[47] the Dominican Republic[48] and Honduras, designs are only protected if they are registered.[49] While the lack of protection in Costa Rica and Honduras is permitted under the optional protection regime of the EU-CA-AA, with regard to the Dominican Republic it breaches the mandatory protection obligation under the EU-CARIFORUM-EPA.

[41] Article 154 IP Law (GT).

[42] Article 75 Patent and Design Law (NI).

[43] Article 31 IP Law (HN).

[44] Article 128(1) IP Law (SV).

[45] Bendaña-Guerrero (1999), p. 296; in England there still exist registered and unregistered (British) design rights, see Cornish et al. (2013) at 15-01 to 15-02.

[46] Article 146(b)4 EU-CARIFORUM-EPA and Article 252.3 EU-CA-AA.

[47] Article 26(2) Patent and Design Law (CR).

[48] Article 57 IP Law (DR).

[49] Article 29 IP Law (HN).

5.2.2 *Term of Protection*

Unregistered designs are protected in Nicaragua and Guatemala for a period of three years.[50] In El Salvador, the provision does not explicitly state the term of protection, however, the term shall comply with the term of registered designs, i.e., a maximum of ten years.[51]

5.2.3 *Rights and Limitations*

In Nicaragua, the scope of protection of unregistered designs is narrower than that of registered designs. Nicaraguan law protects unregistered designs only against (exact) copies or reproductions.[52] Such a restriction of the protection given to registered designs is systematically reasonable and TRIPS-compliant. As *Cornish* points out, only registered rights can obligate third parties, and provide protection, beyond actual copying. Therefore, unregistered designs (like copyrighted works) should only exclude (exact) copying, but not similar reproductions.[53] As TRIPS permits the limitation of design protection to registered designs, if a country provides additional protection for unregistered design, it must be free to restrict the scope of protection, even if the wording of Article 26 TRIPS does not provide for this restriction. Therefore, Article 74 Patent and Design Law (NI) is no violation of TRIPS.

In El Salvador and Guatemala, the articles on rights conferred by designs, providing protection against "products that reproduce the same general impression"[54] and "*similar* reproductions",[55] apply to all designs, including unregistered designs. This scope of protection conflicts with El Salvador's and Guatemala's obligations under Article 252.3 EU-CA-AA, which provides that unregistered designs may be protected only against *copying* the design. This case of non-compliance is noteworthy, because the countries decided not to implement the maximum protection established by the EU-CA-AA, but to leave the excessive existing protection in place.

[50] Article 74 Patent and Design Law (NI); Article 153 IP Law (GT).

[51] Article 125(a) IP Law (SV).

[52] Article 74 Patent and Design Law (NI).

[53] Cornish et al. (2013) at 15-01 to 15-02.

[54] Article 128(1) IP Law (SV).

[55] Article 154 IP Law (GT).

5.3 Topographies of Integrated Circuits

The protection of layout-designs (topographies) of integrated circuits emerged in the 1980ies as a special form of design protection.[56] It was internationally codified in the *Washington Treaty on Intellectual Property in Respect of Integrated Circuits* (Washington Treaty) in 1989.[57] The Washington Treaty has not (yet) entered into force, but was later incorporated into TRIPS.[58] Protection can be provided through existing IP rights or specific statutes.[59] Neither CAFTA-DR nor the EU-CARIFORUM-EPA and the EU-CA-AA contain rules regarding topographies of integrated circuits.

Most countries in Central America decided to create specific legislation following closely the text of the Washington Treaty, *e.g.*, the Law for Protection of Layout Designs of Integrated Circuits in Costa Rica (Integrated Circuits Law (CR))[60] and in Nicaragua (Integrated Circuits Law (NI)).[61] This IP right is only analyzed briefly in this thesis, because it is not governed by CAFTA-DR and does not create significant legal issues relating to other distinctive signs. By way of example, this section briefly describes the protection in Costa Rica.

As a special design right, topography protection requires originality, not novelty.[62] A topography is original if it is "the result of their creators' own intellectual effort and is not commonplace among creators of layout-designs (topographies) and producers of integrated circuits at the time of its creation".[63] Therefore, the independent creation of an existing topography can be protected as well, even though it is not new.[64]

---

[56] Cornish et al. (2013) at 15–54 describe it as "a specially conditioned form of unregistered design right"; in the European Union, it was codified by Directive 87/54/EEC of 16 December 1986 on the legal protection of topographies of semiconductor products.

[57] The treaty was adopted in Washington on 26 May 1989; the text is available at http://www.wipo.int/treaties/en/text.jsp?file_id=295136 (accessed 2 Nov 2024).

[58] According to Article 35 TRIPS, the members have to comply with, but not ratify, the Washington Treaty. Articles 36 to 40 TRIPS contain additional requirements regarding topography protection.

[59] Article 4 Washington Treaty.

[60] Law on the Protection of Layout-Designs of Integrated Circuits (Ley de Protección a Sistemas de Trazados de Circuitos Integrados), Law No. 7961, adopted on 17 December 1999, entered into force on 19 January 2000; the text of the law is available at https://www.wipo.int/wipolex/es/text/126061 (accessed 2 Nov 2024).

[61] Law for Protection of Layout Designs of Integrated Circuits (Ley de Protección a los Esquemas Trazados de Circuitos Integrados), Law No. 324, adopted on 2 December 1999, entered into force on 1 February 2000; available at https://www.wipo.int/wipolex/es/text/128932 (accessed 2 Nov 2024).

[62] Cornish et al. (2013) at 15–54.

[63] Article 3(2)(a) Washington Treaty.

[64] Article 6(2)(c) Washington Treaty; in Central America, see, e.g., Article 12 Integrated Circuits Law (CR).

Central American countries have used the option of Article 7(2) Washington Treaty to require registration of the topography for protection.[65] Unlike in the case of other registered rights, in the case of topographies the right holder enjoys protection from the date of filing the application.[66] By contrast, the Central American countries have not used the option to require that the topography must have already been commercially exploited.[67]

Based on the option in Article 7(2) Washington Treaty, the Central American countries require the registration of topographies within two years after the first commercial exploitation.[68] The IP Register is responsible for topography registrations.[69]

The exclusive right covers the topography itself, the integrated circuits incorporating the topography and the products incorporating these circuits. With regard to these objects, reproducing, importing, selling or otherwise distributing for commercial purposes is illegal.[70] The main limitations of the right are the possibility of reverse engineering,[71] *i.e.*, the analysis of the protected topography and the development of a new topography based on this analysis, the independent creation of the topography[72] and unintentional infringements (*infracción innocente*).[73]

Article 8 Washington Treaty required eight years of protection. Article 38 TRIPS extended the term to 10 years, which is also the term of protection generally granted in Central America.[74]

5.4 Unfair Competition

5.4.1 Introduction

Unlike the Paris Convention and TRIPS, CAFTA-DR does not address unfair competition law. This can be seen as a consequence of the focus of the agreement on proprietary rights protected absolutely, contrary to unfair competition law, which

---

[65] See, e.g., Article 6 Integrated Circuits Law (CR); this requirement does not exist in the EU, see Cornish et al. (2013) at 15–54.

[66] Article 6 Integrated Circuits Law (CR).

[67] This option is provided for in Article 7(1) Washington Treaty.

[68] In Central America, see, e.g., Article 6 Integrated Circuits Law (CR).

[69] See, e.g., Article 2 Integrated Circuits Law (CR).

[70] Article 6(1) Washington Treaty; Article 36 TRIPS; in Central America, see, e.g., Article 8 Integrated Circuits Law (CR).

[71] Article 6(2)(b) Washington Treaty; in Central America, e.g., Article 11 Integrated Circuits Law (CR).

[72] Article 6(2)(c) Washington Treaty; in Central America, e.g., Article 12 Integrated Circuits Law (CR).

[73] See, e.g., Article 13 Integrated Circuits Law (CR).

[74] In Central America, e.g., Article 7 Integrated Circuits Law (CR).

provides only relative protection against certain business practices. The EU-CARIFORUM-EPA requires protection against unfair competition in relation to geographical indications,[75] but contains no substantive requirements in relation to unfair competition. Article 229.3(b) EU-CA-AA provides that, "as regards unfair competition, protection will be granted in accordance with Article 10*bis* of the Paris Convention for the Protection of Industrial Property (Stockholm Act, 1967)". This requirement does not go beyond Article 2(1) TRIPS, which incorporates Articles 1 through 12 and 19 Paris Convention. However, in Central America the protection against unfair competition plays an important practical role, not least as an alternative way to litigate IP cases.[76] In addition, the protection of know-how, in particular test data, and unregistered trademarks developed out of unfair competition law. Therefore, it is important to analyze unfair competition law as an area of law supplemental or even complementary to IP law.

5.4.2 General Principles of Unfair Competition

Unfair competition law protects the results of business efforts to protect the consumer and to promote dynamic competition. It shares the latter objective with IP rights. But unlike IP rights, it is not based on absolute rights relating to such results, but on relative protection against certain abusive or unfair commercial practices.[77]

The following section focuses on the protection of IP through unfair competition rules, because this study focuses on IP protection, especially those areas covered by CAFTA-DR, which do not include unfair competition rules.

There exist in principle two legal systems of unfair competition law. In the restrictive English tradition, the law of "passing off" was created by the courts to protect, *e.g.*, unregistered trademarks. It does not constitute a comprehensive supplement to IP protection which can be easily extended to new subject matter and business relationships.[78] This restrictive approach was based on the assumption that the right to imitate was fundamental to a competitive economy.[79] In the USA and in civil law countries, which used to have a less competitive and more mercantilist economic system (*e.g.*, Spain, Portugal and their colonies in Latin America), broader

[75] According to Article 154.B.3(a) EU-CARIFORUM-EPA, geographical indications shall be protected against "any other use which constitutes an act of unfair competition within the meaning of Article 10bis of the Paris Convention".

[76] In Guatemala, the Ministry of Economy is explicitly charged with combating unfair competition, see Article 32(a) Ley 114-97 del Organismo Ejecutivo, available http://www.mem.gob.gt/wp-content/uploads/2015/06/12._Ley_del_Organismo_Ejecutivo_Decreto_114_97.pdf (accessed 2 Nov 2024).

[77] On the relationship between unfair competition and intellectual property see Henning-Bodewig (2013), p. 6.

[78] Cornish et al. (2013) at 1–15.

[79] Cornish et al. (2013) at 1–15.

systems of protection emerged.[80] In many of these countries a general clause prohibits unfair competition.[81] Central American legislation also provides for such broad unfair competition protection.[82]

5.4.3 Specific Areas of Unfair Competition

5.4.3.1 Trademarks and Advertising

Because unfair competition and trademark law share the objective of protecting the consumer, often unfair competition law may cover trademark-related cases. In Nicaragua, for example, the infringement of a trademark can be the basis for an unfair competition claim.[83] In El Salvador, unfair competition litigation is also an important option for right holders.[84]

Important in Central America is the regulation of marketing practices such as misleading advertising (*publicidad engañosa*).[85] This type of unfair competition covers also the dilution of trademarks which does not constitute a trademark infringement because the use does not indicate a connection between the two signs. Also, there is no legal difference with regard to damages between trademark law and the broader unfair competition provisions.[86]

5.4.3.2 Case Study: Juan Valdez

A good example for the practical application of unfair competition law is the "Juan Valdez" case in Costa Rica. Juan Valdez is the trademark of the Colombian coffee producers' association (*Federación*), protected as a name and as a symbol. For years, its competitor, the Costa Rican producer *Café Britt*, used the slogan "Juan Valdez drinks Costa Rican coffee" in its advertisements and on merchandise.

In January 2006, the *Federación* demanded the merchandise being withdrawn from the market, a demand with which Café Britt complied. In June 2006, the

[80] Cornish et al. (2013) at 1–17.

[81] See, in relation to Brazil, Böttger and Quarch (2013), pp. 146–148 and generally Cornish et al. (2013) at 1–17; in Central America, these general clauses are usually based on Article 10bis (2) Paris Convention, which provides that "any act of competition contrary to honest practices in industrial or commercial matters constitutes an act of unfair competition", see, e.g., Article 172 IP Law (GT); in Germany, unlike in Central America, unfair competition is even protected in a special Unfair Competition Law (UWG).

[82] See, e.g., Article 172 IP Law (GT).

[83] Alvarado (2016).

[84] Romero (2016), p. 83.

[85] See, e.g., Article 272 Criminal Code (NI).

[86] See for example Article 184 IP Law (GT).

Federación filed an unfair competition claim against Café Britt in the town of Heredia, Costa Rica, where Café Britt is domiciled, arguing that the slogan was comparative advertising, constituting *unfair competition*.[87] A claim based on the protection of Juan Valdez as a *well-known mark* was not pursued, probably because Costa Rican trademark law requires at least a *connection* being created with the well-known mark,[88] while in the Juan Valdez case the point of the slogan was the *differentiation* between Colombian and Costa Rican coffee. Café Britt also argued that the use of the slogan was not illegal, because it was a widely known expression in Costa Rica.[89] In retaliation, Café Britt filed a criminal defamation complaint against Gabriel Silva, the CEO of the *Federación*.[90] These lawsuits occurred in the context of the entry of Colombian coffee into the Costa Rican market in early 2007. In late 2008, however, the *Federación* has apparently withdrawn from the Costa Rican market and all lawsuits have been settled sometime afterwards.[91]

This case is instructive for several reasons. First, *Café Britt* did comply with the demand of its competitor without litigation, which corresponds to the observation of many practitioners that the notification of an (alleged) infringement is often sufficient and injunctive relief unnecessary.[92] Second, it shows the practical importance of the broad unfair competition protection as compared to trademark law. And finally, both parties used trademark protection and IP lawsuits as part of their competitive strategy in the Costa Rican market. This was a strategic and sophisticated use of the legal system, and not surprisingly the case concerns coffee, one of Central America's most important commodities.

5.4.3.3 Patents and Know-how/Undisclosed Information

A special type of prohibited marketing practices is the false claim of patent protection or patent ownership, which in addition to civil liability is criminalized in Nicaragua.[93]

Undisclosed information, know-how or business secrets (*secreto empresarial*) are protected against unfair competition under Article 39(1), (2) TRIPS in connection with Article 10*bis* of the Paris Convention (1967). In contrast to TRIPS,[94] in

---

[87] See the newspaper reports available at http://www.nacion.com/archivo/Cafeteros-Cafe-Britt-Juan-Valdez_0_842315798.html (accessed 2 Nov 2024), http://www.ticotimes.net/2006/07/07/lawsuit-filed-over-juan-valdez-and-his-mule (accessed 2 Nov 2024), http://www.ticotimes.net/2006/11/17/coffee-controversy-heats-up (accessed 2 Nov 2024).

[88] Article 35 (c) Trademark Law (CR).

[89] See http://www.ticotimes.net/2006/11/17/coffee-controversy-heats-up (accessed 2 Nov 2024).

[90] See https://www.nacion.com/economia/britt-demanda-a-federacion-colombiana-por-difamacion/IHPGJKDW6BBMNJT2FP3IX6VUJQ/story/ (accessed 2 Nov 2024).

[91] See https://es.wiki2.org/wiki/Juan_Valdez (accessed 2 Nov 2024).

[92] The civil enforcement of IP is further discussed in Sect. 7.3.

[93] The criminal enforcement of IP is further discussed in Sect. 7.7.

[94] Article 39 (1), (2) TRIPS.

CAFTA-DR undisclosed information in general is not regulated. The national legislation in Central America, therefore, still reflects the TRIPS provisions.[95] Undisclosed information is protected, if

- it is secret in the sense that it is not, as a body or in the precise configuration and assembly of its components, generally known among or readily accessible to persons within the circles that normally deal with the kind of information in question,[96]
- it has commercial value because it is secret,[97] and
- it has been subject to steps reasonable under the circumstances, by the person lawfully in control of the information, to keep it secret.[98]

The Guatemalan legislation is a typical example for the scope of protection in Central America. Know-how is protected against the acquisition, exploitation, communication or disclosure by third parties,[99] if it was obtained through the breach of a confidentiality contract, the abuse of confidence, the violation of loyalty obligations or means contrary to honest business practices.[100]

In Central America, undisclosed information plays an important practical role. Because IP protection does not work as effectively as in other jurisdictions, companies often rely on secrecy measures and confidentiality contracts to protect their technology.[101] This protection has the additional procedural advantage that most courts are more familiar with acts of unfair competition than with the infringement of IP rights.[102]

5.4.4 *Procedure*

In Costa Rica, for example, unfair competition claims can be brought in civil proceedings in accordance with Article 17 Law No. 7472.[103] To the extent

[95] E.g., literally identical to the TRIPS provisions, Article 174 IP Law (GT).

[96] Article 39(2)(a) TRIPS, Article 174(a) IP Law (GT), Article 2(a) Undisclosed Information Law (CR), Article 177 IP LAW (SV).

[97] Article 39 (2)(b) TRIPS, Article 174 (chapeau) IP Law (GT), Article 2(c) Undisclosed Information Law (CR), Article 177 IP LAW (SV); see also the definition of know-how in the EU Directive 2016/943 of 8 June 2016 on the protection of undisclosed know-how and business information (trade secrets) against their unlawful acquisition, use and disclosure.

[98] Article 39 (2)(c) TRIPS, Article 174(b) IP Law (GT), Article 2(b) Undisclosed Information Law (CR), Article 177 IP LAW (SV).

[99] Article 175 IP Law (GT).

[100] Article 176 IP Law (GT).

[101] Interview with *Ana Catalina Monge Rodríguez*.

[102] See Sect. 5.4.5.

[103] Law for the promotion of competition and effective defense of the consumer (Ley de Promoción de la Competencia y Defensa Efectiva del Consumidor), Law No. 7472, as amended by Article

consumers are affected by the respective acts constituting unfair competition, administrative and criminal measures may be initiated in addition to civil litigation.[104]

5.4.5 *Practical Relevance*

Practitioners in Central America often prefer litigating IP cases under unfair competition rules; in particular claims based on trademark infringements are often brought as unfair competition claims.[105] One reason is that courts are usually not familiar with the infringement of IP rights.[106]

5.4.6 *Unfair Competition Law and IP Law*

5.4.6.1 Overview

On the statutory level, *e.g.*, in Guatemala, unfair competition is regulated in the IP Law (GT) and is, therefore, formally part of the IP system. In addition, the utilization of goods protected by IP is not only an infringement according to the sections on specific rights, but also constitutes an act of unfair competition.[107] Only if the action is covered by a special criminal provision is the application of the unfair competition provision excluded.[108]

While the double protection under IP law and unfair competition law does not raise practical concerns in cases where both systems complement each other, double protection should not be applied in cases where the *special* IP rules exclude protection. The limitations on the subject matter, rights and term of protection of IP draw the line between the legitimate private protection and the necessary access of competitors and the public. To use unfair competition as the basis for additional protection in such cases overrides the policy decision of the legislator regarding the special patent and design protection and has the potential to permanently restrict competition.[109]

557 of the Code of Civil Procedure of 2016; the text is available at https://www.wipo.int/wipolex/es/legislation/details/21675 (accessed 2 Nov 2024).

[104] Ibid.

[105] Alvarado (2016); see also Romero (2016), p. 83.

[106] As explained above in Sect. 2.5.4, practitioners in Costa Rica noted that the absence of specialized courts poses a challenge, since civil judges are not familiar with IP laws.

[107] Article 173(d) IP Law (GT).

[108] Article 173(d) IP Law (GT).

[109] Ann (2022) § 2 nr 62; Ohly and Sosnitza (2023) Introduction (D) Nr 84.

In Central America, however, the broad utilization of unfair competition law creates the risk of bypassing special industrial protection.[110] The fundamental problem in these cases is the application by the court of the general unfair competition rules which might be considered barred by the special principles of patent or trademark law.

5.4.6.2 Case Study: Sildenafil (Viagra)

A prominent example in Central America for relying on unfair competition law instead of patent or other special protection is the litigation relating to Viagra (or more specifically generic versions using the active pharmaceutical ingredient "Sildenafil").

In Nicaragua, the originator company was able to prevent market entry of a generic competitor by successfully claiming that the statement of bio-equivalence with the originator drug [in a submission for marketing authorization] constitutes an act of unfair competition.[111] Based on the available information one cannot conclusively determine whether this approach circumvented the special protection for originator drugs established by test data protection rules.[112] This case was decided before the adoption of CAFTA-DR rules and before test data protection was introduced in accordance with CAFTA-DR requirements. However, at the time Nicaragua had signed a bilateral agreement with the USA requiring test data protection for five years. Unfortunately, the available reports on this case do not specify whether the court took these rules into account and, more broadly, considered the relationship between general unfair competition rules and specific test data protection.[113]

In El Salvador, the originator company sued a competitor under unfair competition law who sold a generic version of Viagra that not only had the same composition, but also the same form and color. The CSJ (SV) held that the generic drug sales did not constitute unfair competition, because the consumer bought the packaged drugs, not the individual pills, and, therefore, would not be misled by the identical pills.[114]

In the Dominican Republic, by contrast, enforcement was based on a patent covering Sildenafil. This represents the first case in the country in which the CSJ found a patent to be valid and infringed. However, this example serves as an example

---

[110] See Sect. 5.4.3.1 regarding trademarks and Sect. 5.4.6.2 regarding test data protection.

[111] Suescum (2006), p. 13, citing Bendaña-Guerrero, Guy, Estudio de las nuevas leyes de propiedad industrial. UAM, 2003. pp. 96–98.

[112] The international discussion regarding the relationship between unfair competition law and test data protection is discussed in Sect. 3.4.2.

[113] See Suescum (2006), p. 13, citing Bendaña-Guerrero, Guy, Estudio de las nuevas leyes de propiedad industrial. UAM, 2003. pp. 96–98.

[114] CSJ (SV), Sala de lo Civil, 21 December 2007, Pfizer Products Inc. v Ronasa, S.A. de C.V.; for a critical assessment of the court's reasoning see Rangel Ortiz (2011), p. 325.

why right holders may prefer to base their claims on unfair competition. First, the decision was rendered 10 years after the complaint was filed and four years after the expiry of the patent. Second, in a procedurally novel approach the CSJ agreed to hear an appeal of the defendant in a plenary session, in which the original decision was overturned.[115]

References

Alvarado FJ (2016) Trademark protection in Nicaragua, available at https://alvaradoyasociadoslegal.com/blog/trademark-protection-in-nicaragua/. Accessed 2 Nov 2024

Ann C (2022) Patentrecht, 8th edn. C. H. Beck, Munich

Beldiman D, Blanke-Roeser C (2015) European design law: considerations relating to protection of spare parts for restoring a complex product's original appearance. IIC 2015:915–919

Bendaña-Guerrero GJ (1999) *Curso de Derecho* de Propiedad Industrial. Hispamer, Managua, Nicaragua

Böttger F, Quarch T (2013) Brazil. In: Henning-Bodewig F (ed) International handbook on unfair competition. Nomos, Baden-Baden

Cornish W, Llewelyn D, Aplin T (2013) Intellectual property: patents, copyright, trade marks and allied rights, 8th edn. Sweet & Maxwell (cited as Cornish et al. (2013))

Fernández Rodríguez (2015) República Dominicana: la protección de patentes a través de su historia. In: ASIPI, Derecho Farmacéutico y Propiedad Intelectual en América Latina, 2015

Henning-Bodewig F (2013) Unfair competition law - an introduction to a complex topic. In: Henning-Bodewig F (ed) International handbook on unfair competition. Nomos, Baden-Baden

Ohly A, Sosnitza O (2023) Gesetz gegen den unlauteren Wettbewerb, 8th edn. C. H. Beck, Munich

Patent Examiner Manual (2006) Manual de Organización y Examen de Solicitudes de Patentes de Invención de las Oficinas de Propiedad Industrial de los paises del Istmo Centroamericano y la República Dominicana, available at http://www.rnp.go.cr/propiedad_industrial/Documentos/PI_Servicios_Formularios/PI_Manualpatentes.pdf. Accessed 2 Nov 2024

Rangel Ortiz H (2011) La observancia de los derechos de propiedad intelectual - Jurisprudencia, available at http://www.wipo.int/edocs/pubdocs/es/intproperty/627/wipo_pub_627.pdf. Accessed 2 Nov 2024

Romero JR (2016) El Salvador. In: Eckhartt C (ed) Trademarks 2016 (on file with the author)

Suescum A (2006) ANÁLISIS DEL ENTORNO JURÍDICO Y OBSERVANCIA EN NICARAGUA DE LAS DISPOSICIONES DEL CAPÍTULO 15 DEL CAFTA-DR SOBRE LOS DERECHOS DE PROPIEDAD INTELECTUAL - RECOMENDACIONES Y PROPUESTAS PARA PRÓXIMOS PASOS, https://pdf.usaid.gov/pdf_docs/pnadp883.pdf. Accessed 2 Nov 2024

Thomas K (2012) Intellectual property law and the ethics of imitation in Guatemala. Anthropol Q 85(3):785–814

USTR, Special 301 Report 2008., available at https://ustr.gov/about-us/policy-offices/press-office/reports-and-publications/archives/2008/2008-special-301-report. Accessed 2 Nov 2024 (cited as USTR, Special 301 Report 2008)

[115] Fernández Rodríguez (2015), p. 236.

Chapter 6
Genetic Resources and Traditional Knowledge

In this part, Sect. 6.1 analyzes the protection of genetic resources, while Sect. 6.2 addresses specific issues of traditional knowledge protection.

6.1 Genetic Resources

6.1.1 Introduction

The legal protection of *genetic resources*, found in biodiversity-rich countries like Costa Rica, and of *traditional knowledge* of indigenous communities related thereto, *e.g.*, of Maya tribes in the Guatemalan highlands, is usually discussed within the context of the conservation of biodiversity, especially in developing countries. Both issues are not addressed by CAFTA-DR, and only in generic terms by the EU-CARIFORUM-FTA and the EU-CA-AA. However, these issues play a significant role in relation to IP, because of the links to patent law (in particular, the disclosure of origin requirement) and because *sui generis* protection systems are established based on exclusive rights that share common features with traditional IP rights. In Central America, biodiversity protection is of particular relevance, because the region is one of the most biodiversity-rich (also called "mega-biodiversity") areas on earth.[1]

[1] Huettmann (2015), p. 5.

F. Böttger, *CAFTA-DR, European Free Trade Agreements and the Industrial Property System in Central America*, Munich Studies on Innovation and Competition 21, https://doi.org/10.1007/978-3-031-93440-7_6

6.1.2 Policy Considerations

6.1.2.1 Biodiversity

One way to protect biodiversity is to grant a sui generis proprietary right. The policy problem with granting protection to existing subject matter is that it does not provide an incentive for future research. However, *sui generis* protection can be justified because biodiversity should be preserved as a resource used in such future research. This necessity of protection is acknowledged by many countries and legal scholars.[2]

It is generally assumed that appropriate protection cannot be achieved within the current IP system. Special *sui generis* protection is considered necessary, because the subject matter is not new and not eligible for patent protection. Therefore, special mechanisms have been created which provide a substantive and procedural framework, mainly by the Convention on Biological Diversity (CBD).[3]

6.1.2.2 Benefit-Sharing

The utilization of genetic resources and biodiversity-related traditional knowledge has become an issue for developing countries, especially in economic and technological terms. These countries are worried that more innovative developed countries utilize their resources and knowledge without sharing the economic and technological benefits, (ab)using the lack of protection for this subject matter, which does not fit into the classical concepts of IP. Developing countries expect economical compensation for granting access and exploitation rights, and participation with regard to the developed technology.

This issue is discussed under the term "benefit sharing". The concern in this regard is that the universities and companies doing the research and—in some cases—making the money are based in developed countries, while using the genetic resources obtained in developing countries. Biodiversity has, therefore, become one of the battleground issues between "North" and "South" in the international debate about the evolution of the IP system.[4] Many observers see *biopiracy*[5] as evidence that IP protection is systematically discriminating developing countries. Developing countries argue that developed countries appropriate their knowledge through "piracy" or "robbery", while they are excluded from the technology of the developed countries.[6] This is perceived as a new form of colonialism.[7] Some observers,

---

[2] Bucher (2008), p. 70; see Sect. 6.1.5 for further references.

[3] The CBD provides in particular for Prior Informed Consent (PIC) and Access and Benefit Sharing (ABS), see Sect. 6.1.3.

[4] Similarly, Bucher (2008), p. 37.

[5] The origin of the term "biopiracy" is discussed in Sect. 6.1.2.4.

[6] See Sect. 6.1.2.4.

[7] Bucher (2008), p. 45, citing Keating, 87 (2005) J. Pat. & Trademark Off. Soc'y 525, 530.

however, see potential benefits of (traditional) IP protection for the developing countries in relation to biodiversity and their (traditional) knowledge.[8]

The typical scenario underlying the discussion is the use of genetic resources and the knowledge of local tribes by pharmaceutical companies to identify medically useful plants and then exploit these plants without compensating these tribes or contributing to the preservation of biodiversity.

6.1.2.3 Ethical Considerations

Finally, some appropriation practices raise *ethical considerations* related to the privatization of subject matter derived from nature. In addition to the ethical problem of patenting (plant) life, there are also practical concerns. Plant variety protection is criticized because it permits business models which might make small farmers dependent on large agro-businesses that sell seeds which are genetically modified to disable propagation, thus requiring recurring annual purchases, which may also contribute to environmentally dangerous monocultures as farmers increasingly rely on the same seeds.[9]

6.1.2.4 Definitions

"Biological diversity", or in short *biodiversity*, means the variability among living organisms from all sources including *inter alia* terrestrial, marine and other aquatic ecosystems and the ecological complexes of which they are part. This includes diversity within species, between species and of ecosystems.[10] Biodiversity comprises genetic diversity, diversity of species and diversity of ecosystems.[11] The distinction between genetic and other biological resources results in different forms of legal protection. The general law of property applies to the (physical) biological resources, special provisions apply to genetic resources.[12]

As an element of biodiversity, "genetic resources" are particularly relevant for research. The term "genetic resource" refers to genetic material of actual or potential value.[13] Considering the scope of the CBD, relevant is the economic and scientific value.[14] The economically important element of the material is the genetic code, *i.e.*, the genetic information.[15] Because this information as an immaterial element of an

[8]See Hilpert (1998), p. 91 and Rott (2003), p. 107; see also Bucher (2008), p. 79.

[9]Henne (1998), pp. 62–63; see for further references Bucher (2008), p. 310.

[10]Article 2 CBD.

[11]Bucher (2008), p. 27, with further references.

[12]Bucher (2008), p. 47.

[13]Article 2 CBD.

[14]Bucher (2008), p. 27.

[15]Hassemer (2003), p. 153.

organism constitutes its economic value, the system of protection is so closely related to IP protection.[16] Genetic resources can be divided into three subgroups, animal genes, plant genes and micro-organism genes.[17]

The appropriation of these genetic resources by international companies has become generally known under the term *biopiracy*.[18] The term includes broadly speaking three distinct, but related issues: "Piracy" indicates that these resources are taken *without consent* of the host country or community and without compensation. But the term also indirectly expresses the concern over the *aggressive nature* of exploitation practices, which in some cases include legal measures to exclude the host community from further using the genetic resource or the plants which contain it. Finally, it reflects the *moral objection* to the appropriation of elements of nature, which in this view should not be privatized through the legal means of traditional IP rights.

6.1.2.5 Stakeholders

In contrast to some traditional areas of IP, the protection of genetic resources and traditional knowledge is not only controversial on the international level between developed and developing countries, but also on the national level between special business interests and the indigenous communities. As biodiversity is a global public good, its conservation is the priority of many international NGOs. National and local stakeholders are more concerned with benefit-sharing and ethical issues.

On the international level, the protection and maintenance of a diverse biological environment is supported by public interest groups for environmental and ethical reasons. Developing countries have a special interest in protection, because they are the host countries of most of the global biodiversity and, under international law, they are the owners of the genetic resources.[19] They expect to profit from the sharing of economic benefits and to maintain their own access. International opposition comes *inter alia* from pharmaceutical companies and some developed countries. These stakeholders argue against the regulation of access to genetic resources, because the additional administrative and financial obligations increase their research costs. To discourage regulation, they claim that bio-prospecting is not an important business model and not worth the legislative and administrative effort (as the evidence in Costa Rica shows, this claim is not unfounded).[20] *Bucher*

---

[16] Bucher (2008), p. 56, argues that this information does not result from human intellectual activity and, therefore, does not qualify for IP protection.

[17] Henne, Genetische Vielfalt als Ressource, 1998, p. 42.

[18] On the origin of the term "biopiracy" see Drahos (2000), p. 245; see also Bucher (2008), pp. 72–73, and the references in Cabrera Medaglia et al. (2014), p. 19.

[19] See, e.g., Articles 3 and 15(1) CBD.

[20] As discussed in more detail in Sect. 6.1.8, the value derived from a healthy, biodiverse environment through ecotourism appears considerably bigger than the revenue generated by the Costa Rican ABS system.

suggests that regulation might discourage cooperation activities and thus be counter-productive in promoting the commercialization of biodiversity. Such activities might be the reason why the USA has not yet ratified the CBD.[21]

In Central America, the rural, especially indigenous communities who traditionally manage and depend on the local biodiversity are the direct beneficiaries of any system of biodiversity protection. Their interests can directly be addressed by rights relating to traditional knowledge, because these can belong to the indigenous communities themselves. In relation to genetic resources, which are owned by the state, they could be included in benefit-sharing mechanisms, because they have the most direct and vital interest in preserving the environment, which is the basis of their livelihood. These communities have a genuine interest in the protection of biodiversity.

In Latin America, indigenous communities have traditionally been politically weak, but lately have increased their influence and forcefully claim more and effective rights.[22] The protection of traditional knowledge and plant varieties has been an important element of this movement.[23] It coincided with the development of genetic research, which increased the potential economic value of plant genetic resources and the interest in their legal appropriation.[24] Examples for this development in Latin America were the protests in Costa Rica against CAFTA-DR in 2008[25] and the violent protests by indigenous communities in Peru in 2009. In Peru, the protesters opposed the implementation of the FTA with the USA, because of its impact on these communities and protected areas, and succeeded in forcing the government to suspend the implementation.[26]

Opposition against the protection of genetic resources on the national level comes from domestic *business sectors* seeking to exploit natural resources with as little financial or legal restraint as possible. In Central America, especially the farmers' associations are opposing the indigenous groups.[27] The farming industry is responsible for roughly 65% and the logging industry for 25% of the deforestation in Latin America.[28] As a result, in Guatemala, a large part of the *Petén* rainforest has disappeared.[29] This conflict is also a result of the appropriation and privatization

---

[21] Bucher (2008), p. 94.

[22] Bucher (2008), p. 25.

[23] Bucher (2008), p. 65.

[24] Bucher (2008), p. 34 with further references.

[25] See Sect. 2.2.1.

[26] See *New York Times*, Peru Overturns Decrees That Incited Protests, 18 June 2009, available at https://www.nytimes.com/2009/06/19/world/americas/19peru.html?scp=3&sq=peru&st=nyt (accessed 2 Nov 2024).

[27] Morales Marroquín et al. (2023), p. 2.

[28] See, regarding Brazil, Henne (1998), p. 55; these numbers probably apply in roughly the same way to the similarly structured Central American societies.

[29] See the study by Hughell and Butterfield (2008), which also provides graphical illustrations of the affected areas and information on land use and protection of the Petén rainforest.

of public or indigenous territories during and after the colonization.[30] As a consequence of this development, the current owners of bio-diverse land are often no longer interested in its conservation. These businesses are usually well-organized and, therefore, politically more influential than indigenous communities.

There is also an *ethnic dimension* to this issue, as the businesses are usually operated by the *mestizo* population (with partly European ancestry) and the biodiversity-rich rural areas are often inhabited by the indigenous population. Ethnic conflicts still affect the process of nation-building in many Central American countries, and some observers are concerned that the claim to special legislation and autonomous protection even in the limited sphere of biodiversity is considered dangerous, because it might lead to claims for more political autonomy as well.[31] Several Central American countries, especially Guatemala, with its large and geographically concentrated indigenous population, as well as El Salvador, have experienced severe internal conflicts caused by ethnic tensions.[32] These countries are still trying to build multi-ethnic nation-states and are sensitive about any policy measure with the potential of creating conflict. Any legislation in these countries would also have to take this ethnic dimension into account.

Costa Rica is, not surprisingly, the only country in Central America which developed a comprehensive statutory and institutional system for the protection of genetic resources and codified the protection of indigenous rights in the area of biodiversity. Here, the relevance of the ethnic issue and the power of the farmers were more balanced than in other countries in the region. The percentage of indigenous people in Costa Rica is the smallest in Central America and the ethnic homogeneity the highest.[33] Maybe in part because of this homogeneity, the country has a strong civil society to balance special economic interest and has not undergone ethnic conflicts and civil wars as other countries. Because of the smaller impact of the opposing interests, ecological movements emerged already in the 1970ies and achieved tangible success, especially in reforestation and the creation of protected areas.[34] In 1994, the country initiated the project for the systematic registration of the diversity of species in the *Guanacaste* region and adopted its *National Biodiversity Program*.[35] Today, the ecological awareness of the public extends also to the value of the country's considerable biodiversity and its genetic resources, complemented by the importance of ecotourism.[36] The possible negative effects of CAFTA-DR on

[30] Stoll and von Hahn (2003), p. 14.

[31] Stoll and von Hahn (2003), p. 29.

[32] See Sect. 1.3.

[33] Dutfield (2004), p. 148.

[34] Bucher (2008), pp. 252–253.

[35] Bucher (2008), p. 307.

[36] The economic relevance of ecotourism in Costa Rica is further discussed in Sect. 6.1.8; there is widespread public awareness in relation to the importance and value of biodiversity and the necessity of legal protection in Costa Rica, according to the author's own experience.

biodiversity protection were pointed out frequently by the opposition in the national debate on the agreement.[37]

6.1.3 International Legal Framework

6.1.3.1 Multilateral Agreements

As the protection of biodiversity, especially genetic resources, serves economically the interests of developing countries, international protection was created within the framework of the UNO, where they have more political weight, not within the WTO, which is dominated by the developed countries. The issue is addressed in particular by the Convention on Biological Diversity, the International Treaty on Plant Genetic Resources for Food and Agriculture of the FAO (FAO Plant Treaty), the Convention Concerning Indigenous and Tribal Peoples in Independent Countries of the ILO (Indigenous Peoples Convention) and the (not binding) United Nations Declaration on the Rights of Indigenous Peoples of 2007 (DRIPS).[38]

The issue is primarily regulated by the CBD. It introduced basic concepts of the *sui generis* system, such as the Prior Informed Consent (PIC), the system of Access and Benefit Sharing (ABS) and the disclosure of origin within the process of patent examination. It has been ratified by all Central American countries in the mid-1990ies (except Nicaragua, which ratified it in 2015), but not by the USA.[39] As supplement to the CBD, the parties adopted the *Nagoya Protocol on Access to Genetic Resources and the Fair and Equitable Sharing of Benefits Arising from their Utilization (ABS) to the Convention on Biological Diversity* (Nagoya Protocol) in 2010.[40] Until 2016, it had been ratified by the Dominican Republic, Guatemala and Honduras.[41] Nicaragua became a party in 2020.[42] Costa Rica has signed but not ratified the Nagoya Protocol.[43]

[37] E.g., as observed by the author, local generic drug manufacturers, who used this issue to argue against CAFTA-DR generally.

[38] See Bucher (2008), p. 94.

[39] Costa Rica did so on 26 August 1994, Dominican Republic on 25 November 1996, El Salvador on 8 September 1994, Guatemala on 10 July 1995, Honduras on 31 July 1995 and Nicaragua on 20 November 2015, see http://www.cbd.int/convention/parties/list/ (accessed 2 Nov 2024).

[40] The Nagoya Protocol way adopted on 29 October 2010 in Nagoya, Japan and entered into force on 12 October 2014, see https://www.cbd.int/abs/about/ (accessed 2 Nov 2024); the text of the Nagoya Protocol is available at https://www.cbd.int/abs/doc/protocol/nagoya-protocol-en.pdf (accessed 2 Nov 2024).

[41] See the list of parties available at https://www.cbd.int/abs/nagoya-protocol/signatories/ (accessed 2 Nov 2024).

[42] Nicaragua has ratified the Nagoya protocol on 12 June 2020 and became a party on 10 September 2020, see the list of parties available at https://www.cbd.int/abs/nagoya-protocol/signatories/ (accessed 2 Nov 2024).

[43] Cabrera Medaglia (2020), p. 2.

It provides a framework for the fair and equitable sharing of benefits arising out of the utilization of genetic resources, in particular it regulates the access to genetic resources[44] and access to traditional knowledge.[45] The parties must implement these provisions into their national legislation.

Also relevant is the *FAO Plant Treaty*, which has been ratified or accepted by all Central American countries around 2005, except the Dominican Republic.[46] The Dominican Republic ratified the FAO Plant Treaty in 2022.[47] By the acceptance, the respective country becomes bound in the same way as by ratification.[48] The treaty recognizes the importance of genetic resources and of the conservation efforts of indigenous people, but provides that the protection of traditional knowledge[49] and benefit-sharing in relation to the use of genetic resources[50] belongs to the national level and is not mandatory.[51] In any case, the treaty applies only to a limited number of resources, which are all in the public domain.[52] This prevents conflicts with IP rights and TRIPS.[53]

In 1989, the International Labor Organization (ILO) adopted the Indigenous Peoples Convention. It was ratified by 18 countries, in particular from Latin America, including Costa Rica, Guatemala, Honduras and since 2010 Nicaragua.[54] Substantially, it protects the indigenous peoples' rights regarding their land and the resources in it.[55] The broad wording suggests that biological resources are included.[56] Procedurally, it requires the consultation of indigenous peoples, if their rights are directly affected.[57]

---

[44] Article 6 Nagoya Protocol.

[45] Articles 7 and 12 Nagoya Protocol.

[46] Costa Rica, El Salvador and Guatemala by ratification; Honduras and Nicaragua by acceptance, see https://www.fao.org/plant-treaty/countries/membership/en/ (accessed 2 Nov 2024).

[47] Ibid.

[48] See Article 14 (2) Vienna Convention on the Law of Treaties.

[49] Article 9(2)(a) FAO Plant Treaty.

[50] Article 9(2)(b) FAO Plant Treaty.

[51] "[T]he responsibility for realizing Farmers' Rights, as they relate to plant genetic resources for food and agriculture, rests with national governments. In accordance with their needs and priorities, each Contracting Party should, as appropriate, and subject to its national legislation, take measures to protect and promote Farmers' Rights […]", Article 9(2) FAO Plant Treaty.

[52] Article 11(2) FAO Plant Treaty.

[53] Bucher (2008), p. 101.

[54] El Salvador and the Dominican Republic are not members, see the list of ratifications available at http://www.ilo.org/dyn/normlex/en/f?p=1000:11300:0::NO:11300:P11300_INSTRUMENT_ID:312314 (accessed 2 Nov 2024).

[55] Article 14 Nr. 1 and Article 15 Nr. 2 ILO Indigenous Peoples Convention.

[56] von Hahn (2004), p. 91; similarly, Bucher (2008), p. 67.

[57] Article 6 and 7 Indigenous Peoples Convention.

The implementation of this consultation process in Costa Rican national law was the basis for the invalidation by the CSJ in 2008 of the draft CAFTA-DR reform law, which had been approved without consultation of affected indigenous peoples.[58]

6.1.3.2 Application of Multilateral Agreements

The application of these agreements is conditioned in two ways. First, they provide only for rights of parties, not individuals. The implementation is, therefore, in the discretion of each country.[59] In Costa Rica, however, international treaties have a higher rank than ordinary laws,[60] and are as such taken into consideration by the courts.

Second, the application in Central America must take into account the obligations under other international treaties, especially TRIPS and CAFTA-DR. Practically, in cases of conflict between agreements pertaining to genetic resources, such as the CBD and Indigenous Peoples Convention on the one hand and TRIPS and bilateral FTAs on the other hand, the latter can be expected to have more weight: In most countries, the environmental and biodiversity laws have been passed in the late 1990ies, while TRIPS and bilateral FTAs were implemented later, and, therefore, the latter enjoy priority under the *lex posterior* principle[61] Practically, the stronger dispute settlement mechanism gives the WTO agreements more impact than the UN treaties.[62]

Also, CAFTA-DR recognizes (only) the importance of and mutual supportiveness in relation to multilateral environmental agreements to which *all* CAFTA-DR members are party.[63] This reflects Article 30 para 4 Vienna Convention on the Law of Treaties, that specifies that a posterior agreement only prevails over a prior one if all relevant countries are members to the respective agreement. As the US has not ratified the CBD,[64] this conversely means that in relation to the USA the Central American countries cannot rely on their rights and obligations under the CBD to justify any non-compliance with CAFTA-DR.

Costa Rica and El Salvador are not parties to the Nagoya Protocol, so between them and the other Central American countries, only TRIPS and the CBD itself are applicable; here the posterior agreement depends on a case-by-case analysis, as the CBD was ratified by Costa Rica before, but by the other countries after the

[58] See Sect. 3.1.4.4.

[59] Bucher (2008), p. 96.

[60] Cabrera Medaglia (2004), pp. 101 and 117.

[61] Article 30 Vienna Convention on the Law of Treaties.

[62] Bucher (2008), p. 97.

[63] Article 17.12 CAFTA-DR, on the agreement's "Relationship to Environmental Agreements".

[64] See Sect. 6.1.3.1; for details regarding the USA and the CBD, see the CBD country page available at http://www.cbd.int/countries/?country=us (accessed 2 Nov 2024).

ratification of TRIPS. As between the other Central American countries, the Nagoya Protocol is the posterior agreement.

This raises the question whether TRIPS and the CBD (including the Nagoya Protocol) are compatible. While some Latin American and African countries argue that both agreements cannot be reconciled, most observers assume compatibility.[65] The CBD covers genetic resources, *i.e.*, *existing* knowledge, while TRIPS covers inventions, *i.e.*, *new* knowledge.[66] Therefore, the CBD is only a balance to TRIPS, not a conflicting system.[67] This view is supported by the text of the CBD, which recognizes the importance of IP protection for technology transfer.[68] Still, some observers consider changes to the patent law provisions of TRIPS necessary to implement the CBD.[69]

In particular, an amendment requiring the disclosure of the origin of inventions relating to biodiversity as part of a patent application has been proposed in the form of an amendment of TRIPS.[70]

6.1.3.3 CAFTA-DR

The inability of the USA and several Latin American countries to find a compromise on biodiversity protection was one of the reasons why the project for the Free Trade Agreement of the Americas (FTAA) failed.[71] Biodiversity protection was also one of the major obstacles for the ratification of CAFTA-DR in Costa Rica.[72] Because of the position of the USA on the matter, the environmental chapter of CAFTA-DR does not recognize the CBD or the substantive issue of protecting biodiversity-related knowledge as such.[73] However, the investment chapter contains a reference to the ABS system: "*Provided that such measures are not applied in an arbitrary or unjustifiable manner (and) do not constitute a disguised restriction on international trade or investment*", CAFTA-DR does not exclude "*measures related to the conservation of living or non-living exhaustible natural resources*".[74] Such

[65] Bucher (2008), p. 98, with further references.

[66] Hassemer (2003), p. 171.

[67] Hassemer (2003), p. 182.

[68] Article 16(2) and (3) CBD.

[69] E.g., the EU and Brazil, see Bucher (2008), p. 98.

[70] See Sect. 3.1.6.2.

[71] Bucher (2008), p. 71.

[72] The effects of CAFTA-DR on biodiversity protection were a contentious issue before the signature of the agreement, but also impeded the statutory implementation of the IP provisions, see Sect. 3.1.4.4.

[73] See Article 17.12 CAFTA-DR.

[74] Article 10.9(3)(c)(iii) CAFTA-DR.

measures can include the *requirement "to transfer a particular technology, a production process, or other proprietary knowledge"*.[75]

Countries may, therefore, mandate the transfer of technology as part of their system of access and benefit sharing, which would normally be excluded because technology is a protected investment. Apart from this exception, there are several possible tensions between CAFTA-DR and the national legislation, parallel to the conflicts between TRIPS and the CBD. One concern is the relationship between the UPOV Convention and the protection of genetic resources. While Article 15.1.5 CAFTA states that there is no conflict, this legal fiction is practically questionable, because the UPOV Convention does not foresee mechanisms to prevent the protection of plant varieties obtained illegally. It is also unclear whether investments made in relation to bio-prospecting fall under the investment chapter and whether, therefore, the termination of the permission for bio-prospecting would constitute an illegal expropriation.[76] Finally, the text of Article 15.9 CAFTA-DR regarding patent procedure is ambiguous in relation to the exclusion or permission of requirements for the disclosure of origin.[77]

6.1.3.4 EU-FTAs

The EU-CARIFORUM-EPA is more considerate in relation to genetic resources (and traditional knowledge). It states that (i) traditional knowledge shall be protected, subject to the domestic legislation of the parties,[78] and (ii) the patent provisions of the EU-CARIFORUM-EPA and the Convention on Biological Diversity shall be implemented in a mutually supportive way.[79]

In the EU-CA-AA, the parties recognize (i) that the EU-CA-AA shall not prevent the parties from adopting or maintaining measures to promote the conservation of biological diversity, the sustainable utilization of its components and the fair and equitable participation in the benefits arising from the utilization of genetic resources[80] and (ii) the importance of respecting, preserving and maintaining the indigenous and local communities' knowledge, innovations and practices that involve traditional practices related to the preservation and the sustainable use of biological diversity.[81]

[75] Article 10.9(1)(f) CAFTA-DR.

[76] Cabrera Medaglia (2008), sec. 2.

[77] See Sect. 3.1.6.2.

[78] Article 150(A) EU-CARIFORUM-EPA.

[79] Article 150(C) EU-CARIFORUM-EPA.

[80] Article 229.4 EU-CA-AA.

[81] Article 229.5 EU-CA-AA.

6.1.3.5 Regional Agreements

On the regional level, within the Central American Integration System (*Sistema de la Integración Centroamericana*, SICA) the Central American countries (including Belize and Panama) created the Central American Commission for Environment and Development (Comisión Centroamericana de Ambiente y Desarrollo, CCAD).[82]

The CCAD drafted a Convention for the Conservation of Biodiversity (*Convenio para la Conservación de la Biodiversidad y Protección de Áreas Silvestres Prioritarias en Ámerica Central)*, which entered into force on 5 June 1992.[83] However, this Convention provides only for measures of environmental protection, not for mechanisms to exploit biodiversity, as contemplated by the CBD.

One of its subsequent projects, initiated by the ministries responsible for environmental protection, was the draft of the Central American Agreement/Protocol on Access to Genetic and Biochemical Resources and Related Traditional Knowledge (*Acuerdo/Protocolo Centroamericano de Acceso a los Recursos Genéticos y Bioquímicos y al Conocimiento Tradicional Asociado*, ACARG) created in 2000.[84] This draft provides for the PIC and ABS procedures as foreseen in the CBD[85] and, in addition, for *sui generis* protection of individual and collective traditional knowledge, including the right to object the utilization of protected subject matter by third parties for moral reasons.[86] However, this draft has not (yet) entered into force.[87]

6.1.4 National Legal Framework

6.1.4.1 Costa Rica

In Central America, a *sui generis* framework was adopted by Costa Rica, were legislation for both areas of protection, genetic resources and traditional knowledge, has been passed.

As already mentioned, the most developed system for the protection and management of genetic resources exists in Costa Rica, where a *sui generis* framework was adopted and legislation for both areas of protection, genetic resources and

---

[82] On the activities of this institution see http://www.sica.int/ccad/ (accessed 2 Nov 2024).

[83] The text is available at https://www.sica.int/busqueda/busqueda_archivo.aspx?Archivo=leys_6920_1_27032006.pdf (accessed 2 Nov 2024).

[84] See the summary on the CBD website, at https://www.cbd.int/abs/measures/measure.shtml?id=8165 (accessed 2 Nov 2024).

[85] Articles 12 to 27 ACARG.

[86] Article 28 to 35 ACARG.

[87] In 2009, this legislative project was still in the draft stage, see Aguiñada Arévalo et al. (2009), p. 49.

traditional knowledge, has been passed.[88] The central piece of legislation is the Biodiversity Law (CR) (*Ley de Biodiversidad*), which implements the CBD.[89] It protects genetic resources and related traditional knowledge and creates an access and benefit sharing system, which includes financial benefits and technology transfer. The Biodiversity Law (CR) also provides that the respective system must benefit not only the current stakeholders but also future generations.[90]

Articles 7, 78, 80 and 81 Biodiversity Law (CR) were reformed to implement CAFTA-DR, because they directly or indirectly affect patent law. The articles contain in particular the following provisions:

Article 7 Biodiversity Law (CR) contains a list of definitions; the definition of "microorganisms" was specified (without material substantive change) by the CAFTA-DR Reform Law I (CR), in connection with the change of Article 78-(3) Biodiversity Law (CR).

Article 78 Biodiversity Law (CR) contains exclusions from patentability: In subsection (3), the term "microorganisms which are not genetically modified" (original Biodiversity Law (CR)) was replaced with "microorganisms as found in nature" (CAFTA-DR Reform Law I (CR)).

In subsection (6), "inventions essentially derived from traditional knowledge" are excluded. The draft of the second CAFTA-DR reform law and later the Regulation 34959-MINAET-COMEX added "as long as they do not meet the patentability requirements" of the Patent and Design Law (CR), but, as discussed, the draft law and the regulation were subsequently invalidated by the *Sala IV* of the CJS (CR) on 14 December 2012, because the changes exceeded the CAFTA-DR requirements without the necessary consultation of indigenous communities.[91] Therefore, the original wording remains valid.

In subsection (7), the exclusion of "inventions which affect agricultural processes or product considered essential for the food supply and health of the national citizenry" was broadened by CAFTA-DR Reform Law II (CR) to encompass "inventions whose commercial exploitation must necessarily be prevented to protect public order or morality, or to protect the health or lives of persons or animals or to preserve plants, or to avoid serious damage to the environment.". This change is notable because this exception is not limited to patents in the field of biodiversity nor are the exceptions necessarily related to biodiversity consideration. While this raises the question whether this clause is therefore "out of scope" for a biodiversity law, practically the wording is identical to Article 1(4)(a) Patent and Design Law (CR) and therefore the clause seems to be simply a restatement without specific application.

---

[88] This legislation is discussed in detail by Bucher (2008), p. 26.

[89] The text of the law is available at https://www.wipo.int/wipolex/en/legislation/details/896 (accessed 2 Nov 2024).

[90] The objectives of the law are analyzed in detail by Bucher (2008), p. 259.

[91] Boletín Judicial N° 137 of 17 July 2013.

Article 80 Biodiversity Law (CR) requires the RPI to consult the Technical Office of CONAGEBIO during the patent examination procedure in case the respective patent includes elements of biodiversity. The Regulation 34958-MINAET-COMEX limited the grounds for opposing the patent application to patentability requirements, meaning that the non-compliance with requirements of the Biodiversity Law (CR), such as prior informed consent or benefit sharing, were excluded. The Regulation regarding Article 80 was invalidated by the CSJ on 5 December 2012 because the indigenous peoples had not been consulted as required.[92]

Article 81 Biodiversity Law (CR) grants a compulsory license to patents in the field of biodiversity to the state without financial compensation. This mechanism was limited to patents relating to "national" biodiversity by CAFTA-DR Reform Law II (CR).

Regulation 31514-MINAE-CR[93] further defines the access and benefit-sharing regime, the role of the National Commission for the Management of the Biodiversity (*Comisión Nacional para la Gestión de la Biodiversidad*, CONAGEBIO), a governmental agency under the Ministry for Environment and Energy,[94] and provides for an elaborate list of definitions.[95] In particular, the Regulation 34958-MINAET-COMEX establishes the participation of CONAGEBIO in the patent examination procedure.

6.1.4.2 Nicaragua

In Nicaragua there used to be only indirect regulation on genetic resources in the general environmental legislation. The Environment Law (NI)[96] and related statutes focus on protected areas and the sustainable exploitation of forests, and on the exportation of plants and animals.[97] The Environment Law (NI) deals with biodiversity and the national genetic heritage (*Biodiversidad y el Patrimonio Genético Nacional*) in Chapter II and only indirectly addresses the protection of genetic

[92] CSJ (*Sala IV*), decision of 5 December 2012, Acción de inconstitucionalidad contra el Decreto Ejecutivo N° 34958 MINAET-COMEX, 10-000782-0007-CO, Decision No. 2012-017058, Boletín Judicial N° 111 of 11 June 2013.

[93] The text of the decree is available at https://www.wipo.int/edocs/lexdocs/laws/es/cr/cr019es.pdf (accessed 2 Nov 2024).

[94] Article 13 Biodiversity Law (CR).

[95] Regulation 31514-MINAE of 3 October 2003 (Decreto N° 31514-MINAE de 03 de octubre 2003, Normas Generales de Acceso a los Elementos y Recursos de la Biodiversidad Genética y Bioquímica), available at http://www.wipo.int/edocs/lexdocs/laws/es/cr/cr019es.pdf (accessed 2 Nov 2024).

[96] Environment and Natural Resource Law (Ley General del Medio Ambiente y de los Recursos Naturales), Law No. 217, adopted on 27 March 1996, entered into force 6 June 1996, available at http://legislacion.asamblea.gob.ni/Normaweb.nsf/($All)/1B5EFB1E58D7618A0625711600561572 (accessed 2 Nov 2024).

[97] Pérez (2008), p. 102.

resources via the protection of species. The Environment Law (NI) mandates the adoption of an executing regulation for access procedures,[98] and required the government to propose a biodiversity law by November 1996.[99] Despite this statutory obligation, the Nicaraguan government for a long time did not pass such a biodiversity law. An inter-institutional commission had drafted a proposal in 2006, but the draft was "not implemented for limitations of different types".[100] Nevertheless, in 2012, the Conservation and Sustainable Utilization of Biological Diversity Law (*Ley de Conservación y Utilización Sostenible de la Diversidad Biológica*) (Biodiversity Law (NI)) was finally adopted, which covers in particular the protection of genetic resources and establishes *sui generis* protection for traditional knowledge.[101] During the long consultation and negotiation process, civil society representatives were invited to participate through the multi-stakeholder "technical commission".[102] The *Directorate General of Natural Resources and Biodiversity* (Biodiversity Directorate) of the Ministry of the Environment and Natural Resources (MARENA) is responsible for implementing the law.[103] Between 2013 and 2014, MARENA conducted an assessment and planning program for a national strategy regarding the status of biodiversity and its sustainable use in Nicaragua.[104]

6.1.4.3 Other Countries

In other Central American countries, there is no specific legislation regarding genetic resources and traditional knowledge. These issues are only covered, in rudimentary fashion, in the general environmental protection and cultural heritage legislation.

In El Salvador, the general environmental law provides for the future development of specific ABS regulations, however, the draft of a detailed ABS law, which had been developed several years earlier, had not been submitted to the parliament for approval until 2014.[105]

In Honduras, Article 108 Forest Law (HN) (*Ley Forestal, Áreas Protegidas y Vida Silvestre*)[106] provides that the National System of Protected Areas and Forest

---

[98] Article 63 Environment Law (NI).

[99] Article 70 Environment Law (NI); the Environment Law (NI) entered into force on 2 May 1996. Article 70 Environment Law (NI) requires a proposal within 6 months.

[100] Pérez (2008), p. 103.

[101] Ley No. 807, passed by the parliament on 5 September 2012 and entered into force with the publication in the official gazette on 19 October 2012, available at http://www.wipo.int/edocs/lexdocs/laws/es/ni/ni049es.pdf (accessed 2 Nov 2024).

[102] Cabrera Medaglia et al. (2014), p. 37.

[103] Article 11 Biodiversity Law (NI).

[104] See the final report available at https://faolex.fao.org/docs/pdf/nic167166.pdf (accessed 2 Nov 2024).

[105] Cabrera Medaglia et al. (2014), p. 53.

[106] The text of the law is available at https://faolex.fao.org/docs/pdf/hon77556.pdf (accessed 2 Nov 2024).

Life (SINAPN) shall supervise investigations regarding biodiversity, taking traditional practices of local communities into account. In addition, the General Directorate of Biodiversity, a division of the SERNA agency (*Secretaria de Estado en los Despachos de Recursos Naturales y Ambiente*), is responsible for coordinating actions for the conservation, protection and sustainable use of biodiversity.[107] Honduras ratified the Nagoya Protocol on 28 May 2013 by Decree Nr. 41-2013, but has not yet created implementing legislation.[108]

Similarly, Guatemala developed a comprehensive regulatory and institutional framework for ABS between 2012 and 2014. The framework was intended to protect traditional knowledge associated with the sustainable use of biodiversity as well as genetic resources.[109] However, the application of the Nagoya Protocol (ratified in 2014 by Decree 6-2014) and the proposal for a "Law for the protection of biological diversity and the biocultural heritage of indigenous groups and local communities of Guatemala" in 2018 met with strong political and public opposition and were unsuccessful.[110]

6.1.5 Sui Generis *Protection*

6.1.5.1 Introduction

The fundamental legal question regarding the protection of genetic resources is whether to create such protection within the IP system or by a *sui generis* system.

The protection of genetic resources through the existing IP system is difficult, because no IP right really fits to the specific necessities. The patent system only grants protection for (new) inventions.[111] The information contained in the genetic resources already existing in nature does not meet the novelty requirement and is thus not patentable. In addition, the publication of the knowledge and the limited term of protection will often not be in the interest of the indigenous communities.[112] Other IP rights might be suitable for specific cases: The protection of *plant varieties* through the *sui generis* protection under the UPOV Convention can be more

---

[107] See the entity's website, https://portalunico.iaip.gob.hn/390/ (accessed 2 Nov 2024).

[108] The text of Decree Nr. 41-2013 is available at https://absch.cbd.int/api/v2013/documents/21760536-F250-7DC7-EC23-7F7CA597F758/attachments/203625/decreto%2041%202013%20ratificacion%20Protocolo%20de%20Nagoya.pdf (accessed 2 Nov 2024).

[109] Cabrera Medaglia et al. (2014), p. 53; this system is developed as part of the 2013 National Biodiversity Strategy and Action Plan, see CONAP, V Informe Nacional de Cumplimiento a los Arcuerdos del Convenio sobre Diversidad Biológica, 2014, p. 26, https://www.cbd.int/doc/world/gt/gt-nr-05-es.pdf (accessed 2 Nov 2024).

[110] Heinrich et al. (2020), p. 9.

[111] On the utilization of patent law for traditional knowledge see Taubman and Leistner (2003), p. 65; Dutfield (2004), p. 105; Bucher (2008), pp. 80–81 and 90.

[112] Bucher (2008), p. 103.

practically viable, because it does not require absolute novelty.[113] There are (even though few) examples that traditional knowledge can be indirectly protected through distinctive signs, especially *collective marks*.[114] Traditional knowledge may be protected as *undisclosed information*. Such protection requires that the knowledge is kept secret by native and indigenous communities and is of technological and economic value. Such knowledge is protected against unfair competition,[115] which allows contractual solutions and thus commercial exploitation through licensing.

Nevertheless, this still leaves the usual cases of genetic resources without proper protection, as the information contained in the genetic resources is not protected by the traditional IP rights.[116] Because of these problems with IP protection, it is considered necessary to create a special *sui generis* system for the protection of traditional knowledge and genetic resources, to provide control over the access and ensure compensation.

There exist several options regarding the design of *sui generis* regimes of protection. Some focus more on the protection against misappropriation by developed countries and ethical concerns of exploiting nature, *e.g.*, the proposal by *Carlos Correa*.[117] Such systems address primarily the *biopiracy* concerns and appeal specifically to developing countries. Proposals originating in developed countries usually focus more on the management and exploitation mechanisms, *e.g.*, the regime developed by *Peter Drahos* based on a "Global Bio-collecting Society".[118]

6.1.5.2 Policy Considerations

The protection of genetic resources and traditional knowledge addresses several policy objectives, most importantly:

- the restriction of the access of third parties in order to create an incentive to conserve biodiversity, to ensure the sharing of economic benefits between developed and developing countries and to prevent the possible abuse of "sensitive" knowledge, and
- the maintenance of the domestic use by the host countries and local communities and preventing the exclusion from the resources by third parties.

The restriction of the access of third parties is achieved by a proprietary right to exclude third parties from using genetic resources and the maintenance of the domestic use by safeguards of the right to use against exclusion from third parties.

---

[113] The utilization of the protection of plant varieties for traditional knowledge is discussed in more detail in Sect. 3.3 above.

[114] On the possible use of collective marks for traditional knowledge see Sect. 4.3.

[115] Dutfield (2003), p. 39.

[116] Bucher (2008), p. 43.

[117] See Correa (2001), pp. 18–19, on the "misappropriation option".

[118] Drahos (2000), p. 247.

Any comprehensive system of protection of genetic resources and traditional knowledge should include both of these elements, *i.e.*, the rights of local communities to use it and to prevent the monopolization by third parties, and the rights to exclude the access by third parties and ensure benefit-sharing.[119]

6.1.5.3 Protection of Biodiversity

One aspect of the problem of biodiversity protection is the exploitation of biodiversity by users who do not invest in its conservation. Simply put, those who profit do not protect, and those who protect do not profit. *Cabrera Medaglia* describes it as follows: The country providing the research material gets nothing, the country or company doing the research gets everything.[120] This asymmetry threatens the sustainable use of biodiversity. In Central America, as elsewhere, both the loss of rainforest areas and the use of monocultures contribute to the limitation of biodiversity. To reverse this situation, it is considered necessary to create some form of protection for the host country to ensure that the economic benefits derived from the exploitation of these resources are shared. By protecting genetic resources as an element of biodiversity, its use could be made more profitable for those responsible for and capable of protecting it, thus creating an incentive to conserve biodiversity.[121] There are several ecological and socioeconomic *reasons for conservation*. The protection of genetic resources may help to maintain the biological material which is used directly by 80% of the population in developing countries for their medical treatment and as the basis for future medical research.[122] It enables the breeding of new crop varieties, *e.g.*, crops immune to diseases or more nutritious to improve food security, from a large genetic pool. This makes biodiversity also an important element of economic growth.[123] In her study on biodiversity protection in Latin America, *Bucher* refers to former US president *Thomas Jefferson*, who stated that the greatest gift to a country was to add a useful plant to its society.[124] The protection of biodiversity also has spill-over benefits in supporting the preservation of (rain)forests, which play an important role in the global climate system, including the control of the carbon dioxide level in the atmosphere.[125]

Legal protection shall contribute to the equitable sharing of benefits deriving from the use of genetic resources and of traditional knowledge. The CBD opted for the creation of a property right with regulated access for genetic resources. But while control over the exploitation of the physical biological material, without isolation of

[119] Similarly, Bucher (2008), pp. 71 and 78.

[120] Cabrera Medaglia (2004), pp. 101–102.

[121] Article 11 CBD.

[122] Bucher (2008), p. 33 with further references.

[123] Bucher (2008), p. 25.

[124] Ibid.

[125] UNEP-WCMC (2016), p. 93.

genetic information, can be achieved by the protection of the (physical) organism, the protection of the knowledge contained therein is more difficult. The basis of the system of protection of *genetic resources* is the establishment of a proprietary right for the host country.[126] The condition for access for third parties is the prior informed consent (PIC) given by the host country.[127] The host country, therefore, must establish a system of protection and in particular decide whether to create public or private property and under which conditions to grant access.[128] The access must take place under mutually agreed terms.[129] The legal protection of (secret) *traditional knowledge* is not required by the CBD, but is possible according to general principles of protection of undisclosed information or know-how.[130] This is compatible with the legal opinion of some local indigenous communities in Central America, who still today consider secret medical knowledge to be private property.[131]

The exclusive right shall protect economic, technological and moral interests. The main goal of an *access and benefit sharing* system is the sharing of the *economic* benefits derived from the exploitation of the genetic resources[132] through the negotiation of license fees for granting access to genetic resources. This creates the financial incentive to protect biodiversity. Nevertheless by some it is criticized as selling biodiversity and legalizing *biopiracy*.[133]But benefit sharing can include also the access to and *transfer of technology* derived from the use of genetic resources to the host country[134] and other forms of participation, such as joint research or professional training of local workers.[135] This mechanism of the CBD was subsequently included in the benefit sharing system of Article 13.2(b)(i) FAO Plant Treaty.[136] However, the transfer of technology appears to be secondary in practice. This reflects the fact that especially in Latin America research and knowledge-based industries and public institutions have only a limited capacity to absorb transferred technology.[137] The protection would also enable the owner(s) to restrict the use of genetic resources for *ethical or cultural* considerations. It is argued that life—

[126] Articles 3 and 15(1) CBD.

[127] Article 15(3) CBD.

[128] Götting (2004), pp. 731, 734; Bucher (2008), pp. 45 and 71.

[129] Article 15(4) CBD.

[130] See Sect. 5.4.

[131] For example, the Miskito healers in Nicaragua consider their cures private property, see Dutfield (2001), p. 246, citing Dennis, Philip A, Herbal Medicine Among the Miskito of Eastern Nicaragua, 42 Econ. Botany 16 (1988).

[132] Article 15(7) CBD.

[133] For further references see Bucher (2008), p. 258.

[134] Article 16(3) CBD.

[135] Hassemer (2003), p. 184; Bucher (2008), p. 94.

[136] On the FAO Plant Treaty see Sect. 6.1.3.1.

[137] This may be partly due to the fact there is relatively little cooperation between universities and the private sector in Latin America in general Bucher (2008), p. 39.

including genetic resources, plants and medicines derived from these—should not be patented and monopolized for medical and ethical reasons. The *sui generis* right would give the affected indigenous communities a choice between sharing the knowledge, also for the benefit of the environment and the indigenous community itself, or to keep their traditional knowledge secret and prevent its exploitation, if the community does not want to share "sacred" knowledge with outsiders.[138]

It is also important to provide for effective sanctions in cases of infringement, because the unauthorized appropriation of genetic resources and traditional knowledge (as any other type of information) is relatively easy.[139] The *cancellation* of exclusive rights for third parties would protect domestic users, if the original (unmodified) information or resource is misappropriated. However, the sanction for the non-compliance with the rules relating to the access to biodiversity does not necessarily have to be the cancellation of the rights of third parties. To enforce the sharing of benefits, it would be sufficient to provide for *compensation* if the violation is detected. This sanction could be used for any results generated using genetic resources illegally. As far as traditional knowledge constitutes undisclosed information, it is also protected against unfair commercial use.

6.1.5.4 Access to Biodiversity

From the perspective of developing countries, it is a priority to maintain *access* and prevent third parties from obtaining exclusive rights to biodiversity. Rights to traditional knowledge and genetic resources must, at least, provide for the right to utilization by the respective communities themselves. This utilization is often the main basis of the economic activities of these communities, especially in relation to agriculture and health.[140] In addition, the ongoing utilization of traditional methods of treating medical and agricultural plants contributes to the maintenance of biodiversity.[141]

The (mis-)appropriation of the information derived from genetic resources usually includes the patenting of at least some of this information, which gives the right holder the possibility to exclude others from using it. In biodiversity cases, this means that traditional plants or treatments can no longer be commercialized in those countries where patent protection has been obtained. Theoretically, because of the novelty requirement, only the added innovation can be protected, and, therefore, the genetic resources and traditional knowledge as such would not be affected.[142]

---

[138] While this goes against the objective of patent law to publish and ultimately diffusing knowledge, it corresponds with the protection of undisclosed information and test data under traditional IP law.

[139] Bucher (2008), p. 104.

[140] Bucher (2008), p. 55.

[141] Ibid.

[142] Bucher (2008), pp. 72–73.

One element of protecting genetic resources is, therefore, preventing third parties from illegally obtaining IP rights in relation to biodiversity-related knowledge for themselves, both in the host country and/or abroad, and thus excluding users in the host country from using it domestically or exporting it.[143]

Such protection in third countries could result from patenting genetic resources domestically or abroad. While traditional knowledge is usually not patentable for lack of novelty, restrictions in the examination process regarding the relevance of oral sources for the state of the art or small changes to the patent claims could help third parties to obtain a patent.[144]

In practice there have been cases in which applicants abused the fact that the respective (local) knowledge normally is not part of the (global) state of the act consulted by foreign patent offices. Thus, the applicants were able to obtain patent protection for the original plant:

- The best-known case relates to the Indian *Neem* tree, whose properties were patented in India and subsequently the right holder moved against the small local farmers traditionally using this plant.
- In Latin America, a well-known example is the *Enola* bean from Mexico. After it was patented in the USA, the patent owner subsequently obtained an injunction against the importation of these beans by competitors and, as a consequence, the US market was closed for imports from the host country. Depending on the patent prosecution strategy, even the use by the indigenous community in the host country could be restricted.
- Other examples are the *Ayahuasca* plant from Ecuador and the *Quinoa* plant from Peru.[145]

Such practices could be prevented systematically by voluntary amendments to the respective national laws or a TRIPS reform, *e.g.*, requiring the consideration of biodiversity during the patent examination.[146] One way to enforce this right could be the mandatory *disclosure of origin* of an invention, in particular genetic sources, in the patent application. If the application is based on prior art, the registration could be denied or cancelled.[147]

A practical solution could be the creation of public or secret databases, as established in Peru.[148] *Public* databases effectively destroy novelty of patent applications. *Secret* databases may be protected as a trade secret. However, they require legal certainty and, therefore, may be unsuitable for countries with high levels of

[143] Bucher (2008), p. 74.

[144] See Sect. 3.1.6.2 regarding the inclusion of traditional knowledge in the patent application process; see also Bucher (2008), p. 92.

[145] On these cases see Bucher (2008), pp. 75–77.

[146] The procedural implementation of the disclosure of origin in patent law is discussed above in Sect. 3.1.6.2.

[147] See Sect. 3.1.6.2.

[148] Bucher (2008), p. 93.

corruption.[149] If the confidentiality of registries or databases cannot be safeguarded, the possibility of trade secret protection is lost.[150]

In Central America, so far foreign patent owners never tried to prevent domestic use of plants or traditional knowledge.[151] However, this might be due to the generally weak protection of patents in the region. Because of the economic importance of biodiversity for traditional agriculture, it nevertheless seems reasonable to take precautions, *e.g.*, by including the requirement of the disclosure of origin explicitly in the scope of patent examination.

6.1.6 Protection of Biodiversity in Central America

6.1.6.1 Costa Rica

Right Holder

The definition of the *right holder* can be problematic, because it is difficult to attribute traditional knowledge or access procedures regarding genetic resources to an individual or a limited group of persons, as required by traditional IP rights.[152]

In Costa Rica, genetic resources are public property and the right holder is the state.[153] The state, therefore, controls the access to genetic resources. This raises the question whether or how rights for private third parties, especially IP rights, can be attributed to the physical and intellectual results of research performed in connection with these resources.[154]

Exclusive Right to Use

The control of the state over genetic resources is exercised by CONAGEBIO, which grants access based on individual benefit-sharing agreements. The procedure of granting access is provided for in two regulations regarding access to in-situ and ex-situ genetic resources. The regulations establish three types of permits, (1) basic research permits, (2) bio-prospection permits and (3) temporary or permanent economic exploitation permits. The access requirements depend on the type of

[149] Ibid.

[150] Taubman and Leistner (2003), p. 61.

[151] Dutfield (2004), p. 56; Bucher (2008), p. 74.

[152] Bucher (2008), p. 103.

[153] Articles 2 and 6 Biodiversity Law (CR); such public property, according to Article 121.14 Costa Rican Constitution, must serve the public and is subject to administrative systems of protection and access, see Bucher (2008), pp. 265 and 303.

[154] Cabrera Medaglia (2004), pp. 101, 114; Bucher (2008), p. 303.

permit.[155] This distinction has been criticized as artificial, because the economic exploitation is usually the ultimate objective and should, therefore, be included in the access agreements from the start[156] and projects require repeated authorization and negotiation, which might deter potential users.[157] From a practical perspective this should not pose significant problems, because then the access agreements could be structured according to the subsequent phases of research, development and exploitation, with different benefit sharing mechanisms which would be triggered if the respective project reaches this step.[158] CONAGEBIO was given a mandate to establish a new access regime.[159]

In 2018, MINAE a reform regulation was adopted.[160] However, Article 7 of the regulation still maintains the three types of permits existing under the current regime.

The granting of a permit by CONAGEBIO requires also an existing agreement between the provider (mostly INBio, which is managing the protected areas) and the person requesting access, based on prior informed consent (PIC). The agreement must include the monetary benefits, up to 10% of the value of the project and up to 50% of the profits made by products resulting from the bio-prospection.[161] The current contracts were mainly concluded between INBio and universities.[162]

Two limitations safeguard the freedom of academic research: First, only research, bio-prospection and commercialization are considered "access", which enables the establishment of inventories without permit.[163] This clause is complemented by the statutory purpose of INBio (see below) to create such an inventory. It is not specified whether such inventories cover both public and secret databases. Second, Article 4(3) Biodiversity Law (CR) provides for the possibility for universities to establish facilitated access systems to genetic resources if the research is not profit-oriented. In practice, however, the domestic universities apparently use the general access system.[164]

As already discussed, sanctions are of particular importance.[165] However, the enforcement system in Costa Rica is weaker than the comparable systems of Panama

---

155 Article 7 Regulation 31514-MINAE.

156 Cabrera Medaglia (2004), pp. 101, 115.

157 Bucher (2008), p. 298.

158 This structure is used for research and development cooperation between biotech and pharmaceutical companies. Down payments, milestone payments, revenue sharing etc. can be designed in a flexible way, so as to ensure sufficient compensation of the host country if the project is successful, while minimizing the financial commitment of the applicant.

159 Article 62 Biodiversity Law (CR).

160 The text of the current regulation is available at https://www.wipo.int/wipolex/en/legislation/details/21977 (accessed 2 Nov 2024).

161 Aguiñada Arévalo et al. (2009), p. 59.

162 Bucher (2008), p. 306 with further references (based on the situation in January 2006).

163 Article 7 Biodiversity Law (CR); Bucher (2008), p. 263.

164 Bucher (2008), p. 262.

165 See Sect. 6.1.4.3.

and Venezuela.[166] Unauthorized access to biodiversity or exploitation of elements of biodiversity can be sanctioned with a fine ranging from one to 12 monthly minimum salaries.[167] The Biodiversity Law (CR) also contains a framework for other sanctions, *e.g.*, for the non-compliance with formal access requirements, but sanctions have not been established in the law.[168] Costa Rica adopted the administrative *Regulation 39341-MINAE* in 2016 which establishes procedures for such sanctions.[169] Sanctions can be imposed by the Technical Office of CONAGEBIO *ex officio* or based on a *denunciation* by a third party.[170]

Monitoring the Right to Access During Patent Examination

CONAGEBIO elaborated a process for its participation in the patent examination for inventions relating to biodiversity and has conducted trainings with the IP Register and other stakeholders to implement the process.[171] The participation had been established in more detail by the Regulation 34958-MINAET-COMEX, which had been adopted in December 2008 and invalidated in December 2012.[172] The regulation in part ensured that no local genetic resources or traditional knowledge are patented[173] and to prevent third parties from obtaining patents on biodiversity-related knowledge as such. The IP Register and the National Seeds Office (*Oficina Nacional de Semillas*)[174] were required to consult CONAGEBIO before granting protection for inventions involving biodiversity of Costa Rica. In particular, CONAGEBIO examined the compliance with the ABS system established by the Biodiversity Law (CR)[175] and the patentability with regard to the biodiversity sources.[176] If the examination by CONAGEBIO revealed a violation of the access

[166] Cabrera Medaglia (2003), p. 8 Fn 19.

[167] Article 112 Biodiversity Law (CR).

[168] Cabrera Medaglia et al. (2014), p. 25.

[169] Regulation for the Application of Administrative Sanctions regarding non-authorized Access to Genetic and Biochemical Resources established in the Biodiversity Law (*Reglamento para la Aplicación de las Sanciones Administrativas en Materia de Acceso No Autorizado a los Elementos y Recursos Genéticos y Bioquímicos, Establecidas en Ley de Biodiversidad N° 7788) No. 39341-MINAE*), published in the Official Gazette on 16 March 2016, entry into force on 16 September 2016, available at https://absch.cbd.int/api/v2013/documents/1B13B1F7-6561-73FD-1302-522657ADA733/attachments/203745/Decreto%20Ejecutivo%2039341-MINAE%20Reglamento%20para%20la%20aplicaci%C3%B3n%20de%20las%20sanciones%20administrativas.pdf (accessed 2 Nov 2024).

[170] Article 6 Regulation 39341-MINAE.

[171] Jorge Cabrera Medaglia (2010), pp. 7–8.

[172] See Sect. 6.1.4.

[173] Article 2 Regulation 34958-MINAET-COMEX.

[174] The National Seeds Office is responsible for managing plant variety registrations, see Sect. 3.3.6.

[175] Article 4 Regulation 34958-MINAET-COMEX.

[176] Article 3 Regulation 34958-MINAET-COMEX.

regime, *i.e.*, that elements of Costa Rica's biodiversity have been used and the requirements for access to it have not been complied with, it informed the IP Register. While its opinion was communicated to the IP Register, it did not affect the patentability or prevent or delay the granting of the patent.[177] Therefore, the patent had to be granted, giving the right holder (at least theoretically) the possibility to exclude others, including the host community, from use. In addition, the applicant was given a "reasonable period of time" to comply with the requirements of the Biodiversity Law (CR). In case of ongoing non-compliance, the respective applicant was sanctioned with a fine for every day of non-compliance which increases over time to a maximum of one monthly minimum salary per day.[178]

The patent application could only be opposed if the claimed invention does not meet the patentability requirements, especially if, considering the underlying genetic resources and traditional knowledge, it lacked inventive step or novelty.[179] The result of the examination by CONAGEBIO had to be submitted within nine months, and its opposition sent to the applicant for response.[180] Both the opposition and the response were *considered* before the resolution of the substantive examination by the IP Register.[181] It is unclear whether an opposition by CONAGEBIO (based on the lack of patentability) was binding or not. The decision by CONAGEBIO was considered binding by *Cabrera Medaglia*, ("shall prevent").[182] The regulation went into force in December 2008. A comparison of Articles 3 and 4 Regulation 34958-MINAET-COMEX also suggests the binding nature of the decision, because Article 4 stated explicitly that non-compliance with formal access requirements (permission by CONAGEBIO) did not affect patentability or delay the grant. This suggests that conversely a violation of Article 3 Regulation 34958-MINAET-COMEX could affect the grant, as no similar statement was included. On the other hand, the reference in Article 4 Regulation 34958-MINAET-COMEX related to an issue which under TRIPS cannot be grounds for refusing a patent, and, therefore, the statement had no specific effect. Moreover, the word "consider" strongly indicates a non-binding observation. In addition, if the observations of CONAGEBIO were binding, this would override the jurisdiction of the IP Register. While this is theoretically possible, in practice one would expect a clear statement to this effect. In this regard, the participation of CONAGEBIO in relation to the patentability requirements is different from its role in the access management regime. In these cases, the decision of CONAGEBIO did not affect patentability requirements, and, therefore, the decision did not affect the jurisdiction of IP Register, excluding the

[177] Article 4 Regulation 34958-MINAET-COMEX.

[178] Ibid.

[179] Article 3 Regulation 34958-MINAET-COMEX in connection with Article 2 Patent and Design Law (CR).

[180] Article 3(1) and (2) Regulation 34958-MINAET-COMEX.

[181] Article 3(5) Regulation 34958-MINAET-COMEX.

[182] Cabrera Medaglia (2020), p. 6.

possibility of conflicting decisions on the same issue by different administrative agencies.

It appears that the Regulation 34958-MINAET-COMEX has so far not been replaced with a new regulation. Therefore, the consultation process of CONAGEBIO is based on the general provision of Article 80 Biodiversity Law (CR).[183] Accordingly, the consultation of the Technical Office of CONAGEBIO during the patent examination procedure in case the respective patent includes elements of biodiversity is still required and the patent is rejected if a well-founded objection is made.[184] The provision does not clarify if the patent application could also be rejected based on non-compliance with ABS requirements. However, by 2020, no patent applications have been identified that were based on national genetic resources.[185] Therefore this question has not yet been addressed.

6.1.6.2 Nicaragua

Exclusive Right to Use

The protection of genetic resources in Nicaragua is based on Chapter II Environment Law (NI). Article 64 Environment Law (NI) provides that the right holder of the "national genetic heritage" is the state, which corresponds to the principles of the CBD and the legislation in other Central American laws. Genetic resources and the native species are "registered and patented" for the state for its "exclusive or preferential use".[186]

According to *Bendaña-Guerrero*, the protection of genetic resources violates the principle that biological subject matter cannot be patented as found in nature. Such protection would not promote industrial application, the goal of patent protection. He concludes that the expression "patented" only refers to the creation of an inventory.[187] However, this interpretation is questionable if one considers the history and wording of the provision: The creation of an inventory is already provided for by the term "registered", so according to *Bendaña-Guerrero* the term "patented" does not have any specific meaning. In addition, in Nicaragua (like in other Central American countries) the term "patented" is widely used to indicate exclusive rights, but not necessarily IP rights.[188] More importantly, Article 64 explicitly refers to "exclusive

[183] Cabrera Medaglia (2020), p. 5, reports the invalidation of Regulation 34958-MINAET-COMEX and describes the consultation process solely based on Article 80 Biodiversity Law (CR) in April 2020.

[184] Article 80 Biodiversity Law (CR).

[185] Cabrera Medaglia (2020), p. 6.

[186] Article 64 Environment Law (NI).

[187] Bendaña-Guerrero (1999), p. 232.

[188] In this sense the term "patent" simply means "license", e.g., to operate a business; regarding the usage of the term "patent" see Sect. 3.1.

use" of the subject matter, which implies the legal effects of protection similar to an (invention) patent. The interpretation that Article 64 Environment Law (NI) creates an exclusive, patent-like property of the state is reinforced by the historic purpose of the law to implement the CBD, which provides for such exclusive protection.

The ownership of genetic resources by the state is restated in Article 3 Biodiversity Law (NI), which provides that "the state exercises sovereign rights over the biological diversity in its territory. The main categories for the utilization of biological diversity are

- environmental permits for utilization,[189]
- incentive promotion,[190] *i.e.*, incentives for the sustainable use of biodiversity, *e.g.*, compensation for maintaining forests, and
- access and utilization of genetic resources.[191]

The process of granting permits and ensuring compliance with PIC and ABS principles is largely similar to the system in Costa Rica. However, some features in the Nicaraguan system are noteworthy: Any bio-prospection or other access of biodiversity activity requires only one permit and one agreement between the applicant and the government.[192] This avoids the complicated three-phase process established in Costa Rica.[193]

The participation of a Nicaraguan scientist must be foreseen in the contract for any bio-prospection or other access to biodiversity,[194] to ensure the technology transfer and the technological participation of the host country.

The permit shall be granted by the Biodiversity Directorate together with representatives of the region and shall include as a party to the access agreement the responsible authority of indigenous or afro-descended peoples, if the genetic resources are located in their territory.[195] This clause is particularly significant, as it ensures that the affected local communities do not depend on the central government to negotiate the access agreement and the ABS commitments on their behalf, but can control the outcome of the negotiations themselves.

---

[189] Article 16 Nr. 3 Biodiversity Law (NI); the term "utilization" is not defined in Article 16 Nr. 3 Biodiversity Law (NI). However, it should apply to physical exploitation (e.g., logging or extraction of seeds), because the access and utilization of genetic resources is regulated separately in Article 56 Biodiversity Law (NI).

[190] Article 16 Nr. 4 Biodiversity Law (NI).

[191] Article 56 Biodiversity Law (NI).

[192] Article 57 Biodiversity Law (NI).

[193] See Sect. 6.1.6.1.

[194] Article 72 Nr. 1 Biodiversity Law (NI).

[195] Article 77 Biodiversity Law (NI).

Right to Access

The protection of biodiversity against monopolization by third parties in Nicaragua relies on disclosure of origin requirements[196] and the participation of the Biodiversity Directorate in the patent examination process. The guarantee (*aval*) regarding the biological origin submitted by the applicant is sent to the Biodiversity Directorate, which certifies the disclosure of origin.[197] If the disclosure requirements have not been fulfilled or if false information is submitted by the applicant, the patent application is rejected or, if the patent has already been granted, cancelled. In addition, administrative sanctions can be imposed.[198]

This mechanism is significantly stricter than the mechanism established in Costa Rica.[199] There, in case of non-compliance with the disclosure of origin requirements, the patent must be granted and only administrative sanctions can be imposed, if the non-compliance is not remedied. In Nicaragua, the patent application is rejected, without possibility of the applicant to remedy. This sanction has the advantage of being a real risk for the applicant if it does not comply with the formal requirements from the beginning and, therefore, creating an incentive to disclose.

6.1.6.3 Other Countries

In the other Central American countries, the biodiversity protection is less developed both on the statutory level and practically. Therefore, the protection of genetic resources is only briefly discussed in relation to Guatemala, as an example. In Guatemala, according to the National Council of Protected Areas (*Consejo Nacional de Áreas Protegidas*, CONAP), which is responsible for managing biodiversity in Guatemala, regarding the access to genetic resources "some participation mechanisms for the elaboration of a law proposal have been outlined" in 2006.[200] In other words, it had not even been decided who should be responsible for drafting the law proposal. In 2012, Guatemala initiated a process of developing a comprehensive regulatory and institutional framework for ABS as part of its 2013 National

[196] See Sect. 3.1.6.2.

[197] Article 84 Biodiversity Law (NI).

[198] Article 85 Biodiversity Law (NI).

[199] See Sect. 6.1.6.1.

[200] CONAP, III Informe Nacional de Cumplimiento a los Arcuerdos del Convenio sobre Diversidad Biológica (CDB), February 2006, p. 167, available at https://www.cbd.int/doc/world/gt/gt-nr-03-p1-es.pdf (accessed 2 Nov 2024).

Biodiversity Strategy and Action Plan.[201] However, this and subsequent initiatives have been unsuccessful.[202]

6.1.7 Management of Genetic Resources

6.1.7.1 Costa Rica

Responsible for the *management* of biodiversity in Costa Rica is CONAGEBIO and for the *exploitation* through bio-prospecting INBio.

CONAGEBIO

CONAGEBIO is composed of representatives of public entities and private interest groups, including indigenous groups and farmers' associations.[203] Since its creation, CONAGEBIO faced institutional, financial and legal challenges: Because of its small budget, the technical bureau consists only of the managing director and a staff of four public employees.[204] Finally, the creation of CONAGEBIO was delayed and the legal certainty regarding its activities was limited because its establishment was challenged before the CSJ (CR) in 1998.[205] The constitutional challenge did not suspend the execution of the law, but delayed the effectiveness CONAGEBIO politically.[206] The CSJ (CR) rejected the constitutional challenge on 5 June 2006.[207]

CONAGEBIO has successfully claimed an active role in biodiversity system, despite these challenges. This is underlined by the fact that its responsibilities have been extended to the participation in the patent examination procedure.[208]

The technical bureau is responsible for CONAGEBIO's operations, namely processing the applications for access to genetic resources and reviewing the

[201] See Sect. 6.1.4.3; the need to improve the institutional framework and management of biodiversity has been identified by CONAP, see CONAP, V Informe Nacional de Cumplimiento a los Arcuerdos del Convenio sobre Diversidad Biológica, 2014, p. 26, https://www.cbd.int/doc/world/gt/gt-nr-05-es.pdf (accessed 2 Nov 2024).

[202] Heinrich et al. (2020), p. 9.

[203] Bucher (2008), p. 268.

[204] Its main source of income is a fixed share of the entrance fees to national parks, see Bucher (2008), p. 269 with further references.

[205] Unconstitutionality action nr *98-006524-007-CO-M*; on this case see Ruiz Muller (2006), p. 34.

[206] Cabrera Medaglia (2006), p. 34.

[207] Cabrera Medaglia (2010), p. 15.

[208] See Sect. 6.1.6.1.

bio-prospecting contracts.[209] In addition, it is charged with creating and coordinating the access regime and advising public and private institutions and indigenous groups with regard to biodiversity and bio-prospection.[210] Article 80 Biodiversity Law (CR) establishes its participation in the patent examination process for inventions relating to biodiversity.[211]

There are still uncertainties in the participation process, *e.g.*, the question when an invention is related to biodiversity.[212] Also, the institutions involved need training and have to establish practical cooperation.[213] However, this formalized consideration of biodiversity is an important improvement of the protection of biodiversity-related knowledge, not least because it helps to detect violations of the access regime and sanction them.

Unlike in the patent examination procedure, CONAGEBIO is not included in the process of marketing approval for pharmaceuticals.[214] Based on the exclusive protection of test data mandated by CAFTA-DR, pharmaceutical companies might rely primarily on the exclusive marketing approval for protection, making this process almost an alternative mechanism to patent protection. Accordingly, an effective control of the compliance of approved pharmaceuticals with the ABS system could require the participation of CONAGEBIO in the marketing approval process.

INBio

Most of the bio-prospecting in Costa Rica is conducted by INBio. It was created in 1989 as a non-governmental, non-profit association. Among the advantages of this private model are more flexibility and less bureaucracy, and the absence of conflicts between the stakeholders as experienced by CONAGEBIO.

Since May 1992 there exists a formal agreement between INBio and MINAE that outlines the two main activities of INBio, namely (1) the creation and maintenance of a specific national *inventory or database* for genetic resources, enabled by the "inventory exception" of Article 7 Biodiversity Law (CR), and (2) the *use of the country's biodiversity* and manage bio-prospecting by concluding contracts with third parties to economically exploit biodiversity to foster the sustainable use of

---

[209] Article 17 Biodiversity Law (CR); however, the access agreements concluded before the establishment of CONAGEBIO have not yet been evaluated for lack of staff and resources, see Bucher (2008), p. 268.

[210] Bucher (2008), p. 267.

[211] See Sect. 6.1.6.1.

[212] Cabrera Medaglia et al. (2014), p. 32.

[213] Such trainings have been taking place e.g. between CONAGEBIO and the IP Register, see Cabrera Medaglia (2010), p. 10.

[214] The role of CONAGEBIO in the patent examination procedure is discussed in Sect. 6.1.6.1.

Costa Rican biodiversity.[215] The management of bio-prospecting was initiated in 1991 and has resulted in 40 bio-prospection agreements until 2004.[216] Subsequently, however, there was no longer a "market" for bio-prospecting by private pharmaceutical companies.[217] Now INBio is focusing more on cooperation with universities.[218] Between 2005 and February 2014, INBio granted 348 permits, mostly for basic non-commercial research.[219] In 2016 and 2019 two permits for commercial use have been granted.[220]

Among the current challenges for INBio are the lack of resources (which is similar to CONAGEBIO), the increased expectation of more tangible technological value by customers, and the competition by bio-prospection institutions in third countries. Especially pharmaceutical companies expect more tangible value, because the publicity benefit for companies derived from such cooperation is decreasing and there are more and more alternative sources for bio-prospecting.[221]

While the system of bio-prospection may not be perfect, it can nevertheless be considered to be a success, because it produced technological and financial benefits for Costa Rica, increased the awareness regarding the value of biodiversity and not least resulted in the establishment of an extensive biodiversity database.[222] Also, while competition from third countries in bio-prospecting is an issue for Costa Rica and INBio, from a broader perspective it demonstrates the dissemination of the Costa Rican model as a form of "best practice" and the increased awareness of the issue of biodiversity.

Case Study: Merck & Co.

The best-known example for bio-prospection cooperation is probably the research agreement between INBio and the pharmaceutical company *Merck & Co.*[223] It was concluded in September 1991 and was the first contract between a pharmaceutical

---

[215] Hassemer (2003), p. 206.

[216] Bucher (2008), p. 331.

[217] While between 1990 and 2000, most bioprospecting agreements were concluded with pharmaceutical and other private companies, between 2005 and 2014 agreements were almost exclusively with academic partners, Cabrera Medaglia et al. (2014), pp. 28–30.

[218] Bucher (2008), p. 331.

[219] Cabrera Medaglia et al. (2014), p. 31.

[220] The first permit has been granted in 2016 to Chanel and the second in 2019 to the Costa Rican company Lisan Natura for natural product development, Cabrera Medaglia (2020), p. 3.

[221] The analysis of the significant collaborative research agreements shows, there were no research activities by large pharmaceutical companies after 2006, see the list of agreements provided by Cabrera Medaglia et al. (2014), pp. 28–30.

[222] As has been noted, the public awareness in Costa Rica is remarkable, and may well be due partly to the activities of INBio.

[223] See, e.g., Hassemer (2003), p. 206.

company and a biodiversity-rich developing country.[224] It was renewed several times until it was discontinued after eight years in 1999.

For Merck, the agreement did not only produce useful innovations which resulted in 27 patents owned exclusively by Merck, but also good publicity.[225] INBio received *upfront* payments in the amount of 1,135 million USD and (undisclosed) license fees (estimated around 1-3% of net sales),[226] 50% of which benefited the protected areas.[227] It also received publicity as an entity offering bio-prospection opportunities in Costa Rica and gained experience in relation to its operations.[228]

Still, it is controversial whether the project was a success. Article 16 CBD requires that the payments by the company conducting the bio-prospection should cover the administrative costs and provide an incentive for conservation. In addition, technology transfer should take place. Whether the total sum received by INBio satisfies these requirements is questioned.[229] However, in favor of Merck one has to acknowledge that there were technological risks relating to the project and that the medicinal viability of such projects is unclear, as underlined by the fact that only few products by Merck are based on bio-screening (not only from Costa Rica).[230] In this context one can also point to the fact that even if a compound is found, the likelihood of producing a successful drug is small.

6.1.7.2 Nicaragua

In Central America, apart from Costa Rica, only the Nicaraguan legislation contains specific rules on the management of biodiversity: Article 62 Environment Law (NI) provides for the general obligation of the state and the citizens for conservation and *appreciation* of genetic resources. The wording "*aprovechamiento*", which indicates also utilization, suggests that exploitation including bio-prospecting is explicitly permitted. Bio-prospecting is subject to administrative authorization according to Article 63 Environment Law (NI). Article 63 Environment Law (NI) guarantees that, if indigenous communities provide genetic resources, their use shall be allowed according to "conditions determined in consultations with them". The meaning of the term *consultations* is ambiguous, because it only requires discussions between the administration and the indigenous communities, but creates no obligations for the administration to adopt the conditions requested by these communities.

---

[224] Bucher (2008), p. 321 with further references.

[225] Ibid, p. 330.

[226] Asebey and Kempenaar (1995), p. 727.

[227] Asebey and Kempenaar (1995), p. 728 fn 127.

[228] Bucher (2008), p. 330.

[229] Bucher (2008), p. 328; Asebey and Kempenaar (1995), p. 726.

[230] Bucher (2008), p. 326 with further references.

Certain aspects regarding the biodiversity management are specified by the Biodiversity Law (NI) of 2012. It provides that MARENA is responsible for implementing the law and for developing the necessary actions to protect, conserve and utilize biological diversity.[231] Between 2013 and 2014, MARENA conducted an assessment and planning program for a national strategy regarding the status of biodiversity and its sustainable use in Nicaragua.[232]

Article 12 Nr. 21 Biodiversity Law (NI) explicitly charges MARENA with supervising and regulating bio-prospection and access to genetic resources. Such regulation shall be made in form of the "National System of Licenses and Permits".[233] However, such a system has apparently not yet been established.

6.1.7.3 Other Countries

In the other Central American countries, as already noted, the biodiversity protection is less developed. Therefore, the protection of genetic resources is only briefly discussed in relation to Guatemala as an example. In Guatemala, even though there is no regulation on the matter, it seems commonly accepted that the state is the owner of genetic resources.[234] As the right holder, the state is responsible for the management of the exploitation of genetic resources. Because genetic resources are an element biodiversity, CONAP is responsible for their management, but as noted above, there have been no activities yet.[235] In particular, there have been no initiatives in Guatemala to create databases relating to genetic resources. Guatemala had started developing a more comprehensive ABS system between 2012 and 2014, to provide more detailed rules on the management of genetic resources.[236] However, this and subsequent initiatives have been unsuccessful.[237]

6.1.8 Evaluation

6.1.8.1 Necessity of Protection

The introduction of proprietary rights needs to be justified from a policy perspective. This also applies to exclusive rights relating to genetic resources. The protection of genetic resources for indigenous communities or their host countries creates the

[231] Article 11 Biodiversity Law (NI).

[232] See Sect. 6.1.4.2.

[233] Article 56 Biodiversity Law (NI).

[234] Interview with *Gabriela Contreras Aguilera.*

[235] See Sect. 6.1.6.3.

[236] Regarding this project see Cabrera Medaglia et al. (2014), p. 53.

[237] Heinrich et al. (2020), p. 9.

same exclusivity as patents do for international companies. Therefore, in principle, the concerns regarding the restriction of the genetic pool for further research and breeding[238] and the danger for food security through the privatization of seeds[239] also apply. But even though the protection raises the same questions as the protection of other existing knowledge, *e.g.*, the retroactive extension of patent or test data protection, the widespread support for protection is understandable.[240] Most importantly there are social-cultural and ecological-economic reasons. *Culturally*, the biodiversity-related knowledge is embedded into an identifiable ethno-cultural and geographical context which merits protection.[241] This includes the creation of non-economic rights, *e.g.*, the right to prevent utilization which contravenes moral or religious beliefs of the affected indigenous population. Article 35 ACARG could be used as a model for national legislation, even though it is only a draft provision.[242] Such non-economic, moral rights would be in line with principles of IP law.[243] *Economically*, the benefit sharing mechanism would link the exploitation of biodiversity with an incentive for its preservation. It also seems equitable to ensure economic participation of the host countries or communities, because the genetic resources provide economic advantages for third party users, who should, therefore, contribute to the preservation of biodiversity.

6.1.8.2 Effectiveness of Protection

However, the effective implementation of biodiversity protection faces political, legal and economic challenges.

While many developing countries advocate the protection of their indigenous peoples and their knowledge vis-à-vis developed countries, the internal implementation of such protection in most Central American countries is blocked by conflicting political interests and the skepticism toward special legal rights for indigenous peoples. These problems are common in Latin America.[244] Interestingly, the statutory protection of indigenous peoples is most developed in Costa Rica, where the share of the indigenous population in the total population is lowest.[245]

---

[238] Henne (1998), p. 71.

[239] Hassemer (2003), p. 158.

[240] Bucher (2008), p. 70 with further references.

[241] Taubman and Leistner (2003), p. 53.

[242] As the analysis of the regional activities regarding biodiversity has shown (Sect. 6.1.3.5), in this field it seems more likely that protection systems can be successfully established on the national level.

[243] There are also accepted moral elements to patent law and copyright, see for example Article 6 IP Law (SV), which recognizes the moral right of the author.

[244] Bucher (2008), p. 343.

[245] Dutfield (2004), p. 148.

The effective conservation of genetic resources requires *legal certainty* regarding not only the intangible property directly relating to biodiversity, but also the real estate property relating to bio-diverse areas and access rights, either for the state, for indigenous people or other stakeholders. In other words, the incentive for conservation of biodiversity not only depends on rights protecting genetic resources or the biodiverse areas incorporating them, but also requires that these rights are perceived as certain and effective. In some Central American countries, however, some observers have noted considerable uncertainty regarding real estate ownership and access and usage rights.[246] This could also limit the effectiveness of any (future) system of biodiversity protection.

The Costa Rican example shows that, even if the legal framework and corresponding administration are in place, there remain practical problems. The bio-prospection system is well-established in this country, as the following numbers show: By 2014, INBio concluded more than 60 bio-prospecting agreements and from 2005 until early 2014, 348 permits were granted, 300 for basic non-commercial research, and 48 for commercial research and bio-prospecting.[247] However, the exploitation of genetic resources by INBio and its partners has not yielded the expected technological and economic benefits.[248] Only few of the prospected substances turned out to have medical effects, and even these require costly further research and development.[249] This limits the economic value of genetic resources used as input for the development process. In addition, while traditional knowledge was long considered to increase the success rate of medical research based on plants by 200% to 300%, progress in screening methods has made technology-based methods a viable alternative to the input of traditional knowledge.[250] Therefore, the utility of genetic resources depends on the industry and the stage of the development process.[251]

Another practical problem is the administrative procedure of the access and benefit sharing process. In Costa Rica, the negotiations of the access agreements with CONAGEBIO are made more complicated by the system of specific financial benefit sharing, which prevents other forms of benefit sharing, *e.g.*, training, technology transfer or other measures.[252] Another obstacle is the requirement that two agreements must be concluded by the prospecting company or university, the agreement with the provider, including the prior informed consent of the provider,

[246] The situation appears most problematic in Nicaragua, where the USDOS commented in July 2018 that "considerable uncertainty remains in securing property rights in Nicaragua", see USDOS, Nicaragua - Investment Climate Statements for 2018, 19 July 2018, available at https://www.state.gov/reports/2018-investment-climate-statements/nicaragua/ (accessed 2 Nov 2024).

[247] Cabrera Medaglia et al. (2014), p. 31.

[248] Bucher (2008), p. 326.

[249] Bucher (2008), p. 36 with further references.

[250] von Hahn (2004), p. 225; Bucher (2008), p. 53.

[251] Bucher (2008), p. 54.

[252] Cabrera Medaglia (2004), pp. 101, 114; Bucher (2008), p. 299.

and the benefit sharing agreement concluded with CONAGEBIO. The responsibilities and beneficiaries of the results are unclear.[253] The approval of contracts granting access to genetic resources by CONAGEBIO, provided for in Article 74(1) Biodiversity Law (CR), also does not specify the scope of the review. One the one hand is it practically difficult to evaluate the negotiation of such contracts ex-post, on the other hand the participation of CONAGEBIO must allow for a meaningful exercise of its control authority regarding access.[254]

6.1.8.3 Policy Options

Despite these obstacles, positive if limited economic benefits have been obtained in Costa Rica in the amount of several million USD per year. In addition, one can note the increased awareness regarding biodiversity, as displayed in the public debate surrounding the effect of the CAFTA-DR implementation in the field of biodiversity. Finally, even if other mechanisms are more economically effective, the protection against "bio-piracy" and the principle of benefit-sharing seem justified and should not be neglected solely based on short term utilitarian grounds. Nevertheless, other ways to help conserve biodiversity, *e.g.*, ecotourism, are very effective and could complement this protection. Bio-prospecting activities in Costa Rica account for around 5 million USD in annual revenues[255] and ecotourism accounts for 600-700 million USD in annual revenues.[256] So even if one also considers additional benefits in technology transfer, training and infrastructure improvements,[257] the exploitation of genetic resources through bio-prospecting can only be one (and a minor) contribution to environmental and biodiversity protection.[258] Given the limited "market" for genetic resources and bioprospecting revenues, it is important to also utilize alternative mechanisms and to see this kind of protection as part of broader strategy.[259] The other Central American countries share many geographical similarities with Costa Rica in relation to the viability of biodiversity protection, in particular the similar size of the national territory, affecting the possibility to control access to the rich biodiversity. However, the indigenous communities are often larger, *e.g.*, in Guatemala, increasing the possible political obstacles for establishing a system of biodiversity protection. Protection also requires the establishment of new and effective institutions, like CONAGEBIO and INBio. While theoretically INBio could

[253] Ibid.

[254] Cabrera Medaglia (2004), pp. 101, 114.

[255] Cabrera Medaglia (2003), section IV.A, p. 10; Cabrera Medaglia et al. (2014), p. 31.

[256] Bucher (2008), p. 308; Cabrera Medaglia et al. (2014), p. 31.

[257] Cabrera Medaglia et al. (2014), p. 31.

[258] Similarly, Bucher (2008), p. 308, based on the situation in the year 2005, and subsequently Cabrera Medaglia et al. (2014), p. 31.

[259] Bucher (2008), p. 341; Cabrera Medaglia (2004), pp. 101, 119; Cabrera Medaglia et al. (2014), p. 31.

extend its activities to other Central American countries and thus contribute its know-how, this option is practically unlikely, because of the traditional difficulties in regional integration. For the same reasons it seems unlikely that regional institutions will be established. Any policy directed at preserving biodiversity should involve local communities, as foreseen in Nicaragua by the Biodiversity Law (NI),[260] because they are the stakeholders with the highest incentive to preserve their environment. This is exemplified by projects in Guatemala, where local communities were given the possibility to exploit designated areas of rainforest and have done so in a very sustainable way.[261]

6.2 Traditional Knowledge

6.2.1 Introduction

Traditional knowledge is commonly understood as "knowledge, innovations and practices of indigenous and local communities embodying traditional lifestyles relevant for the conservation and sustainable use of biological diversity".[262]

CAFTA-DR does not address this issue. The EU-FTAs, which contain general provisions on genetic resources and traditional knowledge, utilize similar language.[263] Traditional knowledge protects "the enormous contribution (of) local and indigenous communities and farmers [...] for the conservation and development of plant genetic resources which constitute the basis of food and agriculture production throughout the world".[264] From this definition follow two observations. First, the term does not comprise traditional knowledge related to areas unrelated to biodiversity, such as craftsmanship (*artesania*), which may be protected by designs, or art (traditional cultural expressions), which may be protected by copyright. The protection of these artistic expressions is, therefore, not analyzed here.[265]

Second, the term is limited to knowledge developed over generations by indigenous peoples.[266] According to the Costa Rican law, it is "acquired, shared and used

[260] See Sect. 6.1.6.2.

[261] See the study by Hughell and Butterfield (2008), which also provide graphical illustrations of the affected areas and information on land use and protection of the Petén rainforest.

[262] Article 8(j) CBD.

[263] Article 250.1 EU-CARIFORUM-EPA; Article 229.5 EU-CA-AA.

[264] Article 9.1 FAO Plant Treaty.

[265] For a detailed analysis of the protection of traditional cultural expressions in Latin America see Busch (2015); the protection of traditional cultural expressions is subject to controversial political discussions and legal research. On the terminology and distinction from traditional knowledge see also Bucher (2008), p. 48.

[266] This generation-based, traditional aspect of traditional knowledge is based on the ILO Indigenous Peoples Convention; therefore, sometimes the term "indigenous knowledge" is used synonymously for "traditional knowledge", see Bucher (2008), p. 49.

through a social process of learning unique to every indigenous culture and local community".[267]

6.2.2 *Substantive Protection of Traditional Knowledge in Central America*

6.2.2.1 Costa Rica

Costa Rica was the first country in Central America to adopt genuine traditional knowledge legislation, which, however, is much less comprehensive than the legislation relating to genetic resources.

Article 1 Biodiversity Law (CR) establishes *sui generis*, collective "intellectual rights" in relation to traditional knowledge. While the collective nature is emphasized and the term "property" is avoided, individual property rights in traditional knowledge are possible.[268] These rights are based on the registration of the traditional knowledge and prevent the grant of other IP rights in relation to the protected subject matter.[269] Therefore, the registration serves as an inclusion of the knowledge into the state of the art.[270]

Article 82(2) Biodiversity Law (CR) provides that national or international law, especially IP rights, must not infringe traditional customs of indigenous communities, in effect subjecting international law to such traditional customs. This conflicts with Article 9(3) Biodiversity Law (CR), which states that the Biodiversity Law (CR) must comply with the international legal framework, and more importantly the principle of superiority of international obligations, which is part of public international law and the Costa Rican constitutional system, both of which are of higher rank than the Biodiversity Law (CR). To solve the conflict, one has to assume that Article 82(2) Biodiversity Law (CR) restricts IP laws and rights only insofar as this permitted under international law.[271]

[267] Article 6(j) Regulation 31514-MINEA-CR.

[268] Cabrera Medaglia (2003), p. 6.

[269] Article 84(3)(1) Biodiversity Law (CR).

[270] Bucher (2008), p. 291.

[271] Bucher (2008), p. 294.

6.2.2.2 Nicaragua

The Nicaraguan Heritage Law (NI),[272] being 15 years older than the Guatemalan and Honduran laws[273] and preceding the international debate on biodiversity and traditional knowledge and the CBD, does not address the issue of traditional knowledge.

The Biodiversity Law (NI) passed in 2012 establishes *sui generis* protection for traditional knowledge by establishing community intellectual rights to traditional knowledge related to the conservation and sustainable use of biodiversity.[274] In the Biodiversity Law (NI), traditional knowledge is defined as

- all knowledge, innovation and practice,
- individual or collective,
- tangible or intangible,
- of indigenous, afro-descended or local communities,
- with actual or potential value associated with biological resources, and
- developed through the centuries based on the community's experience and transmitted from generation to generation.[275]

While this wording is very detailed, the first four criteria are very broad and only the last two are practically relevant, i.e., the link to biological resources and the development over generations, in line with the ILO Indigenous Peoples Convention and similar wording in the Costa Rican legislation.[276]

6.2.2.3 Other Countries

In Guatemala, the Heritage Law (GT)[277] protects primarily *tangible* objects like archaeological sites, historic artifacts etc.,[278] but also traditional knowledge ("medical traditions" and traditional cultural expressions) as *intangible* cultural heritage.[279] This type of protection was described by *Taubman* and *Leistner* as a "mere "public good" approach", because it only provides protection against harm,

---

[272] National Cultural Heritage Protection Law (*Ley para la proteccion del patrimonio cultural de la nación*), Law No. 1142, adopted on 22 November 1982, entered into force on 2 December 1982; the text of the law is available at http://legislacion.asamblea.gob.ni/normaweb.nsf/3133c0d121ea38970 62568a1005e0f89/390a1d09807cdb9606258744005e90f2?OpenDocument (accessed 2 Nov 2024).

[273] See Sect. 6.2.2.3.

[274] Cabrera Medaglia et al. (2014), p. 41.

[275] Articles 10.3 and 10.9 Biodiversity Law (NI).

[276] On the Indigenous Peoples Convention see Sect. 6.1.3.

[277] National Cultural Heritage Protection Law (Ley para la proteccion del patrimonio cultural de la nación), Law No. 26-97, adopted on 29 April 1997, entered into force on 20 May 1997; the text of the law is available at www.wipo.int/edocs/lexdocs/laws/es/gt/gt032es.pdf (accessed 2 Nov 2024).

[278] Article 3(1) Heritage Law (GT).

[279] Article 3(2) Heritage Law (GT).

but no incentive for its commercial utilization.[280] However, the substantive provisions of the Heritage Law (GT) regarding property and protection only apply to tangible objects as defined by Article 3(1) Heritage Law (GT) and exclude the intangible traditional knowledge protected by Article 3(2) Heritage Law (GT). Therefore, there is some debate about creating more effective statutory protection either via copyright law or through *sui generis* protection.[281] Either way, absent special provisions on property, such traditional knowledge would belong not to the state, but the respective individuals or communities.

In Honduras, Article 2(9) Heritage Law (HN)[282] refers to "knowledge and techniques" of indigenous peoples, establishing legal protection for traditional knowledge. The types of property belonging to the state are enumerated in Article 3(1) Heritage Law (HN). Because this list does not include indigenous "knowledge and techniques", traditional knowledge remains private or communal property according to Article 3(3) and (4) Heritage Law (HN). But even though such knowledge is not legally excluded from protection, as in Guatemala, the provisions on protection and trade of subject matter protected by the Heritage Law (HN) are clearly designed for physical objects and are practically not applicable to traditional knowledge.[283] Therefore, the legal protection of traditional knowledge has no practical effect.

6.2.3 Procedure

In Costa Rica, the Biodiversity Law (CR) establishes a system of fines and a framework for sanctions.[284] Article 83 Biodiversity Law (CR) charged CONAGEBIO with the elaboration of a *sui generis* administration system, with the participation of the indigenous peoples and farmers' associations, but because of controversial interests of the stakeholders no system could yet enter into force.[285] The Biodiversity Law (CR) provides neither for sanctions for the violation of such rights nor for institutions responsible for the enforcement.[286]

[280] Taubman and Leistner (2003), p. 138.

[281] Interview with *Gabriela Contreras Aguilera*.

[282] National Cultural Heritage Protection Law (Ley para la protección del patrimonio cultural de la nación), Law No. 220-1997, adopted on 29 December 1997, entered into force on 21 February 1998; the text of the law is available at https://www.wipo.int/wipolex/es/legislation/details/10180 (accessed 2 Nov 2024).

[283] See in particular the wording of the sanctions established by Articles 37 to 44 Heritage Law (HN).

[284] Cabrera Medaglia et al. (2014), p. 31.

[285] Cabrera Medaglia et al. (2014), p. 25; Bucher (2008), p. 289.

[286] Bucher (2008), p. 304.

Costa Rica established procedures for sanctions in an administrative regulation in 2016.[287] Sanctions can be imposed by the Technical Office of CONAGEBIO.[288]

Since genetic resources are not protected in Nicaragua under the Heritage Law (NI), there are also no related institutions or procedures in this law. Accordingly, there are also no institutions or procedures for protecting traditional knowledge. Under the Biodiversity Law (NI), the indigenous, ethnic and local communities are granted a strong procedural position. Similar to the rules regarding access to genetic resources,[289] they have the right to decide whether their traditional knowledge is used and it can only be utilized after the respective community grants PIC.[290]

While the Heritage Law (GT) in Guatemala and the Heritage Law (HN) in Honduras provide for the registration of cultural heritage, including "knowledge and techniques" of indigenous peoples, the registration procedure for heritage subject matter is designed for physical objects.[291] In addition, there is no practical necessity for its registration, because traditional knowledge cannot effectively be protected.[292]

6.2.4 Evaluation

As the discussion has shown, traditional knowledge is not effectively protected in most Central American countries. In El Salvador, traditional knowledge is not recognized as protected subject matter at all. The legislation in Guatemala and Honduras recognizes intangible cultural heritage, which includes traditional knowledge, but does not provide for the registration or protection of traditional knowledge. Only in Costa Rica and Nicaragua, the statutory protection of traditional knowledge is reinforced on the institutional level by the establishment of a corresponding administration and enforcement mechanisms.

---

[287] Regulation for the Application of Administrative Sanctions regarding non-authorized Access to Genetic and Biochemical Resources established in the Biodiversity Law (CR) (Reglamento para la Aplicación de las Sanciones Administrativas en Materia de Acceso No Autorizado a los Elementos y Recursos Genéticos y Bioquímicos, Establecidas en Ley de Biodiversidad N° 7788) No. 39341-MINAE, adopted on 16 March 2016, and entered into force 16 September 2016.

[288] Article 6 Regulation 39341-MINAE.

[289] See Sect. 6.1.6.2.

[290] Article 82 Biodiversity Law (NI); see also Cabrera Medaglia et al. (2014), p. 41.

[291] Articles 23 and 24 Heritage Law (GT); Articles 11 to 13 Heritage Law (HN).

[292] See Sect. 6.2.2.3.

References

Aguiñada Arévalo S, Ortiz Aguilar C, Cabrera Medaglia J (2009) Acceso a recursos genéticos y participación en los beneficios: una propuesta de ley consensuada para El Salvador. San Salvador, FUNDE

Asebey EJ, Kempenaar JD (1995) Biodiversity prospecting: fulfilling the mandate of the biodiversity convention. Vand J Transnatl Law 28:703

Bendaña-Guerrero GJ (1999) *Curso de Derecho* de Propiedad Industrial. Hispamer, Managua, Nicaragua

Bucher S (2008) Der Schutz von genetischen Ressourcen und indigenem Wissen in Lateinamerika – Eine Untersuchung am Beispiel der Andengemeinschaft, Brasiliens und Costa Ricas. Nomos, Baden-Baden

Busch AF (2015) Protection of traditional cultural expressions in Latin America - a legal and anthropological study. Springer-Verlag, Berlin Heidelberg

Cabrera Medaglia JA (2003) Access to *genetic resources*, protection of traditional knowledge and intellectual property rights: lessons learned from the Costa Rican experience. Gene Conserve, no. 10, 128–151, available at http://cro.ots.ac.cr/rdmcnfs/datasets/biblioteca/pdfs/nbina-2270.pdf. Accessed 2 Nov 2024

Cabrera Medaglia JA (2004) Costa Rica: legal framework and public policy. In: Carrizosa S, Brush SB, Wright BD, McGuire PE (eds) Accessing biodiversity and sharing the benefits: lessons from implementation of the Convention on Biological Diversity. IUCN, Gland, Switzerland and Cambridge, UK

Cabrera Medaglia J (2006) Costa Rica. In: Lewis-Lettington RJ, Mwanyiki S (eds) Case studies on access and benefit-sharing. International Plant Genetic Resources Institute, available at https://www.cbd.int/financial/bensharing/several-case-IPGRI.pdf. Accessed 2 Nov 2024

Cabrera Medaglia JA (2008) Trade (in particular Free Trade Agreements) and access to genetic resources and benefit sharing: exploring some the linkages. Asian Biotechnology and Development Review, vol 10, No. 3, July 2008

Cabrera Medaglia JA (2010) The Disclosure of Origin Requirement in Central America, ICTSD Programme on Natural Resources, International Trade and Sustainable Development, Issue Paper No. 3. International Centre for Trade and Sustainable Development, Geneva, Switzerland

Cabrera Medaglia JA (2020) Costa Rica ABS legislation and practice after the Nagoya Protocol, April 2020, available at https://www.researchgate.net/publication/340952956_COSTA_RICA_ABS_LEGISLATION_AND_PRACTICE_AFTER_THE_NAGOYA_PROTOCOL. Accessed 2 Nov 2024

Cabrera Medaglia JA, Perron-Welch F, Phillips F-K (2014) Overview of national and regional measures on access and benefit sharing, challenges and opportunities in implementing the Nagoya Protocol, 3rd edn. CISDL Biodiversity & Biosafety Law Research Programme, available at https://www.cisdl.org/wp-content/uploads/2018/04/Global-Overview-of-ABS-Measures_FINAL_SBSTTA18.pdf. Accessed 2 Nov 2024

Correa CM (2001) Traditional knowledge and intellectual property, available at http://quakerservice.ca/wp-content/uploads/2011/07/TKcol3.pdf. Accessed 2 Nov 2024

Drahos P (2000) Indigenous knowledge, intellectual property and biopiracy: is a global biocollecting society the answer. E.I.P.R. 22(6):245–250

Dutfield G (2001) TRIPS-related aspects of traditional knowledge. Case West Res J Int Law 33:239

Dutfield G (2003) Protecting traditional knowledge and folklore. A review of progress in diplomacy and policy formulation, Issue Paper No. 1, UNCTAD / ICTSD, Geneva

Dutfield G (2004) Intellectual property, biogenetic resources and traditional knowledge. Earthscan, United Kingdom

Götting H-P (2004) Biodiversität und Patentrecht. GRUR Int 2004:731–736

Hassemer M (2003) Genetic resources. In: von Lewinski S, von Hahn A (eds) Indigenous heritage and intellectual property: genetic resources, traditional knowledge and folklore. Wolters Kluwer Law

Heinrich M, Scotti F, Andrade-Cetto A, Berger-Gonzalez M, Echeverría J, Friso F, Garcia-Cardona F, Hesketh A, Hitziger M, Maake C, Politi M, Spadafora C, Spadafora R (2020) Access and benefit sharing under the Nagoya Protocol—Quo Vadis? Six Latin American case studies assessing opportunities and risk. Front Pharmacol 11:765. https://doi.org/10.3389/fphar.2020.00765

Henne G (1998) Genetische Vielfalt als Ressource - Die Regelung ihrer Nutzung. Nomos, Baden-Baden

Hilpert HG (1998) TRIPS und das Interesse der Entwicklungsländer am Schutz von Immaterialgüterrechten in ökonomischer Sicht. GRUR Int 1998:91–99

Huettmann F (ed) (2015) Central American Biodiversity: conservation, ecology, and a sustainable future. Springer, New York

Hughell D, Butterfield R (2008) Impact of FSC Certification on Deforestation and the Incidence of Wildfires in the Maya Biosphere Reserve, Rainforest Alliance (on file with the author)

Morales Marroquín JA, Zucchi MI, Pinheiro JB (2023) Biodiversity and environmental policy challenges in Central America towards natural resource governance, Conference Paper, United Nations 8th Multi-stakeholder Forum on Science, Technology and Innovation for the Sustainable Development Goals, available at https://www.researchgate.net/publication/370630509_Biodiversity_and_environmental_policy_challenges_in_Central_America_towards_natural_resource_governance. Accessed 2 Nov 2024

Pérez AM (2008) Biodiversidad en Nicaragua: contexto y estado actual, Encuentro 2008 / Año XL, N° 79, 96-104, available at http://www.bio-nica.info/biblioteca/Perez2008BiodiversidadEnNicaragua.pdf. Accessed 2 Nov 2024

Rott P (2003) TRIPS-Abkommen, Menschenrechte, Sozialpolitik und Entwicklungsländer. GRUR Int 2003:103–118

Ruiz Muller M (2006) Central America. In: Lewis-Lettington RJ, Mwanyiki S (eds) Case studies on access and benefit-sharing. International Plant Genetic Resources Institute, available at https://www.cbd.int/financial/bensharing/several-case-IPGRI.pdf. Accessed 2 Nov 2024

Stoll P-T, von Hahn A (2003) Indigenous peoples, indigenous knowledge and indigenous resources in international law. In: von Lewinski S, von Hahn A (eds) Indigenous heritage and intellectual property: genetic resources, traditional knowledge and folklore. Wolters Kluwer Law

Taubman A, Leistner M (2003) Traditional knowledge. In: von Lewinski S, von Hahn A (eds) Indigenous heritage and intellectual property: genetic resources, traditional knowledge and folklore. Wolters Kluwer Law

United Nations Environmental Programme - World Conservation Monitoring Centre (UNEP-WCMC) (2016) The State of Biodiversity in Latin America and the Caribbean: a mid-term review of progress towards the Aichi Biodiversity Targets, available at https://www.cbd.int/doc/meetings/cop/prepcop-2016-04/other/prepcop-2016-04-outlook-grulac-en.pdf. Accessed 2 Nov 2024

von Hahn A (2004) Traditionelles Wissen indigener und lokaler Gemeinschaften zwischen geistigen Eigentumsrechten und der "public domain". Springer, Heidelberg

Chapter 7
Enforcement

As the previous analysis has demonstrated, CAFTA-DR raised the level of protection of IP rights in several ways beyond TRIPS, and this level has largely been implemented in the national IP legislation. However, the practical impact of this increased protection depends on the effective enforcement of IP rights. Stricter enforcement provisions have, therefore, been a key element in post-TRIPS FTAs such as CAFTA-DR.

7.1 Introduction

7.1.1 TRIPS-Plus Enforcement Rules

7.1.1.1 Background

Foreign companies have increasingly been concerned about enforcement in developing countries such as Central America, because it was practically very difficult to prosecute even plain violations such as the sale of fake pharmaceuticals or the import of counterfeit brand-name apparel. The Special 301 Reports of the USTR regularly find and expresses concern with the weak enforcement of IP rights in Costa Rica, the Dominican Republic and Guatemala. However, this assessment does not necessarily mean that enforcement in El Salvador, Honduras and Nicaragua is better from the perspective of the USTR. Rather, the Special 301 Reports of the USTR focuses more on economically relevant markets than legally relevant non-compliance, which might be due to the fact that the input for these Special 301 Reports partly comes

F. Böttger, *CAFTA-DR, European Free Trade Agreements and the Industrial Property System in Central America*, Munich Studies on Innovation and Competition 21, https://doi.org/10.1007/978-3-031-93440-7_7

from industry groups which would understandably focus on bigger markets.[1] More effective enforcement was, therefore, a major objective behind TRIPS,[2] because the Paris Convention only required (non-binding) undertakings to enforce rights.[3]

7.1.1.2 CAFTA-DR

This objective on improving the legal position of the right holder is even more visible in the enforcement section of CAFTA-DR, which focuses on the right holder, while the procedural position of the user is not specifically considered. The enforcement rules of CAFTA-DR cover the enforcement of IP rights comprehensively, *i.e.*, civil, administrative and criminal enforcement, and especially provisional and border measures.

A particular concern for right holders is the possibility to enforce rights in case of *exportation*. Under TRIPS, civil remedies, criminal remedies and border measures are required only for the *importation* of infringing goods.[4] CAFTA-DR extends the scope of enforcement to *exportation*. However, the wording of CAFTA-DR is ambiguous. With regard to border measures and criminal remedies it uses the definition of TRIPS regarding counterfeit and pirated goods, which refers only to "the law of the country of importation".[5] This might conversely be interpreted to mean that exportation is not included as an illegal activity. On the other hand, the provisions on border measures explicitly cover the exportation of infringing goods[6] and criminal remedies are also explicitly extended to exportation.[7] These provisions were specifically included, while the definition mentioned above was merely copied in the footnote. Therefore, the CAFTA-DR parties apparently intended to include exportation generally in relation to enforcement measures. This interpretation is reinforced systematically by the fact that the provisions of CAFTA-DR explicitly extend civil remedies to exportation activities, and it would be inconsistent to provide for civil measures against exportation, but not provide for border measures against the same activity.

The extension of enforcement to exportation has the practical advantage for the right holder that it is more effective to police the shipment of bulk infringing

[1] See, e.g., USTR Special 301 Report (2007), p. 38; subsequent Special 301 Report contain similar assessments; Honduras was mentioned in the Special 301 Report 2016, where it was "applauded" by the USTR for adopting an IP Action Plan, see USTR Special 301 Report (2016), p. 8.

[2] See, e.g., Díaz (2008), p. 75.

[3] Article 10*ter* Paris Convention.

[4] Regarding civil remedies see Article 44(1) TRIPS, regarding border measures and criminal remedies see fn 14 to Article 51 TRIPS.

[5] Fn 18 to Article 15.11.20 of CAFTA-DR is literally identical to fn 14 to Article 51 TRIPS and only refers to importation.

[6] Article 15.11.24 (3) of CAFTA-DR.

[7] Article 15.11.26 (a) of CAFTA-DR.

products while they are in transit, i.e., closer to the source, rather than to await their distribution in the market, i.e., the destination.[8]

However, it also it indirectly extends the substantive level of IP protection of the exporting or transit country to the importing country by preventing the supply of goods or services even if it doesn't constitute IP infringement under the local law of the importing country. This extension implies that Article 51 TRIPS, which refers to an infringing act in the "country of importation" as the basis for border measures, also encompasses "transit countries" in this definition.[9]

7.1.1.3 EU-FTAs

The EU-CARIFORUM-EPA by contrast also contains rules protecting, *e.g.*, the defendant in infringement cases. However, the EU-CARIFORUM-EPA only addresses questions of civil and administrative, but not criminal enforcement.[10]

The EU-CA-AA was concluded between the EU and Central America only a few years after the EU-CARIFORUM-EPA was concluded with the Dominican Republic and other EU-CARIFORUM countries. Nevertheless, in the enforcement section, it differs significantly from the EU-CARIFORUM-EPA. Like the EU-CARIFORUM-EPA, it also contains rules protecting the defendant. For example, according to the EU-CA-AA, in relation to provisional measures judicial authorities must have the authority to require the right holder to provide reasonable evidence and to order the right holder to provide a reasonable security.[11] On the other hand, the EU-CA-AA contains strict obligations in relation to criminal enforcement, similar to CAFTA-DR.

7.1.2 IP Enforcement in Central America

7.1.2.1 Overview

The level of infringing activity in relation to IP rights in Central America is, broadly speaking, high regarding copyright and trademarks and low regarding patents.[12] Enforcement activities in the area of IP correspondingly focus on trademark

---

[8] Blakeney (2005), p. 37.

[9] This issue is discussed in more detail by Grosse Ruse-Khan (2011), p. 659, who raises the question whether Article 51 TRIPS could be interpreted as a "ceiling" for IP protection in effect preventing transit countries from enforcing their IP regime.

[10] The authority of the European Commission to legislate or negotiate criminal law matters is disputed. As a result, such sanctions have been omitted in the European Directive 2004/48/EC of 29 April 2004 on the enforcement of intellectual property rights ("Enforcement Directive") and in the EU-FTAs, which were modelled after the Directive.

[11] Article 265(2) EU-CA-AA.

[12] *El Periodico* (Guatemala), 21 September 2008, pp. 16–17 (on file with the author).

infringements. A study of Guatemalan case-law covering the mid-1980ies until 2002 included 20 trademark cases, one design case and no patent cases.[13] Practitioners also stress the paramount importance of trademark cases.[14] Because trademark counterfeiting is practically by far the most relevant type of infringement, the restriction of many mandatory enforcement provisions of CAFTA-DR to counterfeit trademark goods and the flexibility for the Central American countries with regard to other infringements and other IP rights is, therefore, of limited practical consequence. The effect of this differentiation is further limited by the fact that generally the Central American laws do not differentiate between different IP rights with regard to enforcement measures. The main exception to this "one size fits all" enforcement approach are the more restrictive criminal provisions.[15]

There are very few patent infringement cases litigated as such.[16] Because there are few patents, *e.g.*, in Costa Rica and the Dominican Republic, attorneys based their cases regarding inventions on other grounds, *e.g.*, confidentiality agreements or unfair competition.[17] In addition, patent infringement cases are frequent mainly in countries with large markets or technologically sophisticated manufacturing capabilities, which in Central America by and large do not exist.

7.1.2.2 Practical Restrictions

Enforcement of IP rights in Central America is generally less effective than the administration of IP rights.[18] This is due to several institutional and legal reasons.

Regarding institutions, enforcement agencies are often not adequately equipped or motivated to help the right holder. The motivation appears to be higher and enforcement works better if it relates to health risks, *e.g.*, against counterfeit food products and medicines.[19] This focus reflects the internationally acknowledged risks to public health that counterfeit medicines pose.[20]

---

[13] de Leon Molina (2002).

[14] Interview with *Gabriela Contreras Aguilera.*

[15] See Sect. 7.7.

[16] For example, there are no patent cases reported in the presentations on case-law in Guatemala at WIPO, see, e.g., de Leon Molina (2002).

[17] Interview with *Ana Catalina Monge Rodríguez.*

[18] The assessment that enforcement in Central America is relatively weak(er) is shared by many observers, while the evaluation whether this is positive or negative depends on the general view on IP protection; for example, USTR (2010), p. 30 highlights this as a significant problem in relation to the Dominican Republic, while Roffe and Genovesi (2011), pp. 98–99 also note that law enforcement agencies in the region often have other enforcement priorities.

[19] For example, according to USTR Special 301 Report (2011), the interagency working group on IP rights in Guatemala focuses its training efforts on counterfeit medicines. The USTR also reported a successful enforcement action against a counterfeit medicines manufacturing and distribution network in the Dominican Republic, see USTR Special 301 Report (2016), p. 59.

[20] See, e.g., WHO (2018); see also IMPACT (2011), p. 24.

Another impediment of effective enforcement, even though its effect is hardly quantifiable, is the *legal uncertainty* resulting from the absence of established precedent. Theoretically, prior decisions have effect as precedent, but only from the constitutional and highest courts and only after a certain number of rulings.[21] This limits the deterring effect of enforcement. In addition, even if a judge intended to consider precedent, it will often be difficult to research applicable precedent, because in the area of IP law, there are relatively few cases which are concluded by a judicial decision, and those decisions are not systematically published and accessible to practitioners.[22]

Practically, enforcement activities in Central America mainly concern trademark counterfeiting and usually consist of three phases:

- The process starts with enforcement actions against the *retailer or the street vendor*, when the infringing goods become publicly available and visible for the first time;
- The retailer leads (ideally) to the *distributor*, who is often needed only for the testimony against the producer;
- The enforcement focus is on the *producer*, if it can be identified during the preceding steps.[23]

7.1.2.3 Adhesion Procedure and Conciliation

While CAFTA-DR and the national IP laws are based on *adversarial* procedures, the Central American enforcement practice is more comprehensive and *cooperative*, and disputes are often resolved through *conciliation* between the parties or in criminal cases deals.[24]

Adhesion Procedure

Unlike the separate regulation of civil and criminal enforcement in CAFTA-DR, in Central America many right holders opt for the *adhesion* procedure,[25] because criminal procedures are often quicker and the additional enforcement means of the

[21] See, in relation to Guatemala and Mayora (2022).

[22] The collection of Guatemalan case-law reported by de Leon Molina (2002) at a WIPO seminar is a good example. For a period of about 20 years, it includes 20 trademark cases, one design case and no patent cases. While the collection is not necessarily exhaustive, it is one of the few collections of case-law in the region.

[23] E.g., the USTR emphasizes the importance of enforcement actions against manufacturers, see USTR (2010), p. 33, but also acknowledges that such actions are not as common or successful as against "small scale" sellers, as reported by Thomas (2012), p. 791.

[24] See Sect. 7.1.2.

[25] E.g., Article 208 IP Law (GT).

Ministerio Público facilitate actions against infringers.[26] In such cases, the right holder provides the *Ministerio Público* with evidence, based on which the *Ministerio Público* may initiate further investigations, sometimes with the help of the right holder. Criminal proceedings are then initiated against the alleged infringer by the *Ministerio Público*, to which the right holder joins by adhesion and in this way introduces the civil infringement claims into the criminal proceedings. In such cases, civil claims such as injunctions and damages can be granted by the criminal judge.[27] If the civil damages are paid, additional criminal sanctions might not be imposed by the judge, as part of a comprehensive conciliation or deal.

It should be noted that similar procedures exist also in other countries, especially in Europe. They are practically relevant in the area of commercial disputes particularly in countries with strong formalistic, mercantile traditions such as Spain and Portugal, which influenced the Central American legal systems.[28]

The adhesion procedure also exists in Germany, but has been little used.[29] There was a discussion in Germany in 2009 about the removal of IP crimes from the list of cases in which the adhesion procedure applies, to relieve the criminal enforcement system from defending private commercial interests.[30] However, the German legislator decided to keep the adhesion procedure available in IP cases.[31]

Conciliation

Conciliation can often be reached before the trial. The right holder can inform the alleged infringer about the infringement by sending a warning letter (*carta de apercibimiento*) with the demand to desist.[32]

During a criminal trial, the *Ministerio Público* usually tries to make a deal, including the settlement of civil claims between the parties.[33]

---

[26] Escoto (2004), pp. 32–34.

[27] See, e.g., Article 124 IP Law (GT).

[28] On the adhesion procedure in Portugal in relation to unfair competition claims see Ascensão (2005), pp. 207–208.

[29] In Germany, § 395(2) Nr. 2 Code of Criminal Procedure (*Strafprozessordnung*), explicitly provides for the adhesion procedure in IP cases.

[30] Article 1 Nr. 22 *Gesetzentwurf der Bundesregierung zur Stärkung der Rechte von Verletzten und Zeugen im Strafverfahren (2. Opferrechtsreformgesetz)* proposed the removal of the adhesion procedure; this proposal has been criticized by the IP Committee of the German Lawyers' Association, see Deutscher Anwaltverein (2009).

[31] The adhesion procedure available in IP cases is now codified in § 395 (1) Nr. 6 Code of Criminal Procedure (Strafprozessordnung).

[32] For Costa Rica, see Chambers & Partners, Practical Guide Trademarks 2024, part 8.6, available at https://practiceguides.chambers.com/practice-guides/trade-marks-copyright-2024/costa-rica (accessed 2 Nov 2024).

[33] See the description of this collaborative criminal procedure by Escoto (2004), p. 50 (called "Alternative Dispute Settlement").

Sometimes not only the *Ministerio Público* and the court, but also the *IP Register* is part of this procedure. This again underlines the comprehensive Central American approach to enforcement, and particularly in Central America this seems a practical approach, because the IP Registers arguably have the most expertise in the IP field.[34] If a deal is reached between the parties, the *Ministerio Público* abstains from the criminal charges and the judge closes the case.[35]

The abstention by the *Ministerio Público* is optional, but there is practically little interest of the *Ministerio Público* to prosecute IP cases after a deal also involving the right holder has been reached. Such a deal covers both the civil and the criminal aspects of the case, but the incentive for the infringer to accept it usually is based on the waiver of criminal sanctions in exchange for the compliance with the civil claims (compensation of damages).[36] Only if the conciliation or deal does not work, the case is pursued further by the *Ministerio Público*.[37]

This conciliation approach does not align easily with the *adversarial* procedure envisioned by CAFTA-DR. However, neither international agreements nor CAFTA-DR require specific IP enforcement procedures[38] and, therefore, countries can establish procedures for the enforcement of IP rights in accordance with the foundations of their own legal system.[39]

The conciliation approach used within the IP system in Central America has several advantages for the parties involved in the process. In particular, it provides the possibility to involve the IP Register, which can provide its unique expertise on IP matters, which courts may lack.[40] Also, early resolution saves resources of the *Ministerio Público* and the courts, while long trials would probably not lead to a significantly better result for the right holder. It must also be noted, as will be further discussed below in relation to criminal sanctions, that the law enforcement institutions in most Central American countries must deal with significant challenges posed by other types of crime and it is legitimate for them to allocate their resources in this way.[41]

---

[34] Local practitioners repeatedly confirmed this situation, which is also shown by the numerous outreach activities organized by the IP Registers; in Nicaragua, the IP Register was formally charged with such outreach activities by an executive order, see Executive Decree regarding the Promotion and Protection of IP Rights of the People of Nicaragua (Decreto sobre la Promoción, Fomento y Protección de los Derechos de Propiedad Intelectual del Pueblo Nicaragüense), Decree No. 18-2012 of 27 April 2012; the text of the regulation is available at http://www.wipo.int/edocs/lexdocs/laws/es/ni/ni044es.pdf (accessed 2 Nov 2024).

[35] See, e.g., Article 208 IP Law (GT).

[36] Escoto (2004), pp. 32–34.

[37] However, US right holders reported that, e.g. in Costa Rica, often there is a "lack of interest" to prosecute IP cases to the end, see https://www.state.gov/reports/2020-investment-climate-statements/costa-rica/ (accessed 2 Nov 2024).

[38] Article 41(5) TRIPS.

[39] Article 15.11(1) CAFTA-DR.

[40] See Sect. 2.5.3.

[41] See Sect. 7.7.

However, while this procedure is in the interest of the parties involved, it reduces the number of formally adjudicated cases and thus slows down the development of the law through case-law and may increase the legal uncertainty for the lack of formal and publishable application of the respective statutes.

7.2 General Provisions

Article 41(3) TRIPS and Article 15.11(3) CAFTA-DR impose general enforcement standards on the domestic legal systems regarding the judicial procedures and decisions on the merit.[42]

7.2.1 Procedural Requirements Generally Applicable to Enforcement

7.2.1.1 Due Process

According to Article 41(2) TRIPS, the procedures shall be generally fair and balanced. Specifically, this includes the written notice to the defendant substantiating the claim, representation by independent legal counsel[43] and the opportunity of the parties to be heard in relation to the evidence on which the final decision is based.[44] As these due process provisions are primarily designed to protect the defendant, there are no corresponding requirements in CAFTA-DR, which is generally limited to provisions protecting the right holder. Under CAFTA-DR, enforcement must only conform to the principles of due process.[45]

7.2.1.2 Effectiveness

According to 41(1) and 41(2) TRIPS, the judicial procedures must fulfill several substantive criteria to enable the right holder to enforce the right. Specifically, they must (i) be effective and expeditious, (ii) not be unnecessarily complicated or costly and (iii) not have unreasonable time-limits or unwarranted delays. As there are generally no court fees for judicial procedures in Central America, they are obviously not unnecessarily costly, and the procedures also are not especially

[42] Such requirements, absent in the Paris Convention, had previously been included in Chapter 17 NAFTA.

[43] Article 42 TRIPS.

[44] Article 41(3) TRIPS.

[45] Article 15.11.1(a) CAFTA-DR.

complicated.[46] However, there are concerns regarding the effectiveness and expediency of the enforcement procedures in Central America. There has been criticism of the long duration of procedures in Guatemala in this regard.[47] In Nicaragua, there are civil cases regarding the violation of IP rights which have been pending in the first instance for more than five years. One case was still pending after 13 years and then was settled.[48] Many administrative appeals were abandoned after pending for several years in the second instance. Such enormous delays in adjudication have been considered by foreign right holders to be a practical denial of protection.[49] However, all Central American countries struggle with the lack of resources for law enforcement, and Nicaragua, being the poorest country, maybe most.

7.2.1.3 "Resource Exception" Under Article 41(5) TRIPS

Weak law enforcement is, however, not limited to IP rights, but is a problem for the legal system in general. This is largely due to the current challenges the Central American countries face with regard to their legal systems and law enforcement. Against the background of these challenges in other areas of crime, in particular violent crimes and drug trafficking, it seems understandable that in many Central American countries the political and legal institutions in general and the *Ministerio Público* in particular do not give priority to infringements of IP rights.[50]

In this context it must be noted that both Article 41(5) TRIPS Article 15.11.2 (b) CAFTA-DR state that countries are not required to allocate special resources for the protection of IP, meaning that IP enforcement does not have to be better than other areas of enforcement. In the case "*China—Measures Affecting the Protection and Enforcement of Intellectual Property Rights*", the WTO Dispute Settlement Body had a chance to review Article 41(5) TRIPS.[51] While it rejected China's claims on the specific issues of Chinese IP practice, the panel, by taking up the issue per se, implicitly recognized that resource constraints can justify non-compliance with TRIPS enforcement obligations.[52]

Therefore, one cannot conclude that the practical deficiencies in Central America *per se* constitute a violation of Article 41 TRIPS.

---

[46] For civil procedures, see Sect. 7.3.

[47] USTR Special 301 Report (2016), p. 59.

[48] Interview with *Ricardo Bendaña.*

[49] PhRMA (2007), p. 26. This criticism by PhRMA was not included by the USTR in the final USTR Special 301 Report (2007), however, this was probably not because the USTR disagreed with PhRMA's assessment, but because the USTR usually selected only Costa Rica, the Dominican Republic and Guatemala for its Special 301 Reports during this period.

[50] Regarding the current situation of organized crime in Central America see United Nations (2012).

[51] WTO Dispute Settlement Body, Panel Report, China—Measures Affecting the Protection and Enforcement of Intellectual Property Rights, Decision of 26 January 2009, WT/DS362/R.

[52] Yu (2011), p. 780.

7.2.1.4 Deterrence

While the practical lack of efficiency does not constitute a violation of the legal efficiency requirement, the question becomes whether such enforcement procedures can deter infringements.

According to Article 41(1) TRIPS and Article 15.11.8, 15.11.26 (b) (i) CAFTA-DR, the remedies shall constitute a deterrent to further infringements. It has been argued that the "rampant" infringement of IP in Central America shows that the current enforcement procedures have no deterring effect and, therefore, violate TRIPS (and CAFTA-DR).[53] This argument is problematic for two reasons: First, in order to determine whether there is a deterring effect of enforcement procedures, one should not ask how much infringement still takes place, but how much infringement did not take place that otherwise would have if the enforcement procedures had not existed. It should be sufficient for compliance if the enforcement procedures have *some* deterring effect, because there is no absolute reduction of IP infringement required by either TRIPS or CAFTA-DR. Second, Article 15.11.8 and 15.11.26(b) (i) CAFTA-DR do not require deterring individual decisions, but general procedures, policies or guidelines for criminal and civil enforcement that have a deterring effect. Given the judicial independence, this relates primarily to the legislative level. One possibility to evaluate Central American legislation is the comparison with other countries, because it is practically difficult to establish the appropriate policies necessary for deterrence. Here we find that the level of enforcement provided for in Central American legislation is fairly typical. For example, the statutory penalties for IP crimes for example are very similar to those in Germany, a country which probably can be considered having a sufficiently deterring legislation.[54]

7.2.1.5 Statistics

Accordingly to TRIPS, information that a country collects on its efforts to provide effective enforcement of IP rights shall be published.[55] However, while some enforcement agencies seem to collect statistical information, they publish very little about their activities.[56] Most of the statistical information available on the Internet comes from the IP Register and, therefore, relates to the administration, not the enforcement.[57]

---

[53] PhRMA (2007), p. 26.

[54] See Sect. 7.7.

[55] Article 41(4) TRIPS.

[56] The USTR proposed that the Costa Rican government should publish "detailed information" about IP enforcement, see USTR Special 301 Report (2016).

[57] See for example the reports submitted to WIPO by the IP Registers of Costa Rica and Guatemala, i.e., Registro de la Propiedad Industrial de Costa Rica (2006) and Registro de la Propiedad Intelectual de Guatemala (2006).

7.2.1.6 Judicial Review

In order to prevent or remedy errors and abuses in the civil enforcement system, TRIPS requires control mechanisms. Procedurally, it mandates the adequate *indemnification* of the defendant in cases of an abuse of enforcement measures.[58] It also requires the possibility to appeal to a judicial authority against final administrative decisions and against first instance judicial decisions, at least regarding the legal aspects of the decision.[59] Accordingly, appeals against intermediate procedural decisions are not required, but permitted. Such appeals might enable parties to delay the final resolution of proceedings, because appellate cases take very long.[60] It is reasonable that Article 41(4) TRIPS does not require this type of review, which makes room for reforms in this area to speed up procedures in simple cases. There exist possibilities for appeals against intermediate procedural decisions in Central America, *e.g.*, in Nicaragua.[61] In Guatemala, there are two different appellate procedures for wrong application of the law and non-application of the law.[62] Appeals in trademark cases were denied because they did not clearly and consistently state whether the lower court had applied a legal provision not correctly or not at all.[63]

7.2.2 Requirements Regarding Decisions on the Merits

7.2.2.1 Writing

According to Article 41(3) TRIPS, decisions on the merits shall *preferably* be in writing. Article 15.11(3) CAFTA-DR extends the scope of this obligation, because at least final decisions shall be in writing *without exception*. This obligation is designed to improve the transparency of the proceedings, and is certainly helpful with regard to the final decision. In Central America decisions are generally in writing and, therefore, comply with these requirements.

7.2.2.2 Publication

However, judicial decisions must be made available to the *other party* under Article 41(3) TRIPS, but not published. According to Article 15.11(3) CAFTA-DR, judicial decisions have to be published or made publicly available for *governments* and *right*

[58] Article 48 TRIPS.

[59] Article 41(4) TRIPS.

[60] In Nicaragua about four years, interview with *Ricardo Bendaña*.

[61] Interview with *Ricardo Bendaña*.

[62] See CSJ (GT), decision of 16 March 1993 - [Industrial Design].

[63] See CSJ (GT), Case No. 112-96, decision of 30 January 1997 - DETECTO.

holders. This clause does not include the other party of the proceeding or third parties, *i.e.*, the general public. However, in practice these parties will also be able to access published, publicly available decisions.

7.2.2.3 Reasoning

According to Article 41.3. TRIPS, "decisions on the merits of a case shall preferably be (…) reasoned". Article 15.11(3) CAFTA-DR mandates the statement of the relevant facts and the legal considerations (the reasoning or the legal basis), but limits this requirement to final decisions. The term "stated" suggests that these elements have to be included in the final decision itself, and that it is not enough to make reference to prior decisions. This interpretation is reinforced by the fact that, according to Article 15.11(3) CAFTA-DR, only final decisions have to be published. If such a decision makes reference to the prior decision, which does not have to be published, the governments and right holders could not get acquainted with its relevant content. It is questionable whether the current structure of final judicial decisions in Central America always fulfils these requirements. For example, in some countries at least some appellate decisions do not restate the relevant facts or the legal reasoning of the first instance decision comprehensively, even if it is based on them. It merely makes references to the facts, so that the appellate decision is not understandable in and out of itself, but only if read together with the reviewed decision.[64] In Guatemala, a study in 2016 (on judicial decisions generally, not limited to IP) found that many decisions lacked a statement of the relevant facts and the legal arguments were so abstract that it was not clear how they exactly related to the specific case.[65]

7.2.2.4 Judicial Review

Article 41(4) TRIPS requires the possibility of judicial review "of at least the *legal* aspects of initial judicial decisions on the merits of a case". However, such review may be limited to important cases. The CAFTA-DR enforcement section does not contain additional rules.[66] In Central America, the judicial procedure generally allows appeals against the decisions of the civil, administrative and criminal courts

[64] Observation by the author in 2008.

[65] Garro (2016).

[66] The TRIPS requirements apply to all decisions, those in favor and those against the right holder. Therefore, the possibility of an appeal may also benefit the user and/or infringer of IP rights. This may explain why the right holder-friendly CAFTA-DR did not provide for further obligations in this area.

of first instance. Second instance decisions can usually be appealed to the Supreme Court (CSJ), which, as in the USA, is not only responsible for constitutional issues, but also the review of other legal issues.[67] The possibility of judicial review is extremely important. The lack of expertise with regard to IP issues in the judiciary is of particular concern in Central America, because many first instance judges received little or no training in IP matters.[68] This, together with the factual complexity of many IP cases, increases the risk of incorrect decisions. The second instance courts may have the possibility to acquire more experience in the field by specialization of some judges.

7.3 Civil Enforcement

7.3.1 Introduction

Article 42 TRIPS requires civil judicial procedures concerning the enforcement of IP rights covered by TRIPS. Article 15.11(6) CAFTA-DR extends this obligation to *any IP right*. This extension was necessary to include the rights introduced by CAFTA-DR, *e.g.*, test data.[69] Civil enforcement of IP rights is available in all Central American countries. However, its utilization varies in practice. Practitioners point to several advantages of civil enforcement, including the availability of provisional measures and the possibility of more complex litigation, *e.g.*, in cases of trademark infringement based on confusion, with the option of unfair competition litigation.[70] Civil litigation is especially important for right holders in countries like Costa Rica, where only very limited criminal enforcement measures exist and authorities are reluctant to assist right holders in enforcing IP rights.[71] But civil litigation is also considered slower and more expensive than criminal proceedings in countries like El Salvador and Honduras, where criminal proceedings are well-established and offer the possibility to obtain preliminary injunctions.[72]

---

[67] de Leon Molina (2002), p. 2.

[68] See Sect. 2.5.4.

[69] The most important additional subject matter is material protected by digital rights management (DRM) measures, see Article 15.10 CAFTA-DR and Sect. 5.2., above, which is not analyzed here, because this study is limited to industrial property.

[70] See Sect. 5.4.

[71] See the quite explicit comments of the Costa Rican CSJ reported by Escoto (2004), pp. 27–28.

[72] According to Mejia (2016), p. 101 and Romero (2016), p. 84, in El Salvador and Honduras criminal procedures seem to provide slight advantages to right holders in terms of timing and costs. However, such assessments are obviously difficult to generalize and could easily change over time, and to the author's knowledge there are no studies in this regard.

7.3.2 Remedies

7.3.2.1 Injunctive Relief

The possibility for the right holder to enforce the rights through civil remedies was a priority for foreign businesses and accordingly, civil remedies, especially injunctions (discussed in this section) and damages[73] were provided for in detail in Articles 44 to 46 TRIPS and Articles 15.11(17), 15.11(18) CAFTA-DR. *Internationally*, the obligation to provide for injunctive relief is contained in Article 44 TRIPS. In relation to infringing goods, it requires the authority "to prevent the *entry* into the channels of commerce [...] immediately after customs clearance". This means that civil jurisdiction seamlessly takes over after the administrative jurisdiction for border measures. It also easier for the right holder to intervene at this stage than to get the products "of the shelves" once they have been distributed into the market. In addition, CAFTA-DR provides for the possibility for injunctions to prevent *exportation*. This reflects the experience that border measures in the importing country are not sufficient to combat counterfeiting. This new provision allows for the policing of infringing activities closer to the source.[74] In *Central America*, the obligation to provide for injunctive relief was included in the laws implementing TRIPS (*e.g.*, Article 172(a) IP Law (SV)). In Central America, injunctions are the primary objective of infringement cases.[75] However, the injunction sometimes cannot be effectively enforced, because especially small local distributors and vendors find alternative ways to commercialize the infringing goods simply by relocating their street market.[76]

Both the TRIPS and CAFTA-DR provisions only require the *authority* for the courts to order an injunction, not an *obligation* for the courts to issue such orders in specific cases. This is due to the fact that most jurisdictions, including the USA, allow for exceptions to injunction orders. One might question whether CAFTA-DR allows for statutory exceptions, given that the TRIPS exceptions are not repeated. However, in Article 15.1(7) CAFTA-DR the parties have affirmed their TRIPS rights, which include these exceptions. In addition, CAFTA-DR generally leaves provisions restricting the position of the right holder to the national legislature. TRIPS provides for three exceptions:

- good faith infringements (Article 44(1) second sentence TRIPS),
- compulsory licenses and (Articles 44(2) first sentence with 31 TRIPS),
- cases in which this remedy would be "inconsistent with a member's law" (Article 44(2) second sentence TRIPS), which leaves a lot of flexibility for

[73] This remedy is discussed in Sect. 7.3.2.2.

[74] The extension of border measures to exports and goods in transit is discussed further in Sect. 7.6.2.

[75] For example, Palacios (2016), p. 94 reports that in Guatemala an injunction can be ordered at the beginning of civil proceedings, after which the infringement case is then comprehensively litigated.

[76] Thomas (2012), p. 791.

implementation, and could cover, *e.g.*, the denial of an injunction based on equity as in US case-law.[77] In this case, declaratory judgments and adequate compensation shall be available.

In the Central American legislation, the granting of injunctive relief is not accompanied by statutory exceptions. For example, in El Salvador and Nicaragua, the laws provide for a list of remedies, starting with injunctive relief, but without any broad exception based on equity (In fact without any explicit exceptions).[78] These clauses are similar to the legislative approach of continental European laws, e.g., Article 139 of the Spanish Intellectual Property Law.[79]

7.3.2.2 Damages

Compensatory Damages

Compensatory damages are required by Article 45(1) TRIPS and provided for by all the national laws in Central America. In relation to *requirements*, Article 45(1) TRIPS mandates compensatory damages in cases where the infringer acted "knowingly, or with reasonable grounds to know". Article 15.11(7) and 15.11 (8) CAFTA-DR do not further specify the requirements for the claim to damages. Therefore, the Central American countries are able to determine "reasonable grounds" nationally and also may require actual knowledge of the infringement for awarding other, *e.g.*, pre-established damages. In Central American legal practice, damages are sometimes not awarded because judges construe "rationale motives" for the infringement which exclude liability.[80] For the *calculation of damages* there are generally three options, (1) the compensation of the damage to the right holder, (2) the profits of the infringer and (3) the license analogy. In Central America, national legislation provided for compensatory damages based on the *damages to the right holder*, either following the TRIPS formulation of "injuries [...] suffered" like in Guatemala[81] or by granting "lost profits" like in Costa Rica[82] and Nicaragua,[83] or

[77] The US Supreme Court used the equity exception in the decision *eBay v. MercExchange,* 547 U.S. 388, of 15 May 2006 *to deny an injunction because of disproportionate effects, see* von Mühlendahl (2007), p. 337.

[78] Article 172(a) IP Law (SV) and Article 106(a) Patent and Design Law (NI); in Costa Rica and Guatemala, injunctive relief is not explicitly listed in the remedies section, but included by reference to the substantive IP and civil procedure rules and accordingly also does not provide for explicit exceptions.

[79] Unlike the Central American legislation, Article 139(4) of the Spanish Intellectual Property Law provides for an exception to injunctive relief in relation to infringing goods acquired in good faith for personal use.

[80] Interview with *Ricardo Bendaña.*

[81] Article 184(a) IP Law (GT).

[82] Article 40 IP Enforcement Law (CR).

[83] Article 107(a) Patent and Design Law (NI); Article 99(a) Trademark Law (NI).

both like in El Salvador.[84] In Nicaragua, the provisions on damages were modified during the process of implementing CAFTA-DR to explicitly include lost profits.[85] Article 15.11.7 (b) CAFTA-DR states that "inter alia the value of the infringed-upon good or service based on a legitimate measure of value that the right holder presents" shall be considered by the courts. This formulation means that the provision does not have to be included in the national law, as long as the courts practically calculate the damage accordingly. It is optional to award the *profits of the infringer* under Article 45(1) TRIPS and Articles 15.11.7 and 15.11(8) CAFTA-DR. Article 15.11(7)(a)(ii) CAFTA-DR requires the authority of the courts to order the payment of profits attributable to the infringement, at least in cases of trademark counterfeiting. The respective provisions already existed in the Central American legislation prior to CAFTA-DR.[86] In practice, *e.g.* in Nicaragua, damages were in legal practice awarded based on the benefits obtained by the infringer already prior to CAFTA-DR.[87] Practitioners have questioned the necessity of legislative change which now includes also "lost profits", as it is perceived as resulting in an identical amount.[88] Damages can finally be calculated in an analogy to the price the infringer would have to pay for a *contractual license*, following the example of many European jurisdictions, taking into account the commercial value of the infringed right and existing licenses.[89] The practical relevance of damage claims varies in the CAFTA-DR countries. In Nicaragua, damages are sought and granted only in a minority of cases, because the right holders' priority is the injunction.[90] In El Salvador and Guatemala, right holders claim both an injunction and damages more often.[91]

Special Focus: El Salvador

The implementation of Article 15.11(7) CAFTA-DR in El Salvador is a good example or the difficulties including TRIPS-plus provisions into an existing national law. Even though appropriate damages were already available, El Salvador modified its law as part of the CAFTA-DR implementation. According to Article 173(c) (old) IP Law (SV), damages could be calculated based on the "benefits resulting from the infringing acts". The reform law introduced a new sentence at the end of the article

[84] Articles 172(b), 173(a),(b) IP Law (SV).

[85] Article 107(a) Patent and Design Law (NI); Article 99(a) Trademark Law (NI).

[86] Article 40 IP Enforcement Law (CR), Articles 172(a), 173(c) IP Law (SV), Article 184(b) IP Law (GT), Article 107(b) Patent and Design Law (NI).

[87] Interview with *Ricardo Bendaña*.

[88] Interview with *Ricardo Bendaña*.

[89] Article 40 IP Enforcement Law (CR), Articles 172(a), 173 IP Law (SV), Article 184(c) IP Law (GT), Article 163 IP Law (HN), Article 107(c) Patent and Design Law (NI).

[90] Interview with *Ricardo Bendaña*.

[91] Interview with *Carlos Castillo*.

providing "additionally" for the payment of "profits attributable to the infringement".[92] There was no apparent need for this change because literally there appears to be no difference between "benefits" and "profits" as well as "resulting from" and "attributable to" or "infringing act" and "infringement".

In addition, there already exists a "safeguard" clause in Article 173(e) IP Law (SV), which provides additionally for "any convenient type" of damages. It seems likely that this modification, like the addition of "injuries [...] suffered" to the "lost profits", has been included to ensure the expedient and literal compliance with CAFTA-DR, without the intent to introduce any substantive change. Accordingly, while the change renders the entire provision more complicated and partly redundant, it does not seem to provide any additional legal benefit to the right holder.

Pre-Established Damages

While under Article 45(1) TRIPS pre-established damages are optional, they are mandatory under Article 15.11(8) CAFTA-DR, at least in cases of trademark counterfeiting. They have to be provided for in domestic law, and shall be determined by the courts in an amount "sufficient to constitute a deterrent to future infringements". In Article 160 of the EU-CARIFORUM-EPA, pre-established damages are optional, which is now irrelevant for the Dominican Republic given the obligation under CAFTA-DR. Similarly, in Article 267 EU-CA-AA, pre-established damages are optional, which also does not grant any practical flexibility to the Central American countries because of the mandatory provision of Article 15.11 (8) CAFTA-DR. Nevertheless, in Central America, several countries did not implement the requirement for pre-established damages, *e.g.*, Guatemala.[93] It is one of the very few IP provisions of CAFTA-DR not implemented in Central America, and interestingly the USA accepted the implementation as complete without this provision. Given the practical problems in relation to damage claims in general, this approach by the USA was probably reasonable. Pre-established damages exist explicitly in the Dominican Republic for copyright infringements.[94] More broadly, Costa Rica introduced pre-established damages for trademark and copyright infringements as part of its CAFTA-DR implementation legislation in 2008 as Article 40bis IP Enforcement Law (CR). El Salvador does not explicitly provide for pre-established damages, but under Salvadoran law the court can award "any convenient type" of damages,[95] which also enables judges to set fixed damages as a deterrent for future infringements.

[92] Article 95 CAFTA-DR Reform Law (SV), amending Article 173 IP Law (SV).

[93] See Article 184 IP Law (GT).

[94] Article 177 Copyright Law (DR); the text of the law is available at www.wipo.int/wipolex/es/details.jsp?id=1191 (accessed 2 Nov 2024).

[95] Article 173(e) IP Law (SV).

7.3.2.3 Remedies Related to Infringing Goods

Whereas the rules concerning the *treatment of infringing goods* in Article 46 TRIPS apply to all IP rights, the rules in Article 15.11(11) CAFTA-DR are restricted to trademarks and copyright. However, this is of no practical consequence, because the enforcement rules in the national statutes in Central America normally do not differentiate between rights. Therefore, changes to specific remedies are automatically extended to all rights. Even in countries like Nicaragua, where patents and trademarks are codified in two separate laws, the rules on civil remedies are practically identical. In addition, practically trademark and copyright infringements are by far the most relevant types of infringement.[96] According to both CAFTA-DR and the national statutes in Central America, the infringing goods have to be disposed outside the channels of commerce.[97] This is stricter than Article 46 TRIPS, which allows the disposition into channels of commerce in exceptional cases. As *types of remedies*, Article 15.11(11) CAFTA-DR foresees the *destruction* of the infringing goods as the standard procedure, "in accordance with the foundations of (each country's) own legal system". This limitation resembles the "constitutional requirements" clause in Article 46 TRIPS. The Central American statutes allow for the destruction, but not as the standard procedure, but as one possibility.[98] It is therefore in the discretion of the judge to choose the appropriate remedy. Such provisions are compliant with Article 46 TRIPS, which requires the authority of the courts to order the destruction of infringing goods, but not necessarily as the only option.[99] In practice, infringing goods are often destroyed.[100] The other possibility in trademark cases is the *charitable donation* after the removal of the trademark.[101] In Nicaragua there exists also the possible *attribution of the property of the infringing good* to the right holder, Article 98(e) Trademark Law (NI).

7.3.2.4 Remedies Related to Materials Used in the Manufacture (Equipment)

CAFTA-DR substantially broadens the remedies that have to be available to the courts in cases of trademark counterfeiting with regard to equipment. Two steps have to be distinguished: The court first has to decide whether the material in question is

---

[96] See Sect. 7.1.

[97] See, e.g., Article 185(c) IP Law (GT).

[98] In Guatemala goods shall be destroyed especially if they may be harmful to health or the environment, Article 185(a) GT; see also Article 41 IP Enforcement Law (CR).

[99] WTO Dispute Settlement Body, Panel Report, China—Measures Affecting the Protection and Enforcement of Intellectual Property Rights, Decision of 26 January 2009, WT/DS362/R; see also Yu (2011), p. 780.

[100] In relation to Costa Rica, see Escoto (2004), pp. 47–48.

[101] See, e.g., Article 41 IP Enforcement Law (CR), Article 185(d) IP Law (GT), Article 172(c),(e) IP Law (SV).

equipment and should be subjected to one of the remedies. If yes, secondly the appropriate remedy has to be chosen. Whereas Article 46 TRIPS restricted equipment to material *predominantly* used for infringement, Article 15.11(11) CAFTA-DR applies to *any material* related to the infringement. Because CAFTA-DR is not limited to material which has been predominantly used for the infringing activity, and the material has normally to be destroyed, it previews a more severe remedy for material with weaker links to the infringement. The broader scope of application is accompanied by procedural restrictions. Therefore, the consideration of the proportionality becomes especially important and should be mandatory and as broad as possible. The Costa Rican legislation is inconsistent with these obligations, as Article 41 IP Enforcement Law (CR) (2000) provides only for the disposition or destruction of the infringing merchandise, but not of materials (equipment), and thus violates both TRIPS and CAFTA-DR. Also the Guatemalan provision, which is limited to "materials and instruments used predominantly" for the infringement, is inconsistent with Article 15.11(11) CAFTA-DR.[102] This provision has not been amended by the legislation implementing CAFTA-DR. These provisions on remedies relating to material are practically relevant because *e.g.*, in El Salvador enforcement measures are extended in practice also to manufacturing material, *e.g.*, computer hardware.[103] Article 46 TRIPS *mandates* the consideration of the proportionality, the seriousness of infringement and the interests of third parties in general, not only those holding interests with regard to the material in question. If the court exercises its authority to order the disposition or destruction of the respective material, it is required to make those considerations, also with regard to the interests of third parties. These requirements constitute minimum procedural protection for the infringer and mandatory limitation of the protection of the owner of the infringed right. Article 15.11(11) CAFTA-DR reduces the proportionality consideration to a mere *option* and refers only to the gravity of infringement and to interests of third parties holding ownership, possessory, contractual or secured interests. A literal, restricted implementation of this provision would fall below the minimum requirements of Article 46 TRIPS. However, according to Article 1(1) TRIPS more extensive protection may not contravene TRIPS provisions, including those containing mandatory limitations like Article 46 TRIPS. Article 15.11 (11) CAFTA-DR arguably violates Article 1(1) TRIPS, as it also permits to not consider proportionality. It would have been more consistent with TRIPS to retain the provision of Article 17.11(12)(c) US-Chile-FTA, which indicates that authorities *shall* take into account the need for proportionality between the seriousness of the infringement and the remedies ordered as well as the interests of third Parties. In Central America, the requirement of "proportionality between the gravity of infringement, the remedy ordered and the rights of third parties", in accordance with Article 46 TRIPS, was literally implemented, *e.g.*, in Article 185 IP Law (GT).

---

[102] Article 185(b) IP Law (GT).

[103] For example in the "Caterpillar" case, interview with *Carlos Castillo*.

7.3.3 *Procedure*

TRIPS addresses several procedural issues of civil enforcement, including some provisions with mandatory protection of potential infringers. According to Article 42 TRIPS defendants shall be notified in writing, timely and in sufficient detail, including the basis of the claims. The parties shall be allowed to be represented by independent legal counsel, and procedures shall not impose overly burdensome requirements concerning mandatory personal appearances. In this section however only the provisions on evidence and costs will be analyzed, as they are elaborated by CAFTA-DR.

7.3.3.1 Evidence

It is important for the right holder to obtain relevant information, especially in cases against the vendor, where information about the distribution chain can be the primary objective of enforcement measures. Article 15.11(12) CAFTA-DR extends the requirements compared to TRIPS in several ways, as shown in Table 7.1.

CAFTA-DR broadens the access of the right holder to information on all levels: The authority of the courts to order the infringer to inform the right holder in relation to the infringement is mandatory, not optional. Also, more information must be provided on a broader group of persons. Furthermore, CAFTA-DR does not contain exceptions based on proportionality. Finally, it introduces sanction, which did not exist in TRIPS.

Even though CAFTA-DR does not provide for a proportionality requirement as a limitation, it is not excluded either and could be included based on Article 47 TRIPS. The wording "may provide [...] unless" in Article 47 TRIPS can be read as "may not provide if", meaning that there shall not be authority for an order that "would be out

Table 7.1 Information as a Civil Remedy

	Article 47 TRIPS	Article 15.11(12) CAFTA-DR
Application	*may* provide the authority to order the infringer to inform the right holder …	*shall* provide the authority to order the infringer to provide to the right holder
Personal Information	… of the identity of persons involved in the production and distribution and …	… any information regarding any person involved in any aspect of the infringement and …
Other Information	… of their channels of distribution …	… regarding the means of production (and) the distribution channel …
Limitations	… unless this would be out of proportion to the seriousness of the infringement	–
Sanctions	–	Courts "shall have the authority to impose sanctions, in appropriate cases", if a party does not comply

of proportion to the seriousness of the infringement". Under this interpretation Article 47 TRIPS would create a minimum limitation to the procedural rights of the right holder similar to the proportionality requirement for the destruction of material used in the manufacture of counterfeit goods.[104]

In addition, given the broad scope of Article 15.11(12) CAFTA-DR, covering *any* information on *any* person related to *any* aspect of the infringement, the possibility to balance this authority seems necessary.

However, in Central America the implementation of the provision often consisted in the substitution of the TRIPS text with the CAFTA-DR text, without proportionality requirement.[105] The remaining safeguard is the discretion of the court to issue such an order. Whether the discretion will be exercised is not easy to predict. While the statute does not provide for proportionality, the courts in the region use proportionality to limit damage claims, and could apply such restrictions also to claims for information are reported.

Courts have the authority to order a party to produce evidence which it controls necessary to substantiate a claim of the opposing party,[106] subject to the protection of confidential information.[107] If the party refuses, courts may be given the authority to make a decision against that party based on the available evidence.

According to Article 15.11(10) CAFTA-DR, in cases of trademark counterfeiting courts shall have the authority to order the seizure of suspected infringing goods, related material and documentary evidence.[108] Even though not explicitly stated, this authority has to take into account Article 42 TRIPS, which requires the protection of confidential information.

7.3.3.2 Costs

According to Article 45(2) TRIPS, the defendant must bear the expenses of the prevailing right holder and may be required to pay appropriate attorney's fees. Article 15.11(9) CAFTA-DR extends the requirement to bear costs to cases in which somebody else—especially the defendant—prevails. This is noteworthy, because it is one of the rare examples where CAFTA-DR is not restricted to strengthen the right holder's position. Costs for experts, if bourn by the parties, shall be appropriate and not unreasonably deter recourse to proceedings.[109]

---

[104] See Sect. 7.3.2.4.

[105] Article 172 IP Law (SV); it should be noted however that the proportionality requirement was also omitted in some of the legislation implementing TRIPS, see, e.g., Article 98 Trademark Law (NI).

[106] Article 43 TRIPS; see also Article 39(1) IP Enforcement Law (CR).

[107] Article 43 TRIPS; see also Article 39(2) IP Enforcement Law (CR).

[108] This requirement was already of the regional legislation, see Article 98(c) Trademark Law (NI) and Article 172(c) IP Law (SV).

[109] Article 15.11(16) CAFTA-DR.

The FTAs of the US and the EU provide for very different specifications within this framework. The EU-CARIFORUM-EPA (in the Dominican Republic) contains a rather simple mechanism, the successful party in a proceeding regarding any IP right is entitled to all costs. Under CAFTA-DR, the parties may implement three different cost regimes:

- trademark counterfeiting cases: court and attorney's fees
- patent infringement cases: only attorney's fees
- all other cases (*e.g.*, trademark confusion or design infringement): only expenses of the party

In *Central America* there are no or very low court or litigation fees (*aranceles*).[110] Therefore, the differentiation in CAFTA-DR between trademark counterfeiting and other cases has limited practical effect. The attorney's fees are paid by the losing party in principle, but the national practices are slightly different. The attorney's and experts' fees are sometimes awarded, but not always (e.g., in Honduras).[111] In Costa Rica, the statutory attorney's fees depend on the value of the dispute (similar to the German civil law cost system).[112]

7.4 Provisional Measures

Provisional measures are important for enforcing rights in Central America, because of the importance to obtain expedient injunctions against the infringement of IP rights.[113]

7.4.1 Scope

Under Article 50 TRIPS, provisional measures shall be available at least (a) to prevent the infringement of any IP right, in particular to prevent the entry into the channels of commerce[114] and (b) to preserve relevant evidence. Unlike other provisions, Article 50 TRIPS is applicable to *any* IP right and not restricted to those included in the agreement. Accordingly, it also extends to those rights introduced by

[110] Interviews with *Gabriela Contreras Aguilera* and *Carlos Castillo*; in Nicaragua, the only costs arise from the requirement to purchase officially stamped paper and copies, interview with *Ricardo Bendaña*.

[111] Mejia (2016), p. 1015.

[112] Castro-Chavarría and Valverde-Gutiérrez (2017), p. 49.

[113] This is due to the nature of especially trademark counterfeiting cases in general; therefore, it is similar to the situation in Europe.

[114] Article 50(1)(a) TRIPS, see also Article 174 (a) IP Law (SV).

CAFTA-DR, which, therefore, did not have to especially require provisional measures for such rights.

In Central America, provisional measures are also available to prevent infringement and to preserve evidence.[115]

The *Salvadoran* reform law introduced "the prohibition of importation, exportation or *transit* of infringing goods" as a third ground for provisional measures.[116] The purpose of this amendment is unclear, because CAFTA-DR does not contain a corresponding provision, and the Salvadorian provision appears unnecessary, because importation and exportation constitute infringements which are already ground for provisional measures. *E.g.*, importation will typically constitute an entry into the channels of commerce.[117] On the other hand, the prohibition of the *transit* of infringing goods may broaden protection of IP rights too much. Transit cases have been a very contentious issue, *e.g.*, in Europe, and the prohibition of transit has been questioned because transit does not in itself have an impact on the market where the respective IP right is protected. This extension was not directly mandated by CAFTA-DR and is, therefore, a good example of a national implementation that created even stronger protection than required by CAFTA-DR.

7.4.2 Procedure

7.4.2.1 Procedure Before the Order of Provisional Measures

As required by Article 50(2) TRIPS, Central American courts have the authority to order provisional measures without hearing of the defendant (*inaudita altera parte*).[118] Article 15.11.17 CAFTA provides that "[e]ach Party shall act on requests for relief *inaudita altera parte* and execute such requests, in accordance with its rules of judicial procedure". The provision requires the *parties* to act, and not like the other enforcement provisions requires the establishment of legislative *authority* for the *courts* to act. Given that the rules of judicial procedure in Central America like in most other countries authorize the courts to order such measures, this wording does not have an institutional effect, and probably also was not intended that way. As the clause is probably not intended to directly affect the institutional setting, the focus of the clause is probably not on the action by the party, but on the obligation to order provisional measures *ex parte*. "Party" must, therefore, be understood to refer to the courts responsible for grating provisional measures. Whereas the normal wording providing for "authorization" leaves room for discretion, the wording suggests that the "execution" of provisional measures is mandatory. However, the parties to

[115] See, e.g., Article 174(b) IP Law (SV); Article 50 CAFTA-DR Reform Law (HN).

[116] Article 174(c) IP Law (SV).

[117] See Article 50(1)(a) TRIPS; in Central America, e.g., Article 174(a) IP Law (SV).

[118] Article 186 IP Law (GT); Article 51 CAFTA-DR Reform Law (HN).

CAFTA-DR have the possibility to provide for reasonable legal requirements for such provisional measures, because the execution shall be made "in accordance with its rules of judicial procedure".

Article 15.11(18) and 15.11(19) CAFTA-DR contain *obligations for the petitioner* to provide evidence relating to the infringement and (financial) security for the alleged infringer, the only rules in the enforcement section apparently protecting the alleged infringer. The comparison with TRIPS however reveals that this exceptional protection is in fact designed to further restrict the defendant's rights. While Article 50(3) TRIPS states that judicial authorities shall have the right to require evidence that "*the applicant is the right holder* and that the applicant's right is being infringed or that such infringement is imminent", CAFTA-DR only refers to the authority to require evidence regarding the (imminent) infringement. The systematic interpretation of the CAFTA-DR provision could mean that there *shall not* be authority to require other evidence, especially evidence that the petitioner is the right holder, and indeed this CAFTA-DR provision would have no consequence if not interpreted in this narrow way. But the wording does not explicitly exclude other requirements, and generally the parties retain the right to further specify their procedure, so the broader interpretation is possible from the wording. However, only the broad interpretation is TRIPS-compliant. TRIPS *mandates* that the authorities must have the right to require evidence that the applicant is the right holder. The narrow interpretation of CAFTA-DR only allowing evidence regarding the infringement would result in a violation of TRIPS obligations, which are affirmed by Article 15.1 (7) CAFTA-DR. An interpretation in compliance with TRIPS should prevail over one violating it, if both are literally possible, even if this leaves the CAFTA-DR provision without specific effect. The clause of CAFTA-DR has, therefore, to be interpreted broadly permitting the authority to require evidence regarding ownership in accordance with Article 50(3) TRIPS. The Central American laws implementing CAFTA-DR mostly follow this view. In Guatemala, the old requirement of evidence regarding both ownership and imminent infringement was left unchanged.[119] The *Honduran* law, while usually literally copying the CAFTA-DR provisions, specifically included the requirement of evidence of ownership.[120] Only in El Salvador, the modified provision does not explicitly require evidence of ownership,[121] but this does not necessarily mean that in practice the court could not require evidence to establish that it is the plaintiff's right which is infringed.

With regard to the right in question, the Central American reform laws include the CAFTA-DR provision of a rebuttable presumption regarding the validity of patents.[122]

[119] Article 186 IP Law (GT).

[120] Article 51 CAFTA-DR Reform Law (HN).

[121] Article 174 IP Law (SV).

[122] Article 15.11(19) CAFTA-DR, Article 174 IP Law (SV), as amended by the CAFTA-DR IP Reform Law (SV); Article 186(4) IP Law (GT), as amended by the CAFTA-DR Reform Law (GT); Article 52 CAFTA-DR Reform Law (HN).

According to Article 50(3) TRIPS a reasonable financial security from the plaintiff can be required, to protect the defendant and to prevent abuse. Article 15.11(18) CAFTA-DR includes some protection for the plaintiff here as well by additionally requiring that such security shall not "unreasonably deter recourse to (provisional measures)", *i.e.*, shall not be prohibitively high. The two provisions are compatible, as TRIPS in effect mandates a minimum amount and CAFTA-DR a maximum amount. This provision has been implemented literally as well in Central America.[123] The practical application of the security requirement is often criticized by practitioners. In El Salvador, despite the fact that securities are optional,[124] they are always required by the courts irrespective of the circumstances.[125] In Nicaragua securities are mandatory,[126] but the amounts are considered to be excessive so as to deter the recourse to such measures.[127] The latter practice would practically contravene the restriction imposed by CAFTA-DR. Whether the inclusion of this restriction to reasonable securities, *e.g.*, in the reformed Guatemalan law,[128] will be effective against such practices remains to be seen. The reformed Guatemalan law also includes the restriction of the counter-security payable by the defendant to avoid the provisional measure to a "reasonable" amount.[129] This was not required by CAFTA-DR, as it is an additional protection for the (potential) infringer. But as a matter of procedural fairness it seems appropriate to provide for the same restriction for both petitioner and defendant.

7.4.2.2 Procedure Following the Order of Provisional Measures

If provisional measures have been adopted without hearing, the affected party shall be notified and shall have the right to a hearing after the order.[130] The measures shall be revoked either if proceedings leading to a decision on the merits are not initiated—in Central America within 15 business days - or if there was no infringement or threat of infringement.[131] In this case appropriate compensation for the defendant can be ordered upon request.

[123] See, e.g., Article 174 IP Law (SV).
[124] Article 174 IP Law (SV).
[125] Interview with *Carlos Castillo*.
[126] Article 114 Patent and Design Law (NI).
[127] Interview with *Ricardo Bendaña*.
[128] Article 186(1) IP Law (GT).
[129] Article 188 IP Law (GT).
[130] Article 50(2) TRIPS; Article 115 Patent and Design Law (NI).
[131] Article 50(6) and 7 TRIPS; Article 174 IP Law (SV); Article 116 Patent and Design Law (NI).

7.4.3 *Practical Relevance*

In Costa Rica, the IP Register has the authority to order provisional measures.[132] Between 2002 and 2005, IP Register received on average 14 such measures per year, of which 40% were granted, 25% were rejected and only 10% were settled.[133] In Guatemala, the judge is required to issue provisional measures within two days.[134] In legal practice, they are usually applied for to secure evidence.[135] In Nicaragua, where the normal civil procedure takes up to five years, provisional measures take from three to eight months; especially in the majority of counterfeit cases this is too long, which is why many petitioners desist.[136] In El Salvador, the CAFTA-DR Trademark Reform Law (SV) introduced the authority of criminal courts to order provisional measures.[137]

7.5 Administrative Enforcement

7.5.1 *Introduction*

Neither TRIPS nor CAFTA-DR contain provisions for administrative procedures as such, except for the especially regulated border measures.[138] TRIPS and CAFTA-DR only regulate procedures following an administrative decision, namely the mandatory judicial review, provisional measures and civil procedures. The implementation in Central America is briefly discussed with regard to Costa Rica only, because the issue of administrative enforce is of minor importance under TRIPS and CAFTA-DR.

7.5.2 *Procedure*

Article 41(4) TRIPS requires *judicial review* of final administrative decisions. In Central America, this is relevant especially for the decisions of the IP Register on applications and oppositions. In most countries, administrative courts have

[132] Article 3 IP Enforcement Law (CR); these provisional measures are issued by the Director of the IP Register, see Registro de la Propiedad Industrial de Costa Rica (2006), p. 33.

[133] Registro de la Propiedad Industrial de Costa Rica (2006), p. 34.

[134] Article 186 IP Law (GT).

[135] See Article 186(1) first sentence IP Law (GT).

[136] Interview with *Ricardo Bendaña.*

[137] Article 113 Trademark Law (SV), as amended by the CAFTA-DR Trademark Reform Law (SV).

[138] Article 51 TRIPS and Article 15.11.20-25 CAFTA-DR; see Sect. 7.6.

jurisdiction for such review.[139] Costa Rica established the TRA as the specifically responsible administrative court for the review of decisions of the IP Register.[140]

Article 50(8) TRIPS states that for *provisional measures* following an administrative procedure "shall conform to principles equivalent [...] to those (of the ordinary provisional measures)". However, it does not require that provisional measures are available in relation to administrative procedures. Similarly, *civil procedures* following an administrative procedure "shall conform to principles equivalent [...] to those (of the ordinary civil procedure)".[141] These requirements have no specific relevance in Central America, because provisional measures and civil procedures are regulated without regard to other, prior procedures. Administrative enforcement mechanisms are provided for in Costa Rica for cases of unfair competition.[142]

7.5.3 Practical Relevance

This administrative enforcement is considered faster than civil proceedings and the preferred enforcement mechanism by some practitioners.[143] In Costa Rica, the IP Register is not only responsible for the administrative procedures, but is also involved in other enforcement proceedings.[144]

7.6 Border Measures

7.6.1 Introduction

In principle, border measures are one of the most convenient ways to enforce industrial property rights. Goods entering or leaving the country usually are inspected anyway, providing a possibility to detect infringing goods. Once the goods have entered the internal channels of commerce, they become much harder to locate. Border measures have been provided for already by Article 9 Paris Convention and Article 51 TRIPS. CAFTA-DR contains additional procedural

---

[139] In Guatemala for example the Administrative Court (Tribunal Contentioso Administrativo), see the list of cases reported by de Leon Molina (2002).

[140] While the TRA has jurisdiction regarding all departments of the CNR, in practice most cases relate to IP.

[141] Article 49 TRIPS; Article 15.11(13) CAFTA-DR.

[142] Article 3 IP Enforcement Law (CR).

[143] Interview with *Ana Catalina Monge Rodríguez*.

[144] In particular the IP Register can issue provisional measures, see Sect. 7.4; see also Registro de la Propiedad Industrial de Costa Rica (2006), pp. 15, 33.

requirements.[145] These provisions have been implemented in all Central American countries, making border authorities responsible for enforcement.

The Dominican Republic created the "Intellectual Property Registry" to facilitate border measures against IP infringements.[146] This was established within the customs authorities, distinct from the IP Register, which in the Dominican Republic is named "National Industrial Property Office" (*Oficina Nacional de la Propiedad Industrial*), not "Intellectual Property Register" (*Registro de Propiedad Intelectual*).

7.6.2 Scope

Under TRIPS border measures are required against trademark counterfeiting and copyright piracy in cases of *importation*,[147] but optional for exportation.[148] Under CAFTA-DR *exportation* is mandatory as well.[149] Petty cases can be excluded, such as personal belongings of travelers.[150]

But there are practical restrictions to the use of border measures: Under TRIPS, a country is not required to provide for border measures if it forms a *customs union* with the neighboring country.[151] In Central America, Guatemala and El Salvador have significantly reduced their border controls. Even though these countries do not from a customs union and thus are not legally dispensed, border measures are difficult for practical reasons, without border authorities on site.

Article 273(2) EU-CA-AA and Article 163.1 EU-CARIFORUM-EPA exceed the scope of CAFTA-DR by providing for border measures not only in cases of importation or exportation, but also if goods infringing trademarks or copyrights are placed in a "free zone" or a "free warehouse". This extension is practically very relevant in Central America, because many countries have created free trade zones.

In addition, Article 273(2) EU-CA-AA provides that border measures must be available also in case of "entry or exit"[152] or "transit" in relation to trademarks and copyright.[153] The EU-CARIFORUM-EPA requires that border measures must be available in case of "entry or exit", if initiated by the right holder.[154]

---

[145] Article 15.11.20-25 CAFTA-DR.

[146] European Commission, Executive Agency for Small and Medium-sized Enterprises (2019b), p. 9.

[147] Article 51 TRIPS.

[148] Article 60 TRIPS.

[149] Article 15.11.24 (3) CAFTA-DR.

[150] Article 60 TRIPS; Article 190 IP Law (GT).

[151] Fn to Article 51 TRIPS.

[152] If initiated by the right holder, Article 273(2) EU-CA-AA.

[153] If initiated ex officio, Article 273(4) EU-CA-AA.

[154] Article 163.1 EU-CARIFORUM-EPA.

As noted, the extension of enforcement to exportation and goods in transit has the practical advantage for the right holder that it is more effective to enforce IP rights while goods are in transit.[155] However, it also implies that Article 51 TRIPS, which refers to an infringing act in the "country of importation" as the basis for border measures, also encompasses "transit countries" in this definition.[156]

Article 273(2) EU-CA-AA reflects the border measures framework in the EU. Following WTO complaints from India and Brazil against the seizure of generic drugs in transit in the Netherlands in 2010, the EU agreed to limit border measures in relation to patents in 2011 (which settled the WTO proceedings). However, in 2013 new EU legislation in relation to trademarks did not contain such limitations.[157] In the same way, Article 273(2) EU-CA-AA does not contain any limitations on border measures, but is limited to trademarks and copyright.

7.6.3 *Procedure*

7.6.3.1 *Ex Officio* Suspension

International law provides for border measures which are initiated by the right holder or *ex officio* by the administration. However, TRIPS limits the obligation to provide for border measures to *right holders*,[158] and with regard to *ex officio* border measures requires only that, if such measures are established, both parties (right holder and infringer) have to be notified—thus also protecting the alleged infringer.[159] Article 15.11(20) CAFTA-DR and Article 273(2) EU-CA-AA provides for more details regarding the initiation by the right holder, as the obligation as such is already stated by TRIPS. Article 15.11(23) CAFTA-DR and Article 273(4) EU-CA-AA then expressly requires the possibility of initiation *ex officio*. Article 163 EU-CARIFORUM-EPA omits such a requirement.

In Central America both options have been established on the statutory level. *Ex officio* initiation is often possible by the *Ministerio Público* and other competent authorities.[160] in particular the fiscal authorities responsible for border controls. Considering the reluctance or even refusal of many Central American authorities it seems unlikely whether border measures will be initiated *ex officio* on a regular basis. However, just as in other countries, good relations between the right holder and the

---

[155] See Sect. 7.1; see also Blakeney (2005), p. 37.

[156] This issue is discussed in more detail by Grosse Ruse-Khan (2011), p. 659, who raises the question whether Article 51 TRIPS could be interpreted as a "ceiling" for IP protection in effect preventing transit countries from enforcing their IP regime.

[157] On these complaints and the EU measures see Senftleben (2016), sec. 3 and Grosse Ruse-Khan (2011).

[158] Articles 51, 52 TRIPS.

[159] Article 58 (b) TRIPS.

[160] See, e.g., Article 190 (a) IP Law (GT).

border authorities might help for individual cases.[161] If measures are taken ex officio, the importer must be notified.[162] Beyond the international obligations, in some countries the licensee may also initiate border measures.[163] Guatemala permits *ex officio* measures to be requested by the fiscal administration (*Superintendencia de Administración Tributaria*, SAT).[164] However, Guatemalan customs officers do not have the authority to seize and destroy counterfeit goods themselves, such measures must be ordered by a court.[165]

In the Dominican Republic, the customs agency in 2010 created the "Intellectual Property Registry", where IP right holders can record trademarks and copyrights with the customs agency.[166] Such a registry significantly facilitates the implementation of border measures ex officio by the customs agency, because right holders can register their rights without having to monitor infringements and the customs agency has an easy search tool to determine infringement.

The petitioner must provide evidence regarding the infringement and the suspected goods. It can be ordered to provide other evidence. TRIPS and CAFTA-DR limit the obligation to provide for *ex parte* border measures and, as a consequence, the evidence requirements to *right holders*.[167] In countries like Guatemala, where such procedures can be initiated by *licensees*, the provisions on evidence apply also generally to all petitioners.[168] The terminology regarding the evidence is inconsistent. Regarding the *infringement*, TRIPS and the English CAFTA-DR text require *adequate* evidence,[169] the Spanish CAFTA-DR text requires *sufficient* evidence and, *e.g.*, the Guatemalan law requires *reasonable* evidence.[170] Regarding the *suspected goods*, TRIPS requires that the evidence make the suspected goods *readily* recognizable, the English CAFTA-DR text *reasonably* recognizable.[171] Under the Spanish CAFTA-DR text and, *e.g.*, the Guatemalan law, the suspected goods must be *easily* (*fácilmente*) recognizable.[172] The wording in the Guatemalan legislation could be seen as establishing a higher burden of proof that the CAFTA-DR text, because, for example, even if goods are not *easily* recognizable and thus would not meet the Guatemalan standard, they could still be recognizable using *reasonable* effort. However, these differences probably are not strong enough to have practical

[161] Keupp et al. (2009) p. 217.

[162] E.g., Article 192 IP Law (GT).

[163] Article 191 IP Law (GT).

[164] Arenales and Skinner-Klee (2010), p. 111.

[165] Ibid.

[166] See Sect. 7.6.1.

[167] Article 52 TRIPS, Article 15.11(20) CAFTA-DR.

[168] Article 191 IP Law (GT); this provision was amended by the CAFTA-DR Reform Law (GT) of 2006.

[169] Article 52 TRIPS, Article 15.11(20) CAFTA-DR.

[170] Article 191(a) IP Law (GT), as amended by the CAFTA-DR Reform Law (GT) of 2006.

[171] Article 52 TRIPS; Article 15.11(20) CAFTA-DR.

[172] Article 191(b) IP Law (GT), as amended by the CAFTA-DR Reform Law (GT) of 2006.

consequences. In any case, the wording of TRIPS and CAFTA-DR must be taken into account for the interpretation of the national law, and with regard to CAFTA-DR, both languages are equally authoritative. Therefore, the Guatemalan law is in conformity with CAFTA-DR as it provides for a requirement level with the Spanish text, even if this requirement is more stringent than the English text. CAFTA-DR restricts the requirements regarding the evidence relating to the suspected goods to the benefit of the right holder. The requirements must not unreasonably deter recourse to border measures.[173] According to CAFTA-DR the identification of the suspected goods can also be substantiated by information other than the description. However, the TRIPS provision for the petitioner to supply a description is a minimum requirement, which is mandatory according to Article 1(1) TRIPS. Therefore, CAFTA-DR may not establish a lower standard. The Guatemalan law implementing CAFTA-DR, therefore, correctly requires a description in all cases, in accordance with TRIPS.[174] Beyond this description, the law provides that the requirements must not unreasonably deter recourse to border measures.[175]

The border authorities have the authority to require a right holder initiating procedures for suspension to provide a financial security. This requirement is subject to a number of conditions. The security

– shall protect the defendant and the competent authorities and prevent abuse;[176]
– shall be reasonable;[177]
– shall not unreasonably deter recourse to these procedures[178] and
– may take a form of an instrument issued by a financial services provider.[179]

As required by CAFTA-DR, the Central American countries provide that where an application fee or merchandise storage fee is assessed in connection with border measures to enforce an IP right, the fee shall not be set at an amount that unreasonably deters recourse to such measures.[180] Neither the provisions on securities nor storage fees include practical criteria for reasonable amounts. Even though abstract terms in international agreements can be concretized and are, therefore, enforceable, the respective amounts depend on the practical case to be decided by the court.[181] Therefore, it might have been helpful to include some guidance for the application,

---

[173] Article 15.11(20) CAFTA-DR.

[174] Article 191(b) IP Law (GT), as amended by the CAFTA-DR Reform Law (GT) of 2006.

[175] Article 191(a) IP Law (GT), as amended by the CAFTA-DR Reform Law (GT) of 2006.

[176] Article 53(1) TRIPS Article 15.11.21. CAFTA, Article 195*quater* IP Law (GT).

[177] Article 15.11.21. CAFTA, Article 195*quater* IP Law (GT).

[178] Article 53(1) TRIPS, Article 15.11.21. CAFTA, Article 195*quater* IP Law (GT).

[179] Article 15.11.21. CAFTA, Article 195*quater* IP Law (GT).

[180] Article 15.11.25. CAFTA, Article 195*ter* IP Law (GT).

[181] WTO Dispute Settlement Body, Panel Report, China—Measures Affecting the Protection and Enforcement of Intellectual Property Rights, WT/DS362/R, 26 January 2009, reviewed administrative *de minimis* thresholds, which as a general policy were considered as not being TRIPS-compliant; see Yu (2011), p. 780.

e.g., an amount in relation to the value of the goods. Otherwise it is possible that the security required for border measures may in some cases be as excessive as the security sometimes required for provisional measures.[182] TRIPS also provides for the release of the suspended gods if the defendant pays a counter-security sufficient to protect the right holder for any infringement and subject to certain procedural requirements.[183] As this possibility benefits the defendant, CAFTA-DR does not contain additional provisions.

7.6.3.2 Resolution After the Order of Suspension

After the goods have been seized, the competent authorities may give the right holder and the importer or exporter sufficient opportunity for the *inspection* of the goods.[184] In Guatemala, the respective provision was extended to include exporters by the CAFTA-DR Reform Law (GT), because before border measures had only been available against imports.[185] Some national laws in addition require the presence of the judicial authorities and the invitation of the other party.[186] Both parties (right holder and importer) shall promptly receive *notification* of the suspension of the release of goods.[187] If proceedings leading to a decision on the merits have been initiated, a review, including a right to be heard, shall take place upon request of the defendant.[188] Article 57 TRIPS and Article 15.11(22) CAFTA-DR also regulate the *information* of the right holder of the names and addresses of the consignor, the importer and the consignee and of the quantity of the goods in question. This issue shows that not only CAFTA-DR usually contains protection beyond TRIPS, but also that during the implementation of CAFTA-DR in the national law the protection is sometimes raised even further, *e.g.*, in the case of Guatemala. As shown in Table 7.2,

- under TRIPS, it is optional for the members to establish in their national legislation the authority for the customs agency to require such information,
- under CAFTA-DR, it is mandatory for the Central American countries to establish in their national legislation the authority for the customs agency to require such information, but it is optional for the customs agency to require such information in an individual administrative decision,
- however, under Guatemalan law, it is mandatory for the customs agency to require information from the respective persons.

[182] See Sect. 7.4.
[183] Article 53 TRIPS.
[184] Article 57 TRIPS.
[185] Article 194 IP Law (GT).
[186] Article 194 IP Law (GT).
[187] Article 54 TRIPS.
[188] Article 55 TRIPS.

Table 7.2 Information of the Right Holder about the Defendant and the Infringing Goods

	Art. 57 TRIPS	Art. 15.11 (22) CAFTA-DR	Art. 194 (2) GT
Establishment of legislative basis	Optional	Mandatory	n/a
Decision by customs agency to require information in a specific case	Optional	Optional	Mandatory

The EU-FTAs do no address this issue. However, Article 163.2 EU-CARIFORUM-EPA provides that the provisions of Articles 52 to 60 TRIPS shall be applicable and thus restates the rules under Article 57 TRIPS.

Regarding the *treatment of the goods*, while TRIPS only required the authority for the courts to order the destruction of infringing goods,[189] destruction is mandatory under CAFTA-DR and the subsequent national law, unless the right holder consents to an alternate disposition.[190] CAFTA-DR also introduced requirements for the charitable donation of infringing goods. It is only permitted for counterfeit trademark goods and only for use outside the channels of commerce.[191] The implementation in some national laws is even more restrictive by making the donation conditional upon the authorization by the right holder.[192] In no event shall authorities allow the exportation of infringing goods, except in exceptional circumstances.[193]

If the border measures do not lead to procedures on the merits or if the decision on the merits is against the petitioner, the restitution of the defendant is required by *release* of the goods and indemnification. The goods shall be released if, within 10 working days the customs authorities have not been informed that proceedings leading to a decision on the merits of the case have been initiated.[194]

Whereas the *indemnification* (*indemnización*)[195] of the defendant for any loss or damage resulting from the wrongful detention of goods has to be an option for the relevant authorities under Article 56 TRIPS, it must be ordered under Article 15.11 (21) CAFTA-DR. While this protection of the defendant seems unusual for CAFTA-DR, as it protects the defendant, one must remember that here the situation is different from the common piracy scenario. The indemnification applies in cases where the imported goods are not infringing, *i.e.*, are original. This provision, therefore, also covers cases in which domestic competitors tried to block legitimate importation and thus practically protect the foreign right holder and its licensees.

[189] Article 59(1) TRIPS.

[190] Article 15.11(24) CAFTA-DR; Article 195*bis* IP Law (GT).

[191] Article 15.11(24) CAFTA-DR.

[192] Article 195bis IP Law (GT).

[193] Article 59(2) TRIPS, Article 15.11(24) CAFTA-DR, Article 195bis IP Law (GT).

[194] Articles 55, 56 TRIPS.

[195] Article 195 IP Law (GT).

Central American laws not always limit the indemnification to cases of substantively legitimate importation,[196] but also grant it for procedural reasons and thus might also include cases where the right holder is the plaintiff and thus be obliged to pay the indemnification.[197] In Guatemala there arises a specific problem after the implementation of CAFTA-DR. While the indemnification is payable for substantive and procedural reasons, under the new provision the security supplied by the petitioner is required to remedy the losses or damages only in substantive cases, *i.e.*, when the imported good was not infringing.[198] If the authorities apply this clause literally, the defendant would have to claim the indemnification in a separate proceeding in procedural cases, *e.g.*, if the petitioner did not pursue proceedings on the merits.[199]

7.6.4 Practical Relevance

Customs authorities are responsible for enforcement and have the right to act *ex officio* in all Central American countries. However, in practice, border measures usually require the initiative of the right holder, because customs authorities will often not always have the technical and contact information required for a successful *ex officio* action.[200]

7.7 Criminal Enforcement

Criminal sanctions for the infringement of IP are maybe the most controversial option for enforcement. Even in developed countries, they are sometimes excluded for the infringement of patent rights, to avoid the increased chilling effect on competition caused by the threat of criminal punishment.[201]

---

[196] Article 195(b) and (c) IP Law (GT).

[197] Article 195(a) IP Law (GT).

[198] Article 195*quater* IP Law (GT); see Sect. 7.6.3.2.

[199] Article 195(a) IP Law (GT).

[200] Regarding El Salvador, Guatemala, Honduras and Nicaragua, see European Commission, Executive Agency for Small and Medium-sized Enterprises (2019a), p. 12.

[201] The Directive 2004/48/EC of 29 April 2004 on the enforcement of intellectual property rights ("Enforcement Directive"), Recital 28, provides for criminal sanctions as an enforcement means only in appropriate cases; in the proposal from the European Commission for a Directive (EU) on criminal measures aimed at ensuring the enforcement of intellectual property rights (2005/0127/COD), criminal enforcement was foreseen also for the infringement of patent rights, but this section was deleted in subsequent drafts discussed by the European Parliament; regarding the policy considerations see Lamping et al. (2014), p. 12.

7.7.1 Introduction

According to Article 61 TRIPS, "[m]embers shall provide for criminal procedures and penalties to be applied at least in cases of willful trademark counterfeiting or copyright piracy on a commercial scale.

CAFTA-DR further specified the international obligations existing under TRIPS and prioritizes criminal enforcement to achieve a deterring effect. This objective is typical for post-TRIPS bilateral agreements, which are based on the perception that the criminal enforcement provisions under TRIPS are insufficient.[202]

While Article 41(1) TRIPS only requires remedies that constitute a deterrent to further infringements, Article 15.11.26(b) CAFTA-DR specifically provides for "policies or guidelines that encourage penalties" to that effect. This literally not only means that the deterrence must come from the criminal sanctions per se, irrespective of civil or administrative sanctions, but also that general guidelines must be in place, while it would be insufficient only to rely on individual criminal decisions imposing penalties that create a deterring effect. Such sentencing guidelines for judges however might conflict with legal principles, *e.g.*, the independence of the judiciary. In addition, especially in Central America, many judges consider themselves independent from precedent from higher courts, so it seems uncertain how effective administrative or judicial guidelines would be.[203] It might also affect the adoption of *de minimis* policies not to prosecute certain types of minor infringements.

Some *Central American* countries used the flexibility remaining under CAFTA-DR, which does not provide for specific punishments, to *reduce criminal sanctions* for IP infringements in order to mitigate the impact of mandatory stricter enforcement in other areas, *e.g.*, civil law and border measures, and of the broader scope of IP protection, *e.g.*, the introduction of test data exclusivity. These measures reflect the fact that the Central American countries do not prioritize the criminal enforcement of IP rights, except for counterfeit medicines.[204]

During or following the implementation of CAFTA-DR, Costa Rica and Nicaragua significantly modified their criminal provisions: In Nicaragua, the provisions of the special IP laws were replaced with new articles in an "industrial property" chapter in the new criminal code with harmonized and reduced punishments.[205] In Costa Rica, crimes and punishments for IP infringements were restricted in several areas after the implementation of CAFTA-DR to balance the stronger overall IP

---

[202] On the historical development of criminal enforcement of IP rights under international law see Geiger (2016), pp. 646–648.

[203] See Sect. 2.5.

[204] For example, according to USTR Special 301 Report (2011), p. 35, the interagency working group on IP rights in Guatemala focuses its training efforts on counterfeit medicines.

[205] The Criminal Code (NI) (Codigo Penal), Law Nr. 641, was passed on 13 November 2007 and entered into force on 4 July 2008, the text is available at http://www.wipo.int/wipolex/es/details.jsp?id=9796 (accessed 2 Nov 2024).

protection required by CAFTA-DR. Considering this implementation of the criminal provisions, CAFTA-DR will probably not lead to more or tougher criminal convictions in Costa Rica in the field of IP, but it did lead to more political opposition against IP in general, which in turn lead to the restrictions which were included in the legislation implementing CAFTA-DR.[206]

In Central America, practitioners prefer criminal procedures for trademark counterfeiting cases not primarily for the deterring effect, but for reasons of expediency. Criminal procedures can be fast, provided the right holder assists with the proceeding (e.g. by gathering evidence.[207]

But these cases are substantially different from criminal procedures in other countries, e.g., Germany. First, the civil claims are introduced into the proceedings through the adhesion mechanism. The objective of the entire procedure is mainly to stop the infringement, not to get a conviction. Especially small-scale infringements by end users or street vendors, who make their living almost exclusively on the sale of goods infringing foreign rights, are not considered criminal, and also enforcement officials consider it a minor crime. Therefore, deals are frequent and convictions rare.[208] Second, one has to note that the right holder is practically often forced to collect the necessary evidence and maybe even support searches and arrests, because of the restrictions in resources, personnel and motivation of the enforcement agencies.[209]

7.7.2 Crimes

7.7.2.1 Crimes Related to Inventions, Trade Secrets and Designs

Under *international law* the Central American countries are not required to impose criminal sanctions for infringements of patents, designs etc. Moreover, while Article 61 TRIPS mentioned the option to provide for penalties in cases other than trademark and copyright piracy, and thus clearly referred to patent infringements, this reference was noticeably omitted in Article 15.11(26) CAFTA-DR. This is probably due to the fact that the USA itself does not provide for penalties for patent

---

[206] Escoto (2004), pp. 27–28, reports the opinion given by the CSJ (CR) on strengthening criminal enforcement relating to IP infringement, which reflects the view that IP right holders are predominantly foreign and can afford to enforce their rights themselves in civil proceedings: "*the excessive protection which is claimed to be provided against criminal acts such as those resulting from the infringement of intellectual property appears to us to be disproportional, since most of the criminal acts endanger rights not of a general or collective nature but that are from a sector which is characterized precisely in that it has greater resources than certain sectors in Costa Rican society*".

[207] Escoto (2004), pp. 32, 38.

[208] See Sect. 7.1.2.

[209] On these agencies see Sect. 2.5.

infringements.[210] On the *policy* level, penalties for patent infringements have been criticized for their possible chilling effect on competitors trying to work in the public domain "around patented inventions". Unlike in trademark and copyright cases the questions of validity and infringement are hard to establish without (costly) expert advice, and especially small companies may choose not to compete to avoid the financial and reputation risk associated with criminal proceedings.[211]

Despite these concerns some *Central American* countries, namely Guatemala and Nicaragua, make infringements of patents, trade secrets and design a crime. But is unclear whether this reflects a conscious policy decision. The list of crimes includes:

- producing or commercializing products protected by patents or utility models and using patented processes;[212]
- producing or commercializing protected designs;[213]
- utilizes or commercializes material protected by plant varieties;[214]
- using or revealing trade secrets (undisclosed information)[215] and
- pretending that a product is patented or that oneself is a patent right holder.[216]

Criminal sanctions relating to patents were abolished in Costa Rica and restricted in Nicaragua in the implementation process of CAFTA-DR. In Nicaragua, the old provision on crimes relating to patents, designs and trade secrets (undisclosed information) in the Patent and Design Law (NI)[217] has been revoked by the new Criminal Code. The new Article 253 *Criminal Code* (NI) only covers crimes relating to patents and designs, but not to trade secrets. This specific exclusion of trade secrets is probably connected to the new exclusive protection of test data as a specific form of trade secrets. In Costa Rica, crimes relating to the infringement of patents and trade secrets (undisclosed information) were abolished entirely. This is permitted under Article 61 TRIPS and Article 15.11 CAFTA-DR and it is one of few examples for balancing efforts during the implementation of CAFTA-DR.

In effect, the changes in Costa Rica and Nicaragua mean that test data infringements do no lead to criminal sanctions. Unlike the reduction of some penalties,[218] the targeted elimination of crimes related to trade secrets (undisclosed information) in both countries is probably not just supposed to compensate the broader overall

---

[210] Correa (2007), p. 450.

[211] Ibid.

[212] Article 275(k) and (l) *Criminal Code* (GT) and Article 253(a) to (d) *Criminal Code* (NI); the Guatemalan provision only refers to "patents", so based on a narrow literal interpretation one might consider utility models excluded. However, Article 275 refers to the IP Law (GT) for interpretation, which in Articles 142 to 146 IP Law (GT) states that the right conferred is a "patent", and "utility model" a special subgroup of patents.

[213] Article 253(d) *Criminal Code* (NI); Article 275(m) *Criminal Code* (GT).

[214] Article 254 *Criminal Code* (NI).

[215] Article 275(h) to (j) *Criminal Code* (GT).

[216] Article 254 *Criminal Code* (NI); 252 *Criminal Code* (NI).

[217] Article 132(b)-(d) Patent and Design Law (NI).

[218] See Sect. 7.7.3.

protection and stronger procedural rules. Pharmaceutical test data are protected as trade secrets. Given the fact crimes related to patents or trade secrets have never been practically relevant and that the introduction of test data protection was highly controversial, because of the potential impact on the local pharmaceutical industry, it seems possible that the elimination of the respective criminal provisions shall minimize the chilling effect on this industry.

7.7.2.2 Crimes Related to Distinctive Signs

Internationally, Article 61 TRIPS requires penalties at least in cases of willful trademark counterfeiting on a commercial scale. According to Article 15.11.26 (a) CAFTA-DR this shall include not only trafficking or distribution of counterfeit goods in domestic commerce, but also the "willful importation or exportation". Therefore, penalties are required at least for (1) willful (2) counterfeiting activity, including domestic and cross-border commerce, (3) on a commercial scale. Article 15.11.26(a) CAFTA-DR requires penalties only in "significant" cases of copyright piracy. Even though this provision does not apply directly to cases of trademark counterfeiting, it raises the question whether there can be "insignificant" cases of counterfeiting on a commercial scale. As *significance* of the infringement is not required in trademark cases, any limitation would have to be based on the interpretation of the "commercial scale" requirement. This term is not defined more clearly in TRIPS or related, *e.g.*, preparatory documents. Therefore, the members have some flexibility regarding its application (in accordance with Article 1(1) TRIPS). However, the WIPO Dispute Settlement Body in the case "*China – measures affecting the protection and enforcement of intellectual property rights*" provided some guidance with respect to the interpretation: "[W]hat constitutes a commercial scale for counterfeiting or piracy of a particular product in a particular market will depend on the magnitude or extent that is typical or usual with respect to such a product in such a market, which may be small or large. The magnitude or extent of typical or usual commercial activity relates, in the longer term, to profitability".[219] Therefore, Central American countries could exclude infringing activities with a commercial purpose, but which involve a number of infringing items smaller than the usual size.

The Central American legislation is generally broader that the international minimum and criminalizes commercial activities relating to trademarks themselves, trade names and packaging displaying trademarks.[220]

---

[219] WTO Dispute Settlement Body, Panel Report, China—Measures Affecting the Protection and Enforcement of Intellectual Property Rights, Decision of 26 January 2009, WT/DS362/R, section 7.577; this decision and the discussion in legal literature as to its impact on the effectiveness of IP enforcement under international IP law see Geiger (2016), pp. 650–652.

[220] Article 275(a) – (g) *Criminal Code* (GT).

In Nicaragua, the new provisions on counterfeiting no longer requires commercial activity in all cases.[221] Only Article 255(c) *Criminal Code* (NI), relating to misleading packaging, requires "commercial purposes", which reversely indicates that the crimes in Article 255(a) and (b) *Criminal Code* (NI), relating to counterfeiting, do not contain a commercial element. The provisions criminalizing the use of packaging displaying trademarks are usually restricted to cases where they are used to confuse the consumer about the content of the package, i.e., serve to pretend that it contains the original product.[222] Such activities appear to be a great practical problem, because the respective provision was specifically added in the new Nicaraguan law.

In Guatemala, however, it is also a crime to re-use packaging displaying trademarks for any purpose and even outside of commerce and without relation to the consumer.[223] The confusion of the consumer was probably not required because the provision only applies to the use of the sign itself, not similar signs. In such cases confusion is presumed.[224] However, this would literally cover entirely private use such as refilling a coke bottle with tap water at home or large equipment packaging for private storage. The provision should, therefore, be interpreted narrowly, analogous to Article 35(g) IP Law (GT), which provides that provisional measures against the re-use of packaging require commercial objectives and the intent to mislead the consumer of the user. A broad interpretation would not only conflict with the purpose of trademark law to identify the origin of goods, but also mean that criminal remedies are provided against conduct against which civil remedies do not exist. If private re-use is permitted under civil law, it should also be permitted under criminal law. In Honduras, it is a crime to "produce or offer for sale products which [...] can be confused with similar products registered for the name of another person".[225] It is also a crime to use *in commerce* a false geographical indication.[226] In correspondence to the scope of protection of geographical indication this covers also cases where a translation is used or if the geographical indication is accompanied with expressions like "kind", "type" etc., or the true origin is indicated.

7.7.3 Penalties and Sanctions

7.7.3.1 Penalties with Regard to the Offender

Internationally, Under Article 61 TRIPS, which is not further specified by Article 15.11(26) CAFTA-DR, parties are very flexible with regard to the type and the level

[221] Article 255 *Criminal Code* (NI).

[222] Article 275(e), (g) Criminal Code (GT); Article 255(c) Criminal Code (NI).

[223] Article 275(f) Criminal Code (GT).

[224] See Article 15.2.3. CAFTA-DR; Article 35(a), (c)(1) IP Law (GT).

[225] Article 249 *Criminal Code* (HN).

[226] Article 275(ñ) Criminal Code (GT) and Article 255(d) Criminal Code (NI).

of the penalties they impose on infringements of IP rights. The parties can provide for imprisonment or monetary fines or both. Any level can be chosen as long as it can serve as a deterrent against future infringements.[227] While this excludes arbitrary or completely disproportionate punishments, one has to bear in mind several practical restrictions to the determination of the required penalties in practice:

- It is unclear as a matter of fact which level of punishment is an effective deterrent;
- The likelihood of punishment is probably more significant than the punishment itself;
- Every nation is free to decide which crimes are "of a corresponding gravity".

The penalties provided for in Central America seem in compliance with these international obligations, bearing these flexibilities and restrictions in mind, see Table 7.3. As CAFTA-DR does not provide any specific level of punishment, Costa Rica and Nicaragua used the opportunity of legislative implementation of the agreement to reduce the penalties for trademark and (only in Nicaragua) patent crimes. In Nicaragua the prison time was reduced from four to six years to one to three years.[228] Practically, in El Salvador, which generally provides relatively strong protection, there have been criminal convictions for the infringement of trademarks.[229] In Costa Rica, the courts generally are not favorable to prison or other strict criminal sentences, because IP infringements are considered minor crimes not affecting public interests, but economic interests of parties who also have other legal remedies at their disposal.[230] In addition, many criminal cases are concluded without any punishment after the parties have reached a deal (*conciliación*) including an injunction.[231]

7.7.3.2 Sanctions with Regard to Crime-Related Objects

Article 61 TRIPS requires the authority to order the destruction of infringing goods, but not the destruction in specific cases.[232] CAFTA-DR requires that already during the criminal procedure, *suspected goods* and related materials, evidence and assets can be seized.[233] In addition, courts shall have the authority to order the forfeiture

[227] Article 15.11.26(b) CAFTA-DR.

[228] Article 132 Patent and Design Law (NI) (version of 2000), Article 102 Trademark Law (NI) (version of 2000), Articles 253 and 255 Criminal Code (NI) (version of 2008).

[229] European Commission, Executive Agency for Small and Medium-sized Enterprises (2020), p. 11.

[230] Escoto (2004), p. 29.

[231] Escoto (2004), p. 30; however, it must be noted that also in developed countries criminal enforcement of IP is often not very tough and rarely includes prison sentences.

[232] WTO Dispute Settlement Body, Panel Report, China—Measures Affecting the Protection and Enforcement of Intellectual Property Rights, Decision of 26 January 2009, WT/DS362/R.

[233] Article 15.11.26 (b) CAFTA-DR.

Table 7.3 Penalties for IP Crimes in Central America

Country	Legal Basis	Crime	Prison	Monetary Fine
Costa Rica	Article 44(a) IP Enforcement Law (CR)	Trademark infringement (value less than 5 *base salaries*)	no	5 to 20 *base salaries*
	Article 44(b) IP Enforcement Law (CR)	Trademark infringement (value 5 to 20 *base salaries*)	0.5 to 2 years	20 to 80 *base salaries*
	Article 44(c) IP Enforcement Law (CR)	Trademark infringement (value 20 to 50 *base salaries*)	1 to 4 years	80 to 200 *base salaries*
	Article 44(d) IP Enforcement Law (CR)	Trademark infringement (value above 50 *base salaries*)	3 to 5 years	200 to 500 *base salaries*
Dom. Rep.	Article 166 IP Law (DR)	All crimes	3 months to 2 years	50 minimum salaries[a]
El Salvador	Article 228 Criminal Code (SV)[b]	Commercial patent / design infringement	1 to 3 years	n/a
	Article 229 Criminal Code (SV)	Commercial trade-mark infringement	2 to 4 years	n/a
Guatemala	Articles 275, 358 Criminal Code (GT)[c]	All crimes	1 to 4 years	1000–500,000 Q.
Honduras	248, 249 Criminal Code (HN)[d]	Trademark infringement	3 to 6 years	L. 50,000.00–L. 100,000.00
Nicaragua	252 Criminal Code (NI)	Pretense of patent ownership	1 to 2 years	90 to 300 days' fine[e]
	253 – 256 Criminal Code (NI)	All other crimes	1 to 3 years[f]	300 to 500 days' fine

[a]The statutory "minimum salary" is calculated as one third of the minimum salary of the public sector (*la tercera parte del salario mínimo del sector public*), see Article 1 Criminal Code (DR)
[b]The text of the law is available at www.wipo.int/wipolex/en/details.jsp?id=3773 (accessed 2 Nov 2024)
[c]The text of the law is available at www.wipo.int/wipolex/en/details.jsp?id=2013 (accessed 2 Nov 2024)
[d]The text is available at http://www.wipo.int/wipolex/es/details.jsp?id=2144 (accessed 2 Nov 2024)
[e]The amount corresponding to 1 day's fine is 1/3 of the actual daily income or 1/3 of the official minimum daily salary, Article 64 Criminal Code (NI); the minimum daily salary in 2023 was set at the equivalent of about USD 6-10, see https://blplegal.com/es/nuevos-salarios-minimos-2023-nicaragua/ (accessed 2 Nov 2024)
[f]By comparison, crimes related to cattle brands (marcas de ganado) are punishable by 3–7 years, Article 222 Criminal Code (NI)

and destruction of *infringing goods*,[234] without compensation of any kind to the defendant.[235] These sanctions are available under Central American law.[236] In practice, these sanctions are sometimes, but not always applied.[237] The charitable donation of infringing goods is still possible, because the destruction is not mandated by TRIPS or CAFTA-DR (only the authority to order the destruction).

Article 61 TRIPS also requires the possibility to forfeit materials and implements (*equipment*) which have been *predominantly* used for the infringement. Article 15.11.26(b) CAFTA-DR requires also the possibility to destroy *all* materials and implements, irrespective of the nature of their use, but only with respect to willful *copyright* piracy. The new Guatemalan law, absent any obligation under CAFTA-DR, partly implemented this provision for criminal measures also against *industrial property*. In addition, Article 207*bis*(1) IP Law (GT) authorizes only the forfeiture, not the destruction, but for *all* materials and implements.

7.7.4 Procedure

CAFTA-DR requires that criminal procedures can be initiated by the right holder, *ex officio* or by interested third parties.[238] Central American laws mostly provide for the initiation by the competent authority or interested persons including consumer and industry associations,[239] which constitutes legally the same scope. Only in the Dominican Republic can criminal procedures by initiated only by the right holder.[240] While the possibility of *ex officio* action is not self-evident in other cases of crimes against private rights, it is helpful in IP cases because it is much more difficult for the right holder to learn about infringements of intangible property. Article 15.11.26(b) (iv) CAFTA-DR mandates that the prosecutor and the police must have the possibility to act *ex officio* "at least in cases of suspected trademark counterfeiting", "at least for the purpose of preserving evidence or preventing the continuation of the infringing activity". The "or" between these two activities could literally be cumulative or alternative. However, in the context of the "at least" requirement and the fact that one activity is preventive in nature and the other repressive, *i.e.* there is no correlation between the two, it has to be understood cumulatively as an "and". But this question is not likely to become relevant as most Central American laws (except

[234] Article 61 TRIPS.

[235] Article 15.11.26 (b) CAFTA-DR.

[236] See, e.g., Article 207bis IP Law (GT).

[237] This is in accordance with TRIPS, which does not require the destruction of goods in specific cases.

[238] Article 15.11.26(b) CAFTA-DR.

[239] Article 206 IP Law (GT); Article 103 Trademark Law (NI).

[240] Article 167 IP Law (DR).

in the Dominican Republic) allow for *ex officio* actions for all IP crimes and for preventive and repressive measures.[241]

However, the *Ministerio Público* is not required to initiate procedures, but decides on the basis of expediency (*oportunidad*).[242] And as a practical matter the *Ministerio Público* will normally act on the petition of the right holder and rarely on its own.[243]

Regarding judicial review, under TRIPS, as an exception to the general obligation to provide for legal review of initial judicial decisions on the merits of a case, countries may exclude the review of acquittals in criminal cases.[244] This option is not restricted in CAFTA-DR, even though this is beneficial for the (alleged) infringer.

7.7.5 Evaluation

In Costa Rica, crimes and punishments were restricted in several areas after the implementation of CAFTA-DR to balance the stronger overall IP protection required by CAFTA-DR. Considering this implementation of the criminal provisions, CAFTA-DR will probably not lead to more or tougher criminal convictions in Costa Rica in the field of IP, but it did lead to more political opposition against IP in general, which in turn lead to the restrictions which were included in the legislation implementing CAFTA-DR.[245] In other countries, the enforcement provisions of CAFTA-DR were implemented without such balancing efforts on the statutory level. However, the institutional challenges regarding IP enforcement in Central America and the general framework of law enforcement, *e.g.*, the emphasis on conciliatory settlements of disputes instead of pursuing criminal procedures to the end significantly reduce the practical application of the TRIPS-plus rules created by CAFTA-DR. Practically, criminal procedures are often initiated by right holders in counterfeit cases, because these procedures allow for the adhesion of civil claims and the involvement of the *Ministerio Público* facilitates enforcement measures.[246]

[241] See, e.g., Article 206 and 207 IP Law (GT); in Nicaragua, Article 103 Trademark Law (NI), enabling the initiation of procedures by the right holder, ex officio or by associations, was not revoked by the new Criminal Code (NI), unlike the substantive provision of Article 102 Trademark Law (NI) on crimes related to trademarks.

[242] In Costa Rica, the ex officio action was introduced as part of the CAFTA-DR legislative reforms, but was limited to the minimum required by Article 15.11.26(b)(iv) CAFTA-DR, i.e., "for the purpose of preserving evidence or preventing the continuation of the infringing activity", and not to obtain a criminal conviction.

[243] Regarding the procedural advantages for the right holder to initiate and participate in criminal investigations see Escoto (2004), pp. 32–34.

[244] Article 41 TRIPS.

[245] Interview with *Néstor Morera*.

[246] In the adhesion mechanism, the right holders may have to provide support to the Ministerio Público to advance the process, see Sect. 7.1.2.

References

Arenales & Skinner-Klee (2010) World Trademark Review, Anti-counterfeiting 2010 – A Global Guide – Guatemala, p. 111 (on file with the author)

Ascensão JdeO (2005) Das Recht des unlauteren Wettbewerbs in den Mitgliedsstaaten der Europäischen Wirtschaftsgemeinschaft, Band VIII: Portugal, C.H. Beck, Munich

Blakeney M (2005) Guidebook on enforcement of intellectual property rights. Queen Mary Intellectual Property Research Institute, London. Available at https://www.academia.edu/1185442/Guidebook_on_Intellectual_Property_Enforcement. Accessed 2 Nov 2024

Castro-Chavarría R, Valverde-Gutiérrez S (2017) Costa Rica. In: Claus Eckhartt (ed) Trademarks 2017, Getting the Deal through (on file with author)

Correa CM (2007) Trade related aspects of intellectual property rights, A commentary on the TRIPS agreement. Oxford University Press

de Leon Molina R (2002) Informe de Guatemala: Jurisprudencia sobre Derechos de Propiedad Intelectual, Seminario regional sobre Propiedad Industrial para Jueces y Fiscales de America Latina, WIPO Doc. OMPI/PI/JU/MAD/02/1 GT, 18 to 22 November 2002, Available at https://www.wipo.int/meetings/en/doc_details.jsp?doc_id=18766. Accessed 2 Nov 2024

Deutscher Anwaltverein, Stellungnahme Nr. 30/2009, April 2009. Available at https://anwaltverein.de/de/newsroom/id-2009-30?file=files/anwaltverein.de/downloads/newsroom/stellungnahmen/2009/30.pdf. Accessed 2 Nov 2024

Díaz Á (2008) América Latina y el Caribe: La propiedad intelectual después de los tratados de libre comercio, Comisión Económica para América Latina y el Caribe, CEPAL), Santiago de Chile

Escoto CM (2004) Intellectual Property Rights and Trade Enforcement Procedures in Costa Rica. Available at http://www.wipo.int/edocs/mdocs/enforcement/en/wipo_ace_2/wipo_ace_2_www_33725.doc. Accessed 2 Nov 2024

European Commission, Executive Agency for Small and Medium-sized Enterprises (2019a) Latin America IP SME Helpdesk – Central America IP country factsheet, Publications Office, 2019, https://data.europa.eu/doi/10.2826/267757. Accessed 2 Nov 2024

European Commission, Executive Agency for Small and Medium-sized Enterprises (2019b) Latin America IP SME helpdesk – Dominican Republic, Publications Office, 2019, https://data.europa.eu/doi/10.2826/96734. Accessed 2 Nov 2024

European Commission, Executive Agency for Small and Medium-sized Enterprises (2020) Latin America IP SME Helpdesk, El Salvador IP country factsheet, Publications Office of the European Union, 2023, https://data.europa.eu/doi/10.2826/422379. Accessed 2 Nov 2024

Garro AM (2016) Estilo Judicial y su Relevancia para Apoyarse en la Jurisprudencia como Pauta Orientadora para Resolver Causas Sustancialmente Similares. Available at https://iuristec.com.gt/index.php?title=Articulo:0132. Accessed 2 Nov 2024

Geiger C (2016) Towards a balanced international legal framework for criminal enforcement of intellectual property rights. In: Ullrich H, Hilty RM, Lamping M, Drexl J (eds) TRIPS Plus 20: from trade rules to market principles. Springer-Verlag, Berlin Heidelberg

Grosse Ruse-Khan H (2011) A Trade agreement creating barriers to international trade? ACTA Border Measures and Goods in Transit. Am Univ Int Law Rev 26(3):645–672

IMPACT (International Medical Products Anti-Counterfeiting Taskforce) (2011) Handbook, Available at https://www.aifa.gov.it/documents/20142/516919/final_handbook_for_the_web.pdf. Accessed 2 Nov 2024

Keupp MM, Beckenbauer A, Gassmann O (2009) How managers protect intellectual property rights in China using de facto strategies. R&D Management 39:211

Lamping M et al. (2014) Declaration on Patent Protection - Regulatory Sovereignty under TRIPS, 45 IIC 2014, 679 (cited as Lamping M et al., Declaration on Patent Protection)

Mayora EA et al. (2022) Doing Business in Guatemala, https://uk.practicallaw.thomsonreuters.com/9-554-4025?transitionType=Default&contextData=(sc.Default). Accessed 2 Nov 2024

Mejia RA (2016) Honduras. In: Eckhartt C (ed) Trademarks 2016 (on file with the author)

Palacios MA (2016) Guatemala. In: Eckhartt C (ed) Trademarks 2016 (on file with the author)

PhRMA (2007) Special 301 Submission 2007 (on file with the author)
Registro de la Propiedad Industrial de Costa Rica (2006) Situación actual de la Propiedad Industrial en Costa Rica, WIPO document OMPI/JPI/BUE/06/2 CR. Available at http://www.wipo.int/edocs/mdocs/lac/es/ompi_jpi_bue_06/ompi_jpi_bue_06_2_cr.doc. Accessed 2 Nov 2024
Registro de la Propiedad Intelectual de Guatemala (2006) Situación actual de la propiedad industrial en Guatemala, OMPI/JPI/BUE/06/2 GT. Available at http://www.wipo.int/edocs/mdocs/lac/es/ompi_jpi_bue_06/ompi_jpi_bue_06_2_gt.doc. Accessed 2 Nov 2024
Roffe P, Genovesi LM (2011) Implementación y Administración de los Capítulos de Propiedad Intelectual en los Acuerdos de Libre Comercio con los Estados Unidos: La Experiencia de Cuatro Países de América Latina", Banco Interamericano de Desarrollo, Vicepresidencia de Sectores y Conocimiento Sector de Integración y Comercio, Inter-American Development Bank, Sector of Integration and Trade, Policy Brief (No. IDB-PB-129), available at https://publications.iadb.org/bitstream/handle/11319/1400/Implementaci%c3%b3n_y_administraci%c3%b3n_de_los_cap%c3%adtulos_de_propiedad_intelectual_en_los_acuerdos_de_libre_comercio_con_Estados_Unidos.pdf?sequence=5. Accessed 2 Nov 2024
Romero JR (2016) El Salvador. In: Eckhartt C (ed) Trademarks 2016 (on file with the author)
Senftleben M (2016) Wolf in sheep's clothing? Trade mark rights against goods in transit and the end of traditional territorial limits. Int Rev Intell Prop Compet Law (IIC) 47(8):941–959
Thomas K (2012) Intellectual property law and the ethics of imitation in Guatemala. Anthropol Quart 85(3):785–814
United Nations (2012) Office on Drugs and Crime, Transnational Organized Crime in Central America and the Caribbean: A Threat Assessment, September 2012, Available at https://www.unodc.org/documents/data-and-analysis/Studies/TOC_Central_America_and_the_Caribbean_english.pdf. Accessed 2 Nov 2024
USTR, Special 301 Report 2007, available at https://ustr.gov/sites/default/files/asset_upload_file230_11122.pdf (accessed 2 Nov 2024) (cited as USTR, Special 301 Report 2007)
USTR, Special 301 Report 2010, available at https://ustr.gov/sites/default/files/uploads/gsp/speeches/reports/2010/301/2010%20Special%20301%20Report%20(3).pdf (accessed 2 Nov 2024) (cited as USTR, Special 301 Report 2010)
USTR, Special 301 Report 2011, available at https://ustr.gov/sites/default/files/uploads/gsp/speeches/reports/2011/301/2011%20Special%20301%20Report.pdf (accessed 2 Nov 2024) (cited as USTR, Special 301 Report 2011)
USTR, Special 301 Report 2016, available at https://ustr.gov/sites/default/files/USTR-2016-Special-301-Report.pdf. Accessed 2 Nov 2024 (cited as USTR, Special 301 Report 2016)
von Mühlendahl A (2007) Enforcement of intellectual property rights - is injunctive relief mandatory? IIC 38:377
WHO (2018) Fact Sheet SSFFC Medicines. Available at https://www.who.int/en/news-room/fact-sheets/detail/substandard-and-falsified-medical-products. Accessed 2 Nov 2024
Yu PK (2011) TRIPS enforcement and developing countries. Am Univ Int Law Rev 26(3):727–778

Chapter 8
Evaluation and Recommendations

This section evaluates the main research questions of the TRIPS-plus debate discussed in the introduction[1] based on the findings regarding the implementation of CAFTA-DR, the EU-CA-AA and the EU-CARIFORUM-EPA in Central America. CAFTA-DR is analyzed in more detail in most subsections, because it had the overall bigger impact in the IP system in the region, in particular on the statutory level.

8.1 Impact of Including IP Rules in a *Trade* Agreement

8.1.1 Effect of the "Trade Deal" on the Negotiation of the FTA

The examples of CAFTA-DR and the EU-FTAs show that the linkage with market access rules has a significant impact on the negotiation of IP provisions in an FTA. This is shown by the fact that the changes made in the IP chapter of CAFTA-DR during the negotiations in comparison to similar FTAs concluded by the USA around the same time were minimal. One example for such a change is the ratification of the Protocol relating to the Madrid Agreement (Trademarks), which is mandatory for Korea,[2] but CAFTA-DR only requires "reasonable efforts".[3] Similarly, the final text of the EU-CA-AA reflects largely the negotiation objectives of the EU. It not only includes a detailed section on the protection of geographical indications, for instance, but also an extensive list of geographical indications

[1] See Sects. 1.5 and 1.6.

[2] Article 18.13(e) KORUS.

[3] Article 15.1(6) CAFTA-DR.

F. Böttger, *CAFTA-DR, European Free Trade Agreements and the Industrial Property System in Central America*, Munich Studies on Innovation and Competition 21, https://doi.org/10.1007/978-3-031-93440-7_8

which had to be registered in Central America before the EU-CA-AA could go into effect, despite strong opposition from the Central American countries during the negotiations.[4] There are several (possibly cumulative) explanations why, during the negotiation of CAFTA-DR and the EU-FTAs, the trade interests were so clearly dominating the public policy interests in preventing significant increases of the level of IP protection. Frist, trade interests have a particularly powerful role in Central America. As has been described in this study, exports play an especially large role for the economies in Central American countries, which is not surprising given the small size of the markets.[5] Also, trade relations with the USA and US-American business interests are of particular political significance.[6] Second, as discussed, the public interest of the general population often has less political impact than the special economic interests of small groups.[7] Third, the USTR established a template of IP requirements in its FTAs, which has been developed and elaborated over time with each new FTA. Comparable to a large corporation using template contractual "terms and conditions", the USA strongly opposed any major changes to its model rules in the IP chapter. The Central American negotiation teams probably realized that there was very little leverage to achieve changes in the IP chapter during the negotiations of CAFTA-DR. The *ideal* solution for countries negotiating and implementing TRIPS-plus rules in bilateral FTAs, would be to assess the impact of changes to their IP system on the statutory level on their public policy goals and the financial and other costs of the implementation before agreeing to such rules.[8] For such assessment, they should obtain input from a broad range of stakeholders and experts to minimize the influence of special interests on the fact-finding and decision-making process.[9] However, from a *practical* perspective, it seems unlikely that, as part of the negotiations of an FTA between large developed countries (or regions) and smaller developing countries, the developed FTA partner countries would be willing to seriously negotiate the IP section originally proposed by the developed countries (or regions) or that the developing countries would try to negotiate significant changes to an IP chapter. Public policy interests, therefore, need to be protected outside the system of bilateral FTAs. One solution would be to negotiate IP rules within the multilateral legal framework (WTO and TRIPS), to leverage the collective bargaining power of developing countries, and address emerging IP issues in specific multilateral agreements in IP-specific fora, *e.g.*, WIPO, in order to reduce the impact of stronger, but not IP-related economic interests.[10] Another option is balancing the TRIPS-plus rules after the respective

---

[4] See Sect. 4.4.6.

[5] See Sect. 1.3.1.

[6] See Sect. 1.3.

[7] See also above Sect. 1.5.3.

[8] See MPI Principles (2013), Nr. 16.

[9] See MPI Principles (2013), Nr. 10; see Sect. 8.3.

[10] This was the traditional approach to IP policy development, e.g., in the Paris Convention and Berne Convention and subsequent international agreements, such as the Budapest Treaty, Lisbon

FTA has entered into force, at which point the economic pressure is reduced. This solution has been used with some success in Central America with regard to several TRIPS-plus requirements in CAFTA-DR, *e.g.*, by introducing limitations during the statutory implementation and by minimizing the effectiveness of the new rules on institutional and practical level.[11]

8.1.2 Effect of the "Trade Deal" on the Statutory Implementation

The "trade deal" framework also affects the implementation of the IP requirements of CAFTA-DR in the domestic legislation, though to a lesser degree.[12] The legislation in the USA implementing CAFTA-DR expressly states that the implementation of the provisions of the agreement, including the IP rules, in Central America is a condition for the entry into force of the agreement and, therefore, the improved access to the US market through lower tariffs.[13] The "successful" implementation is determined formally by the US President, in practice by the USTR. To avoid the delay of the entry into force of CAFTA-DR, the Central American countries mostly opted for a literal implementation of the IP rules in their national legislation, to the extent that sometimes rules were copied into national laws without alignment with existing provisions, even where such an alignment would have been in compliance with CAFTA-DR, as illustrated by the amendment of the trademark infringement provisions in Guatemala[14] and the additional categories for damages for IP

Treaty or the TLT, and the *Marrakesh Treaty* to Facilitate Access to Published Works for Persons Who Are Blind, Visually Impaired or Otherwise Print Disabled adopted in 2013; the text of the agreement is available at http://www.wipo.int/treaties/en/ip/marrakesh/ (accessed 2 Nov 2024).

[11] See Sects. 8.6 and 8.7; the Central American countries also balanced the implementation of the EU-FTAs. However, as noted by Drexl (2018) Nr 50, in particular the EU-CARIFORUM-EPA intends to foster sustainable development as well as IP protection. This results in more balanced IP rules than CAFTA-DR and, therefore, there was less need and opportunity for such balance on the statutory level. On the institutional level, the balancing possibilities were also more restricted, because in particular the EU-CA-AA contains some strict implementation requirements that had to be fulfilled before the agreement could enter into force, namely the registration of European geographical indications, see Sect. 4.4.5.3.

[12] This section discusses the implementation of CAFTA-DR generally; the implementation of specific requirements is analyzed in more detail in Sect. 8.6.

[13] Section 101(b) Dominican Republic-Central America-United States Free Trade Agreement Implementation Act states: "Conditions for Entry Into Force of the Agreement. – At such time as the President determines that countries listed in subsection (a)(1) have taken measures necessary to comply with the provisions of the Agreement that are to take effect on the date on which the Agreement enters into force, the President is authorized to provide for the Agreement to enter into force with respect to those countries that provide for the Agreement to enter into force for them"; see Roffe (2013), pp. 935–936.

[14] See above Sect. 4.1.8.

infringements in El Salvador.[15] Honduras even implemented the requirements in a separate implementation law, without the attempt to integrate these rules into the structure of existing laws and specific provisions, as illustrated by the CAFTA-DR Reform Law (HN).[16]

The remaining flexibilities contained in CAFTA-DR were also often not utilized and optional protection was often included in the implementing legislation, as exemplified by the protection of scent marks protection in the Dominican Republic and Guatemala, which is optional according to Article 15.2(1) CAFTA-DR.[17] In Honduras, the legislator excluded the possibility to limit the use of trademarks by labeling requirements to use the common name of a product *in any way*, even though such an exclusion is not mandated by CAFTA-DR.[18] Such "excess" implementation of CAFTA-DR rules occurred in particular in relation to the enforcement provisions. One example is the obligation to provide information to the right holder about the infringer and the infringing goods in the course of enforcement proceedings.[19] Under Article 15.11(22) CAFTA-DR, courts can be given discretion to require the defendant to provide such information, but in Guatemala, under Article 194 (2) IP Law (GT), courts are required to issue such an order. Similarly, the Salvadoran CAFTA-DR IP Reform Law (SV) introduced "the prohibition of importation, exportation *or transit* of infringing goods" as a basis for provisional measures, even though the extension of provisional measures to goods in transit was not mandated by CAFTA-DR.[20]

Compared to the negotiation of the rules of the IP chapter in an FTA, the political and policy considerations change when these rules are implemented on the national level. The implementation does not affect the "template" character of the IP chapter, but directly affects the domestic IP system. This increases the policy incentive and political feasibility of implementing TRIPS-plus rules in a balanced way. However, compliance with the IP requirements on this level is still necessary to secure the entry into force of the FTA and the corresponding trade benefits. The fact that the Central American countries mostly opted for a literal implementation of the IP rules of CAFTA-DR and, to a lesser extent the EU-FTAs, demonstrates that the "carrot" of market access and the linkage of IP requirements with trade rules also strongly affected the level of statutory implementation. This is shown in particular by excessive statutory implementation benefiting right holders, which had no consequences in relation to the *trade deal*. The Central American countries often have chosen implementing even optional protection as the most expedient and pragmatic approach to avoid any risk of non-compliance with the FTA requirements. Interestingly, some cases of incomplete statutory implementation had no consequence in

[15] Article 173(e) IP Law (SV), as amended; on this issue see Sect. 7.3.2.2.

[16] See above Sect. 2.5.6.

[17] See also Sect. 4.1.2.7.

[18] See above Sect. 4.1.7.

[19] See Sect. 7.6.3.2.

[20] Article 174 (c) IP Law (SV).

relation to the *trade deal*, *i.e.*, were not considered (or at least not declared) an incomplete statutory implementation of the respective FTA by the IP-demanding FTA party and, therefore, did not impede the entry into force of the FTA.[21] However, several examples regarding CAFTA-DR and the EU-FTAs show the willingness of the USA and the EU to actually delay the entry into force of the respective FTA, if key IP provisions are not implemented. While not every case of non-compliance triggered such a response, it is clearly risky for the respective country to try. When the reform legislation amending Articles 78 and 80 Biodiversity Law (CR) in Costa Rica was invalidated by the CSJ (CR), for instance, the USTR demanded that another reform was passed before CAFTA-DR could enter into force in relation to Costa Rica. This reform had a particular relevance, because it affected the scope of the patentability requirements, which had been used extensively by Costa Rica to deny patent protection to (foreign) pharmaceutical patent applications. The Costa Rican government had to use the "shortcut" of adopting executive decrees shortly before the implementation deadline expired to ensure compliance with CAFTA-DR.[22]

From the perspective of developing countries, it may, therefore, be safer in a *trade deal* scenario to fully comply with the requirements under an FTA, which mainly address the statutory level, and focus efforts to balance TRIPS-plus rules on the institutional level, after the FTA has entered into force. There are several examples where Central American countries have used this approach. Notably, after CAFTA-DR had entered into force, in Costa Rica the *Sala IV* of the CSJ (CR) invalidated the executive decrees amending Articles 78 and 80 Biodiversity Law (CR), which did not trigger any response from the USA.[23] Therefore, based on the Central American experience, it seems unpractical and unlikely for a country to take the risk of balancing the TRIPS-plus rules during the statutory implementation in a way that could be considered non-compliant with the FTA.

8.1.3 Effect on the Institutional and Practical Implementation

The implementation of the IP rules under CAFTA-DR led to relatively few changes on the institutional level, because most requirements affecting the institutional level were only non-binding commitments, *e.g.*, the electronic registration of trademarks ("work to provide").[24] Moreover, Article 15.11(2) CAFTA-DR explicitly states that

[21] See Sect. 8.6.

[22] See above Sect. 3.1.4.4.

[23] For instance, it was not mentioned in any subsequent Special 301 Report of the USTR, which has been repeatedly used to highlight cases of CAFTA-DR implementation issues; see above Sect. 3.1.4.4.

[24] See above Sect. 4.1.4.2.

the agreement does not create certain institutional obligations, namely to establish a special judicial system or to allocate certain resources for IP enforcement. As a result, for instance, the restrictive registration of pharmaceutical patents in Costa Rica and the Dominican Republic continued after the implementation of the IP rules under CAFTA-DR, even though to a lesser extent.[25] Also, in the Dominican Republic, the IP Register practically does not grant patent extensions, even though they have been included in the IP Law (DR).[26]

The EU-CARIFORUM-EPA and the EU-CA-AA also do not contain many binding institutional or practical requirements, with the important exception of the registration of the Established Geographical Indications according to Article 245 EU-CA-AA.[27] This issue was identified by the EU as a "must have", even though it was heavily opposed by the Central American countries.[28] Initially, some of these Established Geographical Indications were not registered in Costa Rica and El Salvador, because of oppositions filed against the respective applications. The EU postponed the provisional application of the EU-CA-AA in relation to Costa Rica, when the registration of only 6 out of 120 Established Geographical Indications (i.e., 5%) had not been completed within the original timeline. The implementation was "approved" by the European Union, and the EU-CA-AA became (provisionally) applicable, only after some of these outstanding cases were resolved and further negotiations between the EU and Central America had taken place.[29] In a report on the implementation of the CARIFORUM-EPA by the European Commission in 2021, the authors found shortcomings on the CARIFORUM side relating to the commitments on intellectual property rights and on the EU side regarding technology transfer and benefits for the CARIFORUM states regarding market access.[30]

It is understandable from a Central American perspective that there was little incentive to strengthen the institutional and practical level of IP protection and exceed the binding commitments made under CAFTA-DR and the EU-FTAs, because this would require significant efforts without providing economic or other benefits. This lack of institutional impact significantly restricts the feasibility of bilateral FTAs (in the current form) as a tool for developing IP policy. Based on the Central American experience, as the example of the Established Geographical Indications shows, also changes on the institutional and practical level require political and economic incentives.

[25] See above Sect. 3.1.7.

[26] See above Sect. 3.1.8.

[27] This issue is further discussed in Sect. 4.4.6.

[28] The Central American countries initially rejected the list, because some of the geographical indications conflict with existing trademarks from local and US-American right holders, see Sect. 4. 4.5.

[29] See Sect. 4.4.5.

[30] European Commission, Ex-post evaluation of the EPA between the EU and its Member States and the CARIFORUM Member States - Final Report, 2021, available at https://circabc.europa.eu/ui/group/09242a36-a438-40fd-a7af-fe32e36cbd0e/library/a64ce9fb-d24b-435f-a162-68eb0d1ea298/details (accessed 2 Nov 2024).

However, it is questionable whether such an approach would be practically suitable for broader application. The institutional structures of the IP systems on the national level are even more heterogeneous than on the statutory level, making it difficult to establish a set of institutional requirements suitable for a variety of countries. Moreover, while it is relatively easy to review the implementation of statutory requirements in national legislation, the review on the institutional level is more difficult, because this requires an analysis on a case-by-case basis.[31] While, for instance, the statistical data of patent registrations suggests that Costa Rica and the Dominican Republic for a long time applied an restrictive approach during patent examination, because the grant rate was about half of the grant rate of patent offices in developed countries and significantly lower than the grant rate in other Central American countries, it would have been necessary to review specific cases to make a determination reliable enough to be the basis for meaningful consequences, *e.g.*, the suspension of trade benefits. Even if a legal mechanism could be found, developing countries cannot be expected to agree to binding institutional commitments which require additional financial or other resources to strengthen IP-relevant institutions without support from developed FTA partner countries, international institutions or interested stakeholders. Therefore, institutional requirements would have to be accompanied by specific support commitments of FTA partner countries. However, it is uncertain whether the USA would be willing to commit to specific (and possibly long-term) measures, despite the significant challenges regarding IP protection in Central America.

8.2 Trade Benefits for the Central American Countries Under CAFTA-DR

As already noted, this study focuses on the impact of CAFTA-DR and the EU-FTAs on the IP system in Central America, but not the economic impact in general. However, it is necessary to briefly address this issue, because the economic benefits allegedly provided by these FTAs are considered to be one justification for the commitments to increased IP protection. This section focuses on the effects of CAFTA-DR, because it has been in force longer and, therefore, provides a better long-term perspective.[32] In order to assess whether CAFTA-DR provides the expected trade benefits, two categories must be considered. First, direct trade benefits, in particular better access to the US market, and second, indirect

[31] However, as the analysis has shown, there are many cases where the interpretation of the national legislation in Central America is not clear and it is, therefore, not possible to determine with certainty whether national law is compliant with international requirements without further clarification by jurisprudence.

[32] Also, there is significantly more empirical analysis which has been published on CAFTA-DR, compared to the EU-FTAs.

advantages, in particular through the harmonization of the global and regional trade and IP systems.

8.2.1 Market Access

The experience of the Central American countries after CAFTA-DR with the "privileged" access to the US market and other specific trade benefits is mixed. In particular, the available studies suggest that the USA benefited more from CAFTA-DR than Central America from an economic perspective.[33] This shows that the concerns raised by critics regarding the ability of Central American countries to fully utilize the better access to the US market and realize the expected economic benefits from CAFTA-DR seem valid. Therefore, while the expectation of trade benefits created a strong incentive for Central American countries to accept higher levels of IP protection during FTA negotiations, these countries seemingly did not enjoy these trade benefits as expected in the long term, while the new IP rules remain permanently part of the national legislative regimes. Based on the example of CAFTA-DR, the justification of TRIPS-plus rules as part of a trade deal, therefore, is doubtful. Trade and IP negotiations should, therefore, be un-coupled by negotiating IP issues separately, *e.g.*, as part of the negotiations of multilateral WIPO agreements. If IP rules remain part of trade deals like CAFTA-DR, the respective parties should consider introducing the option of similar "emergency" IP restrictions. Such a mechanism could help level the playing field between the FTA partners. In effect, it would work as a mechanism to alleviate trade imbalances, similar to the possibility of "cross-retaliation".[34] Another option to alleviate trade imbalances could be the use of compulsory licenses. From an IP policy perspective, compulsory licenses should not be issued for fiscal or similar economic reasons such as trade deficits; however, it is not illegal under TRIPS, CAFTA-DR or the EU-FTAs to do so.[35] But it must be noted that, even though this option already exists, it has so far never been used in Central America,[36] and there is no indication that it is becoming more politically or practically viable in the future.

8.2.2 Trade Harmonization

It seems doubtful whether CAFTA-DR and similar FTAs concluded by the USA, together with the FTAs concluded by the EU, provide economic advantages by

[33] See above Sect. 2.2.2.5.

[34] See Sect. 2.2.6.

[35] Böttger (2008a), pp. 889–890.

[36] See Sect. 3.1.11.2.

creating more regional and global trade harmonization. CAFTA-DR did harmonize the trade framework on the *regional* level in Central America by establishing lower tariffs on a broad range of goods and services and by creating specific dispute settlement mechanisms applicable in the region, also applicable among the Central American countries themselves.[37] As expected by the supporters of CAFTA-DR, after implementation of CAFTA-DR, regional trade between the Central American parties of CAFTA-DR increased significantly.[38] From a *global* perspective, however, it must be noted that each FTA creates a specific system of trade preferences and market access rules. Specifically, regarding Latin America, *Granados* and *Cornejo* argue that the "aggressive proliferation" of bilateral FTAs in the Americas and the "decentralized and uncoordinated process" threatens the hemispheric trading system.[39] Therefore, CAFTA-DR and the EU-FTAs contributed to the patchwork of trade preferences and rules. Also, CAFTA-DR and similar FTAs concluded by the USA, together with the FTAs concluded by the EU, fracture rather than harmonize the regional and global IP framework.[40] This might offset the economically benefits attributed to the harmonization of the IP framework by levelling the legal and economic playing field.[41] The FTAs negotiated or implemented subsequently, such as the TPP, TTIP or the modernization of the FTA between Mexico and the EU, could further disintegrate the IP system. Effective global trade harmonization can probably be achieved better through multilateral agreements, in order to avoid the current patchwork of tariffs and market access rules. However, initiatives such as TPP and TTIP, suggest that US and EU trade policy continues to focus on a bilateral approach. This might lead to less rather than more harmonization in the fields of market access rules. Likewise, in order to achieve more harmonization of the global IP system, rules should be agreed upon in multilateral IP agreements, rather than in bilateral FTAs.[42]

8.3 Fairness, Transparency and Inclusiveness of the FTA Process

The negotiations of FTAs are viewed by critics as "unfair" not only because the economic benefits under the trade deal are doubtful, but also because the structure of the negotiations is perceived as fundamentally biased. However, it is important to

[37] See above Sect. 3.1.11.2.

[38] See Centralamericadata, Costa Rica Files Arbitration against Dominican Republic, available at www.centralamericadata.com/en/article/home/Costa_Rica_Files_Arbitration_against_Dominican_Republic (accessed 2 Nov 2024).

[39] See above Sect. 1.5.2.2.

[40] This issue will be discussed in more detail in Sect. 8.4.

[41] See above Sect. 2.2.2.1.

[42] The policy options for global IP harmonization are analyzed in more detail in Sect. 8.4.

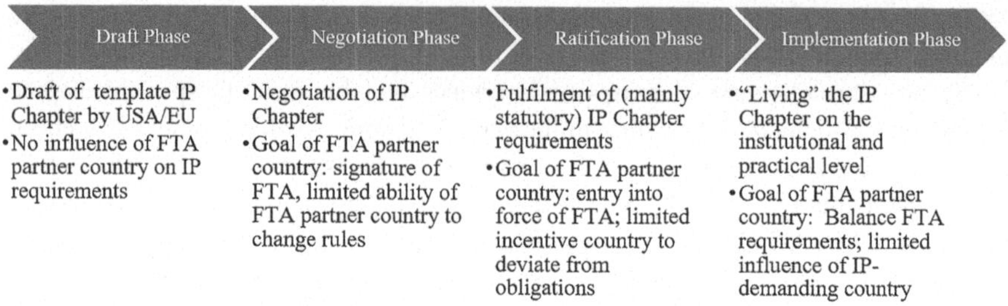

Fig. 8.1 Life Cycle of FTA Provisions (prepared by the author)

widen the lens and also take the preceding drafting phase and the subsequent implementation phase into view: The outcome of the drafting phase provides the basis of the text being negotiated and frames the subsequent negotiations, while during implementation, the level of IP protection established by a bilateral FTA can either be exceeded or reduced.[43] The implementation phase can be divided into two sub-phases, the ratification phase after the signing and before the entry into force of the agreement and the implementation phase after the entry into force.[44] As this and the following sections will show, a different legal and political framework exists at each stage which influences the way the IP rules are created and implemented. The following Figure 8.1 summarizes in a simplified way the life cycle of IP provisions in bilateral FTAs.

8.3.1 Draft Phase

While the procedural analysis of TRIPS-plus in bilateral FTAs focuses mostly on the negotiation phase, it is necessary to take a broader perspective regarding the participation of stakeholders and their influence of the negotiations of FTAs. The IP provisions of an FTA are not primarily determined during the negotiations. It is important whether, before the negotiations of an FTA commence, there is a meaningful possibility for all stakeholders to influence the draft of the standard set of IP rules developed and proposed by the developed country. The standard set of IP rules in CAFTA-DR, as in similar FTAs, established before the start of the negotiations, largely reflects the policy priorities of right holders of developed countries.[45] While the interests of the right holders already influence the drafting phase, the interests of the future FTA partner countries cannot yet impact this stage. Accordingly, at this stage procedural safeguards should be in place to ensure the meaningful

[43] Díaz (2006), p. 6 Nr 7.

[44] Díaz (2006), p. 25, describes them as "short term" and "medium term" implementation.

[45] See Sect. 1.4 and Sect. 2.2.1.

consideration of balancing interests. One example that this can be effective in practice are the changes made to the "standard" US FTA required by the *Bipartisan Trade Deal*.[46]

8.3.2 Negotiation and Ratification Phases

The negotiation of the IP chapters of CAFTA-DR and the EU-FTAs did not permit a meaningful discussion on the IP provisions. Also, the participation of local Central American stakeholders, namely those demanding limitations to IP provisions in the public interest, had little impact. The greater influence of special economic interests on the negotiations of CAFTA-DR and the EU-FTAs is not surprising, because of the underlying "economics" of political decision-making.[47] But the power imbalance between the participating countries and the lack of influence of various stakeholders from the Central American countries had a negative effect not only on achieving a balanced negotiation result. The perception of the fairness and inclusiveness of the negotiation process (or lack thereof) by the stakeholders, including IP agencies and the general population, affects the perception of the legitimacy of the outcome of the negotiations, which in turn affects the acceptance of the national IP rules adopted based on this outcome and ultimately affects the effective application of these rules in the respective country. The IP rules of CAFTA-DR are perceived in Central America as being "imposed" upon their countries because of the one-sided negotiation process, and not as the result of a sovereign national policy debate. Local practitioners observe that the IP rules under CAFTA-DR are rejected, because they are perceived as imposed.[48] This perception of IP rules being imposed by the USA may be reinforced by the historic experience of the USA using its power and influence to shape the economic and political framework of Central American countries to further its business interests.[49] Some observers are even concerned that this apparent lack of legitimacy may not only lead to the rejection of the legislation implementing the TRIPS-plus rules, but may also undermine the recognition of the potential benefits of the IP system in general and the enforcement of IP rights, in particular trademarks, because it is seen as only benefitting foreign companies.[50] This is of course neither a surprising nor novel concern. The possibility of national parliaments and stakeholders to participate in and influence the negotiations of international agreements that create obligations for domestic legislation is an issue of national sovereignty which has always been

[46] USTR (2007), p. 3.

[47] See Sect. 1.5.3.

[48] As described by, e.g., Montero Sequeira (2003), many locals consider IP protection to be beneficial only for foreign right holders.

[49] See Sect. 1.3.3.

[50] See, e.g., Montero Sequeira (2003).

relevant. It is noteworthy that the USA itself rejected the establishment of an International Trade Organization in 1950 because of concerns of infringement of national sovereignty.[51] The same concerns are now brought forward by critics of the current process of negotiating FTAs. To alleviate these concerns, the negotiation process could be structured in a more transparent way that provides a meaningful opportunity to all stakeholders, including the interested public in the negotiating countries, to influence the negotiation process.[52] This could also allow countries facing IP demands to develop their own IP agenda.[53]

However, *practically* the result of the negotiations of CAFTA-DR and the EU-FTAs was, at least in the IP field, largely predetermined by the standard set of IP rules proposed by the USA and the EU and the negotiation bias created by the *trade deal* structure. As the Central American experience shows, even though other stakeholders were formally able to participate in the negotiation of the FTAs, this participation had no meaningful effect. The Central American countries have also not been able to achieve any of their (few) negotiation objectives in relation to IP, e.g., reject the registration of Established Geographical Indications from Europe.[54] From a practical perspective, therefore, the participation of the various stakeholders earlier during the draft phase and later during the implementation phase of the FTA process has probably more impact and is more important than the participation during the negotiation phase as such.

8.3.3 Implementation Phase

Practically, the impact of the TRIPS-plus provisions depends strongly on the statutory and institutional implementation.

Special economic interests where dominant also during the implementation phase. Even in Costa Rica, where concerns by anti-CAFTA-DR stakeholders were voiced most strongly, the pro-CAFTA-DR economic interests ultimately, though narrowly, prevailed in the referendum. However, the experience in Costa Rica shows that, during the implementation phase, stakeholders who were unable to affect the process at an earlier stage had a better standing to influence decision-making at this stage. Not only was the outcome of the referendum on CAFTA-DR a very narrow decision, also in parliament supporters and opponents were evenly matched, which was the reason why the referendum was necessary in the first place. After the referendum, the legislative implementation in Costa Rica was based on the compromise to ratify and implement CAFTA-DR in line with the outcome of the referendum, but which demanded that the implementation did not exceed the requirements

[51] Stiglitz (2006), p. 75.

[52] MPI Principles (2013), Nr. 12.

[53] MPI Principles (2013), Nr. 13.

[54] See above Sect. 4.4.5.3.

of CAFTA-DR.[55] As a result, the implementation legislation included targeted balancing measures in the field of IP, such as the abolition of criminal sanctions for patent and business secret infringements to mitigate the practical effect of test data protection.[56]

Generally speaking, one option to ensure a more balanced outcome of FTA negotiations could be to make the negotiation process more transparent and inclusive[57] and to establish formal procedures for a meaningful possibility of stakeholders to influence the implementation of an FTA.[58] In Costa Rica, the participation of a broader range of stakeholders was a result of the specific political situation in the country during the time of the ratification and implementation of CAFTA-DR, but this participation led to a more balanced outcome. As the example of Costa Rica clearly shows, such steps complicate and prolong the implementation of FTAs. However, on the national level there are well-established procedures to publish draft laws and to invite interested parties to contribute to the fact-finding and policy-making process. Therefore, more transparency and participation are customary in the normal legislative process and should be politically viable also in relation to the implementation of bilateral FTAs. Better participation mechanisms could also increase the acceptance of the negotiation outcomes by affected stakeholders and the public, which may facilitate the effective implementation of FTA requirements.[59]

However, the implementation of CAFTA-DR in Costs Rica shows the practical limits of such an approach. In Costa Rica, where participation of indigenous peoples during the legislative procedure is required by the Constitution, the government chose to sidestep this requirement in order to expedite the implementation of CAFTA-DR. Also, even if formal participation rules are complied with and all stakeholders submit comments, the dynamics of political influence could still in the end result in the bigger impact of special interests, while public interests are disregarded. Similarly, regarding the EU-FTAs, the implementation of requirements identified by the EU as important, namely the registration of European geographical indications, was not affected by the critical participation even of local and foreign trademark owners.

Therefore, negotiating international IP rules on the multilateral level in special, multilateral IP agreements seems more likely to achieve a balanced result by bringing more countries and more special interests to the negotiation table. *E.g.*, it was difficult for the generic pharmaceutical industry in Central America on its own to impact the negotiation of patent and test data rules under CAFTA-DR.[60] However, in the negotiations of a multilateral IP agreement, it would not have to negotiate

[55] See the discussion of the referendum and the implementation in Sect. 2.2.1.2.

[56] See Sect. 7.7.

[57] MPI Principles (2013), Nr. 14 and 15.

[58] MPI Principles (2013), Nr. 10.

[59] See also the discussion in Sect. 8.3.1.

[60] On the activities of the local generic pharmaceutical industry see Sect. 8.8.1; on the ability of the Central American countries to impact the CAFTA-DR negotiations see Sect. 2.2.1.

simply against the Central American export industry, but could be negotiating together with similar special interest groups, *e.g.*, generic drug industries of other countries, which may be bigger and more influential in their respective countries.

The multilateral setting also balances the negotiation power of developed and developing countries, as shown by the adoption of the Doha Declaration under TRIPS.

Finally, while the IP chapter of FTAs such as CAFTA-DR is seen by many local observers as "imposed" by the USA, IP rules developed in a multilateral setting could be more easily accepted as a balanced and "legitimate" compromise.

8.4 Contribution to a Harmonized and Coherent IP System

One argument put forward to support TRIPS-plus rules is the harmonization of IP rules on the global or at least regional level. At first glance, CAFTA-DR appears to harmonize the regional IP system by establishing common statutory requirements for the Central American countries. In addition, these requirements are similar to the requirements included in the IP chapters of other FTAs concluded by the USA.[61] However, a closer look reveals that CAFTA-DR, in conjunction with similar FTAs concluded by the USA with other countries and the FTAs concluded by the EU, practically fractures the IP systems from an international, regional and national perspective more than it harmonizes them.

8.4.1 Global Harmonization

While bilateral FTAs are sometimes considered to contribute to the harmonization of the IP system globally, the US- and EU-FTAs in practice fracture it. While the harmonization of the IP system can have advantages,[62] CAFTA-DR and the EU-FTAs had only a moderate harmonization effect. While CAFTA-DR is largely coherent in structure and content with subsequent FTAs concluded by the USA, one cannot conclude it had a strong "multilateralization" effect.

First, the IP provisions in these FTAs evolve and change over time.[63] This has been shown in this study for the US-FTAs and various types of EU-FTAs. In addition to this existing "patchwork" of international requirements for IP rules, the FTAs negotiated or planned subsequently, such as the TPP, TTIP or the modernization of the FTA between Mexico and the EU, could further fracture the global IP

[61] E.g., the US-Peru-FTA.

[62] See the discussion in Sect. A.II.4.

[63] See Sects. 2.2.4 and 2.3.4.

system. In addition, these FTAs divide the international IP system into countries bound by different layers of FTAs:

- Some countries are subject to both US and EU requirements.[64]
- Some countries are required to apply only the set of IP rules established in either the US-FTAs or the EU-FTAs.[65]
- Some countries are not bound by IP rules under bilateral FTAs at all (in Latin America for example Brazil).[66]

The resulting matrix of different obligations actually makes the harmonization of internal IP law more difficult.

CAFTA-DR also had only a moderate effect on the accession of Central American countries to multilateral IP agreements: First, several agreements had already been adopted prior to CAFTA-DR. Second, the ratification of some agreements is optional under CAFTA-DR and the Central American countries typically opted to not ratify these agreements. Finally, some agreements were not ratified by the Central American countries despite their obligation under CAFTA-DR to do so. The Central American countries became parties to international IP agreements specifically because of CAFTA-DR only in a few cases, namely the Patent Cooperation Treaty,[67] the Budapest Treaty and the Trademark Law Treaty (1994).[68]

It must be noted that the US-FTAs and the EU-FTAs also sometimes supplement each other. For example, the EU-FTAs do not contain requirements regarding the protection of test data. However, with regard to the Dominican Republic and the Central American countries, European pharmaceutical companies benefit from the protection of test data required by CAFTA-DR based on the MFN principle.[69] Similarly, under the EU-CA-AA, only Panama was required to "adhere to the Patent Cooperation Treaty",[70] presumably because it is not part of CAFTA-DR and the

[64] Not only in Central America, but also in neighboring countries like Mexico, Peru and Colombia, two or three "layers" of FTAs apply, resulting in different levels of IP protection.

[65] In some Pacific nations, such as Australia and Singapore, only FTAs with the USA are in force. Several African countries such as Cameroon, South Africa and Zimbabwe concluded an FTA only with the EU; for the full list of bilateral FTAs concluded by the European Union see https://policy.trade.ec.europa.eu/eu-trade-relationships-country-and-region/negotiations-and-agreements_en (accessed 2 Nov 2024).

[66] Several of the largest economies, namely Brazil, China, India and Russia, have not concluded any FTAs containing an IP chapter with either the USA or the EU.

[67] Costa Rica and Nicaragua, however, had already been parties to the Patent Cooperation Treaty prior to CAFTA-DR.

[68] The Trademark Law Treaty had been adopted by all Central American countries except Guatemala, which has not yet ratified the agreement. The impact of the Trademark Law Treaty (1994) is practically limited to procedural questions in Central America, because CAFTA-DR exceeds the substantive level of protection established by the Trademark Law Treaty (1994). Article 2(1)(b) Trademark Law Treaty (1994) does not require the protection of sound and scent marks, whereas this is mandatory under CAFTA-DR.

[69] See Sect. 3.4; see also Drexl (2018) Nr 120.

[70] Article 276.2 EU-CA-AA.

US-Panama-TPA was not yet in force when the EU-CA-AA was negotiated; therefore, Panama was not obliged to adopt the Patent Cooperation Treaty under any existing FTA. The other Central American countries had already ratified the PCT as part of the implementation of CAFTA-DR (or earlier, in the Case of Costa Rica and Nicaragua) and were excluded from the requirement.[71]

The experience with CAFTA-DR and the EU-FTAs strongly suggests that the IP system on the international level cannot effectively be harmonized by bilateral FTAs.[72] The harmonization of the IP system can be better achieved through multilateral agreements, because they avoid the uneven geographical scope of FTAs and the diverging sets of IP rules and the resulting conflicts between FTAs concluded by, *e.g.*, the USA and the EU.

In particular, the trademark and geographical indication rules under CAFTA and the EU-FTAs are to some extent mutually exclusive.[73] Therefore, a coherent international policy should be developed on the multilateral level, because the conflict between the USA and the EU in this area creates a significant legal dilemma for the FTA partner countries.[74]

8.4.2 Regional Harmonization

CAFTA-DR also did not increase the harmonization of the IP systems regionally, even though many IP rules contained in CAFTA-DR were implemented literally in most Central American countries.[75] The process of fragmentation in Central America already began as a consequence of TRIPS.[76] In particular, it terminated the process of introducing the Central American Convention (Patents) and as a consequence led to the adoption of national patent laws, with even diverging definitions of patentable inventions.[77] Also, the Central American countries decided to replace the American Convention (Trademarks) with national statutes.[78] This created, for example, different definitions for geographical indications (and denominations of origin) in each country, partly based on TRIPS, partly on the Lisbon Agreement and partly establishing autonomous definitions.[79] However, the implementation of the

---

[71] See Sect. 2.1.1.4.

[72] See also Drexl (2016), pp. 65 and 69.

[73] See Sect. 4.4.6; see for other examples outside the scope of this analysis Drexl (2016), p. 65.

[74] In the negotiations of the EU-CA-AA, the Central American countries proposed to exclude geographical indications from the agreement and move discussions to the multilateral level, to avoid conflicts with CAFTA-DR, see Sect. 4.4.2.1.

[75] See Sect. 8.1.

[76] See Sect. 2.4.1.

[77] See Sect. 3.1.2.

[78] See Sect. 2.1.4.1 above.

[79] See Sect. 4.4.1.

CAFTA-DR and EU-FTA requirements significantly increased these differences. First, as noted above, fragmentation is caused by the coexistence of CAFTA-DR with conflicting EU-FTAs. CAFTA-DR, the EU-FTAs and multilateral agreements contain different requirements in various fields, for example, in relation to the protection of well-known marks[80] and the prevention of abusive licensing activities.[81] Most importantly, TRIPS, CAFTA-DR and the EU-FTAs contain conflicting obligations in relation to trademarks and geographical indications:[82] For example, the relevant "priority date" for the geographical indication under Article 15.3 (7) CAFTA-DR must be the date of registration in the *country of protection*, while Article 24.5(b) TRIPS provides for the option to refer to the date of protection in the *country of origin*. Both the EU-CA-AA and the EU-CARIFORUM-EPA restrict the refusal of the registration and protection of a geographical indication to cases of confusion with a well-known trademark.[83] These provisions conflict with Article 15.3(7) CAFTA-DR, which excludes the registration and protection of a geographical indication *confusingly similar* to any prior trademark.[84] Finally, Article 23 TRIPS and Article 246.4. EU-CA-AA provide for different dates to determine acquired trademark rights in relation to absolute protection of geographical indications, because each agreement refers to its respective date of entry into force. Article 64 Trademark Law (SV) addresses this problem by referencing "the date set by international agreements", which avoids any openly conflicting wording, but creates legal uncertainty.[85]

In neighboring countries, there exist yet other applicable FTA layers. For example, Mexico concluded the NAFTA agreement with the US in 1994 and an Economic Partnership, Political Coordination and Cooperation Agreement on 1 July 2000 with the EU. Both agreements reflect an earlier stage of international IP protection compared to CAFTA-DR and the EU-FTAs. Mexico and the EU officially initiated talks on 30 May 2016 to modernize their agreement, which lead to an amended agreement in 2020.[86]

Second, while CAFTA-DR and the EU-FTAs created the same IP obligations for all Central American countries, their *implementation* into national law differed considerably and increased existing differences in the IP legislation across the region. Procedurally, there are differences regarding the way IP rules were implemented. Most countries integrated IP requirements in their respective IP laws. Honduras, on the other hand, drafted the CAFTA-DR Reform Law (HN) as

[80] See Sect. 4.2.

[81] See Sect. 3.1.11.2.

[82] See Sect. 4.4.6.

[83] Article 248.2 EU-CA-AA; Article 145.D.1 EU-CARIFORUM-EPA.

[84] See Sect. 4.4.6.4.

[85] See Sect. 4.4.8.

[86] The text of the agreement (as amended in 2020) is available at https://eur-lex.europa.eu/legal-content/EN/TXT/?uri=CELEX%3A02000A1028%2801%29-20200301 (accessed 2 Nov 2024).

a separate implementation law.[87] Substantively, the Central American countries utilized the flexibilities under CAFTA-DR to a varying degree. Some countries implemented the IP rules under CAFTA-DR scrupulously, often including the optional IP protection or increasing the level of protection even further, *e.g.*, the (temporary) test data protection for 15 years instead of five years in Guatemala.[88] Other countries implemented the CAFTA-DR requirements restrictively or even included additional balances to this new IP protection. For example, Costa Rica abolished criminal sanctions for infringements of patents and undisclosed information to balance the creation of test data protection.[89] Also, there are several cases in which CAFTA-DR rules were not implemented into national law, *e.g.*, the requirement for pre-established damages.[90]

The implementation of the EU-FTAs further fragmented the IP laws, because some countries created absolute protection for geographical indications and others did not.[91] In addition, El Salvador, Honduras and Guatemala, in their respective laws implementing the EU-CA-AA, replaced the entire or large parts of the section on geographical indications. During this process, the continuing requirements under CAFTA-DR were sometimes considered and sometimes not.

It is instructive to compare this development in Central America with the Andean Community, which had created a distinct IP legislation (Decision 486), which was, as discussed above, accompanied by a regional court.[92] Two members, Colombia and Peru, concluded FTAs with the USA including IP chapters which were incompatible with Andean Community IP law. To enable these two countries to sign the FTAs, the Andean Community, in a highly controversial procedure, introduced the option for national legislation diverging from the Andean Community IP legislation in *Decision 689*.[93] Like TRIPS and CAFTA-DR in Central America, the implementation of trade agreements in the Andean Community fractured a previously harmonized IP system.

Regional harmonization of IP laws in Central America could provide significant advantages, as exemplified by the Central American Convention (Trademarks). However, the legislative fragmentation which resulted from the implementation of TRIPS, CAFTA-DR and the EU-FTAs will probably be difficult to overcome. Specific solutions agreed upon on a flexible basis, such as creation of the Patent Examiner Manual, seem to be the most feasible option. The Patent Examiner Manual

[87] See section 2.4.6; the EU-CA-AA Reform Law, on the other hand, amended the existing IP Reform Law (HN). However, it did not also incorporate the IP provisions of the EU-CA-AA Reform Law into the IP Reform Law (HN), which, therefore, sometimes refers to the provisions of the EU-CA-AA Reform Law that apply cumulatively.

[88] See Sect. 3.4; the implementation of the IP rules of CAFTA-DR is analyzed in detail in Sect. 8.1.

[89] See Sect. 7.7.

[90] See Sect. 7.3.

[91] See Sect. 4.4.

[92] See Sect. 2.5.2.3.

[93] Böttger (2008b), p. 974.

has significant practical effect and is a useful tool to enable the IP Registers to discuss matters related to patent registration on a common regional basis. Accordingly, it seems practical that the EU is pursuing the further amendment of the registration procedure for geographical indications in "a harmonized approach at regional level", within the Sub-Committee on Intellectual Property established under the EU-CA-AA.[94]

8.4.3 Coherence on the National Level

The implementation of CAFTA-DR also had a negative impact on the coherence of the national legislative IP framework in several Central American countries. The first instructive example is the establishment of IP provisions outside the IP Law (HN) in Honduras following the implementation of CAFTA-DR. There are formally two IP laws in Honduras, the IP Law (HN) and the IP provisions in the CAFTA-DR Reform Law (HN), which have to be applied in parallel.[95] This situation was further complicated following the implementation of the EU-CA-AA through the EU-CA-AA Reform Law (HN), which *amends* the existing provisions in the IP Law (HN), but also refers to the IP provisions in the CAFTA-DR Reform Law (HN), thereby perpetuating the parallel application and in the process creating ambiguities regarding the relationship between the two laws.[96]

Second, the CAFTA-DR requirements were sometimes simply added to the existing provisions, instead of modifying them. The most striking example are the trademark infringement provisions in Guatemala, which became extremely complex and partly redundant.[97]

Finally, the necessity to implement a substantial list of rules into various national laws in a short period of time also led to what may be described as legislative glitches. For example, the original wording of Article 126*bis*(b) IP Law (GT), mandating that the patent term extension for delays during the marketing approval process was calculated not based on the application for marketing approval, but on the patent application, a mistake which had to be corrected in a subsequent amendment to the IP Law (GT).[98]

[94] European Commission (2015), p. 8.

[95] As explained in Sect. 2.5.6, the CAFTA-DR Reform Law partially amends the existing provisions in the IP Law (HN), but also contains provisions on a variety of IP rights which do not modify the IP Law (HN), but apply separately.

[96] See Sect. 2.5.6.

[97] See Sect. 4.1.8.

[98] See Sect. 3.1.8.

8.5 Review and Change Procedures

CAFTA-DR does not provide for any formal review and change procedure regarding the IP chapter.[99] The Sub-Committee on Intellectual Property created by the EU-CA-AA is only responsible to review the implementation of certain aspects of the agreement, but not to discuss changes, which have to be agreed by the parties. Accordingly, in its first meetings, which take place once a year, this body mainly discussed general issues related to geographical indications.[100] The EU-CARIFORUM-EPA also does not create specific institutions to implement or monitor the provisions in the IP Chapter. The absence of a formal review and change process is typical for bilateral FTAs. Under CAFTA-DR and the EU-FTAs, the parties need to agree on changes on a case-by-case basis. The experience with similar bilateral FTAs suggests that, even if IP policy changes take place that the parties intend to practically implement, no formal changes to FTAs are made. For example, the *Bipartisan Trade Deal* adopted by the US Congress in May 2007 provides for more flexibility for developing country FTA partners of the USA in relation to the protection of test data, restoring patent terms to compensate for processing delays and "the types of procedures that developing country partners may implement to prevent the marketing of patent-infringing products" (*i.e.*, patent linkage).[101] However, these flexibilities were not explicitly granted retroactively under existing FTAs, such as CAFTA-DR, and it remains unclear whether the *Bipartisan Trade Deal* can be seen as an implicit waiver in relation to CAFTA-DR. However, the fact that non-compliance with test data and term extension requirements under CAFTA-DR by Costa Rica and the Dominican Republic were explicitly identified in the Special 301 Report 2016 suggests that the USTR does not consider the *Bipartisan Trade Deal* as a waiver of the respective obligations in relation to pre-existing bilateral FTAs.[102]

Even if a formal change process is in place, it can appear too cumbersome for the parties to use it. The implementation of CAFTA-DR and the EU-FTAs and the monitoring activities of the USTR and the European Commission suggest that, after a bilateral FTA entered into force, the parties "move on" politically to other issues. The implementation actions that occurred in Central America after CAFTA-DR entered into force did not lead to practical consequences, not even a reference in the Special 301 Report issued by the USTR (with a few key exceptions, such as test data protection), even if these actions were clear violations of the obligations under the FTAs.[103]

[99] See European Commission (2015), p. 8.

[100] European Commission (2015), p. 8. The focus on geographical indications is not surprising, because the registration of the Established Geographical Indications in Central America was one of the key objectives of the EU in relation to this agreement, on this issue see Sect. 4.4.5.

[101] USTR (2007), p. 3; see Roffe (2013), p. 937.

[102] USTR Special 301 Report (2016), p. 59.

[103] These cases of con-compliance with FTA requirements are discussed in more detail in Sect. 8.6.

This approach can be seen as an implicit waiver of certain FTA obligations by the USA, in some cases based on the subsequent international or domestic legal development. However, it is less transparent and provides less legal certainty to the parties than the formal revision of the FTA. Also, the formal change of the FTA could signal the possible need of a corresponding change on the national level in other countries. It could also help the right holders by clarifying the scope of their rights in practice. Such a process could also facilitate the adaptation of the IP provisions on the FTA level and national level to changes of the global IP system or national policy needs. However, the Central American experience suggests that formal revisions of an FTA are unlikely for political reasons, even if legal developments strongly indicate such revisions. Accordingly, the proposed possibility of countries to request the extension of concessions regarding exceptions and limitations to IP rights obtained by other countries in similar situations, i.e., a "most favored nation" mechanism with regard to flexibilities or limitations relating to IP protection,[104] may not be used, and even if it were used, may be rejected by the IP-demanding FTA party. One solution to this problem could be some form of "most favored nation" estoppel concept, which would enable an FTA party to implement flexibilities or limitations by preventing the FTA partners to claim a breach of the FTA, if the same flexibilities or limitations have been granted to other countries, without the need for a prior request or revision of the FTA. Such an estoppel concept could be included in bilateral FTAs as a general limitation in the IP chapter.

8.6 Implementation on the Statutory Level

This section focuses on the implementation of CAFTA-DR. While also the EU-FTAs required legislative changes, mainly in the field of geographical indications, the required revisions were much more limited, partly because these agreements contain generally less binding statutory commitments, and partly because some requirements were already implemented into national law as part of the CAFTA-DR implementation process. The legislative changes made in Central America following CAFTA-DR were supposed to "eliminate all possibility of contradiction which could create confusion and legal uncertainty" between CAFTA-DR and national law,[105] to ensure compliance with CAFTA-DR, so that CAFTA-DR could enter into force and the Central American countries could subsequently enjoy the trade benefits granted by the agreement. This objective has been largely achieved. Almost all statutory requirements of CAFTA-DR were implemented in the national legislation in the field of IP. The USTR, therefore, considered the reforms compliant with CAFTA-DR and the agreement went into

[104] MPI Principles (2013), Nr. 26.

[105] CAFTA-DR Reform Law I (DR), Consideration 2.

force in relation to all Central American countries.[106] Nevertheless, there are several notable cases of non-compliance or insufficient implementation.

- Regarding patents, there are many examples of non-compliance in Costa Rica. Microbiological processes, for instance, are excluded from patentability, in violation of Article 27(3)(b) TRIPS and Article 15.9(2) CAFTA-DR.[107] Also, the Regulation 34959-MINAET-COMEX relating to traditional knowledge and patentability requirements, which had been considered indispensable for CAFTA-DR compliance by the USTR and had been adopted in 2008, was invalidated by the CJS (CR).[108] In addition, Honduras did not create a statutory basis for patent term extension at all and most other Central American countries created limitations on patent term extension for procedural delays, which is not foreseen by CAFTA-DR.[109]
- Regarding plant varieties, Guatemala repealed the plant variety law and suspended the process of becoming a member of the UPOV Convention following massive popular protests in 2014, in an evident violation of Article 15.1.5 (a) CAFTA-DR.[110] Likewise, Honduras and Nicaragua are in breach of CAFTA-DR for the failure to ratify the UPOV Convention (1991).
- Test data protection has not been implemented on an administrative level in the Dominican Republic, which does not comply with CAFTA-DR.[111]
- Regarding trademarks and geographical indications, Costa Rican legislation is also not fully compliant with CAFTA-DR, because it only protects trademarks against the registration, but not the use of identical or similar signs for related goods.[112] Costa Rica also failed to comply with Article 23 TRIPS and Article 246 EU-CA-AA, both of which require absolute protection of (certain) geographical indications.[113] Nicaragua did not implement the "exception from the exception" regarding the exclusion of generic distinctive signs for geographical indications protected in the country of origin, as required by the EU-CA-AA.[114]
- Unregistered designs are protected in El Salvador and Guatemala against "products that reproduce the same general impression"[115] and "*similar* reproductions",[116] while Article 252.3 EU-CA-AA provides that unregistered designs may only be protected against *copying* of the design. This case of

[106] See Sect. 2.2.1.

[107] See Sect. 3.1.4.3.

[108] See Sect. 3.1.4.4.

[109] See Sect. 3.1.8.

[110] See Sect. 3.3.

[111] See Sect. 3.4.

[112] See Sect. 3.1.6.

[113] Article 80 Trademark Law (CR); see Sect. 4.4.8.

[114] Articles 58(1) and 47 of the Trademark Regulation (NI), see Sect. 4.4.4.2.

[115] Article 128(1) IP Law (SV).

[116] Article 154 IP Law (GT).

non-compliance is especially noteworthy, because the countries decided to exceed the maximum protection established by the EU-CA-AA.

– Regarding enforcement, the requirements of CAFTA-DR regarding pre-established damages for the infringement of IP rights were not fully implemented in several Central American countries.[117]

Interestingly, none of these cases of non-compliance led to any sanctions or similar measures by the USA or the EU. With regard to the CARIFORUM-EPA, a review five years after the signing found that key elements of the provisions on IP have only been partially implemented.[118] However, this assessment apparently did not lead to specific sanctions or measures. Regarding CAFTA-DR, even though the USTR repeatedly identified shortcomings and challenges related to the implementation of the agreement in the Special 301 Reports, this also did not result in specific actions.

Several explanations for this lack of response are possible. These issues may be considered as practically insignificant from the US or EU perspective. However, regarding the Regulation 34959-MINAET-COMEX in Costa Rica, the US government demanded the adoption of such regulation as a condition for the entry into force of CAFTA-DR. Also, the non-compliance regarding the protection of test data has been repeatedly criticized by PhRMA[119] and has been explicitly mentioned as an area for improvement by the USTR.[120] This suggests that these issues have been identified as important by the USA. The position by the USA also cannot be attributed to the more restrictive approach regarding IP protection expressed in the *Bipartisan Trade Deal.* It in particular calls for more flexibility regarding test data protection, but the USTR explicitly identified this as an area for improvement.[121]

This suggests that other factors exist which caused the USTR not to pursue the dispute settlement procedure under CAFTA-DR or take other measures. Legally, the dispute settlement procedure can be used for any violation of CAFTA-DR, but initiating the procedure is nevertheless a politically relevant decision which may not be opportune in the broader context of political relations (e.g., with a view to the collaboration in the war on drugs or illegal immigration). Accordingly, the USTR may prefer to exert pressure to amend national laws in Central America after the entry into force of CAFTA-DR through other, informal channels. Also, while these issues may *per se* be significant, insufficient IP protection in Central America has less economic impact on US businesses than insufficient IP protection in larger markets and, therefore, may be de-prioritized by the USTR.[122]

[117] See Sect. 7.3.

[118] Singh (2014), p. 53.

[119] See, e.g., PhRMA (2014), p. 190.

[120] USTR Special 301 Report (2016), p. 59.

[121] USTR Special 301 Report (2016), p. 59.

[122] The priorities reflected in the Special 301 Reports support this view. For example, in the Special 301 Report 2016, the sections on China and India are about seven pages each, on Argentina and Brazil one page each and on Costa Rica, the Dominican Republic and Guatemala one page in total, see USTR Special 301 Report (2016). Also, Honduras and Nicaragua are not included in the watch

The implementation of CAFTA-DR shows that the approach of changing the IP system by detailed statutory requirements has several disadvantages. From the perspective of the implementing country, it reduces options for structuring the IP legislation and substantively balancing relevant policy needs. The implementation can also conflict with the existing legislative structure and content. In Central America, this led to a number of cases of non-compliance, despite the overall goal of the Central American countries to ensure compliance and the entry into force of CAFTA-DR. From the perspective of the "IP-demanding" country, statutory changes to the IP system required by an FTA alone have limited impact. As will be discussed in Sect. 8.7, the statutory strengthening of IP protection will only have a material practical impact if it is accompanied by changes on the institutional level.

The utilization of the statutory approach to strengthen the IP system in developing countries in bilateral FTAs is appealing at first glance. Developed countries can create a template of statutory "terms and conditions" that can be re-used in several bilateral FTAs. Furthermore, implementation can be monitored relatively easily. However, because of the significant practical problems just explained, this approach should be used in a more targeted and restricted manner. In areas where the scope of protection is debated on the international level and legal changes appear possible in the future, policy space should be left on the national level, because it is difficult to subsequently adapt an FTA in case of policy changes. For example, the Central American countries implemented the broad scope of test data protection and the patent term extension requirements of CAFTA-DR in their national legislation, but when the US Congress adopted the *Bipartisan Trade Deal*, the respective flexibilities were not included in either CAFTA-DR or the national laws in Central America. Similarly, if at some point a global compromise is reached on the relationship between trademarks and geographical indications, the current obligations under the different FTAs could restrict the possibility of Central American countries to implement such a compromise. Also, if developed countries draft the IP chapter of an FTA based on an established set of statutory rules, they should consider using it not as a template to be implemented completely, but as a "toolbox" from which appropriate elements can be selected. For example, pre-established damages are a problem in many civil law countries, not only in Central America. Even from a right holder's perspective, omitting this requirement in CAFTA-DR would not significantly have weakened the level of IP protection, but facilitated the implementation of CAFTA-DR. Finally, the lack of practical implementation had no tangible consequences, e.g., economic or other sanctions imposed by the USA. However, if these rules are ultimately no "deal-breakers", it may have been better to use the time and resources for implementation to strengthen the local IP systems in other, practically more effective ways.

---

list, even though the level of IP protection in general does not seem to be higher than in other Central American countries and these countries are also non-compliant with CAFTA-DR in certain areas. The references to Central American countries in the Special 301 Reports are shown by Díaz (2006), p. 45.

8.7 Effectiveness of Statutory Protection and Impact on the Institutional Level

The focus of many FTAs, including CAFTA-DR and the EU-FTAs, on statutory protection raises the question whether this approach is effective, or whether more consideration needs to be given to institutional challenges regarding IP policy.

8.7.1 Institutional Impact of Bilateral FTAs

The discussion of TRIPS-plus rules is often limited to the analysis of the legislative requirements in the text of the respective FTA and assumes that these requirements are fully implemented on a legislative and institutional level. For example, *Roffe* notes that "the new obligations often require a substantial reinforcement of the country's institutional base in terms of recruiting competent staff to meet the stipulations of the agreement, and employing professionals duly qualified in the management of the system".[123] This view is widespread in the international literature. The underlying assumption that these institutional requirements are met, however, is usually not empirically validated.

As the analysis of CAFTA-DR and the EU-FTAs has shown, many FTA requirements are not effectively implemented on the institutional level and therefore remain practically ineffective. Examples are the backlogs of patent applications in Costa Rica and the Dominican Republic, which for many years almost amounted to a practical denial of protection for pharmaceutical inventions,[124] and the failure of the Dominican Republic to adopt the regulation necessary to implement test data protection.[125]

This limited implementation is due in part to the fact that bilateral FTAs are often explicitly restrictive with regard to institutional obligations. CAFTA-DR makes reference to institutional aspects mainly to underline that it does not create any obligations in this regard. Article 15.11(2) CAFTA-DR states that no special courts have to be established and that the parties are free in their allocation of resources to IP entities. In particular, there is no obligation "with respect to the distribution of resources for the enforcement of IP rights and the enforcement of law in general".[126] Some of the few provisions regarding the institutional level relate to the protection of pharmaceuticals, first the obligation for the IP Registers and health agencies to implement the "patent linkage" mechanism[127] and second the protection of test

[123] Roffe (2013), p. 937.

[124] See Sect. 3.1.7.

[125] See Sect. 3.4.2.2.

[126] Article 15.11.2. (b) CAFTA-DR.

[127] See Sect. 3.1.9.

data, which requires procedural changes at the health agencies.[128] Most of the other institutional provisions are non-binding commitments to institutional cooperation[129] or the commitment to provide "to the maximum degree practical [...] a system for the electronic application, processing, registration, and maintenance of trademarks".[130] This restrictive approach regarding institutions corresponds to most international IP agreements, which explicitly state that no institutional requirements are imposed beyond a general effectiveness obligation.[131]

The EU-FTAs, especially the EU-CA-AA, on the other hand, include more provisions affecting the institutional and practical level.

- Article 245 EU-CA-AA requires the *registration* of a list of Established Geographical Indications in Central America prior to the entry into force of the agreement.[132]
- Under the EU-CARIFORUM-EPA, the parties *must* create publicly available electronic databases of trademark applications and trademark registrations.[133]
- The EU-CA-AA requires the establishment of competition agencies.[134]
- Also, the EU-CARIFORUM-EPA and the EU-CA-AA provide for cooperation in the areas of competitiveness and innovation,[135] science and technology,[136] information society and information and communication technologies[137] and eco-innovation and renewable energy.[138]

This "institutional" approach better reflects the fact that, as the foregoing analysis has shown, the insufficient (from the right holder's perspective) IP protection and enforcement in Central America is not due to shortcomings in the legislation, but to institutional deficits. The USTR, for example, identified a broad range of institutional challenges in Central America, including resource constraints, lack of coordination, lack of IP expertise and lack of emphasis from the *Ministerio Público* and the judiciary.[139]

[128] See Sect. 3.4.

[129] Article 15.1(16) CAFTA-DR.

[130] Article 15.2(7) CAFTA-DR.

[131] See, e.g., Article 41(5) TRIPS.

[132] Under Article 245.1(b) EU-CA-AA, the registration process is also considered completed if a geographical indication was not registered because an opposition was raised. However, practically the Central American countries tried to resolve such oppositions before the entry into force of the EU-CA-AA (see Sect. 4.4.6).

[133] Article 144.A EU-CARIFORUM-EPA; this obligation exceeds the CAFTA-DR requirements. While Article 15.2 CAFTA-DR only requires activities toward the establishment of an electronic system, the EU-CARIFORUM-EPA creates a binding obligation.

[134] See Sect. 2.6.1.

[135] Article 135 EU-CARIFORUM-EPA.

[136] Article 136 EU-CARIFORUM-EPA.

[137] Article 137 EU-CARIFORUM-EPA.

[138] Article 138 EU-CARIFORUM-EPA.

[139] USTR Special 301 Report (2016), pp. 58–60.

However, even in areas where bilateral FTAs focus more on institutional requirements, this does not guarantee implementation. For example, some Central American IP registers still do not provide easily accessible, user-friendly electronic databases to search patents and trademarks and the respective applications.[140] Similarly, even though the EU-CARIFORUM-EPA obliged the Dominican Republic to create an electronic application system for trademarks, such system was only created in 2019.[141] Also, Guatemala has not yet created a competition authority.[142]

There are several factors which explain why the impact of the IP rules under CAFTA-DR and the EU-FTAs on the institutional and practical level in Central America was so little. First, under the existing bilateral FTAs, the Central American countries have little incentive to substantially increase their efforts in relation to IP protection and enforcement. Institutional changes were mostly not necessary to secure the trade benefits under CAFTA-DR, because the IP requirements under CAFTA-DR were largely limited to the statutory level. While the implementation of CAFTA-DR required significant legislative efforts and resources, the institutional flexibilities under CAFTA-DR (and similarly the EU-FTAs) enable the Central American countries and their law enforcement agencies to prioritize other areas. Second, the institutions dealing with IP issues face significant budget constraints (as do other public entities).[143] Third, the standard rules in the respective IP chapters, which are used in FTAs with various partner countries around the globe, cannot address country-specific challenges in Central America. For example, the rules on patent linkage cannot be very effective in Costa Rica and the Dominican Republic, as long as the number of granted pharmaceutical patents remains low. Also, the focus on criminal enforcement legislation is obviously impractical considering that in Central America the *Ministerio Público* (understandably) has other priorities. Importantly, the enforcement provisions of CAFTA-DR are based on the US legal system and do not align with the civil law structure or the practical realities of IP enforcement in Central America.[144]

The IP system in Central America can, therefore, only be effectively changed by focusing on institutional challenges, taking the specific needs of each country into account. After the implementation of CAFTA-DR, the USTR seems to move in this direction. In relation to the Dominican Republic, for example, the Special 301 Report 2009 addressed (among other things) the insufficient implementation of the patent linkage mechanism, but ignored the lack of patent protection as such.[145] The reports

[140] See Sect. 2.5.3.3.

[141] See Sect. 2.5.3.3.

[142] See Sect. 2.6.1.

[143] This issue is analyzed in more detail in Sect. 8.7.

[144] An illustrative example is the clear separation of civil, administrative and criminal enforcement under CAFTA-DR on the one hand and the hybrid adhesion procedure in Central America on the other hand, see Sect. 7.1.2.

[145] USTR Special 301 Report (2017), p. 24.

in 2016 and 2017 replaced the reference to patent linkage with a demand to reduce the backlog of patent applications.[146]

Another major institutional issue is criminal enforcement. Even before CAFTA-DR, several countries had made special commitments to strengthen the IP system, namely by creating specific IP units in the *Ministerio Público*.[147] In Central America, this has broader enforcement implications, because right holders often rely on criminal procedures and the adhesion mechanism to enforce their rights.[148] Nevertheless, CAFTA-DR only addressed criminal enforcement on the statutory level, but not the institutional challenges. While, for instance, Honduras re-established its specialized IP unit within the *Ministerio Público* in 2010, in other countries it is difficult to show that specifically the implementation of CAFTA-DR strengthened criminal enforcement in practice in Central America.[149]

However, the obligation to make institutional changes, as such, is not sufficient to successfully transform the IP system, as evidenced by the examples of institutional requirements in the EU-FTAs that have not been implemented in Central America. Therefore, additional measures are necessary.

8.7.2 Resource Allocation

A major reason for the practical problems relating to IP protection and enforcement is the lack of resources of IP institutions. Most IP Registers in Central America have little budget autonomy and face resource constraints.[150] The *Ministerio Público* (understandably) allocates the available resources often to other areas of criminal enforcement, e.g., organized crime, drug trafficking and violent crime.[151] These institutions, therefore, sometimes practically require logistical support from the right holders in order to take action. However, this lack of resources does not necessarily constitute a breach of the obligations under the bilateral FTAs. In the case "*China - Measures Affecting the Protection and Enforcement of Intellectual Property Rights*", the WTO Dispute Settlement Body acknowledged (at least implicitly) that Article

[146] USTR Special 301 Report (2016), pp. 58–60; USTR Special 301 Report (2017), p. 64.

[147] See Sect. 2.5.5.

[148] See Sect. 7.1.2.

[149] See Sect. 2.5.5; at least from the perspective of the US government, criminal enforcement in Central America is still not satisfactory; regarding the situation in Costa Rica, for instance, see USTR Special 301 Report (2016).

[150] See Sect. 2.5.3.

[151] See Sect. 2.5.5. It must also be noted that also in many developed countries, e.g., Southern Europe, trademark counterfeiting is commonplace and criminal enforcement is not used as a meaningful deterrent. In Germany, the criminal enforcement of IP rights also plays only a secondary role. Therefore, even by international standards, one cannot say that the Central American countries display a particular lack of efforts to protect and enforce IP, considering the respective level of development.

41(5) TRIPS can justify weak IP enforcement in case a country faces general resource constraints.[152] Similarly, Article 15.11.2(b) CAFTA-DR creates no obligation with respect to the distribution of resources for the enforcement of IP rights and the enforcement of law in general. In Central America, there can be no doubt about such lack of resources generally, and while the Special 301 Reports repeatedly urge the Central American countries to provide more resources to IP enforcement, they noticeably never allege a violation of the TRIPS or CAFTA-DR obligations.[153] The bilateral FTAs do not mitigate this resource problem. To the contrary, the implementation of bilateral FTAs requires financial and human resources and, therefore, burdens the legislative, administrative and judicial infrastructure of the implementing country.[154] The World Bank estimated that Mexico spent more than 30 million USD to upgrade IP laws and enforcement because of TRIPS, even though the existing legislation was already at a higher level than in many other developing countries.[155]

Central America is a case in point. The implementation of, *e.g.*, CAFTA-DR requirements like sound and scent marks protection require considerable administrative and training efforts and resources.[156] It may also require particular efforts to implement the new legislation within the relevant institutions.[157] Especially courts, which do not deal with IP issues on a regular basis (with the exception of the TRA in Costa Rica) will require training in order to implement the new legislation. Also, personnel of the IP Registers received training on plant variety protection under the UPOV Convention.[158] Last but not least, the registration of a multitude of Established Geographical Indications required significant resources (including lawyer's fees and the efforts related to the oppositions by the owners of conflicting trademarks).[159] The development of the IP system on the multilateral or bilateral level should consider these institutional ramifications, because they strongly impact the overall success of such development. International agreements should provide sufficient flexibility to allow each country to implement the agreement in balanced way.[160] However, it is also necessary to take the limited resources of developing countries into account. One solution that has been suggested is financial and technical support from developed countries. However, this creates the risk that

---

[152] WTO Dispute Settlement Body, Panel Report, China—Measures Affecting the Protection and Enforcement of Intellectual Property Rights, Decision of 26 January 2009, WT/DS362/R.

[153] For example, in relation to Guatemala, see USTR Special 301 Report (2016), p. 59, in relation to Costa Rica, see USTR Special 301 Report (2011), p. 33.

[154] MPI Principles (2013), Nr. 9.

[155] Finger (2000), p. 427.

[156] See Sect. 4.1.2.7.

[157] In the Dominican Republic, the IP Register created a cooperation with the National Music Conservatory to examine sound marks, see Sect. 4.1.2.7.

[158] See Sect. 8.7.4.

[159] Regarding Established Geographical Indications, see Sect. 4.4.5.

[160] MPI Principles (2013), Nr. 24.

such support is used to further increase the practical level of IP protection.[161] So far, such support in Central America has been limited mainly to training.[162] A practical solution used by enforcement agencies in Central America is to require financial and logistical support from right holders for enforcement actions.[163]

8.7.3 Regional Cooperation

In Central America, regional harmonization and cooperation activities have been an important element of IP policy.[164] However, the bilateral FTAs of the USA and the EU do not support such activities. Article 141 EU-CARIFORUM-EPA states abstract commitments to foster regional harmonization and integration, but under this agreement no direct support measures for harmonization have been adopted. CAFTA-DR and the EU-CA-AA contain no provisions relating to regional harmonization or cooperation. In the case of the EU-CA-AA, this is surprising, because the EU expressly concluded the agreement with Central America as a region to promote regional integration.[165] Practically, the EU has supported regional harmonization by organizing a training by the EPO for the users of the Patent Examiner Manual in 2010.[166] Incentivizing and supporting regional cooperation and integration in Central America can be a significant way to strengthen the national and regional IP framework. One must note that all Central American countries and their economies are relatively small. As a consequence, few IP rights are registered by both national and international right holders (compared to Mexico, for example) and there is relatively little case law in this field.[167] The harmonization of IP laws and regional cooperation can, therefore, help "aggregate" IP experience and strengthen the IP system.

8.7.4 Training and Support by the USA and the EU

Another reason why the practical IP prosecution and enforcement does not work effectively is the lack of public awareness and institutional capacity building. Specific measures proposed, in addition to training for IP institutions, are the education of the public already in schools, the publication of enforcement measures

---

[161] MPI Principles (2013), Nr. 13.

[162] Training measures are further discussed in Sect. 8.7.4.

[163] See Sect. 2.5.5.

[164] See Sect. 2.5.2.

[165] See Sect. 2.3.1.

[166] WTO (2011), p. 51.

[167] See Sect. 2.5.2.

and measures improving the innovative capacities of society.[168] While the focus of CAFTA-DR was on statutory requirements and the TCB Committee did not achieve any specific results in the field of IP, there have been training activities targeting the institutional level that coincided with CAFTA-DR and the EU-FTAs, especially by organizations from the USA or Europe.[169] These activities can be considered an indirect impact of the CAFTA-DR implementation process, because of this coincidence. For example, the courts and specialized IP units of the *Ministerio Público* receive training from the IP Registers, *e.g.*, in Nicaragua,[170] or from abroad, in particular from institutions in the USA and EU and from WIPO.[171] In October 2008, the German GIZ organized a seminar on patent law for local practitioners in San Salvador.[172] Also in October 2008, a Seminar on IP law was organized in San José, Costa Rica, with about 100 mostly local lawyers participating (but also many visitors from other Central American countries).[173] In addition, the CAFTA-DR implementation process as such and the controversies surrounding specific IP provisions increased the public awareness and led to an increase in legal and other publications and documentation on the issue.[174] Unlike CAFTA-DR, the EU-FTAs explicitly provide for training in the field of IP. In connection with the ratification and implementation of these agreements, a number of training activities have been conducted.[175]

While trainings and similar activities are important means to improve IP protection in Central America, the fact that such trainings are often organized by institutions of developed countries or right holder organizations raises concerns. This sponsorship entails the likelihood that such training emphasizes strong protection of IP.[176] However, support by "IP-demanding" countries should not reduce the available policy space of the implementing country regarding IP protection.[177] To manage this issue, training could be planned not solely by the USA or the EU or entities selected by them, but FTA partner countries could be allowed to request

---

[168] See for example Díaz (2006), p. 13; USTR Special 301 Report (2016), pp. 58–60.

[169] See Sect. 2.5.3.4.

[170] Registro de la Propiedad Intelectual de Nicaragua (2006), p. 22.

[171] Registro de la Propiedad Intelectual de Nicaragua (2006), p. 18; WTO, Technical Cooperation Activities: Information from Members, European Union, IP/C/W/550/Add.7, 1 June 2011, p. 51.

[172] Material on this seminar is on file with the author.

[173] Material on this seminar is on file with the author.

[174] See Sect. 1.2.4; there are also numerous publications on specific issues, mainly those areas of IP affected by CAFTA-DR. It should be added that one can observe a larger number of academic papers on IP issues originating from Central American universities, which speaks to the increasing relevance of and interest in IP in the region.

[175] See Sect. 2.3.4.3.

[176] While training on some topics can only be provided by specialized entities, e.g., patent offices in relation to examination and registration of patents, in addition to the USPTO or the EPO, there are also regional patent offices, e.g., from Mexico or Brazil, capable of conducting trainings for Central American IP Registers.

[177] MPI Principles (2013), Nr. 27.

trainings depending on their needs. This procedure conforms with Article 67 TRIPS, which provides that "developed countries shall provide, *on request* (…), technical and financial cooperation". Training performed or organized by international organizations can be more balanced. WIPO, for example, has developed information material to help developing countries implement international IP obligations in a way that does not practically restrict the remaining policy options further, but instead helps the respective countries to utilize flexibilities and protects public policy goals.[178]

8.7.5 Legal and Social Framework

The effective implementation of IP rules in Central America is further impeded by the fact that many local stakeholders reject strong(er) IP protection. However, this negative attitude is starting to change, because, *e.g.*, local entities increasingly utilize trademarks and geographical indications to protect their businesses, in particular, if they expand their economic activities internationally.[179] Implementation difficulties can also be attributed to differences in the legal culture which impede the practical implementation of these rules. A study by *Kedron Thomas* on the apparel industry in Guatemala found that the harmonization of IP law is practically limited by the political and cultural differences among countries.[180] For example, the enforcement provisions of CAFTA-DR clearly distinguish between civil, criminal and administrative enforcement, whereas legal practice in Central America is based on a hybrid model, which combines criminal and civil enforcement in the adhesion procedure and (in Costa Rica) civil and administrative enforcement by authorizing the IP Register to grant provisional measures.[181] Similarly, while under Article 15.2 (10) CAFTA-DR, recordal of trademark licenses may not be required to assert any rights in a trademark, in Central America it is practically difficult to assert rights based on a license in court, if the license is not registered.[182] Generally, the enforcement section of CAFTA-DR is based on a system of adversarial judicial proceedings, whereas in Central America IP disputes are preferably resolved by conciliation.[183]

---

[178] WTO, Technical Cooperation Activities: Information from Members, European Union, IP/C/W/550/Add.7, 1 June 2011, p. 51.

[179] See Sect. 2.5.7.

[180] Thomas (2009), p. 6; regarding criminal IP enforcement, she cautions that the idea that criminalizing certain activities will automatically have a deterring effect and reduce illicit activities is "misguided", see Thomas (2011), pp. 195–199.

[181] See Sect. 7.1.2 (adhesion procedure) and Sect. 7.4 (provisional measures).

[182] See Sect. 4.1.6.1.

[183] See Sect. 7.1.2.

The negative perception of the legitimacy and relevance of IP protection could be addressed by returning international IP policy-multilateral level and ensuring a balanced rule-making process. However, a fundamental shift in the perception of IP protection in Central America probably also requires the increasing use of IP rights by domestic entities and a change of perception of the relevance of the IP System. Only if the economy of Central America is transformed from a commodity-based to a more innovation-based economy will IP protection significantly contribute to the economic success of local businesses. As long as the number of patents granted to local applicants in the entire region remains in single digits annually and as long as there are relatively few successful examples of local companies that build their success on strong brands, the skepticism is unlikely to significantly change. Possible measures on the national level to actively facilitate the use of the IP system by local entities may be reduced filing, examination and annual maintenance fees for local SMEs. Depending on the criteria for "SMEs", many local businesses could benefit from such a fee structure. Focusing more on institutional improvements in bilateral FTAs could also help reduce frictions caused by statutory requirements that do not align with principles of the domestic legal systems, e.g., pre-established damages.[184]

8.8 Support of IP Policy Objectives

While the TRIPS-plus debate addresses many procedural aspects of IP protection in bilateral FTAs, such as negotiation imbalances, participation of stakeholders and general statutory and institutional implications, at its core lies the concern that the TRIPS-plus level of IP protection and enforcement creates "overprotection" which is detrimental to the objectives of IP protection.

8.8.1 Local Innovation

Compared to CAFTA-DR, the EU-FTAs did not significantly affect patent protection and, therefore, are not separately discussed in this section.

Under CAFTA-DR, the patentability requirements, scope of protection (*e.g.*, compulsory licenses) and registration procedure established by TRIPS have been modified only in a few narrow areas, *e.g.*, regarding the patentability of inventions related to animals and other biological subject matter.[185] However, CAFTA-DR introduced or broadened several mechanisms which strengthen patent protection,

[184] See Sect. 7.3.2.2.

[185] See Sect. 3.1.4.3.

notably patent term extensions,[186] patent linkage[187] and the protection of test data of pharmaceuticals.[188] Practically, the effect of these TRIPS-plus provisions has been limited in Central America, because especially in these areas the statutory and institutional implementation reduced the level of protection established in the agreement. As has been described in Sect. 8.6, several cases of non-compliance with CAFTA-DR in Central America were identified regarding the patentability of biological subject matter (microbiological processes and traditional knowledge), patent term extension and test data.[189] Also, Costa Rica used the flexibility under CAFTA-DR regarding the enforcement of patents by modifying its criminal law to exclude illegal test data use from the list of criminal activities.

The regional technological and socio-economic framework limits the incentive created by patent protection existing under the level of protection established by TRIPS.[190] This is shown by the data available in relation to the years after the implementation of TRIPS.[191] This framework was not modified by CAFTA-DR, which suggests that also the implementation of CAFTA-DR did not significantly impact local inventive activity. The practical experience in Central America more than ten years after the implementation of CAFTA-DR supports the assumption that the higher level of patent protection had a positive effect on local inventive activity.

An indicator of inventive activity is the number of patent applications originating locally. Immediately after the implementation of CAFTA-DR, the number of patent applications originating from Central America stagnated or even decreased.[192] This corresponds to the global trend in smaller developing countries, but it shows that the Central American countries, during the first years after the implementation of CAFTA-DR, did not increase their innovative capacity (as measured by patent applications) in relation to comparable countries. This suggests that the increase in patent protection introduced by CAFTA-DR did not lead to a stronger incentive to innovate or that, irrespective of the existence of such an incentive, the socio-economic framework in Central America does not support more innovative activity. There has been a slight increase in patent filings originating from the region between 2011 and 2014, but the data basis is too small to determine whether this was caused by the changes in IP policy due to CAFTA-DR or is simply a temporary spike.[193] More data over a longer term is necessary. However, from a practical

[186] See Sect. 3.1.8.

[187] See Sect. 3.1.9.

[188] See Sect. 3.4.

[189] Test data protection has not been implemented on an administrative level in the Dominican Republic (see Sect. 3.4.2). Also, Honduras did not create a statutory basis for patent term extension and most countries created limitations on patent term extension for procedural delays, which is not foreseen by CAFTA-DR (see Sect. 3.1.8.2).

[190] See Sect. 1.3.4.

[191] This is evident from the number of patent applications originating from Central America, see Sect. 3.1.7.

[192] See Table 3.4.

[193] See Sect. 3.1.7.

perspective, it seems unlikely that the implementation of patent rules under CAFTA-DR is the main cause of the increase. The stronger protection relates mainly to pharmaceutical patents by protecting test data and creating patent linkage, therefore, one would expect the increased number of patent applications to originate from the pharmaceutical industry. However, the local pharmaceutical industry is focused on importing generic compounds to manufacture finished products, and seems an unlikely candidate for suddenly filing a significant number of patent applications. The additional protection mandated by CAFTA-DR in relation to test data and patent linkage practically benefits predominantly foreign right holders, particularly the pharmaceutical industry. This corresponds to the prediction of economic models indicating that, in a given country, the economic benefit of a higher incentive for innovation by stronger patent protection is lower than the welfare gain of more competition and lower prices by lower levels of patent protection.[194] This expectation was shared by local Central American businesses. In Costa Rica and Guatemala, the generic pharmaceutical industry strongly endorsed the national and international opposition against CAFTA-DR and especially the data exclusivity provisions to protect its business model.[195] The experience of the Central American countries with CAFTA-DR suggests that developing countries could, *e.g.*, during the negotiation of an FTA, justifiably reject the claim that stronger patent protection will foster local inventive activity irrespective of the local socio-economic framework. Institutional measures, *e.g.*, better education and the introduction of an innovative and patent-friendly culture at universities, are necessary to practically improve the capacity to innovate.

8.8.2 Global Innovation

While from a local perspective, developing countries such as the Central American countries are usually net "consumers" of innovation and, therefore, benefit from a low level of patent protection, it is less clear whether there is a welfare benefit of weaker patent protection also from a global perspective. It is generally assumed that patent protection contributes to inventive activity (if calibrated appropriately).[196] Therefore, theoretically, a low level of patent protection even in small developing countries reduces the incentive to innovate globally. However, there is no empirical evidence whether small developing countries practically contribute to the global incentive to innovate.[197] The economic models discussed above indicate that, in developing countries, the welfare gain of more competition and lower prices outweighs the economic benefit of a higher incentive for inventive activity by stronger

[194] See, e.g., the study by Klaus Liebig, discussed in Sect. 1.6.2.2 and Sect. 3.1.1.1.

[195] See Sect. 2.5.7.

[196] See Sect. 3.1.1.

[197] See Sect. 3.1.1.

patent protection. However, they do not show that such incentive for inventive activity does not exist. However, assuming that patent protection in Central America can contribute to global inventive activity, it is difficult from an economic perspective to determine the equitable level of contribution from developing countries to global inventive activity. The level of patent protection generally requires a balance between maximizing the incentive to innovate and minimizing the "trade-off" of restricting users of inventions. Determining the "trade-off", i.e., the extent to which the use of inventions is restricted, will vary between different countries.[198] It will depend in particular on the level of development and economic strength of each country, e.g., the ability to bear the economic costs created by price premiums. Therefore, it is appropriate to allow a different level of IP protection depending on the level of development.

This approach is used in TRIPS, which contains provisions with different obligations for countries in different "tiers", *i.e.*, developed, developing and least developed countries. Both TRIPS and the Doha Declaration grant more flexibility to low-income countries, but only limited flexibility to middle-income countries in relation to the restriction of patents to facilitate access to medicines, thus overcoming the simplistic distinction between developed and developing countries. This "tiered" system is also used in the EU-CARIFORUM-EPA, which provides for modified IP provisions in relation to least-developed countries.[199] While, therefore, low levels of IP protection are justified in least-developed countries, more advanced developing countries should accept an intermediate level of IP protection.[200] Middle-income countries like Costa Rica can be expected to contribute more to the creation of knowledge as a global public good than low-income countries, but less than high-income countries. Accordingly, TRIPS requires Costa Rica to comply with stricter obligations under international law. However, the earlier policy of Costa Rica (and similarly the Dominican Republic) not to grant patent protection for pharmaceuticals resulted in free-riding even beyond relatively poorer countries such as, for instance, Guatemala.[201] Such an approach conflicts with the IP system created by TRIPS and may pose an obstacle for the creation of an appropriate global balance between IP protection and public access.

The Costa Rica approach raises also another issue. On the one hand, the country has established an elaborate system for the protection and use of its natural genetic resources (biodiversity) through the access and benefit sharing (ABS) system, which includes the analysis of the properties of these genetic resources by international pharmaceutical companies. This system works on the assumptions that (a) Costa Rica has a proprietary right in the information contained in genetic resources and

---

[198] Drexl (2016), pp. 70–71.

[199] Article 140 EU-CARIFORUM-EPA; the distinction between least-developed countries and other countries was not included in CAFTA-DR and the EU-CA-AA, because neither any of the Central American countries not the Dominican Republic are least-developed countries.

[200] Böttger (2008a), p. 889.

[201] See Sect. 3.1.7.

(b) these companies can protect their results by patents to recuperate their investment. The Costa Rican patent office for years effectively denied patent protection for pharmaceutical inventions. Costa Rica, therefore, relies on patent protection in other countries as an incentive for pharmaceutical research and (indirectly) as a source of ABS revenues, while at the same time not (or only in a limited way) participating itself in this system.

However, patent protection also should not enable rent-seeking strategies that do not contribute to inventive activity. One area of concern in this regard is the term extension for delays during patent examination and marketing approval, which enables (especially pharmaceutical) companies to longer exploit existing products.[202] An obvious rent-seeking strategy is the fact that the increased patent protection under CAFTA-DR also applies *retroactively* to existing inventions, which the incentive rationale of patent protection does not apply. The fact that international pharmaceutical companies have specifically monitored whether the laws implementing CAFTA-DR are retroactive, as evidenced by their submission to the USTR in 2007, further supports this view that rent-seeking was part of the reason of including stronger patent protection in CAFTA-DR.[203]

8.8.3 Public Health

Several aspects suggest that CAFTA-DR will not have the strong impact on public health that critics claim it will. The general patent law provisions in CAFTA-DR will probably not have a material practical effect in public health, because the legislation existing in Central America prior to CAFTA-DR already provided for the patentability of pharmaceutical inventions and for statutory enforcement measures. Also, the small number of granted pharmaceutical patents in particular in Costa Rica and the Dominican Republic limit their impact on public health. Finally, in relation to less developed countries like Nicaragua, it must be noted that the availability and affordability of medicines is generally low[204] and that there are fundamental issues such as access to clean water that may affect public health more.[205] However, some factors could contribute to an increased impact in the medium or long term: The number of granted patents increased substantially in most Central American countries, which could also increase the practical impact of stronger, longer and broader statutory patent protection required by CAFTA-DR.[206] In addition, the protection of

[202] See Sect. 3.1.8.

[203] PhRMA (2007), p. 2.

[204] Based on WHO statistical data for the year 2019, the monthly per capita total expenditure on health in Nicaragua in 2013 was around 12.50 USD, while it was around 75 USD in Costa Rica, available at http://www.who.int/gho/countries/en/ (accessed 2 Nov 2024).

[205] See Sect. 3.1.1.4.

[206] See the data provided in Sect. 3.1.7.

test data and the provisions regarding patent linkage required by CAFTA-DR could have a significant impact. However, these systems do not (fully) operate in several countries on an administrative level.[207] The empirical evidence regarding the actual impact of these rules on public health in Central America is inconclusive. While the available studies, covering Guatemala and Costa Rica, show that to some small extent they enabled pharmaceutical companies to keep generic competitors off the market for specific medicines, they did not show that this practically affected treatment options or the public healthcare budget.[208]

A significant public health issue globally, that is typically not the focus of TRIPS-plus analysis, is the access to safe drugs, be they original or generic drugs. "Sub-standard, spurious, falsely labelled, falsified and counterfeit" (SSFFC) medicines usually fail to have the desired curing effect, and sometimes might even include unhealthy substances.[209] Access to safe drugs is a particular concern in developing countries and in particular in Latin America.[210] Here, organized crime organizations are not only trafficking coca-based drugs, but also false pharmaceutical drugs (SSFFC).[211] The effective protection especially of trademarks could help combat the distribution of false products and thus can improve the safety of consumers. Stricter enforcement of IP rights, namely trademarks, could therefore be a contribution to public health in the area of access to safe medicines. The problem of drug safety also exists in Central America, where enforcement measures in this field are prioritized by local law enforcement.[212] Therefore, more effective IP protection may be beneficial for public health by removing potentially dangerous fake drugs from the market.

The analysis of CAFTA-DR shows why test data protection and patent linkage are particularly critical issues in the TRIPS-plus debate. Both mechanisms do not rely on IP enforcement to prevent generic drugs from entering the market, but utilize public health agencies to protect the right holder from generic competition. In this way, the monitoring of the generic competition does not have to be performed by the right holder, but is done *ex officio* by the public agencies. It creates the possibility of the right holder to protect the exclusivity through additional means. In addition, the protection of test data provides exclusivity even without patent protection, *e.g.*, if the originator company decides not to file for patent protection or if the patent grant is

[207]It is noticeable that the discussion regarding the protection of pharmaceutical patents has shifted from patent protection as such, e.g., the low number of patents granted in the Dominican Republic (which improved subsequently) to the denial of patent term extensions and test data protection on the administrative level, see PhRMA (2007), p. 26; see also USTR Special 301 Report (2016), p. 59.

[208]These studies are discussed in more detail in Sects. 3.1.2 and 3.4.7.

[209]WHO (2018).

[210]Mackey et al. (2015), pp. 59–67.

[211]Mackey et al. (2015), pp. 59–67.

[212]For example, according to USTR Special 301 Report (2011), the interagency working group on IP rights in Guatemala focuses its training efforts on counterfeit medicines; see also the enforcement action related to counterfeit medicines in the Dominican Republic, Sect. 7.1.2.2.

delayed in the Central American country.[213] So far the Central American countries have not experienced any significant effect on access to medicines, because of the incomplete administrative implementation, in particular of test data protection and patent linkage. Also, the effects will always be mitigated to a considerable extent by the balancing measures of Costa Rica's Ministry of Health and because in some countries many people do not have access to or cannot afford any kind of medicine. However, more effective IP protection systems could limit the supply of reliable generic drugs and thereby negatively affect access to medicines. In addition to higher prices or delayed access, it might also practically benefit the large black market of counterfeit pharmaceuticals that exists in Central America.[214] These counterfeit pharmaceuticals pose an enormous health risk.[215] The black market exists despite existing patent and trademark protection and would likely continue to exist despite test data protection and patent linkage. In other words, better patent protection can in practice improve public health, but the statutory changes introduced by CAFTA-DR do not achieve this objective.

One issue that the studies on patents and public health analyzed in this thesis have not clarified is the impact of the practically low level of IP protection in Central America on investments in endemic diseases. Such investments rely on the existence of a market also in more developed countries and activities of global (e.g., WHO) or non-profit organizations (e.g., the Gates Foundation).[216] It would be useful for the policy discussion to better understand if and to what extent developing countries could contribute to the incentive to innovate in this field. However, the studies analyzed do show the difficulties in demonstrating any clear link.[217]

8.8.4 Protect Fair Competition

In the small markets of Central America, effective competition is a particular concern.[218] The possible anti-competitive effect of TRIPS-plus provisions in CAFTA-DR is restricted by the institutional limitations of IP protection. However, some provisions have the potential of substantially increasing the market power of right holders, if the provisions become more effective, especially the test data rules, which not only restrict competitors but also facilitate the flexible entry in the local

[213] See the more detailed discussion in Sect. 3.4.

[214] The availability of counterfeit drugs in Latin America is discussed by Mackey et al. (2015), pp. 59–67.

[215] WHO (2018).

[216] See, e.g., https://www.gatesfoundation.org/What-We-Do/Global-Health/Neglected-Tropical-Diseases (accessed 2 Nov 2024).

[217] The various and partly inconclusive empirical studies regarding the effect of patent protection in general show the limits of the empirical economic approach, see Sect. 3.1.1.

[218] See Sect. 1.3.2.

market of the originator company.[219] In order to the mitigate the risk of anti-competitive effects, the countries implementing TRIPS-plus provisions should therefore strengthen domestic competition laws and policies. As discussed above, however, the process of strengthening the competition law framework in Central America is slow.

8.8.5 Consumer Protection and Combating Counterfeit Products

Regarding *trademarks*, the pre-CAFTA-DR legislation in Central America already contained rules protecting the right holder and consumers against counterfeiting and unfair competition. CAFTA-DR increased the level of protection, in particular by providing for criminal sanctions against counterfeiting.[220] This increase in protection was justified in part as consumer protection.[221] However, the TRIPS-plus provisions in CAFTA-DR and the EU-FTAs do not address the institutional and social factors underlying the insufficient IP enforcement, in particular the lack of resources and incentives.[222] The analysis shows that the increase of statutory protection under CAFTA-DR had little practical impact on trademark counterfeiting in Central America, which is still widespread.[223] On the other hand, there were (limited) enforcement activities and specialized IP enforcement units have been created, both before and after the implementation of CAFTA-DR.[224] This also suggests that CAFTA-DR had no significant impact on IP enforcement and combatting counterfeit products. The available statistics on trademark applications also suggest that registering trademarks in Central America has not become more attractive for right holders.[225] Accordingly, bilateral FTAs and multilateral agreements should avoid imposing new statutory requirements, *e.g.*, with regard to the possibility of *ex officio* enforcement measures or specific criminal sanctions, because these measures will probably have little practical effect and could absorb implementation resources needed elsewhere. The analysis also suggests that previous institutional reforms, such as the creation of specialized IP units by the *Ministerio Público* and trainings by various international and foreign institutions, did not have a strong impact. However, improvements on this level, such as the establishment of the "Intellectual Property Registry" to facilitate border measures against IP

[219] See Sect. 3.4.
[220] See Sect. 7.7.
[221] See Sect. 1.6.2.3.
[222] See Sect. 1.3.
[223] Thomas (2011), p. 50.
[224] See Sect. 2.5.5.
[225] See Sect. 4.1.6.

infringements in the Dominican Republic may have a significant practical effect on trademark counterfeiting.[226]

8.8.6 *Biodiversity*

CAFTA-DR impacts the protection of biodiversity in several ways. The agreement requires the accession of the Central American countries to the UPOV Convention (1991), establishing strong protection of plant varieties. This type of protection has been criticized for restricting traditional business models of local farmers, especially regarding the re-use of seeds, by restricting the farmer's privilege.[227] It also supports the extensive use of new, genetically modified organisms (GMO) as a business model, which could led to monocultures and ultimately harm *biodiversity*, as the use of traditional and diverse types of crops could be discontinued.[228] The latter issue was a major concern in "mega-diverse" Central American countries such as Costa Rica.[229] The protection of local biodiversity is further restricted by Article 15.9 (10) CAFTA-DR, which suggests that applicants cannot be required during the patent examination process to disclose the biological origin of the invention.[230] While the disclosure of origin is seen by many countries and scholars as necessary to fully implement the access and benefit sharing rules of the Convention on Biological Diversity,[231] in Central America only Nicaragua requires the disclosure of origin in Article 84 Biodiversity Law (NI) since 2012.[232] However, CAFTA-DR also clarifies that the agreement does not exclude "measures related to the conservation of living or non-living exhaustible natural resources", including the requirement "to transfer a particular technology, a production process, or other proprietary knowledge".[233] This statement can be the basis for balancing the more restrictive provisions with the requirements of establishing a viable system of biodiversity protection. The EU-CARIFORUM-EPA and the EU-CA-AA state that countries shall retain the flexibility to protect genetic resources and traditional knowledge and promote biodiversity protection.[234] However, both agreements do not provide for any specific statutory or institutional measures. Only Costa Rica and Nicaragua have established a statutory (and institutional) framework for the protection of

---

[226] See Sect. 7.6.1.

[227] See Sect. 3.3.9.

[228] See Sect. 6.1.2.3.

[229] See Sect. 3.3.1.

[230] See Sect. 3.1.6.2.

[231] *WTO* General Council, Trade Negotiations Committee, Council for Trade-Related Aspects of Intellectual Property Rights (2006); see Sect. 3.1.6.2.

[232] See Sect. 6.1.6.2.

[233] Articles 10.9(3)(c)(iii) and 10.9(1)(f) CAFTA-DR.

[234] See Sect. 6.1.3.

biodiversity, while all other countries refer to biodiversity only in very general terms in their environmental legislation. Both CAFTA-DR and the EU-FTAs to some extent consider the protection of biological diversity, as has been suggested as a way to balance TRIPS-plus requirements.[235] However, the evidence from Central America clearly shows that the respective clauses had no practical impact. Specific systems for protecting biodiversity have been created only in Costa Rica and Nicaragua, but the system in Costa Rica was established long before CAFTA-DR and the system in Nicaragua long thereafter, in 2012, with no visible connection to the EU-CA-AA concluded around the same time. In all other countries, no corresponding activities were generated following the ratification of the EU-FTAs. This raises the question whether instead of simply creating a contractual possibility to protect biodiversity, the FTAs should have provided for mandatory rules, for example, "maximum protection" or "ceilings" for patent protection by requiring the disclosure of origin or establishing an ABS system, to support the development of the respective systems in these countries.[236] However, the restrictive and, therefore, flexible approach is probably advantageous in this case. As the example of Costa Rica has shown, the development of a functioning system on the national level is complex and must take many legal, institutional and practical factors into account. Also, the system of promoting biodiversity and protecting genetic resources and traditional knowledge related to it is still evolving on the international level. Even the well-intentioned establishment of a specific system would restrict the adaptation of a national system to the evolving framework of protection. In addition, El Salvador, Guatemala and Honduras initiated projects with the goal of developing national ABS systems, without being obliged under a bilateral FTA.[237]

8.9 Balancing of Minimum Protection, Flexibilities and Maximum Protection

8.9.1 Minimum Protection

CAFTA-DR establishes additional "minimum protection" for the right holder compared to TRIPS (*i.e.*, TRIPS-plus). The wording of CAFTA-DR is limited to the interests of the right holder even in cases like the publication of court decisions in IP matters, which are also—if not primarily—relevant for the general public.[238] Another example is the judicial review of administrative decisions, which is only required for the *refusal* to register a trademark, i.e., the decision negatively affecting

[235] MPI Principles (2013), Nr. 20, see Sect. 1.6.3.

[236] See Sect. 6.1.6.

[237] See Sect. 6.1.6.

[238] Article 15.1(11) CAFTA-DR.

the right holder.[239] It remains the responsibility of each party to include balancing provisions in the public interest in the national implementation legislation.

The TRIPS-plus protection in CAFTA-DR was justified in part as making the vague TRIPS provisions clearer and more practical.[240] Indeed, several provisions in CAFTA-DR specify provisions contained in TRIPS, *e.g.*, the term of test data protection is set at a minimum of ten years. However, if examined closely, this term is not really a clarification, because no fixed term is set in Article 39(3) TRIPS. Rather, the minimum term of protection is set at ten years by Article 15.10 CAFTA-DR. But even if one would consider TRIPS-plus as (also) "TRIPS-clear", this effect is offset in many cases by the way CAFTA-DR was implemented in Central America. The national legislation implementing TRIPS sometimes was not amended by the legislation implementing CAFTA-DR, the new provisions were simply added to the existing rules. The trademark infringement provisions in Guatemala and the separate CAFTA-DR implementation law in Honduras are maybe the most striking examples.[241]

This minimum protection mechanism creates a number of problems. First, the inclusion of this mechanism in TRIPS and bilateral FTAs has created subsequent layers of *ever-increasing* protection, which is permitted under TRIPS. One example in CAFTA-DR is the obligation to provide information about the defendant and the infringing goods to the right holder in the course of enforcement proceedings.[242] It is optional under Article 57 TRIPS, but mandatory under Article 15.11(22) CAFTA-DR to provide for the statutory basis for courts to order the defendant to provide such information. Regarding non-traditional trademarks,

- under TRIPS neither sound nor scent marks had to be protected,
- under CAFTA-DR sound mark protection is mandatory, while scent mark protection is optional,[243] and
- under the subsequent US-Peru-TPA, also scent mark protection is mandatory.[244]

Second, CAFTA-DR contains several provisions or sections which no longer represent the "state of the art" of IP protection, even from a US perspective, and illustrate the "policy freeze" effect of bilateral FTAs.[245] The *Bipartisan Trade Deal* adopted by the US Congress in May 2007 provides for flexibility of developing country FTA partners of the USA in relation to the protection of test data, to restoring patent terms to compensate for processing delays and "the types of procedures that developing country partners may implement to prevent the marketing of

[239] Article 15.2(6) CAFTA-DR; see Sect. 4.1.4.

[240] See Sect. 1.4.3.

[241] See Sects. 4.1.8 and 2.4.6.

[242] See Sect. 7.6.

[243] Article 15.2(1) CAFTA-DR.

[244] Article 16.2(1) US-Peru-TPA.

[245] On this issue, see Sect. 1.6.3.

patent-infringing products" (*i.e.*, patent linkage).[246] However, the new rules were created after the signature of CAFTA-DR and were not explicitly granted retroactively to the parties of CAFTA-DR or other bilateral FTAs concluded earlier by the USA.[247] Another example, in the field of patent law, is the Doha Declaration. It was included in CAFTA-DR by way of a *Side Letter* and explicitly included in subsequent bilateral FTAs. However, it is not part of the bilateral FTAs concluded by the USA prior to the adoption of the Doha Declaration.[248] A good example in the field of copyright law is digital rights management (DRM). US entertainment companies had argued strongly for rules on DRM, which was subsequently included in great detail in CAFTA-DR. The DRM section in CAFTA-DR was hailed "state-of-the-art" by the USTR in 2005. But by the time CAFTA-DR was ratified by Costa Rica in 2008, business representatives had already publicly questioned the viability of the DRM system.[249] However, the adaptation of IP laws in Central America to new developments is restricted by the minimum requirements imposed by CAFTA-DR and the EU-FTAs (with regard to geographical indications), which could only be altered through the cumbersome process of renegotiation. None of these FTAs contains a change mechanism that would allow for a simplified mechanism to adjust IP requirements.[250]

Third, CAFTA-DR and the national legislation implementing it are partly not aligned with relevant multilateral agreements.[251] For example, it is ambiguous regarding the implementation of the CBD and the creation of a disclosure of origin requirement in the patent examination process.[252] More difficult to resolve is the relationship of the TRIPS-plus rules in CAFTA-DR with the provisions of TRIPS protecting the public interest, namely Article 7 TRIPS. These clauses refer to policy flexibilities in an abstract and general way, while CAFTA-DR provides for specific requirements of IP protection. At what exact point does IP protection become detrimental to social and economic welfare? The answer can only be practically given in the national context. For example, the public health system and the relevance of patented medicines is different in, e.g., Costa Rica and Guatemala.[253]

To address these problems, FTAs could establish a mechanism to incorporate limitations and balances agreed to by the IP-demanding country after the FTA has

---

[246] USTR (2007), p. 3.

[247] See Sect. 3.1.9.1.

[248] See Sect. 3.1.11.2.

[249] The discussion started in February 2007 with the article "Thoughts on Music" by Steve Jobs, available at https://macdailynews.com/2007/02/06/apple_ceo_steve_jobs_posts_rare_open_letter_thoughts_on_music/ (accessed 2 Nov 2024).

[250] This issue is further discussed in Sect. 8.5.

[251] On this issue, see Sect. 1.6.3.

[252] See Sect. 3.1.6.2.

[253] See Sect. 3.1.1.4.

been concluded.[254] This would avoid the situation in Central America, where the USTR demands that the countries implement, for example, the provisions regarding patent term extension, despite the flexibilities introduced with regard to other bilateral FTAs following the Bipartisan Trade Deal.

8.9.2 Flexibilities and Differentiation of the Level of Protection

One solution often suggested to avoid the problems associated with minimum protection is the inclusion of flexibilities in multilateral agreements and bilateral FTAs.

CAFTA-DR contains very few flexibilities, which relate in particular to transition periods,[255] the Doha Declaration[256] and the right of the parties to establish enforcement procedures and remedies in accordance with the foundations of the respective national legal system.[257] However, the increase of the minimum protection in many areas means that flexibilities or optional protection contained in TRIPS are made mandatory by CAFTA-DR. As already mentioned, while neither sound nor scent marks had to be protected under TRIPS, under CAFTA-DR sound mark protection has become mandatory, while scent mark protection is optional.[258] Also, while TRIPS does not make reference to it, Article 15.1.6(b) CAFTA-DR contains a requirement to make *reasonable efforts* to ratify the Hague Agreement Concerning the Registration of Industrial Designs (1999).[259] Interestingly, however, no CAFTA-DR country has ratified it. Article 15.9(2) CAFTA-DR provides that the parties do not have to *introduce* patent protection for animals, but shall *maintain* such

[254]The MPI Principles (2013), Nr. 23, propose that if "a country has agreed to a specific exception or limitation to IP protection or enforcement in a bilateral or regional agreement, it should make this available to any other country with which it has concluded a bilateral or regional agreement, if that other country is at a similar stage of development as the country to which the exception or limitation is granted."

[255]Article 15.1.5(a) CAFTA-DR grants Nicaragua, as the probably least developed country in the region, the longest period for ratifying the UPOV Convention. However, as the provision also grants Costa Rica a longer ratification period than the other countries, even though it is probably the most developed country in the region, it is unclear if this clause can be seen as a flexibility based on the level of development.

[256]See Sect. 3.1.11.2.

[257]Article 15.11.1(b) CAFTA-DR.

[258]Article 15.2(1) CAFTA-DR; by comparison, under the US-Peru-TPA, scent mark protection has also become mandatory (16.2(1) US-Peru-TPA).

[259]The ratification was also optional in the earlier US-Peru-TPA and Colombia-TPA (Article 16.1 (4)(b) US-Peru-TPA, Article 16.1(4)(b) Colombia-TPA); the Geneva Revision of 1999 of the Hague Agreement has been ratified by only 21 countries as of 2008. By 2016, this number has increased to 51 members and by 2024 to 73 members, see https://www.wipo.int/export/sites/www/treaties/en/docs/pdf/hague.pdf (accessed 2 Nov 2024).

protection if it already exists. While this clause affords some level of policy flexibility to Central American countries to maintain existing exemptions to patentability, it also perpetuates differences in the local patent laws, restricts the possibility to harmonize Central American IP laws and acts as other minimum protection clauses by "casting in stone" protection and restricting policy changes. CAFTA-DR also introduced mandatory protection in areas that were explicitly optional under TRIPS.[260] In comparison, the EU-FTAs are generally more "flexible" than CAFTA-DR and include references to the Doha Declaration and Article 8 TRIPS. Similarly, the EU-FTAs make reference to the flexible application of IP rules. Namely, Article 139(2) EU-CARIFORUM-EPA states that the enforcement of IP rights should provide a balance of rights and obligations between right holders and users and allow the parties to protect public health and promote access to medicines.[261] The EU-FTAs also reflect the need to differentiate the level of IP protection based on the level of technological and economic development of the respective country. Article 228(a) EU-CA-AA explicitly provides that the parties shall "ensure an adequate and effective protection of IP rights in the territories of the Parties, taking into consideration the economic situation and the social or cultural need of each Party".[262] However, the EU-FTAs in some cases also reduce the flexibility remaining under TRIPS. While Article 16(3) TRIPS requires protection of a well-known mark in case of related goods and services only if the well-known mark is registered, Article 240 EU-CA-AA states that the EU-CA-AA parties "may" extend the protection to unregistered well-known marks, which opened the possibility of including such protection in the national legislation during implementation.[263]

Differentiation in the level of IP protection is particularly appropriate for Central America.[264] Considering the technology gap and the level of technological development of the local industries, generally a lower level of IP protection seems justified. Higher levels of IP protection might not be feasible for the current development level in some countries, *e.g.*, Nicaragua, but more so for Costa Rica. Less developed countries like Nicaragua might focus more on an IP framework facilitating the absorption of simpler foreign technology, while countries with an established technology base like Costa Rica could benefit from stronger protection by encouraging both the transfer of technology through patent and know-how license agreements and domestic research. These examples also demonstrate that the optimal level of IP protection in a country may, therefore, change over time. As the countries develop further, the levels of protection can be adapted and, if

[260] For example, the optional inclusion of pre-established damages under Article 45(2) TRIPS is required under Article 15.11(8) CAFTA-DR; similarly, the optional right of information against an infringer under Article 47 TRIPS is obligatory under Article 15.11(12) CAFTA-DR.

[261] This issue is discussed in more detail in Sect. 2.3.4.2.

[262] See Sect. 2.3.4.1.

[263] In this particular case, such implementation did not occur in Central America, because the implementation legislation was limited to the requirements relating to geographical indications.

[264] Roffe (2013), p. 937.

appropriate, increased, as envisioned by Article 131.2 EU-CARIFORUM-EPA. This approach further highlights the need for flexible IP rules.

While flexible and differentiated rules can help balance the "minimum protection" approach, the experience in Central America also illustrates certain practical shortcomings associated with this approach. As the example of CAFTA-DR shows, even mandatory provisions are implemented in Central America in different ways, but the approach in the region regarding the implementation of flexibilities is even more divergent, as shown for example in relation to the optional protection of scent marks.[265] Another risk is that the flexibilities in international agreements are not used effectively by developing countries. If international agreements provide for limitations or utilize vague terms, these flexibilities leave policy space for the national legislator.[266] However, based on the example of the implementation of CAFTA-DR in Central America, the concern that flexibilities are not utilized is justified, at least within the framework of the implementation of a bilateral FTA. While not explicitly stated, CAFTA-DR left considerable policy space to the national legislator in several areas, because these areas were not regulated by CAFTA-DR. However, this space was used only in few cases. Nevertheless, there are a few examples where countries have implemented statutory or practical limitations to IP rights to offset the effects of the CAFTA-DR statutory reforms that almost exclusively strengthen the position of the right holder. The maximum limitations of the patent term extension created in Central American legislation, which deviates from CAFTA-DR requirements, is one of the few cases in which balancing provisions were included in the implementation laws which did not have some basis in explicitly stated flexible TRIPS or CAFTA-DR flexibilities or prior national laws. Only Costa Rica implemented balancing provisions more broadly. In addition to the limitations of the patent term extension, for example, patent infringements were de-criminalized to offset the increase in the scope of patent (and related) protection.

In addition, explicitly permitted, but not mandatory, limitations were sometimes not implemented. Even though Article 15.1(15) CAFTA-DR gave the possibility to adopt "measures necessary to prevent anticompetitive practices", no Central American country introduced legislation enabling the administration to adopt such measures. Similarly, Article 131 EU-CARIFORUM-EPA, referring to "increasing levels of protection *appropriate* to their levels of development", has been identified as a positive example of balancing a county's level of development and the scope of IP protection.[267] However, this clause has also not resulted in any specific legislative or

[265] See Sect. 4.1.2.7.

[266] According to Appellate Body case-law, countries have some flexibility in interpreting their TRIPS obligations, see, in relation to enforcement obligations, WTO Dispute Settlement Body, Panel Report, China—Measures Affecting the Protection and Enforcement of Intellectual Property Rights, Decision of 26 January 2009, WT/DS362/R; on this decision Wallot (2016), p. 215.

[267] Roffe (2013), p. 937.

other policy measures in Central America. Finally, biodiversity provisions in the EU-FTAs had no impact in Central America.[268]

This behavior may have been caused by a lack of the time and expertise needed to draft balanced legislation.[269] If this is correct, then international agreements will only contribute to a meaningful improvement of national competition legislation if they provide more specific guidance. However, considerable divergence also exists between developed jurisdictions as to the most appropriate balancing rules.[270] Therefore, it may be difficult to agree on suitable specific guidance. From this point of view, the approach of Article 15.1(15) CAFTA-DR regarding competition policy, stating that "[n]othing in this Chapter shall be construed to prevent a Party from adopting measures necessary to prevent anticompetitive practices that may result from the abuse of the intellectual property rights", seems pragmatic. The implementation of CAFTA-DR in Central America also shows the potential for abuse created by flexibilities. The relative level of IP protection is not always reflective of the relative level of development. For example, Costa Rica made broader use of statutory flexibilities remaining under CAFTA-DR and, practically, reduced the level of IP protection, by granting patents more restrictively, than other Central American countries with a lower level of development.[271]

These risks illustrate that flexibilities are not always the superior tool for IP regulation. A careful evaluation is necessary whether using a flexibility is the best approach and if so, which type of flexibility is best suited. In case of public policy issues which are strongly affected by specific development circumstances of each country, a specific provision or limitation could practically restrict national policy options and the inclusion of flexible references to broadly defined public interests, such as "health" or "technology transfer" might be an appropriate approach.[272] However, in this case one must consider the drafting problems developing countries may experience during the implementation of such clauses and the protection of such clauses against limitation by more specific minimum protection in subsequent agreements. In addition to simply making reference to public policy objectives, such a clause could identify examples of specific minimum protection provisions that can legitimately be limited based on such exception. In this regard, the explicit reference to, *e.g.*, patent term extension in the *Bipartisan Trade Deal* of 2007, provides an instructive example.[273] Alternatively, the issue could be left entirely to

---

[268] See Sect. 2.3.4.2.

[269] Implementation requires time, see Finger (2000), p. 426. However, under CAFTA-DR, the trade deal structure created political and economic pressure that was not conducive to a deliberate policy debate.

[270] Drexl (2007), p. 21.

[271] See Sect. 3.1.7.

[272] Regarding Articles 7 and 8 TRIPS see, for example, Article 131 EU-CARIFORUM-EPA.

[273] The Bipartisan Trade Deal does not mandate the inclusion of specific wording in an FTA, but only requires that the substantive considerations are reflected in an FTA. However, the drafting approach could also be used for the wording of an FTA as such.

the national legislature, because explicit flexibilities can lead to subsequent mandatory "clarifications" in bilateral FTAs or national legislation.

If an international consensus has emerged or there is a risk that a flexible rule may not be implemented or circumvented by bilateral FTAs, a mandatory limitation may be more effective. As the implementation of CAFTA-DR and the EU-FTAs has shown, optional flexibilities are often not utilized during an implementation process, while mandatory requirements (both minimum protection and limitations) are routinely included in reform legislation.

8.9.3 Maximum Protection (Ceilings) and Limitations Outside IP Law

CAFTA-DR is not designed as a "model law" broadly regulating the field of IP law, but focuses on minimum protection in areas relevant to the USA. Similarly, the EU-CA-AA focuses particularly on the protection of geographical indications relevant to the EU. In CAFTA-DR, the focus on strengthening the position of the right holder becomes even more visible if we consider the notable absence of limitations. The agreement provides not only for few limitations, but also restricts the possibility to introduce limitations. For example, exceptions to the rights conferred by a trademark must be (a) limited and (b) take account of the legitimate interest of the owner of the trademark and of third parties.[274] There are only few provisions in CAFTA-DR that can be considered limitations of IP protection. These "true" limitations mostly relate to geographical indications, which are limited to protect US-American trademarks against European geographical indications, and cannot be considered limitations aimed at balancing IP protection.

Some clauses in the enforcement section of CAFTA-DR seem to protect the defendant in enforcement proceedings, *i.e.*, the infringer of the IP right. Since CAFTA-DR aims at reforming the Central American IP system, the typical infringer will be a national of these countries. However, these provisions cannot be considered evidence for an attempt to balance the legal position of these persons against the rights of the typically US-American right holders. The restrictive wording of these "mandatory limitations" rather serves to restrict the limitations to the wording in CAFTA-DR and practically establishes "maximum limitations".[275] Moreover, these

[274] Article 15.2(4) CAFTA-DR.

[275] For example, Article 15.2(4) CAFTA-DR provides that "(e)ach Party may provide limited exceptions to the rights conferred by a trademark, such as fair use of descriptive terms (…)". The term "such as" clarifies that other exceptions could be introduced as well. However, by slightly modifying the wording to read "(e)ach Party may provide limited exceptions to the rights conferred by a trademark to permit the fair use of descriptive terms […]", this would exclude limitations for other purposes. As the implementation of CAFTA-DR Central America has shown, there is, for various reasons, a tendency to implement FTA provisions literally. Accordingly, there is a material risk that an open list of limitation examples becomes during the implementation process a closed list

provisions protecting the defendant reflect international legal standards, not an attempt to include particular balances in the IP chapter.

In addition, the example of the implementation of CAFTA-DR and the EU-FTAs in Central America shows that FTA obligations are often implemented like model laws, "as is", without additional balancing provisions, even when these are permitted. Optional flexibilities are often not implemented. Maximum protection clauses could, therefore, have facilitated the implementation of these bilateral FTAs in Central America. As a caveat it must be noted, however, that the Central American experience also shows that this approach does not always work. El Salvador and Guatemala protect unregistered designs against "products that reproduce the same general impression"[276] and "*similar* reproductions",[277] even though Article 252.3 EU-CA-AA establishes maximum protection by requiring that unregistered designs be protected only against *copying* of the design.

Generally, however, the USA and EU had no incentive to include such provisions and the Central American countries do not have the necessary bargaining position in trade deal negotiations to achieve such a goal, as evidence by the failed attempt to exclude geographical indications from the negotiations of the EU-CA-AA.[278] Therefore, the forum for creating maximum protection clauses should be the multilateral level. The Doha Declaration and the CBD are examples for successful developments regarding IP rights on the multilateral level.[279]

Considering the difficulties in including maximum protection of IP rights in bilateral or multilateral agreements, countries seeking to balance their IP system should also take limitations outside IP law into account. Competition law in particular can help mitigate the anti-competitive effect high levels of IP protection created by TRIPS-plus rules could have.[280] The protection of especially large companies from developed countries inhibits the emerging local competition in developing countries.[281] This is especially true for CAFTA-DR, where the strengthening of IP protection applies retroactively.[282] Procurement law is an area of law that receives much less attention as a countermeasure in the TRIPS-plus debate, but is practically very useful for balancing the strong exclusive position created by TRIPS-plus type IP laws.[283] In Central America, two instructive examples are the procurement principles for medicines used by the CCSS (CR) in Costa Rica, which limits the

of enumerated limitations. Even without this effect, mandatory limitations limit the policy space for the national legislator, who can no longer design the IP system according to its specific needs, which may include not providing for certain limitations.

[276]Article 128(1) IP Law (SV).

[277]Article 154 IP Law (GT).

[278]See Sect. 4.4.

[279]On the Doha Declaration, see Sect. 3.1.1.4, on the CBD, see Sect. 6.1.2.

[280]On this issue see Drexl (2006–2007), p. 534.

[281]Light (2007), pp. 232–245.

[282]Article 15.1(11) CAFTA-DR, see Sect. 2.2.4.4.

[283]See Sect. 3.1.1.4.

budgetary effect of patented drugs,[284] and the purchase of corn seeds by the Salvadoran government, which was challenged by the US government on behalf of Monsanto under procurement rules of CAFTA-DR.[285]

8.9.4 Transition Periods

CAFTA-DR and the EU-FTAs include transition periods for specific countries, in case of CAFTA-DR with different periods for different countries. For example, in relation to Nicaragua, Article 15.12(2) CAFTA-DR provides for relatively short transition periods in relation to specific obligations of one, one and half, two, three and four years.[286] By contrast, Article 131(2) EU-CARIFORUM-EPA refers to "increasing levels of protection appropriate to [the] levels of development". Procedurally, the CARIFORUM-EC Trade and Development Committee has the possibility to modify the deadline for implementing the EU-CARIFORUM-EPA requirements, "taking into account the development priorities and levels of development".[287] Transition periods have been suggested as an important element in bilateral FTAs to enable developing countries to balance the effect of TRIPS-plus requirements.[288] However, the effect of transition periods in Central America reveals two significant problems with this approach. First, in the case of CAFTA-DR, the utilization of transition periods would require the respective country to pass several implementation laws in (from a legislative perspective) short succession and thereby significantly increase the burden on administrative and human resources. Second, the transition periods in CAFTA-DR are granted for a predetermined length of time and are not adjustable if the legal, institutional or social conditions in the respective country, which originally had been the reason for not immediately imposing the deferred obligation, continue. Therefore, transitional periods should not be used as a policy tool in IP agreements as a compromise for controversial IP provisions. Before using transitional periods, the following questions should be clarified:

- If the respective obligation does not have be implemented immediately, should it be required at all?
- Will the circumstances underlying the transition period have changed by the end of the period?
- Are any specific measures required in relation to these circumstances, *e.g.*, technical or financial assistance to the country concerned?

---

[284] See Sect. 3.1.1.4.

[285] See Sect. 3.3.10.

[286] In addition, it may also increase the political costs, as for each reform law a legislative majority must be organized.

[287] Article 139(4) EU- CARIFORUM-EPA.

[288] MPI Principles (2013), Nr. 22, see Sect. 1.6.3.4.

If the respective obligation depends on higher levels of development in the broad sense, a flexible obligation may be more appropriate than fixed transition periods. In this regard, the mechanism established by the EU-CARIFORUM-EPA seems practical.

8.10 Conclusion

As one local practitioner put it, Central American IP law is "under construction".[289] The implementation of international trade agreements resulted in three waives of major legislative changes, around 2000 (TRIPS), 2006 (CAFTA-DR) and 2013 (EU-CARIFORUM-EPA and EU-CA-AA). As legislative reforms take many years to be practically implemented, it is estimated that the effects of the changes will only become clear over time.[290] Nevertheless, more than ten years after the implementation of the IP requirements of CAFTA-DR and more than five years after the implementation of the EU-CARIFORUM-EPA and the EU-CA-AA, there is enough empirical material to evaluate these bilateral FTAs and their effects on the Central American IP system and recommend policy alternatives.

8.10.1 Shortcomings of the TRIPS-Plus Approach in Bilateral FTAs

The analysis of these agreements and their implementation in Central America confirmed some of the critical observations made with regard to TRIPS-plus rules in bilateral FTAs. Procedurally, the negotiation of CAFTA-DR, the EU-CARIFORUM-EPA and the EU-CA-AA showed the superior bargaining power of developed countries and the pressure created by the inclusion of IP provisions in a *trade deal*. This limits the possibility of the partner countries and their stakeholders to participate in the negotiation or the implementation in a meaningful way.[291] Substantively, CAFTA-DR, and to a lesser extent the EU-CARIFORUM-EPA and the EU-CA-AA, require the implementation of a number of TRIPS-plus provisions which are not aligned with the specific policy needs of developing countries, *e.g.*, test data protection, and reduce policy space on the national level by requiring the allocation of resources to certain types of protection, *e.g.*, non-traditional trade-marks, irrespective of whether such protection is suitable in Central America.[292] The provisions of CAFTA-DR, compared to earlier US-FTAs, show the trend of

[289] Interview with *Néstor Morera.*

[290] Interview with *Ricardo Bendaña.*

[291] See Sects. 8.1 and 8.3.

[292] See Sect. 8.8.3.

ever-increasing protection established by bilateral FTAs.[293] The EU-CA-AA and the EU-CARIFORUM-EPA resulted in less TRIPS-plus rules being implemented in Central America. However, this is partly due to the fact that certain rules had already been implemented previously in the CAFTA-DR implementation legislation and in the case of the EU-CA-AA, the stronger focus on practical, not statutory implementation in relation to the mandatory registration of Established Geographical Indications. The Central American countries were left with the difficult task of balancing the protection of geographical indications as required by the EU-FTAs with the trademark requirements under CAFTA-DR.[294] The minimum protection structure and lack of review and change procedures in all of these bilateral FTAs also inhibits the adaptation of national legislation to changing policy needs, even if an international consensus has emerged, as exemplified by the ongoing political pressure to comply with patent term extension requirements of CAFTA-DR despite the more flexible approach mandated by the US Congress in the *Bipartisan Trade Deal*.[295]

However, the analysis also revealed some additional issues regarding the effects of bilateral FTAs that so far have not been sufficiently considered in the TRIPS-plus debate. Most importantly, many contributions do not take into account that *institutional challenges and socio-political and fiscal constraints* in developing countries significantly reduce the practical effect of statutory TRIPS-plus obligations mandated by bilateral FTAs. The effectiveness of the Central American IP system often suffers not from insufficient legislation, but, *e.g.*, the lack of specialized and independent IP institutions or the education of relevant stakeholders regarding IP. In other words, despite the statutory over-protection in some areas created by bilateral FTAs, in Central America practical under-protection is still commonplace.[296] The focus on statutory protection in bilateral FTAs enables developing countries to avoid overprotection of IP in practice without risking non-compliance with the respective agreements and, as a consequence, the trade benefits they offer. The implementation activities also show that, to a varying degree, the Central American countries carefully introduced measures on the statutory and especially the institutional level to balance the increased protection. To phrase it differently, while the interests necessary to balance the IP system "are not, or not sufficiently, taken into account in international trade negotiations",[297] they clearly balance the institutional IP system on the national level, once the statutory implementation has been completed and the trade benefits have been "locked in". This is particularly visible with regard to patent protection, which affected public policy concerns in the region most strongly. While CAFTA-DR mandates a very high level of protection, including patent term extension, patent linkage and test data protection, which were mostly implemented on the statutory level, some Central American countries reduced the

[293] See Sect. 8.9.1.

[294] See Sect. 4.4.6.

[295] See Sects. 8.9.1 and 8.9.2.

[296] See Sect.8.6.

[297] Drexl (2016), p. 62.

practical impact, *e.g.*, by simply not granting term extensions on the administrative level and keeping the number of granted patents low.[298] Interestingly, these measures, which are in some cases clear violations of CAFTA-DR, did not result in any sanctions from the USA. However, while the practical effects are limited, implementing a higher level of statutory IP protection still absorbs substantial resources, without providing significant benefits even to the right holders. IP Registers, for example, must allocate financial and human resources to create the technical infrastructure for the protection of sound (and in some countries scent) marks and receive training on plant variety protection under the UPOV Convention. Using the available resources for the creation of easily accessible, user-friendly electronic databases for patents and trademarks and the reduction of the backlog of patent applications in some countries may be better for right holders and other users of the Central American IP system.[299] The institutional challenges in Central America suggest that an effective IP reform should, therefore, focus more on the practical improvement of the IP system. One way to achieve this is by providing training options, preferably by neutral, *e.g.*, international organizations.

Also, these bilateral FTAs, in combination with TRIPS, had a strong negative effect on the *coherence and harmonization of the IP system* in Central America. While in particular trademark law was regionally harmonized by the Central American Convention (Trademarks) prior to TRIPS, harmonization efforts in the field of IP were suspended following TRIPS and replaced by national laws in the late 1990ies. The different approaches to implementing the varying layers of statutory requirements under CAFTA-DR and the EU-FTAs in each country increased the differences of the IP legislation in structure and content, an effect not balanced in a meaningful way by the partially identical literal implementation of certain specific clauses.[300] While Article 141 EU-CARIFORUM-EPA contains abstract commitments to foster regional harmonization and integration, few if any specific support measures for harmonization have resulted from it. One practically relevant harmonization measure in Central America, the regional Patent Examiner Manual, was developed independently from the reforms following the bilateral FTAs.[301] This fracturing of regional IP law diminishes the level statutory playing field and has the potential to distort competition. In addition, it complicates the regional, cross-border approach of the legal community which is traditional in Central America.

[298] See Sects. 8.8.1 and 8.8.2.

[299] See Sect. 8.7.2.

[300] See Sect. 8.4.2.

[301] See Sect. 2.5.2.3.

8.10.2 A New Approach for Bilateral FTAs

Overall, this study shows that bilateral FTAs in their current form are not a useful tool for shaping the IP system in developing countries, neither from a right holder nor from a user perspective. The TRIPS-plus provisions could create overprotection, if they would be effectively applied in practice, while the statutory focus fails to address the institutional and practical challenges underlying the IP systems in these countries. The experience in Central America suggests that the approach with regard to the use of bilateral (or regional) FTAs to change IP policy should be modified. The process of concluding and implementing new FTAs between the USA and the EU on the one hand and developing countries on the other hand is still ongoing. In May 2016 the EU and Mexico started negotiations for a new (or "modernized") FTA. In addition, the USA has been negotiating the Trans-Pacific Partnership (TPP) with several Asian and Latin American countries and the USA and the EU are conducting negotiations on the Transatlantic Trade and Investment Partnership (TTIP) since 2013.[302] However, if more bilateral FTAs are concluded in the future, they should use the possibility of the bilateral setting to address protection and enforcement issues specifically in relation to the respective countries instead of relying on a standard set of TRIPS-plus requirements. This could mean, for example, if the country so far has barely granted pharmaceutical patents, removing patent linkage clauses and focusing instead on support activities to reduce the backlog of patent applications, or identifying the necessary measures to establish a publicly available database of trademarks rather than requiring the registration of scent marks.[303] During the drafting and negotiation process, the parties should also consider that FTAs are designed as contracts and focus on rights which are of special interest to one party, and not on complementary provisions to balance such rights, but that FTAs are mostly implemented as "model laws" and, therefore, should be drafted in a more balanced way.[304] To address this issue, these TRIPS-plus rules could be complemented and balanced by mandatory limitations and flexible provisions. However, the implementation of the bilateral FTAs in Central America revealed several drafting and policy problems relating to the use of flexibilities and maximum protection ("ceilings") in multilateral and bilateral agreements. Both flexibilities and ceilings require careful consideration in the drafting and implementation phase, to avoid the risk that such provisions are not effectively utilized or become the basis for future increases in minimum protection or mandatory restrictions of flexibilities, as exemplified by several CAFTA-DR provisions.[305] In addition, the "minimum protection" legal framework of TRIPS and other international IP agreements make it unlikely that ceilings will be widely accepted.[306]

[302] See the information on these agreements available at http://trade.gov/fta/ (accessed 2 Nov 2024).

[303] See Sect. 8.7.2.

[304] See Sect. 8.9.3.

[305] See Sect. 8.9.2.

[306] Drexl (2016), p. 61.

Bilateral FTAs face legitimacy problems because of the asymmetrical negotiating power of the trade partners. The widespread perception in Central America that CAFTA-DR was imposed by the USA and not negotiated further undermines the relatively low support both from local authorities and the public at large, which is felt most strongly in the weak enforcement of IP rights in practice.[307] The participation and inclusion of the various stakeholders in the negotiation of IP rules in an FTA will practically not be meaningful, if these rules are based a standard set of IP rules developed by the USA (or similarly the EU), because this will invariably predetermine the outcome of the negotiations. Also from this perspective, therefore, the IP-demanding parties should be open to discussing specific issues introduced by the FTA partner countries.

8.10.3 A Return to Multilateral Solutions

The USA and the EU still focus on bilateral or regional FTAs, such as TPP and TTIP. However, they should consider making more and better use of the multilateral approach to develop the global IP framework. The skepticism of "IP-demanding" countries is largely due to the fact that it has been difficult to reach an international consensus on a high level of IP protection. However, at least in Central America, the use of bilateral FTAs has not resulted in a significantly higher level of IP protection in practice. The analysis of the IP systems in Central America suggests that countries will find a way to adjust the practical level of IP protection to their policy needs, irrespective of the statutory level of protection required by international agreements. A return to the multilateral "arena", therefore, would not necessarily reduce the level of IP protection, but could lead to the development of more sustainable global and national IP systems, not least because multilateral negotiations could balance the bargaining power of the developed countries with the bargaining power of large developing countries and be more participatory and transparent than bilateral FTAs and, therefore, could lead to more legitimacy and acceptance of the negotiation outcome.[308]

Substantively, patent-related protection, *e.g.*, patent term extension, patent linkage and test data protection, and the balance between the protection of trademarks and geographical indications should be addressed on the international level, to relieve individual countries from the pressure to develop a solution which complies with (sometimes conflicting) requirements from IP-demanding countries, but takes into account local policy priorities.

[307] See, e.g., Sects. 8.7.5 and 8.8.4.

[308] See Sect. 8.3.

8.10.4 More Focus on Institutional and Practical Improvements

Unless there is a compelling need for international regulation to create clarification and balance, generally a more "passive" approach to international IP rule-making should be considered. It seems unlikely that the call for a moratorium on bilateral agreements[309] will be successful. However, given the limited practical effectiveness of the constant increase in statutory protection, the significant implementation costs and the impact on the public perception of the IP system in general, it seems preferable to identify specific, particularly institutional issues on a country-by-country or regional basis, involving all relevant stakeholders, and openly discuss if and how the respective challenges could be addressed. In Central America, for instance, this could mean support for further regional collaboration in patent examination or help with setting up the necessary infrastructure for electronic patent and trademark applications and databases of IP rights.

An intesting example in this regard is the validation agreement negotiated between Costa Rica and the EPO in 2023 that would enable applicants to validate patents examined by the EPO also in Costa Rica without additional examination, could facilitate patent prosecution significantly.[310]

In short, in order to improve the IP system, it may be more effective to reduce legislative activity on the international and national level, regarding both increases and limitations of IP protection, and focus more on specific institutional and practical measures. Less may be more.

References

Böttger F (2008a) Zwangslizenzen im Patentrecht - Eine systematische Bewertung der neueren Praxis insbesondere im Bereich der öffentlichen Gesundheit. GRUR Int 2008:881–891

Böttger F (2008b) Internationales – Andengemeinschaft genehmigt Umsetzung des Freihandelsabkommens zwischen Peru und den USA. GRUR Int 2008:974

Díaz Á (2006) TLC y propiedad intelectual: Desafíos de Política Pública - en 9 países de América Latina y el Caribe, preliminary and unedited version, https://repositorio.cepal.org/server/api/core/bitstreams/44194f7d-0b13-41f0-be93-3553029996f6/content. Accessed 2 Nov 2024

Drexl J (2006–2007) IP in Bilateral Trade Agreements. Some ideas on how they promote market power and distort international competition. In: Ghidini G, Genovesi LM (eds) Intellectual Property and Market Power, ATRIP Papers 2006–2007. Universidad de Buenos Aires, Buenos Aires

Drexl J (2007) Responding to the challenges with a competition-oriented approach. In: Barton JH, Abbott FM, Correa CM, Drexl J, Foray D, Marchant R (eds) Views on the future of the intellectual property system, International Centre for Trade and Sustainable Development. Geneva, Switzerland

[309] Drexl (2007), p. 21.

[310] See Sect. 2.5.3.

Drexl J (2018) In: Beck CH (ed) Internationales Immaterialgüterrecht, Münchener Kommentar zum BGB, vol 12, 7th edn, Munich

Drexl J (2016) The concept of trade-relatedness of intellectual property rights in times of post-TRIPS bilateralism. In: Ullrich H, Hilty RM, Lamping M, Drexl J (eds) TRIPS plus 20: from trade rules to market principles. Springer-Verlag, Berlin Heidelberg

European Commission (2015) Annual Report on the Implementation of Part IV of the EU-Central America Association Agreement, COM(2015) 131 final, 18 March 2015. Available at https://eur-lex.europa.eu/legal-content/EN/TXT/PDF/?uri=CELEX:52015DC0131. Accessed 2 Nov 2024

Finger JM (2000) The WTO's special burden on less developed countries. Cato J 19(3):425–437. Available at https://www.cato.org/sites/cato.org/files/serials/files/cato-journal/2000/1/cj19n3-9.pdf. Accessed 2 Nov 2024

Grosse Ruse-Khan H, Drexl J, Hilty RM, Kur A, Bakhoum M, Jaeger T et al (2013) Principles for intellectual property provisions in bilateral and regional agreements. IIC 2013, 878–883 (cited as MPI Principles (2013))

Light DW (2007) Globalizing restricted and segmented markets: challenges to theory and values in economic sociology. Ann Am Acad Polit Soc Sci 610(1):232–245

Mackey TK, Liang BA, Kubic T (2015) Counterfeit drug penetration into global legitimate medicine supply chains: a global assessment. Am J Trop Med Hyg 92:59–67. Available at https://pmc.ncbi.nlm.nih.gov/articles/PMC4455087/pdf/tropmed-92-59.pdf. Accessed 2 Nov 2024

Montero Sequeira A (2003) Propiedad intelectual: espina del Cafta, El Financiero, 24 March 2003 (on file with the author).

PhRMA, Special 301 Submission 2007 (on file with the author)

PhRMA, Special 301 Submission 2014 (on file with the author)

Registro de la Propiedad Intelectual de Nicaragua (2006) Situación Actual de la Propiedad Industrial en Nicaragua, OMPI/JPI/BUE/06/2 NI. Available at http://www.wipo.int/edocs/mdocs/lac/es/ompi_jpi_bue_06/ompi_jpi_bue_06_2_ni.doc. Accessed 2 Nov 2024

Roffe P (2013) Free Trade Agreements and the Americas. IIC 2013:932–943

Singh RH et al (2014) Monitoring the Implementation & Results of the CARIFORUM – EU EPA Agreement, Final Report, September 2014

Stiglitz J (2006) Making globalization work. Norton, New York

Thomas K (2009) Structural adjustment, spatial imaginaries, and "Piracy" in Guatemala's apparel industry. Anthropol Work Rev 30(1):1–10

Thomas K (2011) An Ethnography of Brand Piracy in Guatemala, Doctoral dissertation. Harvard University

USTR (2007) Bipartisan Agreement on Trade Policy, May 2007. Available at https://ustr.gov/sites/default/files/uploads/factsheets/2007/asset_upload_file127_11319.pdf. Accessed 2 Nov 2024

USTR, Special 301 Report 2011. Available at https://ustr.gov/sites/default/files/uploads/gsp/speeches/reports/2011/301/2011%20Special%20301%20Report.pdf. Accessed 2 Nov 2024 (cited as USTR, Special 301 Report 2011)

USTR, Special 301 Report 2016. Available at https://ustr.gov/sites/default/files/USTR-2016-Special-301-Report.pdf. Accessed 2 Nov 2024 (cited as USTR, Special 301 Report 2016)

USTR, Special 301 Report 2017. Available at https://ustr.gov/sites/default/files/301/2017%20Special%20301%20Report%20FINAL.PDF. Accessed 2 Nov 2024 (cited as USTR, Special 301 Report 2017)

Wallot M (2016) The proportionality principle in the TRIPS Agreement. In: Ullrich H, Hilty RM, Lamping M, Drexl J (eds) TRIPS Plus 20: from trade rules to market principles. Springer-Verlag, Berlin

WHO (2018) Fact Sheet SSFFC Medicines. Available at https://www.who.int/en/news-room/fact-sheets/detail/substandard-and-falsified-medical-products. Accessed 2 Nov 2024

WTO, Council for Trade-Related Aspects of Intellectual Property Rights (2011) Technical Cooperation Activities: Information from Members, European Union, IP/C/W/550/Add.7, 1 June

2011, Available at https://docs.wto.org/dol2fe/Pages/SS/directdoc.aspx?filename=Q:/IP/C/W550A7.pdf. Accessed 2 Nov 2024

WTO General Council, Trade Negotiations Committee, Council for Trade-Related Aspects of Intellectual Property Rights (2006) Communication from Brazil, China, Colombia, Cuba, India, Pakistan, Peru, Thailand and Tanzania, Doha Working Programme - The Outstanding Implementation Issue on the Relationship between the TRIPS Agreement and the Convention on Biological Diversity, *WT/GC/W/564/*Rev. 2, TN/C/W/41/Rev. 2, IP/C/W/474, 5 July 2006, Available at https://docs.wto.org/dol2fe/Pages/SS/directdoc.aspx?filename=Q:/IP/C/W474.pdf&Open=True. Accessed 2 Nov 2024

Table of Legislation

Multilateral Intellectual Property Agreements

F. Böttger, *CAFTA-DR, European Free Trade Agreements and the Industrial Property System in Central America*, Munich Studies on Innovation and Competition 21, https://doi.org/10.1007/978-3-031-93440-7

Title	Adoption (and revisions)	CAFTA-DR countries	Signature	Ratification/accession	Entry into force
Beijing Treaty on Audiovisual Performances (Beijing Treaty)	24 June 2012 (Beijing)	Costa Rica	26 June 2012	13 November 2020	13 February 2021
		Dominican Republic	n/a	5 June 2018	28 April 2020
		El Salvador	7 November 2012	10 October 2016	28 April 2020
		Guatemala	27 May 2013	No	No
		Honduras	4 October 2012	No	No
		Nicaragua	26 June 2012	No	No
		USA	26 June 2012	No	No
Berne Convention for the Protection of Literary and Artistic Works (Berne Convention)	9 September 1886 (Berne) Revisions: 4 May 1896 (Paris), 13 November 1908 (Berlin), 20 March 1914 (Berne), 2 June 1928 (Rome), 26 June 1948 (Brussels), 14 July 1967 (Stockholm), 24 July 1971 (Paris), 28 September 1979	Costa Rica	n/a	3 March 1978	10 June 1978
		Dominican Republic	n/a	24 September 1997	24 December 1997
		El Salvador	n/a	18 November 1993	19 February 1994
		Guatemala	n/a	28 April 1997	28 July 1997
		Honduras	n/a	24 October 1989	25 January 1990
		Nicaragua	n/a	23 May 2000	23 August 2000
		USA	n/a	16 November 1988	1 March 1989

Brussels Convention Relating to the Distribution of Programme-Carrying Signals Transmitted by Satellite (Brussels Convention)	21 May 1974 (Brussels)	Costa Rica	n/a	March 25, 1999	25 June 1999
		Dominican Republic	n/a	No	No
		El Salvador	n/a	April 22, 2008	22 July 2008
		Guatemala	n/a	No	No
		Honduras	n/a	January 7, 2008	7 April 2008
		Nicaragua	n/a	December 1, 1975	25 August 1979
		USA	May 21, 1974	December 7, 1984	7 March 1985
Budapest Treaty on the International Recognition of the Deposit of Micro-organisms for the Purposes of Patent Procedure (Budapest Treaty)	28 April 1977 (Budapest) Revisions: 26 September 1980	Costa Rica	n/a	30 June 2008	30 September 2008
		Dominican Republic	n/a	3 April 2007	3 July 2007
		El Salvador	n/a	17 May 2006	17 August 2006
		Guatemala	n/a	14 July 2006	14 October 2006
		Honduras	n/a	20 March 2006	20 June 2006
		Nicaragua	n/a	10 May 2006	10 August 2006
		USA	April 28, 1977	24 September 1979	19 August 1980
Convention on Biological Diversity	Adoption: 22 May 1992 Entry into force: 29 December 1993	Costa Rica	13 June 1992	26 August 1994	24 November 1994
		Dominican Republic	13 June 1992	25 November 1996	23 February 1997
		El Salvador	13 June 1992	8 September 1994	7 December 1994
		Guatemala	13 June 1992	10 July 1995	8 October 1995

(continued)

(continued)

Title	Adoption (and revisions)	CAFTA-DR countries	Signature	Ratification/accession	Entry into force
		Honduras	13 June 1992	31 July 1995	29 October 1995
		Nicaragua	13 June 1992	20 November 2015	18 February 1996
		USA	4 June 1993	No	No
Nagoya Protocol on Access to Genetic Resources and the Fair and Equitable Sharing of Benefits Arising from their Utilization	Adoption: 29 October 2010 Entry into force: 12 October 2014	Costa Rica	6 July 2011	No	No
		Dominican Republic	20 September 2011	12 November 2014	11 February 2015
		El Salvador	1 February 2012	No	No
		Guatemala	11 May 2011	18 June 2014	12 October 2014
		Honduras	1 February 2012	12 August 2013	12 October 2014
		Nicaragua	n/a	12 June 2020	10 September 2020
		USA	No	No	No
International Treaty on Plant Genetic Resources for Food and Agriculture (FAO Plant Treaty)	3 November 2001	Costa Rica	10 June 2002	14 November 2006	12 February 2007
		Dominican Republic	11 July 2002	1 February 2022	2 May 2022
		El Salvador	10 June 2002	9 July 2003	29 June 2004
		Guatemala	13 June 2002	1 February 2006	2 May 2006
		Honduras	n/a	14 January 2004	29 June 2004
		Nicaragua	n/a	22 November 2002	29 Jun 2004
		USA	1 November 2002	13 December 2016	13 March 2017

Hague Agreement Concerning the International Registration of Industrial Designs (Hague Agreement)	6 November 1925 (Hague) Revisions: 2 June 1934 (London) 28 November 1960 (the Hague) 18 November 1961 (Monaco) 14 July 1967 (Stockholm) 2 July 1999 (Geneva)	Costa Rica	No	No	No
		Dominican Republic	No	No	No
		El Salvador	No	No	No
		Guatemala	No	No	No
		Honduras	No	No	No
		Nicaragua	No	No	No
		USA	6 July 1999	13 February 2015	May 13, 2015
Indigenous and Tribal Peoples in Independent Countries Convention (Indigenous Peoples Convention)	27 June 1989 (Geneva)	Costa Rica	n/a	2 April 1993	Yes
		Dominican Republic	n/a	No	No
		El Salvador	n/a	No	No
		Guatemala	n/a	5 June 1996	Yes
		Honduras	n/a	28 March 1995	Yes
		Nicaragua	n/a	25 August 2010	Yes
		USA	n/a	No	No
Lisbon Agreement for the Protection of Appellations of Origin and Their International Registration (Lisbon Agreement)	31 October 1958 (Lisbon) Revisions: 14 July 1967 (Stockholm) 28 September 1979 20 May 2015 (Geneva)	Costa Rica	n/a	30 April 1997 (Stockholm); 13 October 2015 (Geneva)	30 July 1997 (Stockholm)
		Dominican Republic	n/a	n/a	17 January 2020 (Stockholm)
		El Salvador	No	No	No
		Guatemala	No	No	No
		Honduras	No	No	No
		Nicaragua	n/a	15 March 2006 (Stockholm); 21 May 2015 (Geneva)	15 June 2006 (Stockholm)
		USA	No	No	No

(continued)

(continued)

Title	Adoption (and revisions)	CAFTA-DR countries	Signature	Ratification/accession	Entry into force
Madrid Agreement for the Repression of False or Deceptive Indications of Source on Goods [Madrid Agreement (Indications of Source)]	April 14, 1891 Revised: 2 June 1911 (Washington) 6 November 1925 (the Hague) 2 June 1934 (London) 31 October 1958 (Lisbon)	Costa Rica	No	No	No
		Dominican Republic	n/a	23 June 1950	6 April 1951
		El Salvador	No	No	No
		Guatemala	14 April 1891	No	No
		Honduras	No	No	No
		Nicaragua	No	No	No
		USA	No	No	No
Madrid Agreement Concerning the International Registration of Marks [Madrid Agreement (Trademarks)]	14 April 1891 Revisions: 14 Dec. 1900 (Brussels) 2 June 1911 (Washington) 6 November 1925 (the Hague) 2 June 1934 (London) 15 June 1957 (Nice) 14 July 1967 (Stockholm) 28 September 1979	Costa Rica	No	No	No
		Dominican Republic	No	No	No
		El Salvador	No	No	No
		Guatemala	14 April 1891	No	No
		Honduras	No	No	No
		Nicaragua	No	No	No
		USA	No	No	No
Marrakesh Treaty to Facilitate Access to Published Works for Persons Who Are Blind, Visually Impaired or Otherwise Print Disabled (Marrakesh Treaty)		Costa Rica	n/a	9 October 2017	9 January 2018
		Dominican Republic	No	No	5 September 2018
		El Salvador	n/a	1 October 2014	30 September 2016
		Guatemala	n/a	29 June 2016	30 September 2016
		Honduras	n/a	29 March 2017	29 June 2017

		Nicaragua	No	No	16 April 2020
		USA	No	No	8 May 2019
Nairobi Treaty on the Protection of the Olympic Symbol (Nairobi Treaty)	26 September 1981 (Nairobi)	Costa Rica	No	No	No
		Dominican Republic	No	No	No
		El Salvador	n/a	14 September 1984	14 October 1984
		Guatemala	n/a	21 January 1983	21 February 1983
		Honduras	No	No	No
		Nicaragua	No	No	No
		USA	No	No	No
Nice Agreement Concerning the International Classification of Goods and Services for the Purposes of the Registration of Marks (Nice Agreement)	15 June 1957 Revisions: 14 July 1967 (Stockholm) 13 May 1977 (Geneva) 28 September 1979	Costa Rica	No	No	No
		Dominican Republic	No	No	No
		El Salvador	No	No	No
		Guatemala	No	No	No
		Honduras	No	No	No
		Nicaragua	No	No	No
		USA	n/a	23 February 1972	25 May 1972
Paris Convention for the Protection of Industrial Property (Paris Convention)	20 March 1883 Revisions: 14 December 1900 (Brussels) 2 June 1911 (Washington) 6 November 1925 (Hague) 2 June 1934 (London) 31 October 1958 (Lisbon) 14 July 1967 (Stockholm) 28 September 1979	Costa Rica	n/a	28 July 1995	31 October 1995
		Dominican Republic	n/a	20 October 1884	11 July 1890
		El Salvador	n/a	18 November 1993	19 February 1994
		Guatemala	n/a	18 May 1998	18 August 1998

(continued)

(continued)

Title	Adoption (and revisions)	CAFTA-DR countries	Signature	Ratification/accession	Entry into force
		Honduras	n/a	3 November 1993	4 February 1994
		Nicaragua	n/a	3 April 1996	3 July 1996
		USA	n/a	18 March 1887	30 May 1887
Patent Cooperation Treaty (Patent Cooperation Treaty)	19 June 1970 (Washington) Revisions: 28 September 1979 3 February 1984 3 October 2001	Costa Rica	n/a	3 May 1999	3 August 1999
		Dominican Republic	n/a	28 February 2007	28 May 2007
		El Salvador	n/a	17 May 2006	17 August 2006
		Guatemala	n/a	14 July 2006	14 October 2006
		Honduras	n/a	20 March 2006	20 June 2006
		Nicaragua	n/a	6 December 2002	6 March 2003
		USA	19 June 1970	26 November 1975	24 January 1978
Protection of Producers of Phonograms against Unauthorized Duplication of their Phonograms (Phonograms Convention)	29 October 1971	Costa Rica	n/a	1 March 1982	17 June 1982
		Dominican Republic	No	No	No
		El Salvador	n/a	25 October 1978	9 February 1979
		Guatemala	n/a	14 October 1976	1 February 1977
		Honduras	n/a	16 November 1989	6 March 1990
		Nicaragua	29 October 1971	10 May 2000	10 August 2000
		USA	29 October 1971	26 November 1973	10 March 1974

Patent Law Treaty (PLT)	1 June 2000 (Geneva)	Costa Rica	No	No	No
		Dominican Republic	No	No	No
		El Salvador	No	No	No
		Guatemala	No	No	No
		Honduras	No	No	No
		Nicaragua	No	No	No
		USA	2 June 2000	18 September 2013	18 December 2013
Rome Convention for the Protection of Performers, Producers of Phonograms and Broadcasting Organizations (Rome Convention)	26 October 1961	Costa Rica	n/a	9 June 1971	9 September 1971
		Dominican Republic	n/a	27 October 1986	27 January 1987
		El Salvador	n/a	29 March 1979	29 June 1979
		Guatemala	n/a	14 October 1976	14 January 1977
		Honduras	n/a	16 November 1989	16 February 1990
		Nicaragua	n/a	10 May 2000	10 August 2000
		USA	No	No	No
Singapore Treaty on the Law of Trademarks (Singapore Treaty)	27 March 2006 (Singapore)	Costa Rica	28 March 2006	No	No
		Dominican Republic	28 March 2006	No	No
		El Salvador	No	No	No
		Guatemala	No	No	No

(continued)

(continued)

Title	Adoption (and revisions)	CAFTA-DR countries	Signature	Ratification/accession	Entry into force
		Honduras	No	No	No
		Nicaragua	No	No	No
		USA	28 March 2006	1 October 2008	16 March 2009
Strasbourg Agreement Concerning the International Patent Classification (Strasbourg Agreement)	24 March 1971 Amendment: 28 September 1979	Costa Rica	No	No	No
		Dominican Republic	No	No	No
		El Salvador	No	No	No
		Guatemala	No	No	No
		Honduras	No	No	No
		Nicaragua	No	No	No
		USA	24 March 1971	21 December 1973	7 October 1975
Trademark Law Treaty (Trademark Law Treaty)	27 October 1994 (Geneva)	Costa Rica	18 October 1995	17 July 2008	17 October 2008
		Dominican Republic	28 October 1994	13 September 2011	13 December 2011
		El Salvador	n/a	14 August 2008	14 November 2008
		Guatemala	n/a	12 September 2016	12 December 2016
		Honduras	n/a	22 January 2008	22 April 2008
		Nicaragua	n/a	22 June 2009	22 September 2009
		USA	28 October 1994	12 May 2000	12 August 2000

Trade-Related Aspects of Intellectual Property Rights Agreement (TRIPS)	15 April 1994 (Marrakesh, Morocco)	Costa Rica	n/a	n/a	1 January 1995
		Dominican Republic	n/a	n/a	9 March 1995
		El Salvador	n/a	n/a	7 May 1995
		Guatemala	n/a	n/a	21 July 1995
		Honduras	n/a	n/a	1 January 1995
		Nicaragua	n/a	n/a	3 September 1995
		USA	n/a	n/a	1 January 1995
UPOV Convention for the Protection of New Varieties of Plants (UPOV Convention)	2 December 1961 (Paris) Revisions: 10 November 1972 (Geneva) (1972 Act) 23 October 1978 (Geneva) (1978 Act) 19 March 1991 (Geneva) (1991 Act)	Costa Rica	n/a	12 December 2008	12 January 2009 (1991 Act)
		Dominican Republic	n/a	16 May 2007	16 June 2007 (1991 Act)
		El Salvador	No	No	No
		Guatemala	No	No	No
		Honduras	No	No	No
		Nicaragua	n/a	6 August 2001	6 September 2001 (1978 Act)
		USA	n/a	22 January 1999	22 February 1999. (1991 Act)

(continued)

(continued)

Title	Adoption (and revisions)	CAFTA-DR countries	Signature	Ratification/accession	Entry into force
Treaty on Intellectual Property in Respect of Integrated Circuits (Washington Treaty)	26 May 1989 (Washington)	Costa Rica	No	No	No
		Dominican Republic	No	No	No
		El Salvador	No	No	No
		Guatemala	31 May 1989	No	No
		Honduras	No	No	No
		Nicaragua	No	No	No
		USA	No	No	No
WIPO Copyright Treaty (WCT)	20 December 1996 (Geneva)	Costa Rica	2 December 1997	23 May 2000	6 March 2002
		Dominican Republic	n/a	10 October 2005	10 January 2006
		El Salvador	n/a	20 October 1998	6 March 2002
		Guatemala	n/a	4 November 2002	4 February 2003
		Honduras	n/a	20 February 2002	20 May 2002
		Nicaragua	n/a	6 December 2002	6 March 2003
		USA	12 April 1997	14 September 1999	6 March 2002
WIPO Convention (Convention Establishing the World Intellectual Property Organization) (WIPO Convention)	14 July 1967 (Stockholm) Revision: 28 September 1979	Costa Rica	n/a	10 March 1981	10 June 1981
		Dominican Republic	n/a	27 March 2000	27 June 2000
		El Salvador	n/a	18 June 1979	18 September 1979

		Guatemala	n/a	31 January 1983	30 April 1983
		Honduras	n/a	15 August 1983	15 November 1983
		Nicaragua	n/a	5 February 1985	5 May 1985
		USA	14 July 1967	25 May 1970	25 August 1970
WIPO Performances and Phonograms Treaty (WPPT)	20 December 1996 (Geneva)	Costa Rica	2 December 1997	23 May 2000	20 May 2002
		Dominican Republic	n/a	10 October 2005	10 January 2006
		El Salvador	n/a	20 October 1998	20 May 2002
		Guatemala	n/a	8 October 2002	8 January 2003
		Honduras	n/a	20 February 2002	20 May 2002
		Nicaragua	n/a	6 December 2002	6 March 2003
		USA	12 April 1997	14 September 1999	20 May 2002
General Inter-American Convention for Trade Mark and Commercial Protection (Inter-American Trademark Convention)[a]	20 February 1929 (Washington)	Costa Rica	20 February 1929	No	No
		Dominican Republic	20 February 1929	No	No
		El Salvador	No	No	No
		Guatemala	20 February 1929	30 December 1929	2 April 1930
		Honduras	20 February 1929	29 November 1935	29 November 1935
		Nicaragua	20 February 1929	7 June 1935	6 June 1935
		USA	20 February 1929	17 February 1931	17 February 1931

[a]The contracting parties are available at www.oas.org/juridico/english/sigs/b-7.html (accessed 2 Nov 2024)

Bilateral and Regional Intellectual Property and Trade Agreements

Agreements with the USA

Title	Parties	Signature	Ratification	Entry into force
Dominican Republic—Central America—United States Free Trade Agreement (CAFTA-DR)[a]	Costa Rica	5 August 2004	7 October 2007	1 January 2009
	Dominican Republic		6 September 2005	1 March 2007
	El Salvador		17 December 2004	1 March 2006
	Guatemala		18 May 2006	1 July 2006
	Honduras		3 March 2005	1 April 2006
	Nicaragua		10 October 2005	1 April 2006
	USA		2 August 2005	*See above per country*
North American Free Trade Agreement (NAFTA)[b]	Canada	17 December 1992	8 December 1993	1 January 1994
	Mexico		8 December 1993	
	USA		8 December 1993	
United States-Chile Free Trade Agreement (US-Chile-FTA)[c]	Chile	6 June 2003	2 November 2003	1 January 2004
	USA		2 November 2003	
United States-Colombia Trade Promotion Agreement (US-Colombia-TPA)[d]	Colombia	22 November 2006	1 July 2008	15 May 2012
	USA		12 October 2011	
United States-Korean-Free Trade Agreement (KORUS)[e]	Korea	30 June 2007	22 November 2011	15 March 2012
	USA		12 October 2011	
United States—Nicaragua Agreement concerning Protection of Intellectual Property Rights (US-Nicaragua IP Agreement)[f]	Nicaragua	7 January 1998	30 June 1998	1 July 1999
	USA		n/a	
United States-Panama Trade Promotion Agreement (US-Panama-TPA)[g]	Panama	28 June 2007	11 July 2007	31 October 2012
	USA		12 October 2011	

(continued)

(continued)

Title	Parties	Signature	Ratification	Entry into force
United States-Peru Trade Promotion Agreement (US-Peru-TPA)[h]	Peru	12 April 2006	n/a	1 February 2009
	USA		n/a	

[a]The text of the agreement is available at https://ustr.gov/trade-agreements/free-trade-agreements/cafta-dr-dominican-republic-central-america-fta/final-text (accessed 2 Nov 2024); the negotiation timeline is available at http://www.sice.oas.org/TPD/USA_CAFTA/USA_CAFTA_e.ASP#Articles (accessed 2 Nov 2024)
[b]The text of the agreement is available at http://sice.oas.org/trade/nafta/naftatce.asp (accessed 2 Nov 2024)
[c]The text of the agreement and more information are available at https://www.ustr.gov/trade-agreements/free-trade-agreements/chile-fta (accessed 2 Nov 2024)
[d]The text of the agreement and more information are available at https://ustr.gov/trade-agreements/free-trade-agreements/colombia-tpa (accessed 2 Nov 2024)
[e]The text of the agreement is available at https://ustr.gov/trade-agreements/free-trade-agreements/korus-fta/final-text (accessed 2 Nov 2024)
[f]The text of the agreement is available at http://www.wipo.int/wipolex/en/other_treaties/details.jsp?group_id=23&treaty_id=491 (accessed 2 Nov 2024)
[g]The text of the agreement is available at http://www.ustr.gov/trade-agreements/free-trade-agreements/panama-tpa/final-text (accessed 2 Nov 2024)
[h]The text of the agreement is available at https://ustr.gov/trade-agreements/free-trade-agreements/peru-tpa/final-text (accessed 2 Nov 2024)

Agreements with the EU

Title	Parties	Signature	Ratification	Entry into force
European Union-CARIFORUM Economic Partnership Agreement (EU-CARIFORUM-EPA)[a]	Dominican Republic	15 October 2008	n/a	29 December 2008 (provisional application)
	CARICOM		n/a	
	EU		n/a	
European Union-Central American Association Agreement (EU-CA-AA)[b]	Costa Rica	29 June 2012	Ratification in progress (the agreement is provisionally applied)	1 October 2013
	El Salvador			1 October 2013
	Guatemala			1 December 2013
	Honduras			1 August 2013
	Nicaragua			1 August 2013
	EU			*See above*

(continued)

(continued)

Title	Parties	Signature	Ratification	Entry into force
European Union-Chile Association Agreement (EU-Chile-AA)[c]	Chile	18 November 2002	n/a	1 February 2003 (pro-visional application) 1 March 2005 (full a.)
	EU		n/a	

[a]Official Journal of the European Union, Nr. L 289 of 30 October 2008; the text of the agreement is also available at http://www.sice.oas.org/Trade/CAR_EU_EPA_e/careu_in_e.ASP (accessed 2 Nov 2024)

[b]The text of the agreement and background information is available at https://trade.ec.europa.eu/access-to-markets/en/content/eu-central-america-association-agreement (accessed 2 Nov 2024); the EU-CA-AA was ratified by the Guatemalan parliament on 26 June 2013

[c]The text of the agreement is available at http://eur-lex.europa.eu/resource.html?uri=cellar:f83a503c-fa20-4b3a-9535-f1074175eaf0.0004.02/DOC_2&format=PDF (accessed 2 Nov 2024)

Regional Agreements

Title	Parties	Signature	Ratification	Entry into force
Mexico-El Salvador, Guatemala and Honduras-Free Trade Agreement (Mexico-Northern Triangle-FTA)[a]	El Salvador	29 June 2000	n/a	15 March 2001
	Guatemala		n/a	15 March 2001
	Honduras		n/a	1 June 2001
	Mexico		n/a	*See above*
CARICOM-Dominican Republic-Free Trade Agreement (CARICOM-DR-FTA)[b]	Dominican Republic	22 August 1998	n/a	5 February 2002
	CARICOM		n/a	*Various dates*
Chile-Central America- Free Trade Agreement (Chile-CA-FTA)[c]	Costa Rica	18 October 1999	n/a	15 February 2002
	El Salvador		n/a	3 June 2002
	Guatemala		n/a	7 December 2007
	Honduras		n/a	18 July 2008
	Nicaragua		n/a	19 October 2012
	Chile		n/a	*See above*
Central America—Dominican Republic Agreement[d]	Costa Rica	16 April 1998	n/a	7 March 2002
	Dominican Republic		n/a	*See above/ below*
	El Salvador		n/a	4 October 2001

(continued)

(continued)

Title	Parties	Signature	Ratification	Entry into force
	Guatemala		n/a	3 October 2001
	Honduras		n/a	19 December 2001
	Nicaragua		n/a	3 September 2002
Colombia-Costa Rica-Free Trade Agreement (Colombia-Costa Rica-FTA)[e]	Colombia	22 May 2013	6 April 2016	1 August 2016
	Costa Rica		5 May 2014	

[a]The text is available at http://www.sice.oas.org/Trade/mextnorte/Mex_TNorte_s.asp#a1601 (accessed 2 Nov 2024)
[b]The text of the agreement is available at http://www.sice.oas.org/trade/ccdr/English/Ccdr_in.asp (accessed 2 Nov 2024)
[c]The text of the agreement is available at http://www.sice.oas.org/trade/chicam/chicamin.asp (accessed 2 Nov 2024); background information on the ratification process is available at http://www.sice.oas.org/TPD/CACM_CHL/CACM_CHL_e.ASP (accessed 2 Nov 2024); the agreement entered into force for each Central American country in relation to Chile and the other Central American countries on the date specified in this line
[d]The text of the agreement is available at http://www.sice.oas.org/trade/camdrep/indice.asp (accessed 2 Nov 2024); the agreement entered into force for each Central American country in relation to the Dominican Republic on the date specified in this line
[e]The text of the agreement and background information are available at http://www.sice.oas.org/TPD/COL_CRI/COL_CRI_e.asp (accessed 2 Nov 2024)

Other Agreements

Title	Parties	Signature	Ratification	Entry into force
Free Trade Agreement between the Republic of China (Taiwan), the Republic of El Salvador and the Republic of Honduras (Taiwan-El Salvador-Honduras-FTA)[a]	Honduras	7 May 2007	n/a	15 July 2008
	El Salvador		n/a	1 March 2008
	Taiwan		n/a	1 January 2008
China-Costa Rica Free Trade Agreement (China-Costa Rica-FTA)[b]	China	8 April 2010	n/a	1 August 2011
	Costa Rica		n/a	
Central America-Korea Free Trade Agreement[c]	South Korea	21 February 2018	n/a	n/a
	Costa Rica		5 March 2019	n/a
	El Salvador		28 May 2018	n/a
	Honduras		n/a	n/a

(continued)

(continued)

Title	Parties	Signature	Ratification	Entry into force
	Nicaragua		n/a	1 October 2019
	Panama		n/a	n/a
	Guatemala	Not signed	n/a	n/a

[a]The text of the agreement is available at http://www.sice.oas.org/Trade/SLV_HND_TWN_FTA_e/Index_e.asp#FULLTEXT (accessed 2 Nov 2024)

[b]The text of the agreement is available at http://www.sice.oas.org/Trade/CRI_CHN_FTA/Texts_Apr2010_e/CRI_CHN_ToC_e.asp (accessed 2 Nov 2024)

[c]More information on this agreement and the text of the agreement is provided by SICA, available at http://www.sice.oas.org/TPD/CACM_KOR/CACM_KOR_e.ASP (accessed 2 Nov 2024)

National Legislation in Central America

Costa Rica

Title in English	Title in Spanish	Abbreviation	Number	Adoption	Entry into force	Revisions/comments
Constitution	Constitución Política de la República de Costa Rica	Constitution (CR)	n/a	7 November 1949	8 November 1949	
Patents, Designs and Utility Models Law	Ley de Patentes de Invención, Dibujos, Modelos Industriales, Modelos de Utilidad	Patent and Design Law (CR)	6867	25 April 1983	13 July 1983	Law No. 7979 of 6 January 2000, Law No. 8632 of 25 March 2008, Law No. 8686 of 21 November 2008
Law on Marks and other Distinctive Signs	Ley de marcas y otros signos distintivos	Trademark Law (CR)	7978	22 December 1999	1 February 2000	Law No. 8020 of 28 August 2000, Law No. 8632 of 25 March 2008
Undisclosed Information Law	Ley de información no Divulgada	Undisclosed Information Law (CR)	7975	4 January 2000	18 January 2000	Law No. 8686 of 21 November 2008
Plant Variety Protection Law	Ley de Protección de las Obtenciones Vegetales	Plant Variety Law (CR)	8631	6 March 2008	19 March 2008	Law No. 8686 of 21 November 2008
Law on Procedures of Enforcement of IP Rights	Ley de Procedimientos de Observancia de los Derechos de Propiedad Intelectual	IP Enforcement Law (CR)	8039	6 January 2000	31 January 2000	Law No. 8686 of 21 November 2008; Law N° 8834 of May 3, 2010; Law Nr. 9524 of 7 March 2018

(continued)

(continued)

Title in English	Title in Spanish	Abbreviation	Number	Adoption	Entry into force	Revisions/comments
Trademark Law, Patent and Design Law and Biodiversity Law Reform	Modificación de Varios Artículos de la Ley de Marcas y Otros Signos Distintivos, de la Ley de Patentes de Invención, Dibujos y Modelos Industriales y Modelos de Utilidad, y de la Ley de Biodiversidad	CAFTA-DR Reform Law I (CR)	8632	25 March 2008	25 April 2008	n/a
Law amending, adding or repealing various Rules on Matters pertaining to Intellectual Property	Reforma, Adición y Derogación de varias normas que regulan materias relacionadas con Propiedad Intelectual	CAFTA-DR Reform Law II (CR)	8686	21 November 2008	26 November 2008	n/a
Biodiversity Law	Ley de Biodiversidad	Biodiversity Law (CR)	7788	30 April 1998	27 May 1998	Law No. 8632 of 25 March 2008
Law regarding the identification of Costa Rican bananas in international markets	Ley para identificar el banano de Costa Rica en los mercados internacionales	Banana Law (CR)	8063	20 December 2000	17 April 2001	
Law for the promotion of competition and effective defense of the consumer	Ley de Promoción de la Competencia y Defensa Efectiva del Consumidor	Competition Law (CR)	7472	20 December 1994	19 January 1995	Law No. 9072 (5 October 2012)
Law on the Protection of Layout-Designs of Integrated Circuits	Ley de Protección a los Sistemas de Trazados de los Circuitos Integrados	Integrated Circuits Law (CR)	7961	17 December 1999	19 January 2000	

Law No. 7982, Approving the Protocol of the Central American Agreement for the Protection of Industrial Property (Trademarks, Trade Names and Advertising Slogans or Signs)	Aprobación del Protocolo al Convenio Centroamericano para la Protección de la Propiedad Industrial (Marcas, Nombres Comerciales y Expresiones o Señales de Propaganda)		7982	14 January 2000	2 February 2000	Repeals the Central American Convention (Trademarks)
Code of Civil Procedure	Código Procesal Civil		7130	16 August 1989	3 November 1989	Law No. 7979 of 6 January 2000
Constitutional Jurisdiction Law	Ley de la Jurisdicción Constitucional	Constitutional Jurisdiction Law (CR)	7135	5 October 1989	10 October 1989	
Brand Law	Ley de Marcas de Ganado	Brand Law (CR)	2247	7 August 1958	1 January 1959	
Judiciary Law	Ley Organica del Poder Judicial	Judiciary Law (CR)	7333	n/a	5 May 1993	Amended by the Judicial Reorganization Law (*Ley de Reorganizacion Judicial*) 7728 of 15 December 1997
Regulation regarding Article 78 of the Biodiversity Law (CR)	Reglamento al Artículo 78, Inciso 6) de la Ley de Biodiversidad	Regulation 34959-MINAET-COMEX	34959-MINAET-COMEX	11 December 2008	1 January 2009	
Regulation regarding Article 80 of the Biodiversity Law	Reglamento al Artículo 80 de la Ley de Biodiversidad	Regulation 34958-MINAET-COMEX	34958-MINAET-COMEX	11 December 2008	1 January 2009	Invalidated by the CSJ on 5 December 2012

(continued)

(continued)

Title in English	Title in Spanish	Abbreviation	Number	Adoption	Entry into force	Revisions/comments
Regulation of the Law of Patents, Designs and Utility Models	Reglamento de la Ley de Patentes de Invención, Dibujos y Modelos Industriales y Modelos de Utilidad	Patent Regulation (CR)	15222-MIEM-J—34758-J-COMEX	12 December 1983	12 December 1983	Decree No. 17602 of 11 May 1987; Decree No. 34758-J-COMEX of 18 September 2008; Decree No. 38308-JP of 12 February 2014
Generals Rules for the Access to elements and Genetic and Biochemical Resources of Biodiversity	Normas Generales para el Acceso a los elementos y Recursos Genéticos y Bioquímicos de la Biodiversidad	Regulation 31514-MINAE	31514-MINAE	3 October 2003	n/a	
Regulation for the Application of Administrative Sanctions regarding non-authorized Access to Genetic and Biochemical Resources established in the Biodiversity Law	Reglamento para la Aplicación de las Sanciones Administrativas en Materia de Acceso No Autorizado a los Elementos y Recursos Genéticos y Bioquímicos, Establecidas en Ley de Biodiversidad N° 7788	Regulation No. 39341-MINAE	39341-MINAE	16 March 2016	16 September 2016	
Patent and Design Regulation (CR)	Reglamento de la Ley N° 6867 de 25 de Abril de 1983 de Patentes de Invención, Dibujos y Modelos Industriales y Modelos de Utilidad	Patent and Design Regulation (CR)	15222-MIEM-J		12 December 1983	amended by regulation 38308-JP, adopted on 12 February 2014 and entered into force on 24 April 2014

Dominican Republican

Title in English	Title in Spanish	Abbreviation	Number	Adoption	Entry into force	Revisions/comments
Constitution of the Dominican Republic	Constitución de la República Dominicana	Constitution (DR)	n/a	26 January 2010	26 January 2010	
Law of Industrial Property	Ley de Propiedad Industrial	IP Law (DR)	20-2000	4 April 2000	10 May 2000	CAFTA-DR Reform Laws I & II (DR)
Law on the Protection of the Plant Breeder's Rights	Ley de Protección de los Derechos del Obtentor de Variedades Vegetales	Plant Variety Law (DR)	450-06	6 December 2006	6 December 2006	
Copyright Law	Ley de Derecho de Autor	Copyright Law (DR)	65-00	26 July 2000	21 August 2000	Law No. 2-07 (2007) Law No. 493-06 (2007)
Criminal Code	Código Penal	Criminal Code (DR)	n/a	20 August 1884	20 August 1884	Law No. 12-07 of 5 January 2007
CAFTA-DR Implementation Law	Ley de Implementación del Tratado de Libre Comercio, entre la República Dominica, Centroamérica y los Estados Unidos de América	CAFTA-DR Reform Law I (DR)	424-06	20 November 2006	1 March 2007	CAFTA-DR Reform Law II (DR)
Amendment Law to the CAFTA-DR Implementation Law	Ley que modifica los Articulos 6,49,58 y 62 de la Ley N° 424-06 […]	CAFTA-DR Reform Law II (DR)	493-06	22 December 2006	22 December 2006	

El Salvador

Title in English	Title in Spanish	Abbreviation	Number	Adoption	Entry into force	Revisions/comments
Constitution of the Republic of El Salvador	Constitución de la República de El Salvador	Constitution (SV)	n/a	15 December 1983	20 December 1983	
Intellectual Property Promotion and Protection Law	Ley de Fomento y Protección de la Propiedad Intelectual	IP Law (SV)	604	15 July 1993	15 October 1993	CAFTA-DR IP Reform Law (SV)
Intellectual Property Promotion and Protection Law Reform	Reformas a la Ley de Fomento y Protección de la Propiedad Intelectual	CAFTA-DR IP Reform Law (SV)	912	14 December 2005	12 January 2006	
Intellectual Property Law Reform	Reformas a la Ley de Propiedad Intelectual		611	15 February 2017	25 May 2017	
Law of Trademarks and other Distinctive Signs	Ley de Marcas y otros Signos Distintivos	Trademark Law (SV)	868	6 June 2002	8/17 July 2002	CAFTA-DR Trademark Reform Law (SV)
Reform of the Law of Trademarks and other Distinctive Signs	Reformas a la Ley de Marcas y otros Signos Distintivos	CAFTA-DR Trademark Reform Law (SV)	913	14 December 2005	12 January 2006	
Law of Trademarks and other Distinctive Signs (2013)	Ley de Marcas y otros Signos Distintivos (2013)	EU-CA-AA Trademark Reform Law (SV)	358	19 April 2013	14 Mai 2013	Restatement of the Law of Trademarks and other Distinctive Signs
Law regarding the use and registration of coffee and balm	Ley para el Uso y Registro de Marcas de Café y Bálsamo		48	29 May 1934	29 May 1934	Decree No. 436 of 18 October 2007; Decree No. 63 of 29 May 2008
Competition Law	Ley de Competencia	Competition Law (SV)	528	26 November 2004	31 December 2004	
Criminal Code	Código Penal	Criminal Code (SV)	1030	26 April 1997	20 April 1998	
Regulations for the protection of test data for new pharmaceuticals	Reglamento para la protección de datos de prueba de nuevos productos farmacéuticos	Test Data Regulation (SV)	65	4 June 2008	4 June 2008	

Guatemala

Title in English	Title in Spanish	Abbreviation	Number	Adoption	Entry into force	Revisions/ comments
Constitution	Constitución Política de la República de Guatemala	Constitution (GT)		31 May 1985	31 May 1985	
Industrial Property Law	Ley de Propiedad Industrial	IP Law (GT)	57-2000	18 September 2000	1 November 2000	
Law on Copyright and Related Rights	Ley de Derecho de Autor y Derechos Conexos	Copyright Law (GT)	33-98	19 May 1998	21 June 1998	consolidated by Copyright Reform Law (GT)
Criminal Code	Código Penal	Criminal Code (GT)	17-73	27 July 1973	15 September 1973	
Law No. 56-2000	Decreto Ley No. 56-2000	Copyright Reform Law (GT)	56-2000	27 September 2000	1 November 2000	
National Cultural Heritage Protection Law	Ley para la protección del patrimonio cultural de la nación	Heritage Law (GT)	26-97	29 April 1997	20 May 1997	Law No. 81-98
IP Law Reform	Decreto N° 30-2005 por el que se reforma la Ley de Propiedad Industrial	CAFTA-DR Reform Law (GT)	30-2005	18 March 2005	19 March 2005	
IP Law Reform	Reformas al Decreto N° 57-2000 del Congreso de la República, Ley de Propiedad Industrial	EU-CA-AA Reform Law (GT)	3-2013	13 June 2013	26 June 2013	
IP Register Regulation	Arancel del Registro de Propiedad Intelectual, en Materia de Propiedad Intelectual		Acuerdo Gubernativo 862-2000	21 December 2000		IP Register Regulation Reform
IP Register Regulation Reform	Reformas al Acuerdo Gubernativo		Acuerdo Gubernativo 148-2014	7 May 2014	16 May 2014	

Honduras

Title in English	Title in Spanish	Abbreviation	Number	Adoption	Entry into force	Revisions/comments
Industrial Property Law	Ley de Propiedad Industrial	IP Law (HN)	12-99-E	12 December 1999	28 February 2000	CAFTA-DR Reform Law
Copyright Law	Ley del Derecho de Autor y de los Derechos Conexos	Copyright Law (HN)	4-99E	13 December 1999	15 January 2000	CAFTA-DR Reform Law
CAFTA-DR Implementation Law	Ley de Implementación del Tratado de Libre Comercio República Dominicana, Centro-américa, Estados Unidos	CAFTA-DR Reform Law (HN)	16-2006	16 / 21 March 2006	24 March 2006	The establishes a separate set of rules; however it contains also changes to the IP Law (HN) in Article 53
Criminal Code	Código Penal	Criminal Code (HN)	144-1983	23 August 1983	12 March 1985	
National Cultural Heritage Protection Law	Ley para la protección del patrimonio cultural de la nación	Heritage Law (HN)	220-1997	29 December 1997	21 February 1998	
Investment Promotion and Protection Law	Ley para la promoción y protección de inversiones		51-2011	3 May 2011	15 July 2011	Article 57 amends the IP Law (HN)
Law No. 219-2012	Ley No. 219-2012	EU-CA-AA Reform Law (HN)	219-2012	18 January 2013	19 March 2013	
Forest, Protected Areas and Sylvan Life Law	Ley Forestal, Áreas Protegidas y Vida Silvestre	Forest Law (HN)	Decree 98-2007			Revised by Decrees 176-2010 and 365-2013
Law for the Defense and Promotion of Competition	Ley para la Defensa y Promoción de la Competencia	Competition Law (HN)	Decree 357-2005	29 December 2005	4 February 2006	

Nicaragua

Title in English	Title in Spanish	Abbreviation	Number	Adoption	Entry into force	Revisions/comments
Patents, Utility Models and Designs Law	Ley de Patentes de Invención, Modelo de Utilidad y Diseños Industriales	Patent and Design Law (NI)	354-2000	1 June 2000	21 November 2000	CAFTA-DR IP Reform Law (NI) and Law No. 634-2007
Law on Amendments and Additions to Law No. 354, Law on Patents, Utility Models and Industrial Designs	Ley de Reformas y Adiciones a la Ley N° 354, Ley de Patentes de Invención, Modelos de Utilidad y Diseños Industriales	CAFTA-DR IP Reform Law (NI)	579-2006	21 March 2006	24 March 2006	
Law on Amendments and Additions to Law No. 354, Law on Patents, Utility Models and Industrial Designs	Ley de Reforma y Adición a la Ley N° 354, Ley de Patentes de Invención, Modelo de Utilidad y Diseños Industriales		634-2007	13 September 2007	12 October 2007	This reform law only created Article 38*bis* Patent and Design Law on patent term extension
Law on Copyright and Related Rights	Ley de Derecho de Autor y Derechos Conexos	Copyright Law (NI)	312-1999	6 July 1999	31 August 1999	Ley N° 577 of 16 March 2006
Law on Marks and other Distinctive Signs	Ley de Marcas y otros Signos Distintivos	Trademark Law (NI)	380-2001	14 February 2001	16 April 2001	
Amendments and Additions to Law No. 380 on Marks and other Distinctive Signs	Reformas y Adiciones a la Ley N° 380, Ley de Marcas y Otros Signos Distintivos	CAFTA-DR Trademark Reform Law (NI)	580-2006	21 March 2006	24 March 2006	
Plant Variety Protection Law	Ley de Protección para las Obtenciones Vegetales	Plant Variety Law (NI)	318	20 October 1999	27 February 2000	
Competition Law	Ley sobre la Promoción de la Competencia	Competition Law (NI)	601-2006	28 September 2006	24 June 2007	

(continued)

(continued)

Title in English	Title in Spanish	Abbreviation	Number	Adoption	Entry into force	Revisions/comments
Criminal Code	Código Penal	Criminal Code (NI)	641	13 November 2007	4 July 2008	
Environment and Natural Resource Law	Ley General del Medio Ambiente y de los Recursos Naturales	Environment Law (NI)	217	27 March 1996	6 June 1996	Law 647 of 13 February 2008
National Cultural Heritage Protection Law	Ley para la protección del patrimonio cultural de la nación	Heritage Law (NI)	1142	22 November 1982	2 December 1982	
Law on the Conservation and Sustainable Use of the Biological Diversity	Ley de Conservación y Utilización Sostenible de la Diversidad Biológica	Biodiversity Law (NI)	807	5 September 2012	19 October 2012	
Law for Protection of Layout Designs of Integrated Circuits	Ley de Protección a los Esquemas Trazados de Circuitos Integrados	Integrated Circuits Law (NI)	324	2 December 1999	1 February 2000	
Regulations to the Law on the Protection of New Plant Varieties	Reglamento de la Ley de Protección para las Obtenciones Vegetales		37	2 May 2000	31 May 2000	
Regulation of the Law on Trademarks and Other Distinctive Signs	Reglamento de la Ley de Marcas y Otros Signos Distintivos	Trademark Regulation (NI)	83-2001	4 September 2001	27 September 2001	
Amendments and Additions to the Regulation of the Law on Trademarks and Other Distinctive Signs	Reformas y Adiciones al Decreto N° 83-2001, Reguladora de la Ley de Marcas y Otros Signos Distintivos	EU-CA-AA Trademark Reform Regulation (NI)	25-2012	20 June 2012	20 June 2012	

Executive Decree about the Promotion and Protection of IP Rights of the people of Nicaragua	Decreto sobre la Promoción, Fomento y Protección de los Derechos de Propiedad Intelectual del Pueblo Nicaragüense		18-2012	27 April 2012	27 April 2012	
Resolution Nr. 115-2006	Resolución Ministerial No. 115-2006 (Ministerio de Salud)		115-2006	22 March 2006	22 March 2006	

Table of Cases

Central American Cases

Jurisdiction	Court/ agency	Date of decision	Title	Case number	Citation
Costa Rica	CSJ (*Sala IV*)	11 September 2008	n/a	2008-13832	Cited in Decision No. 2012-018147
Costa Rica	CSJ (*Sala IV*)	14 December 2012	Acción de inconstitucionalidad contra el Decreto Ejecutivo N° 34959-MINAET-COMEX	09-009870-0007-CO Decision No. 2012-018147	Judicial Bulletin N° 137 of 17 July 2013 *https://vlex.co.cr/vid/499781262*
Costa Rica	CSJ (*Sala IV*)	5 December 2012	Acción de inconstitucionalidad contra el Decreto Ejecutivo N° 34958 MINAET-COMEX	10-000782-0007-CO Decision No. 2012-017058	Judicial Bulletin N° 111 of 11 June 2013
Costa Rica	First Civil Court of San José	6 July 2001	Registered Trade name coinciding with that of a competitor	831-R	Reported by *Escoto* (2004), p. 21
Costa Rica	TRA	10 November 2014	Fontina	VOTO N° 0773-2014	*On file with the author*

(continued)

F. Böttger, *CAFTA-DR, European Free Trade Agreements and the Industrial Property System in Central America*, Munich Studies on Innovation and Competition 21, https://doi.org/10.1007/978-3-031-93440-7

(continued)

Jurisdiction	Court/ agency	Date of decision	Title	Case number	Citation
Costa Rica	TRA	4 November 2011	Super Cola	VOTO No. 698-2011	*On file with the author*
Costa Rica	TRA	15 March 2006	MASATICA CORONA	VOTO N° 058-2006	*On file with the author*
El Salvador	CSJ (Sala de lo Civil)	21 December 2007	Pfizer Products Inc. v Ronasa, S.A. de C.V.		Rangel Ortiz (2011), p. 325
Guatemala	CSJ	17 November 1998	ZAMACORT / SANACORT	135-98	de Leon Molina (2002), pp. 18–19
Guatemala	CSJ	23 August 1995	NATALIN and NATALAC	40-95	de Leon Molina (2002), p. 4
Guatemala	CSJ	30 January 1997	DETECTO	112-96	de Leon Molina (2002), p. 15
Guatemala	CSJ	5 September 1995	CHOW CRUNCHIS / CRUNCH	106-94	*de Leon Molina* (2002), p. 15
Guatemala	CSJ	3 October 1995	BONBOM BUM / BUM	119-94	*de Leon Molina* (2002), p. 17
Guatemala	CSJ	3 March 2010	Canel's	3155-2009	*Turcios Urrutia* (2016), p. 10
Guatemala	CSJ	11 October 1994	QUESIFRITOS	13-94	*de Leon Molina* (2002), p. 20
Guatemala	CSJ	16 March 1994	Oshkosh B'Gosh	73-93	*Barreda Valenzuela* (2003), p. 20
Guatemala	CSJ	20 February 2001	n/a	157-2000	*de Leon Molina* (2002), p. 3
Guatemala	CSJ	19 May 1998	PEPSI	128-97	*de Leon Molina* (2002), p. 18
Guatemala	CSJ	16 March 1993	[Industrial Design]	n/a	*de Leon Molina* (2002), p. 8
Guatemala	CSJ	7 December 2001	El Americano más suave	94-2001	*de Leon Molina* (2002), p. 9
Guatemala	CSJ	9 November 1993	La adequada alimentación para la nueva generación	43-93	*de Leon Molina* (2002), p. 9

(continued)

(continued)

Jurisdiction	Court/ agency	Date of decision	Title	Case number	Citation
Nicaragua	CSJ	12 July 1996	n/a	n/a	Judicial Bulletin 1996, p. 216 *Plata Rivas* (2004), pp. 10–16
Nicaragua	CSJ	9 January 1962	n/a	n/a	Judicial Bulletin 1962, p. 7

Barreda Valenzuela, Roberto Eduardo, Tendencias más recientes sobre la Jurisprudencia en material de Propiedad Intelectual en le Republica de Guatemala, Secundo Seminario Regional sobre Propiedad Industrial para Jueces y Fiscales de America Latina, 2003, available at http://www.oepm.es/cs/OEPMSite/contenidos/ponen/sem_jueces_03/informes/guatemala.pdf (accessed 2 Nov 2024)
Escoto, Carmen María, Intellectual Property Rights and Trade Enforcement Procedures in Costa Rica, 2004, available at http://www.wipo.int/edocs/mdocs/enforcement/en/wipo_ace_2/wipo_ace_2_www_33725.doc (accessed 2 Nov 2024)
Plata Rivas, Hernaldo Alberto, Tendencia de la Jurisprudencia en Nicaragua, Tercer Seminario Regional sobre Propiedad Industrial para Jueces y Fiscales de America Latina, 2004, available at http://www.wipo.int/edocs/mdocs/mdocs/es/ompi_pi_ju_lac_04/ompi_pi_ju_lac_04_3.pdf (accessed 2 Nov 2024)
Turcios Urrutia, José Roberto, El Principio de Uso Obligatorio de la Marca Registrada en Guatemala—The Principle of Compulsory Use of a Trademark, 2016, available at https://dialnet.unirioja.es/descarga/articulo/6088229.pdf (accessed 2 Nov 2024)

International and Foreign Cases

Jurisdiction	Court/ agency	Date of decision	Title	Case number	Citation
Andean Community	Court of Justice	28 September 2001	n/a	89-AI-2000	*Markowski* (2004), p. 44
European Union	CJEU	16 July 1998	Silhouette International Schmied GmbH & Co. KG v Hartlauer Handelsgesellschaft mbH	C-355/96	ECR 1998, I-4799
European Union	CJEU	13 July 2006	GAT v LUK	C-04/03	ECR 2006, I-6509
European Union	CJEU	13 July 2006	Roche	C-539/03	ECR 2006, I-6535
European Union	CJEU	14 February 1978	United Brands v Commission	C-27/76	ECR 1978, 207
European Union	CJEU	13 February 1979	Hoffmann-La Roche	C-85/76	ECR 1979, 461

(continued)

(continued)

Jurisdiction	Court/ agency	Date of decision	Title	Case number	Citation
European Union	CJEU	6 April 1995	Radio Telefis Eireann et al. v Commission ("Magill")	C-241/91 P and C-242/91 P	ECR 1995, I-00743 IIC 1996, 78
European Union	CJEU	6 December 2012	AstraZeneca v Commission	C-457/10 P	ECLI:EU: C:2012: 770
European Union	CJEU	2 July 2009	Bavaria N.V. and Bavaria Italia Srl v Bayerischer Brauerbund	C-343/07	ECR I-5491 (2009) GRUR 2009, 961
European Union	CJEU	12 December 2002	Ralf Sieckmann v Deutsches Patent- und Markenamt	C-273/00	ECR 2002, I-11737 GRUR 2003, 145
European Union	CJEU	18 June 2009	L'Oréal v Bellure	C-487/07	ECR 2009 I-05185
European Union	EUIPO, Fourth Board of Appeal	25 August 2003	Roar of a lion	R 781/1999-4	GRUR 2003, 1054
Germany	Federal Patent Court	31 August 2016	Merck v Shionogi	3 LiQ 1/16 (EP)	GRUR-Prax 2017, 105
International	WTO Appellate Body	1 February 2002	United States—Section 211 Omnibus Appropriations Act of 1998	WT/DS176/ AB/Rv	DSR 2002: II, p. 683
International	WTO Appellate Body	16 January 1998	India—Patent Protection for Pharmaceutical and Agricultural Chemical Products	WT/DS50/AB/ R	DSR 1998: I, 9
International	WTO Appellate Body	12 October 2000	Canada—Term of Patent Protection	WT/DS170/ AB/R	DSR 2000: X, 5093
International	WTO Dispute Settlement Body	7 April 2000	Canada—Patent Protection for Pharmaceutical Products	WT/DS114/R	DSR 2000: V, 2289
International	WTO Dispute Settlement Body	20 March 2009	China—Measures Affecting the Protection and Enforcement of Intellectual Property	WT/DS362/R	DSR 2009: V, p. 2097
International	WTO Dispute Settlement Body	20 April 2005	European Communities—Protection of Trademarks and Geographical Indications for Agricultural Products and Foodstuffs (Complaint by the USA)	WT/DS174/R	DSR 2005: VIII, p. 3499

(continued)

(continued)

Jurisdiction	Court/ agency	Date of decision	Title	Case number	Citation
International	WTO Dispute Settlement Body	20 April 2005	European Communities—Protection of Trademarks and Geographical Indications for Agricultural Products and Foodstuffs (Complaint by Australia)	WT/DS290/R	DSR 2005: VIII, p. 3499 / DSR 2005: X, p. 4603
International	ICSID Tribunal	18 September 2018	Aven and others v. Costa Rica	UNCT/15/3	*www.italaw.com*
International	ICSID Tribunal	29 June 2012	Railroad Development Corporation v Republic of Guatemala	ARB/07/23	*www.italaw.com*
International	WIPO Arbitration and Mediation Center	31 March 2005	Campero International, Corp., Campero International Limited, Campero International, S.A., Campero USA Corp., Pollo Campero, S.A., Pollo Campero, S.A. de C. V., Pollo Campero de Honduras, S.A. de C.V. v. Jordan Data Communication Services Company	D2004-1105	*www.wipo.int/amc/en/domains/*
United States	Supreme Court	15 May 2006	eBay v. MercExchange	05-130	547 U.S. 388
United States	Supreme Court	16 June 1980	Diamond v. Chakrabarty		447 U.S. 303
United States	CAFC	10 September 1992	Atari Games Corp. v. Nintendo of America, Inc.		897 F.2d 1572, 1576
United States	Supreme Court of California	9 July 1990	Moore v. Regents of the University of California		51 Cal. 3d 120
United States	USPTO, Trademark Trial and Appeal Board	8 July 2015	Campero International Limited and Campero Inc. v. Marcelo Paolo Dicunta Servellon and Giovanna Lucrecia Dicunta Servellon—Pollo Campesino	Opposition No. 911 99515	